Recentering the Self

SUNY series in Transpersonal and Humanistic Psychology

Richard D. Mann, editor

Recentering the Self

A Defense of the Ego

MICHAEL WASHBURN

SUNY
PRESS

Published by State University of New York Press, Albany

For information, contact State University of New York Press, Albany, NY
www.sunypress.edu

Library of Congress Cataloging-in-Publication Data

Name: Washburn, Michael, 1943– author.
Title: Recentering the self : a defense of the ego / Michael Washburn.
Description: Albany, NY : State University of New York Press, [2023] |
    Series: SUNY series in transpersonal and humanistic psychology |
    Includes bibliographical references and index.
Identifiers: LCCN 2022059332 | ISBN 9781438494678 (hardcover : alk. paper) |
    ISBN 9781438494685 (ebook) | ISBN 9781438494661 (pbk. : alk. paper)
Subjects: LCSH: Ego (Psychology) | Ego (Psychology)—Religious aspects. |
    Self. | Consciousness.
Classification: LCC BF175.5.E35 W37 2023 | DDC 155.2—dc23/eng/20230624
LC record available at https://lccn.loc.gov/2022059332

10 9 8 7 6 5 4 3 2 1

This book is dedicated to my grandchildren, with love.

Grace Hammer

Michael J. Hammer

Nathan Hammer

Emma Hurley

Luke Hurley

Cayla Kedik

Dominic Kish

Contents

PART III
RETHINKING THE EGO'S ROLE IN SPIRITUAL LIFE

List of Tables

Acknowledgments

I am grateful to Dr. James McGrath and Dr. Jean Raffa, who commented on early versions of the manuscript, to Dr. Thomas Smythe, who offered critical feedback on selected chapters, and to the anonymous readers who evaluated the manuscript when it was under review for publication. The generous efforts of these people helped me correct errors, strengthen arguments, address overlooked perspectives, explore needed research, and improve the formulation of several key theoretical ideas.

I am also grateful to the people at SUNY Press with whom I worked during the process leading to publication. Many thanks to James Peltz, who agreed to review my manuscript and coordinated the review process; to Catherine Blackwell, who also played an important role in the review process; to Diane Ganeles, who efficiently and pleasantly oversaw the production of the book; and to Ivo Fravashi, who did an excellent job of copyediting a long, densely written manuscript.

Finally, I am grateful to Indiana University South Bend for supporting my teaching and research over the course of many years. IUSB, a regional campus of Indiana University, is an excellent school serving an important mission in northern Indiana. It was my good fortune that IUSB hired me in 1970, when I finished graduate school, and was my academic home until 2007, when I retired.

The editors of the *Journal of Consciousness Studies* have allowed me to adapt "Rethinking the Notion of the Ego" (19, no. 3–4 [March/April 2012]: 194–222) for use in this book, primarily in chapter 3.

Introduction

The notion of the ego, long thought to express a signature insight of the modern period, has almost as long been a target of strong criticism. Criticism of the notion picked up pace in the second half of the twentieth century, and many now consider the notion of the ego to be a defining myth, not a signature insight, of the modern period. Responding to this reversal of opinion, *Recentering the Self* undertakes a defense of the ego, a defense that is multidisciplinary in perspective and wide in scope. This defense begins with a rethinking of the notion of the ego (part 1) and then proceeds to a corresponding rethinking of ego development, first within the general context of the human lifespan (part 2) and then within the specific context of spiritual life (part 3).

Part 1 rethinks the notion of the ego by examining its historical origins, by reassessing major criticisms of the notion, and then by formulating a revised conception of the ego designed to meet critical challenges. This revised conception of the ego is here referred to as "RCE."[1] Part 2 rethinks ego development within the general context of the human lifespan by applying RCE to ten well-studied stages of ego development. The purpose of part 2 is to use RCE to highlight basic psychological (cognitive, motivational, behavioral) and philosophical (phenomenological, existential) aspects of the ego's development during the ten stages considered. Finally, part 3 rethinks ego development within the specific context of spiritual life by applying RCE to four broad stages of spiritual development: spiritual preawakening, spiritual awakening, spiritual growth, and spiritual maturity. The purpose of part 3 is to use RCE to clarify the essential role played by the ego in these four stages and thus to defend the ego against the strongly negative accounts of its role in spiritual life prevalent in spiritual literature.

The rethinking of the notion of the ego in part 1 consists of three main tasks. The first is to explain the principal ideas that have been associated with the "traditional" notion of the ego, by which I mean the notion that emerged at the beginning of the modern period. This task is taken up in chapter 1, which presents a brief exposition of René Descartes's account of the soul as a "thing that thinks" (*res cogitans*) or, more precisely, a thing the *only* function of which is to think. In saying that the only function of the soul is to think, Descartes was stressing the point that the soul performs only rational functions and not, as had long been believed, also biological (body-animating, body-regulating) functions.

Descartes divided the rational functions of the soul into two basic types, which he referred to as "perception of the intellect" and "operation of the will."[2] Perception of the intellect is a passive function by which the soul, as a thing that thinks, experiences (Descartes: perceives) whatever arises within consciousness or presents itself to consciousness through the senses. In contrast, operation of the will is an active function by which the soul operates either on ideas or mental images, thus performing active cognitive functions (functions that operate on things in order to know them), or on impulses, the body, or states of affairs in the world, thus performing active practical functions (functions that operate on things in order to regulate, utilize, or change them). In our terminology, that which performs the functions just outlined is the ego.

Descartes's account of the soul as a thing the only function of which is to think thus introduced the notion of the ego into Western intellectual history. Stripped to essentials, the notion he introduced is that of the *subject and executive agency of consciousness*. The ego is the subject of consciousness because it is that which experiences whatever arises within consciousness or presents itself to consciousness through the senses. The ego is thus an "experiencer," a subject that intuits, perceives, observes, senses, and feels. However, the ego is not only a subject or experiencer but also an agency because it performs active, will-initiated—henceforth: "executive"—functions of cognitive and practical sorts. The ego performs cognitive executive functions such as controlling attention, holding things in mind, recalling things to mind, switching between cognitive tasks, and engaging in operational thinking of all types. Additionally, the ego performs practical executive functions such as regulating impulses, moving the body, and undertaking actions in the world. The ego bequeathed to us by Descartes is exclusively passive in its experiencing (Descartes: perceiving) function. The ego is the recipient rather than to any extent the creator of the thoughts, images, impulses, sensations, and sense impressions it experiences.³ In contrast, the ego bequeathed to us by Descartes is exclusively active in its executive (Descartes: will-initiated or volitional) functions. The ego alone initiates and carries out the cognitive and practical functions it performs.

The notion of the ego, once introduced in the seventeenth century, raised perplexing new philosophical questions, questions that became central to the discussion of the traditional notion of the ego. The following questions are among those that came to the fore: Is the ego something real, or is it only a useful fiction or, perhaps, a persistent illusion? If the ego is real, what kind of thing, if a thing at all, is it? How, if at all, can the ego be known to exist? Is the ego a necessary basis of consciousness? How, as the subject of consciousness, does the ego hold consciousness together as one consciousness? How, as the executive agency of consciousness, can the ego be causally efficacious in performing its executive functions? If the ego is causally efficacious in performing its executive functions, is its efficacy confined within consciousness or does it extend to the body and to bodily actions in the world? Chapter 1 presents Descartes's answers to these and other questions about the ego by identifying eleven ideas that are prominent in or assumed by his account of the soul as a thing the only function of which is to think.

The second task in rethinking the notion of the ego is to trace the antecedents and historical emergence of the traditional notion. This task is taken up in chapter 2, which places Descartes's account of the soul in its seventeenth-century context and explains which of its principal ideas were carried over from the premodern past and which broke new ground for the modern future. As we shall see, Descartes's account of the soul emerged from an attempt to satisfy the requirements of both Christian orthodoxy, which held that the soul is incorporeal and immortal, and the new mechanistic paradigm of seventeenth-century science, which held that physical nature, including organic bodies, can be explained exclusively in terms of the motion and contact of physical things. The result of this attempt to satisfy the requirements of both an old religion and a new science was a conception of the soul that in important respects preserved ideas with long histories but that in other respects broke with the past in such a way as to replace the premodern rational-*biological* soul with an exclusively rational-*interior* soul, the subject-agency of which is the ego of the modern period.

The third task in rethinking the notion of the ego is to formulate a revised conception of the ego (RCE) designed to meet critical challenges. This task is taken up in chapters 3 through 5. Chapter 3 sets forth the core ideas of RCE by responding to criticisms of the notion of the ego that were debated between Descartes's time and the end of the nineteenth century. These core ideas are set forth briefly in this introduction, beginning here with the following general idea: the ego is a side of two fundamental dualities of human experience and would be incomplete or could not function without the other sides of these dualities. We call these dualities the "duality of the interior ego and the worldly self" and the "duality of agency and spontaneity."

First, the ego, as the *subject* of consciousness, exists as the interior side of an interior-exterior duality, the exterior side of which is the worldly self. As we explain in chapter 3, the ego, in the very process of its production as the interior subject of consciousness, is already in the process of appropriating and thus forging for itself an exterior or worldly side, a side consisting of its worldly experiences and what it perceives to be its worldly (bodily, mental, social) attributes. Second, the ego, as the *executive agency* of consciousness, functions as the executive, managing, side of an interior-interior duality, the other side of which is the underlying source or sources from which the internally generated contents of the ego's experience spontaneously arise. As we explain in chapter 3, the ego functions as an agency only by giving focus, engagement, and, therefore, guidance to the spontaneity of consciousness, which produces for the ego the thoughts, images, and impulses with which it performs its executive functions. According to RCE, the dualities of the interior ego and the worldly self and of agency and spontaneity are inherent to the constitution of the ego. The ego, as the subject of consciousness, is incomplete apart from its worldly self; and the ego, as the executive agency of consciousness, cannot function apart from the spontaneity of consciousness.

Chapter 4 adds quite a few ideas to RCE by responding to criticisms of the traditional notion of the ego that were debated in the twentieth century. Specifically, chapter 4 responds to criticisms set forth by the following twentieth-century perspectives: *psychoanalysis*, which argued that the traditional view that the ego has complete control of its executive functions and the traditional view that the ego has primacy over the passions are false; *existential phenomenology*, which argued that the traditional view that the ego resides within the interior of the psyche is false; *depth psychology*, which argued that the traditional view that the ego has complete access to the interior of the psyche is false; *symbolic interactionism* and *relational psychoanalysis*, which argued that the traditional view that the ego always has privileged access to itself is false; *postmodernism*, which argued that the traditional view that the ego is the author of its identity in the world is false;[4] *psychoanalytic feminist theory*, which argued that the traditional view that the ego (as conceived in the modern period) is gender-neutral is false; and *physicalism in the philosophy of mind*, which argued that the traditional view that the ego's interior side is something more than physical science can explain is false.

Among the ideas added to RCE in chapter 4, the most general is that the ego, on its interior side, is a bridge that integrates the two fundamental dualities introduced a moment ago. Chapter 4 explains how the ego bridges and integrates the fundamental duality of the interior ego and the worldly self, including, among its specific forms, the duality of interior psychic life and embodied, social life, the duality of self-authorship and social construction of identity, and, generally, the duality of subjectivity (including its phenomenal, intentional, and cultural dimensions) and objectivity (including its physical, functional, and social dimensions). Chapter 4 also explains how the ego bridges and integrates the fundamental duality of agency and spontaneity, including, among its specific forms, the duality of executive and spontaneous (intuitive, creative) cognition and the duality of self-control and the passions.

A major point made in chapter 4 is that the ego's role as bridge and integrator of the dualities just mentioned indicates that neither of the sides of these dualities is inherently dominant over the other. It indicates that, depending on conditions, the sides can be in relatively balanced interaction or can be out of balance (in either direction), with one side exerting dominance across a wide range of possibilities, from slight to extreme, although never complete. Chapter 4, therefore, concludes that the "truth" about the dualities under discussion lies on neither of the sides of these dualities but rather on the middle ground between the sides.

More precisely, chapter 4 concludes that the truth lies on a *wide* and *shifting* middle ground because whether the sides of the dualities are in or out of balance depends on empirical factors, which can vary from one person to another and can change over time for a single person. With this conclusion, chapter 4 challenges both the traditional notion of the ego and its primary antitraditional critics. It challenges the former by rejecting the view that forms of human subjectivity and agency in principle have dominance over their corresponding forms of objectivity and spontaneity; and it challenges the latter by rejecting the view that in principle the dominance goes the other way around. Neither side of these dualities has an inherent primacy over the other. Chapter 4 argues that the truth is determined by empirical factors, not a priori arguments, and that empirical factors indicate that the truth cannot be fixed and is subject to change, lying on a wide and shifting middle ground between the sides of the dualities in question.

Chapter 5 adds two final ideas to RCE by adopting, revising, and integrating the ideas of the *self-system* and the *lifeworld*, the former borrowed from the interpersonal psychoanalysis of Harry Stack Sullivan, and the latter borrowed from existential phenomenology. These two ideas further develop the notion of the exterior, worldly side of the ego, the idea of the self-system explaining what the ego is as an exterior or worldly self and the idea of the lifeworld explaining what kind of world the ego lives in as such a self. The ideas of the self-system and lifeworld play central roles in our account of ego development in parts 2 and 3. The two ideas are set forth more clearly later in this introduction.

The basic ideas of RCE are borrowed from historical sources. One of these sources is Buddhism; the others are major figures or schools in modern European philosophy and psychology, where the modern European period is here understood to extend from the early seventeenth century to the end of the first half of the twentieth century. Primary among the modern European sources are Descartes, Kant, (William) James, classical psychoanalysis, Jungian psychology, and existential phenomenology. Although the ideas borrowed from these sources are part of the historical record, belonging more to the past than to the present, they all still retain their original value. Furthermore, I hope to show that the value of these ideas can be more fully realized if, first, they are revised so that they can withstand criticisms that, like those considered in chapter 4, have emerged in more recent times and if, second, they are adapted to each other so that they work together as cohering ideas of a single theoretical framework, such as RCE.

Regrettably, newly emerging theoretical approaches often supplant rather than supplement older ones, which are then treated as if they have *only* historical significance. This book moves in the opposite direction. Committed to the view that the notion of the ego was a signature insight rather than a defining myth of the modern period, this book is a project of retrieval and rethinking. It reevaluates and, when appropriate, reemploys ideas that played important roles in shaping the traditional notion of the ego. It reevaluates these ideas to determine which among them have withstood the test of criticism. It then reemploys those that have withstood this test, first by revising them so that they fit together in mutually strengthening and clarifying ways, second by grounding them in recent research, and third by demonstrating how, once thus revised and grounded, they can provide both historical perspective and new insights to current debate.

Buddhism, Kant, and James provide RCE with its most prominent ideas. These ideas are set forth in chapter 3 and further developed in chapter 4. From Buddhism RCE adopts two key ideas. The first is that there is a "space of spontaneity" within the psyche, what earlier was described as the underlying psychic source or sources from which arise the thoughts, images, and impulses with which the ego performs its executive functions. According to Buddhism, the more deeply a meditator examines consciousness, the more evident it becomes that consciousness is an open space in which thoughts, images, and impulses arise unpredictably and of their own accord. Meditative awareness of this space reveals that the thoughts, images, and impulses that arise within it are countless in number and that they appear and disappear in a seemingly uninterrupted process of creative production. Buddhists have referred to this space of spontaneity as a "fertile void" or "creative emptiness."

The second key idea adopted from Buddhism is that to experience the space of spontaneity within us is to experience the absence of an ego in that space. According to Buddhism, meditation shows that at the center of consciousness, where a unified, executive ego is supposed to be, there is instead *only* an open space of spontaneity. In our view, the thoughts, images, and impulses that arise within the space of spontaneity are produced spontaneously *for* the ego, which appropriates them and thus relates to them as its own thoughts, images, and impulses when, guided and motivated by them, it performs its executive functions. Buddhism argues otherwise, holding that there is no ego for which these thoughts, images, and impulses are produced or by which they are appropriated for executive purposes. According to Buddhism, the *presumption* that there is such an ego is unmasked as a false belief or persistent illusion once the space of spontaneity is brought meditatively into view. To be aware of the space of spontaneity is to be aware only of thoughts, images, and impulses that arise without having been premeditated by an ego and that come and go without being appropriated or put to functional use by an ego.

According to RCE, awareness of the space of spontaneity does *not* unmask the ego as a false belief or illusion. Rather, it hides the ego, just as awareness of the ego's executive activity hides the spontaneity of consciousness. Sitting silently in Buddhist meditation, it certainly seems as if there is nothing more to consciousness than a space in which thoughts, images, and impulses spontaneously arise, just as, actively engaged in operational thinking or goal-directed action, it certainly seems as if there is nothing more to consciousness than an executive ego thinking its own thoughts and pursuing its own aims. RCE argues that these appearances, although indisputable, are misleading because they hide the fact that the ego and the spontaneity of consciousness work together as opposite, coessential interior sides of consciousness, together making up what earlier was referred to as the duality of agency and spontaneity.

The ego is the side of this duality that experiences what arises within or is presented to consciousness and that performs executive functions of cognitive and practical sorts. In contrast, the spontaneity of consciousness is the side that produces the internally generated content of experience, specifically the thoughts with which the ego thinks, the images with which the ego imagines, and the impulses on which the ego acts. Although, as opposites, the ego in its agency and the spontaneity of consciousness hide and frequently conflict with each other, they more fundamentally, according to RCE, require and complete each other. According to RCE, the ego and the spontaneity of consciousness have coevolved to work together as complementary opposites, each providing for the other what the other cannot provide for itself.

Chapters 3 and 4 explain in some detail how the ego and the spontaneity of consciousness interact, explaining that the spontaneity of consciousness provides the ego with the internally generated content of its experience and that the ego, *when strongly organized, selectively focused, and functionally engaged,* provides the spontaneity of consciousness with guidance in what content to produce. The spontaneity of consciousness does not cease being spontaneous and, therefore, unpredictable in the *specific* thoughts, images, and impulses it produces when under the ego's strong guiding influence. Nevertheless, when under such influence, it does tend to produce thoughts, images, and impulses of *types* that are relevantly responsive to the ego's engaged concerns. Whereas a weak, unfocused, and disengaged ego is witness to the free play of the spontaneity of consciousness, as occurs during reverie and dreams, a strong, focused, and engaged ego "harnesses" the spontaneity of consciousness in such a way that for the most part it produces thoughts, images, and impulses that facilitate the ego's executive functions and thus allow the ego to act effectively in the world. In this account of the interaction between the ego and the spontaneity of consciousness, it becomes clear that the ego bridges and integrates the duality of agency and spontaneity—including the dualities of executive and spontaneous cognition and of self-control and the passions—rather than standing only on the side of agency.

RCE also adopts two ideas from Kant. The first is that the ego is a formal unity of apperception, which means that the ego is (1) an experiencing subject that cannot experience itself directly because, as an experiencing subject, it is empty of intuitable content (a *formal* unity of apperception); (2) an experiencing subject that, because it is itself temporally unified (self-identical over time[5]), unifies its experiences by binding them together under its unified point of view (a formal *unity* of apperception); and (3) an experiencing subject that is aware of itself as that to which its experiences belong, as that which not only unifies its experiences but also appropriates them, thus assuming ownership of them and relating to them as "its" experiences (a formal unity *of apperception*). Kant's idea that the ego is a formal unity of apperception is complex and subtle. However, I hope to show that it is an idea that, if properly unpacked, can be shown to ascribe to the ego no more than we can experience for ourselves as egos.

The second idea adopted from Kant, this one a hypothesis rather than an idea conveying what we can experience for ourselves, is that the ego, as a formal unity of apperception, is the organized form of an activity, not a thing. In adopting this idea, RCE does not accept Kant's account of the activity of which the ego is the organized form. Whereas Kant held that this activity works beyond consciousness to produce both the ego and consciousness, RCE holds that it works within consciousness to produce only the ego. Specifically, whereas Kant held that the activity that produces the ego is a synthesizing process of a "transcendental" (supraempirical) sort, RCE holds that this activity is a synthesizing process of a *neurophenomenological* sort, a synthesizing process that works at once within the neurological bases and the subjective interior of consciousness.[6]

Although RCE does not adopt Kant's account of the activity that produces the ego, it does accept his view that this activity produces the ego in a twofold way, as both the unifying subject and the appropriating owner of consciousness. It produces the ego as the unifying subject of consciousness by creating a temporally unified experiencing point of view under which succeeding experiences are held together and thus unified within one consciousness. Simultaneously, it produces the ego as the appropriating owner of consciousness by attaching the experiences that the ego unifies to the ego in such a way that they belong to it as parts of what it is, thus transforming these experiences from unowned, impersonal experiences into *the ego's* experiences. Because the activity of which the ego is the organized form produces the ego as both the unifying subject and appropriating owner of consciousness, RCE calls it the "unifying-appropriating function."

Taking this Kantian line of thought one step further, RCE holds that the ego, as the organized form of the unifying-appropriating function, can be understood to be not only active in its inherent nature but also active *as an agency,* specifically as an agency that performs executive functions of cognitive and practical sorts. According to RCE, the unifying-appropriating function constitutes the ego as a subject that performs two root functions, an *experiencing* function, which the ego performs as the unifying subject of consciousness, and a *proprietary* function, which the ego performs as the appropriating owner of consciousness. RCE explains in general terms how these two root functions underlie and make possible the ego's executive functions, the experiencing function underlying and making possible the ego's cognitive functions and the proprietary function underlying and making possible the ego's practical functions.

The hypothesis that the ego is the organized form of the unifying-appropriating function is the leading hypothesis of RCE. In chapter 3, we argue that this hypothesis is warranted because it helps to explain important facts and assumptions about the ego that would otherwise go unexplained. We have just proposed that it helps to explain the ego's structure as a formal unity of apperception and the ego's cognitive and practical agency. In chapters 3 and 4, we propose that the hypothesis also helps to explain several other basic, essential features of the ego.

RCE also adopts two ideas from James. These ideas are already implied by the hypothesis that the ego is the organized form of the unifying-appropriating function. Nevertheless, they are ideas that first came to prominence in James's work. The first of these ideas is that everything in the "stream of consciousness" is in ceaseless motion, *including* the ego as interior subject and executive agency of consciousness. The second idea is that the ego has two, interior and exterior, subjective and worldly, sides, which we have referred to as the fundamental duality of the interior ego and the worldly self. James expressed this second idea by saying that the ego is both an interior subject or "I" and an exterior object or "Me." As an interior subject or I, the ego is a temporally unified conscious point of view that has experiences and that performs executive functions; and as an exterior object or Me, the ego is an embodied self defined by the experiences it has and by the worldly attributes with which it identifies.[7]

In adopting these ideas from James, RCE uses the Kantian ideas we have introduced to explain them. RCE explains that the ego on its interior side is in ceaseless motion because it is the organized form of an activity, the unifying-appropriating function. Additionally, RCE explains that the ego has not only an interior but also an exterior side because, as an interior ego with a proprietary function, it appropriates its experiences and what it perceives to be its bodily, mental, and social attributes, thus forging for itself an exterior side by making itself an object or Me in the world. In this way, the ego, in the very process of being constituted on its interior side is already in the process of forging for itself a worldly self. In sum, according to RCE, the interior ego, as subject or I, is an ever-in-motion, ever-reconstituting unifying-appropriating function; and the exterior ego, as object or Me, is the set of worldly experiences and attributes that have been appropriated by the interior side of the ego in the exercise of its proprietary function.

To flesh out the idea of the ego's exterior side, RCE adopts and revises three key ideas from psychoanalysis. One of these ideas, mentioned earlier, is that of the self-system, which is borrowed from Harry Stack Sullivan. The other two ideas are those of the ego ideal and the superego. RCE revises Sullivan's idea of the self-system so that it focuses on self-knowledge and self-motivation rather than, as it does for Sullivan, on self-esteem. Thus revised, the self-system consists of the following four components: (1) the ego on its interior side, as subject and executive agency of consciousness (the self of the self-system); (2) the self-representation (the ego's primary instrument of self-knowledge); (3) the ego ideal (one of the ego's two primary instruments of self-motivation); and (4) the superego (the other of the ego's two primary instruments of self-motivation).[8]

RCE adopts the idea of the self-representation without needing to revise it. According to the general understanding, the self-representation is the mental record on which the ego keeps track of what it believes itself to be as a human being in a material, social world. In adopting this understanding of the self-representation, RCE interprets it in terms of the Kantian and Jamesian ideas just introduced. For RCE, therefore, the self-representation is the mental record on which, in Kantian terms, the ego keeps track of the experiences and attributes that, by exercising its proprietary function, it has appropriated and thus relates to as parts of what it is. In Jamesian terms, the self-representation is the mental record on which the ego, as interior subject or I, keeps track of the experiences and attributes that make up its worldly side, as exterior object or Me.

Whereas RCE adopts the idea of the self-representation without needing to revise it, it adopts the ideas of the ego ideal and the superego only with significant revisions. Specifically, it revises them to clarify their relations to the two chief motivating forces of life, desire (ego ideal) and fear (superego). As defined by RCE, the ego ideal is the ego's desire-elicited, "pulling," or, in Aristotelian terminology, *telic* instrument of self-motivation. Specifically, the function of the ego ideal is to manage the ego's pursuit of desire by encouraging the ego to pursue desires that facilitate or at least do not conflict with its ideal goals. In turn, as defined by RCE, the superego is the ego's fear-driven, "pushing," or, in Aristotelian terminology, *efficient* instrument of self-motivation. Specifically, the function of the superego is to manage the ego's avoidance of fear by pressuring the ego to act in ways that minimize unwanted consequences. Redefined in these ways, it becomes clear that the ego ideal and superego work together in opposite but complementary ways, as telic and efficient motivators of the ego's actions. The ideas of the ego ideal and the superego are among the most important insights of psychoanalysis. The importance of these ideas becomes more evident, I believe, when they are revised, as they are by RCE, in ways that clarify their relations to desire and fear and their opposite but complementary roles as instruments of the ego's self-motivation.

The idea of the self-system just set forth fills out the idea of the ego's exterior side by explaining how the ego not only thinks of itself as a self with worldly experiences and attributes (self-representation) but also motivates itself to act as a self with worldly desires (ego ideal) and fears (superego). The self-representation is a record on which the ego logs everything it has appropriated and thus made part of itself, as worldly object or Me. In turn, the ego ideal and the superego are auxiliary agencies by which the ego motivates itself to act in pursuit of worldly interests, whether by satisfying worldly desires or avoiding worldly fears. Together, the self-representation on the one hand and the ego ideal and the superego on the other provide the ego with both self-knowledge and self-motivation as a self that belongs to and acts in the world.

The idea of the self-system as defined by RCE implies a closely associated key idea, that of the shadow. The idea of the shadow was introduced by Carl Jung. Because Jung wrote on such topics as archetypes, synchronicity, and mysticism, many hold his contributions to psychology in suspicion. However, there is nothing occult about the idea of the shadow, which is simply the idea that there are parts of the ego's life that the ego does not acknowledge because they are highly threatening to it. Whereas the self-representation is a mental record of those parts of the ego's life that the ego has appropriated and thus understands belong to it as parts of what it is, the shadow consists of those parts of the ego's life that the ego has disowned and hidden from view. Whereas the self-representation is the record of the experiences and attributes that the ego relates to as Me, the shadow is an unconscious subsystem underlying the self-system to which the ego has banished the experiences and attributes that it relates to as not-Me.

This brief account of the shadow reveals that the shadow is the negative counterpart of the self-representation: the shadow consists of all those parts of the ego's life, if any, that are excluded from the self-representation. The "if any" qualification was inserted because the fact that a person has a self-representation does not by itself imply that that person has a shadow. As we shall see in chapters 9 and 10, the self-representation emerges before the shadow is formed, the former emerging in the second half of the second year, and the latter emerging, along with the ego ideal and the superego, in the transition from early to middle childhood. Additionally, as we shall see in chapter 17, the shadow is sometimes awakened in adults in a way that leads to its integration within consciousness. Thus integrated, the shadow ceases to exist and what was the shadow becomes part of a more inclusive self-representation.

This point made, the more important point here is that the shadow, once formed in the transition from early to middle childhood, consists of those parts of the ego's life that the ego has excluded from consciousness because they are highly threatening to it. Because the shadow is excluded from consciousness, it is not part of the self-system. Indeed, the shadow is in certain respects the antithesis of the self-system. Nevertheless, because the shadow is the negative counterpart of the self-representation, it is inherently tied to the self-system, as an underlying unconscious subsystem. Tied to the self-system in this way, the shadow, once formed, develops in concert with the self-system, stage by stage over the course of life.

Unfortunately, the idea of the shadow has been a frequent target of criticism. The primary issue is that it is difficult to explain how the ego can hide unwanted parts of itself, thus removing these parts from consciousness and forming the shadow. From the beginning, the explanation has been that the ego accomplishes this feat by so inhibiting the expression of unwanted parts of itself that these parts are expelled from consciousness. This explanation, that the shadow is *the product of repression,* has come under criticism because the idea of repression, especially in its original Freudian formulation, has been called into question, for reasons discussed in chapter 10. To adopt the idea of the shadow, therefore, the idea of repression needs to be reconceived in such a way that it can explain the formation of the shadow without relying on assumptions that have called it into question.

In chapter 10, I propose what I call the "energy-reduction" conception of repression, which, I believe, meets these stipulations. After setting forth this conception of repression, I incorporate it within RCE to explain how the ego creates the shadow—as part of the same process by which it creates the ego ideal and the superego—in the transition from early to middle childhood. Then, in chapter 12, I use the energy-reduction conception of repression to explain how the ego reconstitutes the shadow, as an adult shadow, in early adulthood. Finally, in chapters 11, 13, 16, and 17, I use the energy-reduction conception to explain why shadow awakening is more likely to occur during some developmental stages (adolescence, midlife transition, spiritual preawakening, and spiritual awakening) than during others.

Further to flesh out the idea of the ego's exterior side, RCE adopts two ideas from existential phenomenology, the idea of the existential priority of the world over subjectivity and the idea of the lifeworld. According to the first of these ideas, we live originally and primarily in the world and withdraw into subjectivity only as a "secondary abode." RCE, in adopting this idea from phenomenology, reformulates it to say that the exterior, object or Me, side of the ego has existential priority over the interior, subject or I, side. The exterior side has this priority because the ego, from birth forward, spends most of its time as a bodily self engaged in the material, social world. The ego at the beginning of life is not yet aware of subjectivity as an interior space distinct from the physical, intersubjective, and communal spaces it shares with others. Moreover, after discovering this interior space, the ego withdraws into it only as a secondary abode, as a place for sleep, reverie, introspection, prayer, or meditation.

In following existential phenomenology by assigning the world an existential priority over subjectivity, RCE does not follow existential phenomenology by also assigning the world an ontological priority over subjectivity. According to existential phenomenology, subjectivity, as an interior space set off from the world, is derivative in nature, emerging only in acts of withdrawing from engaged participation in the world. Thus conceived, subjectivity is an emerging and disappearing epiphenomenon, an interior space that is created only in the act of entering it, collapsing and thus vanishing upon return to worldly engagement.

RCE does not accept this view. RCE holds that subjectivity—rooted in and arising from the neurological bases of consciousness—is the place within which the ego is originally formed. This view follows from RCE's idea that the ego is the organized form of the unifying-appropriating function, which, again, works at once within the neurological bases and the subjective interior of consciousness. According to RCE, therefore, the ego is formed within a domain, subjectivity, in which originally and primarily it does not live. However, although subjectivity is not the place in which the ego originally and primarily lives, it is the place in which the ego is formed and, therefore, in which it comes most intimately in touch with itself, as interior subject or I.

In this view, the ego, in the very process of being constituted as the subject and executive agency of consciousness, is already projecting itself outwardly. It is already employing its proprietary function to appropriate its experiences and what it perceives to be its worldly attributes, thus constituting for itself an exterior side. The ego, that is, is already living in the world and establishing itself as a self belonging to the world in the very process of being constituted as an interior subject and agency. RCE thus holds that the ego's interior and exterior sides are both basic, although in different ways. The ego's interior side is basic ontologically, so far as its original constitution as subject or I is concerned; and the ego's exterior side is basic existentially, so far as its lived experience as worldly object or Me is concerned.

As for the second idea that RCE adopts from existential phenomenology, that of the lifeworld, RCE agrees with existential phenomenology that the world in which we originally and primarily live is the world as it is experienced prereflectively by an engaged subject, not the world as it is described by science or as it might exist apart from human experience. RCE incorporates this idea of the lifeworld by redefining it as the world as it is prereflectively experienced by the ego *through the lens of its self-system*. Thus defined, the lifeworld is the world as it is invested with personal meanings by the ego's self-representation and as it is charged with positive and negative values by the ego's ego ideal and superego, respectively. With this conception of the lifeworld, it becomes clear that the lifeworld, like the shadow, is inherently tied to the self-system and, therefore, develops in concert with it.

Using RCE as a guide, part 2 of *Recentering the Self* provides an account of ego development that highlights both the interior and exterior sides of the ego as we have thus far described them. It tracks how the ego develops both as an interior subject and executive agency and as an embodied self with a self-system living originally and primarily in a lifeworld. A primary contribution made by this approach to ego development is that it brings together psychological (psychoanalytic, Jungian, developmental, clinical, neuropsychological) studies and philosophical (Buddhist, Kantian, Jamesian, phenomenological, existential) perspectives, using the former to give scientific grounding to the latter and using the latter to give more human meaning to the former. The result is a whole-life account of how the ego and its executive functions, self-system, shadow, and lifeworld develop in concert stage by stage over the course of life.

Inescapably, the account of ego development in part 2 reflects the author's perspective as a white male who has lived comfortably in the United States in the twentieth and twenty-first centuries. Understanding this fact, I have tried hard to overcome biases and blind spots so that the account of ego development in part 2, although not suited for everyone, might have existential significance for most people. I am hopeful that the account of ego development focusing on the ego's interior side will have such significance because it explains how the ego bridges and integrates opposite sides of inherent dualities of human experience, dualities with which everyone is intimately familiar. It explains how the ego, as an interior subject, forges, monitors, and maintains its outer, worldly self and how the ego, as an interior agency, engages and guides the spontaneity of consciousness.

I am even more hopeful that the account of ego development focusing on the ego's exterior side will have existential significance for most people. It tracks the ego's self-systems and corresponding lifeworlds as they change from stage to stage and thus presents both a "biography" of the ego and a "travelogue" of its journey through the world. I understand that this account of the ego's life and journey, in stressing how we are alike rather than how we differ, goes against the grain of current discussion. I also understand that, despite having tried to make the account as inclusive as possible, unconscious biases and blind spots have inevitably worked against my aim. Nevertheless, I hope that readers will find something of value in the book to the extent that it succeeds in being inclusive, even if they are dismayed to the extent that it does not.

Part 3 of *Recentering the Self* applies RCE to stages of spiritual development with the aim of defending the ego against the widespread view that it plays primarily a negative role in spiritual life. This negative view of the ego is found in Asian traditions such as Advaita Vedanta and Buddhism, which challenge the notion of an abiding individual self (or ego), either because, properly understood, our true self is nothing other than ultimate reality itself (Ātman is Brahman: Advaita Vedanta) or because meditation reveals only ever-changing constituents of consciousness, not an abiding individual self that is the subject and owner of consciousness (*anattā*, meaning no-self in Pali: Buddhism). Either way, these views hold that attachment to the idea of an abiding individual self stands in the way of liberation or enlightenment. A negative view of the ego is also found in Taoism and Zen, which, skeptical of the ego generally, are harshly critical of executive functions associated with the ego. They argue that (operational) thinking interferes with the original fullness of experience and that (intentional) action interferes with the spontaneity of life. That the ego plays primarily a negative role in spiritual life is also frequently advocated within relational traditions, such as the Abrahamic faiths, which hold that the ego in its free will is susceptible to unwholesome urges, tendencies, or social influences or, as main lines of Christianity maintain, is hereditarily predisposed to sin. Finally, the view maintaining the ego's negative role is also widely espoused among transpersonal theorists, many of whom write from one or more of the Asian perspectives just mentioned.

Part 3 begins by dividing spiritual development into the following four broad stages: spiritual preawakening, spiritual awakening, spiritual growth, and spiritual maturity. It then tracks changes in the ego's status, role, self-system, and lifeworld as spiritual development unfolds through these stages. This account of the ego's spiritual development leads to the following four general conclusions: (1) that the ego, as the organized form of the unifying-appropriating function (a self-conscious subject and agency), is real and, therefore, is not something to unmask as a false belief or persistent illusion; (2) that the ego is present in all known spiritual states, even those in which it seems to be absent; (3) that the ego has necessary, positive roles to play in all stages of spiritual development; and (4) that the ego is as essential to the "spirit" of spiritual life as this spirit is to the ego, since it is through the ego's conscious perspective that spirit perceives the world and with the aid of the ego's executive functions that spirit expresses itself in the world. Generally, the position defended in part 3 is that successful spiritual development requires a strong and resilient ego, not an ego that has been dispelled, dissolved, or suppressed, let alone mortified. Successful spiritual development requires that the ego be strong enough to withstand and resilient enough to adapt to awakened spiritual life so that, eventually, it can become a mature vehicle for spiritual life.

In putting the ego at center stage, the account of spiritual development set forth in part 3 opens itself to three main criticisms: that it might represent men's experience better than women's, that it might represent relational spiritual traditions better than nondual traditions, and that it might have little or no relevance for indigenous spiritual traditions. I address these criticisms in chapter 16, where I acknowledge their importance and attempt to respond to them. First, I explain that the account of spiritual development set forth in part 3 can be understood to apply to both women and men once it is understood how marked differences in women's and men's ego development in patriarchal societies help explain corresponding differences in their spiritual development. Second, I propose that the account of spiritual development set forth in part 3 applies to nondual spiritual traditions by presenting a challenge to them, specifically, the challenge of acknowledging the ego's presence and essential role in spiritual life, even in expressions, states, and stages in which it seems to be absent from or resistant to spiritual life. Finally, I acknowledge that the account of ego development set forth in part 3 applies to indigenous traditions only abstractly and uncertainly, if at all. With these responses, I explain the qualifications that must be placed on and the merit that remains for an account of spiritual development that, like the one set forth in part 3, puts the ego at center stage.

I should add a note on scholarship. Part 1 is scholarly in aim. Chapters 1 and 2, which focus on the notion of the ego in historical perspective, are primarily scholarly endeavors. They cite a wide range of sources that help explain how the premodern notion of the soul was transformed into the modern notion of the ego. Chapters 3 through 5, which set forth RCE, are more theoretical than scholarly in aim but nonetheless require frequent references to historical sources and empirical findings, which are cited in the endnotes. Part 2, which sets forth an account of ego development based on RCE, presupposes and thus rests on many more psychological and other scientific studies than could possibly be cited. Part 2 is very wide in scope, seeking to show how RCE can be applied to major stages of the human lifespan. Given this scope, it was necessary in part 2 to be highly selective in referring to supporting literatures. Nevertheless, I have tried in part 2 to cite behavioral, clinical, neuroscientific, and other studies whenever points are made that might raise questions for the reader. Finally, part 3, which applies RCE to four stages of spiritual development, is intended as a proposal rather than as a scholarly exposition or theoretical demonstration. As explained in chapter 16, the account of spiritual development set forth in part 3 is hypothetical only. Moreover, based on RCE, it is an account that to a significant extent is the author's own invention. Scholarly citations are for these reasons provided in part 3 only as required in making explicit references to sources.

A note is also needed on terminology used in part 2 in discussing ego development in childhood and old age. "It" is used when referring to a (single) child instead of alternating between "he" and "she" or using "they." Additionally, "old" is used when referring to people in the last stage of life instead of using words such as "older" or "elderly." These choices were made without intending any disrespect for children (including my younger self) or old people (including my current self).

Part I

Rethinking the Notion of the Ego

Chapter 1

The Birth of the Ego

Descartes's "Thing That Thinks"

The most influential source for what I call the traditional notion of the ego—indeed, the defining source—is René Descartes's seventeenth-century account of the soul (or mind). The traditional notion of the ego is for this reason essentially the modern notion. However, I prefer "traditional" to "modern" because the latter term overly historicizes the notion of the ego, suggesting that its significance is limited to the historical period of its emergence. I also prefer "traditional" to "modern" because the modern notion of the ego itself had a long prehistory, a prehistory that set the context for its formulation and is essential background for its proper understanding. Descartes's conception of the soul was radically new in its time. Nevertheless, the ways in which it departed from the past are best understood in contrast to what it still had in common with accounts of the soul that preceded it.

The task of the present chapter is to introduce the traditional notion of the ego by setting forth a brief exposition of Descartes's conception of the soul. The best way to begin is to explain why Descartes's conception of the soul was daringly and controversially new in its time. Briefly stated, Descartes's conception stood out because it broke away from the long-prevailing (premodern) conception of the soul in the following two major ways: (1) it disjoined the soul from the body, and (2) it markedly reduced the functions of the soul. It disjoined the soul from the body by restricting it to the sphere of interior consciousness. Correspondingly, it reduced the functions of the soul by ridding it of biological functions and limiting it to the rational function of thinking (explained in the next paragraph). For

Descartes's contemporaries, this exclusively interior and rational soul stood in stark contrast to the soul as it had been conceived for centuries, not only by philosophers but also by the Catholic Church, namely, as a principle not only of rational but also of bodily life. According to this premodern conception, the soul is not only that which thinks but also that which works within the body to animate it and regulate its growth and functioning.

The reasons Descartes disjoined the soul from the body, thus ridding it of biological functions, and the theological issues that were raised by this decisive break from the premodern conception of the soul are explored in the next chapter. Here we need to explain what Descartes meant in saying that thinking is the only function of the soul. In *Meditations on First Philosophy,* Descartes said, "I am a thing that thinks: that is, a thing that doubts, affirms, denies, understands a few things, . . . is willing, is unwilling, and also which imagines and has sensory perceptions."[1] As is clear from this famous passage, Descartes understood thinking in a widely inclusive way. To think, for Descartes, is simply to be conscious, whether in a passive (experiencing or perceiving) way or an active (will-initiated) way. One thinks when one passively experiences what is presented to consciousness from sources within or beyond consciousness, for example, when one experiences ideas, mental images, feelings, desires, bodily urges, bodily sensations, or sense impressions. One also thinks when one actively performs will-initiated actions, whether cognitive actions such as doubting, affirming, and denying (along with analyzing, combining, inferring, and so forth) or practical actions aimed at self-control or achieving goals in the world.

With thinking understood in this inclusive way, we can say that the soul, for Descartes, as that which has thinking as its only function, is both an experiencing subject and an agency. It is both a subject that experiences psychomental and physical phenomena and an agency that, by exercising will, performs cognitive and practical functions. More precisely, the soul is this subject and agency, this thinker, *together with all its thoughts,* which is to say, together with all the experiences it has as subject of consciousness and all the actions it performs as executive agency of consciousness.

Any exposition of Descartes's conception of the soul faces terminological difficulties. Descartes was attempting to express what are essentially modern ideas at a time when the Latin and French in which he wrote were not suited to the task. For this reason he had to make do with new constructions, such as "thing that thinks" (Latin: *res cogitans;* French: *chose qui pense*), or with terms that did not yet have their modern meanings, such as "ego" (Latin: *ego,* meaning I or self; French: *je*), or with terms that were laden with misleading inherited meanings, such as "soul" (Latin: *anima;* French: *âme*).

Descartes does use the Latin *ego* to refer to the thing that thinks, but in doing so he assigns a new referent to an old term. In *Meditations,* after concluding that "this proposition, *I am [ego sum], I exist [ego existo],* is necessarily true whenever it is put forward by me or conceived in my mind," he goes on to say that he does not know what this "I" is. After eliminating familiar possibilities (a man, a body, perhaps a soul of wind, fire, or ether), he concludes that this "I" is only a thing that thinks.[2] In thus assigning a new referent to an old term, Descartes initiated a transformation that led to the usage of the old term in an essentially new way, as a term that began to mean not only "I, this human person" but also, especially in philosophical and psychological texts, "I, this interior subject and executive agency of consciousness."

The term that Descartes uses that presents the most difficulty is "soul." Descartes uses this term—along with "mind" (Latin: *mens;* French: *esprit*)—inclusively to refer not only to the thing that thinks (along with its experiences and actions) but also to the interior space within which, he thought, the thing that thinks resides (and within which, he thought, its experiences and actions occur). Our term "consciousness" came to replace "soul" in this usage. For us, the ego is the interior subject and executive agency *of consciousness,* not of the soul. Keeping these meanings in mind, the problem for Descartes in using "soul" was that, as we have noted, that term had long been used to refer to a bodily soul that performs not only rational but also biological functions. Descartes says,

> I . . . have said that the term "soul," when it is used to refer to both these [rational and biological] principles is ambiguous. . . . [The] term must be understood to apply only to the principle in virtue of which we think; and to avoid ambiguity I have as far as possible used the term "mind" for this. For I consider the mind not as a part of the soul but as the thinking soul in its entirety.[3]

The inherited bodily, biological connotation of "soul" was a frustration for Descartes and was the reason he preferred "mind" to "soul," even though of necessity he used both.

Given the close correspondences between Descartes's "thing that thinks" and "ego" and Descartes's "soul" or "mind" and "consciousness," I take the liberty in the ensuing exposition of Descartes's conception of the soul of frequently substituting the latter terms for Descartes's terms. When discussing quoted passages from Descartes, I use his terms, but otherwise I most often substitute "ego" for "thing that thinks" and "consciousness" for "soul" or "mind." The reader can reverse this substitution, going back to Descartes's terms, should that be helpful in clarifying my exposition at any point. This shifting back and forth between terms is inconvenient, but it is to be expected in discussing a philosopher whose thought reached into the future but whose language was rooted in the past.

The exposition of Descartes's conception of the soul in this chapter is divided into two sections. The first section begins by setting forth Descartes's view that the ego, as a thing that thinks, is an incorporeal substance. It then proceeds to formulate six ideas that are implied by this view or that came to be closely associated with it. The second section of the chapter presents a brief inventory of the soul (or consciousness) as Descartes conceived it. The inventory sets forth Descartes's account of the ego as the subject and executive agency of consciousness, focusing specifically on the ego's two principal faculties, three principal types of ideas, two principal types of actions, and two principal types of passions. The inventory also sets forth Descartes's account of the extent to which the ego is in control of consciousness, focusing especially on the extent to which the ego is in control of its actions and its two principal types of passions.

The Ego Is an Incorporeal Substance

According to Descartes, finite or created things are of two types: egos (thinkers with their thoughts) and bodies. Descartes believed that both these types of things are substances, where a substance is a thing that is self-subsistent, capable of existing on its own, independently of other things. Finite substances do depend on God for their existence, according to Descartes. However, as substances, they are self-subsistent in the sense of not depending on any other finite things for their existence.[4]

In being self-subsistent, egos and bodies support attributes in existence. "Attribute" is to be understood widely as including anything that can be predicated of a substance, such as powers and functions, properties and qualities, and states and modes. Descartes held that egos, as substances, are incorporeal (unextended, indivisible) in nature, whereas bodies are material (extended, divisible) in nature. Moreover, according to Descartes, egos and bodies each have an essential or defining attribute. The essential attribute of egos is thinking (in the inclusive sense, already explained); the essential attribute of bodies is extension. Descartes said, "Admittedly I conceive of myself as a thing that thinks and is not extended, whereas I conceive of the stone as a thing that is extended and does not think, so that the two conceptions differ enormously; but they seem to agree with respect to the classification 'substance.'"[5]

In Descartes's terminology, the essential attributes of egos and bodies have many different "modes," which are ways in which their attributes appear. The modes of thinking, the essential attribute of egos, are all the different kinds of thoughts that egos think, whether passively, only by experiencing them (ideas, mental images, feelings, desires, bodily urges, bodily sensations, sense impressions), or actively, by exercising will and thus initiating them (intentional actions of cognitive and practical sorts). The essential attribute of egos does not change, only the modes in which that attribute appears change. As for bodies, their modes, the ways in which the essential attribute extension appears, are length, depth, breadth, shape, position, arrangement, and motion. As with egos, bodies undergo change in the modes in which their essential attribute appears but not in that attribute itself.

It is one of Descartes's signature views that the ego, as a substance, is an *incorporeal* substance, a substance without matter or extension that can in principle exist apart from the human body, which is a material substance. Descartes believed that the ego is paired with a human body during life and depends on it for interacting with the material world but can, and indeed does, continue to exist on its own after the death of the body. Descartes, as a Christian, believed that the ego survives the death of the body and continues to exist in a disincarnate state until the time of the Last Judgment, when, according to Christian doctrine, the body is resurrected. The view that the ego—or, more widely, the soul—is an incorporeal substance that, as such, can in principle exist apart from the body can in the West be traced as far back as the Orphics, Pythagoreans, and Plato. Nevertheless, owing to Descartes's influential formulation of the view, it is most often referred to as "Cartesian dualism."

The idea that the ego is an incorporeal substance is the most controversial idea associated with Descartes's conception of the ego and, therefore, with the traditional notion of the ego. Following Descartes, some philosophers, most notably David Hume, argued that the traditional notion of the ego is untenable because it presupposes this idea, whereas others, most notably Immanuel Kant, argued that the traditional notion *is* tenable but only because it can be reconceived without the idea. The arguments of Hume and Kant are discussed in chapter 3. Here the purpose is more fully to explicate Descartes's idea that the ego is an incorporeal substance. To this end, we briefly set forth six views that were thought, either by Descartes or by those who followed him, to be implied by or otherwise closely associated with the idea that the ego is an incorporeal substance. After Descartes, these six views came to play prominent roles in shaping the traditional notion of the ego.

1. THE EGO IS THE UNIFIER OF CONSCIOUSNESS

Descartes said, "For when I consider the mind, or myself in so far as I am merely a thinking thing, I am unable to distinguish any parts within myself; I understand myself to be something quite single and complete."[6] He also said that the ego is necessarily a unity because we are unable "to conceive of half or a third of a soul. . . ."[7] According to Descartes, the ego is ontologically unitary because, unlike extended (material) substances, it is without parts into which it might be divided. The ego, as an unextended (incorporeal) substance, is inherently "simple." It is something that either exists unitarily or does not exist at all. Given this ontological unity of the ego, it follows that it is the ego that gives unity to thinking or to consciousness. To be the consciousness of one incorporeal substance is to be one consciousness.

Descartes argued that the ego is not only ontologically but also functionally indivisible and, therefore, unitary. As explained in the next chapter, Descartes argued that the ego cannot be divided into functional parts because, unlike the premodern soul, which has both rational and biological functions, it has only one function, the rational function of thinking. This functional indivisibility of the ego, along with its ontological indivisibility, is the basis of the unity of consciousness. Consciousness is the consciousness *of* an indivisibly unitary substance that has only one, indivisible, function: to think.

2. THE EGO IS ALWAYS WHOLE OR COMPLETE

For Descartes, the idea that the ego is whole or complete is the flip side of the idea that it is inherently unitary: that which is ontologically and functionally indivisible and, therefore, unitary must be ontologically and functionally whole or complete. As an incorporeal substance, Descartes said, the ego is "something single and *complete*" (emphasis added). Moreover, as an incorporeal substance the only function of which is to think, the ego is in no danger of losing any of its functions and thus becoming incomplete upon death. For Descartes, although the ego can be more or less alert as the subject of consciousness and more or less active as the executive agency of consciousness, it can never be more or less an ego. It is always indivisible and, therefore, whole, both as an incorporeal substance and as a thing the only function of which is to think.

3. THE EGO IS THE OWNER OF CONSCIOUSNESS

The ego relates to consciousness in a possessive way, as if the consciousness of which it is the subject and executive agency belongs to it and to it alone. That the ego thus plays the role of owner of consciousness is implied by Descartes's view that the ego is an incorporeal substance of which thinking or consciousness is an attribute. Attributes inhere in and thus *belong to* the substances that support them in existence. The size and shape of a stone belong to the stone as "its" size and shape, as, too, does the stone's extension generally, of which size and shape are modes. Correspondingly, the thoughts, the experiences and actions, of an ego belong to the ego as "its" thoughts, as, too, does the ego's thinking or consciousness generally, of which the various types of thoughts are modes. Generally, Descartes's view that the ego is an incorporeal substance implies that the ego is not only that which unifies consciousness but also that which owns consciousness, that which makes consciousness *someone's* consciousness.

4. THE EGO IS A NECESSARY BASIS OF CONSCIOUSNESS

Because they are supported in existence by substances, attributes necessarily presuppose substances. Descartes says, "Thus, if we perceive the presence of some attribute, we can infer that there must also be present an existing thing or substance to which it may be attributed."[8] Accordingly, since thinking, according to Descartes, is an attribute, it follows that there must be a thing or substance to which thinking, and thereby all its modes, can be attributed. Thinking thus requires a substantial thinker, consciousness a substantial ego.[9] Otherwise stated, the ego is a necessary basis of consciousness.

5. THE EGO REMAINS PERMANENT THROUGH CHANGES IN CONSCIOUSNESS

Descartes's view that the ego is an incorporeal substance implies not only that the ego is a necessary basis of consciousness because it supports consciousness in existence but also that the ego remains permanent (uninterrupted in its existence) as particular states of consciousness, particular thoughts, come and go. Ever since Aristotle, it has been part of the meaning of "substance" that a substance is not only something that supports the existence of attributes—of all kinds, whether essential or not—but also something that remains uninterruptedly the same thing as the attributes it supports change. Change, according to this standard view, is change of something that is permanent relative to the changes it undergoes. Descartes, in inheriting the Aristotelian idea of substance, inherited with it the idea of the permanence of a substance relative to its changing attributes.

6. The ego has privileged and full access to itself and, therefore, can in principle know itself completely simply by turning its attention inward

According to Descartes, the ego, as an incorporeal substance, is an interior subject that can know everything about itself simply by looking within its own consciousness. It can know the fact of its existence as a thinking being by direct intuition, in the very act of thinking about it: "I think, therefore I am." It can also, Descartes believed, know the nature of its existence—that it is an incorporeal substance—by direct intuition. Descartes had a "clear and distinct idea" (to be explained) that, as a thinking thing or ego, he was something unextended, indivisible, and, therefore, immaterial, which is to say, an incorporeal substance. Finally, Descartes believed that the ego is able introspectively to know all its thoughts, everything it experiences and does. He says,

> As to the fact that there can be nothing in the mind, in so far as it is a thinking thing, of which it is not aware, this seems to me to be self-evident. . . . If it [something in the mind] were not a thought or dependent on a thought it would not belong to the mind *qua* thinking thing; and we cannot have any thought of which we are not aware at the very moment when it is in us.[10]

In these ways, by direct intuition and introspection, the ego has privileged and full access to itself and, therefore, can in principle know itself completely as an incorporeal thing that thinks. The ego has no need to look beyond its own consciousness or to depend on other consciousnesses to know itself completely as an ego-centered consciousness.

Having set forth Descartes's idea that the ego is an incorporeal substance and six views that came to be closely associated with that idea, we can now turn to our inventory of the soul as Descartes conceived it.

An Inventory of the Cartesian Soul

The most efficient way to present Descartes's conception of the soul is by doing a brief inventory of the principal kinds of faculties, ideas, actions, and passions that either belong to the soul inherently (faculties, some ideas) or that are characteristic of the soul in its agency (basic kinds of will-initiated actions) or that arise or occur within the soul as effects of outer causes (many ideas, almost all passions). Table 1.1 presents such an inventory in summary, preview form.

FACULTIES—INTELLECT AND WILL

Let us begin with the ego's two chief faculties, the intellect and the will. According to Descartes, the intellect is the ego's faculty of perception. He says, "All modes of thinking that we experience within ourselves can be brought under two general headings: perception, or the operation of the intellect, and volition, or the operation of the will. Sensory perception, imagination and pure understanding are simply various modes of perception."[11] The intellect, therefore, is the faculty of perception in the widest sense, since it is the intellect that perceives or intuits both purely intelligible ideas (pure understanding) and actual or possible matters of fact in the world (sense perception, imagination). As a faculty of perception, the intellect is passive, according to Descartes. In perceiving ideas or facts, it does nothing to them; rather, it simply "sees" them.

However, in passively perceiving ideas and matters of facts, the intellect sees them not only in their particularity but also in their meaning, as particulars that convey truths, whether clearly and distinctly or obscurely. For example, in the famous passage in *Meditations* in which Descartes discusses the piece of wax, he states that it is the intellect that discerns the self-evident truth that the malleable wax, as an extended thing, can in principle assume innumerable shapes.[12] The intellect is thus the faculty of *intelligent* perception, a faculty that, in perceiving, cognizes truths, whether, again, clearly and distinctly or only obscurely. Finally, the intellect, like the ego of which it is a faculty, is incorporeal. Although it depends on the body

Table 1.1. The Ego and Its Faculties, Ideas, Actions, and Passions

Ego		
Incorporeal substance that experiences what arises within or is presented to consciousness and that performs what Descartes calls "actions of the soul" or "volitions" (cognitive and practical functions)		
Faculties (or powers)		
Intellect	*Will*	
Faculty by which the ego perceives both rational truths and actual or imagined empirical states of affairs	Power by which the ego performs actions	
Thoughts		
Without Material Causes	With Material Causes	
Innate and Invented Ideas	*Adventitious Ideas*	
Innate: ideas deriving from within the soul or consciousness rather than from the external world *Invented:* ideas that the ego actively constructs from other ideas	Ideas derived from and representing empirical states of affairs as they are presented to the ego through sense perception or bodily sensation	
Actions of the Soul (resulting from ego's exercise of will)	*Passions of the Soul* (resulting from the movement of animal spirits in the nervous system and brain)	
Actions that terminate in the body: actions by the ego that lead to bodily movement or to changes in the external world *Actions that terminate in the soul:* actions by the ego that are performed on contents of consciousness, such as ideas, mental images, feelings, and desires	*Passions that refer to the body:* bodily urges, sensations, and sense impressions *Passions that refer to the soul:* feelings, desires, and spontaneously arising mental images *Exception:* actions of the soul as experienced by the ego in the act of performing them, which, although experienced by the ego as passions, are caused by the incorporeal ego itself rather than by the movement of animal spirits in the nervous system and brain	

for perceiving and imagining material things, it does not depend on the body for its existence; and it does not depend on the body for perceiving purely intelligible ideas (pure understanding).

Whereas the intellect is a passive faculty, the will is an active power. It is the power by which the soul performs actions, whether of cognitive or practical sorts. Like the intellect, the will is incorporeal. Although material things are within the range of its influence, it does not depend on material things, including the human body, for its existence or for its purely incorporeal functioning. That Descartes held these general views about the will is clear enough. However, the remainder of his views on the will are difficult to sort through. Much of the difficulty, I suggest, derives from Descartes's allegiance to conflicting tenets of Christianity and Stoicism.

Descartes, a Catholic, always stressed that his scientific and philosophical views conformed to Church doctrine. Among such doctrines was the Church's conception of the will. We trace the antecedents and the development of this conception—here referred to simply as the "Christian conception of the will"—in the next chapter. For present purposes, it suffices to say that this conception is based on two principal defining ideas. The first is that the will has a dual nature, being both an elective and a desiderative power, a power that is set in motion both electively, by autonomous or self-initiated choice, and desideratively, by being drawn to whatever the intellect discerns to be good. The second defining idea is that the elective component of the will was damaged by original sin. Original sin afflicted humans with an attraction to sin and thus damaged the elective will by rendering it unable to avoid sin and thus unable on its own to choose what is in our best interest. According to Christianity, such a damaged or sin-prone will is passed down hereditarily, generation after generation, from Adam and Eve to all their progeny.

According to the first of these ideas, the will is set in motion both by the soul itself, which sets the will in motion as an agency or efficient cause (the elective component of the will), and by whatever object or aim the intellect discerns to be good, which sets the will in motion as an attractor or telic cause (the desiderative component of the will). Because, according to Christianity, our highest good is restored intimacy with of God, leading ultimately to the beatific vision, it follows that the will as a desiderative power is inherently drawn to and set in motion by God to the extent that the intellect can discern God to be our highest good. According to the Christian conception, the will is both an active and a passive power. It is active insofar as it is set in motion by the soul, whose power it is; and it is passive insofar as it is set in motion by whatever the intellect discerns to be good.

According to the second defining idea of the Christian conception of the will, the elective will was so damaged by original sin that we are powerless by its means alone to achieve our highest good, a repaired, intimate relationship with God. To repair our relationship with God, we must cease being attracted to sin; and according to Christianity, we are powerless on our own to overcome this inherited consequence of original sin. Luther and Calvin disagreed with the Catholic Church on the degree of the elective will's powerlessness in this regard. They held that the elective will is completely in bondage to sin such that only God-conferred faith and not anything the elective will can do, can lead to salvation. In contrast, the Catholic Church holds that, after baptism, the elective will, although still damaged, is enabled by grace to cooperate with grace in working to weaken the power of sin and thus to improve the spiritual character of the soul. This difference notwithstanding, the point remains that, according to Christianity generally, the elective will was damaged by original sin in such a way that we are powerless by its means alone to achieve our highest good.

Most of Descartes's statements about the will agree with the first of the two Christian ideas just set forth. Regarding the first of these ideas, Descartes, in *Meditations*, describes the will as both an elective and desiderative power. He describes it as the "faculty of choice" or "freedom of the will," the power "to do or not do something (that is, to affirm or deny, pursue or avoid)."[13] The will is thus set in motion electively by the ego itself, acting as autonomous agent. However, in the "Objections and Replies" accompanying *Meditations*, Descartes makes it clear that he also holds that the will is inherently inclined toward the good and, therefore, is also set in motion by whatever the intellect deems to be good. He says,

> The will of a thinking thing is drawn voluntarily and freely . . . , but nevertheless inevitably towards a clearly known good.[14]

> But as for man, since he finds that the nature of all goodness and truth is already determined by God, and his will cannot tend towards anything else, it is evident that he will embrace what is good and true all the more willingly, and hence more freely, in proportion as he sees it more clearly.[15]

The will is thus set in motion not only by the ego itself, acting as agent or efficient cause, but also by things discerned by the intellect to be good, acting as attractors or telic causes, where the ultimate attractor or telic cause of the will's motion is God. Clearly, the evidence indicates that Descartes believed, at least in *Meditations*—although perhaps not in his later work[16]—that the will has a dual, elective-desiderative, nature.

Although it is thus clear that Descartes agreed with the Christian conception of the will on the point of the will's dual nature, it is not at all clear that he agreed with the Christian conception on the point of the damage caused to the elective side of the will by original sin. He certainly did not deny this latter view. To do so would have been to adopt the view of Pelagius, whose teaching was rebuked by Saint Augustine and condemned by the Church. Nevertheless, many of the things Descartes says about the will indicate that he believed that the elective will is not damaged in such a way as to need God's help to achieve our highest good. Rather, in these statements, he held that our highest good can be achieved by the elective will alone.

That the elective will on its own can achieve our highest good is clearly indicated in Descartes's (cautious, understated) recommendation of Stoicism as a moral philosophy. Stoicism holds that by our own efforts we can achieve happiness, understood as mastery of the passions and serene peace of mind. Descartes recommends just this view in *Discourse on Method*, again in his correspondence with Princess Elisabeth of Bohemia in 1645, and again in his last philosophical work, *Passions of the Soul*.[17] As we shall see, although Descartes disagreed with the Stoics on the function of the passions and how they should be controlled, he otherwise agreed with the major tenets of Stoic moral philosophy.

The question arises how Descartes could possibly have been both a Christian and a Stoic and, specifically, how he could have held, at least implicitly, a conception of the will that reflects both the Christian view that we are dependent on God's grace for our highest good (restored intimacy with God) and the Stoic view that we are dependent only on ourselves for our highest good (self-controlled serenity).[18] The main sticking point is the Christian conception of the damaged character of the fallen will, according to which we are unable on our own, by exercise of elective will, to do what our highest good requires.

The following passage from *Meditations* provides a possible clue to Descartes's thinking.

> I should like to pause here and spend some time in the contemplation of God; to reflect on his attributes and to gaze with wonder and adoration on the beauty of his immense light, so far as the eye of my darkened intellect can bear it. For just as

we believe through faith that the supreme happiness of the next life consists solely in the contemplation of the divine majesty, so experience tells us that this same contemplation, albeit much less perfect, enables us to know the greatest joy of which we are capable in this life.[19]

This passage suggests that human existence unfolds through two markedly different stages, this life and the afterlife, where the greatest joy of this life, as Descartes consistently described it, is a serene peace of mind based on reason and achieved by a person's own efforts (Stoicism), and where the supreme happiness of the afterlife is a contemplation of the divine majesty based on faith and made possible by grace (Christianity). Corresponding to these two, Stoic and Christian, stages of human existence are, implicitly, two conceptions of the will, one a conception derived from Stoic views, according to which the will as an elective power can achieve the highest good of this life; and the other a conception inherited from Christianity, according to which the will as an elective power is damaged and, therefore, stands in the way of achieving the highest good of the afterlife, needing God's grace for this ultimate end to be realized.

This division of human existence into temporal and eternal stages might have been Descartes's way of separating from each other two otherwise conflicting conceptions of the will (and of our highest good or happiness). Learning from Galileo's experience, Descartes was always on guard to avoid trouble with Church authorities. This caution led him to suppress publication of his early book *The World*, which challenged the Aristotelian physics and cosmology then accepted by the Church. It might also have led him to understate his Stoicism and disguise conflicts between his Stoic views and Church doctrine on the will. We return to the topic of Descartes's conception of the will later in this chapter and again in the next chapter.

IDEAS—INNATE, ADVENTITIOUS, INVENTED

Continuing our inventory of the Cartesian soul, we now turn from the ego and its faculties to the ego's thoughts, beginning with "ideas." As table 1.1 indicates, Descartes divided ideas into three types, innate, adventitious, and invented. According to Descartes, innate ideas are those that are inherent to consciousness and arise entirely from within it rather than being formed within consciousness as effects of external causes. Among innate ideas, Descartes gave primary attention to purely intellectual ideas such as the idea of

God, the basic ideas of mathematics, and the ideas of minds and bodies as opposite types of substances. Descartes focused primarily on innate ideas like these because, as we shall see, he believed they are clear and distinct and, as such, are sources of knowledge in the highest and strictest sense.[20] In contrast to innate ideas, adventitious ideas are those that derive from external causes affecting the senses. These ideas are caused by and represent material things or matters of fact. Examples of adventitious ideas are the idea that the sun is spherical and hot, the idea that birds have two legs and two wings, the idea that horses have four legs and no wings, and the idea that sugar tastes sweet. Finally, invented ideas are those that have been constructed by the ego by combining two or more ideas to form a compound idea. Examples of invented ideas cited by Descartes are those of a siren, a hippogriff, a winged horse, a triangle inscribed in a square, and the idea that the sun is much larger than it appears.[21]

Descartes holds that innate and adventitious ideas are passively perceived by the intellect. He makes this point by contrasting the passive perception of ideas with active willing and by comparing the intellect's passivity in perceiving ideas to the passivity of a piece of wax in being imprinted with a seal.[22] When the ego perceives an innate or adventitious idea, the idea presents itself to the ego as having already been formed by a source beyond the ego, whether by God in creating our minds (purely intellectual innate ideas) or by the material world in affecting our senses and, thereby, our minds (adventitious ideas). The ego is unable in any way to modify how innate and adventitious ideas are perceived by the intellect. When the intellect perceives the innate idea that bodies are extended, it is unable to perceive—or imagine or believe—otherwise. Similarly, when the intellect perceives the adventitious idea that the sun is spherical and hot, it is unable to perceive—although it can imagine and, were it given sufficient evidence to the contrary, believe—otherwise.

According to Descartes, ideas can be divided not only according to the sources from which they derive, the soul or the material world, but also according to how well they are formed and how adequately they convey truths, whether rational or empirical. Descartes held that ideas are well formed when they are clear and distinct, which is to say, when they are forcefully manifested and unambiguously set apart from other ideas.[23] Oppositely, he held that ideas are not well formed to the extent that, lacking clarity or distinctness, they are obscure, which is to say, to the extent that they are faint or indistinguishable from other ideas. In turn, he held that ideas are fully adequate in conveying truths only when they do so self-evidently and with certainty, which is the case only with clear and distinct ideas. Oppositely, he held that ideas are less than fully adequate in conveying truths when they fall short of being self-evident and, therefore, cannot be known with certainty, which is the case with all ideas that are at least to some degree obscure.

Using these distinctions, Descartes held that our innate ideas of God and mathematics and of minds and bodies are clear and distinct. These ideas, which arise from within consciousness and present themselves to the intellect forcefully and unambiguously, are altogether without obscurity and, therefore, are self-evident and knowable with certainty. In being clear and distinct, these ideas convey truths that are so illuminated by an interior intelligible light—which Descartes called the "natural light"—that they cannot be doubted. Descartes was a rationalist whose two chief concerns were whether we can know anything of a nontrivial sort with complete certainty and, if so, what sort or sorts of cognition can provide us with such knowledge. His conclusion was that we *can* know basic truths about God and mathematics and about minds and bodies with complete certainty and that the primary sort of cognition that provides us with such knowledge is the intellect's perception, aided by the natural light, of clear and distinct innate ideas.

The knowledge of the world we obtain through sense perception differs greatly from the knowledge we obtain from clear and distinct ideas. Factual knowledge of the world is based on adventitious ideas, all of which, according to Descartes, are obscure at least to some degree and, therefore, inadequate at least to some extent in conveying truths about the facts they represent. Descartes believed that adventitious ideas for this reason reveal matters of facts only uncertainly and can be false. Recall the idea that the sun is much larger than it appears, which Descartes classified as an invented idea. This idea is counterintuitive, since it contradicts the adventitious idea we receive through sense perception, according to which the sun is spherical and hot but small. Nevertheless, we are justified in believing that the sun is much larger than it appears because there is a line of scientific reasoning that, by bringing mathematical ideas to bear upon observations and measurements of distances, leads to this conclusion as a probable, although not indubitable, truth. Many adventitious ideas can thus be shown to be inadequate as representations, and for this reason we are often justified in believing otherwise than they indicate.

ACTIONS AND PASSIONS OF THE SOUL

Moving forward with our inventory, we can now turn to Descartes's distinction, set forth in *Passions of the Soul*, between actions and passions of the soul. In their most general nature, Descartes says, actions of the soul are "volitions," by which he means actions that issue from the ego's elective exercise of the will. Actions of the soul thus include all actions that the ego as an agency intentionally performs, whatever the objects or aims of the actions might be. In contrast, passions of the soul, except for one type, are passively experienced inner effects of material causes, to wit, feelings, desires, spontaneously arising mental images, bodily urges, bodily sensations, and sense impressions.[24] According to Descartes, actions of the soul are initiated entirely by the incorporeal ego by exercise of will and, therefore, are influenced by the passions only indirectly, whereas (most) passions of the soul are entirely the effects of material causes and, therefore, are influenced by the ego's actions only indirectly. More on this point later.

Descartes divides actions of the soul into two types, those that "terminate in the body" and those that "terminate in the soul." Actions that terminate in the body are those that move bodily parts or limbs and, in doing so, initiate actions in the world. These actions are volitions not only in the wider sense of issuing from the exercise of will but also in the narrower, practical, sense of seeking to effect changes in things, in this case changes to the body's rest or motion or changes to states of affairs in the world. Actions that terminate in the body correspond to one of two main types of what we have called the ego's practical functions. They represent the ego's actions insofar as they have consequences and effect changes in the material world.

In contrast to actions that terminate in the body, actions that terminate in the soul are those that occur when we "apply our mind to some object which is not material."[25] For Descartes, such objects include ideas, mental images, and the passions. Actions of the soul that operate on ideas or mental images are volitions of a cognitive sort, corresponding to what we have called the ego's cognitive functions (more on these actions momentarily). In contrast, actions of the soul that operate on the passions, like those that terminate in the body, are volitions in the narrower, practical, sense of seeking to effect changes in things, in this case changes in the passions they operate on, for example, by cultivating, regulating, or suppressing them. Actions of the soul that operate on the passions are the second of the two main types of what we have called the ego's practical functions.

Together, actions of the soul that terminate in the body and actions of the soul that terminate in the soul correspond to what we have called the ego's executive functions, with actions that operate on ideas and mental images corresponding to the ego's cognitive executive functions and actions that operate on the body and on the passions corresponding to the ego's practical executive functions. Descartes's terminology differs from ours. Nevertheless, it gives unmistakable expression to the modern understanding of the ego as an executive agency that performs cognitive and practical functions.

Actions of the soul that, terminating in the soul, operate on ideas or mental images deserve special attention because they play a more important role in Descartes's account of human knowledge than is generally understood. Unfortunately, Descartes gave less prominent attention to active forms of cognition than he did to the intellect's (passive) perception of innate and adventitious ideas. Nevertheless, he still had a good deal to say about cognition in which the ego plays an active role. We have already discussed his account of invented ideas, which are ideas created by actively combining two or more ideas. Such a joining of ideas to form compound ideas and the reverse, the analysis of compound ideas into their simpler components, are examples of cognitive functions actively performed by the ego. Another example is deductive reasoning, to which Descartes devoted considerable attention in *Rules for the Direction of the Mind*. According to Descartes, deduction is a kind of reasoning that, when used in conjunction with knowledge of clear and distinct ideas, can draw out the implications of the indubitable truths revealed by these ideas without, if the deduction is done properly, any loss of certainty.

In *Rules* and elsewhere Descartes also acknowledged that active scientific reasoning, by applying principles perceived with certainty by the intellect to premises based on sense perception, can proceed logically from such premises to highly probable, although not completely certain, conclusions about unperceived matters of fact.[26] Additionally, Descartes speaks of the ego as actively performing cognitive functions when it fixes its attention on selected objects, when it concentrates in such a way as to bring forth an innate idea from within the mind, when it voluntarily recalls earlier experiences, and when it actively elicits mental images.[27] In all these ways the intellect, or knowing ego, actively performs cognitive executive functions, which, in Descartes's understanding, are ways in which the ego operates on ideas, whether innate or adventitious, and on images.

Although actions of the soul that terminate in the body (bodily movement, pursuit of worldly goals) and actions of the soul that terminate in the soul (active cognition, regulation of the passions) focus on different things for different purposes, they are alike, according to Descartes, in being actions over which the ego has direct and complete control. He says, "Of the two kinds of thought I have distinguished in the soul—the first its actions . . . , and the second its passions . . .—the former are absolutely within its power and can be changed only indirectly by the body."[28] Since actions of the soul are volitions, ways in which the ego exercises the will, it follows from the statement that actions of the soul are absolutely in the ego's power that the ego has absolute control of the will. Although the will can be swayed "indirectly by the body," that is, by bodily passions, it is not set in motion by the body or the passions the body stirs. The ego alone has direct and complete control of the will. For this reason, passions, even very strong ones, are unable to set the will in motion except by persuading the ego to do their bidding. Passions can strongly influence the ego, but they can never compel it to set the will in motion in agreement with their promptings.

Descartes's statement that the soul or ego has absolute control of the will has an important and surprising implication, that the will has no desiderative component. If it is the ego alone that sets the will in motion, it follows that perceived goods cannot be causes of the will's motion, no matter how much indirect sway desire for such goods might have on the ego. This implication is surprising because it seems to be at odds with the account of the will set forth in *Meditations* in 1641. As we have seen, according to that account, the will is set in motion both electively, by the ego acting as agent or efficient cause, and desideratively, by objects or goals that the intellect discerns to be good acting as attractors or telic causes. According to the account in *Meditations,* the will is inherently drawn to objects or goals that the intellect discerns to be good. These objects or goals, and not just the ego, set the will in motion.

In *Passions,* however, there is no discussion of the desiderative component of the will, and everything Descartes says about the will in that work strongly suggests that the will has no desiderative component. Against this interpretation of *Passions,* it might be argued that although Descartes clearly held that the physically caused passions have neither a direct effect on the will nor a compelling effect on the ego, he did not so clearly hold that the same is true regarding purely rational desires, those the aims of which the intellect *clearly and distinctly* perceives to be good. This argument, however, is ruled out on general grounds if we take literally Descartes's statement, in *Passions,* that "the will is by its nature so free that it can never be constrained."[29] Moreover, the argument is ruled out directly in the following passage from a letter to Denis Mesland dated February 9, 1645: "So that when a very evident reason moves us in one direction, although morally speaking we can hardly move in the contrary direction, absolutely speaking we can. For it is always open to us to hold back from pursuing a clearly known good, or from admitting a clearly perceived truth, provided we consider it a good thing to demonstrate the freedom of our will by so doing."[30] Although it would be perverse for the ego to act against a clearly known good, it is in the ego's power to do so.

It seems, therefore, that Descartes meant what he said in *Passions* when he stated that the will—or, in our terminology, the ego's control of the will—can never be constrained. Perhaps the discussion of Stoicism in his correspondence with Princess Elisabeth of Bohemia led Descartes, in working on *Passions,* to rethink his conception of the will in a way that more closely conformed to Stoic teaching. By 1649, the year *Passions* was published, he seems to have been ready publicly to defend the decisive points at issue: that only the ego sets the will in motion and that it suffers no constraints in doing so. Descartes, in *Passions,* does not explicitly reject the conception of the will set forth in *Meditations.* Nevertheless, he seems in *Passions* to have discarded the desiderative component of the will and to have arrived at an exclusively elective conception according to which the will belongs entirely to the ego as its *autonomous instrument of action.*

To avoid misunderstanding, we should note that to say that the ego has complete command of the will is not to say that the ego can always accomplish what it wills. According to Descartes, the ego *can* always accomplish what it wills so long as its actions do not require the cooperation of the body. So, for example, the ego is guaranteed success when it chooses to think about the Pythagorean theorem and then chooses to stop thinking about the Pythagorean theorem and to begin thinking about God's omniscience instead. However, there is no guarantee that the ego will accomplish what it wills when the cooperation of the body is required, as is the case not only with actions that terminate in the body but also with actions that, terminating in the soul, seek to control the passions, which, again, are effects of material causes. However, although the ego for these reasons frequently lacks the power to accomplish what it wills, it does have complete control over the act of willing. Moreover, it has complete control over the success of its willed actions up to the point at which they require the cooperation of the body.

Corresponding to his division of actions of the soul into two types, those that terminate in the body and those that terminate in the soul, Descartes divides the passions of the soul into two types, those that "refer to the body" and those that "refer to the soul." Passions that refer to the body are bodily urges, bodily sensations, and sense impressions. About these passions, Descartes notes that they represent either states of the body (bodily urges, bodily sensations) or, based on information received through the senses, objects or states of affairs in the material world (sense impressions). He also notes that the material causes of these passions are ordinarily easily identified. For example, the material causes of a painful sensation of heat and an intense visual impression of flames are obvious: emissions from a fire to which I have moved too close. Finally, Descartes notes that passions that refer to the body, although passions experienced *by* the ego, are not attributed to the ego as passions *of* the ego. Instead, they are attributed to the body or to the material objects or states of affairs that are their originating causes. Passions that refer to the body are not the chief concern of *Passions,* which focuses primarily on passions that refer to the soul, which are passions in a narrower and to us more familiar sense.

Descartes includes among passions that refer to the soul feelings, desires (other than bodily urges), and spontaneously arising mental images. About these passions, Descartes notes that they are experienced exclusively within the soul rather than within any part or through any organ of the body. He also notes that the material causes of these passions are not evident. For example, the material causes of a spontaneously arising mental image of Abraham Lincoln and a concomitant feeling of admiration, unlike the material causes of the sensation of heat and the visual impression of flames, are not evident. Nevertheless, according to Descartes, passions that refer to the soul do have material, and only material, causes. The causes in his opinion are very subtle but nonetheless merely material animal spirits that, like an air or wind, flow through nerve pathways into and out of the brain. These animal spirits act as transmitters that convey information to the soul about the body and the world and that convey instructions from the soul to the body about actions that the ego has willed the body to perform, with the pineal gland serving as the locus at which this body-to-soul and soul-to-body exchange occurs. Accordingly, when the ego experiences a spontaneously arising image of Abraham Lincoln together with a feeling of admiration, that is because animal spirits are moving in nerve pathways and the brain in precisely the ways and places that produce these passions as effects. Finally, Descartes notes that passions that refer to the soul "refer" or belong to the ego not only in the sense of being passions experienced by the ego but also in the sense of being passions *of* the ego. Experienced by the ego within its own domain, consciousness, these passions give expression more to the ego's interests and values than they do to the body's state or interaction with the world.

Let us now turn to the issue of the ego's control of the passions. On this matter, Descartes says, "[passions of the soul] are absolutely dependent on the [material] actions which produce them, and can be changed by the soul only indirectly."[31] Just as passions have only an indirect influence on the ego's actions, so the ego's actions have only an indirect influence on passions. Just as passions can affect the will only through the ego, by persuading it to exercise the will, so the ego can affect passions only through the material causes that produce them, by somehow altering these causes so that they cease producing distressing passions and begin producing passions that are more agreeable to the ego. The ego, therefore, can control passions only by employing means—if there are such means—that bring about changes in the causes that produce them. Fortunately, the ego does have such means at its disposal, means by which, according to Descartes, the ego can in principle attain "absolute mastery" of the passions.[32]

Before discussing these means, we should note that Descartes, although agreeing with Stoicism for the most part, disagreed with Stoicism on the function of the passions and how they should be controlled. According to Stoicism, passions—except for a few that are of a purely rational sort, such as inner joy and wish or desire for the good—are inherently "perturbations" that trouble the soul and, therefore, that should be eliminated so that inner tranquility can be achieved. In contrast, Descartes held that passions are not inherently troubling and in fact perform positive functions because they inform us about what is helpful and what is harmful to us.[33] Because passions perform these positive functions, they should not be eliminated, Descartes held. Instead, they should be regulated in such a way as to allow them to perform their positive functions but not allow them to become so strong or persistent as to trouble the soul. According to Descartes, it is possible by such a moderating regulation of the passions to enjoy both a beneficial and conflict-free relationship with them, a relationship in which they perform life-supporting and life-protecting functions for the ego without causing the ego any significant distress.

The ego's control of passions that refer to the body, although indirect, is most often unproblematic and accomplished without difficulty. Because the causes of bodily passions are ordinarily well known and easily managed, the ego is most often able to control these passions by controlling their causes. For example, the ego can indirectly produce or remove a bodily urge to eat by fasting or consuming food; it can indirectly produce or remove a bodily sensation of heat by moving closer to or farther from a fire; and it can indirectly produce or remove a visual impression of flames by aiming its line of vision in the direction of or away from a fire. Clearly, the ego cannot produce or remove passions that refer to the body when the body, owing to illness, injury, or deprivation, is unable to cooperate. Just as clearly, the ego cannot avoid all passions that refer to the body, for the body remains a sensorium until death. Still, the ego does have a good deal of control over what bodily urges, bodily sensations, and sense impressions it experiences.

The ego in principle has even more control over passions that refer to the soul, feelings and desires in particular.[34] Control of these passion is important because they tend to exaggerate the importance of their objects or aims and, therefore, if not managed properly, can easily become too strong or persistent.[35] Should they become unruly, passions that refer to the soul can be brought under control in two ways. The first is for the ego to exercise its free, unconstrained will to resist and refuse to act on troublesome passions. The second and more transformative way to control passions that refer to the soul is to forge habits that keep them within proper limits. The ego can begin to forge such habits, Descartes observed, by changing the way it thinks about passions, for example, by thinking about them in terms of their consequences rather than only in terms of their immediately experienced phenomenal qualities.[36] This change in thinking, if sustained, affects the movement of animal spirits in the brain, which eventually respond to the ego's efforts by producing fewer distressing and increasingly more moderate passions. Descartes believed that by these two means—the exercise of will and the forging of good habits—the ego can eventually bring troublesome feelings and desires under control, transforming them so that they perform their positive functions without disquieting the mind. He said, "Even those who have the weakest souls could acquire absolute mastery over all their passions if we employed sufficient ingenuity in training and guiding them."[37]

The Ego Is the Sovereign Power of the Soul

It follows from Descartes's account of the actions and passions of the soul that the ego is the sovereign power of the soul. First, the ego has sovereignty over itself as executive agency of consciousness because it has complete command of the will and, therefore, of all actions of the soul, which is to say, of all the soul's executive functions. Nothing other than the ego, not even very strong passions, can set the will in motion. Passions can exert a great deal of influence on the ego, but the ego always has the power to resist them, even to act contrary to them, if it should so choose. Only the ego can perform actions of the soul. The ego's sovereignty over itself as the executive agency of conscious is thus absolute.

However, the ego's sovereignty extends further, for the ego also has sovereignty over the passions. To be sure, the ego often succumbs to the influence of the passions, thus strengthening their influence. Such capitulation to the passions can go so far as to make it appear as if they, and not the ego, have command of the will. However, such an appearance is contrary to fact because, again, the ego's exercise of the will is absolute, completely unconstrained. Moreover, in addition to being able to resist or even act contrary to passions, should it so choose, the ego can also forge habits that keep passions within proper limits. The ego's inability to control the passions in the direct way it controls its actions means that the ego is not omnipotent within consciousness. However, the ego's ability in principle to gain complete control of the passions indirectly means that it is nonetheless the sovereign power of the soul. It means that the ego has sovereign power not only over the actions but also over the passions of the soul.

Conclusion

The foregoing exposition of Descartes's conception of the soul as consisting of a thinker and its thoughts (experiences and actions) has identified eleven ideas that helped fashion the traditional notion of the ego. The eleven ideas are (1) that the ego is the interior subject of consciousness; (2) that the ego is an executive agency that performs cognitive and practical functions; (3) that the ego is an incorporeal substance; (4) that the ego is that which unifies consciousness; (5) that the ego is always whole or complete, always fully constituted as subject and agency of consciousness; (6) that the ego is the owner of consciousness; (7) that the ego is a necessary basis of consciousness; (8) that the ego remains permanent through changes in consciousness; (9) that the ego has privileged and full access to itself and, therefore, can in principle know itself completely simply by turning its attention inward; (10) that the ego has direct and complete control of the will and, therefore, direct and complete control of its actions, its executive functions; and (11) that the ego, by exercise of will, has only indirect but nonetheless a good deal of control—if not, as Descartes holds, complete control—of the passions.

To these eleven ideas we need to add two more, (12) that the ego is the author of its identity in the world, and (13) that the ego is gender-neutral. These ideas were not themselves explicitly part of the traditional notion of the ego. Nevertheless, they came to be associated with the traditional notion in the second half of the twentieth century, when theorists of postmodern and feminist perspectives criticized the traditional notion of the ego, with postmodernists arguing that personal identity is a social construct, not something authored by an inner ego, and with feminist theorists arguing that the traditional notion of the ego better describes men's than women's subjectivity. Ideas twelve and thirteen, and the postmodern and feminist criticisms of them, are considered in chapter 4, as part of our rethinking of the traditional notion of the ego.

Having set forth Descartes's formulation of the traditional notion of the ego, we now turn our attention to the philosophical, religious, and scientific sources from which it emerged.

Chapter 2

Before the Ego

Greek Philosophy, Christian Doctrine, and the New Physics of the Seventeenth Century

Descartes's formulation of the traditional notion of the ego derived from three principal sources, Greek philosophy (primarily Plato's and Aristotle's conceptions of the soul), Christian doctrine (primarily the Church's teachings on the soul, body, and afterlife), and the new mechanistic paradigm of seventeenth-century science (primarily its implications for biological organisms). To set the context for explaining how these sources influenced Descartes's thinking, we begin with a brief exposition of Plato's and Aristotle's conceptions of the soul followed by a short account of how the mechanistic paradigm of seventeenth-century science challenged Aristotelian natural philosophy. The Christian doctrines that influenced Descartes's formulation of the traditional notion of the ego are introduced later in the chapter, in the sections that pertain to them.

Plato and Aristotle

Premodern authors believed that the human soul differs from the souls of nonhuman animals by performing not only biological but also rational functions. Unlike the souls of nonhuman animals, the human soul cogitates, deliberates, and acts in premeditated ways. Some premodern authors, especially those who, like Saint Augustine, wrote from the perspective of contemplative spirituality, also believed that the human soul is unique by virtue of having a subjective interior into which one can withdraw to engage in self-examination, meditation, or prayer. However, in holding that the human soul differs from the souls of other animals in these ways, premodern philosophers generally held that the human soul is like the souls of other animals in performing biological functions. The most basic functions of all terrestrial souls, according to the premodern view, are to bring life to organic bodies, to guide their growth, and to keep them functioning in ways that sustain their life. For premodern philosophers, the soul is thus active within the body as the principle of bodily life.

That Plato believed that the soul is the principle of bodily life might seem surprising given that he believed that the soul's highest destiny, after many incarnations, is to exist forever completely apart from the body, as an incorporeal contemplator of eternal truths. However, notwithstanding this view, Plato did subscribe to the premodern understanding of the soul's biological functions. The primary texts expressing this view are the *Phaedo* and the *Republic*. In *Phaedo*, Plato argues that the soul is immortal not despite but rather *because* it is the principle of bodily life.[1] The argument is that the soul, as that which brings life to the body, cannot itself die. That which brings life must itself be inherently and, therefore, inextinguishably alive, which is to say, immortal. Plato's conclusion that the soul is immortal is thus based on the premise, to which he subscribed, that the soul is the principle of bodily life.

That Plato believed that the soul is the principle of bodily life is further evident in his account of the tripartite soul in the *Republic*. According to this account, the soul is organized in the same manner as society. Society, Plato held, is made up of three classes, each of which should consist of members possessing the abilities best suited for performing the distinctive function the class. The three classes are (1) a class of rulers, members of which should possess the wisdom needed to make good decision in governing society; (2) a class of auxiliaries (defenders), members of which should possess the strength and courage needed to defend society from danger; and (3) a class of workers, members of which should possess the practical (agricultural, technical) skills needed to provide amply (but not excessively) for society's material needs.

Plato believed that society, thus organized, is "just"—which is to say, properly functioning or healthy—when members of each of the classes not only possess the abilities best suited for performing the function of their class but also devote themselves exclusively to that function and thus perform an essential social function well, whether the function be governing, defending, or providing. Accordingly, a just society is one in which wise rulers devote themselves exclusively to governing and thus perform the governing function well. It is also a society in which strong and courageous auxiliaries devote themselves exclusively to defending society and thus perform the defending function well. Additionally, a just society is one in which skilled workers devote themselves exclusively to providing for society's material needs and thus perform the providing function well. In contrast, an unjust society is one in which members of any of the classes are unable or unwilling to perform their class function or seek to perform functions other than the function of their class. Such a society is not healthy; and should class functions deteriorate enough, it is in danger of disintegrating as a social organism.

Applying this account of society to the soul, Plato divided the soul into three parts, which correspond to the three classes of society. Each of these parts of the soul, Plato held, should have the same abilities and should perform the same function as the corresponding class of society. The three parts of the soul are (1) the rational part, consisting of the intellect, which, like the rulers in society, should possess wisdom; (2) the affective part, consisting of spirited feelings such as anger, pride, honor, and righteous indignation, which, like the auxiliaries in society, should possess strength and courage; and (3) the appetitive part, consisting of the bodily appetites, which, like the workers in society, should possess "practical skills," which here means the biological intelligence needed to provide for the body's needs.

According to Plato, the soul, like the state, is just or healthy when each of its parts not only possesses the abilities best suited for performing its function but also devotes itself exclusively to that function and thus performs an essential function of the soul well. Such a soul is one in which a wise intellect devotes itself exclusively to governing and thus guides the soul toward what is best for it; in which strong and courageous feelings devote themselves exclusively to defending and thus effectively protect the soul from danger; and in which "skilled" bodily appetites devote themselves exclusively to providing for bodily needs and thus sustain life and support the soul in all its functions.

Just as a society is unhealthy if its rulers, defenders, or workers are unable or unwilling to perform their proper functions or seek to perform functions other than their proper ones, so also a soul is unhealthy if the intellect, spirited feelings, or bodily appetites are unable or unwilling to perform their proper functions or seek to perform functions other than their proper ones. Continuing with the analogy, just as a seriously unhealthy society is at risk of disintegrating as a social organism, so also a seriously unhealthy human soul is at risk of disintegrating, if not entirely—since, according to Plato, the rational part of the soul, if not its other parts, is immortal—then at least as a life-conferring, body-regulating soul of a human being. A soul one or more parts of which are not performing their functions well suffers from a pathology that could lead to bodily death. A soul the intellect of which is clouded or ignorant or the feelings of which are wild or weak or the appetites of which are deficient or excessive is in danger of no longer being able to sustain the life of the body, of which it is the soul.

What stands out in Plato's account of the tripartite soul is that the human soul is not only an intellect destined after many lifetimes to leave embodied life behind but is also that which enlivens the body and invests human life with intelligence, feelings, and appetites. For Plato, the three parts of the human soul perform essential functions in bestowing and then sustaining embodied human life, the intellect performing a governing function, spirited feelings performing a defending function, and the appetites performing a providing function. Plato's account of the tripartite soul thus clearly illustrates the premodern assumption that the soul is the principle of bodily life. For Plato, embodied human life just *is* the tripartite soul's functioning within the human body.

Aristotle's conception of the soul provides an even clearer illustration of the premodern assumption under discussion. According to Aristotle, the human soul is the organizing principle—"substantial form"—by which matter is transformed into a living, biologically functioning, percipient, rational animal. Briefly stated, it is the organizing principle by which matter takes on the essential, defining characteristics of a living human being. Aristotle believed that all naturally occurring kinds of things—unlike heaps or collections of things—are brought into being by the activity of organizing principles or substantial forms, which actualize potentialities inherent in matter in such ways as to produce unified things with distinctive features, abilities, and behaviors. For example, the substantial form of an oak tree is the organizing principle that transforms matter into a hardwood tree with deeply grooved bark, lobed leaves, and acorn fruit. The substantial form of a frog is the organizing principle that transforms matter into an amphibian with four legs, protruding eyes, and strong leaping and swimming abilities. Correspondingly, according to Aristotle, the substantial form of a human being is the organizing principle that transforms matter into a rational animal. In sum, Aristotle believed that all natural things are "hylomorphic," consisting of both matter and form, where the forms by virtue of which things belong to natural species or kinds are substantial forms.

For Aristotle, the substantial forms of living things are their souls. Souls, as substantial forms, organize matter in such ways as to give living things not only their distinctive features, abilities, and behaviors but also their life. Common to all living things is a vegetative soul, which gives plants and animals their life and abilities to assimilate nutrition from the environment, to regulate biological processes, to steer growth toward maturity, and to reproduce. Common to all animals is not only this vegetative soul but also a second, sensitive, level of the soul, which gives animals sense organs, appetites, and locomotion and thus endows them with perception, desire for things perceived by the senses, and the ability to move themselves toward objects of desire. Finally, distinguishing human beings from all other animals is a third, rational, level of the soul, which gives humans an intellect and thus endows them with the power of rational thought, the ability to discover truths and deliberate about courses of action. Accordingly, all plants have a one-level vegetative soul; all animals have a two-level sensitive-vegetative soul; and only human beings have a three-level rational-sensitive-vegetative soul. Again, the human soul is the substantial form that organizes matter into human beings, into living, biologically functioning, percipient, rational animals. Clearly, for Aristotle, as for Plato, the soul is the principle of bodily life.

It is unclear whether Aristotle believed that the human soul, in being the principle of bodily life for human beings, is only this or whether he agreed with Plato that the human soul is something that at least in part can exist apart from the body after death. Generally, Aristotle opposed Plato's view that the forms or essences of things can exist apart from the material things of which they are the forms or essences. Given this opposition, it would seem to follow that Aristotle must have believed—and, indeed, he may have believed—that no part of the human soul, as the substantial form or essence of the human body, can exist apart from the human body. However, there is a famous passage in which Aristotle seems to suggest that at least one part of the human soul, that part of the rational level that brings to light fundamental truths and intelligible forms—what later came to be called the "active" or "agent" intellect—might survive the death of the body.[2]

The passage in question has been a focus of debate throughout the history of philosophy, with some arguing that Aristotle was speaking of the divine intellect, not the human, and with others arguing that Aristotle did in fact believe that at least one part of the human soul is immortal. We return to the Aristotelian idea of the active intellect later in the chapter, when we explain the difficulties that Christian philosophers faced in trying to adapt Aristotle's conception of the soul to the Christian doctrine of immortality. For present purposes it suffices to conclude that it is unclear whether Aristotle believed, as Plato did, that the souls of human beings can at least in part transcend bodily life.

Both Plato and Aristotle had a transformative influence on Christianity. Plato had the earlier influence, primarily through the work of Saint Augustine, who adapted Plato's ideas to Christian doctrine from the late fourth century through the first quarter of the fifth century. Aristotle had a later influence, primarily through the work of Saint Thomas Aquinas, who adapted Aristotle's ideas to Christian doctrine in the thirteenth century. Once translations of Aristotle's works began being produced in Europe and, especially, after Aristotle's ideas became central to the work of Albert the Great, Aquinas, and other scholastics in the thirteenth century, they were increasingly accepted not only by philosophers and scientists but also by the Roman Catholic Church. Aristotle's conception of the soul, his hylomorphic natural philosophy, and his geocentric cosmology were increasingly accepted in Europe from the thirteenth century to the beginning of the modern period.

The Beginnings of Modern Science

This preeminence of Aristotle was finally challenged in the early modern period. On grounds of mathematical parsimony, Copernicus challenged the Aristotelian geocentric cosmology (as systematized by Ptolemy in the second century CE). Drawing on a vast amount of data gathered by Tycho Brahe, Kepler challenged the Aristotelian-Ptolemaic view that celestial bodies always move in perfect circles. Using mathematics, observation, and experiment, Galileo challenged not only the Aristotelian-Ptolemaic cosmology but also Aristotelian physics, specifically its account of the motion of terrestrial bodies. Additionally, inspired by the rediscovery of classical atomism, an increasing number of philosophers and scientists proposed mechanistic theories of the natural world, thus challenging Aristotle's hylomorphic natural philosophy.

The rediscovery of Lucretius's *De rerum natura* in the fifteenth century led to the reemergence of atomistic conceptions of physical reality. These conceptions became highly influential in the first half of the seventeenth century in the work of people such as Isaac Beeckman, Sebastian Basso, and Pierre Gassendi. Descartes, although not himself an atomist, was aware of the work of atomists, especially the work of Beeckman, and adopted and further developed the mechanistic paradigm associated with atomism.[3] As a mechanist, Descartes held that everything in the material world can be explained in terms of the size, shape, arrangement, motion, and contact of merely material bodies. This mechanistic perspective led Descartes, like other advocates of the new science, to call into question the prevailing hylomorphic perspective of Aristotle, including the conception of the soul based on it.

Although Descartes's mechanistic physics is fundamentally at odds with Aristotelian natural science, Descartes himself, learning from the experience of Galileo, was cautious not to antagonize authorities by overtly challenging teachings of the Church. We noted in the last chapter that such caution led him to withhold his early work on physics, *The World,* from publication. This caution notwithstanding, Descartes let it be known, especially in correspondence but also in published writings, that he disagreed with basic ideas of Aristotle's natural philosophy, including those on substantial forms and on essential differences between kinds of matter.[4]

Descartes's physics, in explaining the world in exclusively mechanistic fashion, had no use for Aristotelian substantial forms, which in Aristotle's theory of causation are the "formal causes" of things, the organizing principles that give things their essential forms. Having no use for Aristotelian formal causes, neither did Descartes's physics have a use for Aristotelian "telic causes," the presumed natural ends toward which objects tend as they are shaped and guided in their development or movement by their substantial forms. Of the four types of causes distinguished by Aristotle, only the material and efficient (impelling) causes remain in Descartes's physics, and even these are interpreted in minimal ways. Descartes reduced all matter to the same basic type, thus implicitly rejecting the Aristotelian view of essential differences between heavy and light and between terrestrial and celestial matter; and he reduced all efficient causes to merely mechanical causes, causes working exclusively through material contact or collision.

From the Premodern Soul to the Ego of the Modern Period

With this brief review of historical background completed, we can now return to Descartes's conception of the soul to see how, for both scientific and theological reasons, he came to reject the premodern view that the soul is the principle of bodily life. To expedite the discussion, we highlight some of the Cartesian ideas identified in the last chapter, ideas that, whether explicit or only implicit in Descartes, became leading ideas of the traditional notion of the ego.

THE EGO IS THE INTERIOR SUBJECT OF CONSCIOUSNESS

In juxtaposing Descartes's idea that the soul or ego is the interior subject of consciousness with its premodern predecessor, the idea that the soul is the principle of bodily life, the primary questions that arise are (1) Why did Descartes disjoin the ego from the body and restrict its activity to the sphere of interior consciousness? and (2) Why, in doing so, did he redefine the soul not just as interior consciousness generally but as a "thinking thing" within interior consciousness, thus arriving at our ego, the subject and executive agency of consciousness? In answering these questions, it will be useful to contrast Descartes's turn to interior consciousness with Saint Augustine's turn to the interior of the soul to understand why, although similar in striking respects, these well-known "subjective turns" were more fundamentally different than they were similar.

Descartes's subjective turn is based primarily on two views, one metaphysical and the other epistemological. The metaphysical view is that the soul or mind is exclusively interior or subjective in nature. The epistemological view is that direct inspection of interior consciousness provides us with knowledge of an indubitable sort, knowledge that, in its complete certainty, can serve as the foundation for all other knowledge. In this section, we contrast Descartes and Augustine on the first of these views. Later in the chapter, we contrast them on the second view.

Striking similarities in some of Descartes's and Augustine's views have led to a debate about whether these similarities are superficial or deep, expressing minor convergences or major affinities in their views. Good cases have been made on both sides of this debate. Some similarities do seem to run deep, enough so to make Augustine look like an early Cartesian or Descartes like a late Augustinian.[5] Other similarities, however, do not run as deep as they might seem. I suggest that the similarities considered in this chapter are of this latter sort. I argue that similarities in Descartes's and Augustine's subjective turns are outweighed by greater differences and that only Descartes's subjective turn led to the modern conception of subjectivity and self-knowledge.

Augustine made his subjective turn for psychological and spiritual reasons. He focused on the interior life both because he himself had an extraordinary interior life, on which he reflected in his *Confessions,* and because he was drawn within in search of divinely illumined knowledge and a closer relationship with God. With subjectivity thus playing such an important role in his life, Augustine, more than others before him, stressed the interior side of human life. Developing a distinction found in the Pauline epistles, Augustine stressed that there is not only an "outer man" of bodily and social life but also an "inner man" of psychological and spiritual life.[6]

It is important for us to understand that Augustine, in turning to subjectivity, did not, as Descartes did, disjoin the soul from the body, thus making subjectivity the whole of the soul rather than only one side. Augustine, in turning his attention inward, did so from the standpoint of an embodied soul. He considered the inner man and the outer man to be two sides of the same soul. Additionally, the soul of which the inner man and the outer man are sides is, as he said, a soul that animates the body and empowers its senses.[7] Furthermore, as a Christian, Augustine held that the soul is inherently the soul of a specific body, a body that will be resurrected and reunited with the soul just before the Last Judgment. Finally, according to Augustine, whereas God is the "life of lives," the soul is the "life of bodies."[8] Clearly, Augustine's subjective turn did not call into question the premodern assumption that the soul is the principle of bodily life.

It was decisively otherwise with Descartes, who made his subjective turn for scientific and theological rather than for psychological and spiritual reasons, and who, given his scientific reasons, had no choice but to reject the premodern assumption that the soul is the principle of bodily life. Postponing consideration of the theological reasons for Descartes's subjective turn until later in the chapter, let us here consider the primary scientific reason for the turn.

The primary scientific reason is that Descartes, in adopting the new mechanistic paradigm for explaining the physical world, applied it not only to inanimate matter but also to organic bodies. This extension of the mechanistic paradigm to living things led Descartes to the following three conclusions: (1) that, because living things (other than human beings) are only mechanical systems, they do not need souls—Aristotelian substantial forms—to explain their aliveness, distinctive features, and abilities; (2) that plants and nonhuman animals for this reason do not have souls; and (3) that the human soul is not, as previously had been thought, active within the body performing biological functions but is rather active only within subjectivity, interior psychic space, where it performs only one function, the rational function of thinking.

Regarding the first of these consequences, Descartes's mechanistic view implied that no such thing as a soul is needed to explain how an organic body comes to life, develops, functions, or dies and that, with the exception of the human body, no such thing as a soul is needed to explain how an organic body moves or behaves. Mechanical causes, not a soul, give an organic body life; mechanical causes, not a substantial form, give an organic body its distinctive features and abilities; mechanical causes, not an indwelling organizing principle, regulate biological functions; and mechanical causes, not the deterioration or departure of a soul, bring about bodily death. Additionally, except for the human body, mechanical causes alone govern how an organic body moves or behaves. Living bodies are physical systems consisting exclusively of material parts, the size, shape, arrangement, motion, and contact of which completely explain their life, features, abilities, and, except for human bodies, their motions or behaviors.

Regarding the second consequence, it was Descartes's view that plants and nonhuman animals are nothing more than their mechanical bodies. Descartes's mechanistic account of living bodies divested plants of the vegetative soul that had been thought to govern their growth and functioning; and it divested nonhuman animals of the sensitive-vegetative soul that had been thought to govern their growth and functioning. Now, since plants and nonhuman animals were not thought to perform rational functions, the consequence of the reduction of vegetative and sensitive functions to mechanical operations was the stripping of plants and nonhuman animals of souls altogether.

Turning to the third consequence, Descartes believed that the human body, as a material substance, must, like all other organic bodies, be a mechanical system. It must, therefore, be a thing the biological functions of which are mechanical operations, operations occurring without conscious awareness or volitional intervention. Descartes makes this point clearly in *Description of the Human Body* (unfinished treatise, written between 1647 and 1648), where he said,

> It is true that we may find it hard to believe that the mere disposition of the bodily organs is sufficient to produce in us all the movements which are in no way determined by our thought. So I will now try to prove the point, and to give such a full account of the entire bodily machine that we will have no more reason to think that it is our soul which produces in it the movements which we know by experience are not controlled by our will than we have reason to think that there is a soul in a clock which makes it tell time.[9]

As a mechanical system without the need of a soul to give it life, guide its growth, or regulate its functioning, the human body is the same as any other organic body.

Descartes made this point with specific reference to the vegetative and sensitive levels of the soul in a letter sent to Henricus Regius in May, 1641, where he said,

> There is only one *soul* in human beings, the *rational soul;* for no actions can be reckoned human unless they depend on reason. The *vegetative power* and the *power of moving the body,* which are called the *vegetative* and *sensory souls* in plants and animals, exist also in human beings; but in the case of human beings they should not be called *souls,* because they are not the first principle of their actions, and they belong to a totally different genus from the *rational soul. . . .* The *vegetative power* in human beings is nothing but a certain arrangement of the parts of the body which, etc. . . . The *sensory power,* etc. . . . So these two are simply, in the human body, etc. . . . And since the *mind,* or *rational soul,* is distinct from the body, etc., it is with good reason that it *alone* is called *soul.*[10]

As Descartes says, the vegetative and sensitive "souls" are merely arrangements of the parts of the body and, therefore, do not truly belong to the soul. Rather than belonging to the soul, they are "in the body" in the sense of being ways in which the body operates entirely on its own, in a mechanical fashion.

Descartes concludes from this discussion that the human soul, no longer a rational-sensitive-vegetative soul at work within the body, is an exclusively rational soul at work within its own sphere, an exclusively subjective sphere apart from the body. This exclusively rational-subjective soul, because it exists within its own sphere, must act *on* the body rather than, as did the Aristotelian soul, *within* the body. The same is true for the body, which must act on rather than within the soul. With the soul and the body thus interacting, each from its own separate sphere, the soul affects the body by causing its intentional motions and actions, and the body affects the soul by causing its passions, its feelings, desires, sensations, and sense impressions.

Descartes in this way transformed the premodern rational-*biological* soul into a rational-*interior* soul, a soul that is restricted to only one function, the rational function, and that, disjoined from the body, is restricted to subjective or psychic space. Descartes's mechanistic physics applied to organic bodies thus led him to an account of subjectivity that departed from tradition in a much more extreme way than Augustine's account did. For Descartes, the human soul is no longer the principle of bodily life. It is no longer, as it was for Augustine, a two-sided (interior-exterior), multifunctional (rational, biological, social) soul active in the body but is rather a one-sided (interior), unifunctional (rational) soul restricted to subjectivity. Descartes, in turning *to* subjectivity, turned *away* from the body. Augustine did not. Descartes's application of the mechanistic paradigm to organic bodies thus transformed the soul from the principle of bodily life into an interior "thing" the only function of which is to think.

What is this thing that thinks? It cannot be the embodied person because Descartes's subjective turn disjoined the soul from the body and confined it within subjectivity. However, neither can the thing that thinks be all of subjectivity, since that which thinks must be distinguished from the "thoughts" it thinks. As noted in the last chapter, Descartes did use "soul" (and "mind") to refer to subjectivity in this wide sense, using these terms in much the same way we use "consciousness." However, he also used "soul" (and "mind") more narrowly to refer specifically to that thing within subjectivity that does the thinking, thus distinguishing this "thinking thing" from its "thoughts." With this narrower usage in mind, the question becomes, "What is this thinking thing within subjectivity," or, as Descartes asked, "this 'I' (Latin: *ego*) that thinks?" As we learned in the last chapter, Descartes, without a good term available, decided upon the expression "res cogitans." This res cogitans, this interior thing or subject that thinks, is what became the ego of the modern period.

In sum, in applying the mechanistic paradigm to organic bodies, Descartes was led to reject the premodern view that the soul is the principle of bodily life. For this reason, he, unlike Augustine, arrived at a one-sidedly subjective and exclusively rational conception of the soul, a conception that transformed the human subject into an exclusively subjective "thing" the only function of which is to think. As we shall see later in the chapter, Descartes believed that this new conception of the soul was superior to previous, premodern, conceptions not only in meeting the requirements of mechanistic science but also in helping to explain doctrines of the Christian faith.

The Ego Is an Executive Agency that Performs Cognitive and Practical Functions

For Descartes, the ego, as a thing that thinks, is not only an interior subject that has experiences but also an interior agency that performs "volitions" or "actions of the soul," what we have called the ego's cognitive and practical executive functions. The ego is that which performs cognitive functions such as controlling the focus of attention, holding thoughts in mind, recalling thoughts to mind, guiding the imagination, combining parts into wholes, analyzing wholes into parts, applying ideas to objects, comparing objects with each other, following out logical implications, and deliberating about means to ends. Additionally, the ego is that which performs practical functions such as regulating the passions, initiating and controlling bodily movements, and undertaking actions in the world.

In this section, we focus only on the ego's cognitive functions, exploring the background against which Descartes arrived at his conception of them. The major point of the section is that Descartes's account of the ego's cognitive functions, although ushering in the modern conception of these functions insofar as he assigned them to the ego as an interior subject and agency, otherwise conceived these functions in ways that remained squarely within the tradition of premodern epistemology.

Let us recall that Descartes gave a good deal of attention to forms of intuitive cognition, specifically to the intellect's perception of innate and adventitious ideas. Descartes referred to the intellect's perception of innate ideas as "pure understanding" (*puram intellectionem*) and held that this type of cognition—henceforth "intellectual intuition"—provides us with indubitable knowledge of God, mathematics, and basic features of minds and bodies. In contrast, he believed that the intellect's perception of adventitious ideas—henceforth "sense perception"—provides us with only fallible beliefs about contingent matters of fact. As forms of intuitive cognition, intellectual intuition and sense perception are ways in which we receive information about the world. According to Descartes, intellectual intuition is the source of rationally guaranteed, indubitable knowledge of the world; in contrast, sense perception is the source of empirically grounded, probable belief about the world.

Let us recall as well that Descartes gave less attention and assigned a subordinate status to forms of cognition that are actively carried out by the ego. Again, these forms of cognition are what we have called the ego's cognitive executive functions. For the sake of efficient exposition, we shall here refer to these forms of ego-active cognition simply as forms of executive cognition. In Descartes's terms, executive cognition consists of actions of the soul that operate on ideas or images for the purpose of extracting truths or information present in them. In discussing the formation of compound ideas, deductive inference, empirical scientific reasoning, and guided imagining, Descartes made it clear that these forms of executive cognition are only adjunct to intellectual intuition and sense perception. Whereas intellectual intuition and sense perception provide the content of knowledge or belief, executive cognition is nothing more than a set of actions by which the ego operates on this content, to clarify, rearrange, or apply it or to elicit it from mind or memory. In sum, Descartes's view was that intellectual intuition is the highest form of cognition, that sense perception, in being fallible, falls below intellectual intuition, and that the ego's executive cognition, in acting on cognitive content without itself being a source of such content, falls below both intellectual intuition and sense perception.

Descartes's account of the subordinate status of executive cognition has deep roots in premodern thought, finding its initial formulations in the work of Plato and Aristotle. Plato held that the intellect possesses a power of vision that is analogous to the eye's power of sight, with the difference that, whereas the eye perceives physical things by means of the sun's light, the intellect intuits universal truths by means of a nonphysical light. For Plato, the universal truths intuited by the intellect are what he called "Forms" (or "Ideas"), which are perfect exemplars of things existing in a timeless, unchanging, immaterial realm. Chief among these Forms are those of mathematics (e.g., line, circle, sphere, equality, number, odd, even), those of natural kinds of things (e.g., water, fire, horseness, humanness), and those of art and morality (e.g., beauty, goodness, virtue). These Forms are innately available to the intellect because, Plato believed, the intellect intuited them before this lifetime, if not in a previous lifetime then between lifetimes. The intellect can for this reason regain its previous knowledge of the Forms through a process of "recollection" (*anámnēsis*).

Such recollection is made possible by the fact that sensible things in the natural world are, according to Plato, imperfect images (*eikasia*) of the Forms, images that "participate" in the reality of the Forms to some degree (participation: *méthexis*). For example, an equilateral triangle drawn in the sand is an imperfect image that to some degree participates in the Form of an ideal equilateral triangle, and a perceived horse is an imperfect image of the Form of an ideal horse. Such images, although imperfect, material, and subject to change, have features that resemble, albeit remotely, their corresponding perfect, immaterial, and unchanging Forms. Such images, therefore, stir the intellect's memory, setting it on a course that can lead to recollection proper, intellectual intuition of the Forms.

However, recollection proper is not easily achieved. It requires not only familiarity with sensible images of the Forms but also rigorous intellectual training. In the *Republic,* Plato recommends that future philosopher rulers spend ten years studying mathematics, which, as an exercise in abstract thinking, helps detach the intellect from the senses and thus prepares it for the intuition of purely intelligible Forms. He then recommends that future philosopher rulers spend an additional five years practicing dialectic (a form of thinking designed to arrive at definitions), which, by trying verbally to define Forms, brings the intellect closer to them. By means of such training, the intellect is freed from reliance on the senses and redirected toward the Forms and is thus readied for intellectual intuition of the Forms. Intuition of the Forms now begins and evolves in stages of contemplation. Ultimately, as this contemplation deepens, the intellect is led to an intuition of the Form of the Good, the highest of all intelligible realities and the source of the nonphysical light that renders Forms visible to the intellect.

Both mathematical demonstration and dialectical thinking are forms of executive cognition. For us, although not Plato, they are cognitive functions performed by the ego. Plato describes mathematical demonstration as a type of discursive thinking (*dianoia*), which means that it is a type of executive thinking that proceeds by steps to get from a starting point to an end point.[11] Specifically, mathematical demonstration proceeds by deductive steps to get from axioms to theorems. Dialectic, too, is a type of discursive thinking, since it proceeds by dialectical steps (definition, refutation of definition, revised and improved definition) to get from an initial definition of a Form to increasingly more accurate definitions. In contrast to both mathematical demonstration and dialectic, intellectual intuition (*noêsis*) does not involve steps and is a passive or receptive rather than an active form of cognition. It is an immediate and infallible seeing of a universal truth, a Form.

Clearly, for Plato, mathematical demonstration and dialectical thinking are adjunct to intellectual intuition, at least in the sense of being cognitive exercises that prepare one for intellectual intuition. Mathematical demonstration and dialectic are exercises that help future philosopher rulers ascend to knowledge of the Forms. Mathematical demonstration helps future philosopher rulers by detaching the intellect from the senses and by demonstrating logical relationships between (mathematical) Forms that are not yet immediately evident to intuition. In turn, dialectic helps future philosopher rulers by formulating definitions that bring the Forms being defined into increasingly better intellectual focus. However, the question arises whether, for Plato, other forms of executive cognition—importantly, not just mathematical but deductive thinking generally and not just dialectical (definitional) but classificatory thinking generally—might be adjunct to intellectual intuition not only in the sense of being cognitive exercises that prepare one for intellectual intuition of the Forms but also in the sense of being cognitive tools for applying knowledge of the Forms to the sensible objects of the natural world.

It is plausible that deductive and classificatory thinking might be used as such tools by employing them to produce reasoned arguments explaining why a sensible object, in exemplifying a Form, must for that reason exemplify another Form or Forms (deductive thinking) or reasoned arguments explaining whether or how well sensible objects instantiate specific Forms (classificatory thinking). Deductive demonstration might be used to infer properties that an object must possess by virtue of exemplifying a Form; for example: "Socrates is a human being and, therefore, must possess the properties 'animal' and 'rational.'" In turn, classificatory thinking might be used to identify and compare objects according to the Forms they exemplify; for example: "that object has [or does not have] the shape of a triangle because . . ." "that animal is [or is not] a rabbit because . . ." or "John is more [or less] brave than Jim because . . ." Form-based arguments of these deductive and classificatory sorts, it seems, would be necessary in Plato's view if there is to be such a thing as scientific knowledge (*epistêmê*) of the natural world rather than only observation-based belief (*pístis*) or, worse, only mere opinion (*dóxa*).

Moreover, just such knowledge of the natural world seems to be a major point of Plato's entire body of work. After all, the future philosopher rulers of Plato's ideal republic are not trained in mathematics and dialectic so that, after achieving intellectual intuition of the Forms, they can lead exclusively contemplative lives. Rather, the purpose of their training is to prepare them to apply the Forms to the world so they can formulate just governing policies and make wise governing decisions. Unfortunately, Plato's views on whether and, if so, how knowledge of the Forms might be applied in the sensible world are unclear. All that can be said with confidence is that, for Plato, executive thinking is a supportive adjunct to intellectual intuition because it provides the cognitive exercises needed for ascending to knowledge of the Forms if not also because it provides the cognitive tools for applying knowledge of the Forms to sensible objects.

Aristotle agrees with Plato that executive thinking is a supportive adjunct to intellectual intuition. However, his account of this point is based on a very different understanding of the ontological status of the truths that the intellect intuits. For Aristotle, these truths—mathematical ideas, substantial forms, and universals (properties, qualities, attributes) generally—do not exist in a higher metaphysical realm but rather exist only in the sensible objects of the natural world. Moreover, in existing only in sensible objects, truths intuited by the intellect do so only in incompletely instantiated ways. Mathematical ideas are ideal properties or relations that exist in sensible objects only to one degree of approximation or another; and substantial forms are essential blueprints of natural kinds of things that exist in sensible objects only to one degree of actualization or another. Similarly, other universals—for example, "smooth," "thin," "soluble," "virtuous," "wise"—are properties, qualities, or attributes that exist in sensible objects only in ways that fall short of what can be conceived ideally. In thus existing only approximately or incompletely in sensible objects, mathematical ideas, substantial forms, and other universals exist in their fully comprehended character—not, as Plato believed, as innately accessible, eternal Forms of a higher realm—but rather only as intuitions occurring within the minds of people well experienced with their presence in sensible particulars.

Like Plato, Aristotle held that intellectual intuition is possible only after stages of thought that prepare for it. However, for Aristotle, these preparatory stages are stages of induction (*epagôgê*) rather than, as they are for Plato, stages of mathematical and dialectical thinking. Today, induction—in the narrower sense of inductive generalization—is a form of executive thinking that proceeds from a comparison of particulars to a conclusion about the universals (forms, properties, qualities, attributes) that the particulars instantiate in common. For Aristotle, induction is this and much more. As a process of generalizing from particulars to universals, it is not only a form of executive thinking of the logical sort just described but also a multistage process of cognitive development. In *Posterior Analytics,* Aristotle describes induction as a learning process that unfolds through four stages, beginning with sense perception of physical objects and culminating in intellectual intuition of scientific first principles, including most importantly mathematical ideas and substantial forms of natural things.

Sense perception is the first stage of Aristotelian induction because Aristotle, like Plato, believed that sensible objects "reflect" (Plato) or embody (Aristotle) forms and, therefore, are the natural starting point for learning about forms. However, whereas Plato interpreted this view to mean that sensible objects are imperfect reflections of perfect transcendent Forms, Aristotle interpreted it to mean that sensible objects are approximate or incomplete instantiations of immanent forms, forms that exist only in the sensible objects of this world and, in a secondary way, in the minds that intuitively grasp them. Despite this difference, the point, again, is that Aristotle agrees with Plato that knowledge starts with perception of sensible objects.

The second stage of Aristotelian induction is memory. In perceiving sensible objects, we retain images of them, and these images merge in such ways as to become increasingly generalized over time. With repeated perception of things of a natural kind, images representing things of that kind increasingly emphasize their common and essential features and de-emphasize features that are uncharacteristic or accidental. This generalization of the data of the senses leads to what Aristotle calls "experience" (*empeiria*), which is the third stage of inductive learning. Experience is an acquired familiarity with things that enables one to distinguish between them according to their kinds. However, this experience-based familiarity is not yet a clear understanding of the essential features that define things according to their kinds, the type of understanding that is required for scientific knowledge. Finally, the work of the first three levels of inductive learning bears fruit in intuitive insight. Such insight occurs when the intellect explicitly grasps what it has learned implicitly through sense perception, memory, and experience, thus apprehending universals—and, ultimately, scientific first principles—in a clear, fully comprehended way.

Regarding the scientific first principles thus known, Aristotle says that they are known in a way that "cannot possibly be otherwise."[12] Scientific knowledge, he says, "must proceed from premises which are true, primary, immediate, better known than, prior to, and causative of the conclusion."[13] That is, it must proceed from first principles that have been intuitively grasped in a clear, fully comprehended—indeed, self-evident—way. Although induction leads to the intuitive grasp of scientific first principles, it does not provide the justification for these first principles. Rather, it is the self-evidence of the first principles to the intellect that grasps them that provides the justification.

Once induction has ascended from sense perception of particulars to intellectual intuition of universals, the intuited universals—most importantly, again, mathematical ideas and substantial forms of natural things—are ready to serve as the first principles of scientific knowledge (*epistêmê*). Unlike induction, which is an ascending learning process, scientific knowledge—or, rather, scientific reasoning—is a descending explanatory process. Specifically, it is a process that, starting with intuitively apprehended first principles, uses deductive syllogisms and chains of demonstrative reasoning to explain the properties and behaviors of natural things. Clearly, for Aristotle, executive thinking, not only as it plays a role in inductive generalization but also as it is used in scientific reasoning, is a supportive adjunct to intellectual intuition. Induction is a learning process leading upward *to* intellectual intuition (of scientific first principles); scientific reasoning is an explanatory tool leading down *from* such intuition.

Although Aristotle disagreed with Plato on the metaphysics of intellectual intuition and the learning process leading to it, he agreed with Plato on what it is like to experience intellectual intuition. For Aristotle, like Plato, such intuition is an immediate seeing of a universal truth as it is illumined by a nonphysical light. The primary difference between Plato and Aristotle on this matter is, again, metaphysical. They disagree on the ontological status of both the truths that are known by intellectual intuition and on the nonphysical light that illumines these truths. We have already seen how Aristotle disagreed with Plato on the ontological status of the truths known by intellectual intuition: whereas Plato held that these truths are transcendent Forms of a higher incorporeal world, Aristotle held that they are immanent forms of this material world. As for the light that illumines these truths, Aristotle disagreed with Plato on corresponding metaphysical grounds. Whereas Plato stressed the otherworldly origin of this light, Aristotle stressed that this light is the intellect's own light. According to Aristotle, there is an active part of the intellect that illuminates universal truths that, in being intuited, are imprinted in a corresponding passive part of the intellect.[14]

With this review of Plato's and Aristotle's accounts of intellectual intuition and its primacy over executive cognition, we can see that Descartes inherited much of his epistemology from premodern thought, from views first formulated by Plato and Aristotle and then further developed by later Platonists, such as Plotinus and Augustine, and later Aristotelians, such as Averroes and Thomas Aquinas. Clearly, the following Cartesian views were inherited from either or both the Platonic and Aristotelian lineages of premodern epistemology: (1) that intellectual intuition is an immediate seeing of universal truths; (2) that the light by which universal truths are illuminated is a nonphysical light, which, as we learned in the last chapter, Descartes called the "natural light"; (3) that intellectual intuition is the highest type of cognition, having priority over sense perception and executive cognition; (4) that intellectual intuition is achieved only after stages of thought that prepare for it, even if, for Descartes, these are stages of radical doubt rather than stages of mathematical, dialectical, or inductive thinking; and, finally, (5) that deductive reasoning, as a form of executive cognition, can be used as a tool for top-down scientific accounts of natural phenomena.

In inheriting these long-standing views, Descartes was much closer to Plato and his lineage than he was to Aristotle and his lineage. Like Plato, he held that universal truths intuited by the intellect have a transcendent origin and are innately available to the intellect. For Descartes, universal truths are created transcendently by God, who implanted them in our souls, thus allowing us to access them innately from within our souls. Clearly, Descartes did not believe in reincarnation and recollection of transcendent truths across lifetimes. Nevertheless, he did believe in innate access to such truths.

An important point on which Descartes differed from both Plato and Aristotle is that he did not include essential forms of natural kinds of things—whether Platonic Forms or Aristotelian substantial forms—among the universal truths known by intellectual intuition. Again, in developing his mechanistic natural philosophy, Descartes broke away decisively from Aristotelian hylomorphism, dispensing with the substantial forms and the corresponding formal and telic causes of Aristotelian natural philosophy. These and other differences notwithstanding, Descartes's account of the primacy of intellectual intuition, the secondary status of sense perception, and the merely adjunct status of executive cognition shares a good deal with both Plato and Aristotle and, thereby, with both of the two main lineages of premodern epistemology. Although Descartes departed from premodern thought in rejecting essential forms of natural things and in assigning executive cognition to the ego in its role as executive agency of consciousness, his epistemological orientation otherwise remained premodern in character.

The major point to draw from the preceding exposition is that Descartes's conception of executive cognition is derived from premodern accounts of the subordinate status of such cognition. This point helps explain why Descartes did not give executive cognition the praise it later came to earn in the modern period. Modern philosophy, following the lead of modern science, challenged the authority of intellectual intuition by making the senses, not the intellect, the final arbiter of truth. With the success of modern science, intellectual intuition came to play a humbler epistemological role. No longer a source of infallible a priori truths, it became a source only of tentative a posteriori hypotheses. With this demotion of intellectual intuition, forms of executive cognition—now understood as cognitive functions performed by the ego—rose to take precedence over it in the modern period. Forms of executive cognition became the tools by which data leading to hypotheses are gathered and by which hypotheses, once formed tentatively, are assessed for consistency and coherence and thus readied for experimental test. No longer only supportive adjuncts to intellectual intuition, forms of executive cognition, especially inductive generalization and hypothetico-deductive reasoning, became the primary instruments of the scientific method. In our terms, the ego's cognitive executive functions became the primary instruments for the acquisition of knowledge.

The Ego Is an Incorporeal Substance

The most disputed part of Descartes's account of the soul is his view that the soul is an incorporeal substance, a substance that can in principle exist on its own, apart from the body. This Cartesian view, controversial throughout much of the modern period, was not controversial in Descartes's time. On the contrary, it, like Descartes's premodern epistemology, was the then-prevailing view, with roots going back at least as far as Plato. We have already seen that, for Plato, the soul, although the principle of bodily life, is something that can exist apart from the body not only intermittently, between lifetimes, but also, after it has achieved knowledge of the Forms during a lifetime, permanently, as a disembodied contemplator of the Forms. Plato, like Descartes, was a metaphysical dualist. For Plato, like Descartes, the soul is an incorporeal substance that can exist apart from the body.

Plato's dualism of soul and body found its way into Christianity primarily through the work of Saint Augustine. In agreement with the general Platonic view, Augustine held that the human soul is incorporeal and can exist apart from the body. However, in accepting Platonic teaching on this central point, Augustine departed from Platonic teaching on the relation of the incorporeal soul to the body. Whereas Plato held that the soul is reincarnated in different bodies until it is finally liberated from incarnate life, Augustine espoused the Christian view that the soul is inherently the soul of the body to which it was joined during its only mortal life and, therefore, exists in an incomplete state when that body dies, continuing in this state until its one-and-only body is resurrected at the time of the Last Judgment. For Christianity, the soul is not only the principle of bodily life but also inherently the soul of a specific body. Accordingly, in contrast to the Platonic view that the soul achieves its highest destiny when, having fully awakened to the Forms, it is liberated from further incarnate life, the Christian view, articulated by Augustine, is that the soul achieves its highest destiny when, having been received into heaven, its body is finally resurrected and restored to it at the end of time. Augustine did allow that the body is a drag on the soul under conditions of fallenness during this life, for original sin corrupted human desires. However, he believed that the body, when resurrected, will be free of corruption and will function in completely supportive union with the soul.

The Christian view that the soul exists in an incomplete state when separated from the body was further developed by Aquinas. Aquinas's formulation of this view was based on a rethinking of Aristotle's three-level (rational-sensitive-vegetative) conception of the human soul. As explained earlier, Aristotle may have entertained the possibility that a part of the rational level of the soul, the active or agent intellect, is separable from the body and immortal. Nevertheless, his more general view was that the substantial and other forms of natural things, including the soul as the substantial form of the body, do not exist apart from the bodies of which they are the forms. Aquinas, adapting Aristotle to Christianity, departed from this more general Aristotelian view in the specific case of the human soul by holding that not only the active intellect but the whole of the human soul, including all three of its levels, can exist apart from the body. In making this point, Aquinas acknowledged that the sensitive and vegetative levels of the soul, in existing apart from the body, do so only in a disengaged way, as bodily organizing principles that have ceased for a time functioning as such.

Aquinas's account of how the soul exists when separated from the body is considered more fully shortly. The point here is that Aquinas held that the soul in its entirety survives the death of the body but does so in an incomplete state because it lacks the body of which it is inherently the form. In Aquinas's view, existence apart from the body is contrary to the soul's nature. It is only when the soul is united with its body that, rather than subsisting in an incomplete state, it exists in a complete, fully engaged state, as the form side of a form-matter substance.

It is clear from this brief historical review that Descartes's idea that the soul is incorporeal was nothing new. Descartes inherited the idea from the Church. What was new with Descartes is that he believed that his conception of the soul was superior to the prevailing Aristotelian conception in explaining the Church's doctrine of the soul's immortality. We already know that Descartes believed that his conception of the soul was superior to Aristotle's from the standpoint of science because his conception, in reducing the soul to an exclusively subjective and rational soul, made it possible to give a mechanistic explanation of the body and its biological functions. Here we can add that Descartes believed that his conception of the soul was also superior to Aristotle's from the standpoint of religion because his conception, in reducing the soul to an exclusively subjective and rational soul, made it more plausible that the soul can survive intact after bodily death.

In his letter dedicating *Meditations* to the theology faculty of the University of Paris, Descartes says that he is presenting his book to the faculty in the hope that they will agree that it provides a strong defense of two fundamental teachings of the Catholic Church, that God exists and that the soul is of such a nature that it can continue to exist after the death of the body. Concerning the latter teaching, Descartes says,

> As regards the soul, many people have considered that it is not easy to discover its nature, and some have even had the audacity to assert that, as far as human reasoning goes, there are persuasive grounds for holding that the soul dies along with the body and that the opposite view is based on faith alone. But in its eighth session the Lateran Council held under Leo X condemned those who take this position, and expressly enjoined Christian philosophers to refute their arguments and use all their powers to establish the truth; so I have not hesitated to attempt this task as well.[15]

Descartes is here saying that *Meditations* demonstrates that the soul is sufficiently different from the body that it can, as the Church teaches, survive the death of the body. Having proved to his own satisfaction that the body, as a mechanism, does not require a soul for its life, he was convinced that he had also proved that the soul, as an exclusively subjective and rational substance, does not require a body for its life. Descartes is here saying that because, in his conception, the soul is not active in the body performing biological functions during life, there is no difficulty in understanding how it can, as the Church teaches, continue to exist apart from the body after life.

The Ego Is the Unifier Consciousness

To recall, Descartes believed that the soul is ontologically unitary because, as an incorporeal substance, it cannot be divided into parts. This account of the soul's unitary character, like the idea of the soul's incorporeality on which it is based, has premodern antecedents going back to Plato. In the *Phaedo,* Plato argued that the soul is like the eternal Forms in being incorporeal, incomposite, and, therefore, indissoluble, which is to say, immortal.[16] Ever since Plato, philosophers who believed that the soul is incorporeal have argued similarly, holding that the notions of incorporeality, indissolubility (or indivisibility), and immortality are mutually implicative. However, if Descartes's account of the soul's unitary character has these premodern roots, it is nonetheless a distinctively modern account for the following two reasons: (1) because it attributes to the soul not only an ontological unity as an incorporeal substance but also a functional unity as a thing the only function of which is to think; and (2) because it attributes both ontological and functional unity not to the soul generally but to the ego specifically, to the thinking thing within the soul, the interior subject and executive agency of consciousness.

That Descartes's account of the soul's unitary character is distinctively modern in these two respects can best be understood against the background of an earlier debate among Christian philosophers on the unity and wholeness of the soul. The debate in question began in the thirteenth century, when Scholastics tried to fit Aristotle's conception of the soul to Christian doctrine. The focus of the debate was on the nature of the intellect and how it is related to the rest of the soul, conceived in Aristotelian fashion as consisting of three levels, not only a rational level but also sensitive and vegetative levels.

Parties to the debate represented one or the other of two primary positions. One of these positions was held by Aristotelians who adopted a conception of the intellect advocated by the twelfth-century Spanish Muslim philosopher Averroes. According to this conception, there is only one intellect, which we all share, and it is only this universal intellect and not any of the other levels of the soul that is immortal. The other position was held by Aristotelians who adopted the conception of the intellect advocated by Saint Thomas Aquinas. According to this conception, there are as many individual intellects as there are human bodies, and it is not only these intellects but also the sensitive and vegetative levels of the soul paired with them during life that are immortal, even though the sensitive and vegetative levels, separated from the body of which they are organizing principles, are for a time disengaged from the object of their activity.

The Aristotelian-Averroistic position, frequently associated with Aquinas's contemporary Siger of Brabant, consists of two chief views. The first of these views was the view of Averroes just set forth, that the intellect is not only incorporeal and immortal but also universal in the sense of being a single intellect shared by all. In this view, the intellect is incorporeal and immortal because it is not dependent on the body for its functioning; and it is universal because, in being incorporeal, it lacks that which, according to Aristotle, individuates forms and other universals into a multiplicity of instances: matter.[17] We have already explained that it is unclear whether Aristotle believed that the intellect, the active intellect in particular, is incorporeal and immortal, let alone universal. However, what is clear is that some of Aristotle's later followers, including Avicenna, Averroes, and later Christian authors influenced by their writing, interpreted Aristotle in such a way as to conceive the active intellect—if not also what came to be called the passive intellect[18]—as having all these attributes.

Added to the Averroistic view affirming an immortal, universal intellect was a second view acknowledging the mortality of the sensitive and vegetative levels of the soul. If it seemed plausible that the intellect could function apart from the body, it seemed obvious that the sensitive and vegetative levels of the soul could not. These levels seemed quite evidently to depend on the body, as the body just as evidently seemed to depend on them, for life and for all biological functions. These levels of the soul were for this reason held to be like the body in being subject to corruption and death.

Bringing the premise of an immortal, universal intellect together with the premise of the mortality of the sensitive and vegetative levels of the soul, the conclusion was drawn that the human soul during life is a composite of universal and individual, incorporeal and corporeal, immortal and mortal levels. The soul insofar as it is universal, incorporeal, and immortal is by no means the complete human soul, nor is it even a personal soul. Rather, it is only one, universal-impersonal, level of a three-level soul the two lower levels of which, in being individual, corporeal, and mortal, are lost along with the body at death. For Siger and others taking a similar position, the three-level Aristotelian soul is unified as a composite whole only during life; in the disembodied state, it is neither unified nor whole.

Aquinas strongly disagreed with this view, both in its Averroistic conception of the intellect as a universal intellect and in its implication that the soul is composite during life and divisible at death. Aquinas held that each person has his or her own numerically distinct intellect, and he stressed that all three levels of the soul belong together indivisibly as one soul.[19] In defense of the indivisible unity of the soul's three levels, Aquinas offered the explanation that lower levels of the soul are nested in higher levels, such that a soul with a rational level or an intellect contains within itself both sensitive and vegetative organizing principles.[20] This preexistence of the sensitive and vegetative levels of the soul within the rational level means that these lower levels, notwithstanding their seeming dependence on the body, do not disappear at death. As organizing principles belonging inherently to the rational level of the human soul, which is incorruptible, the sensitive and vegetative levels of the soul are incorruptible, as organizing principles.[21]

According to Aquinas, the sensitive and vegetative levels of the human soul do cease being "actual" after death in the sense of ceasing for a time to be engaged in regulating the sensitive and vegetative functions of the body from which they have been separated. Nevertheless, he held, these levels of the human soul remain in existence "virtually" or "radically" (in their principle or root: *sicut in principio vel radice*) in the sense of being organizing principles that, nested within the rational level of the soul, can be reengaged and, indeed, will be reengaged once the body is resurrected.[22]

In this way, Aquinas defended the view that the soul is inherently and, therefore, always a unity, even though this unity is sometimes only virtual rather than actual so far as the two lower levels of the soul are concerned.

The Aristotelian assumptions that defined the issues of this thirteenth-century debate continued to define those issues up to Descartes's time. Descartes entered the debate and changed its course dramatically by replacing the Aristotelian hylomorphic natural philosophy with his mechanistic physics and thus in one move dismissing both the Aristotelian-Averroistic and the Aristotelian-Thomistic positions and the difficulties that beset each. It allowed him to escape the difficulties associated with a composite soul that loses two of its functions at death (the Aristotelian-Averroistic position) and the difficulties associated with a unitary soul that, although retaining all its functions at death, retains two of them only in a mysterious, virtual or disengaged, way (the Aristotelian-Thomistic position). Descartes decisively undercut both these positions by arguing that the sensitive and vegetative levels of the soul are neither lost nor mysteriously retained at death for the simple reason that there are no sensitive or vegetative levels of the soul. In reducing the sensitive and vegetative functions of the body to mechanical operations, Descartes transformed the soul from a complex and perhaps divisible unity of three functional levels into a soul that, because it has only one functional level, the rational level, is necessarily unitary, not only ontologically but also functionally.

Descartes in this way escaped difficulties that had arisen in attempting to fit the Aristotelian conception of the soul to the Christian doctrine of immortality. However, in doing so he was immediately faced with other difficulties, a difficulty associated with the phenomenon of psychic conflict and a set of "Platonic" difficulties (discussed in the next section). The difficulty associated with psychic conflict is the seeming impossibility of explaining how a functionally unitary rational soul could ever be at odds with itself. Indeed, it was the phenomenon of psychic conflict that first led to multilevel accounts of the soul like those of Plato and Aristotle. The phenomenon was first addressed by Plato in the *Republic*.[23] Plato gave the example of experiencing a desire to drink while at the same time drawing back from doing so as a reason to think that the soul consists of multiple parts, for instance, an appetitive part that gives rise to the desire to drink and a rational part that, in being able to calculate the consequences of actions, gives rise to drawing back from doing so. The challenge that Descartes had to meet, therefore, was to explain how, given his premise that the soul is a functionally unitary rational soul, conflicts like the one described by Plato can occur.

Descartes's answer to this question, based on his mechanistic account of the human body, was bold. He dismissed appearances and claimed that there are no conflicts within the soul. When, for example, the soul experiences a desire to drink but draws back from doing so, the soul is not in fact in conflict with itself but is rather in conflict with bodily processes affecting the pineal gland and, thereby, the soul. In *Passions* he said, "All the conflicts usually supposed to occur between the lower part of the soul, which we call 'sensitive,' and the higher or 'rational' part of the soul—or between the natural appetites and the will—consist simply in the opposition between the movements which the body (by means of its spirits) and the soul (by means of its will) tend to produce at the same time in the [pineal] gland."[24]

The apparent conflict between the desire to drink and drawing back from doing so is thus truly a conflict between body and soul, not between parts of the soul. It is a conflict between the body's animal spirits, which affect the pineal gland in such a way as to produce the desire to drink, and the rational soul's will, which affects the pineal gland in just the opposite way. Descartes is here saying that passions of the soul such as appetites and bodily urges, which before had been attributed to the sensitive level of the soul, do not properly belong to the soul because they are effects within the soul produced by the body rather than expressions of the soul itself. In this way, Descartes believed that he could preserve the soul's undivided unity as an exclusively rational soul in face of what hitherto were thought to be unity-dividing conflicts within the soul.

In removing biological functions from the soul, Descartes disjoined the soul from the body and thus identified the soul with interior subjectivity. Moreover, in arguing for the functional unity of the soul, as a thing the only function of which is to think, Descartes identified the soul more specifically with an incorporeal thing residing within subjectivity, the ego as subject and executive agency of consciousness. Only such a res cogitans, Descartes thought, can possibly be both ontologically unitary, by virtue of having no extensive parts, and functionally unitary, by virtue of performing only one essential function: thinking.

THE EGO IS ALWAYS WHOLE OR COMPLETE

Descartes believed that the ego is not only ontologically and functionally unitary but also ontologically and functionally whole. The ego's unity and wholeness go together as two sides of the same idea. The ego is not only ontologically unitary but also ontologically whole because, having no extensive parts, it can never come apart; and it is not only functionally unitary but also functionally whole because, having only one, rational, function—which, presumably, does not depend on the body—it remains functionally intact after death. The ego is thus always complete as an ego, both ontologically and functionally. The ego can be more or less alert as the subject of consciousness and more or less active as the executive agency of consciousness, but it can never be more or less an ego. In other words, the ego is always fully constituted as subject and agency of consciousness.

Descartes's arguments for the inherent, inviolable unity and wholeness of the soul provided him with reasons for recommending his conception of the soul as the best possible basis for the Christian doctrine of immortality. Clearly, he thought, his conception of the soul overcame the Aristotelian difficulties discussed in the last section, those of explaining how the soul can be immortal without either losing parts of itself at death or retaining those parts but only in a mysterious way. However, if his conception of the soul overcame these difficulties, it incurred an opposite set of "Platonic" difficulties. These latter difficulties are problems that had arisen in previous attempts to render Plato's conception of the soul compatible with the Christian doctrine of the soul's relation to the body, specifically, the doctrine that the soul is inherently the soul of one and only one human body and for this reason exists in an unnatural, incomplete state when it is separated from that body.[25] According to this doctrine, the soul and its body belong together in an essential rather than merely accidental union.

It is a strength of the Aristotelian conception of the soul that it provides an excellent explanation of just this doctrine. In holding that the soul is the substantial form of the body, indeed, that each soul is the rational-sensitive-vegetative form of a numerically distinct body, the Aristotelian conception provides a clear understanding of how the soul can be necessarily tied to one and only one body in an essential union. Having this strength, the Aristotelian conception of the soul has the equal but opposite weakness of being unable to explain plausibly how the soul, as the substantial form of a body, can exist apart from the body, let alone as a soul that remains unitary and whole in a disembodied state. This weakness is the basis of the Aristotelian difficulties that Descartes believed his conception of the soul avoided.

The strength and weakness of the Platonic conception of the soul with respect to Christian doctrine are opposite to those of the Aristotelian conception. The strength of the Platonic conception is that it, much more easily than the Aristotelian conception, can explain how the soul can exist apart from the body, as a soul that is both unitary and whole. According to Plato, the soul is an immortal intellect that survives the deaths of different bodies until, purified of bodily impediments, it is finally liberated from the cycle of birth and death. For Plato, the soul is not inherently joined to any specific body and is not even inherently in need of being embodied. Clearly, Plato's conception of the soul is supportive of the Church's view that the soul can survive the death of the body. This strength of Plato's conception of the soul with respect to Christian doctrine is, however, at the same time a weakness, for Plato's view seems to be in direct contradiction with the Christian doctrine that the soul exists in an essential union with one and only one body.

Antoine Arnauld observed that Descartes's conception of the soul departed from the Aristotelian conception sufficiently to bring it close to the Platonic conception.[26] Descartes, sensitive to this criticism, took extraordinary measures to show that the soul, although an incorporeal substance fundamentally different in kind from material things, is nonetheless inherently the soul of one and only one body, as the Church required. To press home this point Descartes even went so far as to use the Scholastic terminology of the Church, saying that the rational soul is the substantial form of the body and that, as such, it is an incomplete substance when separated from the body.[27] He said this despite holding that the soul is both ontologically and functionally unitary and whole as an incorporeal substance. In this context, the use of the terms "substantial form" and "incomplete substance" is striking given that Descartes's mechanistic physics had effectively done away with Aristotelian substantial forms, including, presumably, those that might, like the human soul, be thought to exist apart from their corresponding matter.

Descartes's desire to distance his conception of the soul from Aristotle's without thereby moving too far in the direction of Plato's is evident in a letter he sent to Regius in January of 1642. Descartes said,

> He [Gisbertus Voetius] fears that if we deny substantial forms in purely material things, we may also doubt whether there is a substantial form in man, and may thus be in a less happy and secure position than the adherents of forms when it comes to silencing the errors of those [Averroists] who imagine there is a universal world-soul, or something similar.
>
> In reply to this it may be said on the contrary that it is the view which affirms substantial forms which allows the easiest slide to the opinion of those who maintain that the human soul is corporeal and mortal. Yet if the soul is alone recognized as

substantial form, while other such forms consist in the configuration and motion of parts, this very privileged status it has compared with others shows that its nature is quite different from theirs. And this difference in nature opens the easiest route to demonstrating its non-materiality and immortality, as may be seen in the recently published *Meditations on First Philosophy.* Thus one cannot think of any opinion on this subject that is more congenial to theology.[28]

In this communication Descartes is trying to knit together the following three views: (1) that it is the Aristotelian conception of the soul, not his, that encounters the greater difficulties in explaining the incorporeality and immortality of the soul; (2) that, with one exception, there is no need for Aristotelian substantial forms, since such forms, including those attributed to plants and nonhuman animals, are truly only "configuration and motion of parts"; and (3) that the human soul—and here Descartes, having distanced himself from Aristotle, now distances himself from Plato—is an exception because, despite being an incorporeal substance opposite in nature to material things, it is a substantial form that properly fits together with a body in a mutually completing essential union. That the human soul is thus the only substantial form that remains from Aristotelian natural philosophy indicates, according to Descartes, its "privileged status" as something that is essentially tied to a body without thereby being subject to the mortality of this body.

Whereas Descartes's account of how his conception of the soul avoids Aristotelian difficulties in explaining the immortality of the soul has persuasive power, his account of how his conception of the soul avoids the opposite set of Platonic difficulties seems ad hoc, defensive, and, frankly, disingenuous. However, putting this concern aside, the more important point is that Descartes's efforts to explain how his conception of the soul resolves disputed issues in Christian doctrine reveal that Descartes believed that his mechanistic physics, far from being an enemy of the Church, as representatives of the Church believed, was in fact an ally. Specifically, he believed that the reduction of sensitive and vegetative functions to mechanical operations benefited not only science, by opening organic bodies to rigorous scientific investigation, but also the Church, by eliminating long-standing theological difficulties concerning the immortality, unity, and wholeness of the soul. Descartes, in making the human soul meet the requirements of the new science, at the same time, he believed, made it better meet the requirements of the old religion.

The Ego Has Privileged, Full Access to Itself and, Therefore, Can in Principle Know Itself Completely Simply by Turning Its Attention Inward

In the last chapter we learned that Descartes believed that the ego can know itself completely simply by turning its attention inward. By inwardly directed intellectual intuition, the ego can know the fact of its existence as a thing that thinks and the status of its existence as an incorporeal substance. Additionally, by introspection the ego can know everything it experiences as subject of consciousness and all the "actions of the soul" it performs as executive agency of consciousness. The ego of course has all manner of features that come from being associated with a body, and it can know these features only by accessing data provided by sensation or sense perception. However, these features do not belong to the ego inherently, since they are neither the ego itself, as thinker, nor the ego's thoughts, its experiences and actions. They, therefore, cannot be known directly or with the certainty that the ego enjoys in knowing what does belong to itself inherently. The ego for this reason can know itself better than it can know its body or other material things, Descartes believed. In sum, it was Descartes's view that the ego has privileged, full access to itself and, therefore, can know itself completely without needing to rely on anyone or anything beyond its own consciousness.

In an earlier section, we discussed how Descartes's and Augustine's subjective turns led to very different conclusions about the nature and functions of the soul, with Descartes concluding that the soul is a one-sided (exclusively interior) soul with only one (rational) function and with Augustine concluding the soul is a two-sided (interior-exterior) soul with multiple (rational, biological, and social) functions. Here we consider how Descartes's and Augustine's subjective turns led to very different conclusions about self-knowledge, where self-knowledge will here be understood to be knowledge *of the soul.*

As we shall see, thus understood, Descartes's subjective turn led to an account of self-knowledge that is one-sided, complete, and "shallow." It is one-sided because the soul that is known is an exclusively interior soul; it is complete because this exclusively interior soul can in principle be known by the ego in its entirety and with certainty; and it is shallow because nothing within the interior soul is either too deep or too high to be beyond the ego's reach. In contrast, Augustine's subjective turn led to an account of self-knowledge that is two-sided, incomplete, and "vertical." It is two-sided because the soul that is known has both a subjective interior and a bodily, social exterior; it is incomplete because much within the interior side of this soul is hidden or obscure; and it is vertical because the interior side of the soul has both dark depths and only dimly lit heights.

Descartes's account of self-knowledge, based on the view that the soul is exclusively interior or subjective in nature, is strictly speaking only an account of what we can know about ourselves by turning inward. Because, for Descartes, the soul is not active within the body as the principle of bodily life, knowledge of the body and its behaviors is not self-knowledge in the strict sense intended here, knowledge of one's soul. Knowledge of the body and its behaviors, however biographical, is only knowledge of the soul's causal interaction with the material world. Despite his claim that the soul is the substantial form of the body and, therefore, is an incomplete substance when separated from the body, Descartes, in reducing the body to a mechanism, restricted the soul to subjectivity and thus effectively narrowed the scope of self-knowledge to knowledge of an interior thinker and its private thoughts.

For Augustine, in contrast, self-knowledge, as in knowledge of one's soul, is two-sided, being a knowledge of both an inner man, a private subjectivity, and an outer man, a person belonging to the material, social world. According to Augustine, self-knowledge is thus knowledge of the "whole man." For Augustine, just as the soul exists in inherent union with the body, whose indwelling principle of life it is, so the inner man exists in inherent union with the outer man. Self-knowledge for Augustine is thus irreducibly two-sided, being a knowledge of both the soul's interior life and its embodied, social life.

Let us now restrict our focus to self-knowledge insofar as it is knowledge of the interior soul, of human subjectivity, disregarding for the moment that, for Descartes, the interior soul is the whole of the soul, whereas, for Augustine, it is only the interior side of a two-sided soul. Our aim now is to explain how Descartes and Augustine differed on the extent to which the interior soul can be known. With this aim in mind, the first thing that stands out is that Descartes's and Augustine's accounts of interior self-knowledge agree on two striking points, these: (1) that we can know with certainty that we exist as thinkers, and (2) that we can know with certainty that our experiences have the phenomenal character they seem to us to have. Augustine, long before Descartes, explicitly formulated the *cogito* argument ("I think, therefore I am"[29]). Furthermore, he, like Descartes, argued that we would not be mistaken in our beliefs about the phenomenal character of our experiences even if we were deluded about what the senses seem to teach us about the external world.[30] These similarities in Descartes's and Augustine's conceptions of interior self-knowledge are striking, so striking that many have concluded that Descartes, intent on refuting radical skepticism, borrowed, if not directly from Augustine, then from others who were well versed in Augustine's writings.[31]

The similarities just discussed should not mislead us into thinking that Descartes and Augustine had similar accounts of interior self-knowledge overall. The fact is that their accounts are much more different than they are similar. The primary difference is that Descartes's account holds that everything within the interior psyche is in principle fully accessible and evident to the ego, whereas Augustine's account holds that the most important things for which we search in looking within ourselves—our true motives, the reasons for our desires and feelings, the ideal (Platonic) forms of knowledge, and, most importantly, God—are either deeply submerged and, therefore, hidden or remote in their height and, therefore, for us, only dimly lit.

Descartes explicitly argues that consciousness or the soul is immediately accessible and fully knowable to the ego:

> As to the fact that there can be nothing in the mind, in so far as it is a thinking thing, of which it is not aware, this seems to me to be self-evident. For there is nothing that we can understand to be in the mind . . . that is not a thought or dependent on a thought. If it were not a thought or dependent on a thought it would not belong to the mind *qua* thinking thing; and we cannot have any thought of which we are not aware at the very moment when it is in us.[32]

For Descartes, the entire domain of subjectivity, including the ego, innate ideas, and all the ego's thoughts (experiences and actions), are in principle immediately and fully evident to the ego, through intuition or introspection. This idea of a completely knowable subjectivity indicates that, for Descartes, the interior soul is without depths or heights beyond our reach and is in this sense, as noted shortly ago, shallow.

In contrast, for Augustine, what is most striking about human subjectivity is that it has just such depths and heights. As he explains in detail in *Confessions,* many of our motives are unclear to us, and the reasons for our desires and feelings, especially those that resist our will or that are ambivalent or that conflict with each other, often remain elusive even after we have searched the depths within. Moreover, the interior soul has not only these murky depths but also remote and only dimly lit heights. Augustine believed that original sin so dimmed the intellect that the most profound intelligible truths, the eternal forms in the mind of God, are known by us at best only remotely and obscurely. It is only through faith and by the grace of God that we can turn our attention away from desires of the world and begin an interior ascent that, aided by infusions of divine illumination, gradually brings purely intelligible truths more closely and clearly into view.

Explaining his conception of the interior soul with such depths and heights, Augustine says, "The faculty of memory is a great one, O my God, exceedingly great, a vast, infinite recess. Who can plumb its depth? This faculty of my mind, belonging to my nature, yet I cannot myself comprehend all that I am. Is the mind, then, too narrow to grasp itself, forcing us to ask where the part of it is which it is incapable of grasping? Is it outside the mind, not inside? How can the mind not compass it?"[33] For Augustine, subjectivity is a seemingly infinite recess with depths too dark to see and with heights too dimly lit to see clearly.

It was Descartes's subjective turn, with its one-sidedly subjective, complete, and shallow conception of self-knowledge, that set the course for the modern period. Some philosophers disagreed with Descartes on what specifically we can know by looking within, taking aim especially at Descartes's views that we can know that, as egos, we are incorporeal substances and that we can intuit inwardly accessible innate ideas. These differences notwithstanding, the basic Cartesian view that we are fundamentally subjective beings with privileged, full access to ourselves was the predominant view in Europe until, beginning at the middle of the nineteenth century and continuing through the first half of the twentieth century, the one-sidedly subjective, complete, and shallow character of Descartes's account of self-knowledge began to be challenged. We review the more important of these challenges in chapter 4, where we discuss the depth psychologies of Freud and Jung, which challenged the complete and shallow character of Descartes's account of self-knowledge, and existential phenomenology, symbolic interactionism, and relational theories in psychoanalysis, which challenged the one-sidedly subjective character of Descartes's account of self-knowledge.

The Ego Is the Sovereign Power of the Soul

We proposed in the last chapter that Descartes seems to have had two conceptions of the will, one the traditional Christian conception and the other, coming to the fore in the last years of his life, a conception reflecting Descartes's agreement with core tenets of Stoicism. In this section we trace the historical emergence of the notion of the will and explain how the two conceptions found in Descartes's work were rooted in the past and how his later, more Stoic conception, although rooted in the past, helped set the stage for two principal modern conceptions of the will.[34]

There is no mention of anything resembling the will in classical Greek philosophy. In Plato's *Republic,* there is no will that sets the soul in motion and that keeps feelings and appetites obedient to the intellect's governing authority. Plato does say that "spirited" feelings, such as pride and righteous indignation, serve as enforcers of what the intellect deems to be good. However, feelings, even spirited ones, are not what we would call a will. Moreover, the question arises about the means by which spirited feelings are made obedient to the intellect's governing authority. Clearly, for Plato, the answer is not because they are subject to the discipline of a will.

Plato does speak of unruly feelings and appetites, which from our point of view, but not his, suggests that the will is too weak to keep these lower parts of the soul in line. According to Plato, unruly feelings or appetites are characteristic of an unjust (unhealthy) soul, which is a soul in which feelings or appetites, rather than keeping to their proper functions, usurp the function of the intellect by taking command of the soul. For example, spirited feelings like pride and righteous indignation might become over-weening, asserting themselves rashly, or appetites might become excessive, asserting themselves greedily, each in these ways unjustly taking command of the soul. Such unruly feelings and appetites raise the questions of how, if not by weakness of will, Plato thought that feelings or appetites become unruly in these ways and how, if not by strength of will, he thought that unruly feelings or appetites might be brought into obedience with the intellect's authority. The answer to both these questions, implicit in everything Plato says about just and unjust souls, is that it is the intellect on its own, not the intellect in partnership with a disciplining will, that either keeps or fails to keep feelings and appetites in line.

Socrates introduced an intellectualist perspective into ancient Greek philosophy by arguing that knowledge of the good—or at least genuine knowledge of the good—suffices for doing the good. This perspective is not as prominent in Plato's thinking as it is in Socrates's. Nevertheless, without a conception of something that functions like a disciplining will, Plato seems to have believed that the intellect's power to maintain justice and overcome injustice in the soul is the power of the intellect's *knowledge,* not the power of a will working under the intellect's guidance. Without knowledge of the good, feelings and appetites are without proper guidance and, therefore, tend to go astray, causing disorder in the soul. In contrast, with knowledge of the good, feelings and appetites are given proper guidance, guidance to which they somehow inherently respond, without needing to be brought into line by such a thing as the will.

Although Plato does not have a notion of the will, he contributed an essential idea that was later included in the notion of the will: that the soul—or, later, will—aims at the good. In the *Symposium,* Plato presented an account of the soul's itinerary as it is attracted to beauty, first as beauty appears in lower (physical) manifestations and then as it appears in higher (social, intelligible) manifestations and then, finally, as it reveals itself at the highest level as beauty itself, the pure Form of Beauty. For "beauty" we can substitute "good" and understand that for Plato the highest aim of the soul, sometimes achieved only after many incarnations, is an awakening of the intellect to an intuition of the Good itself. Such an intuition is the ultimate object of the soul's desire. This is the *desiderative* component that was later to be incorporated within the notion of the will: the will is the desire for the good.

Like Plato, Aristotle presented no clearly recognizable notion of the will. He spoke of many matters that were later associated with the will without, however, presenting an account of a psychic faculty or power that we would recognize as such. He had a good deal to say about such phenomena as voluntary and involuntary action, reason's leadership of arational feelings and desires, self-mastery versus moral weakness, rational deliberation, and rational desire or wish (*boulêsis*) for the good. Still, he did not bring these will-related phenomena together by explaining how they might be expressions of a single thing, the will.

So far as the history of the notion of the will is concerned, the most important of Aristotle's contributions is his idea of rational wish or desire for the good, which, following Plato's account of the soul's desire for beauty, further developed what would later become the desiderative component of the notion of the will. Aristotle clarifies that the soul's wish for the good, as is implicit in Plato's account of the soul's desire for beauty, is a *rational* wish, a wish for that which the intellect discerns to be *truly* good. Whereas Plato held that this true good is a life lived with knowledge of the Good itself, Aristotle held that this true good is the actualization of our nature as rational animals, which is Aristotle's understanding of the happy life. In either case, Hellenic philosophy set forth the idea that the soul has a rational desire or wish for the good. This idea would be adopted by Christianity and incorporated into its conception of the will.

Moving from the Hellenic to the Hellenistic world, the Stoics made a second contribution to what later would become the notion of the will: the soul's power of assent. According to the Stoics, we possess a power by which we can assent to or withhold assent from our impulses, thus either acting or not acting as they prompt. This power of assent, along with reason or the intellect, which is its guide, distinguishes us from other animals. Other animals are set in motion immediately by their impulses. We, in contrast, although prompted by impulses, are set in motion by assent, which alone allows actions to unfold.

Given this power of assent, we should, the Stoics held, follow the guidance of reason and reserve our assent for what is within our power. If we do not follow this guidance, we render ourselves vulnerable to the vagaries of fortune and to consequent perturbations of the soul. The only thing completely within our power, the Stoics taught, is the soul itself. Accordingly, although we might choose to pursue such worldly boons as good health and good reputation—which, although strictly neither good nor bad, are "preferred" because they can make virtuous actions more effective—we should not, in doing so, assent to them in the sense of staking our happiness on them. Instead, we should assent to them with indifference (*apátheia*), pursuing them without needing them or being attached to them. The only things we should assent to fully are reason, self-control, and virtue (acting in accordance with reason). These things alone are completely in our power, and reserving full assent to them allows us to achieve a self-sufficient happiness of inner tranquility (*ataraxía*).

The Stoics' idea of the soul's power of assent was a precursor to what became the *elective* component of the notion of the will. This component is very much the opposite of the desiderative component. Whereas the desiderative component sets the soul—or, later, will—in motion passively, by attraction to the good, the elective component sets the soul—or, later, will—in motion actively, by, in the Stoics' view, giving consent to actions. Such active assent is most evident in situations in which a choice must be made between two or more equal goods or between two or more equal means to an end. However, active, assent-initiated motion of the soul is necessarily, even if less evidently, present in all other actions as well, according to the Stoics. If assent is not given, at least tacitly, an action does not ensue. The Stoics, like Plato and Aristotle, believed that the soul has a rational wish or desire for what reason deems to be good, which, for Stoics, is ultimately a life of tranquility based on reason, self-control, and virtue. However, they differ from Plato and Aristotle in explaining that more is involved in our actions than rationally guided desire; and that something more is assent, giving a "green light" to an impulse and ensuing action.

Judaism and Christianity, rooted in the Hebrew Bible, contributed another key idea to the notion of the will, the idea of autonomous choice, which was thrown into relief in the context of a people struggling to obey God's commandments. The idea of autonomous choice, like the Stoic idea of assent, helped give definition to the elective component of the notion of the will. The two ideas are alike in holding that there is a source of action apart from impulse or other influencing factors. They differ in that the idea of autonomous choice conceives this source of action as a personal agency that *produces* actions rather than, as does assent, an intellectual authority that *allows* (or disallows) actions. Thus understood, autonomous choice *authors* actions, whereas assent only *authorizes* them. Autonomous choice, in authoring actions, puts a personal tag on them. It emphasizes that the actions belong and give expression to an individual person or self. In contrast, assent, in authorizing actions, emphasizes only that the actions have met a set of certifying requirements.

The Judeo-Christian idea of autonomous choice is rooted in Genesis. Adam and Eve faced the countervailing influences of God's command not to eat the fruit of the tree of the knowledge of good and evil on the one hand and the serpent's temptation to eat this fruit on the other. In succumbing to the temptation of the serpent, Adam and Eve were not just yielding or, perhaps in Stoic fashion, assenting to an impulse. They were at the same time independently choosing to act contrary to divine instruction, thus asserting "self-will" in opposition to God's command. Accordingly, although eating the forbidden fruit may have been in part a concession or assent to temptation, it was at the same time an autonomous choice to disobey God in doing so. Adam and Eve thus made a fateful choice, a choice that, at least in its disobedience, was an expression of their ability to act on their own initiative independently of God. Tragically, this initial exercise of autonomous choice was an act of sin.

According to Christian interpretation, this sin of the first humans hereditarily predisposed their progeny to further acts of sin. Adam and Eve, in acting against God's instructions, cut themselves off from the grace that had enabled them to live immortal lives in harmony with nature and each other. Among the consequences of this loss of God's grace was concupiscence, the damaging of our moral character in such a way as to make sin attractive to us, most immediately sin related to the bodily appetites but more broadly sin related to worldly desires generally. Another consequence of the loss of God's grace was the damaging of the elective will, which was weakened to the point of being unable to resist sin, even when it is known that an act that is about to be committed is contrary to God's commands. In the Christian doctrine of original sin, therefore, the elective component of the will, understood as autonomous choice, entered the historical record already burdened with a highly negative interpretation. As an elective faculty, the will was thought to be damaged in such a way as to make human beings predisposed to sin and, therefore, incapable on their own of repairing their relationship with God and thus achieving their own highest good.

Christianity joined this idea of sin-prone autonomous choice with the Greek idea of rational desire for the good to form the first real conception of the will, which Christian writers referred to as *voluntas,* the Latin rendering of the Greek *boulêsis.* The conception of the will that thus emerged is that of a power of the soul that has both elective and desiderative components, where the elective component was understood as sin-prone autonomous choice, as just explained, and the desiderative component was understood in terms of the Christian conception of the highest good toward which rational desire aspires. Instead of Plato's Form of the Good or Aristotle's actualized human nature or the Stoics' life of rational tranquility, the highest good toward which rational desire aspires according to Christianity is reconciliation and restored intimacy with God, leading ultimately to the beatific vision. God in this way became the highest good or attractor to which the will is drawn, the ultimate telic cause of the will's striving. In thus being called to or beckoned by God, the will (or heart), as Augustine so famously said, "is unquiet until it rests in you."[35] The will as conceived by Christianity is thus at once a sin-prone elective instrument by which we make autonomous choices and a desiderative power by which, ultimately, we are tethered and drawn to God. It is at once a fallen autonomous will and, as Aquinas, echoing Aristotle, said, the "rational appetite for the good."[36]

The Christian will, thus conceived, is clearly divided against itself. It is a will that strives for God and at the same time is prone to disobey God and thus undermine its own striving. This division of the will against itself reflects a conflict within the Christian's soul. The Christian struggles to bring autonomous choice into harmony with longing for God or, otherwise stated, to bring the elective component of the will into harmony with the desiderative component. This notion of a will divided against itself is central to the work of both Saint Paul and Saint Augustine. In *Confessions,*

Augustine describes this conflict by saying that our divided will is like having two wills, a higher will calling us to our true good and a lower will resisting this call.[37]

With the will playing such a central role in Christianity, the question of the will's status within the soul and its relation to other parts of the soul necessarily arose. Generally, the answer that emerged is that the will, although subject to the influence of bodily feelings and desires, is not itself bodily or physical in nature. Rather, as a rational will, it, along with the intellect, is a purely spiritual and, therefore, incorporeal part of the soul. This view is implicit in the Christian belief that God is a purely spiritual being with an omniscient intellect and omnipotent will and that we, although fallible, weak creatures, have been fashioned in the image of God. Our intellect and will reflect, albeit only remotely and obscurely, the divine being who created us.

Saint Augustine explored these ideas in *De Trinitate,* where he suggested that God's nature, in particular the Christian God's triune nature, is reflected in us in our memory, intellect, and will, which, he held, are purely spiritual, incorporeal powers of the soul.[38] Aquinas followed Augustine's lead and also deemed memory (of universal principles and intelligible forms), intellect, and will to be powers that have no reliance on the body and, therefore, belong to a part of the soul that is completely rational and incorporeal in nature.[39] In sum, the will for Augustine and Aquinas and for Christianity generally is an incorporeal power of the soul that functions under the guidance of the intellect and that is at once an autonomous elective power prone to sin and a desiderative power by which we are attracted to the good, ultimately to God.

Let us now return to Descartes, beginning with the fact, discussed in the last chapter, that he seemed to have held two conflicting conceptions of the will, the Christian conception, which he inherited from his faith, and a conception with strong Stoic influences, which he advocated in his writings on moral philosophy, especially in his last work, *Passions of the Soul.* To recall, Descartes kept these two conceptions of the will separate from each other, seemingly applying the Christian conception to the afterlife, where faith and God's grace is needed to behold the beatific vision, and the Stoic conception to this life, where the highest human good is in principle achievable by our efforts alone. Descartes always stressed his Christian orthodoxy and understated the extent of his agreement with the Stoics. Nevertheless, for reasons sketched in the last chapter, we can with justification conclude that his agreement with core tenets of Stoicism, including those in conflict with Christian teaching, was stronger than he acknowledged in his writings.

Descartes's agreement with core tenets of Stoicism is apparent in at least two points that came to the fore in Descartes's later work, especially *Passions*. The two points, both of which are inconsistent with Church teaching, are (1) that the will is an exclusively elective instrument autonomously exercised by the ego, and (2) that this exclusively elective will is a self-sufficient will, a will that needs nothing beyond itself to achieve the highest human good. In this view, the will is set in motion only by the ego's autonomous choices in performing actions of the soul and, rather than being prone sinfully to undermine the achievement of the highest human good, is able under the ego's command to achieve this good by rationally mastering the passions and thus achieving serene peace of mind.

Although Descartes stressed autonomous choice rather than assent, as the Stoics did, he, like the Stoics, believed that we have—or, in Descartes's view, that *the ego* has—complete control of the soul and, therefore, the ability to achieve the highest human good. To repeat, Descartes believed that the ego by exercise of will has direct and complete mastery over its own actions or executive functions and indirect but nonetheless in principle complete mastery over its passions. With this mastery of both its actions and passions, the ego is capable of complete self-mastery, which means, in effect, that it is the sovereign power of the soul. The kinship with Stoicism is striking.

Descartes's elimination of the desiderative component of the Christian conception of the will was representative of one of two opposite conceptions of the will that came to the fore in the modern period. One of these conceptions held that the will, although influenced by the passions, is nonetheless set in motion only electively, by the agency of the ego; and the other conception held that the will, although informed by the intellect, is nonetheless set in motion only desideratively, by the prompting of the passions. Philosophers who espoused the former of these two conceptions of the will include not only Descartes but also Locke, Berkeley, Kant, (Thomas) Reid, C. A. Campbell, and Roderick Chisholm.[40] Philosophers who espoused the latter of these conceptions include Hobbes, Lord Shaftesbury (Third Earl of Shaftesbury), (Francis) Hutcheson, Hume, Schopenhauer, Nietzsche, and Freud, with Hobbes, Schopenhauer, Nietzsche, and Freud stressing that the will is set in motion only by self-regarding (self-satisfying or self-expressing) impulses, and with Hume, Lord Shaftesbury, and Hutcheson stressing that the will is set in motion not only by self-regarding impulses but also by other-regarding (benevolent or compassionate) sentiments. In this way, Descartes's elimination of the desiderative component of the Christian conception of the will is a dramatic example of the fissuring of that conception into two opposite modern conceptions of the will, one stressing the will's exclusively elective character and the other stressing the will's exclusively desiderative character.

Most modern philosophers who stressed the ego's elective role in volition, although often critical of one or more of the Cartesian ideas associated with the traditional notion of the ego, nonetheless agreed with the traditional notion on two fundamental points: (1) that the ego is a unified experiencing subject, and (2) that the ego is an agency that performs cognitive and practical functions. Most also agreed with the traditional notion that the ego, as an executive agency, exercises considerable causal power, including not only complete power over its executive functions but also a good deal of power over the passions, enough to regulate them effectively in most situations if not, as Descartes held, enough in principle to master them completely. In contrast, many among those who stressed that it is the passions that set the will in motion—especially Hobbes, Hume, Schopenhauer, Nietzsche, and Freud—were strong critics of the traditional notion of the ego, arguing that the ego is more "slave" than "master" of the passions if not arguing as well (1) that the ego is not in complete control of its executive functions (Schopenhauer, Nietzsche, Freud), and (2) that the very notion of a unified ego is suspect (Hume, Nietzsche).

Chapter 3

Rethinking the Notion of the Ego, Stage One

From Descartes to the End of the Nineteenth Century

It is now time to move from historical exposition to critical rethinking of the traditional notion of the ego. In this and the next chapter, I use criticisms of and proposed changes to the traditional notion as a guide for reassessing its principal ideas (those identified in chapter 1). In this chapter I discuss criticisms and proposed changes that emerged between the publication of Descartes's *Meditations* in 1641 and the end of the nineteenth century. In the next chapter I discuss criticisms and proposed changes that emerged in the twentieth century. The result of this critical rethinking of the traditional notion of the ego is a set of key ideas for a revised conception of the ego, which are set forth in summarized form in text box 3.2 of this chapter and text box 4.1 of the next chapter. Finally, in chapter 5, I add two more key ideas, ideas that complete the revised conception of the ego and then serve as leading themes for the rethinking of ego development that begins with chapter 6.

Most critical discussion of the traditional notion of the ego from the second half of the seventeenth century to the end of the nineteenth century focused on Descartes's idea that the soul or ego is an incorporeal substance. This idea was the primary focus of attention for two main reasons, one theoretical and one historical. Theoretically, the idea stood out because it was unsupported by experience and yet seemed to be the only idea that could explain the soul's unity, agency, self-identity, and, of concern to religion, incorporeality and immortality. In turn, historically, the idea attracted attention because the rise of science and the corresponding wane of religion increasingly called into question the incorporeality and immortality of the soul. With critical attention thus drawn to the idea that the ego is an incorporeal substance, philosophers began increasingly to reject the idea, tending either, in rejecting the idea, to reject the notion of the ego altogether (if no incorporeal substance, then no ego) or to explore ways in which the ego might be conceived as something other than an incorporeal substance.

This chapter organizes criticisms of and proposed changes to the idea that the ego is an incorporeal substance by focusing on five questions, four of which were at the forefront of discussion during the period from Descartes to the end of the nineteenth century.[1] The questions are these:

1. If the ego is not an incorporeal substance, how can it be the unifying center and owner of consciousness?

2. If the ego is not an incorporeal substance, how can it be the executive agency of consciousness?

3. If the ego is not an incorporeal substance, need it always be fully constituted as subject and executive agency of consciousness?

4. If the ego is not an incorporeal substance, is there any reason to believe that it is a necessary basis of consciousness?

5. If the ego is not an incorporeal substance, how, if at all, can it be self-identical and, perhaps, permanent (uninterrupted in its existence) over the course of a lifetime?

Question 1

IF THE EGO IS NOT AN INCORPOREAL SUBSTANCE, HOW CAN IT BE THE UNIFYING CENTER AND OWNER OF CONSCIOUSNESS?

David Hume challenged Descartes's idea that the ego is an incorporeal substance by reporting that "for my part, when I enter most intimately into what I call *myself*, I always stumble on some particular perception or other. . . . I never catch *myself* at any time without a perception, and never can observe anything but the perception."[2] According to Hume, no substantial self—which is to say, ego—is to be found within consciousness and for this reason the belief that there is such a self is unwarranted. The persistence of this belief, Hume explained, is due to the repeated, habitual ordering of our memories, thoughts, and feelings. Because these types of experience repeat themselves again and again and are associated with each other in familiar, habitual patterns, we are led to believe, without justification, that they are the experiences of a single interior self. We are thus led to superimpose the idea of a unitary ego on what is in fact the unceasing flux of experience. So far as we know, Hume concluded, the Cartesian self, the res cogitans, is a fiction. It is an understandable fiction but, so far as we know, a fiction nonetheless. So far as we know, the self is merely a "bundle of perceptions."

Hume's argument against Descartes's account of the ego rests on the fact that, in examining consciousness, we find only perceptions, never a perceiver, where Hume used "perceptions" in much the same way that Descartes used "thoughts," to include not only ideas or concepts but also mental images, volitions, feelings, desires, sensations, and sense impressions. However, the fact that we never find a perceiver does not by itself warrant a dismissal of the idea that there is an incorporeal, substantial ego at the center of consciousness. It might be the case, as Immanuel Kant argued, that the ego is an incorporeal substance but is inherently unable to experience itself as such. Our inability to find an incorporeal substance at the center of consciousness does not logically exclude the possibility that one is there. This point acknowledged, the logical possibility that the ego is an incorporeal substance is not a good reason for concluding that the ego is in fact such a substance.

Kant responded to Hume's challenge by attempting to reconceive the ego in a way that does not assume that it is an incorporeal substance. His first step was to analyze what we can confidently say about the ego so far as it is experientially evident to us. He concluded that although we cannot confidently say that the ego is an interior thing or substance, let alone an incorporeal thing or substance, we can confidently say that it is a "unity of apperception [of self-consciousness]."[3] By this he meant that we can confidently say two things about the ego. First, we can say that the ego is a temporally unified (self-identical) experiencing point of view in relation to which experiences are held together and thus unified within one consciousness. In making this point about the ego, we are saying that it is a *unity* of apperception.[4] Additionally, Kant's conclusion that the ego is a unity of apperception means that we can confidently say that the ego is an experiencing point of view that is at least implicitly self-conscious in the sense of being aware that the experiences it unifies are "its" experiences. The ego thus relates to the experiences it unifies in a possessive way, as experiences that belong to it as parts of what it is. In making this second point about the ego, we are saying that it is a unity *of apperception,* a self-conscious owner of its experiences. According to Kant, our experience attests that, whatever else the ego might or might not be, it is at least a temporally unified "experiencer" that unifies its experiences and relates to them in a proprietary way. It is that by virtue of which experiences not only occur within one consciousness but also belong to the consciousness in which they occur.

Kant said, "Only because I can comprehend . . . [the manifold of representations] in a consciousness do I call them all together **my** representations; for otherwise I would have as multicolored, diverse a self as I have representations of which I am conscious."[5] For an earlier and a later experience to be related, they must be held together as experiences of a subject that (1) is temporally unified in the sense of being the same (self-identical) subject at both the time of the earlier and the time of the later experience; and (2) is at least implicitly aware that both the earlier and the later experiences are its own experiences, experiences that belong to it as episodes of its experiential history. Were earlier and later experiences not held together in this temporally unified, proprietary-apperceptive way, they would be isolated episodes of a "multicolored, diverse self," experiential islands no more related to each other than are the experiences of two different people.

Kant's account of the ego as a unity of apperception implies that the ego has two basic functions, an *experiencing* and a *proprietary* function. The ego has an experiencing function not only because it is a temporally unified subject that has experiences but also because, in having experiences, it transforms them into experiences of temporally unified objects. With the aid of memory, the ego holds its experiences together in such a way as to bring into focus objects that, rather than being merely momentary phenomena, are objects that, like the ego itself, possess self-identity over of time. Memory allows the ego to see that some phenomena perceived at later times match phenomena perceived at earlier times, thus making it possible for the ego to combine such matched phenomena and to see them as temporally distinct appearances of temporally unified objects. The ego thus brings into focus experienceable objects properly so called, objects that, because they are self-identical over stretches of time, can be observed, studied, and otherwise known. In being a temporally unified unifier of experiences, the ego is at the same time a temporally unified unifier of experienceable objects. Having experiences and combining them into experiences of temporally unified objects are basic to the ego in its experiencing function.

The ego has a proprietary function because, in addition to unifying its experiences, it relates to them possessively, as if they belong to it as parts of what it is. Unlike a mirror, which is unaware of and has no relationship with the images it reflects, the ego is aware of its experiences and has an appropriating-proprietary relationship with them, whether implicitly, in the moments in which they occur, or reflectively, in later thinking about or remembering them. Taking possession of its experiences in this way is basic to the ego in its proprietary function. The ego, therefore, is not only a subject that unifies its experiences into experienceable objects but also a subject that is aware of itself as the owner of its experiences.

This discussion of the ego's experiencing and proprietary functions is highly condensed and only preliminary. We have more to say about these functions later in this and again in the next section of the present chapter. For now, it suffices to have introduced these functions in a preliminary way to help explain the Kantian idea that the ego, as a unity of apperception, is both the unifying subject and appropriating owner of consciousness.

Kant's second step in reconceiving the ego in response to Hume's challenge was to explain that the ego, as a unity of apperception, cannot be known to be anything more than a formal or "empty" unity of consciousness.

> From all this one sees that rational psychology has its origin in a mere misunderstanding. The unity of consciousness, which grounds the categories, is here taken for an intuition of the subject as an object, and the category of substance is applied to it. But this unity is only a unity of **thinking,** through which no object is given; and thus the category of substance, which always presupposes a given **intuition,** cannot be applied to it, and hence this subject cannot be cognized at all. Thus the subject of the categories cannot, by thinking them, obtain a concept of itself as an object of the categories; for in order to think them, it must take its pure self-consciousness, which is just what is to be explained, as its ground.[6]

Kant is here saying that Hume was mistaken in thinking that the inability to find, intuit, an ego within consciousness casts doubt on the existence of the ego. Hume's error was to assume that the ego is something that could in principle be an object of intuition for itself. According to Kant, this assumption is false because the ego can apprehend itself only "in thinking" about itself, only in reflecting on itself as the X that performs experiencing and proprietary functions, not by intuiting this X as an object of consciousness. Based on our own experience as egos, therefore, the ego cannot be known to be anything more than a formal unity of apperception, an experiencing-proprietary subject empty of intuitable content. Hume's error, as P. F. Strawson put it, was to "confound the unity of experience with the experience of unity."[7]

Kant's account of the ego as a formal unity of apperception highlights basic features of the ego that are experientially evident to us as egos. It is, therefore, a report of observable facts about our subjective lives, not an account offering an explanatory hypothesis. It posits no unperceived entities or hidden processes. It says only that the ego is a temporally unified "experiencer" that unifies its experiences and relates to them as its own experiences. All it says about the ego is (1) that it cannot be intuited; (2) that it recognizes itself as being the same (self-identical) subject that, in having experiences in the present, has also had experiences in the past; and (3) that it relates to its experiences in a proprietary way, as "its" experiences. Because Kant's account of the ego as a formal unity of apperception thus reports only what we can experience for ourselves about our egos, it is a good starting point for our revised conception of the ego. Let us, therefore, adopt it as the first key idea of the revised conception.

It is implied by Kant's account of the ego as a formal unity of apperception that the ego, in addition to performing two fundamental functions, has two opposite sides, an experiencing-proprietary side and an appropriated-owned side. The experiencing-proprietary side of the ego is simply the ego as a formal unity of apperception. It is the ego as an unintuitable subject that performs both experiencing and proprietary functions. In contrast, the appropriated-owned side of the ego is the side that results from the ego's exercise of its proprietary function. The appropriated-owned side of the ego, therefore, consists of everything that the ego, in exercising its proprietary function, has appropriated and thus relates to as belonging to it as part of what it is. Most basic among the things that the ego relates to in this way, as Kant explained, are its experiences.

This account of the ego's two sides provides an explanation for the distinction, introduced by William James, between the interior and exterior sides of the ego, which he called the ego as subject or "I" and the ego as object or "Me."[8] James's account of the interior and exterior sides of the ego is presented more fully later in the chapter. The part of the account relevant here is James's inventory of the types of things that belong to the ego on its exterior side. According to James, this side of the ego includes not only the ego's experiences, both present and remembered, but also its bodily, "spiritual" (i.e., mental in the widest sense: cognitive, volitional, emotional), and social life. The ego is a self-aware owner not only of the experiences it has but also of what it perceives to be its bodily, mental, and social attributes. As it does with its experiences, the ego appropriates these attributes and thus relates to them as "its" attributes, as attributes that belong to it as an embodied subject living in the material, social world, as Me.

In better-known terminology, the exterior side of the ego as conceived by James consists of all the experiences and attributes that the ego records in its self-representation, once the self-representation emerges.[9] These are experiences and attributes that the ego has appropriated and recognizes as belonging to itself as parts of what it is. Clearly, as James emphasized, the exterior side of the ego changes over time to reflect changes in the ego's experiences and in its bodily, mental, and social attributes. However, although it is thus subject to change, the exterior side of the ego at any given stage of life ordinarily retains core components long enough to overlap a great deal with the exterior side of stages recently left behind and stages soon to emerge. This fact indicates that the exterior or Me side of the ego ordinarily preserves self-identity over time. We return to this point later in the chapter.

The idea that the ego has both interior (experiencing-proprietary, subject or I) and exterior (appropriated-owned, object or Me) sides can be safely accepted not only because it is implied by the idea, already accepted, that the ego is a formal unity of apperception but also because, like that idea, it conveys no more than we can know about ourselves based on our own experience as egos. We have not yet moved from observable fact to explanatory hypothesis or theory. Our own experience as egos tells us that we relate in a proprietary way not only to the experiences we have but also to bodily, mental, and social attributes, thus creating for ourselves an exterior or Me side. Since our account thus far is based only on facts evident to us as egos, we are, I believe, justified in joining Kant's and James's ideas in the way indicated and, therefore, in adopting the interior-exterior, I-Me duality of the ego as the second key idea of our revised conception of the ego. This duality, which in the introduction we referred to as the duality of "the interior ego and the worldly self," is fundamental to the constitution of the ego.

Having incorporated James's idea of the interior-exterior or I-Me duality of the ego—and, with it, our own idea of the fundamental duality of the interior ego and the worldly self—within the revised conception of the ego, let us return to Kant.

Kant's response to Hume led him to ask how, without falling back on the assumption that the ego is an incorporeal substance, one can explain the fact that the ego is a unity of apperception. The answer Kant proposed is that the ego, as a unity of apperception, is the product of a *synthesizing activity*. "The thought that these representations given in intuition all together belong **to me** means, accordingly, the same as that I unite them in a self-consciousness, or at least can unite them therein . . ."[10] Kant's point is that the ego, as a unity of apperception, is the product of a synthesizing activity that holds experiences together under a unifying point of view and that in doing so appropriates the experiences for this point of view, thus making them "its" experiences, experiences that belong to it as parts of what it is. This proposal, that the ego is the product of a synthesizing activity (or activities), is an explanatory hypothesis, not an observable fact. A synthesis that produces the ego cannot itself be experienced by the ego. Again, as a *formal* unity of apperception, the ego cannot intuit itself—or, in this case, the synthesizing activity that produces it—inwardly.

Although Kant's idea that the ego is the product of a synthesizing activity goes beyond the limits of what we can experience about ourselves as egos, it has merit as a hypothesis. Unfortunately, Kant's account of the synthesizing activity that produces the ego is suspect. Skipping details, his general view was that the synthesizing activity that produces the ego is a "transcendental" (supraempirical) activity that works outside consciousness to produce both the ego and consciousness. Indeed, he held that this activity works outside consciousness to produce not only the ego and consciousness but also the spatio-temporal-causal character of the perceived world! According to Kant, space, time, and causality are a priori structures of human consciousness, our ways of organizing the data of experience, not structures inherent to the world itself. Given this view, it follows that the activity that produces the ego *and* consciousness also produces the spatio-temporal-causal structures of the *experienced* world, the world as it appears to us, not as it exists beyond the organizing structures of human consciousness. Clearly, such a conception of the synthesizing activity that produces the ego is heavily freighted with metaphysics.

To avoid Kantian metaphysics, Kant's hypothesis about how the ego is produced needs to be reinterpreted so that the synthesizing activity that produces the ego is understood to work within rather than beyond consciousness and, of course, within rather than beyond space, time, and causality. The question, therefore, is whether there is a candidate for an activity of this sort. I believe there is. I propose that the synthesizing activity that produces the ego is a *neurophenomenological* activity, an activity that works at once within the neurological bases and phenomenological interior of consciousness.[11] According to this proposal, the synthesizing activity that produces the ego as a formal unity of apperception is an activity that, like consciousness itself, is neither exclusively neurological nor exclusively phenomenological but, rather, both: neurophenomenological.

Further to reduce the risk of unnecessary metaphysics, we should add that the view proposed here holds that the ego, in being the product of a neurophenomenological synthesizing activity, is not a product distinct from this activity. The ego should not be thought of as something that, once produced, is something other than the activity that produces it. Rather, it should be thought of as the *organized form* of this activity. Kant's hypothesis, thus interpreted, implies that the ego just *is* an activity. Accordingly, in our interpretation of Kant (and James), the ego is a neurophenomenological activity that, in its neurological bases, is not yet known and that, in its interior phenomenological expression, has the organized form of a formal unity of apperception, an unintuitable subject that performs both experiencing and proprietary functions and has both interior and exterior sides.

Pursuing our interpretation of Kant's hypothesis, let us refer to the neurophenomenological activity of which the ego is the organized form as the "unifying-appropriating function." This term is apt because it clarifies the relation between the neurophenomenological activity that produces the ego and the ego's two basic functions and two basic sides. The unifying side of the unifying-appropriating function produces the ego in its experiencing function by synthesizing a temporally unified experiencing point of view that holds succeeding experiences—and, therefore, objects insofar as they are known through these experiences—together under its unifying perspective. Concomitantly, the appropriating side of the unifying-appropriating function produces the ego both in its proprietary function and on its exterior side by appropriating the experiences that are in the process of being unified *for* the point of view under which they are being unified, thus attaching these experiences to this point of view as "its" experiences, as experiences that belong to it as parts of what it is, as Me.

The hypothesis that the ego is the organized form of a unifying-appropriating function is here introduced as the third key idea of the revised conception of the ego. This hypothesis is the first and primary hypothesis (as opposed to observable fact) on which the revised conception of the ego rests. For convenience, the hypothesis is henceforth referred to as the "organized-form hypothesis."

Although the organized-form hypothesis goes beyond what we can directly observe about ourselves as egos, it is, I believe, not only plausible but also justified. The justification is twofold, both weak (nondisqualifying) and strong (validating). The hypothesis is justified in a weak or nondisqualifying way because it avoids unnecessary metaphysical assumptions. No incorporeal substances or transcendental syntheses are assumed. All that is assumed is that the ego, organized as a formal unity of apperception, has not only neurological bases but also an interior phenomenological expression. Moreover, the assumption that the ego has an interior phenomenological expression does not presuppose that this expression of the ego is ontologically distinct from its neurological bases. The revised conception of the ego is open to this possibility but takes no position regarding it.

In being open to the possibility that the interior expression of the ego is ontologically distinct from its neurological bases, the revised conception of the ego is also open to the possibility that human subjectivity can in principle be explained by the physical sciences. The organized-form hypothesis and, with it, the revised conception of the ego hew closely to human experience, assuming only that *so far as lived experience is concerned* the interior ego and its neurological bases seem to be irreducibly distinct, whether this appearance correctly or incorrectly reflects the underlying facts. We address this matter more fully in the next chapter, when we discuss the challenge posed to the traditional notion of the ego by physicalists in the philosophy of mind.

The organized-form hypothesis is also justified in a strong or validating way, for the following three reasons (which we here state and then briefly explain): (1) because it can in principle be empirically grounded; (2) because it provides an explanation not only of what the ego is (a unity of apperception or subject of consciousness) but also, as we shall see, of what the ego does in its role as executive agency of consciousness (perform cognitive and practical functions); and (3) because it provides plausible answers to several questions about the ego that are otherwise difficult if not impossible to answer. These three reasons do not validate the organized-form hypothesis in the sense of demonstrating its truth; they do, however, validate it by providing a strong case for accepting it as the best hypothesis available.

As regards the first reason, the idea that the ego is produced by a neurophenomenological synthesizing activity, unlike Kant's idea that it is produced by a transcendental synthesizing activity, can in principle be subject to scientific investigation. It is amenable to such investigation because it is possible to identify and study a neurophenomenological activity in its neurological bases. Neuroscience has already made great strides in identifying the neurological signatures of many conscious states and processes. Some of these signatures are discussed in ensuing chapters. There is, therefore, no reason in principle why neuroscience should not be able to find neurological signatures of the presence and activity of the ego, of the presence of the ego as a unity of apperception and of the activity of the ego as an agency performing cognitive and practical functions. Such a discovery is not imminent and may not be realistic in the foreseeable future. Nevertheless, it cannot be ruled out on principle.

The organized-form hypothesis is also justified in a strong sense because it explains not only what the ego is but also what the ego does. In this section, we have seen how the hypothesis explains what the ego is by explaining that the ego, as the organized form of the unifying-appropriating function, is a formal unity of apperception, an unintuitable subject with two fundamental (experiencing and proprietary) functions and two opposite (interior and exterior, I and Me) sides. In the next section, we shall see how the hypothesis also explains what the ego does by explaining how the unifying side of the unifying-appropriating function, in being the basis of the ego's experiencing function, is also the basis of the ego's cognitive functions generally and how the appropriating side of the unifying-appropriating function, in being the basis of the ego's proprietary function, is also the basis of the ego's practical functions generally.

Finally, the organized-form hypothesis is additionally justified in a strong sense because, as explained in later sections of this chapter, it provides answers to the following difficult questions about the ego: (1) Must the ego always be fully constituted as subject and agency of consciousness, or can it be variable in strength of constitution? (2) Why, as James observed, is the ego in ceaseless motion? And (3) How can the ego, despite being in ceaseless motion, be temporally unified—which is to say, self-identical—over time?

Question 2

IF THE EGO IS NOT AN INCORPOREAL SUBSTANCE, HOW CAN IT BE THE EXECUTIVE AGENCY OF CONSCIOUSNESS?

The ego is not only the subject of consciousness, an experiencer or observer, but also the executive agency of consciousness, an active power that operates on what is presented to it in cognitive and practical ways. The fact that the ego is an executive agency that performs cognitive and practical functions is evident to us from experience. Although we cannot experience the ego directly, we can experience it indirectly. We have already seen that we can experience the ego indirectly as *that* which has experiences, as *that* which relates to experiences and to bodily, mental, and social attributes in a proprietary way, and as *that* which, in thus relating to things, is not only an interior subject or I but also an exterior object or Me. Here we can add that we can also experience the ego indirectly as *that* which performs cognitive and practical functions of a wide variety of sorts. We are indirectly aware of the ego in all these ways, although it is the functional activity of the ego as the executive agency of consciousness that is most evident.

For example, we are aware of the ego's executive activity when we try to concentrate, when we are engaged in sustained operational thinking, when we are examining data to find patterns or themes, when we are restraining or otherwise regulating impulses, when we are deliberating about future actions, and when we are setting ourselves in motion to perform duties or accomplish goals. Because we are aware of the ego as that in us that is active when we are performing functions of these sorts, we can here add the idea that the ego is an executive agency that performs cognitive and practical functions to the revised conception of the ego, as its fourth key idea.

According to the traditional notion of the ego, the ego is the executive agency of consciousness because it is a substantial subject to which consciousness belongs as a subordinate power, a subject, therefore, that has executive authority over consciousness and can act within it as it sees fit. Our account of the ego cannot explain the ego's agency in this way. In our account, the ego, rather than being a substance to which consciousness belongs as a power, is itself only a product of consciousness, specifically a product of a synthesizing activity that occurs within consciousness. The challenge for our account, therefore, is to explain how the ego can be two seemingly incompatible things, a product of consciousness and the executive agency of consciousness.

The ego, I suggest, can be both these things, first, because it is the organized form of an activity and, therefore, is something that is active by its very nature and, second, because the activity of which it is the organized form has the specific character of an agency. Not all activities are agencies. An agency is an activity that operates on things of a certain type or types to produce results of a certain type or types. For example, flowing water is an activity but most often not an agency. However, flowing water can be an agency if, say, it operates on turbines to produce mechanical or electrical power. In general, an agency is an activity that performs functions or does work. Applying this definition to the ego, the question to be answered is how the ego, as the organized form of the unifying-appropriating function, can be understood to be active in a way that performs a function (or functions) or does work.

The ego, I suggest, can be understood to be active in this way because the activity of which it is the organized form already performs primitive cognitive and practical functions in the very process of bringing the ego into existence. The unifying side of the unifying-appropriating function performs a primitive cognitive function because, in producing the ego as a *unity* of apperception, a temporally unified experiencing point of view, it at the same time brings into view temporally unified objects, objects that, with the aid of memory, can be recognized as having been experienced before and, therefore, as possessing self-identity over stretches of time. The unifying side of the unifying-appropriating function in this way brings into view experienced objects properly so called, objects that, because they are not merely momentary phenomena, can be observed, studied, and known. The unifying side of the unifying-appropriating function, in thus producing a temporally unified subject and bringing into view temporally unified objects for this subject to know, lies at the basis of all the ego's cognitive functions. It performs the first and most basic cognitive function, a protofunction that makes possible the ego's experiencing function and that in doing so makes possible the ego's cognitive functions generally.

While the unifying side of the unifying-appropriating function is performing this primitive cognitive function, the appropriating side is performing a primitive practical function, where a practical function is one that acts on things not, as is the case with cognitive functions, to observe, study, or otherwise know them, but rather to transform or utilize them in some way. The appropriating side of the unifying-appropriating function performs a primitive practical function because, in the very process of the ego's ongoing unification, it claims the ego's experiences and worldly attributes for the ego, thus transforming these experiences and attributes by attaching them to and incorporating them within the ego, as parts of what it is. In performing this primitive practical function, the appropriating side of the unifying-appropriating function transforms the ego's experiences and attributes from unbound into bound experiences and attributes, from anonymous into owned experiences and attributes, from no one's into *the ego's* experiences and attributes.[12]

Just as the unifying side of the unifying-appropriating function is twofold, being a synthesis not only of a temporally unified subject but also of temporally unified experienceable objects, so the appropriating side of this function is also twofold. The appropriating side is twofold because, in acting on the incipient ego's experiences and attributes, it transforms not only these experiences and attributes but also the ego itself. It transforms not only the ego's experiences and attributes by making them bound, owned experiences and attributes; it also transforms the ego itself by making it an ego with not only an interior but also an exterior side. The appropriating side of the unifying-appropriating function makes the ego an interior ego *to which have been added experiences and attributes and, therefore, a worldly self.* The appropriating side of the unifying-appropriating function thus transforms the ego by constituting it as a duality, a duality of an interior ego and a worldly self. We can, therefore, conclude that the appropriating side of the unifying-appropriating function, in thus transforming not only the ego's experiences and attributes but also the ego itself, is the first and most basic practical function. It is a protofunction that makes possible the ego's proprietary function and that in doing so makes possible the ego's practical functions generally.

In sum, I suggest, the ego, although a product of consciousness, can be the executive agency of consciousness because the activity of which it is the organized form is itself already functionally active in primitive cognitive and practical ways. The unifying side of the unifying-appropriating function, in producing the ego in its experiencing function, performs a primitive cognitive function in the very process of bringing the ego into existence, that of synthesizing a temporally unified subject aware of temporally unified objects. Correspondingly, the appropriating side of the unifying-appropriating function, in producing the ego in its proprietary function, performs a primitive practical function in the very process of bringing the ego into existence, that of binding experiences and attributes to the ego and thus forging for it an exterior or Me side.

We learned in the previous section that our hypothesis that the ego is the organized form of the unifying-appropriating function can explain why the ego is a formal unity of apperception with two fundamental functions and two opposite sides, and we have learned in this section that it can also explain why the ego is an executive agency that performs cognitive and practical functions. That the organized-form hypothesis can explain these facts about the ego—and that it can do so presupposing only the neurological bases and phenomenological interior of consciousness—goes a long way toward its justification. Granted, it is extremely difficult and perhaps impossible to explain in any detail how the unifying-appropriating function produces the ego as both an experiencing and proprietary subject and, therefore, as an agency that performs both cognitive and practical functions.[13] However, such an explanation is not needed here. All that is needed here is an answer in broad outline to the question of how the ego can be both a product and the executive agency of consciousness.

The account of the ego's agency just set forth has the following important implication: there is no hard-and-fast distinction between the unifying-appropriating function, which is the function by which the ego is constituted, and the executive functions that the ego performs once it is constituted. If the ego just *is* the organized form of the unifying-appropriating function, it follows that the ego's cognitive and practical functions, beginning with its experiencing and proprietary functions, are inherent to the unifying-appropriating function itself, either actually, as is the case with the protocognitive and protopractical functions just discussed, or potentially, as is the case with all of the more developed cognitive and practical functions that will emerge as the ego develops. We track the development of the ego's executive functions, from birth forward, in part 2.

Question 3

IF THE EGO IS NOT AN INCORPOREAL SUBSTANCE, NEED IT ALWAYS BE FULLY CONSTITUTED AS SUBJECT AND EXECUTIVE AGENCY OF CONSCIOUSNESS?

Descartes argued that the ego, as an incorporeal substance, is always ontologically and functionally whole, incapable of being more of an ego at one time and less of an ego at another time. Although the ego can be more or less alert or active, it cannot be more or less an ego, more or less a substance the only function of which is to think. As an incorporeal substance, the ego, Descartes maintained, is always fully constituted as an ego. Kant's account of the ego suggested if not strictly entailed the same: the ego, produced by a synthesizing activity working beyond consciousness, is always already constituted—presumably fully constituted, although Kant does not explicitly state this point—once experiential consciousness is on scene.

Our view, which holds that the ego is the organized form of the unifying-appropriating function, a synthesizing activity working within rather than beyond consciousness, is open to the possibility, contrary to Descartes and Kant, that the ego is variable in strength of constitution. Our view is open to the possibility that the ego is sometimes more strongly constituted and sometimes less strongly constituted, being more strongly constituted when the unifying-appropriating function is more strongly active and less strongly constituted when this function is less strongly active.

The idea that the ego is variable in strength of constitution is defended in this section, in which reasons are given for adopting it as a key idea of the revised conception of the ego. However, before defending this idea, we must first prepare some ground by setting forth a view shared (from very different perspectives) by Buddhists and Jean-Paul Sartre.

As Buddhists discovered millennia ago and as Jean-Paul Sartre rediscovered in the first half of twentieth century, the more one disengages attention and opens awareness to the inner sources of creativity, the more evident it is that at the center of consciousness, where a unified executive ego is supposed to be, there is an open space within which thoughts, images, and impulses spontaneously arise. This intriguing fact presents a serious challenge to the notion of the ego because it seems to indicate that what one finds at the center of consciousness is not just, as Hume reported, the *absence* of an ego but the very *opposite* of an ego. Rather than a unified ego, one finds a void or hole; and rather than an executive ego performing cognitive and practical functions, one finds spontaneously arising psycho-mental phenomena. Buddhists and Sartre are well known for arguing that this space of spontaneity at the center of consciousness reveals that the ego hypothesis is false. This space, in both its openness and its spontaneity, is the very opposite of an ego and, therefore, they have argued, the verified existence of this space where the ego is supposed to be reveals that the ego is an empty concept, a deeply held false belief.

Buddhists believe that the egolessness of consciousness is a good thing. The ego, they believe, seems real only from the perspective of *samsāra*, the realm of conditioned, phenomenal existence. If we are to experience the world from the perspective of *nirvāna*, therefore, it is necessary to let go of the identifications and attachments on which the ego's seeming existence and value are based and thereby, eventually, dissolve the felt sense that we are egos. Fortunately, Buddhists maintain, there is a tool that facilitates the achievement of these ends. The tool is the practice of interior mindfulness (*satipatthāna*) leading to "insight" (*vipassanā*), the meditative practice of steadfast, nonselective, functionally disengaged attention. According to Buddhism, such meditation, if practiced diligently, eventually reveals to the meditator that, rather than there being a unified, executive ego at the center of consciousness, there is instead a "creative emptiness" or "fertile void," from which thoughts, images, and impulses spontaneously arise. This interior emptiness or void is what we have called the space of spontaneity. According to Buddhists, the space of spontaneity at the center of consciousness is the source of creativity and, once belief in the ego has been relinquished, the wellspring of enlightened, liberated life.

Sartre interpreted the egoless spontaneity of consciousness in a completely opposite way. Rather than describing the open space at the center of consciousness as a creative emptiness, he described it as a "hole in being," a frightening "nothingness" through which psychomental phenomena arise of their own accord, without premeditation or regulation. Reporting on this nothingness, Sartre described consciousness as an impersonal spontaneity: "We may therefore formulate our thesis: transcendental consciousness is an impersonal spontaneity. . . . Each instant of our conscious life reveals to us a creation *ex nihilo*."[14]

For Sartre, both the opening within us where the ego is supposed to be and the spontaneity of consciousness expressed through it are bad things. The opening is a rupture at the most intimate point in the fabric of our existence; and the spontaneity of consciousness expressed through it is a spontaneity that is beyond executive control. In Sartre's view the egoless spontaneity of consciousness is for these reasons a source of irrelievable anxiety. It is a spontaneity that undermines both our sense of being and our sense of being in control. Opposite to Buddhists, who see the ego as a false belief that we need to relinquish, Sartre sees the ego as a false belief to which we need to cling.

It is not our concern here whether the space of spontaneity is a good or a bad thing. Rather, our concern is, first, to accept the reports of Buddhists, Sartre, and many others that there *is* such a space and, then, to answer two questions about it. In accepting the reports of Buddhists, Sartre, and others, we are accepting that the space of spontaneity they describe is a confirmable fact about consciousness, not a hypothesis. Admittedly, confirming that there is a space of spontaneity at the center of consciousness is not as easy as confirming the facts about the ego that we have adduced thus far, namely, that it is a formal unity of apperception; that it has two, interior and exterior, sides; and that it is an executive agency that performs cognitive and practical functions. Still, many credible people have observed the space of spontaneity, and many more could if, by meditation or other means, they learned how to experience consciousness in a deep, still, and disengaged way, without thereby becoming drowsy or falling asleep. The point here is that the space of spontaneity, despite being difficult for many to observe, has nonetheless been observed by more than enough credible people to be accepted as a confirmed fact about consciousness. With this point made, let us adopt the idea that there is an open space of spontaneity at the center of consciousness as the fifth key idea of the revised conception of the ego.

We are now ready to begin defending the idea that the ego is variable in strength of constitution by answering the following two questions about the space of spontaneity: (1) Is the existence of this space at the center of consciousness incompatible with an ego also being present at that location, as Buddhists, Sartre, and others argue?, and (2) If not, how is such a conjunction of opposites possible?

The answer to the first question is straightforward, for the following reason: the experience and subsequent memory of a space of spontaneity at the center of consciousness imply the presence of an ego at that location. They do so because an experience implies an experiencer, an experiencing point of view; and a remembered experience requires a proprietary experiencer, an experiencer that relates to the experiences it has (or had and is now remembering) as "its" experiences. In short, to experience and remember a space of spontaneity at the center of consciousness requires a unity of apperception, which is to say, an ego. Clearly, even when a space of spontaneity is evident and the ego is not, the ego *is* still present, *as an experiencing, proprietary point of view to which the space of spontaneity is evident.* Accordingly, despite the paradox of there being both a space of spontaneity and a unified executive ego at the center of conscious, there is good reason to believe that both are in fact present at that location.

This brings us to the second question, about how such a conjunction of opposites is possible. Such a conjunction is possible, I suggest, only if two hypotheses are true. The first is that the space of spontaneity is an opening within the ego itself, specifically an opening that can vary in size by expanding or contracting. The second hypothesis is that the spontaneity of consciousness and the ego in its role as executive agency, although opposites, are fundamentally complementary opposites, opposites that depend on each other as mutually completing interior sides of consciousness. Let us refer to the first of these hypotheses as the "variable-opening hypothesis" and the second as the "complementary-opposites hypothesis."

The paradox that a space of spontaneity and a unified executive ego coexist at the center of consciousness can be broken down into two component paradoxes: (1) that a *space* of spontaneity and a *unified* executive ego coexist at the center of consciousness; and (2) that a space *of spontaneity* and a unified *executive* ego coexist at the center of consciousness. To these paradoxes two more should be added, paradoxes that also arise from the conjunction of a space of spontaneity and a unified executive ego at the center of consciousness. The two additional paradoxes are these: (3) that when the space of spontaneity is evident, the ego is not; and (4) that when the ego is evident, the space of spontaneity is not. I hope to show that the variable-opening hypothesis resolves the first of these four paradoxes, that the complementary-opposites hypothesis resolves the second, and that these two hypotheses together resolve the third and fourth.

Before explaining how the variable-opening and complementary-opposites hypotheses resolve these paradoxes, we need first to provide a provisional account of strongly and weakly constituted ego states. This account is set forth in text box 3.1. Text box 3.1 begins with a statement of the general characteristics of strongly and weakly constituted ego states. It then presents examples of these states. Finally, it provides a brief account of important exceptions, examples of strongly and weakly constituted ego states that lack at least some of the characteristics of the states. It is important to stress that the account of strongly and weakly constituted ego states set forth in text box 3.1 is provisional. It is so because it assumes what we have yet to establish, namely, that there are good reasons for adopting the variable-opening and complementary-opposites hypotheses.

Text Box. 3.1
Strongly and Weakly Constituted Ego States

Characteristics of strongly and weakly constituted ego states: Strongly constituted ego states are those in which the unifying-appropriating function is strongly active, thus producing an ego that is steadfastly alert and that in most cases has contracted boundaries (a small internal opening), a selective focus, and actively engaged executive functions. In contrast, weakly constituted ego states are those in which the unifying-appropriating function is weakly active, thus producing an ego that is unsteady or unalert and that in most cases has expanded boundaries (a large internal opening), an inclusive focus, and less active or disengaged executive functions.

Examples of strongly constituted ego states: Clear examples of strongly constituted ego states are keenly targeted attention, sustained operational thinking, and engaged goal-directed action. In states of these sorts the ego, steadfastly alert, ordinarily has contracted boundaries, a selective focus, and actively engaged executive functions. Using the variable-opening hypothesis, we can say that under these conditions the opening at the center of consciousness, which is an opening within the ego itself, has become so small that it is hidden from view. In other words, the ego's boundaries have contracted almost entirely. Correspondingly, the ego's selective focus and heightened executive activity are such that the spontaneous character of inwardly generated thoughts, images, and impulses is not evident. Such phenomena remain unpredictable, but they tend to be more relevantly responsive to the ego's engaged concerns. Moreover, with the ego's boundaries contracted, such phenomena seem to emerge as if from a place within the ego, as if they had been produced by the ego itself. The ego's small internal opening is like a narrow channel through which, it seems, the ego gives birth to its own thoughts, images, and impulses. Additionally, under the conditions just described, the ego ordinarily forms a strong bond of memory with what it experiences. It does so because the more selectively the ego focuses and the more actively it exercises its executive functions on something, the more information about that thing the ego records to memory.

Exceptions: Strongly constituted ego states that lack at least some of the characteristics of these states: As an exception, ego states can be steadfastly alert, and thus strongly constituted, but nonetheless nonselectively or widely focused and for the most part functionally disengaged. Such strongly constituted ego states are rare outside the practice of what we shall call "opening meditation," which is the practice of giving sustained alert attention to whatever presents itself to consciousness. Opening meditation allows what presents itself to emerge and disappear, allowing what follows to emerge and disappear, and so on, without fixating on, tracking, acting upon, or interacting with any observed phenomena. Opening meditation can be practiced during daily activities (e.g., Buddhist mindfulness meditation [*satipatthāna*] and other practices of being fully present in the moment) or in the context of sitting meditation (e.g., Buddhist insight meditation [*vipassanā*] and Zen "just sitting" meditation [*shikantaza*]). Common to all forms of opening meditation is steadfast alertness that refrains from "doing" anything in response to what presents itself in the moment. Opening meditation thus attempts to maintain alert but nonselective and functionally disengaged attention. The practice of opening meditation during daily activities is said to reveal the phenomena of lived experience in their immediacy and fullness; and as we have seen, Buddhism holds that insight meditation can reveal the space of spontaneity within, the creative source from which thoughts, images, and impulses spontaneously arise. Without the practice of opening meditation of some sort, it is difficult to maintain alert awareness in the moment because attempts to widen the focus of attention and disengage functional activity ordinarily lead not only to more inclusive awareness and to greater stillness of mind but also to loss of alertness, drowsiness, and sleep. It is primarily by practicing a form of opening meditation that one can train oneself to achieve strongly constituted (steadfastly alert) ego states that, by way of exception, are expansively open, inclusively aware, and for the most part functionally disengaged.

Examples of weakly constituted ego states: Clear examples of weakly constituted ego states are most states of reverie, hypnagogic and hypnopompic semisleep, and REM (rapid eye movement) sleep. In states of these sorts the ego, unsteady or unalert, ordinarily has expanded boundaries, a more inclusive focus, and less active executive functions. Using the variable-opening hypothesis, we can say that under these conditions the opening at the center of consciousness is clearly in view, as, too, is the inherently spontaneous character of the phenomena that manifest themselves to the ego through it. These phenomena seem to emerge not from within the ego itself but rather from an open space extending deep within the psyche; and they seem to emerge not as relevant responses to the ego's concerns but rather as unguided or "free" productions of the spontaneity of consciousness. Additionally, under the conditions just described, the ego ordinarily forms only a weak bond of memory with what it experiences (unless the experiences are highly energetic). It does so because the less selectively the ego focuses and the less actively it exercises its executive functions on something, the less information about that thing it records to memory.

Exceptions: Weakly constituted ego states that lack at least some of the characteristics of these states: By way of exception, ego states can be unsteady or unalert, and thus weakly constituted, but nonetheless selective or narrow in focus and functionally engaged. Examples of such states are selectively focused daydreaming and, perhaps, non-REM dreaming (see next section), in which the ego, rather than experiencing the free play of the spontaneity of consciousness, dwells in a perseverative way on matters of personal concern.

With these preliminaries out of the way, it is easy to see how the variable-opening hypothesis resolves the first of the four paradoxes of consciousness set forth earlier, that a *space* of spontaneity and a *unified* ego coexist at the center of consciousness. It resolves this paradox by explaining that the ego's unifying boundaries are not like the fixed boundaries of solid objects or like the dimensionless boundary of a point but are rather like the expanding and contracting boundaries of a camera lens aperture, assuming that the aperture can never be completely closed. Thus conceived, the ego's unifying boundaries can vary across a wide range of aperture sizes. They can contract, thus producing smaller internal openings, as ordinarily happens when the ego narrows its focus and exercises its executive functions. They can also expand, thus producing larger internal openings, as ordinarily happens when the ego widens its focus and disengages its executive functions, thus becoming more receptively and inclusively aware.

Using the aperture analogy, we can say that a space of spontaneity and a unified ego can coexist at the center of consciousness because the space through which the spontaneity of consciousness is expressed is an aperture-like opening within the ego itself, an opening the size of which varies as the ego contracts and expands its boundaries. It is an opening that, with the exceptions noted in text box 3.1, varies in size inversely to the ego's strength of constitution. Even when the ego is strongly constituted and has contracted boundaries and a narrow, selective focus, it still has a (small) opening within itself, a space through which thoughts, images, and impulses reach consciousness and, thereby, the ego itself.

It is also easy to see how the complementary-opposites hypothesis resolves the second paradox, that a space *of spontaneity* and an *executive* ego coexist at the center of consciousness. It resolves this paradox by explaining that the spontaneity of consciousness and an executive ego *must* be joined to each other because neither is complete without the other. As opposites, the spontaneity of consciousness and the ego in its executive activity can and frequently do conflict with each other. However, as *complementary* opposites, they more often and more fundamentally cooperate with each other. They cooperate because they must, because, to modify a point from Kant, the spontaneity of consciousness without the ego would be "blind," and the ego without the spontaneity of consciousness would be "empty" and "idle."

The spontaneity of consciousness without the ego would be blind because it would be without an engaged point of view to guide its production of thoughts, images, and impulses. Without being joined to the ego, the spontaneity of consciousness would be disconnected from a worldly perspective and worldly interests; and its productions would for this reason be not only spontaneous but also random or nearly so. Without the ego, therefore, the productions of the spontaneity of consciousness would be of little or no theoretical or practical value. Oppositely, the ego without the spontaneity of consciousness would be empty and idle because it would be without the thoughts and images that inform its cognition (empty) and without the impulses that motivate its actions (idle). The spontaneity of consciousness and the ego evolved together not to interfere with each other, although they frequently do, but rather to work with each other so that each can provide for the other what the other cannot provide for itself.

Again, although they are complementary opposites, the spontaneity of consciousness and the ego in its executive activity do frequently conflict with each other. The spontaneity of consciousness often misguides the ego with false thoughts or distorted images or distresses the ego with persistent or frightening impulses. Under seriously pathological conditions, the spontaneity of consciousness can even delude and torment the ego, afflicting it with aberrant thoughts, menacing hallucinations, and overpowering impulses. In its turn, the ego's executive activity often restricts the expression of the spontaneity of consciousness, for example, by avoiding or denying unpleasant thoughts or images, by adhering to extreme regimens of self-control, and by repressing threatening impulses or memories. These conflicts between the spontaneity of consciousness and the ego notwithstanding, the more important point, again, is that cooperation between these two interior sides of consciousness is more fundamental than conflict. Joined at the opening at the center of consciousness—which is an opening within the ego itself— the spontaneity of consciousness and the ego are complementary opposites, mutually completing interior sides of consciousness. This fact is what in the introduction we referred to as the duality of "agency and spontaneity." Along with the duality of the interior ego and the worldly self, the duality of agency and spontaneity is fundamental to the constitution of the ego.

Having used the variable-opening hypothesis to resolve the first paradox arising from the conjunction of a space of spontaneity and the ego at the center of consciousness and having used the complementary-opposites hypothesis to resolve the second, we can now use these two hypotheses together to resolve the third and fourth paradoxes. These hypotheses together resolve the third paradox, that when the space of spontaneity is evident, the ego is not, by explaining that the space of spontaneity is evident when the opening within the ego—which just *is* the open space through which the spontaneity of consciousness is expressed—is larger and, correspondingly, the ego has more expanded boundaries, a wider focus, and, ordinarily, less active executive functions. Under these conditions, the ego has little or no awareness of itself as either a unified ego (because its unifying boundaries are expanded) or an executive ego (because its executive functions are less active) and instead is aware almost exclusively of thoughts, images, and impulses that emerge in a conspicuously spontaneous manner from an open space at the center of consciousness. Under these conditions, it certainly seems as if there is nothing more to consciousness than an emptiness or void through which psychomental phenomena arise entirely of their own accord. However, this appearance is misleading because, again, it is the seemingly absent ego that, in its experiencing function, experiences the space of spontaneity and that, in its proprietary function, later remembers this experience as "its" experience. Buddhists and Sartre are wrong to reject the ego. Awareness of a space of spontaneity at the center of consciousness does not expose the ego as a false belief or persistent illusion. It merely hides the ego.

The variable-opening and complementary-opposites hypotheses also resolve the fourth paradox, that when the ego is evident, the space of spontaneity is not. They do so by explaining that the ego is evident when the opening within it is smaller and, correspondingly, it has more contracted boundaries, a narrower focus, and, ordinarily, more active executive functions. Under these conditions, the ego, although not aware of itself directly (because it is an empty, formal unity of apperception), *is* aware of itself as that which performs executive actions. It is aware of itself focusing its attention, holding ideas in mind, performing analyses or inferences, deliberating about means or ends, initiating actions, and the like. When the ego has more contracted boundaries, a narrower focus, and more active executive functions, therefore, it is aware only of what it is observing and doing and for this reason has no awareness of an opening at the center of consciousness through which psychomental phenomena spontaneously arise.

On the contrary, under these conditions the ego, rather than experiencing thoughts, images, and impulses as arising from depths beyond itself as spontaneous productions of consciousness, experiences such phenomena as emerging from a source within itself as relevant responses to its own concerns. When the ego has more contracted boundaries, a narrower focus, and more active executive functions, it seems as if the ego itself "conceives" and gives birth to the thoughts, images, and impulses with which it performs its cognitive and practical functions. It seems as if there is nothing more to consciousness than an ego thinking its own thoughts, entertaining its own images, and pursuing practical aims prompted by its own impulses. However, this appearance is also misleading because the space of spontaneity remains active as a source of the ego's experience, although it is now reduced in size and is more responsive to the ego's concerns. The space of spontaneity continues to be the portal through which the spontaneity of consciousness feeds the ego with the internally generated content of its experience, even though it now seems as though the ego itself has generated this content. Just as awareness of the space of spontaneity hides the ego, so awareness of the ego hides the space of spontaneity.

In sum, the variable-opening and complementary-opposites hypotheses resolve four perplexing paradoxes of consciousness. These paradoxes, if left unresolved, would have seriously counterintuitive implications. They would imply either that there is no space of spontaneity at the center of consciousness or that there is no ego at that location, when both are amply confirmed by our experience. Because the variable-opening and complementary-opposites hypotheses resolve the four paradoxes we have discussed, they deserve, I believe, to be added to the revised conception of the ego, as auxiliary hypotheses supplementing the organized-form hypothesis. To keep count, the variable-opening and complementary-opposites hypotheses are added as the sixth and seventh key ideas, respectively, of the revised conception.

Let us now return to the question posed at the beginning of the section, the question asking whether the ego is always fully constituted as subject and executive agency of consciousness. The foregoing discussion indicates that the answer to this question is "no." The ego is a variable ego, an ego that can be either strongly or weakly constituted over a wide range of values depending on how strongly or weakly the unifying-appropriating function, of which the ego is the organized form, is active. When the unifying-appropriating function is strongly active, it produces a strongly constituted ego, an ego that is steadfastly alert and that ordinarily has a smaller internal opening, more contracted boundaries, a narrower focus, and more active executive functions. Oppositely, when the unifying-appropriating function is weakly active, it produces a weakly constituted ego, an ego that is unsteady or unalert and that ordinarily has a larger internal opening, more expanded boundaries, a wider focus, and less active executive functions.

The foregoing discussion leads us to the conclusion that the ego is variable in strength of constitution. Only a variable ego of the sort described in this section, I suggest, can coexist with a space of spontaneity at the center of consciousness, not only conflicting with it on occasion but also, more importantly, cooperating with it in the manners indicated. Only such an ego can disengage from functional activity and expand its boundaries, thus becoming aware of the space of spontaneity (even if only thereby to lose sight of itself). Additionally, only such an ego can reengage functional activity and contract its boundaries, thus becoming aware of itself as a functional agency (even if only thereby to lose sight of the space of spontaneity). Accordingly, having already adopted the variable-opening and complementary-opposites hypotheses as the sixth and seventh key ideas of the revised conception of the ego, we can here adopt the idea of the ego's variable strength of constitution as the eighth key idea.

Question 4

IF THE EGO IS NOT AN INCORPOREAL SUBSTANCE, IS THERE ANY REASON TO BELIEVE THAT IT IS A NECESSARY BASIS OF CONSCIOUSNESS?

The issue of whether the ego is a necessary basis of consciousness can be approached both theoretically and phenomenologically. The theoretical approach attempts to decide this issue by testing the concept of egoless consciousness for coherence (meaningfulness and consistency). If the concept of egoless consciousness fails the coherence test, the issue of whether consciousness always requires an ego is decided immediately in the affirmative. If the concept of egoless consciousness is incoherent, it follows that the ego can never be absent when consciousness of any sort is present. However, if the concept of egoless consciousness passes the coherence test, the issue of whether consciousness always requires an ego is left undecided so far as the theoretical approach is concerned.

The phenomenological approach focuses on actual states of consciousness that have been said to be egoless. The point of the phenomenological approach is to examine these states to determine if they can truly be known to be egoless. If on examination it is evident that at least one of these states truly is egoless, the issue of whether consciousness always requires an ego is decided immediately in the negative. Confirmation of just one state of egoless consciousness refutes the claim that the ego is a necessary basis of consciousness. However, if on examination it becomes evident that there is after all or at least possibly could be an ego present in all states of consciousness that have been said to be egoless, the issue of whether consciousness always requires an ego is left undecided so far as the phenomenological approach is concerned.

The theoretical approach, in testing the concept of egoless consciousness for coherence, seeks to answer the question of whether it is possible for there to be what I, risking an oxymoron, shall call "unexperienced experiential phenomena." In more familiar terms, the theoretical approach seeks to answer the question of whether it is possible for there to be phenomena such as thoughts, images, impulses, sensations, and sense impressions without an ego present to experience them. Let us return here to Kant, who offered the following reason for denying the possibility of such phenomena: "The **I think** must **be able** to accompany all my representations; for otherwise something would be represented in me that could not be thought at all, which is as much as to say that the representation would either be impossible or else at least would be nothing to me."[15] Kant evidently assumed that the alternatives "impossible" and "nothing to me" are close enough to justify ruling out the possibility of unexperienced experiential phenomena (Kant: unthought representations). Because such phenomena "would either be impossible or would at least be nothing to me," it follows, according to Kant, that anything that can coherently be called "consciousness" must be the consciousness *of* an ego. It must be the consciousness of a subject that not only unifies its experiences but also relates to them in a self-consciously possessive way, thus being able to attach an "I think" to them.

Is Kant correct in thinking that "impossible" and "nothing to me" are close enough to justify ruling out the possibility of unexperienced experiential phenomena? Granting that experiential phenomena that I do not experience are nothing *to me,* does that mean that they are for that reason nothing *without me?* One might attempt to answer this question by arguing that experiential phenomena cannot be present in consciousness without an ego to experience them because, like colors in contrast to light waves and sounds in contrast to sound waves, they are inherently the types of things that an ego experiences. This answer, however, clearly begs the question. It assumes the very point needing to be proved, that things that are inherently the types of things that an ego experiences can exist only if they are in fact being experienced by an ego.

No doubt, the idea of unexperienced experiential phenomena is strongly counterintuitive. It is especially difficult to grasp in the case of experiential phenomena such as thoughts and feelings. It seems almost nonsensical to say that there might be thoughts without a thinker and feelings without a "feeler," although, according to Buddhists and Sartre, precisely this is true. However, there are other experiential phenomena with respect to which it seems less nonsensical, although still strongly counterintuitive, to say that they might pass through consciousness without being experienced. Could not sensory phenomena and inwardly produced sensory-like phenomena (mental images, inner sounds) pass through consciousness without an ego present to experience them, as happens with images and sounds in an empty movie theater? Clearly, we as experiencing egos can treat "nothing to me" as practically equivalent to "impossible." However, this is a fact about us as egos, not about experiential phenomena themselves. To think otherwise seems either to beg the question, as explained, or fallaciously to infer an ontological conclusion (unexperienced experiential phenomena do not exist) from an epistemological premise (unexperienced experiential phenomena are nothing to me).

I do not see how the concept of unexperienced experiential phenomena—or, what is the same, the concept of egoless consciousness—can be dismissed as incoherent. It is one thing to be counterintuitive, another to be meaningless or inconsistent. Accordingly, if the concept of unexperienced experiential phenomena is not incoherent, then such phenomena must be acknowledged to be theoretically possible. Nothing much rests on acknowledging this possibility because it is a possibility that makes no practical difference, a possibility that, again, is nothing to me. Still, acknowledging the possibility makes a theoretical difference. It requires that we conclude that the issue of whether the ego is a necessary basis of consciousness is theoretically undecidable.

Let us now turn to the phenomenological approach and consider some actual states of consciousness that have been said to be egoless. One such state is the sleeping state, which can be divided into dreaming sleep and, should it sometimes happen that all dreaming activity ceases, dreamless sleep. Here we consider only dreaming sleep because it is only sleep with dreams that has been said to be a state of egoless *consciousness,* whereas sleep completely without dreams is ordinarily said to be a state of egoless *unconsciousness.* We consider the possibility of dreamless sleep and what it might imply about the ego in the next section.

The main reason for thinking that the ego is absent in the dreaming state is that the ego weakens rapidly in the transition to sleep. As we move toward sleep, the ego's boundaries tend to expand and loosen; and the ego becomes more widely focused, less active as an executive agency, and less able to recall what it experiences. This weakening of the ego in the transition to sleep suggests that the ego, in crossing the sleep threshold, might lose the last thread of unification, become inactive, and disappear, thus leaving the spontaneity of consciousness to generate psychomental phenomena in an egoless and, therefore, unguided, freely spontaneous way. In terms of the revised conception of the ego, the weakening of the ego in the transition to sleep suggests that, in crossing the sleep threshold, the unifying-appropriating function might come to a halt, thus ceasing the production of the ego and leaving a fully expanded, fully opened space of spontaneity as the "stage" on which the spontaneity of consciousness produces the stuff of dreams.

Three facts stand against this view of what happens in the transition from wakefulness to sleep. The first is that we do sometimes remember our dreams and very likely would remember more if we trained ourselves to do so. People who are awakened from sleep during laboratory experiments are frequently able to remember and report on what they were dreaming. Such reports are made more frequently later in the sleep cycle, during REM (rapid eye movement) sleep, when people report having been dreaming 74 to 80% of the time. However, such reports are also made earlier in the sleep cycle, during the stages of non-REM sleep, when people report having been dreaming 23 to 74% of the time, with more such reports following shallower non-REM sleep and fewer following deeper non-REM sleep.[16] The fact that dreams are frequently remembered strongly suggests that an ego is at least sometimes present during dreaming sleep, an ego that, having experienced dreams, can remember at least some of them, as "its" dreams.

A second fact that stands against egoless dreaming is that some people experience lucid dreams, which are dreams in which there is awareness not only of dream phenomena but also of the fact that one (i.e., the ego) is dreaming. In lucid dreaming, the ego is quite evidently a part of the dreaming experience. Finally, a third fact that stands against egoless dreaming is that the kind of dreams that typically occur during non-REM sleep suggest the presence of an ego engaged in executive activity. To elucidate this last point, we need briefly to clarify important differences between non-REM and REM dreaming.

We are most familiar with REM dreaming because we more often remember REM dreams than we do non-REM dreams and because REM dreams can be gripping and unusual. REM dreams are sensory-like, spontaneous, bizarre, and action-oriented. They are sensory-like because the dreamer experiences phenomena like those that, when we are awake, are generated by the sensory systems. They are spontaneous because these sensory-like phenomena arise unexpectedly, seemingly produced without any control or guidance from the dreamer. They are bizarre because the dream phenomena, although like impressions of the senses, are often surreal, wildly exaggerated, or causally impossible. Finally, they are action-oriented because the dreamer is caught up in dream scenes, responding to them emotionally and feeling impelled to act out physically, unable to do so only because of the protective paralysis that obtains during REM sleep for most people.

In contrast, non-REM dreams tend to be much less sensory-like, spontaneous, bizarre, and action-oriented. They typically involve perseverative thinking about issues of personal concern. This dream thinking, although highly repetitive and cut off from reality testing, is otherwise like our ordinary thinking in being selective in focus and, it seems, active in the examination of real-life issues. Non-REM dreams are for these reasons typically more cognitive than sensory-like, more selectively focused than spontaneous, more commonplace than bizarre, and more self-absorbed than action-oriented. They are more cognitive because the dreamer, mulling over issues of personal concern, primarily thinks rather than senses. They are more selectively focused because the dreamer sticks to specific issues, which tend to be replayed repeatedly. They are more commonplace because the issues dreamt about, as issues of personal concern, are familiar to the dreamer. Finally, they are more self-absorbed because the dreamer, in perseverating on issues of personal concern, is immersed in thought rather than emotionally primed to respond to arising scenes.

This account of REM and non-REM dreams exaggerates their differences. Characteristics of REM and non-REM dreams frequently overlap in transitions through stages of the sleep cycle. Furthermore, non-REM dreams can be said to be selective in focus and ego-active in their examination of issues only in a weak and relative sense. Although the dreamer dwells on matters of personal concern, repeatedly examining them for solutions or implications, he or she is no doubt as much captive to thoughts that replay themselves as actively focused on thoughts that are intentionally pursued. These qualifications acknowledged, the preceding account of the differences between REM and non-REM dreams, although exaggerated, reflects the general findings of dream researchers.[17]

To return to our point, the similarities between non-REM dreams and our ordinary thinking suggests the presence in non-REM dreams of an ego performing executive functions. It seems that an ego is present in non-REM dreams doing what it frequently does when awake: think in a preoccupied way about issues of personal concern. To be sure, this thinking is repetitive and occurs without the reality testing that protects us when we are awake, which may be a reason why night terror sometimes occurs during non-REM sleep. This point acknowledged, it does still seem that an ego, however weakly constituted and barely active, is present in non-REM dreams. Add this fact to the other facts adduced—that people awakened from sleep, both REM and non-REM sleep, often remember their dreams and that some people have lucid dreams—and it is plausible to conclude that at least a weakly constituted ego is frequently if not always present in sleep with dreaming activity. Perhaps crossing the sleep threshold, rather than dissolving the ego, only transforms it from a waking ego into a dreaming ego, a weakly constituted ego unable to test reality and much less able to record experiences to memory.[18] With this possibility in mind, we conclude that the evidence we have reviewed is insufficient to establish that dreaming sleep is ever completely egoless.

Two other conscious states that have been said to be egoless are states of completely opposite sorts. These states sometimes occur on their own but are best known as states produced by meditative practice. The states in question are (1) *expansive openness,* achieved by forms of what we have called "opening meditation" (text box 3.1), which cultivate nonselective, functionally disengaged attention in the present moment; and (2) *deep absorption,* achieved by meditations that concentrate consciousness on and thus absorb it in an object (scene, idea, image, koan, energy, or psychic space), for example, Hindu yoga meditation (leading to absorbed states designated by the Sanskrit word *samādhi*), Buddhist concentrative practice (leading to absorbed states designated by the Pali word *jhāna*), Zen koan meditation (leading to absorbed states designated by the Japanese expression *dai-gidan*), and Christian contemplative practice (leading to absorbed states called "rapture" or "union").

We briefly touched on states of expansive openness when (in text box 3.1) we discussed how opening meditations can create states of alert attention that are inclusively aware and for the most part functionally disengaged. In such states all that seems to be present is whatever presents itself or occurs in the moment. The ego seems to be absent. Again, Buddhist insight meditation, an opening practice, leads to such a state by revealing the space of spontaneity within, the creative emptiness or fertile void from which thoughts, images, and impulses spontaneously emerge. Deep in insight meditation, it does seem that spontaneously arising psychomental phenomena are all that is present and, therefore, that the ego is absent. However, we have already explained that, appearances to the contrary, the ego *is* present in this state of expansive openness. It only seems to be absent because of its low profile, because of its expansive and thus loose unification as a subject and its inactivity (for the most part) as an agency.

What applies to the state of expansive openness produced by insight meditation applies as well to such states produced by other forms of opening meditation. Knowledge that there are such states implies that an ego was present when they occurred, an ego that, because it was present when they occurred, can later remember having experienced them. We conclude, therefore, that the ego may be present in all states of expansive openness and can be known to be present in all such states that are later remembered. It is present in these latter states at least as a bare experiencer that witnesses the states, that appropriates and records to memory its experiences in the states, and then later recalls these experiences as "its" experiences.

States of deep absorption are said to be egoless because the power of the absorption is such as to preclude reflective self-awareness for the duration of the absorption. In such states, it certainly seems as if there is only an object of consciousness (that in which consciousness is absorbed) and no subject of consciousness, no ego. Sustained concentration by a subject on an object so invests that object with energy that it becomes a powerful "cathexis object," an attractor that captivates the subject, thus submerging the subject within the object, seemingly without remainder. The subject, the ego, is thus seemingly dissolved, leaving only the object of meditation, consciously illumined. However, the fact that many people remember having experienced deeply absorbed states indicates that the states remembered, like sleep states and states of expansive openness later remembered, were not without an ego. Recollection of a deeply absorbed state indicates that an ego experienced the state, even though, when it was captive to the absorption, it was not able to reflect on the fact that it was experiencing the state. Such reflective or explicit awareness of the experience becomes possible only after the ego is released from the absorption, thus remembering a state that has since disappeared.

This brief review of presumptive states of egoless consciousness is inconclusive. Is dreaming consciousness ever truly egoless or is an ego always present but so weakly constituted and so limited by altered neurological conditions that it has difficulty remembering what it dreamed? Are states of expansive openness ever truly egoless or is an ego always present but so inwardly open, expansively unified, inclusively focused, and functionally disengaged as to appear absent? Are states of deep absorption ever truly egoless or is an ego always present but in such a captive condition that it cannot explicitly apperceive the experience of absorption until later, when it remembers the experience as "its" experience? We have given reasons for concluding that an ego could be present in all these states and can be known to be present in all that are later remembered. Still, it is possible that there are instances of these states in which no ego is present. Moreover, there may be other types of conscious states in which there is no ego. For these reasons, the phenomenological approach as it has been pursued here is unable to decide the issue of whether the ego is a necessary basis of consciousness.

In sum, neither the theoretical nor the phenomenological approach has decided the issue addressed in this section. Neither approach has shown either that the ego must always be present when consciousness of any sort is present or that the ego can on occasion disappear without taking the rest of consciousness—the space of spontaneity, experiential phenomena—with it. Accordingly, having failed to decide the issue of whether consciousness always requires an ego, we leave the issue undecided and bracket it so far as the revised conception of the ego is concerned.

Question 5

IF THE EGO IS NOT AN INCORPOREAL SUBSTANCE, HOW, IF AT ALL, CAN IT BE SELF-IDENTICAL AND, PERHAPS, PERMANENT (UNINTERRUPTED IN ITS EXISTENCE) OVER THE COURSE OF A LIFETIME?

This question combines two questions, one about self-identity and the other about permanence. Self-identity and permanence are not the same. Permanence implies self-identity but self-identify does not imply permanence. If something remains uninterruptedly in existence from time A to time B (permanence), that implies that it remains one and the same thing over that stretch of time (self-identity). However, as we shall see, if something remains one and the same thing from time A to time B, that does not imply that it remains uninterruptedly in existence over that stretch of time.

We noted earlier that the ego ordinarily possesses self-identity on its exterior or Me side because this side of the ego, although always undergoing change, ordinarily changes in ways that leave core constituent elements much the same over significant stretches of time. Many memories and many bodily, mental, and social attributes recorded in the self-representation either do not change much at all over significant stretches (e.g., early memories, body type, skin color, language, nationality) or change slowly enough (e.g., overall physical appearance, social roles, beliefs, values) to preserve a good deal of overlap between the self-representation of an earlier time and the self-representation of a later time.

That self-identity is thus ordinarily preserved on the ego's exterior side is an uncontroversial fact that we all take for granted in our daily lives. One can imagine science fiction stories in which people change so totally, bizarrely, or abruptly that the notion of exterior-side self-identity is undermined. However, in our lives, the changes we undergo are ordinarily not of this type. We ordinarily change in ways that are partial rather than total, commonplace rather than bizarre, and gradual rather than abrupt. Changes of the types we undergo, rather than undermining the notion of exterior-side self-identity, are both consistent with and explained by it. For us, the notion of exterior-side self-identity highlights the fact that we remain on balance the same as we undergo changes in our lives. With these considerations in mind, let us add exterior-side self-identity to the revised conception of the ego, as its ninth key idea.

We have thus far spoken of the ego as if it possesses self-identity not only on its exterior or Me side but also on its interior or I side. In introducing the notion of the ego as a unity of apperception, we described the ego as a temporally unified experiencing subject, where "temporally unified" just means that the ego, as an interior subject, is at least self-identical if not also permanent over time. However, the issue of the ego's interior-side self-identity, unlike that of its exterior-side self-identity, presents difficulties. It does so because the possibility of interior-side self-identity seems to be contradicted by the fact, stressed by William James, that everything within consciousness is in ceaseless motion, as part of what James (and Alexander Bain before him[19]) called the "stream of consciousness."

James's point is that when we look within ourselves, we find only things in motion. Nothing remains constant from one moment to the next, not even the interior ego. Experiential phenomena morph and succeed each other rapidly; and with each such change there is a corresponding change in the interior ego, which must keep up with the ever-changing contents of its experience. Although we are not aware of the interior ego directly, we *are* aware of its executive activity as it shifts attention from one thought, image, impulse, sensation, or perception to the next, almost always responding in some way, whether to scan, think about, facilitate, resist, or simply disengage itself from whatever has become the focus of its attention. So far as introspection attests, the interior ego, along with consciousness generally, is always in motion.[20] Let us for this reason accept James's point that the interior side of the ego is in ceaseless motion as the tenth key idea of the revised conception of the ego.

Accepting James's point about the ceaseless motion of the interior ego raises the following two questions: (1) Why is the ego on its interior side in ceaseless motion?, and (2) How can the ego on this side possess self-identity over time if it is in ceaseless motion? James does not answer these questions. His account of the ego is exclusively empirical in a phenomenological sense. He reports the observable fact that the interior ego is in ceaseless motion without offering a hypothesis about the underlying nature of the interior ego that would explain its motion, let alone its self-identity despite its motion.

The revised conception of the ego does offer such a hypothesis: the organized-form hypothesis, the hypothesis that the ego on its interior side is the organized form of the unifying-appropriating function. This hypothesis, which earlier earned its justification by providing explanations of the ego's basic form, sides, and functions, here earns additional justification by providing answers to the two questions just posed. It provides an answer to the first question, asking why the interior ego is in ceaseless motion, by explaining that the interior ego is an activity and, therefore, must always be in motion. As the organized form of the unifying-appropriating function, an activity, the interior ego is *inherently* in motion. Additionally, the organized-form hypothesis provides an answer to the second question, asking how self-identity is possible for an interior ego in ceaseless motion, by explaining that such an ego can possess self-identity *if* the activity of which it is the organized form can itself possess self-identity. If the unifying-appropriating function can possess self-identity *as an activity*, then so, too, can its organized form, the ego on its subject or I side.

To explain more fully how the interior ego can possess self-identity as an activity, we need first to discuss how activities generally possess self-identity. Briefly, we recognize an activity as possessing self-identity over time when it meets these conditions: (1) the location of the activity either remains the same or moves in a way that is characteristic of an activity of a certain type (e.g., tornadoes move in distinctive ways, without losing self-identity); (2) the causes of the activity remain generally the same over time; (3) the distinctive organized form of the activity remains generally the same over time; and, if the activity ceases and then resumes, (4) the intervals between cessation and resumption are short enough to indicate that an earlier activity has resumed rather than that a new activity has begun. Significantly, permanence (uninterruptedness of the activity) is not on this list of conditions.[21]

We frequently ascribe self-identity to activities that are interrupted. Take, for example, Old Faithful, the geyser that erupts in Yellowstone National Park in Wyoming. The location of this activity remains the same, in Yellowstone's Upper Geyser Basin. The causes of the activity are volcanic magma and heated underground water, which remain generally the same over time. The organized form of the activity consists of jets of steam and hot water, which remain generally the same over time. Finally, the intervals between cessation and resumption of the activity are between 94 and 68 minutes (+/– 10 minutes).[22] Considering these facts, we assume that Old Faithful is one intermittent geyser rather than a succession of different geysers. The location remains the same; the causes of the geyser remain generally the same; the organized form of the activity remains generally the same; and the intervals between cessation and resumption have not yet been so long as to raise the question of whether Old Faithful has been replaced by a new geyser.

Can the unifying-appropriating function meet the conditions for the self-identity of activities? The answer, I believe, is "yes." Let us consider a hypothetical case, which can be called "John." *Location of activity:* In John's case, the location of the unifying-appropriating function would be twofold. It would be in both John's brain and the phenomenological interior of John's consciousness. Both John's brain and, by association, his interior consciousness change location as John moves from place to place. In doing so, however, they both remain in the same location relative to John. *Causes of activity:* The causes of the unifying-appropriating function in John's case would be the neurons, axons, dendrites, synapses, neurochemicals, and so forth in John's brain. *Organized form of activity:* The organized form of the unifying-appropriating function in John's case, like the location, would be twofold. In the neurological bases of John's consciousness, it would be the distinctive pattern of brain activities that signals the presence and activity of the ego. Correspondingly, in the phenomenological interior of John's consciousness, it would be the distinctive configuration identified by Kant as a formal unity of apperception, together with the cognitive and practical agency inherent to this configuration. *Intervals of activity:* The intervals between cessation and resumption of the unifying-appropriating function in John's case, if any, would be short enough, we can assume—unless, perhaps, John were to fall into a lengthy coma—that the question of whether John might have two or more interior egos successively rather than only one ego intermittently would not arise.

Briefly, regarding the organized-form condition, we should note that neuroscientists might someday be able to track the neurological signatures of the presence and activity of the ego in John's brain. They might be able to confirm that, rather than being erratic or chaotic, these signatures remain roughly stable in their organized form, fluctuating in strength and definition in ways that reliably reflect the degree of John's alertness and functional activity. Correspondingly, John himself can confirm by interior observation that the interior side of his ego, despite being in ceaseless motion, remains roughly stable in the organized form of a unity of apperception and cognitive and practical agency.

John's case, although entirely hypothetical, indicates that there is nothing *conceptually* problematic about the unifying-appropriating function remaining self-identical over time, perhaps even over an entire lifespan. This finding is important because it is the necessary first step in answering the more important question of whether we would be justified in adopting the hypothesis that the unifying-appropriating function—and, therefore, the ego on its interior side—*is* self-identical over time. Let us now consider the extent to which the adoption of this hypothesis—henceforth, the "interior-side–self-identity hypothesis"—might be justified.

At the present time, justification for the interior-side–self-identity hypothesis must be primarily theoretical. Like John, we can attest that our interior egos remain roughly stable as unities of apperception and cognitive and practical agencies. The interior-side–self-identity hypothesis thus has phenomenological support. However, it does not yet have scientific support because neuroscience does not yet know the neurological signatures of the unifying-appropriating function. As for empirical support, therefore, the interior-side–self-identity hypothesis is justified only on phenomenological grounds. However, the scientific support that is currently missing may someday become available.

Turning to theoretical considerations, the primary point in favor of the interior-side–self-identity hypothesis is that the only alternative hypothesis is plagued with conceptual difficulties. The only alternative—let us call it the "succession-of-subjects hypothesis"—holds that the interior ego is not self-identical and, therefore, is a succession of ontologically distinct subjects rather than being one and the same subject over time. This hypothesis is prima facie suspect because it flies in the face of our deep-seated assumption to the contrary. Fundamentally, we assume that we, people generally, possess not only exterior-side but also interior-side self-identity. Doubts about interior-side self-identity might occur when people have just awakened from lengthy comas or have lost all personal memory or suffer from multiple personality disorder or, perhaps, believe they are possessed by spirits or demons. These doubts notwithstanding, our default assumption is that interior-side self-identity—indeed, lifelong interior-side self-identity—obtains for people generally. It would be disconcerting in the extreme if we had to take seriously the possibility that people we know, including most especially ourselves, possess only exterior-side self-identity and not also interior-side self-identity, as experiencing subjects.

Perhaps this difficulty is not so serious. After all, would not a new subject replacing earlier subjects be effectively if not ontologically the same as its predecessors by virtue of having access to their experiences? This conjecture seems promising; however, it suffers from conceptual difficulties. One such difficulty is that it is unclear how it is possible for a new subject to access the experiences of earlier subjects. First, how would a new subject, without any earlier experiences of its own, know that earlier experiences are available for access? Second, even if a new subject somehow knew that earlier experiences were available for access, how would it, without any earlier experiences of its own, know which earlier experiences to look for? Third, even if, despite these difficulties, a new subject succeeded in accessing earlier experiences, how would it know that all or even most of the experiences it accessed derived from its own predecessors, from earlier subjects belonging to its own succession-of-subjects lineage, rather than from a subject or subjects that were not among its predecessors? The fact that experiences are recorded in the brain, which, according to the succession-of-subjects hypothesis, would be shared by subjects belonging to the same lineage, might go some way toward answering these questions. However, it is unlikely that it would lead to satisfactory answers to them all.

Let us for the moment set aside the difficulties just set forth and assume that a new subject arrives on scene automatically supplied with the experiences (and only the experiences) of its own predecessors. Does this assumption make the succession-of-subjects hypothesis tenable? It does not, for we now face the much more serious problem that the new subject would not recognize the experiences it thus inherits as its own earlier experiences. For the new subject, these experiences would be new experiences, not its own earlier experiences, now reexperienced. These earlier experiences, therefore, would not be memories. The new subject for this reason could exercise its proprietary function only on the (second-order) experience of the earlier experiences, not on the earlier experiences themselves. For example, if a new subject were somehow to access an experience that a previous subject had in 2014 in Italy, it could not appropriate this experience as "the experience I had in 2014 in Italy" but rather would have to access it as "the 2014 Italy experience that I am having now in [add the current location]." A new subject would thus relate to the experiences of predecessor subjects only as experiences *from* other times and places, not as its own experiences *of* other times and places. Not being able to appropriate these experiences as its own earlier experiences, it would necessarily relate to them as someone else's experiences.

Thus far, we have established that it is conceptually possible for the ego, as the organized form of an activity, to possess interior-side self-identity.

Furthermore, our own interior experience offers phenomenological support for such self-identity. Finally, and perhaps decisively, we have just seen that the only alternative possibility, that the interior ego, rather than being self-identical over time, is a succession of different subjects, is prima facie suspect and plagued with conceptual difficulties. Given these considerations, we are, I believe, justified in choosing the interior-side–self-identity hypothesis over the succession-of-subjects hypothesis, not as a statement of fact known to be true, but rather as the best hypothesis available. Let us, therefore, add the interior-side–self-identity hypothesis to our revised conception of the ego, as its eleventh key idea.

We can now turn from the issue of interior-side self-identity to the issue of interior-side permanence. The issue now is whether there is reason to think that the interior ego is not only self-identical over time but also permanent, uninterrupted in its existence, through time. This issue of ego permanence, like the issue of whether the ego is a necessary basis of consciousness, can be approached both theoretically and phenomenologically.

The theoretical approach to the issue of ego permanence focuses on the concept of ego impermanence and tests it for coherence. If this concept fails the coherence test, the issue of whether the ego is permanent or impermanent is decided immediately in the favor of permanence. Indeed, it is decided in favor of *immortality,* for a currently existing ego whose nonexistence, however brief, is inconceivable must always remain in existence. However, if the concept of ego impermanence passes the coherence test, as it does easily, I argue, the issue of whether the ego is permanent or impermanent is left undecided so far as the theoretical approach is concerned.

The phenomenological approach to the issue of ego permanence examines actual states that are assumed to be completely unconscious, states in which, therefore, the existence of the ego would be interrupted. To clarify, there can be no ego present in completely unconscious states because the ego, by definition, is a conscious subject, an experiencer. The ego, therefore, is inherently conscious, no matter, in our view, how weakly constituted and thus barely conscious it might be. Although there might be consciousness without an ego, this being the matter we left undecided in the last section, there cannot be an ego without consciousness. Accordingly, if on examining states that are said to be completely unconscious, it turns out that at least one such state can be known truly to be completely unconscious and, therefore, without an ego, the issue of ego permanence is decided immediately in favor of impermanence. However, if on examination of these states, it cannot be established that at least one is completely unconsciousness and, therefore, without an ego, the phenomenological approach will have accomplished all it can without deciding the issue of ego permanence. Let us begin with the theoretical approach.

From the perspective of the revised conception of the ego, testing the concept of ego impermanence for coherence is straightforward, and the outcome is clear: the concept is coherent. If, as the revised conception of the ego holds, the ego is the organized form of an activity, the unifying-appropriating function, then there is nothing conceptually problematic about the possibility that this activity occasionally ceases and then resumes. Indeed, this possibility becomes plausible when one adds, as we have, that the unifying-appropriating function is a variable activity, an activity that can be more or less strongly active and, therefore, that can produce an ego that is more or less strongly constituted. Assuming this variable character of the unifying-appropriating function, why cannot the function sometimes become so weakly active that it completely ceases as an activity from time to time, thus ceasing altogether to produce an ego from time to time? The variable character of unifying-appropriating function and, therefore, of the ego implies a point of minimal ego constitution, where the theoretical minimum is zero, no ego at all.

Although the revised conception of the ego thus provides an explanation of how ego impermanence is possible and, therefore, of why the concept of ego impermanence is coherent, it does not provide any reason for thinking that the ego is in fact impermanent. It may be that the unifying-appropriating function sometimes approaches the zero minimum without ever reaching it. It may be that the unifying-appropriating function never altogether ceases being active so long as a person is alive. The revised conception of the ego establishes only that there is a way to understand how ego cessation might occur, not that it ever does occur. With this point made, we conclude that the theoretical approach is unable to decide the issue of ego permanence.

Turning to the phenomenological approach, there are four principal states that are sometimes said to be completely unconscious and, therefore, without an ego: deep non-REM sleep (stage 3), deep anesthesia, coma, and the vegetative state. Regarding deep non-REM sleep—that is, sleep in which slow delta waves predominate—the case for complete unconsciousness rests on the significantly altered neurological profile of this kind of sleep and on the fact that people awakened from deep non-REM sleep most often report disorientation and blankness of mind, as if they were returning from a state in which nothing was experienced, presumably because no ego was present to do the experiencing. We noted earlier that people awakened from non-REM sleep report having dreamed 23 to 74% of the time, with more such reports following shallower non-REM sleep and fewer following deeper non-REM sleep. Perhaps this indicates that in deepest non-REM sleep dreaming activity—and with it, the ego and consciousness of any sort—disappears, even if only briefly.

Acknowledging the possibility that deep non-REM sleep might sometimes be completely dreamless, it is difficult to know how one could be justified in holding that this type of sleep is ever in fact completely dreamless. The blankness of mind upon awakening might be due to highly altered brain activity rather than to an interruption of dreaming during these states. Some anesthetics allow consciousness during a medical procedure but induce amnesia thereafter. Furthermore, a major fact about sleep, chemically induced or not, is that it interferes with memory. These considerations suggest the possibility that the deepest level of sleep disallows, not dreaming, but only the memory of dreaming. Perhaps dreams do always occur in deep non-REM sleep but cannot be remembered because the recording or later retrieval of them is prohibited by the neurological conditions of such sleep.

Given what we know, I do not think we can rule out either that dreaming always continues or that it sometimes ceases during deep-REM sleep. However, let us for the moment assume that dreaming *does* sometimes cease during such sleep and consider the implications for ego permanence or impermanence. Would cessation of dreaming during deep non-REM sleep imply that such dreamless sleep is completely unconscious and, therefore, without an ego? The answer, I suggest, is "no." It is of course possible that cessation of dreaming leads to a cessation of all consciousness and, therefore, to a cessation of the ego. However, it is also possible that the ego, and therefore consciousness, remains in sleep states altogether without dreaming. Such an ego would not engage in thinking about matters of personal concern, as is characteristic of much of non-REM sleep; nor would it witness any spontaneously arising sensory-like phenomena, as is characteristic of REM sleep. Both the ego's executive functions and the spontaneity of consciousness would be arrested, or nearly so.

In such sleep, the ego would be only blankly conscious and, except for such activity of the unifying-appropriating function as is minimally necessary to keep it in existence, would be inactive. It would not in any perceivable way be active as an executive agency performing cognitive or practical functions. Moreover, it would not be aware of any thoughts, images, or impulses arising within the space of spontaneity, which would thus be devoid of content. The ego would approach being a bare, motionless experiencer; and the space of spontaneity, which the ego would experience, would approach being a dormant void. The ego would be aware, although only barely so, and the psychic space of which it would be aware would be empty. Awakening from such a state would understandably leave one with blankness of mind.

The possibility of dreamless sleep of the sort just described might seem far-fetched. However, some meditation-based schools of Asian philosophy maintain that sleep of this sort does occur. According to these schools, deepest sleep is a state in which dreaming ceases but consciousness—bare awareness of emptiness—remains.[23] Vedanta especially stresses this point, maintaining that dreamless sleep is one of four major states of consciousness, the other three being waking consciousness, dreaming consciousness, and liberated or pure consciousness (*turiya*).

Whether deep sleep always has some dreaming activity or is sometimes dreamless but not egoless, as just described, or is sometimes both dreamless and egoless is extremely difficult and perhaps impossible to know. Moreover, the same, I suggest, is true with respect to deep anesthesia, coma, and the vegetative state. Although some are of the opinion that these states are completely unconscious and, therefore, without an ego, it is possible that ego-consciousness of some sort is present in them. The ego could possibly be present in these states, despite their radically altered neurological profiles, despite the lack of any response to external stimuli, and despite the blankness of mind upon awakening from the states (if awakening occurs). Granted, it would be accurate to say that "effectively" or "so far as we know" there is no awareness of any sort in these states. However, even this statement is an admission that we cannot be sure about the matter. As with deep non-REM sleep, it is extremely difficult and perhaps impossible to know whether deep anesthesia, coma, and the vegetative state are ever completely unconsciousness and, therefore, without an ego. We conclude, therefore, that the phenomenological approach, at least as it has been pursued here, cannot decide the issue of ego permanence.

Having failed to decide the issue of ego permanence by either the theoretical or the phenomenological approach, we leave the issue undecided and bracket it so far as the revised conception of the ego is concerned. Accordingly, just as the revised conception takes no position on whether the ego is a necessary basis of consciousness, neither does it take a position on whether the ego is permanent throughout a lifetime. The most plausible view, I believe, is that the ego *is* a necessary basis of consciousness but is *not* permanent, that conscious experiencing cannot occur without an ego as experiencer but that there are intervals in people's lives that are without an ego and, therefore, without consciousness. In this view, the ego could still be self-identical over time even though it would occasionally go out of existence, taking consciousness with it. This view, however, is only a guess. The revised conception of the ego leaves the issues of the ego's necessity and permanence undecided.

Conclusion

The revised conception of the ego as it has been formulated thus far is built on Buddhist, Kantian, and Jamesian ideas. We have borrowed two ideas from each of these sources. From Buddhism we have borrowed the idea that there is a space of spontaneity at the center of consciousness and the idea that when this space is evident the ego appears to be absent. From Kant we have borrowed the idea that the ego is a formal unity of apperception and the idea that the ego is the product of a synthesizing activity. Finally, from James we have borrowed the idea that the ego has both an interior (subject or I) side and an exterior (object or Me) side and the idea that the interior side of the ego is in ceaseless motion.

The integration of these ideas within the revised conception of the ego has required us to reject, reinterpret, or make additions to Buddhist, Kantian, and Jamesian views. We have rejected the Buddhist view that the space of spontaneity contradicts the ego hypothesis by explaining why a unified executive ego can—indeed, must—coexist with a space of spontaneity at the center of consciousness. We have reinterpreted Kant's hypothesis that the ego is the product of a synthesizing activity by replacing Kant's view that it is the product of a transcendental synthesizing activity with the view that it is the organized form of the unifying-appropriating function, a neurophenomenological synthesizing activity. Finally, we have added to James's view that the ego on its interior side is in ceaseless motion the hypothesis that the ego is the organized form of the unifying-appropriating function, thus answering the following two questions that James's views raised but could not answer: (1) Why is the interior ego in ceaseless motion?, and (2) How can the interior ego possess self-identity despite its ceaseless motion?

In this chapter we have attempted to answer five questions that pose challenges to the traditional notion of the ego. These questions raise issues most of which (the issues raised by question 3 being the exception) came to the fore after Descartes but before the twentieth century. In attempting to answer these questions, eleven key ideas for the revised conception of the ego have emerged. These ideas are restated in text box 3.2.

Text Box 3.2
Key Ideas of the Revised Conception
of the Ego: First Set

NOTE: This summary of key ideas indicates for each idea whether it refers to an *observation* (something we can know about the ego based on our own experience as egos), a *justified hypothesis* (something we can justifiably say about the ego because it provides the best available explanation of an observation or because it resolves paradoxes or other difficulties that have plagued the notion of the ego), or a *conclusion* (something we can justifiably say about the ego because it is implied by an observation or a justified hypothesis).

1. *Observation: The ego is a formal unity of apperception.* The ego is an unintuitable subject with two basic functions, an experiencing function and a proprietary function. In its experiencing function, the ego is the unified-and-thus-unifying subject of consciousness, a subject that unifies consciousness under its experiencing point of view so that it can observe what arises within or is presented to consciousness. In its proprietary function, the ego is the appropriating owner of consciousness, a subject that appropriates its experiences and worldly attributes and thus relates to them in a proprietary way, as "its" experiences and attributes, as experiences and attributes that belong to it as parts of what it is.

2. *Conclusion (implied by no. 1), which is also knowable by observation: The ego has two, interior and exterior, sides.* The ego's two basic functions imply, what we can ourselves observe, that the ego has two basic sides, an interior side, referred to by William James as the ego as subject or "I," and an exterior side, referred to by James as the ego as object or "Me." The interior side of the ego is the ego in its experiencing and proprietary functions (and in all its executive functions). The exterior side of the ego consists of everything that the ego, in the exercise of its proprietary function, has appropriated and thus attached to itself as part of what it is, including not only present and remembered experiences but also bodily, mental, and social attributes. The self-representation is the mental record on which the ego keeps track of its exterior side. That the ego is fundamentally two-sided in the way just described is what we have called the "duality of the interior ego and the worldly self." This duality is constitutive of the ego. The interior side of the ego, the ego as subject or I, is incomplete without the exterior side.

3. *Justified hypothesis: The ego is the organized form of a unifying-appropriating function (organized-form hypothesis).* The primary hypothesis of the revised conception of the ego is that the ego on its subject or I side is the organized form of a neurophenomenological activity, which we have called the "unifying-appropriating function." This hypothesis is justified because it explains (a) why the ego on its subject or I side is organized as a formal unity of apperception with both experiencing and proprietary functions; (b) how the ego, in the exercise of its proprietary function, creates for itself an object or Me side; (c) why the ego is an agency that performs cognitive and practical functions; (d) why the ego on its subject or I side is in ceaseless motion; and (e) why the ego on its subject or I side can possess self-identity despite being in ceaseless motion.

4. *Conclusion (implied by no. 3), which is also an observation: The ego is an agency that performs cognitive and practical functions.* The organized-form hypothesis also explains the following observable fact about the interior side of the ego: it is a functional agency, specifically an agency that performs executive functions of cognitive and practical sorts. The organized-form hypothesis explains this fact about the ego because the unifying-appropriating function already performs primitive cognitive and practical functions in the very process of producing the ego as its organized form. The unifying side of the unifying-appropriating function performs a primitive cognitive function by synthesizing the ego as a temporally unified subject that, with the help of memory, can be aware of temporally unified objects, objects that it can observe, study, and thus know. At the same time, the appropriating side of the unifying-appropriating function performs a primitive practical function by laying claim to the ego's experiences and worldly attributes in the very process of the ego's unification as subject and executive agency of consciousness, thus making these experiences and attributes *the ego's* experiences and attributes and making the ego not just an interior ego but an interior ego *with an exterior side,* with a worldly self.

5. *Observation: There is a space of spontaneity at the center of consciousness.* Buddhist meditators and many others who have looked within consciousness report that, rather than finding an ego at the center of consciousness, they have instead found an open space through which thoughts, images, and impulses spontaneously arise.

6. *Justified hypothesis: The space of spontaneity is a variable opening within the ego (variable-opening hypothesis).* The revised conception of the ego adopts the hypothesis that the space of spontaneity is a variable opening within the ego, an opening that can contract or expand, thus decreasing or increasing in size. When the ego contracts its boundaries, thus narrowing its focus and, ordinarily, engaging its executive functions, the opening within it decreases in size. Under these conditions the ego becomes aware of itself, specifically of its selective focus and engaged executive activity, but only by losing awareness of the space of spontaneity. Oppositely, when the ego expands its boundaries, thus widening its focus and, ordinarily, disengaging its executive functions, the opening within it increases in size. Under these conditions the ego becomes aware of the space of spontaneity, but only by losing awareness of itself. The variable-opening hypothesis is justified because, along with the complementary-opposites hypothesis (below), it explains four perplexing paradoxes of consciousness.

7. *Justified hypothesis: The spontaneity of consciousness and the ego are complementary interior sides of consciousness (complementary-opposites hypothesis).* The revised conception of the ego adopts the hypothesis that the spontaneity of consciousness and the ego in its role as executive agency work together as complementary interior sides of consciousness, each side providing for the other what it cannot provide for itself. The spontaneity of consciousness provides the ego with the internally generated content of its experience, the thoughts, images, and impulses that it experiences, appropriates as its own, and acts on in performing its executive functions. In turn, the ego provides the spontaneity of consciousness with an experiencing point of view and, when focused and functionally engaged, guidance in the types of thoughts, images, and impulses to produce. The complementary-opposites hypothesis is justified because, along with the variable-opening hypothesis, it explains four perplexing paradoxes of consciousness. The complementary-opposites hypothesis is also justified because it explains the fundamental duality of agency and spontaneity. This duality, like the duality of the interior ego and the worldly self, is constitutive of the ego. Just as the interior ego as subject of consciousness is incomplete without its worldly self, so the interior ego as executive agency of consciousness cannot function apart from the spontaneity of consciousness.

8. *Conclusion (implied by nos. 6 and 7): The ego is variable in strength of constitution.* The ego, rather than always being fully constituted as subject and executive agency of consciousness, is variable in strength of constitution. When the unifying-appropriating function is more strongly active, it produces a more strongly constituted ego, an ego that ordinarily has more contracted boundaries, a more selective focus, and more active executive functions. Oppositely, when the unifying-appropriating function is less strongly active, it produces a less strongly constituted ego, an ego that ordinarily has more expanded boundaries, a more inclusive focus, and less active executive functions.

9. *Observation: The ego ordinarily possesses self-identity on its exterior side.* The core features of the self-representation ordinarily change slowly enough that features at later times significantly overlap with features of earlier times, thus preserving exterior-side self-identity over time.

10. *Observation: The subject or I side of the ego is in ceaseless motion.* As subject and executive agency of consciousness, the subject or I side of the ego is always in motion and undergoing change. This observed fact about the ego is explained by the organized-form hypothesis, which explains that the subject or I side of the ego is always in motion because it is the organized form of an activity, the unifying-appropriating function.

11. *Justified hypothesis: The ego ordinarily possesses self-identity on its subject or I side (interior-side–self-identity hypothesis).* The revised conception of the ego adopts the hypothesis that for most people the unifying-appropriating function meets the conditions for self-identity of activities and, therefore, that most people possess not only object- or Me-side but also subject- or I-side self-identity. This hypothesis has the advantage of agreeing with our intuitions about ourselves as subjects and of avoiding conceptual difficulties that plague the alternative hypothesis, that the ego on its subject or I side is a succession of ontologically distinct egos.

NOTE: The revised conception of the ego takes no position on whether the ego is a necessary basis of consciousness or on whether the ego on its subject or I side is permanent (uninterrupted) in its existence over the course of life.

Chapter 4

Rethinking the Notion of the Ego, Stage Two

The Twentieth Century

The traditional notion of the ego was a target of criticism for many schools of thought in the twentieth century. Representatives of classical psychoanalysis, existential phenomenology, depth psychology, symbolic interactionism, relational psychoanalysis, postmodernism, feminism, and physicalism in the philosophy of mind all took aim. This chapter considers the criticisms presented by these schools and uses them as a guide for the second stage of our revision of the traditional notion of the ego. The criticisms are discussed in the context of attempting to answer the following seven questions:

6. How is the traditional view that the ego has the power to regulate the passions to be evaluated in response to Freudian psychoanalysis, which provided both a theory of psychopathology and clinical evidence demonstrating that the ego is prey to the passions in many ways?

7. How is the traditional view that the ego exercises direct and complete control of its executive functions to be evaluated in response to advances in our understanding of psychopathologies of thought and action and in response to philosophical views stressing the spontaneity of consciousness?

8. How is the traditional view that the ego resides within the interior of the psyche to be evaluated in response to phenomenological accounts of the primacy of embodiment and being-in-the-world?

9. How is the traditional view that the ego has full, privileged access to itself to be evaluated in response to depth psychology, symbolic interactionism, and relational psychoanalysis?

10. How is the traditional view that the ego is the author of its identity to be evaluated in response to postmodernists' accounts of the socially constructed self?

11. How is the traditional view that the ego is gender-neutral to be evaluated in response to the argument that the notion of the ego as it has emerged in patriarchal societies more accurately represents men's subjectivity than women's?

12. How is the traditional view that the ego is ontologically distinct from the body to be evaluated in response to advances in cognitive science, artificial intelligence, and neuroscience?

Question 6

HOW IS THE TRADITIONAL VIEW THAT THE EGO HAS THE POWER TO REGULATE THE PASSIONS TO BE EVALUATED IN RESPONSE TO FREUDIAN PSYCHOANALYSIS, WHICH PROVIDED BOTH A THEORY OF PSYCHOPATHOLOGY AND CLINICAL EVIDENCE DEMONSTRATING THAT THE EGO IS PREY TO THE PASSIONS IN MANY WAYS?

The traditional notion of the ego holds that the ego exercises a good deal of causal power. To recall, Descartes held that the ego has direct and complete control of "actions of the soul," its executive functions, indirect but nonetheless in principle complete control of the passions, and indirect, incomplete, but still considerable control of its body and actions in the world. Descartes's account of the ego's mastery of the passions, which is close to the Stoic view, is too extreme to be representative of the traditional view. Nevertheless, the traditional view does hold that the ego has enough power over the passions to regulate them reasonably well on most occasions; and it otherwise agrees generally with Descartes's assessment of the ego's causal powers.

The question of the extent to which, if any, the ego has control of the passions was debated throughout the modern period. Figures such as Hobbes, Hume, Schopenhauer, and Freud opposed the traditional view by arguing that it is the passions that control the ego—assuming, as Hume did not, that there is such a thing as an ego—not the ego that controls the passions. According to these critics of the traditional view, the will is set in motion only desideratively, by inclinations, not electively, by the ego's choices. It is not the ego's choices that cause its actions; rather, it is the most influential, the most recent or powerful, inclinations that cause its actions. The question of which has control of the other, the ego control of the passions or the passions control of the ego, was in this way debated repeatedly in the modern period without resolution. The question is considered here, as a question in the second stage of our rethinking of the notion of the ego, because it was not until early in the twentieth century that a new approach was introduced that made significant progress toward answering the question. This new approach was Freudian psychoanalysis.

Freud was a staunch antitraditionalist, holding that the ego is the servant of the instinctual demands of the id. However, it was not Freud's account of the relation of the ego to the id that introduced a new approach to answering the question about the relation of the ego to the passions. Rather, it was his theory of psychopathology and his clinical case studies that did so. His writings on these subjects explained how people, owing to a wide variety of psychological disorders, can be assailed by feelings and desires over which they have little control. Moreover, these writings shed light on the fact that even people free of serious psychological disorders can, owing to early traumatic experiences or harsh upbringings, be chronically vulnerable to feelings such as anxiety, fear, guilt, and shame. Freud's writings and the subsequent psychoanalytic literature focusing on mental disturbances made it unmistakably clear that people suffer from a wide range of conditions that allow passions, if not to enslave them, at least to prey on them persistently. Whatever one might think of Freud's theories of the structure of the psyche; the roles of the ego, superego, and id; the Oedipus complex; and psychosexual development, one must acknowledge his groundbreaking role in the history of clinical psychiatry and psychology. Thanks to Freud and those who were heir to his contributions, it has now long been established that there are many circumstances under which the ego has little control of the passions.

Acknowledging this point, it might be argued that people who are free of psychological disorders and who do not suffer from the effects of early trauma or a harsh upbringing might be able to control their passions, at least most of their passions most of the time. This possibility seems plausible. However, it does so only because the ego, in controlling the passions, is most often supported by a hidden defense system, a fact revealed and explained in detail by Freud. According to Freud, the ego's control of the passions is to a great extent based on unconscious defenses, most importantly on repression but also on mechanisms such as reaction formation, isolation, undoing, projection, introjection, turning against the self, reversal, and sublimation.[1] Freud's insight was that much of the power the ego has over the passions is predicated on unconscious defense mechanisms that hide, mute, or disguise the passions.

Defense mechanisms, Freud explained, are psychodynamic, cognitive, or behavioral maneuvers by which the ego shields itself from psychic materials that pose a threat to it, especially to its executive control of consciousness. Psychodynamically, defense mechanisms are forms of internal inhibition or redirection of threatening psychic forces by which the ego denies or resists their expression or diverts their expression to safer outlets (e.g., repression, suppression, sublimation, displacement). Cognitively, these mechanisms are mental stratagems by which the ego protects itself by disavowing, misattributing, misclassifying, or misinterpreting threatening psychic materials so that the dangers they threaten either go unacknowledged (e.g., denial, dissociation) or are imputed to others (e.g., projection, reaction formation, splitting) or are safely separated from other psychic materials (e.g., compartmentalization, isolation) or are seen in a less threatening light (e.g., rationalization, intellectualization, idealization). Finally, behaviorally, defense mechanisms are actions by which the ego protects itself from threatening psychic materials by doing the opposite of what they prompt or by engaging in rituals that keep them at bay (e.g., undoing, reversal, obsessive-compulsive rituals).

The ego's strength with respect to the passions is thus to a great extent predicated on unconscious defenses that in a variety of ways lessen the destructive or destabilizing effects that passions can have on the ego. When the ego's defenses are strong, the ego's strength with respect to the passions is greater, since it is less beset with passions that would pose a threat to it. However, when the ego's defenses have been undermined or fail, passions from which the ego had been protected can begin to prey on it. Although some of the defense mechanisms described by Freud have been critically questioned within psychiatry and clinical psychology, repression especially, Freud's general idea that such mechanisms undergird the ego's executive powers remains basic to these fields.

In sum, Freud and those who followed him changed the debate between traditional and antitraditional views on the ego's relation to the passions by offering a new challenge to the traditional view. Freud demonstrated that people who suffer from psychological disorders or who have been subject to trauma or who have had harsh upbringings or who are dependent on defenses that might fail can easily fall prey to the passions. Freud thus demonstrated that the traditional view naively overestimates the ego's power in relation to the passions. However, in demonstrating this much, Freud did not thereby demonstrate the truth of his own extreme antitraditional view, that the ego is only a servant of the id. Freud needed to be corrected on the matter of the ego's causal power. The correction was soon to come.[2]

It came in the 1930s in the work of Heinz Hartmann and other psychoanalytic ego psychologists. Hartmann made a strong case for the view that the ego has not only defensive but also considerable "conflict-free" or autonomous power. He held that the ego has energy at its disposal that it can use for purposes other than protecting itself against threatening psychic materials.[3] Specifically, Hartmann held that the ego has energy with which it can perform autonomous functions, functions, such as disciplined thinking, self-regulation, and intentional action, that are needed for meeting the challenges of the world. These autonomous ego functions are executive functions of the same cognitive and practical sorts that had been assigned to the ego throughout the modern period.

Additionally, Hartmann's ego psychology brought forth a new understanding of ego strength. A strong ego in Hartmann's view is not only an ego that has sound defenses and, therefore, is free of serious internal conflict; it is also, and indeed primarily, an ego that has a good deal of conflict-free energy available to perform nondefensive executive functions. Such energy, Hartmann held, can be increased by a process of neutralization, which strips libidinal and aggressive energies of their instinctual aims and makes them available to the ego as energy to be used for its aims. For Hartmann, a strong ego is of course an ego that is psychologically healthy and has good defenses; but even more it is an ego with ample reserves of autonomous energy, energy with which it can perform cognitive and practical functions as the executive agency of consciousness.

With the wide acceptance of this conception of the ego's autonomous powers, Freud's antitraditional view on the ego's power with respect to the passions was replaced with a more balanced view, a view that locates the truth on a middle ground between traditional and antitraditional positions. According to this view, although the passions have considerable power over the ego, the ego itself has considerable power, which it exercises not only in defending itself against threatening passions but also in regulating the passions in more positive ways and in additionally performing executive functions in thinking about and acting in the world.

How might this middle ground be understood? An analogy will be helpful. Let us compare the ego to a feudal king. The king rules with the presumption of sovereignty over the whole of his domain, including his vassals, peasants, and territory. However, the king's vassals sometimes refuse his orders and may even plot against him, causing the king to react with uncontrollable rage and violence. The peasants also pose challenges to the king's authority. They frequently disregard the laws and sometimes rise in rebellion, causing the king forcibly to suppress them. Furthermore, the king is wary of enemies that might invade his kingdom should perimeter defenses fail. The king is thus subject to many limitations on and threats to his power, limitations and threats of types like those to which the ego is subject according to Freud. This fact notwithstanding, the king ordinarily has enough power to survive occasional plots, rebellions, and invasions, to enforce the laws under most circumstances, to implement essential policies, and in these ways to retain his crown and reign reasonably well.

That is, the king ordinarily has enough power to do these things *if* he has the resources to survive domestic challenges and to keep foreign enemies at bay (Freud: a strong ego is free of psychological disorders and is well defended against threatening psychic materials), *if* he is himself a strong enough leader to provide for social needs and achieve social goals (Hartmann: a strong ego has not only a sound defense system but also autonomous strength as an executive agency), and *if* he is self-disciplined and has good habits (Descartes: an ego can achieve self-control if it practices good psychological hygiene).

The middle ground on which the ego "presides" over the passions, I suggest, is like the kingdom just described. The ego, as the executive agency of consciousness, is like the king in acting on the presumption of sovereignty, despite many limitations on and threats to its power. The ego is also like the king in being unable to maintain complete control of its "subjects," the passions with which it is familiar in everyday life. The ego frequently succumbs to anger, guilt, shame, desire, or fear. Furthermore, should the ego's defense system be compromised at a deep level, the ego's domain, its "kingdom"—which is to say, consciousness—is vulnerable to being invaded by strong impulses over which the ego may have no control. However, despite these limitations and threats, the ego is also like the king in ordinarily having enough power to "keep its crown" and "reign" reasonably well. That is, the ego is ordinarily able to do these things *if* it has the resources to survive strong challenges from the passions and to keep deeper, more dangerous impulses at bay, *if* it has the autonomous strength needed to provide for personal needs and achieve important life goals, and *if* it is self-disciplined and has good habits.

The middle ground depicted by our analogy indicates that the ego's presumption of sovereignty, although overreaching its actual power, is by no means wholly delusory.[4] The ego does have significant causal power. Its power over the passions specifically, although limited, is real and can be considerable if all the aforementioned conditions are met. The ego's power over the passions is real to the extent that the ego is psychologically healthy and has a good defense system. Moreover, the ego's power over the passions can be considerable if, in addition to being psychologically healthy and having a good defense system, the ego possesses autonomous strength, is well disciplined, and is supported by good habits. It is possible for the ego, if lacking autonomous strength, self-discipline, or good habits, to struggle mightily with the passions; and it is possible for the ego, if suffering from a serious psychological disorder or lacking a good defense system, to succumb to the passions almost entirely. However, it is also possible for the ego, if all the conditions we have been discussing are met, to have a great deal of control over the passions and to be little troubled by them. This view, I suggest, best explains why people differ so greatly in the extent to which they control their passions, with some controlling them to a great extent (stoics, ascetics), with others controlling them almost not at all (people suffering from serious psychological disorders), and with still others, the majority, controlling them adequately although sometimes losing control to them.

The discussion thus far points to the conclusion that the most reasonable view on the issue of the ego's control of the passions is that the truth lies on a *wide* and *shifting* middle ground between the positions represented by advocates and critics of the traditional notion of the ego. This middle ground is wide because it must have room for all the people mentioned at the end of the last paragraph. Moreover, this middle ground is shifting because most people, wherever they might ordinarily be located on this ground, can change their position, moving significant distances toward either more or less control of the passions, depending on changes in the conditions we have discussed: mental health, soundness of the defense system, autonomous strength, self-discipline, and good habits. Only a middle ground that is thus both wide and shifting, I suggest, can accommodate the different and changing ways in which we relate to the passions.

A larger point that emerges from the discussion in this section is that the ego is a bridge that integrates an inherent duality of human experience, that of self-control and the passions. The two sides of this duality, as opposites, frequently conflict with each other. Self-control is sometimes overridden by surges of the passions; and the passions are sometimes suppressed or repressed by self-control. Such conflicts notwithstanding, self-control and the passions, as opposite sides of a duality inherent to human experience, are fundamentally coessential, complementary opposites, opposites that depend on and complete each other. Self-control depends on the passions for motivated, energetic response to the world; and the passions depend on self-control for regulation and cultivation. Together, they make possible responses to the world that are motivated, energetic, and properly measured.

In the introduction and again in the last chapter we explained that there are two dualities that are fundamental to the constitution of the ego, that of the interior ego and the worldly self, and that of agency and spontaneity. The duality of self-control and the passions is a specific form of the latter of these two dualities. Another specific form of this fundamental duality is the duality of executive and spontaneous (intuitive, creative) cognition, that is, of actively performed thought on the one hand and suddenly emergent insight or ideation on the other. The duality of executive and spontaneous cognition is not discussed here. However, its general character should become evident from the exposition in the next section, which focuses on the fundamental duality of agency and spontaneity.

Gathering what we have learned in this section, we arrive at the following, twelfth, key idea for our revised conception of the ego: the ego is situated on a wide and shifting middle ground between the sides of the duality of self-control and the passions.

Question 7

HOW IS THE TRADITIONAL VIEW THAT THE EGO EXERCISES DIRECT AND COMPLETE CONTROL OF ITS EXECUTIVE FUNCTIONS TO BE EVALUATED IN RESPONSE TO ADVANCES IN OUR UNDERSTANDING OF PSYCHOPATHOLOGIES OF THOUGHT AND ACTION AND IN RESPONSE TO PHILOSOPHICAL VIEWS STRESSING THE SPONTANEITY OF CONSCIOUSNESS?

Again, it was Descartes's view and was generally assumed by advocates of the traditional notion of the ego that the ego, by exercise of will, has direct and complete control of its executive functions. According to the traditional view, although the ego's control of the passions and the body is subject to material conditions over which the ego does not have direct or complete control, the ego's control of its own internal actions, its own thinking and willing, is not subject to these or any other limiting conditions. This view that the ego has direct and complete control of its executive functions is no longer as plausible as it once seemed. Indeed, from today's perspective, there are good reasons to believe that the view is false.

As was the case with the issue of whether the ego has control of the passions, Freud led the way in setting forth a debate-changing challenge to the traditional view. Beginning with Freud and continuing throughout the first half of the twentieth century, psychiatrists and clinical psychologists gathered evidence that psychopathologies are disorders not only of mood or emotion but of thinking and acting as well. For example, obsessive-compulsive disorder gives rise to obsessive thinking and compulsive acting, depression gives rise to negative thinking and nonacting, bipolar disorder gives rise to manic thinking and impulsive acting, and schizophrenia gives rise to delusional thinking and senseless acting. In all these psychopathologies, the ego's executive functions, its actively initiated, intentional thinking and acting, have been wrested from the ego's control in ways that reflect the psychopathologies that have taken control.

For example, a person suffering from obsessive-compulsive disorder is compelled to think about imagined dangers and to repeat rituals that are thought to ward off those dangers. A person suffering from depression cannot escape from negative loops of thought and cannot get out of bed. A person suffering from bipolar disorder cannot stop hatching grandiose schemes and engaging in risky behavior. A person suffering from schizophrenia is captive to inner voices and sometimes feels compelled to act out what these voices say. It is by now a long- and well-established fact that psychopathologies like these and others of less serious sorts can take command of the ego's cognitive and practical functions, each in its own way. Under conditions of psychopathology, the ego's executive functions and its agency generally are to a significant extent no longer in its control.

Acknowledging these damaging effects of psychopathology, might not it at least be true that a psychologically healthy and strong ego has direct and complete control of its executive functions? The answer to this question is also negative, for reasons set forth in the last chapter in discussing the spontaneity of consciousness. Although the idea of the spontaneity of consciousness—understood as the spontaneous production not only of motivating impulses but also of thoughts and images—is most closely associated with Buddhism, it has been championed in the West, most famously by Friedrich Nietzsche, who repeatedly stressed the idea near the end of the nineteenth century, and, as noted in the last chapter, by Jean-Paul Sartre, who wrote about the idea in dramatic fashion in the 1940s. Nietzsche famously observed that the thoughts and images with which we think and the impulses on which we act are not products of a subject or I, the ego, but are rather things that arise spontaneously within consciousness. With respect to thoughts, he said, "I shall never tire of emphasizing a small terse fact, . . . that a thought comes when 'it' wishes, and not when 'I' wish, so that it is a falsification of the facts of the case to say that the subject 'I' is a condition of the predicate 'think.' *It* thinks; but that this 'it' is precisely the famous old 'ego' is, to put it mildly, only a supposition, an assertion, and assuredly not an 'immediate certainty.' "[5]

Nietzsche's observation is simple but compelling: the ego, if there is one, thinks with thoughts and images and acts on impulses that are produced *for* it rather than *by* it. Specifically, his point is that the ego, rather than producing its own thoughts, images, and impulses, receives them from an underlying psychic source, from which they spontaneously arise. Sartre took this line of thought to its limit, arguing that deep inspection of consciousness reveals that there is no ego at the center of consciousness, only an impersonal spontaneity of upwelling psychomental content.

In returning here to the idea of the spontaneity of consciousness, our point is to respond to Nietzsche and Sartre by looking more closely at what in the last chapter we referred to as the "complementary-opposites hypothesis," the hypothesis that the ego and the spontaneity of consciousness are coessential, mutually completing interior sides of consciousness. Briefly, this hypothesis can be used to respond to Nietzsche and Sartre as follows: the fact that the ego's thoughts, images, and impulses are produced for it by the spontaneity of consciousness reveals, not that the ego's agency is a fiction, but rather that the ego's agency is a *cooperative* rather than autonomous agency. It reveals that the ego's agency is one that, centered in the ego, works only in interaction with the spontaneity of consciousness.

According to the complementary-opposites hypothesis, the ego and the spontaneity of consciousness complete each other by each providing for the other what the other needs to make its distinctive contribution to psychic functioning. We know from the foregoing discussion that the spontaneity of consciousness provides the ego with the thoughts, images, and impulses that inform and motivate it in the exercise of its executive functions. Now we can add that the ego provides the spontaneity of consciousness with the focus and engagement that guide it in its production of psychic content. It is only when the ego is strongly constituted, selectively focused, and functionally engaged that the spontaneity of consciousness is focused and engaged. Without a strongly constituted ego thus to focus and engage it, the spontaneity of consciousness produces psychic content in a more random way. Accordingly, although the spontaneity of consciousness produces the ego's thoughts, images, and impulses, the ego, when strong, focused, and engaged, guides the spontaneity of consciousness in the types of thoughts, images, and impulses it produces. The ego, when strong, focused, and engaged, "harnesses" the spontaneity of consciousness, thus putting its creativity to work for useful purposes.

The spontaneity of consciousness does not cease being spontaneous when it is thus harnessed by the ego. Rather, it is transformed from being a more random spontaneity into being a more predictable spontaneity. Although it is never possible to predict exactly which thoughts, images, and impulses the spontaneity of consciousness will produce, it is possible, when the ego is strongly constituted, selectively focused, and functionally engaged, to predict how likely it is that certain *types* of thoughts, images, and impulses will be produced. Types that are more relevant to the ego's engaged concerns are more likely to be produced, and types that are less relevant are less likely to be produced—according to their degree of relevance. Clearly, the thoughts, images, and impulses produced when a carpenter is building a cabinet are much more likely to be of a "cabinet-building" type than they would be when, say, the carpenter is jogging in a park with a disengaged mind. Somewhat like quantum indeterminacy, which allows statistical predictions of outcomes that might be measured, the spontaneity of consciousness, when harnessed by the ego, allows rough-guess predictions of the likelihood of types of thoughts, images, or impulses that might be experienced.

In sum, the fact that the ego receives its thoughts, images, and impulses from the spontaneity of consciousness does not overturn the idea that the ego is an agency. It does, however, imply that the ego's agency is neither autonomous nor constant in degree of efficacy. The ego's agency is not autonomous because it works only in partnership with the spontaneity of consciousness; and the ego's agency is not constant because it waxes or wanes depending on the ego's strength of constitution, selectivity of focus, and degree of engagement. On the one hand, when the ego is strong, focused, and engaged, it asserts itself vigorously as an agency, thus harnessing the spontaneity of consciousness in such a way that this creative source produces psychic content that is relevant to the ego's concerns. On the other hand, when the ego is weak, unfocused, and disengaged, it ceases for the most part exerting itself as an agency, thus unharnessing the spontaneity of consciousness and becoming primarily a passive witness to its free play.

The discussion in this section leads to the thirteenth key idea of the revised conception of the ego, which can be stated as follows: the ego's ability to control its executive functions, its agency, varies across a wide and shifting middle ground between the sides of a fundamental duality of human experience, that of agency and spontaneity. Sometimes the ego has little control of its agency, either because it suffers from a psychological disorder or because it is weak, unfocused, or disengaged. At other times, however, the ego has a great deal of control of its agency, specifically, when it is psychologically healthy, strongly constituted, selectively focused, and functionally engaged.

The conclusion of this section agrees with the conclusion of the last section. Both hold that the ego is situated on a wide and shifting middle ground between the sides of an inherent duality of human experience, one side of which has been advocated by representatives of the traditional notion of the ego and the other side by antitraditional critics. Just as the ego bridges the duality of self-control and the passions rather than residing only on the side of self-control, so the ego also bridges the more fundamental duality of agency and spontaneity rather than residing only on the side of agency.

Question 8

HOW IS THE TRADITIONAL VIEW THAT THE EGO RESIDES WITHIN THE INTERIOR OF THE PSYCHE TO BE EVALUATED IN RESPONSE TO PHENOMENOLOGICAL ACCOUNTS OF THE PRIMACY OF EMBODIMENT AND BEING-IN-THE-WORLD?

Descartes's mechanistic account of the material world removed the soul from the body and confined it within psychic space as the interior subject and agency of consciousness, the ego. The result of this inward confinement of the ego is what came to be called the "egocentric predicament," which is the twofold difficulty of explaining (1) how the ego, existing exclusively within its own interior sphere, can know for sure that there is an external, public world; and, assuming that there is an external world, (2) how the ego can ever get beyond the confines of subjectivity and truly participate in that world, as an embodied, social being. The egocentric predicament, inherent to the traditional notion of the ego, was finally challenged decisively by a school of thought that arose in the first half of the twentieth century, existential phenomenology. Important representatives of existential phenomenology are Martin Heidegger, Jean-Paul Sartre, and Maurice Merleau-Ponty.

In his magnum opus, *Being and Time* (1927), Heidegger challenged the traditional notion of the ego by arguing that human beings are not interior egos living in psychic space, thus faced with the problem of reaching beyond this space into the world, but are rather beings living originally and primarily in the world. Furthermore, the world in which humans thus live is not only the material world but also and more importantly the interpersonal and social worlds of shared human experience. Instead of speaking of the ego, therefore, Heidegger spoke of Dasein (literally, "there-being"), a being whose existence is inherently rooted in the world. Dasein is inherently "outside itself," engaged in worldly activities, especially those that occur within the context of everyday life, such as activities using tools to produce goods or perform services and activities using language to communicate with others about the tasks of the day. Human existence, Heidegger held, is prereflective "being-in-the-world" (*In-der-Welt-sein*).

Heidegger was not saying that we are always engaged in worldly activities. He was not denying that we sometimes withdraw from worldly engagement by adopting a theoretical or introspective perspective, as, for example, occurs when we ponder something not yet understood or observe thoughts, images, and impulses as they arise within consciousness. However, it was Heidegger's view that, in adopting a theoretical or introspective perspective, we are withdrawing from a prereflective way of living (being-in-the-world) that not only precedes these perspectives but is also their necessary basis. There can be no theoretical or introspective perspectives without the prereflective consciousness from which they withdraw. The implication is clear: for Heidegger, a self-enclosed, exclusively interior psychic space is impossible. He says, "The idea of a subject which has intentional experiences merely inside its own sphere and is not yet outside it but encapsulated within itself is an absurdity which misconstrues the basic ontological structure of the being that we ourselves are."[6] The concept of an exclusively interior psychic space of thought or introspection—the kind of space in which the traditional ego is supposed to reside—fundamentally misconceives the nature of our existence, Heidegger maintained.

In his two major early philosophical works, *Transcendence of the Ego* (1936) and *Being and Nothingness* (1943), Sartre adopted many of Heidegger's ideas, giving them a provocatively negative twist. Sartre agreed with Heidegger that consciousness is originally and primarily in the world.

He stressed that consciousness is immediately present in the body, where, in his negative interpretation, it is vulnerable to bodily needs; that consciousness is intimately present in human relationships, in which, in his negative interpretation, it is engaged in irresolvable conflict; and that consciousness is directly present on the stage of social life, where, in his negative interpretation, it is burdened with the responsibility of freedom. Sartre, in thus agreeing with Heidegger that consciousness is originally and primarily in the world, agreed with Heidegger as well that theoretical and introspective perspectives are based on prereflective consciousness and, therefore, that an exclusively interior psychic space is impossible.[7]

In *Phenomenology of Perception* (1945), Maurice Merleau-Ponty presented a less negative, more balanced account of the topics that Sartre treated in *Being and Nothingness*. Most relevant here is his account of the ego. Unlike Sartre, Merleau-Ponty held that there *is* an ego but that it is an ego of a different sort and residing in a different place than the Cartesian ego that Sartre looked for within consciousness and could not find. According to Merleau-Ponty, the ego is not an exclusively psychic ego residing at the center of interior consciousness. Instead, he argued, it is a *body* ego, an ego that is originally and primarily the ego of an embodied person engaged in the world and only secondarily an ego that sometimes withdraws from the world to reflect or introspect.

That the ego is thus inherently a body ego engaged in the world brought Merleau-Ponty to the same conclusion that Heidegger and Sartre had reached, namely, that there can be no such thing as a self-enclosed or exclusively interior psychic space. He said, "The most important lesson which the reduction teaches us is the impossibility of a complete reduction," where "reduction" refers to Edmund Husserl's method for studying intentional meanings and choices by suspending commitment to the existence of the external world.[8] Merleau-Ponty's point is that although the ego can disengage from embodied life in the world and withdraw into psychic space, it can never do so completely. It can never withdraw into a self-enclosed, exclusively interior psychic space. It cannot do so because the psychic space into which it withdraws is an emergent interior enclave within a body ego, an ego that is not "detachable" from the body and world in which it lives.

Of the ideas of Heidegger, Sartre, and Merleau-Ponty just reviewed, three stand out as candidates for adoption as key ideas for the revised conception of the ego. These ideas are (1) that the world, not interior psychic space, is our—and, therefore, the ego's—original and primary abode; (2) that interior psychic space derives ontologically from prereflective engagement in the world in the sense of coming into existence emergently only when the ego withdraws inwardly from such engagement; and (3) that interior psychic space is never a completely self-enclosed sphere. The ensuing discussion explains why the revised conception of the ego should adopt the first and third of these ideas but not the second.

The first idea, that the world, not interior psychic space, is the ego's original and primary abode, can be restated to say that the ego, from the beginning of life and for the most part throughout life, is a worldly self, an embodied subject that interacts with material things, participates in relationships, communicates with others in a common language and culture, and performs social roles. From a Jamesian perspective, this idea can be restated to say that the ego lives originally and primarily as an embodied object or Me in the world and withdraws into interior subjectivity only subsequently and secondarily.

In yet other terms, the first idea can be restated to say that, for the ego, the world has *existential priority* over interior life. The world is the ego's original and primary abode because it is the dwelling place of which we are originally aware, in which we spend most of our time, and in which we conduct the primary business of life. In contrast, the psychic space of interior life is only a subsequent and secondary abode because it is a dwelling place of which we are originally unaware, in which, when awake, we spend much less time, and in which we perform only a few select tasks, such as sleep, reflection, reverie, introspection, meditation, and prayer. That the world thus has existential priority over the interior of the psyche is an observed fact about where we originally find ourselves and how we split our time between two distinct, worldly and psychic, domains of our existence. In thus conveying a matter of fact of importance to our topic, the idea that the world has existential priority over the psyche, that the world is the ego's original and primary abode, can be adopted by the revised conception of the ego, as its fourteenth key idea.

The second idea, that interior psychic space derives ontologically from prereflective engagement in the world, does not report an observed fact and is not accepted by the revised conception of the ego. It is not accepted because it is incompatible with the primary hypothesis of the revised conception, that the ego is the organized form of the unifying-appropriating function. According to the revised conception, the ego is produced by a neurophenomenological activity working within consciousness, indeed, by an activity that, on its interior or phenomenological side, works at the center of consciousness. For this reason, although psychic space is existentially only the ego's secondary abode, it is ontologically the ego's place of origin. According to the revised conception of the ego, psychic space is not an interior "bubble" that expands into existence only when the ego withdraws from prereflective engagement in the world and then deflates into nonexistence when the ego returns to such engagement. Rather, it is an interior space that preexists—or, more precisely, that from the beginning coexists with—the world, as the place in which the ego is constituted as a unity of apperception and executive agency.

In sum, the revised conception of the ego, in accepting the existential priority of the world over interior consciousness, does not accept a corresponding ontological priority of the world over interior consciousness. According to the revised conception, it is interior consciousness, not the world, that has ontological priority so far as the ego is concerned. The phrase "so far as the ego is concerned" is needed because the idea that interior consciousness has ontological priority over the world has nothing to do with metaphysical idealism. The idea holds only that the *ego,* not the world, is constituted within interior consciousness. Mindful of this clarification, we can say that the ego, although originally and primarily a body ego in the world, is not for that reason ontologically more of a worldly than a psychic ego. On the contrary, if, existentially, the ego is primarily a bodily, worldly ego, that is because, in the process of its production as an *interior* subject or I, it is already appropriating bodily and worldly experiences and attributes, thus forging for itself an exterior, object or Me, side.

Existential phenomenologists explain their account of the priority of being-in-the-world by using Heidegger's notion of "thrownness" (*Geworfenheit*), saying that human beings are originally and primarily thrown—i.e., projected—into the world. However, from our point of view this existential-phenomenological notion of thrownness is incomplete because, although it correctly stresses the place *into which* the ego is thrown, the world, it has nothing to say about the place *out of which* the ego is thrown. In our view, the ego is thrown into the world because it is thrown out of the psyche. The fact that the ego discovers interior psychic space only after it has been living in the world does not mean that this interior space is ontologically derivative in relation to prereflective engagement in the world. It means only that, because the ego reaches outward in the very process of its production, it cannot visit the place in which it originates until after it has lived in the world and then learned how to turn its attention inward.

The third idea under consideration, that interior psychic space is never a self-enclosed sphere, is accepted by the revised conception of the

ego but not for the reason it was originally advanced by existential phenomenologists. According to the revised conception, psychic space is never
a self-enclosed sphere not because it is an epiphenomenon that emerges by
withdrawing from prereflective engagement in the world but rather because
the ego, despite originating within the psyche, always has an "open door"
to the world, its original and primary abode. Because it lives originally and
primarily in the world, the ego has and always retains birthright access to
the world. However, because it originates within the psyche, the ego also has
and always retains birthright access to the psyche. According to the revised
conception of the ego, the ego is always open to both the world and the
psyche. Being a body ego in the world never closes the ego to the psyche,
and being the interior subject and executive agency of consciousness never
closes the ego to the world.

There is for this reason no egocentric predicament: the ego is never
locked within psychic space. Neither is there a world-centric predicament:
the ego is never exiled to the world. Once the ego discovers psychic space
within itself, it is always able thereafter to enter it and then return to the
world and then reenter psychic space and then return to the world again,
and so forth. The ego thus has two abodes that share an opening that is
never closed: the world, an ontologically secondary but existentially primary abode that opens in to the psyche, and the psyche, an ontologically
primary but existentially secondary abode that opens out to the world. Let
this point be added to the revised conception of the ego, as its fifteenth
key idea. The point can be stated as follows: the psyche and the world are
always open to each other.

The revised conception of the ego thus differs from both traditional and
antitraditional perspectives on the ego's psychic or worldly character by taking
a both-and rather than an either-or approach. Rather than prioritizing the
interior psyche, as do Descartes and other representatives of the traditional
notion of the ego, or the world, as do existential phenomenologists, the
revised conception prioritizes both, although in different ways, prioritizing
the psyche ontologically and the world existentially. The psyche, the location
of the ego's interior life, and the world, the location of the ego's exterior
life, make up another inherent duality the sides of which the ego bridges
and integrates. This duality is a specific form of the more fundamental
duality of the interior ego and the worldly self, other forms of which are
discussed in ensuing sections.

Echoing the conclusions of the preceding two sections, we can here
conclude that the ego is situated on a wide and shifting middle ground

between the sides of an inherent duality, one side of which has been advocated by representatives of the traditional notion of the ego (the psychic realm of the ego's interior life) and the other side of which has been advocated by antitraditional critics (the embodied, social world of the ego's exterior life). The revised conception of the ego stakes out a wide middle ground between the sides of this duality because, for the ego, both the interior psychic realm and the embodied, social world are native ground, ground to which the ego has birthright access. Furthermore, according to the revised conception, this wide middle ground between psyche and world is shifting because, existentially, the ego moves back and forth between the two sides of this ground. Such movements occur not only when the ego falls asleep and then returns to wakefulness but also when the ego, without falling asleep, withdraws into reflection, reverie, introspection, meditation, or prayer and then, concluding such interior musings, returns to affairs of the world. Again, the ego, rather than being or residing on only one side of an inherent duality, is the bridge that integrates the two sides. Let us, therefore, add our conclusion that the ego lives on a wide and shifting middle ground between the sides of the duality of the interior psyche and embodied life in the world to the revised conception of the ego, as its sixteenth key idea.

Question 9

HOW IS THE TRADITIONAL VIEW THAT THE EGO HAS FULL, PRIVILEGED ACCESS TO ITSELF TO BE EVALUATED IN RESPONSE TO DEPTH PSYCHOLOGY, SYMBOLIC INTERACTIONISM, AND RELATIONAL PSYCHOANALYSIS?

A third challenge to the traditional notion of the ego that emerged in the twentieth century came from representatives of depth psychology, symbolic interactionism, and relational psychoanalysis. Representatives of these perspectives challenged the traditional view that the ego has full, privileged access to itself and, therefore, can in principle know itself completely simply by looking inward. Focusing their criticisms on this traditional view, depth psychologists on the one hand and symbolic interactionists and relational psychoanalysts on the other hand challenged the view in different ways. Depth psychologists argued that the ego does not have full access to itself because many of its thoughts and feelings are obscured by or hidden in psychic depths. In contrast, symbolic interactionists and relational psychoanalysts argued that the ego does not always have privileged access to itself because the ego is frequently dependent on others for knowledge of itself.

As depth psychologists, Freud and Jung both defended the view that there is more to the psyche than the ego knows. They provided reasons to believe that the psyche consists not only of the region of which the ego is aware, interior consciousness, but also of underlying strata of which the ego is unaware, the unconscious. Specifically, they argued that there are two underlying unconscious strata of the psyche, a deeper stratum, about which they disagreed on essential points, and a shallower stratum, about which they agreed for the most part. Let us call the deeper stratum the "deep unconscious" and, following Jung, call the shallower stratum the "personal unconscious."

The deep unconscious consists of the underlying sources of what we have called the spontaneity of consciousness. These are the sources from which thoughts, images, and impulses spontaneously arise. Freud and Jung agreed that the deep unconscious is primarily a product of evolution. They also agreed that this stratum of the unconscious consists of inherited drives and an image-producing process that gives expression to these drives. However, in agreeing on these points, Freud and Jung disagreed on the nature of the drives belonging to the deep unconscious and, therefore, on the kind of images produced by the image-producing process. According to Freud, the deep unconscious, which he called the "id," consists exclusively of instinctual drives. Conceiving the deep unconscious in this exclusively instinctual way, Freud held that the image-producing process that gives expression to the deep unconscious, which he called the "primary process," produces images of objects that would satisfy instinctual drives (or desires derived from them). In contrast, according to Jung, the deep unconscious, which he called the "collective unconscious," consists not only of instinctual drives but also of a "spiritual" drive, the "transcendent function," which pulls us toward psychic wholeness. Thus attributing not only instinctual drives but also this spiritual drive to the deep unconscious, Jung explained that the image-producing process that gives expression to the deep unconscious produces not only images of objects that would satisfy instinctual drives but also images or "archetypes" that guide us on the path toward psychic wholeness.

Both these conceptions of the deep unconsciousness are controversial. Many commentators have criticized both Freud and Jung for underestimating cultural influences on this stratum of the unconscious. Moreover, commentators have criticized Freud for overemphasizing the instinctual character of this stratum (instinctual reductionism) and Jung for overemphasizing the spiritual character (spiritual "elevationism"). In previous works, I have argued that, if interpreted as accounts of different developmental organizations of the underlying sources of the spontaneity of consciousness rather than as accounts of the inherent and unchanging constitution of these sources, Freud's and Jung's conceptions of the deep unconscious can be integrated in broad outline.[9] This book, however, is not the place for reconsidering such a reconciliation of Freud and Jung.

Whatever one thinks of Freud's and Jung's conceptions of the deep unconscious, it seems undeniable that, for the ego, the underlying sources of the spontaneity of consciousness are unfathomably deep. The ego is conscious of the thoughts, images, and impulses produced by these sources, since they appear to the ego through the open space of spontaneity, which, according to our "variable-opening hypothesis," is an opening within the ego itself. However, the ego is not and almost certainly cannot be aware of the processes by which thoughts, images, and impulses are spontaneously formed. Deeper levels of Buddhist insight meditation are said to move into deeper levels of the space of spontaneity, at which the meditator observes increasingly fine and increasingly many thoughts, images, and impulses as they "bubble up" in the space of spontaneity. One might here be said to see thoughts, images, and impulses in earlier stages of their release from the sources of spontaneity. Still, even at the deepest levels of meditation, one is not privy to the processes that produce the phenomena that rise into consciousness spontaneously. This fact places an unsurpassable limit on the ego's self-knowledge. The ego, rooted in the spontaneity of consciousness, can observe only the products of this spontaneity and not the processes at work within it. The depths from which the ego's thoughts, images, and impulses arise are, in Jung's terminology, psychoid rather than psychic. As such, they are inherently inaccessible to the ego.

There is more agreement between Freud and Jung on the matter of the shallower stratum of the unconscious. The reason for using Jung's expression "personal unconscious" for this stratum is that it aptly indicates that this stratum is more a product of the ego's personal history than, as is the case with the deep unconscious, the species' evolution. Specifically, it is the product of the ego's attempts to protect itself by excluding from conscious everything in its personal life (impulses, action tendencies, thoughts, memories) that it has found too threatening to allow further expression.[10] We have used Jung's term "the shadow" to designate this part of the unconscious even though, in Jung's conception, the shadow has not only personal but also archetypal or deep, collective elements.[11] In any case, the Jungian personal unconscious as it concerns us here consists of all parts of the ego's personal history that the ego has banished from consciousness because it found them too threatening to allow them further expression. Freud's term for the personal unconscious is "dynamic unconscious," which gives expression to the fact that the ego must mobilize its internal resources defensively—specifically, repressively—to keep threatening parts of itself out of view. Clearly, the personal unconscious is more individually formed than biologically inherited; it is more biographical than evolutionary in derivation.

Whereas the deep unconscious is a part of the psyche that is inherently hidden from the ego, the personal unconscious is a part that the ego hides from itself. The ego is unaware of the contents of the personal unconscious not because it cannot in principle be aware of them but rather because, out of anxiety, guilt, or shame, it does not allow itself to be aware of them. Conceptual difficulties arise in attempting to explain how the ego can hide parts of itself from itself. We discuss these difficulties in chapter 10. For the moment, let us conclude that twentieth-century depth psychology strongly challenged the traditional assumption that the ego has full access to itself. Depth psychology revealed to us that there is a deep stratum of the psyche that is inherently hidden from the ego and a shallower stratum that, although not inherently hidden from the ego, is hidden nonetheless because the ego does not allow it to come into view.

Whereas depth psychologists challenged the traditional view of the ego's self-knowledge by arguing that the ego does not have full access to itself, symbolic interactionists and relational psychoanalysts have challenged the traditional view by arguing that the ego does not always have privileged access to itself. They have argued that the ego, rather than being able in principle always to know itself on its own, frequently cannot know itself without the help of others. Others are needed either because self-knowledge sometimes requires the validating feedback of others (symbolic interactionism) or because self-knowledge is sometimes possible only in the context of engaged exchanges with others (relational psychoanalysis). According to both symbolic interactionists and relational psychoanalysts, self-knowledge is not simply a matter, as Descartes believed, of looking inside oneself to examine one's consciousness or even a matter of looking outside oneself to observe one's attributes as an embodied, social self in the world. For both symbolic interactionists and relational psychoanalysts, self-knowledge is often something that can emerge only because of or during interactions with others.

Symbolic interactionism emerged in the first half of the twentieth century in the work of George H. Mead and Charles H. Cooley and was developed in the second half of the twentieth century by Herbert Blumer, Erving Goffman, and others. Symbolic interactionism holds that people arrive at self-knowledge by interpreting how their actions are perceived and judged by others. The self, symbolic interactionists hold, is not something pregiven but is rather a construct based on the validating feedback of others. This perspective is nicely captured in Cooley's notion of the looking-glass self, which, as formulated by sociologist Robert Bierstedt, holds that "I am not what I think I am and I am not what you think I am. I am what I think you think I am."[12] According to symbolic interactionists, self-knowledge is frequently cooperative rather than independent in derivation; and it is frequently interpretive rather than exclusively factual in character. For symbolic interactionists, the self—or at least the self-representation—is a construct that arises out of interpretive exchanges with other people.

Relational psychoanalysis arose in response to classical "one-person" psychoanalysis, which focused on the individual psyche, explaining it in terms of instinctual drives, the ego's mechanisms of defense, the ego's mediating role in relation to the superego and the id, and the ego's autonomous functions. In contrast, relational psychoanalysis focuses on human relationships, explaining that psychic structures emerge in the context of relationships and that psychotherapy is an intersubjective exchange. Forerunners of the relational perspective are psychoanalytic object-relations theorists such as Melanie Klein, Donald Winnicott, and Ronald Fairbairn and interpersonal psychoanalyst Harry Stack Sullivan. These theorists explained that psychic structures, including original representations of self and others, emerge only in the context of relationships, first and most importantly in the context of the infant-caregiver relationship, and then in the context of the growing child's relationships with parents and other people.

In 1983 Jay R. Greenberg and Stephen A. Mitchell published *Object Relations in Psychoanalytic Theory*, which distinguished between the original one-person, drive-focused model of psychoanalysis and the more recent relational models. The book was highly influential and led to the establishment of relational psychoanalysis as a new psychoanalytic paradigm. Relational psychoanalysis grew rapidly in the 1990s and thereafter and now has many prominent theorists, including Lewis Aron, Donnel Stern, and Jessica Benjamin. Robert D. Stolorow and George E. Atwood, representing a parallel (intersubjective) perspective, should also be mentioned.

Applying the relational perspective to psychotherapy, recent relational psychoanalysts have stressed that therapeutic self-insight arises not from within the analysand but out of the relationship between the analysand and the analyst, specifically when unconscious tendencies are played out in this relationship. These theorists hold that the psychotherapeutic relationship is a form of intersubjectivity that is greater than the sum of its parts. The analyst assists the analysand in achieving self-insight less by offering expert interpretations or empathically attuned responses than by engaging and reacting to tendencies that are enacted in the relationship. In such exchanges between the analyst and analysand, the analyst looks for patterns of speech or behavior that are repeated in problematic ways and, therefore, pose issues for therapeutic attention. The analyst then explores with the analysand sources from and circumstances in which these issues arise and how they might be resolved. Problematic tendencies that previously were unknown can in this way be brought to light, acknowledged, and worked through.

Robert D. Stolorow and George E. Atwood have formulated a psychoanalytic theory of intersubjectivity that presses any relational view to its limits. They argue that individual subjectivities are always organized only through intersubjective exchanges, such that, following the first such exchange between infant and caregiver, subsequent exchanges are played out between participating subjectivities that have already been organized by previous intersubjective exchanges. Furthermore, subsequent exchanges are played out between participating subjectivities that are open to further reorganization in these exchanges. Applying this account of intersubjectivity to psychotherapy, Stolorow and Atwood argue that the relationship between analysand and analyst is fully mutual, with each party engaging the other in reorganizing and potentially enlightening ways. According to Stolorow and Atwood, there is no such thing as an isolated mind.[13] Subjectivities are organized, reorganized, and expressed only in relationships with each other.

Together, symbolic interactionists and relational psychoanalysts have established that the ego, rather than always having privileged access to itself, is often dependent on others for its self-knowledge. Clearly, we can know a great deal about ourselves on our own, without the help of others. Much if not most of what we know about ourselves we know by the following four independent means: (1) *direct observation* (e.g., "I have brown hair," "I live in a two-story house"); (2) *independent investigation* (e.g., "My blood type is O positive," "I am descended from French Huguenots"); (3) *introspective examination* (e.g., "That was a memory image of my high school graduation," "I just experienced an impulse to tell a lie"); and (4) *self-reflection* ("I exist," "I have both interior and exterior and both agentic and spontaneous sides"). However, it is to the credit of symbolic interactionists and relational psychoanalysts to have shown that we possess attributes that we cannot knowingly ascribe to ourselves by any of these independent means. Specifically, they have shown that we possess attributes that are so tied to others that we cannot know we possess them without the help of others.

Symbolic interactionists have focused on personal features that reflect how we are judged by others, whether the others doing the judging are individuals or certifying committees, boards, or institutions. Examples of such features are being attractive or unattractive, likable or unlikable, or reliable or unreliable (as judged by individuals with whom we interact) and features such as being a college graduate, a licensed private investigator, or a published author (as judged by certifying boards, committees, or institutions). Clearly, features like these are inherently dependent on the judgments of others. For this reason, we can knowingly ascribe features like these to ourselves only after receiving validating feedback from others. In turn, relational psychoanalysts have focused on behavioral tendencies that are played out in relationships, especially, from a psychotherapeutic perspective, tendencies that replay in the present problematic relationships from the past. Clearly, such behavioral tendencies have an inherently relational character. We can knowingly ascribe them to ourselves only after they have been enacted with others and have thus elicited responses that bring them to light.

Having now completed our review of twentieth-century challenges to the traditional notion of the ego's self-knowledge, we can conclude by once again situating the ego on a wide and shifting middle ground. In this case the middle ground lies between two opposing positions on the ego's self-knowledge, one advocated by representatives of the traditional notion of the ego and the other by antitraditional critics. It is important to note that the opposing positions here, unlike those discussed in earlier sections, do not align with sides of an inherent duality of human experience. Traditionalists arguing in favor of full, always-privileged self-knowledge and antitraditionalists arguing in favor of limited or relationally dependent self-knowledge, although clearly arguing in favor of opposing sides of a theoretical issue, are not thereby clearly arguing in favor of opposite sides of an inherent human duality.

This point made, it remains true that the middle ground between the traditional and antitraditional views on the ego's self-knowledge is wide and shifting. This middle ground is wide because, despite our limited access to underlying strata of the psyche and our dependence on others for much of our self-knowledge, there is still a great deal we can know about ourselves, whether by using one or more of the independent means listed earlier or by learning from the judging or revealing responses of others. However, in saying that the ego can thus know a great deal about itself, the emphasis is on "can," since self-knowledge is an achievement, not a given. The ego, we are saying, can know a great deal about itself *to the extent that* it avails itself of independent means of self-knowledge and *to the extent that* it heeds the judging or revealing responses of others. Self-knowledge thus ranges on a wide middle ground between the possibility of knowing a great deal about oneself, as did the highly self-aware Siddhartha Gautama, Socrates, and Saint Teresa of Avila, and the possibility of knowing very little about oneself, as is the case with people who are incurious, resistant to introspection, unreflective, or unheedful of the responses of others. Let us, therefore, state as a preliminary conclusion that, so far as self-knowledge is concerned, the ego is situated on a middle ground that is very wide indeed.

The fact that self-knowledge is an achievement means that it is something that can be gained *and lost.* It can be gained by the independent and interpersonal means already discussed, and it can be lost by failure to take advantage of these means and by the effects of illness or cognitive decline. Adding this fact about gain and loss to the preliminary conclusion just stated gives us the following, final, conclusion for this section: that, so far as self-knowledge is concerned, the ego is situated on a middle ground between traditional and antitraditional positions that is not only wide but also shifting. This middle ground is wide because it has room both for people with a great deal of self-knowledge and for people with very little self-knowledge, and it is shifting because it allows for both significant increases and significant decreases in self-knowledge over the course of life. Let us add this version of the "wide and shifting" conclusion to the revised conception of the ego, as its seventeenth key idea.

Question 10

How is the traditional view that the ego is the author of its identity to be evaluated in response to postmodernists' accounts of the socially constructed self?

Another major challenge to the traditional notion of the ego came from postmodernism, a movement in both European and English-speaking countries that became a major cultural force in the last quarter of the twentieth century. Although the term "postmodern" had already been in use to describe styles of literature, music, and architecture, it was not until the publication of Jean-François Lyotard's *The Postmodern Condition* in 1979 that the term began to be used widely to describe any perspective skeptical of basic assumptions of the modern historical period, such as that freedom is the goal of historical development and that comprehensive, completely objective knowledge of the world is the goal of scientific development. Two major perspectives that came to be described as postmodern are, first, poststructuralism in cultural studies (e.g., Jacques Lacan, Michel Foucault, Gilles Deleuze, Julia Kristeva), including as a subtype deconstructionism in literary theory (Jacques Derrida); and, second, versions of social constructionism in the social sciences that evolved from Peter L. Berger and Thomas Luckmann's *The Social Construction of Reality* (1966) and from various strands of postmodern thought (notably, Kenneth Gergen).

Common to these perspectives is a challenge to the idea that language conveys stable, clearly demarcated meanings and the closely related idea that the meanings conveyed by language are derived from and, therefore, reflect reality as it exists beyond human society and culture. According to postmodernism, language is a historically evolving social phenomenon, and the meanings conveyed by language can be understood only in relation to other meanings to which they are tied in the social practices within which they play expressive, descriptive, persuasive, and other roles. The terms of everyday discourse and even the carefully crafted ideas of scientific theory, therefore, always bear the imprint of their historically derived, socially embedded character. They are inextricably a part of the larger web of evolving language and are inherently tied to the social interests responsible for their formation. For these reasons, the language we use in communicating with each other and in describing the world never gives expression to essential meanings or wholly objective facts. Precisely these notions are called into question by postmodernism.

Postmodernists have criticized the traditional notion of the ego by arguing that the self, rather than being a unified subject centered within consciousness, is a complex construct reflecting a multitude of social determining factors, many of which stand in changing, obscure, and conflicting relations with each other. The voices of the human subject, which emerge only with the learning of language, are not the voices of a single, centered subject; rather, they are voices that give expression to a congeries of desires, feelings, and values that have been elicited in response to diverse social influences. With the learning of language, we become speaking subjects able to give expression to ourselves, without, however, thereby being able to bring either our voices as subjects or the socially grounded parts of ourselves for which our voices speak into unity. Given this lack of an interior unifying center, the self, according to postmodernists, is more like an assemblage of selves; it is a self that is prone to what social psychologist Kenneth Gergen called "multiphrenia."[14]

This postmodern account of the socially constructed self stands in stark contrast to the existentialist conception of self-authorship, according to which we author our worldly identity by our free choices and actions. Although Sartre, who most famously advanced this view of individual "self-creation," denied the existence of the ego, it is understandable that postmodernists, in setting their sights on the traditional notion of the ego, would have set their sights as well on this notion as it had begun to be reconceived in existentialist fashion, as a unified interior subject that authors its worldly identity.

In thus setting their sights on the ego, postmodernists have argued that the idea of an interior subject that authors its worldly identity is not only mistaken but is the opposite of the truth. They have argued that the self, rather than being constructed "from the inside out" by an interior ego, is instead constructed "from the outside in" by social influences. Again, according to postmodernism, the elements of the self are rooted in social circumstances and are resistant to efforts to unify them. The self, rather than being a unified, centered interior self, is a complex, decentered social construct. Clearly, there is a wide gulf between traditional (ego-authored) and antitraditional (socially constructed) views on the notion of the human self.

The postmodern account of the self poses a major challenge to our revised conception of the ego. Nevertheless, if properly qualified—indeed, if qualified in a major way—the postmodern account can be made compatible with the revised conception and can provide balancing counterpoint to it, as, I believe, the revised conception can provide balancing counterpoint to the postmodern account. The qualifications to the postmodern account of the self needed to make it compatible with the revised conception of the ego are (1) that it needs to be restricted in application to the exterior, object or Me, side of the ego; and (2) that even with this restriction, it needs to be understood as applying to the exterior side of the ego only incompletely, even if to a great extent.

Regarding the first of these qualifications, the postmodern account of the self needs to be restricted to the exterior side of the ego because the interior side as we have conceived it is precisely what the postmodern account rejects. According to the revised conception of the ego, the ego on its interior side is a subject and agency that observes and initiates changes in the world. Moreover, the revised conception holds that the ego, as an interior subject (if not yet also as an agency), is present at birth. Beginning in chapter 6, we discuss developmental and neuroscientific studies that provide evidence both (1) that the ego is present at birth, at least in its role as subject or observer; and (2) that this subject begins performing executive functions, if not at birth, then very soon thereafter, at least by three or four to six months of age, when precursors of voluntary control of attention emerge. This is not the place to discuss these studies further, other than to say that, to the extent that they confirm the account of the interior side of the ego as it was formulated in chapter 3, they imply that the postmodern account of the self does not apply to the ego on its interior, subject or I, side.

If the ego on its interior side is present at birth, it is on scene before any social shaping of the exterior side of the ego can have occurred. That said, the ego, from birth on, is already being shaped on its exterior side. As we learned in chapter 3, the interior and exterior sides of the ego arise together, with the interior, subject or I, side already appropriating for itself an exterior, object or Me, side in the very process of its production as the interior subject and agency of consciousness. Moreover, social shaping of the exterior side of the ego begins, if not at birth, then immediately thereafter. The great majority of what we as children learn about ourselves as embodied, social subjects we learn from others. Moreover, many of the features that define us as such subjects are features that reflect our relationships and social circumstances. These features are shaped under the influence of the original caregiver, family members, teachers, role models, television programs, social media sites, and the like. Accordingly, the debate about a self-authored or socially constructed self is primarily a debate about the extent to which the exterior side of the ego is an intentional creation of an interior ego and the extent to which it is the product of relational exchanges and social influences.

Without question, social construction of the exterior side of the ego far outweighs self-authorship at the outset of life. Indeed, intentional self-authoring is impossible early in life because, as young children, our cognitive functions are too immature to entertain the idea of such an endeavor and our practical functions are too immature, were the idea of self-authoring entertained, effectively to act on it. That children are not engaged in intentional self-authoring might be challenged by adducing the facts that, in middle childhood, girls and boys (1) make choices that change and thus help shape what they are, (2) begin thinking about what they might be when they are adults, and, perhaps most to the point, (3) begin speaking to themselves in an inner, self-narrating voice. Using this voice, they make observations about their likes and dislikes, about what they have said and done, about what others have said about or done to them; and about what they might be when they grow up.

However, in speaking to themselves in these ways, girls and boys are for the most part only keeping a record of their lives; they are not yet attempting to *author* their lives. The choices they make that bring about changes in their lives are choices made in response to changing life circumstances, not choices made *for the purpose of giving shape, meaning, and purpose to their lives.* Their imaginings about what they might be when they grow up are simply that, imaginings. They are not initial plans, let alone concrete preparations, for becoming what they imagine they might be. In sum, the inner self-narration of girls and boys during middle childhood is for the most part only verbal documentation of past, present, and possible futures facts about themselves. It is not yet a narration of a life that is in the process of being shaped and given meaning and purpose.

As we shall learn in chapter 11, it is only in adolescence that inner self-narration evolves from simple autobiographical self-documentation into the narration of a *life story,* which is not only an account of past, present, and possible future facts about oneself but also an existentially significant reflection on who and what one is as a person and on who and what one might become as a member of adult society. However, once adolescents awaken to the possibility of authoring a life story, they find that they have already been shaped and defined, primarily by relational and social influences over which they had little if any control. In beginning to think about authoring a life story, they find that they already have socially constructed selves.

For these reasons, the debate about a self-authored or socially constructed self needs to be focused on older adolescents and adults, people old enough to have awakened to the idea of self-authoring and old enough to be in command of executive functions that can effectively undertake such a project. With the focus thus set, the point here is that, by the time intentional self-authoring begins, previous relational and social circumstances have already produced a script that will be the original draft and starting point for self-authoring. The project of self-authoring thus consists of accepting, revising, and changing this script as desired and to the extent possible. To get an idea of the scope and limits of self-authoring given such a prewritten script, let us map in rough outline four types of identity elements—calling them "features," as in features of the self-representation—that characteristically might be part of a self-authored or socially constructed self.

First type: Features that are created by conscious choice or effort (possible examples: "mother," "teacher," "socialist"). *Second type:* Features that are inherited or imposed by society or by the actions of others but are nonetheless affirmed or at least not resisted (possible examples: "male," "Army veteran," "grandfather"). *Third type:* Features that are inherited or imposed by society or by the actions of others, that are unwanted, and that might be removed by exercise of will (possible examples: "brown-haired," "poor," "refugee"). *Fourth type:* Features that are inherited or imposed by society or by the actions of others, that are unwanted, and that rarely if ever can be removed by exercise of will (possible examples: "slave," "convicted felon," "sexual abuse victim"). Let us briefly consider whether and, if so, to what extent the ego might reasonably be said to engage in free and responsible self-authorship in the case of each of these types of identity features.

The most plausible assessment of the ego's authorial freedom and responsibility with respect to features of these types is, I suggest, as follows. *First type:* The ego has a good deal of freedom and responsibility so far as features of this type are concerned. After all, the ego chooses these features. *Second type:* The ego has little freedom but nonetheless a significant degree of responsibility so far as features of this type are concerned. After all, although the ego does not choose these features, it affirms or at least does not resist them. *Third type:* The ego has limited freedom and, should it make no effort to exercise this freedom, at least some responsibility so far as features of this type are concerned. After all, although the ego does not choose these features, it accrues some responsibility by omission if it makes no effort to remove them. *Fourth type:* The ego has little or no freedom and anywhere from complete to no responsibility so far as features of this type are concerned. After all, although the felon does not want the judicially imposed "convicted felon" feature of his identity, he (assuming guilt) deserves it, whereas the slave and the sexual abuse victim share no responsibility for and do not deserve these features of their identities.

Clearly, the ego is far from being able to author its identity in any way it pleases. Postmodernists rightly stress the ways in which we are fashioned by society. Still, reflection on the above types of identity features strongly suggests that the ego, despite many constraints, does play a free and responsible role in shaping its identity. Although many, perhaps most, of the features making up the ego's identity are inherited or imposed by society or by the actions of others, many others are not. Moreover, many of the features that the ego does not choose it nonetheless affirms or at least does not resist, and some of the features that the ego neither chooses nor affirms could be removed if the ego tried to remove them. Granted, as postmodernists have stressed, a person's identity is to a great extent determined by social factors such as nationality, class, race, gender, and material means. However, this fact does not preclude self-authorship. Social factors impose constraints on self-authorship, sometimes greatly restricting the range of choices a person can make. Nevertheless, they never dictate a person's life script entirely and most often leave a good deal of room for genuine self-authoring.

The existentialist view that we are free to live lives almost entirely of our own choosing seems naïve today. However, the postmodern view that we are defined by social circumstances seems cynical. As argued here, the more plausible view is that both the existentialist and postmodern views exaggerate essential truths about us as egos with real but limited self-authoring powers. For a few people, especially a privileged few, the future presents itself as an open field for self-exploration and self-creation. For most others, the realities of nationality, class, race, gender, and material means place serious constraints on self-authorship, constraints that greatly limit the extent to which self-authorship is possible. Complicating matters is the fact that, on both sides of this divide, there are both people who are predisposed to individualism and people who are predisposed to conformism, people who are motivated to exercise their self-authoring powers to the greatest extent possible given the opportunities and constraints they face and people who are content to cede their self-authoring powers to society, thus allowing society to script their lives for them.

Once again, we see that the ego has significant leeway in where it positions itself between the sides of an inherent duality of human experience, in this case the duality of self-authorship and the social construction of identity, which is a specific form of the fundamental duality of the interior ego and the worldly self. Once again, therefore, we arrive at a "wide and shifting" conclusion, in this case the conclusion that the ego is situated on a wide and shifting middle ground between sides of a duality represented by traditional and antitraditional positions on the ego's role in the formation of personal identity. Let us add this conclusion to the revised conception of the ego, as its eighteenth key idea.

Question 11

HOW IS THE TRADITIONAL VIEW THAT THE EGO IS GENDER-NEUTRAL TO BE EVALUATED IN RESPONSE TO THE ARGUMENT THAT THE NOTION OF THE EGO AS IT HAS EMERGED IN PATRIARCHAL SOCIETIES MORE ACCURATELY REPRESENTS MEN'S SUBJECTIVITY THAN WOMEN'S?

Contemporary feminist theory, which emerged in the 1960s and came to the fore in intellectual circles and the academy in the 1970s, provided another major twentieth-century challenge to the traditional notion of the ego. There are many different perspectives within feminist theory. Here we consider psychoanalytic feminist theory as it arose to prominence in the 1970s in both France and the Anglo-American world. We consider this perspective because it focuses specifically on ego development in women and men. Psychoanalytic feminist theorists have explained that in patriarchal societies ego development unfolds in markedly different ways for women and men, with the consequence that the traditional notion of the ego more accurately represents men's subjectivity than women's.

French psychoanalytic feminist theory arose out of and in response to the work of Jacques Lacan, who rejected psychoanalytic ego psychology and rethought psychoanalysis from a poststructural perspective. Luce Irigaray and Julia Kristeva are two important feminist writers whose work draws on and responds to Lacan. Two of Irigaray's most important works are *Speculum of the Other Woman* and *This Sex Which Is Not One*. In *Speculum,* Irigaray discussed major figures in the history of philosophy and psychoanalysis, revealing the many ways in which these *men,* in thinking that they were writing from a universal human standpoint, were in fact writing from a male perspective that excludes women. In *This Sex Which Is Not One,* Irigaray discussed, among other things, the misinterpretation of female sexuality in psychoanalysis, the absence of understanding of female sexuality in patriarchal society, and the exploitation of women as objects of exchange in patriarchal society.

As for Kristeva, perhaps best known among her writings are *Revolution in Poetic Language* and *Powers of Horror: An Essay on Abjection*. In *Revolution,* Kristeva set forth an account of the semiotic (preverbal) communication of the body and how it exists in dialectical tension with the symbolic structures of language. In *Powers of Horror,* Kristeva developed the important idea of abjection, which is the idea of casting off part of oneself as alien, only to recoil in revulsion when what was cast off makes its presence felt in ways that seem to undermine one's worldview, destabilize one's identity, or dissolve one's boundaries.

Anglo-American psychoanalytic feminist theory arose out of psychoanalytic object-relations theory, which, as noted earlier, turned away from the one-person model of psychoanalysis to focus on how psychic structures emerge and are formed in the context of relationships, especially the relationship between the child and the caregiver in the first years of life. Dorothy Dinnerstein and Nancy Chodorow are two important feminist writers in this object-relational lineage. Dinnerstein's major work is *The Mermaid and the Minotaur: Sexual Arrangements and Human Malaise,* in which she analyzed how the fact that women almost alone have had the responsibility of caring for young children has been a primary cause of disadvantages that women experience in relation to men. Chodorow's major work is *The Reproduction of Mothering*, in which she analyzed how women's mothering of young children has contributed both to differences in women's and men's ego development and to the "reproduction of mothering," the shaping of women in such a way as to predispose them to continue being the caregivers of the young.

The feminist theories of Irigaray and Kristeva presuppose an understanding of Lacan's account of early childhood development. Translated into standard psychoanalytic terminology, Lacan's account can be simplified to say that development proceeds from the outset of life to a "mirror" stage (approximately 6 to 18 months), a stage during which the child creates the ego by falsely identifying with the reflected image of its own body.[15] This mirror stage is a turning point at which development changes course fundamentally, somewhat as follows: (1) imaginary order (preoedipal stage, roughly): life is rooted in the body, instincts, vague imaginings, and intimacy with the caregiver as original object of desire; (2) mirror stage (within preoedipal stage): the child, previously experiencing a sense of fragmentation, creates the ego, an illusory sense of wholeness and coherence, by identifying with the image of its unified body; (3) entry into symbolic order (the oedipal stage, roughly): the child separates from the caregiver, submits to the "law of the father," and begins being defined in language-based symbolic terms;[16] and (4) adult life: the child, having submitted to the shaping influence of the symbolic order, makes progress in acquiring language and conforming to social norms, thus preparing for adult membership in the world of symbolic discourse.

Unfolding in this basic direction, early childhood development moves from a life anchored in the body and the imagination to a life centered in language-based symbolic thought, from a life of unrestrained instincts and feelings to a life held in check by the exercise of will, from a life not yet fully differentiated from the caregiver to a life clearly marked off by ego boundaries, and, generally, from a preverbal, intimately relational life focused on the caregiver as object of desire to a symbolic, fully individuated life obedient to social standards. Overall, since women primarily have performed the role of caregiver in the preoedipal stage and since male authority has been dominant in the oedipal stage and in the adult symbolic world, the direction of early childhood development has been away from a "primitive" preverbal world that has been gendered female to a "civilized" symbolic world that has been gendered male.

This account of early childhood development is clearly a reflection of patriarchal society, which has assigned women the role of caregivers of children and has conferred on men the right to govern. According to Kristeva, the movement of early childhood development away from the preoedipal caregiver and toward the male-dominant symbolic world is first evident in the mirror stage, which, in the terms she uses, is the first step in "thetic" development because it is the stage in which the child first posits itself as an object ready to be defined and thus reconstituted by the symbolic discourse of others.[17] Specifically, the child in the mirror stage posits itself as a presymbolic, merely imaginal object by identifying itself with its reflected bodily image. In thus objectifying itself, the child presents itself as a blank slate to be shaped by the categories and governed by the imperatives of the symbolic world, including, importantly, gender categories and imperatives. This symbolic reconstitution of the child then accelerates when the child, following the oedipal stage, is subject to socializing influences, which further imprint the categories and imperatives of male-dominant society on the soul. From this perspective, early childhood development is a time when children are prepared for and then reconstituted symbolically by male authority so that they can become members of "man's" world.

Irigaray and Kristeva make this point by saying that patriarchal society recognizes only male subjects, where by "subject" is meant, as per Lacan, a language user or speaking subject. As Irigaray says, "Any theory of the subject has always been appropriated by the masculine."[18] In patriarchal society, that is, any theory of the subject is a theory of the male subject. A female subject, as female, is not recognized. This male subject, produced by and for patriarchal society, has a characteristic form. It is one-sidedly identified with logically structured symbolic thought ("reason"), with volition that aims at mastery of self, objects, and others, and with individuating boundaries that not only mark it off but that also distance it from others. Equally but oppositely, this subject is to a significant extent alienated from the preverbal body, from the immediacy and felt power of fully embodied life, and from boundary-dissolving intimacy with others. According to Irigaray and Kristeva, subjects who approximate, however well or poorly, this one-sidedly rational-volitional-individuated model are the only subjects acknowledged by patriarchal society.

It follows from the fact that patriarchal society recognizes only male subjects that women in patriarchal society are considered subjects only to the extent that their subjectivity is thought to be like men's. However, because patriarchal society defines women in otherness to men, it can acknowledge that women's subjectivity is like men's only by perceiving it to be an inferior copy of men's. Specifically, patriarchal society can acknowledge that women's subjectivity is like men's only by perceiving it to be a subjectivity that in its rationality is less reasonable than men's, that in its volition is weaker than men's, and that in its individuation is less well defined than men's. Furthermore, were women to overcome these perceived shortcomings, the reward would not be equality with men as *female* subjects but only equality with men as male subjects. Irigaray says, "Instead of saying, 'I do not want to be the other of the masculine subject and, in order to avoid being that other, I claim to be his equal,' I say, 'The question of the other has been poorly formulated in the Western tradition, for the other is always seen as the other of the same, the other of the subject itself, rather than an/other subject [*un autre sujet*], irreducible to the masculine subject and sharing equivalent dignity.'"[19] If patriarchal society considers women to be lesser subjects than men, that, in the view of Irigaray and Kristeva, does not mean that, in seeking to be subjects equal to men, women should strive to be the same kind of subjects as men. Their idea of equality is an equality with men that preserves their differences and dignity as women.

According to Irigaray and Kristeva, women, in being defined in otherness to men, are defined not only as inferior men but also as the opposite of men. In being defined in this latter way, women are perceived as representatives of that which the ego was forced to reject during its patriarchal formation: embodied preoedipal life. Perceived thus, women are disparaged not only for being less rational, volitional, and individuated than men but also for being irrational, captivating, and engulfing. This disparagement of women is most dramatically evident when women are associated with features of the preoedipal caregiver that, in addition to having been devalued, are frightening. For example, as Irigaray notes, women, in being associated with the preoedipal caregiver, are sensed to have the power to devour others, as if to reincorporate them within the maternal body.[20] In general, in being perceived as embodiments of preoedipal life, women are considered attractive, mysterious, and powerful, but only in negative ways. They are considered attractive in an ensnaring, enervating way; mysterious in a primitive, irrational way; and powerful in a destructive, consuming way. In their otherness to men, women are thus perceived both as inadequate men and as primitive, dangerous opposites of men.

Additionally, women, in being associated with the preoedipal caregiver, are perceived not only to be attractive, mysterious, and powerful in negative ways but also to be horrific in nature. They are perceived as beings whose bodies are not only dangerous (reengulfment) but also hideous or odious to the "body-transcended" male ego. According to Kristeva, boys' separation from the preoedipal caregiver in early childhood is not just a rejection of a being perceived to be dangerous but an *abjection* of a being perceived to be repugnant. This sense that women are repugnant, thus having its origin in early childhood, becomes a pathology of men's (but not women's) treatment of women in patriarchal society. Kristeva clarifies that degrading one's love object is primarily a male perversion. Women do not relate to the presymbolic caregiver as a love object that was rejected in disgust but rather as a love object that was relinquished with sadness.[21]

With these views, Irigaray and Kristeva have proposed strategies for cultivating women's subjectivity. Perhaps most importantly, they have sought ways to revalue aspects of preoedipal life that have been devalued. Kristeva's best-known contribution in this vein is her account of the preverbal, bodily self-expression that underlies symbolic discourse. This "semiotic" self-expression initially consists of the bodily movements, gestures, and sounds by which the infant communicates its instinctual needs to the caregiver. Such preverbal bodily communication, in play at the outset of life, does not disappear when it is overwritten by symbolic discourse. Instead, according to Kristeva, it remains active beneath symbolic discourse, challenging its formal structures, energizing it, and grounding it in bodily felt significance. According to Kristeva, semiotic self-expression and symbolic discourse, although in unresolved dialectical tension with each other, require and complement each other.[22]

Another strategy used by Kristeva for cultivating women's subjectivity has been to reevaluate the maternal role. She has sought to do this by describing the maternal role in its humanness, without idealizing or devaluing it. She has thus sought to describe the maternal role as it is experienced by women as they adjust to the destabilizing effects of pregnancy, as they deal with the reality of being responsible for a new life, as they grow to love the human being who is emerging within them, and, finally, as they are willing to relinquish this loved one when its independence requires that it separate itself from its caregiver. In thus describing the maternal role as requiring both love of great intimacy and the strength to let go, Kristeva avoids both idealizing the role as a superhuman self-sacrifice and devaluing it as a subhuman biological function.[23]

Irigaray's strategies for cultivating women's subjectivity include exploring how women's bodies and sexuality might be imagined apart from how they have been imagined by men and how women's relationships with other women might be transformed apart from the influence of men. Regarding the latter strategy, Irigaray has given special attention to the mother-daughter relationship, which she believes has great potential for bringing about positive social and cultural change. "In our societies, the mother/daughter, daughter/ mother relationship constitutes a highly explosive nucleus. Thinking it, and changing it, is equivalent to shaking the foundations of the patriarchal order."[24]

Another strategy proposed by Irigaray is to explore how spirituality might have a locus in the body. Patriarchal society projects spirituality on high in the form of an unseen transcendent mind and will, an all-knowing judge. We need to think in another way, Irigaray proposes, and explore how spirituality can be visibly manifest in the body. She says, "The law creates invisibility, so that God (in his glory?) cannot be looked upon. What happens to seeing, to flesh, in this disappearance of God? Where can one's eye alight if the divine is no longer to be seen? And if it does not continue to dwell in the flesh of the other in order to illuminate it, to offer up to the look the other's flesh as divine, as the locus of a divine to be shared?"[25] Such a rethinking of spirituality as manifest within the body, Irigaray says, would make spirituality an immediately present "sensible transcendental" rather than, as it has been, a remote invisible transcendental.

As feminists, both Irigaray and Kristeva agree that much work needs to be done on economic, social, and political levels to overcome women's disadvantages and to improve their opportunities. However, as *psychoanalytic* feminists, they also agree that much work needs to be done on the level of subjectivity, most importantly work that unmasks men's and cultivates women's subjectivity. As the strategies mentioned in the previous paragraphs indicate, Irigaray and Kristeva believe that the patriarchal character of the symbolic order, although deeply entrenched, is not something inherent to it. Change is possible on all levels, the level of subjectivity being their primary concern.

Some critics have alleged that Irigaray's and Kristeva's proposals for cultivating women's subjectivity presuppose essentialism, the view that there are inherent rather than only socially constructed differences between women and men. Irigaray has responded to this claim by explaining that her proposals have been meant only as exploratory strategies, strategies for investigating women's subjectivity without assumptions about where the strategies will lead. The point, she says, is not to define the essential feminine but rather to free women from patriarchally imposed definitions and roles, which "imprison us in enclosed spaces where we cannot keep on moving, living, as ourselves."[26] As for Kristeva, she has responded that her proposals have been set forth with respect for the diverse constituencies of the women's movement and with an understanding that, as it matures, the movement will increasingly shift its focus from the experience of women generally and even from the differing experiences of racial, social, or cultural groups of women to the experience of individual women.[27]

Dorothy Dinnerstein, in *The Mermaid and the Minotaur*, and Nancy Chodorow, in *The Reproduction of Mothering*, have perspectives that differ significantly from those of Irigaray and Kristeva and that lead to conclusions that, although similar to Irigaray's and Kristeva's in many ways, are also importantly different. The primary difference between Dinnerstein's and Chodorow's perspectives on the one hand and Irigaray's and Kristeva's on the other is that Dinnerstein and Chodorow, characteristic of psychoanalytic object relations theory, give primary attention to the preoedipal child-caregiver relationship. Dinnerstein and Chodorow trace the beginnings of differences in girls' and boys' development primarily to that stage rather than, as Irigaray and Kristeva do, to the oedipal stage.

For Dinnerstein and Chodorow, the most important fact underlying differences between girls and boys and, therefore, between women and men is that, historically, women almost exclusively have played the role of caregivers of young children. This arrangement is not so nearly universal now as it was in the 1970s, when Dinnerstein's and Chodorow's books came out. Since the 1970s, men have increasingly begun to help care for infants and toddlers, and the inequities underlying traditional gender arrangements have become much more widely understood. Nevertheless, women's traditional role as caregivers of young children has remained in place more than it has given way, and it still has the kinds of consequences that Dinnerstein and Chodorow describe. Given the importance of female caregiving at the outset of life to Dinnerstein's and Chodorow's analyses, we shall for the rest of this section use the terms "preoedipal mother" and "mothering" in the place of "preoedipal caregiver" and "caregiving."

Dinnerstein and Chodorow argue that women's role in caring for the young is the primary cause of differences in girl's and boy's gender development. The fact that girls are the same gender as the mother and that boys are opposite in gender to the mother causes the mother to treat them in opposite ways. Mothers develop closer relationships with girl children, with whom they identify for reasons of gender, and more distant relationships with boy children, from whom they disidentify for reasons of gender. Furthermore, mothers hold girl children in close relationship longer, thus slowing their separation and individuation; and they push boy children out of close relationship sooner, thus quickening their separation and individuation. In this way, in the first year of life girls are already being shaped to identify with relationship and openness to others, whereas boys are already being shaped to identify with separateness and independence from others. Additionally, girls are already being shaped so that throughout life they will associate themselves with the preoedipal mother and everything she represents, and boys are already being shaped so that throughout life they will dissociate themselves from the preoedipal mother and everything she represents.

Dinnerstein and Chodorow agree with Irigaray and Kristeva that the oedipal stage is the pivot stage during which the child finally turns away from the mother and submits to male authority, which they conceive in more traditional fashion as the authority of a literal father figure. In the transition from love of the mother to submission to the father, both boys and girls turn away from the bodily, instinctual, emotional, and relational world of the preoedipal mother and submit themselves to the norms of rationality, agency, independence, and obedience imposed by the oedipal father and patriarchal society. However, in thus turning away from the mother and submitting themselves to the father, girls retain a greater remaining connection with the mother than boys do and, therefore, both turn away from the mother and submit themselves to the father less completely and decisively than boy's do. Chodorow says, "Because mothers are the primary love object and object of identification for children of both genders, and because fathers come into the relational picture later and differently, the Oedipus complex in girls is characterized by the continuation of preoedipal attachments and preoccupations, sexual oscillation in an oedipal triangle, and lack of either absolute change of love object or absolute oedipal resolution."[28] As Chodorow also says, girls, owing to their continuing gender link with the mother, repress the preoedipal mother and her world less completely than boys do and find regression to modes of preoedipal life less threatening than boys do.[29]

With their analyses being quite similar thus far, Dinnerstein and Chodorow diverge on the conclusions they draw. Dinnerstein's conclusions are primarily about how the asymmetries of preoedipal development lead to systematic disadvantages for women in adult life. The two primary types of disadvantages she writes about are the same as the two primary types that Irigaray and Kristeva write about. The first is that women, in being perceived to be like men, are seen as inferior men; and the second is that women, in being perceived to be opposite to men, are seen as representatives of embodied preoedipal life in its devalued forms.

Dinnerstein explains that the disadvantages that women suffer because they are perceived to be like, but inferior, to men are those that are part of the double standard that makes it more difficult for women to do many of the things that men do. According to Dinnerstein, this double standard afflicts women (1) by making them unwelcome in spheres that have been dominated by men, allowing them to participate in these spheres primarily in a vicarious way, through their men; (2) by making them objects over which men have authority; (3) by making them less able than men (in heterosexual relationships) to recreate the love relationship they first enjoyed with the preoedipal mother; (4) by making them more constrained than men are in giving expression to erotic desire; and (5) by making them more conflicted in their relationships with other women than men are in their relationships with other men. About these various forms of the double standard that afflicts women, Dinnerstein says, "So: as long as it is women who are mainly in charge of children the double standard will survive. The harsh truth is that no societal compromise which changes other features of women's condition while leaving her role as first parent intact will get at the roots of asymmetric sexual privilege."[30] According to Dinnerstein, the women's movement must work on many levels; however, it will never be completely successful so long as it is almost exclusively women who care for young children.

Dinnerstein explains that women also suffer disadvantages in being perceived to be opposite to men because, in being perceived in this way, they are seen to represent not just embodied preoedipal life but embodied preoedipal life as it was devalued when the child was struggling for separation from the mother. In discussing disadvantages of this type, Dinnerstein notes (1) that women are perceived to be primitive and insentient, only half human, more "it" than "I"; (2) that women are perceived in the same split way as the preoedipal mother, fluctuating between "an omniscient goddess and a dumb bitch";[31] (3) that women are perceived as mysterious, alien, and dangerous; (4) that women, as in Kristeva's account of abjection, are perceived to be repugnant; and (5) that women, in being associated with the body and, therefore, with the transient, mortal world, are perceived as a threat to the immortality quest (the denial of death), which is deeply rooted in male-dominant culture. As with the double standard that afflicts women, these disadvantages that accrue to women as perceived representatives of preoedipal life cannot, Dinnerstein believes, be finally overcome so long as the traditional gender division of labor in parenting remains intact.[32]

Chodorow's analysis, like Dinnerstein's, explores the consequences that mothering has for women. However, her focus is different. Without dismissing the disadvantages that mothering creates for women, Chodorow focuses more on how women in their role as mothers shape girls' and boys' egos differently and, in doing so, predispose girls, and only girls, to perform the mothering role. Regarding how women as mothers shape girls' and boys' egos differently, Chodorow argues that mothers, in identifying with girl children and in holding them in close relationship longer, create girls with egos that are defined more in terms of relationship and, therefore, that have boundaries that are more permeable and open to others. Oppositely, Chodorow argues that mothers, in disidentifying from boy children and in pushing them out of close relationship sooner, create boys with egos that are defined more in terms of independence and, therefore, that have boundaries that are more sharply marked off from and closed to others. More generally, Chodorow argues that women's mothering role shapes girls with egos that, in being more relational, are more empathic, fluid, and continuous with others and shapes boys with egos that, in being more independent, are more assertive, rigid, and discontinuous from others.[33] Furthermore, once the oedipal stage forces the turn from the mother and her world to the father and his world, it creates girls with egos that are more complex and ambivalent (because, in turning from mother to father, girls do so less decisively, retaining more affiliation with and affection for the mother) and boys with egos that are less complex and ambivalent (because, oppositely, in turning from mother to father, boys do so more decisively, retaining less affiliation with and affection for the mother).[34]

Chodorow argues that women's mothering, in creating these differences in girls' and boys' egos, creates corresponding differences in how women and men are disposed toward mothering. Specifically, it creates women who feel a need to re-create the original mother-child bond because, still identified with the preoedipal mother and her role, women can reexperience the satisfactions of the mother-child bond not only in their adult love relationships but also and especially in their relationships with their own children. In contrast, it creates men who are not disposed to re-create the mother-child bond because, in being opposite in gender to the preoedipal mother and in having separated themselves more decisively from her, men are prone to reexperience the satisfactions of the mother-child bond only in their adult love relationships. Chodorow says,

> The psychoanalytic account of male and female development, when reinterpreted, gives us a developmental theory of the reproduction of female mothering. Women's mothering repro-

duces itself through differing object-relational experiences and differing psychic outcomes in women and men. As a result of having been parented by a woman, women are more likely than men to seek to be mothers, that is, to relocate themselves in a primary mother-child relationship, to get gratification from the mothering relationship, and to have psychological and relational capacities for mothering.[35]

Chodorow acknowledges the obvious biological facts that have tied women to mothering: that they, not men, get pregnant and give birth to children and that they, not men, lactate and thus provide nourishment for children. However, she holds that these facts are malleable.[36] Her point is that even if women were not tied to mothering by biological facts, they would be prone to perform the mothering role by virtue of having themselves been cared for by women.

This exposition of psychoanalytic feminist theory leads to the following conclusion: the notion of the ego has not been gender-neutral and throughout most of history has more accurately represented men's than women's subjectivity. To avoid misunderstanding, we should stress that this conclusion is a comparative statement. It says "only" that the notion of the ego has reflected, facilitated, and valued men's subjectivity more than women's and that it has hidden, obstructed, and devalued women's subjectivity more than men's. It does not say that the notion of the ego has reflected, facilitated, and valued only men's subjectivity or that it has hidden, obstructed, and devalued only women's subjectivity. It does not, therefore, say that the notion of the ego has been misapplied to women. As a comparative statement, all our conclusion says is that the ego as it has been shaped in patriarchal society has been a much better fit for men than it has been for women.

Clearly, women, like men, have always had interior-exterior, subject-object, I-Me egos. Women have always been interior subjects and executive agencies, even if in patriarchal society they have been taught to identify with their status as subjects and agents less strongly than men do. Additionally, women, like men, have always had exterior, object or Me, sides, sides that reflect their DNA, their upbringing, and their socialization. That woman, like men, have always had exterior, object or Me, sides is in no way contradicted by the fact that women in patriarchal society have, on their exterior sides, been less well defined *as women* than men have been defined *as men* and even if, as feminist theory has demonstrated, they have been defined contradictorily, as both lesser men and the opposite of men.

All that is implied by these facts is that *some* features—indeed, some very important features—that have been imposed on women's self-representations have to a significant extent hidden, obstructed, or devalued their subjectivity. To avoid misunderstanding, therefore, we should repeat that the conclusion stated above is only comparative, not absolute.

We can now consider our conclusion as the comparative statement it is, as a statement holding that the notion of the ego, although applying to both men and women, has applied to men better than it has to women. Thus understood, our conclusion raises the following question: Is it possible that circumstances could be changed so that the notion of the ego would apply equally well to men and women, even if it applied to them differently? The answer to this question is, I believe, clear enough in the abstract.

The answer is, yes, circumstances could in principle be changed so that the notion of the ego no longer advantaged men and disadvantaged women. Among circumstances that would need to be changed are (1) that women's subjectivity, as Irigaray and Kristeva propose, would need to be better understood and more highly valued; (2) that the parenting of young children, as Dinnerstein and Chodorow propose, would need to cease being primarily the work of women; (3) that society would need to become more aware and accepting of nonbinary, diverse expressions of sexuality and gender; and, generally, (4) that the male-dominance of society would need to disappear. If we assume that such changes could be accomplished—and, thanks to the women's and LGBTQ movements of the last fifty-plus years, these changes have begun, if only begun, to be accomplished—then we can conclude that the notion of the ego could in principle apply to women as well as it does to men. This conclusion is "too easy" in the sense that it presupposes deep changes throughout society that may never be accomplished. Nevertheless, the conclusion, I believe, is no less justified as an abstract statement for this reason.

With these considerations, we arrive at the following final conclusions: (1) that the notion of the ego applies, and has always applied, to both women and men; (2) that the ego might not be gendered at birth but has always become gendered soon thereafter; (3) that the traditional notion of the ego has been a much better fit for men than it has been for women and, therefore, much more advantageous and less disadvantageous for men than it has been for women; and (4) that the notion of the ego could apply equally well, even if differently, to women and men if the distorting imprint of patriarchy on development, language, society, and culture were eliminated. These four points will be combined and added to the revised conception of the ego, as its nineteenth key idea.

The reader might have noticed that we have made no mention of a wide and shifting middle ground in this section. The reason is that in this section the opposing traditional and antitraditional positions discussed have not represented opposite, coessential sides of an inherent duality of human experience or even, as was the case in the section on self-knowledge, opposing sides of a theoretical debate each side of which presents an important but only partial truth. Instead, in this section the traditional and antitraditional positions have represented only a false traditional assumption—that, historically, the notion of the ego has been gender-neutral—and an antitraditional criticism that has demonstrated the falsity of that assumption.

Question 12

How is the traditional view that the ego is ontologically distinct from the body to be evaluated in response to advances in cognitive science, artificial intelligence, and neuroscience?

Another major challenge to the traditional notion of the ego in the twentieth century came from those advocating physicalism in the philosophy of mind, where by "physicalism" is meant any view that holds that only the entities, forces, and properties studied by the physical sciences exist, thus denying that interior consciousness is ontologically distinct from physical reality. Physicalism presents a challenge to the traditional notion of the ego because it is open to the notion of interior consciousness—and, therefore, to the notion of an ego within interior consciousness—only if, as seems very difficult, it can be shown that interior consciousness is an exclusively physical system functioning according to the laws of the physical sciences.

Physicalism, under the traditional name "materialism," has an ancient history in philosophy. It was always a minority view until the second half of the twentieth century, when it became a prominent view in the philosophy of psychology and the philosophy of mind, especially in Britain and the United States. It entered the mainstream with the emergence of behaviorism in the philosophy of psychology, which opened the possibility of explaining mental states and functions in terms of behaviors or dispositions to behave. It then became the prevailing view in the academic community with the emergence of computational and neuroscientific theories in the philosophy of mind, which opened the possibility of explaining mental states and functions in computational terms, especially in terms of the activity of neural networks in the brain.

Critics of physicalism have argued that explanations of consciousness in exclusively physical terms, although essential for understanding the physical substratum of consciousness, are unable to explain or at least fully explain some fundamental aspects of consciousness. Two such aspects often said to be beyond physicalistic explanation are (1) intentionality, the fact that many mental states are "about" something in the sense that they represent and thus refer to things or states of affairs beyond themselves; and (2) qualia, the phenomenal features of many mental states, the "what it is like" to experience or be in these states.

The problem posed by intentionality is that it is difficult to understand how something exclusively physical in character might be said to be about or to refer to anything. It is difficult to understand how a physical thing might be about another physical thing and even more difficult to understand how a physical thing might be about a nonphysical, fictional, or impossible thing, for example, about a disembodied soul, Cinderella, or the set of all sets, respectively. Whereas a perception, belief, or desire can be about, say, a new car, a new car, it seems, cannot itself be about or refer to anything beyond itself, not another physical thing and certainly not, it would seem, a nonphysical, fictional, or impossible thing. Franz Brentano, who brought the (medieval) notion of intentionality to modern attention, held that intentionality is a "mark of the mental."[37] Only mental states can be about something, Brentano thought; exclusively physical things cannot.

On this view, an exclusively physical world would be devoid of meaning because it would lack the intentional states that alone give things meaning. This would be true even if such a world were to include computers that spoke fluent English (or some other natural language), for from this point of view the language thus spoken would have no meaning *to the computers*. The computers' output would have only a derivative meaning, a meaning given to the computers by us and understood only by us, not an original meaning, not a meaning created or understood by the computers themselves.[38] However, this intuitively plausible view has not gone unchallenged. Philosophers have explored strategies for naturalizing intentionality by offering proposals for how intentional states might be understood to be present in exclusively physical or biological systems. Whether intentionality can be fully naturalized remains an open question.

The problem posed by qualia is that it is difficult to understand how an exclusively physical thing might be said to experience phenomenal qualities, where phenomenal qualities are such things as the distinctive sound we experience when we listen to a waterfall, the hue of redness we experience when we perceive an apple, the unpleasant feeling we experience when we are in pain, and, perhaps, the surprise we experience in learning that Santa Clause does not exist or that quantum phenomena remain entangled even at great distances. According to critics of physicalism who focus on qualia, phenomenal qualities, unlike mental or cognitive processes of a clearly functional character, are inherently resistant to explanation in exclusively physical terms. No account of behavior or of computationally modeled mental functions or of neural networks can explain what it is like to have experiences or to be in states like those mentioned. This resistance of phenomenal consciousness to physicalist explanation is what David Chalmers famously called the "hard problem" of consciousness.[39]

Chalmers's notion of the hard problem has led to wide-ranging responses. Some have argued that the hard problem is in fact not so hard, either because the problem is a pseudoproblem or because phenomenal qualities upon closer examination might be found to have underlying structures or functions that make them amenable to physical-scientific explanation after all. Others have argued that the hard problem is impossibly hard, either because it points to an unbridgeable gap between the physical and the mental or because it exceeds the abilities of the human mind to solve. Still others have argued that the hard problem, although hard for us now, might become easy for future philosophers and scientists, who might have at their disposal the concepts and evidence needed to solve it. Like the problem of naturalizing intentionality, the possibility of solving (or dissolving) the hard problem of consciousness remains an open question.

It is understandable that philosophers representing the natural and social sciences would want an explanation of homo sapiens that invokes nothing beyond the human organism and its behaviors. Such a desire, however, has always run up against the phenomenon of subjectivity. More precisely, as Ken Wilber has argued, it has always run up against the fact that we have *two* subjective sides, each with a corresponding objective side.[40] Wilber calls these corresponding pairs of sides the four "quadrants" of human existence. The two subjective quadrants are individual subjectivity (interior consciousness) and collective subjectivity (intersubjective relationships and the shared meanings, values, and narratives of human culture). The corresponding objective quadrants are individual objectivity (the human body and its causal connections with the material world) and collective objectivity (society: social groups, social systems, economies).

The two subjective quadrants of human existence have always posed hard problems for sciences devoted to one or the other of the two objective quadrants. It has always been a hard problem for the natural sciences to explain the intentional and phenomenal aspects of consciousness (individual subjective quadrant). It has been left to phenomenology to provide an understanding of these aspects of consciousness. Similarly, it has always been a hard problem for the social sciences to explain intersubjectivity and culture (collective subjective quadrant). It has been left to hermeneutics to provide an understanding of these types of shared subjectivity. In Wilber's terms, a full understanding of humanness requires a "four-quadrant" approach, an approach that, rather than seeking to explain subjectivities in terms of objectivities, gives equal respect to all four quadrants, acknowledging that all are fundamental sides of humanness.

Whether the explanation of subjectivities in terms of objectivities is metaphysically impossible; possible but, owing to our current ignorance, not yet feasible; or inherently beyond human understanding is not important for our concerns. It is not important because the revised conception of the ego is an account of the ego as it lives and experiences its life. From this perspective, the dualities of the subjective and objective sides of human life are *existentially* irreducible, even if future philosophers or scientists might someday find a *theoretical* reduction. Just as we act with the belief that our actions are not completely predetermined, so we also live with the belief that our lives have irreducibly different subjective and objective sides. These beliefs might be false. Nevertheless, they are foundational to our lives as we live them. It is with this understanding that Wilber's four-quadrant account, as applied to the ego, is here adopted as the twentieth key idea of the revised conception of the ego.

Once again, we can conclude that the ego is situated on a wide and shifting middle ground between sides of an inherent duality of human experience, one side of which has been championed by representatives of the traditional notion of the ego and the other side by antitraditional critics. In this case, the middle ground between the two sides of the duality is the existential space bridging, on one side, individual and collective subjectivity and, on the other side, individual and collective objectivity. The ego, we have argued, is neither something exclusively subjective nor something exclusively objective but is rather something that is both subjective and objective. Such a two-sided existence is what we have called the duality of the interior ego and the worldly self, which, we have argued, is fundamental to human experience. Here we can add that this fundamental duality is a two-by-two, four-quadrant duality, as described by Wilber. The ego, I suggest, bridges and lives in all four of Wilber's quadrants, sometimes living primarily in one and other times living primarily in another.

In stating this view, we should add one qualification, which arises from our adoption of the existential-phenomenological view that the world has existential priority over individual subjectivity. The qualification is that the ego, although arising within and frequently returning to the individual subjective quadrant, lives originally and primarily in the three quadrants it shares with others, collective subjectivity and material and social objectivity. For example, when I as ego participate in relationships or communicate with others or join others in acting on shared values or narratives, I live primarily in shared subjective space (collective subjective quadrant). Switching quadrants, when I tend my garden, I live primarily in my body as an object interacting with other objects (individual objective quadrant). Switching quadrants again, when I interact with others as a member of a group or perform job-related or other social roles or produce or consume economic goods, I live primarily in a world of socially organized cooperation (collective objective quadrant). Finally, when I withdraw inwardly from these three shared quadrants, in which I primarily live, I take up residence in interior consciousness (individual subjective quadrant), the space in which I am nearest to myself as subject or I but in which I reside only as a secondary abode. The ego, rooted in the individual subjective quadrant, thus lives on a wide and shifting middle ground between two subjective and two objective sides of its existence.

Conclusion

The signature conclusion of this chapter is that the ego is situated on a wide and shifting middle ground between opposite sides of inherent dualities of human experience, where one side of each of these dualities has been championed by advocates of the traditional notion of the ego and the other side by antitraditional critics. Two sections of this chapter came to different conclusions. The section on self-knowledge did come to a "wide and shifting" conclusion. However, the middle ground under discussion in that section, although lying between opposing sides of a theoretical debate between advocates and critics of the traditional notion of the ego, did not lie between opposite sides of a duality. As for the section on feminist theory, it did not arrive at a wide and shifting conclusion of any sort, since it sided entirely with the antitraditional view that, historically, the notion of the ego has *not* been gender-neutral. However, in all other sections of this chapter, we have arrived at our signature conclusion. Specifically, we have concluded that the ego is situated on a wide and shifting middle ground between these dualities: (1) the duality of self-control and the passions, the duality of executive and spontaneous cognition, and, fundamentally, the duality of agency and spontaneity; and (2) the duality of psyche and world, the duality of self-authorship and social construction of identity, and, fundamentally, the duality of the interior ego and the worldly self (understood from Wilber's four-quadrant perspective).

Here we should restate the reason why the ego is situated on a wide and shifting middle ground between the sides of these dualities: *it is the bridge that integrates the sides of the dualities.* The ego is both a regulator and a vehicle of the passions, both a manipulator and a recipient of arising thoughts and images, and, fundamentally, both an executive agency that harnesses and a partner that is dependent on the spontaneity of consciousness. Additionally, the ego is both a psychic ego and a bodily, social self, both a responsible author of its identity and a subject whose identity is to a great extent the product of social circumstances, and, fundamentally, both an intentional-phenomenal-cultural subject or I and a physical-functional-social object or Me. This proposal that the ego is a bridge that integrates the sides of inherent dualities of human experience can be added to the revised conception of the ego as its twenty-first key idea.

We have seen in this chapter that many twentieth-century schools of thought presented strong challenges to the traditional notion of the ego. Each challenge struck a blow, calling into question if not refuting a main idea or assumption of the traditional notion. The psychoanalytic revolution in psychiatry and psychology struck a blow to the traditional view that the ego has primacy over the passions, although it did so without establishing the antitraditional view that it is the passions that have primacy over the ego. The psychoanalytic revolution also struck a blow—as, too, did Nietzsche and Sartre—to the traditional view that the ego has complete control of its executive functions. Existential phenomenologists exposed the error in the traditional view that interior psychic space is the ego's primary abode. Depth psychologists on the one hand and symbolic interactionists and relational psychoanalysts on the other demonstrated that the traditional account of the ego's self-knowledge is overstated, the former demonstrating that, contrary to the traditional view, the ego does not have full access to itself and the latter demonstrating that, contrary to the traditional view, the ego does not always have privileged access to itself.

Coming to the fore in the second half of the twentieth century, post-modernism called into question the traditional view that assigned to the ego the role of authoring its worldly identity. In their turn, psychoanalytic feminist theorists brought to light many of the ways in which the traditional notion of the ego better applies to men's than to women's subjectivity, thus proving that the traditional notion is not, as had been assumed, gender-neutral. Finally, physicalists in the philosophy of mind challenged the traditional notion of the ego by arguing that the ego's cognitive functions and perhaps even its intentional states and phenomenal experiences can be explained in terms of the functioning of exclusively physical systems.

The challenges posed by these twentieth-century schools have exposed many false or suspect points in the traditional notion of the ego. However, none of these challenges, nor all of them together, we have argued, have demonstrated that the core component ideas of the notion—that the ego is the unifying subject, appropriating owner, and executive agency of consciousness—are mistaken. We have argued that the traditional notion, pared down to remove the false and suspect points exposed by antitraditionalists, survives as an essential insight of the modern period. Descartes's idea of the res cogitans, although laden with historical baggage and metaphysical misconceptions, remains a major contribution to our understanding of ourselves as conscious beings.

However, if, once pared down, the traditional notion of the ego survives as an essential insight of the modern period, it does so only as an *incomplete* insight. The traditional notion of the ego is an incomplete insight because it does not include the idea that the ego is a bridge that integrates inherent dualities of human experience. In this and the last chapter, we have seen that the ego is only one side of two fundamental dualities and, therefore, is incomplete or cannot function apart from the other sides of these dualities. The ego, as the interior subject of consciousness, is incomplete without its exterior or worldly self, which it forges—in response to interpersonal and social influences—in the very process of its production as an interior subject. Additionally, the ego, as the executive agency of consciousness, cannot function apart from the spontaneity of consciousness, on which it depends for the thoughts, images, and impulses it uses in performing its executive functions. The traditional notion of the ego, therefore, needs not only to be properly pared down but also properly built up by clarifying that it is a side of (and bridge between) two fundamental dualities of human experience.

In the last chapter, we set forth eleven key ideas of the revised conception of the ego. We have added ten more key ideas in this chapter. Two final key ideas—those of the ego's self-system and lifeworld—are added in the next chapter. The ten ideas added in this chapter, ideas twelve through twenty-one, are summarized in text box 4.1.

Text Box 4.1
**Key Ideas of the Revised Conception
of the Ego: Second Set**

12. *The ego's ability to control the passions varies across a wide and shifting middle ground between the sides of the duality of self-control and the passions.* The ego is neither master of nor slave to the passions. The ego can have a great deal of or very little control over the passions depending on the extent to which it possesses or lacks psychological health, a sound defense system, autonomous strength, self-discipline, and good habits.

13. *The ego's ability to control its executive functions varies across a wide and shifting middle ground between the sides of the (fundamental) duality of agency and spontaneity.* The ego is never in complete control of its executive functions because its thoughts, images, and impulses are produced for it by the spontaneity of consciousness. Nevertheless, the ego can have a great deal of control over its executive functions if certain conditions are met. When the ego is strongly constituted, selectively focused, and functionally engaged, it exercises guiding influence over the spontaneity of consciousness, which responds by producing thoughts, images, and impulses that are more relevantly responsive to the ego's engaged concerns. However, when the ego is weakly constituted, unselectively focused, or functionally disengaged, it exercises little if any guiding influence over the spontaneity of consciousness, which, therefore, produces thoughts, images, and impulses that are less connected with reality and more nearly random. Accordingly, as the ego's strength of constitution, focus, and engagement vary, so, too, does its control of its executive functions.

14. *The world, not interior psychic space (the individual subjective quadrant), is the ego's original and primary abode.* In the very process of being constituted as an interior subject or I, the ego reaches outward by appropriating its worldly experiences and what it perceives to be its worldly attributes. Originally and primarily, therefore, the ego lives as a body ego in the material,

social world. It takes time for the ego to discover interior psychic space; and after discovering this space, the ego enters it only as a secondary abode, a place in which it sleeps or engages in reflection, reverie, introspection, meditation, or prayer. Although the psyche, as the place in which the ego is constituted, has ontological priority over the world, the world, as the place in which the ego originally and primarily lives, has existential priority over the psyche.

15. *The psyche and the world are always open to each other.* The psyche always opens out to the world, and the world always opens in to the psyche. Ontologically, the ego is thrown *out* of the psyche and *into* the world. The ego is thus native and has birthright access to both the psyche and the world, which, therefore, can never be closed to each other.

16. *The ego lives on a wide and shifting middle ground between the sides of the duality of the interior psyche and embodied, social life in the world.* The ego travels between the two sides of the duality of psyche and world, spending most of its time in the world, in which it originally and primarily lives, but still spending a good deal of time within the psyche, where it sleeps, dreams, and carries on its interior life.

17. *The ego's self-knowledge varies across a wide and shifting middle ground between opposing, traditional and antitraditional, positions.* The ego does not have full, always-privileged access to itself because there are underlying strata of the psyche that are hidden from it and because it frequently cannot know itself without the help of others. Notwithstanding these limitations, the ego does have means at its disposal by which it can know itself: direct observation, independent investigation, introspection, reflection, and heeding the responses of others. Given these means, the ego can know either a great deal or very little about itself depending on the extent to which it avails itself of these means. The ego's self-knowledge thus covers a wide range of possibilities. Furthermore, the ego's self-knowledge is not only thus wide in range but also shifting within this range, since it not only increases when the ego uses the means mentioned but also decreases when it ceases uses these means or when it suffers from illness or cognitive decline.

18. *The ego's self-authoring ability varies across a wide and shifting middle ground between the sides of the duality of self-authorship and social construction of identity.* Although the ego's identity is to a great extent a social construct, it is also to a great extent the product of the ego's self-authoring choices. Some people value individualism, striving as much as possible to be authors of their identity, whereas others are prone to conformism, tending to allow society to script their identities for them. Nevertheless, even the most individualistic people are to a great extent defined by society (and history and DNA); and even the most conformist people are to a great extent the responsible authors of their identities.

19. *The traditional notion of the ego, rather than being gender-neutral, has always been more a notion of a man's than a women's ego.* The notion of the ego has always applied to both men and women. However, in patriarchal societies, the notion has applied better to men than to women. It has highlighted and valorized human features that, although shared by men and women, are more strongly associated with men; and it has hidden and denigrated human features that, although shared by men and women, are more strongly associated with women. Despite this fact, the notion of the ego could apply equally well, even if differently, to women and men *if* women's subjectivity were better understood and valued, *if* women were no longer primarily responsible for the care of young children, *if* the diversity of sexual and gender expressions were better understood and valued, and *if*, generally, patriarchal imbalances and inequities in social arrangements and culture were eliminated.

20. *The ego lives on a wide and shifting middle ground between the sides of the duality of individual and collective subjectivity on the one hand and individual and collective objectivity on the other hand.* The ego is both an interior subject (individual subjective quadrant) and a body in the world (individual objective quadrant); and it is both a participant in relationships and culture (collective subjective quadrant) and a member of a social system (collective objective quadrant). The revised conception of the ego makes no attempt to reduce the two subjective quadrants of the ego's existence to the two objective quadrants but rather embraces all four quadrants as coessential, inherent sides of

human experience. Although the ego lives originally and primarily in the three quadrants it shares with others (individual objective quadrant, collective subjective quadrant, and collective objective quadrant), it spends time in all four quadrants, shifting from one to another according to fluctuations in its focus and desires.

21. *The ego is the bridge that integrates inherent dualities of human experience.* The ego is situated on a wide and shifting middle ground between the sides of inherent dualities of human experience because it is the bridge that integrates the sides of these dualities. The ego bridges and integrates the fundamental duality of the interior ego and the worldly self, including, among its specific forms, the dualities of psyche and world, of self-authorship and social construction of identity, and of (individual and collective) subjectivity and (individual and collective) objectivity. Additionally, the ego bridges and integrates the fundamental duality of agency and spontaneity, including, among its specific forms, the duality of self-control and the passions and the duality of executive and spontaneous cognition.

Chapter 5

The Ego's Self-System and Lifeworld

We need to add two more ideas to the revised conception of the ego, those of the ego's self-system and lifeworld.[1] These ideas are needed to complete our account of the ego on its object or Me side. They also are needed because, beginning with the next chapter, they are primary themes in our account of ego development, which tracks the unfolding of the ego not only on its subject or I side, as the subject and executive agency of consciousness, but also on its object or Me side, as an embodied self in a social world. Of the two ideas set forth in this chapter, the idea of the ego's self-system guides our account of how the ego, as an embodied, social self, is transformed stage by stage over the course of life. The idea of the ego's lifeworld guides our account of how the world, as a world experienced by such a self, is transformed stage by stage in corresponding, closely related ways.

The Self-System

In addition to the ego, which is the self of the self-system, the self-system consists of the ego's instrument of self-knowledge and its two primary instruments of self-motivation. The ego's instrument of self-knowledge is the self-representation, also called "ego identity" (or simply "identity") and "self-concept." The ego's two primary instruments of self-motivation are the ego ideal and the superego. The idea of the self-representation is generally accepted across psychological literatures and can be adopted here without significant revision. It is otherwise with the ideas of the ego ideal and the superego, which, introduced by Freud long ago and used primarily within psychoanalytic literature, need to be reformulated before they can be integrated within the revised conception of the ego. Specifically, they need to be reformulated so that their complementary functions as instruments of self-motivation can be better understood. To this end, we significantly redefine these two ideas by clarifying their relation to the two primary motivating forces of life, desire (to which the ego ideal is tied) and fear (to which the superego is tied).

The self-representation, emerging in the second half of the second year, is the construct by means of which the ego understands itself as a human being belonging to the material, social world.[2] As such, it is the mental record of those things that the ego believes can be ascribed to it as parts of what it is. Items that the ego enters in this record include its experiences and its bodily, mental, and social attributes. Included among its bodily attributes are its height, skin color, hair and eye color, sex, and other physical features. Included among its mental—or, more broadly, psychological—attributes are its beliefs, desires, values, goals, and personality traits. Finally, included among its social attributes are its family relationships, ethnicity, nationality, class, and social roles. In terms of the I-Me distinction, the self-representation can be said to be the ego's record of everything that, as subject or I, the ego believes can be attributed to it as object or Me, most importantly, again, its experiences and its bodily, mental, and social attributes.

The features making up the self-representation have many sources. Although some are products of the ego's free choices (possible examples: "father," "teacher," "atheist"), many are genetically inherited or assigned by social circumstances (possible examples: "blue-eyed," "aristocrat," "poor"), and some are acquired by unanticipated events (possible examples: "widow," "exile," "Nobel laureate"). Of the features of the ego's self-representation, some, such as "father," "teacher," and "atheist," may be both chosen and affirmed; many others, such as "blue-eyed," "aristocrat," and "Nobel laureate," may be unchosen but nonetheless affirmed; and some, such as "poor," "widow," and "exile," may, although acknowledged, be neither chosen nor affirmed. Not everything the ego records in the self-representation and believes to be part of what it is as object or Me is something that it chose to be or wants to be.

In the last chapter, we explained reasons why the self-representation often includes unchosen or unwanted features. We learned that many of the features of the self-representation are grounded in interpersonal exchanges or are products of social circumstances or, just as importantly, are inherited with DNA or are consequences of unforeseen events. Much of what the ego understands itself to be is based on the judgment of others; much else is based on family relationships, ethnicity, nationality, class, social roles, and the like; and much else is based on biology or fortune. The ego, although active and responsible as the author of the self-representation, has only limited control over the features of the self-representation.

Beginning in middle childhood, the ego uses inner speech to keep track of the self-representation. The ego speaks to itself inwardly in a narrator's voice to confirm what it has been, is, and might be. This narrator voice thus becomes the primary tool with which the ego fashions its object or Me side and, beginning in adolescence, authors the story of its life. Because the object or Me side of the ego is always a work in progress, the work of the ego's narrator voice is never finished. The inner narrator is always busy revising the self-representation by adding new experiences and attributes to it and by reinterpreting or deleting old ones.

We should note that the ego's narrator voice is the master voice of the self-system. It is not only the voice that the ego uses in keeping track of the self-representation and in authoring the life story; it is also the voice that the ego uses in managing the self-system as a whole. As we shall see, the ego's narrator voice, as the master voice of the self-system, has precedence over two other voices associated with the self-system, those of the ego ideal and the superego. We describe these other two voices presently. Here it suffices to say that the voices of the ego ideal and the superego, which the ego uses to motivate itself to act, are subordinate to the ego's narrator voice. The voices of the ego ideal and the superego speak as advisers to the ego, advisers that the ego, in its narrator voice, can overrule. It is only in using its narrator voice that the ego, in speaking *to* itself, also speaks *for* itself, using the first person to report on its decisions and actions and more generally on what it understands to be the facts of its life. The ego's narrator voice, which is widely recognized in developmental psychology, is a major focus in our account of ego development.[3]

In contrast to the self-representation, which is the ego's mental record of its actual life, the life the ego believes it has in fact been living, the ego ideal is the ego's fantasized depiction of its ideal life, the life the ego imagines it would most like to live. Specifically, according to the standard account, the ego ideal is the ego's fantasized depiction of the life that would fulfill its highest hopes.[4] The conception of the ego ideal used in this book adopts this standard account but adds to it the stipulation that the ego ideal is the ego's fantasized depiction not just of the life that would fulfill its highest hopes but of the life that, in fulfilling its highest hopes, would satisfy its other desires as well (insofar as satisfying these other desires is compatible with fulfilling its highest hopes).

The added stipulation may be implicit in the standard account of the ego ideal, but it is important to make it explicit because it clarifies the ego ideal's relation to the motivating force of desire. It reveals that the ego ideal helps the ego manage not just its highest hopes but all its desires. The stipulation thus widens the function of the ego ideal, making it the instrument that guides the ego in the pursuit of its positive self-interest generally, where the "positive" in "positive self-interest" refers to the satisfaction of desires as opposed to the avoidance of fears (negative self-interest). Thus understood, the ego ideal is the ego's fantasy of its best possible life, which is the life that, it believes, would fulfill its highest hopes and so far as possible satisfy its other desires as well. The ego's highest hopes are in this account of the ego ideal the governing desires, not the only desires, promoted by the ego ideal. They are the desires in relation to which other desires are ranked.

In addition to its narrator's voice, with which the ego keeps track of its self-representation and authors its life story, the ego also speaks to itself in a voice representing the ego ideal. In this voice, the ego often speaks to itself as "you" rather than as "I," inspiring itself by saying, "You *can* do [get, achieve] X." Using this voice, the ego encourages itself to strive for its ideal goals and for other things it wants in life, urging itself to persevere even when what it aspires to seems remote or out of reach. The ego listens to this inspiring voice and fantasizes about the day when its hoped-for ideal self might become its actual self, the day when what is now its ego ideal might become its self-representation. In thus listening to the ego-ideal voice, the ego listens to itself. Despite often speaking in the second person, the ego-ideal voice, like the ego's narrator voice, is the ego's own voice. The ego is speaking to itself not only when it says "I am an X" or "I will do X" but also when it says "You can do X" or "Wouldn't it be good if you achieved X?"

Unlike the ego ideal, which motivates the ego by inspiring it to act, the superego motivates the ego by impelling it to act, by enforcing discipline. According to the standard account, the superego is an inner agency that enforces rules of right and proper conduct. This account expresses Freud's original exposition of the idea. In Freud's view, the superego is an agency that, formed in the transition from early to middle childhood, enforces rules of conduct prescribed by parents (especially the father) and that later in life enforces rules of conduct prescribed by society. In explaining the origin of the superego, Freud assigned an essential role to the Oedipus complex, holding that the child, in resolving the Oedipus complex, relinquishes its desire for the mother and submits to the authority of the father. In thus submitting to the father's authority, the child, according to Freud, internalizes parental rules of right and proper conduct and begins to discipline itself as its parents do. The superego, thus created as an agency that enforces internalized rules of right and proper conduct, continues to be an agency that performs this function as the child grows and becomes an adult, with the difference that parental rules are replaced with adult social rules once the child has grown into an adult.

The conception of the superego used in this book modifies this standard Freudian account in the following two ways: (1) it explains the emergence of the superego in terms of early childhood splitting and its overcoming rather than in terms of the Oedipus complex and its resolution; and (2) it clarifies the superego's relation to the motivating force of fear by explaining that the superego manages the ego's fear of unwanted consequences generally rather than only those that might result from breaking rules of right or proper conduct. The first of these two modifications is discussed later in the book, in chapter 10. The second is discussed here.

The superego's function is here widened from enforcing rules of morality or propriety specifically to enforcing rules of prudence generally, where by "prudence" I mean the caution that seeks to avoid unwanted consequences, whether the consequences are in some way tied to right or proper conduct or are tied to narrow self-interest only. For example, it is the same inner voice that says, "Tell the truth," "Tell the hosts how much you enjoyed the evening," "Set aside money for retirement," and "Don't get too close to the edge of the cliff." Clearly, "Tell the truth" is a command enforcing a rule of what is considered right, morally required, conduct; and "Tell the hosts how much you enjoyed the evening" is a command enforcing a rule of proper, socially expected, conduct. However, in our account, these commands are not superego commands because they enforce rules of these sorts. Rather, what makes them superego commands is that the ego, in exhorting itself to tell the truth or to compliment the hosts, just as in telling itself to save for retirement or to stay away from the edge of the cliff, is attempting to avoid unwanted consequences. It makes no difference if the unwanted consequences are those that might come from violating rules of right or proper conduct (e.g., punishment, a sense of guilt, damage to one's reputation, embarrassment) or those that might come from imprudently disregarding one's personal interests (e.g., poverty, injury, death). The superego in our account does often speak in a voice of morality or propriety. However, it just as often if not more often speaks in a voice of caution that is exclusively self-interested. The general point is that, in either case, it speaks in a voice that seeks to avoid unwanted consequences.

In contrast to the ego ideal, which motivates by the attracting power of desire, the superego motivates by the coercing power of fear. The admonitions and commands of the superego are laden with fear, however strong or slight, because they carry an implicit alarm about unwanted consequences. In effect, they are saying, "Do [or don't do] this—or else!" Accordingly, whereas the purpose of the ego ideal is to assist the ego in satisfying its desires, the purpose of the superego is to keep the ego from realizing its fears. Whereas the ego ideal motivates the ego to pursue its positive self-interest generally, to maximize the goods in its life, the superego motivates the ego to protect its negative self-interest generally, to minimize the "bads" in its life. Reconceived in these ways, the ego ideal and the superego can be seen to be complementary instruments of self-motivation.

Like the ego ideal, which ranks the ego's desires, the superego ranks the ego's fears. However, the superego ranks the ego's fears by a different criterion than the ego ideal uses in ranking the ego's desires. The difference is this: whereas the ego ideal ranks desires according to their compatibility with the ego's highest hopes, the superego ranks fears simply according to their strength. The superego gives most attention to the ego's strongest fears, irrespective of the reasonableness or unreasonableness of the fears. If the ego's strongest fear is the fear of germs, the primary focus of the superego's discipline will be on hygiene and avoiding germs: "Wash your hands," "Don't touch that." If the ego's strongest fear is the fear of wrongdoing or sin, the primary focus of the superego's discipline will be on meeting obligations, keeping commitments, and avoiding temptation: "Keep your promise," "Say your prayers," "Stay away from that kind of person!" Whatever fears the ego might have, the superego metes out discipline proportional to their strength.

The superego also has a voice, a fact that, since Freud introduced the notion in 1923, has long been known. Almost everyone is familiar with the superego as an inner voice of "conscience" that commands, admonishes, praises, and blames to ensure that our actions are, if not perfect, at least good enough to meet standards of conduct that have been set for us. What needs to be added here is that the superego voice—as we have conceived it, as the voice that manages the ego's fears by alerting the ego to unwanted consequences—is the third voice of the ego's self-system. As the third voice, the superego voice is like the ego-ideal voice in being an advisory, motivating voice that frequently addresses the ego as "you." However, it differs from the ego-ideal voice in speaking warningly, imperatively, praisingly, or blamingly rather than encouragingly. Whereas the ego-ideal voice encourages the ego to pursue what it desires, the superego voice warns or commands the ego to avoid what it fears and then praises or blames the ego depending on whether it succeeds or fails in its efforts.

Again, the ego's narrator voice is the master voice of the self-system; the ego ideal and superego voices are subsidiary voices. The ego uses its narrator voice when, speaking both to and for itself in the first person, it reports on matters of fact about its life. In contrast, the ego uses its ego ideal and superego voices when it advises itself on perceived goods to pursue or on unwanted consequences to avoid. Although the ego listens to the voices of the ego ideal and the superego, digesting their counsel and feeling their motivating influence, it does not make decisions or take action in their voices. It makes decisions and takes action in its first-person narrator voice. Furthermore, after listening to the ego ideal and the superego voices and then making decisions or taking action in its narrator voice, the ego continues to speak to itself in its narrator voice by explaining to itself how the decisions it has made or the actions it has taken have changed its self-representation and, perhaps, life story. In thus speaking in its narrator voice, the ego manages the self-system as a whole.

Because desires and fears are the two principal goads to action, the ego ideal and the superego are the ego's two principal instruments of self-motivation. The ego ideal is the carrot that induces the ego to pursue what it desires; the superego is the stick that prods the ego to avoid what it fears. The ego ideal, working with the attracting power of desire, is a telic cause of action, a cause that motivates the ego to act by inspiring it to seek what it believes will promote its well-being. The superego, working with the coercing power of fear, is an efficient cause of action, a cause that motivates the ego to act by impelling it to avoid what it believes will cause it harm. The ego ideal and superego thus work together in opposite (encouraging-coercing, pulling-pushing, telic-efficient) but complementary fashion. The voices of these two instruments of self-motivation, in dialogue with the ego as narrator, help the ego follow a path that is both ascending and straight, both aspiring and cautious, a path believed to lead in the direction of desired goods and away from unwanted consequences.

Beginning in the next chapter, we track the emergence of the self-system from birth, when the self-system consists of the ego alone, to the beginning of middle childhood, when all four components of the self-system are finally in place. Having thus tracked the early emergence of the self-system, the focus then turns to the ensuing developmental transformations of the self-system. In tracking these transformations, we explain how the components of the self-system and the voices that represent them undergo a succession of stage-related changes in the transitions from middle childhood to adolescence, from adolescence to early adulthood, from early adulthood to midlife, from midlife to retirement, and from retirement to old age. Finally, in the last four chapters of the book (part 3), we discuss four stages of spiritual development and explore changes to the self-system during those stages.

In tracking the emergence of the self-system, this book also tracks the emergence of a psychic structure that, although not part of the self-system, is inherently tied to it. This is the structure that Carl Jung called the "shadow."[5] We explained in the introduction the rationale for adding an account of the shadow to the account of the self-system: it is almost always true that some parts of the ego's life are too threatening to acknowledge consciously. To avoid the distress caused by these parts of its life, the ego banishes them from consciousness, thus excluding them from the self-representation and relegating them to the shadow. The shadow, therefore, is the hidden underside of the self-representation and in many ways its opposite. Whereas the self-representation includes those parts of the ego's life that it acknowledges as Me, the shadow consists of those parts that the ego cannot acknowledge and insists are not-Me.

The idea of the shadow is not without problems. The primary difficulty is that it presupposes the idea of repression, and this idea has been subject to strong criticism. The idea of the shadow presupposes the idea of repression because it is by repression, targeted inhibition, that the ego is said to remove threatening impulses and related cognitive content from consciousness, thus creating the shadow. Discussion of the shadow, therefore, requires that the idea of repression be reformulated in such a way that it can avoid the criticisms that have been brought against it and still be able to explain the formation of the shadow. In chapter 10, I set forth what I call the "energy-reduction" conception of repression, which I believe, meets these stipulations.

In popular psychology the shadow is described as a dangerous place within us that prompts us to act in immoral or improper ways. This account is too narrow for our purposes. It is one-sidedly focused on immorality and impropriety in much the same way as the standard account of the superego is one-sidedly focused on morality and propriety. To recall, the standard account of the superego focuses on morality and propriety because, as Freud discovered, the superego first emerges in the transition from early to middle childhood as an internalizing acceptance of parental expectations regarding required or at least acceptable behavior. Oppositely, as explained in chapter 10, the shadow is most often associated with immorality and impropriety because it emerges in the transition from early to middle childhood as an internalizing acceptance of parental judgments regarding unacceptable behavior. Parents' strong disapproval of the older toddler's raging, defiant, and selfish outbursts eventually lead the child—after the toddling stage, in the preschool period leading to middle childhood—to repress the impulses responsible for those outbursts, thus creating the shadow as an unconscious subsystem in which "bad" or "naughty" impulses (and corresponding cognitive content) are laid to rest. Owing to their origins in the parent-child interaction in early childhood, it is understandable both that the superego would be associated with morality and propriety and that the shadow would be associated with the opposites.

Having widened the idea of the superego from an agency that enforces morality and propriety to an agency that protects the ego from unwanted consequences generally, we should now widen the idea of the shadow correspondingly. Specifically, we should widen it from the idea of an unconscious subsystem containing parts of the ego's life that the ego has removed from consciousness because it deems them immoral of improper to the idea of a subsystem containing parts of the ego's life that the ego has removed from consciousness because it finds them highly threatening and harmful to its sense of self, whether it deems them immoral, improper, or neither.

With this widening of the idea of the shadow, it becomes clear that the contents of the shadow need not always have an immoral or improper character. Although many shadow impulses, if allowed expression, would lead to immoral or improper actions, many others would not; and some would lead to actions with beneficial consequences, at least for the person acting on them if not also for society generally. We discuss examples of beneficial shadow impulses in later chapters. At present, the only point that needs to be made is that shadow impulses (and corresponding forbidden thoughts and fantasies) need not be immoral, improper, or even harmful in some way but need only be highly threatening to the ego, especially to its sense of self. This wider definition of the shadow is not new; it is explicit in Jung and in most accounts that are based on Jung. Nevertheless, it is necessary to stress this wider definition to clarify how the shadow, as the hidden underside of the self-system, is inherently tied to the self-system and, therefore, develops in concert with it.

The shadow also has a voice, which is yet another of the ego's voices. The shadow voice is ordinarily understated compared to the ego's narrator voice and the voices of the ego ideal and the superego, but it does make itself heard, especially when the self-system is unstable or undergoing change, thus allowing the shadow to awaken. As we shall see in ensuing chapters, the shadow voice tends under these conditions to speak at first in a menacing way, as an adversary or tempter seeking to undermine the self-system. However, the shadow voice can evolve into a supportive and guiding voice, especially when shadow impulses are inherent to one's biological or psychological makeup and need to be integrated within the conscious personality. Under these conditions, the shadow voice can begin to speak as a counselor and guide.

Speaking as an adversary, the shadow voice seeks to undermine the self-system by deriding features of the self-representation, goals of the ego ideal, and rules of the superego. Speaking as a tempter, the shadow voice seeks further to undermine the self-system by enticing the ego to act on forbidden impulses. Should the shadow voice evolve into the voice of a counselor and guide, it begins to speak to the ego in ways that give it strength and discernment as it faces, integrates, or at least responsibly manages parts of itself that it had previously been unable to acknowledge. Examples of all these ways in which the shadow voice can speak are provided in ensuing chapters. Here it suffices to describe the shadow voice in a general way so that it is clear how this voice is tied to but differs from the voices of the self-system.

Jung's account of the shadow focused primarily on the shadow of early adulthood, a shadow that ordinarily lies dormant during early adulthood and then sometimes awakens during midlife for people who undergo what Jung called "individuation." Neither Jung nor Jungians generally have had much to say about the shadow as it is formed and either hidden or revealed during other stages of development, most importantly preadult stages. I try to fill this gap by explaining how the shadow is formed along with the ego ideal and the superego in the transition from early to middle childhood, how this childhood shadow is sometimes awakened during adolescence, how the childhood shadow is then reconstituted as an adult shadow in early adulthood, and how, finally, this adult shadow is sometimes awakened during midlife. In part 3 of the book, I also explain how the adult shadow is often awakened during spiritual development, specifically during the stage of spiritual preawakening and then again and for the last time during the stage of spiritual awakening.[6] As we shall see, stage-by-stage transformations of the self-system are at the same time stage-by-stage transformations or possible awakenings of the shadow.

The Lifeworld

This book presents not only a biography of the ego but also a travelogue of its journey through the world. In studying the many developmental transformations of the ego's self-system and underlying shadow, it also studies the many developmental transformations of the ego's *lifeworld*. The lifeworld is not the world as it might exist on its own, apart from human experience; nor is it the world as described from the detached standpoint of science. Rather, it is the world as it is prereflectively experienced by an engaged and motivated subject. In short, it is the world of lived experience.

The notion of the lifeworld is central to the discipline of phenomenology. The notion, although not the term, was introduced by Martin Heidegger in 1927 in *Being and Time*. Heidegger sought to give an account of our everyday "being-in-the-world" (*In-der-Welt-sein*), an account, that is, of how we experience the world when, engaged in tasks and activities, we go about our daily lives. The term "lifeworld" was introduced a few years after the publication of *Being and Time* by Edmund Husserl, Heidegger's mentor and the founder of phenomenology. Serious study of the lifeworld was then undertaken by other authors in the phenomenological tradition, Maurice Merleau-Ponty being chief among them.

As the world of lived experience, the lifeworld is as much "subjective" as it is "objective." It is the objective world *as it is brought into focus by a subject's cognition and as it is brought to life by a subject's personal concerns, most basically its desires and fears*. The subject's cognition brings into focus contents and structures of the world, with primitive cognitive abilities bringing into focus pronounced contents and simple structures and more advanced cognitive abilities bringing into focus more subtle contents and more complex structures. With a subject's cognition thus bringing contents and structures of the lifeworld into focus, a subject's personal concerns charge the lifeworld with positive and negative values, its desires populating the world with attractive objects and possibilities and its fears with threatening objects and possibilities. Once the self-system/shadow complex is fully in place, at approximately five years of age, cognition, desires, and fears become closely associated with components of the self-system. Cognition becomes closely associated with the self-representation; and as we have seen, desires and fears become closely associated with the ego ideal and the superego, respectively.

Cognition becomes closely associated with the self-representation because the self-representation, as we know, is the ego's instrument of self-knowledge. As the record on which the ego keeps track of its experiences and its bodily, mental, and social attributes, the self-representation is the cognitive construct by means of which the ego understands what it is as an entity belonging to the world. The self-representation is for this reason the most important cognitive lens through which the ego brings the world into focus. It is the ego's representation of itself as a *self-in-the-world*. Accordingly, the world as it is experienced by the ego, the lifeworld, is to a great extent the world as it is seen through the lens of the ego's self-representation.

Although the ego can assume the posture of a disinterested observer, its default stance is that of an engaged and motivated participant in the world. The ego is a subject that belongs to the world and performs actions in it that are driven most basically by desires and fears. Once the self-system/shadow complex is in place, the ego's desires and fears come under the supervision of the ego ideal and the superego, respectively. The ego ideal manages the ego's desires by prioritizing them according to their compatibility with the ego's highest hopes, and the superego manages the ego's fears by prioritizing them according to their strength. The ego ideal thus imbues the world with a wide range of attractive objects and possibilities, the most attractive of which are imagined life-fulfilling goals; and the superego imbues the world with a wide range of threatening objects and possibilities, the most threatening of which are imagined life-ruining or life-ending perils. In these ways, the ego ideal and the superego animate the lifeworld with positive and negative values.

The shadow, when it stirs, also plays a role in animating the lifeworld. It does so because what the ego rejects in itself it tends to perceive in others in exaggerated form. Impulses and corresponding forbidden thoughts and fantasies that have been repressed and hidden in the shadow thus tend to be seen writ large in others. This well-known phenomenon, called "projection," is responsible for charging the world with negative values of a specifically alien (not-me, other, evil) sort. It is because of shadow projection that we often experience others as being not only more reprehensible or menacing than they truly are but also as representing the antithesis of what we think we are. The negative values projected by the shadow are especially disturbing to the ego because they threaten to make it aware of parts of itself that it has refused to acknowledge.

Given the central role that the self-representation, ego ideal, super-ego, and shadow play in shaping the lifeworld, it follows that stage-specific transformations of these components of the self-system/shadow complex determine corresponding stage-specific transformations of the lifeworld. The self-system/shadow complex and the lifeworld for this reason unfold not only synchronously but also in ways that mirror each other. As we shall see, at each major stage of development changes in the self-system/shadow complex bring about and are reflected in corresponding changes in the lifeworld.

Conclusion

The ego is the root self. It is a subject that experiences what arises within or is presented to consciousness and an agency that performs cognitive and practical functions. Along with the ego, the self-representation, ego ideal, and superego are components of the self-system. The self-representation is the ego's instrument of self-knowledge. It is the record of the ego's experiences and its bodily, mental, and social attributes. Beginning in middle childhood, the ego uses its inner narrator voice to keep track of the self-representation; and beginning in adolescence, it uses this voice not only to keep track of the self-representation but also to author a closely corresponding life story.

The ego ideal and the superego are the ego's primary instruments of self-motivation. The ego ideal is the ego's instrument of aspiring, telic self-motivation, the function of which is to encourage the ego to satisfy its desires, its highest hopes especially. The superego is the ego's instrument of coercing, efficient self-motivation, the function of which is to ensure that the ego avoids what it fears. Both the ego ideal and the superego have voices, which are voices by which the ego advises itself and motivates itself to act. Speaking in the ego-ideal voice, the ego encourages itself to pursue its highest hopes and to pursue other desires as well insofar as they are compatible with its highest hopes. Speaking in the superego voice, the ego commands itself to avoid what it fears, praising itself when it succeeds and blaming itself when it fails.

Underlying the four components of the self-system is the shadow, an unconscious subsystem in which threatening impulses and corresponding cognitive content, having been repressed, lie hidden. The shadow also has a voice, which most often speaks as an adversary or tempter seeking to undermine the self-system but which can speak as a counselor and guide when shadow impulses, in awakening, need to be integrated within the conscious personality. The shadow is not part of the self-system; however, as the negative counterpart of the self-representation, it is inherently tied to the self-system. Together, the four components of the self-system and the shadow make up the self-system/shadow complex.

Finally, paired with the self-system/shadow complex is the lifeworld, which is the world as it is perceived and enlivened by the self-system, as it is perceived through the lens of the self-representation and as it is enlivened with positive and negative values according to the priorities of the ego ideal and the superego (and shadow). As conceived by the revised conception of the ego, the components of the self-system/shadow complex and the life-world are inherently interconnected and for this reason develop in concert with each other, stage by stage over the course of life.

The accounts of the self-representation, ego ideal, superego, shadow, and lifeworld set forth in this chapter are presupposed in what follows. In later chapters, it will frequently be convenient to speak of the ego ideal and the superego as they are ordinarily understood in psychoanalytic literature, the ego ideal as the representation of the ego's ideal self and the superego as the inner agency enforcing standards of right and proper conduct. The reader should know that these ways of describing the ego ideal and the superego are useful shorthand and should keep in mind the wider functions that these two instruments of self-motivation perform in managing the pursuit of desire (positive self-interest) and the avoidance of fears (negative self-interest), respectively.

Part II

Rethinking Ego Development

Chapter 6

The First Four Weeks

Does the newborn have an ego? It was long thought that the answer is "no." Ever since William James, in *Principles of Psychology*, described the newborn's consciousness as a "blooming, buzzing confusion," it was generally thought that the newborn's experience is only a jumble of sensations and impressions, a "chaos" not yet divided into an experiencing ego on one side and a structured field of experienced objects on the other. The psychoanalytic version of this view, formulated by Freud in *Civilization and Its Discontents*, was that the newborn gestates in an "oceanic feeling," a primitive condition in which consciousness is all-inclusive and undifferentiated, without even a distinction between knower and known.

This long-prevailing view was finally shown to be without basis in fact when, beginning in the 1970s, developmental psychologists began using sophisticated technologies, such as video- and audio-recording equipment, and to devise ingenious experiments, such as those testing for preference for novelty and violation of expectation, to study infants in entirely new ways. The results, relative to the time, were stunning. It soon became evident that infants, even newborns, are much more keenly observant of a world of differentiated objects and much more attuned to others than hitherto had been assumed. Very soon, views like those of James and Freud were exposed as versions of a philosophical myth; and the cognitive and interpersonal intelligence of infants, even newborns, began being extolled.

Heir to the research revolution of the 1970s, we now know that the newborn has a wide range of cognitive and other abilities. It discriminates between visual stimuli of a variety of sorts. It shows preference for the human face. It focuses on salient stimuli and tracks objects as they move. It processes sensory data and records them to memory, thus learning from experience. It matches data across sense modalities (especially sight and touch). It responds to tactile stimuli and, under certain circumstances, responds to images of its body in ways that indicate that it discriminates between its body and other objects, thus exhibiting self-awareness of an initial sort. Additionally, the newborn responds to the caregiver in ways that seem to be on the threshold of interpersonal exchange. In addition to rooting for the caregiver's breast, the newborn orients toward the caregiver's smell, voice, and face. Furthermore, although this finding has been challenged, it seems to imitate the caregiver's facial gestures (e.g., tongue protrusion, mouth opening) and hand and finger movements.[1] Clearly, the newborn's abilities are rudimentary and only minimally developed. Nevertheless, they are extraordinary relative to what was thought possible before the 1970s.

Does the Newborn Have an Ego?

Do these abilities imply that the newborn has an ego? Assuming the conception of the ego introduced in chapter 3, I believe the answer that best fits the evidence currently available is that the newborn does have an ego but that the newborn's ego is only weakly constituted and may not yet be active as an executive agency. Several steps will be needed to explain why this answer best fits current evidence. To begin, let us recall two basic facts about the ego explained in chapter 3. The first is that the ego is a unity of apperception, which is to say, an experiencing subject that unifies its experiences and relates to them in a proprietary way. As a unity of apperception, the ego is an experiencing subject that (1) holds succeeding experiences together under its temporally unified point of view (a *unity* of apperception) and (2) relates to the experiences it thus unifies in an implicitly self-conscious and possessive way, as its own experiences, as experiences that belong to it as parts of what it is (a unity *of apperception*).

The second basic fact about the ego explained in chapter 3 is that it is the executive agency of consciousness, specifically an agency that performs cognitive and practical functions. These functions, as the ego's executive functions, are not reflex responses to stimuli. Rather, they are actions that involve at least some intentionality and self-initiated effort on the part of the ego so that, typically, it can satisfy curiosity or achieve some aim. Combining the two facts about the ego just summarized, we can say that being a unity of apperception is what the ego most basically is and that performing cognitive and practical functions is what the ego most basically does.

It is evident from this summary that the question about whether the newborn has an ego needs to be divided into two questions: (1) Is the newborn a unity of apperception? and (2) Does the newborn perform cognitive and practical functions? The first of these questions, which we deal with first, must itself be divided into two questions: (1) Is the newborn conscious not only neurologically, as an information processor that responds to its environment in intelligent ways, but also experientially, as a subject that has phenomenal experiences of its environment? and (2) If the newborn is conscious not only neurologically but also experientially, does its experiential consciousness have the specific form of a unity of apperception, of an experiencing subject that unifies its experiences and relates to them in a proprietary way? Let us begin with the first of these latter two questions.

It might seem obvious that the newborn is experientially aware of its environment. This possibility is suggested by the remarkable cognitive and other abilities of the newborn, mentioned a moment ago. Even more, this possibility is suggested by our own experience as parents of newborns. When we interact with newborns, it certainly seems that, when they are awake, they are fully, which is to say, experientially, conscious of us, paying alert attention to our expressions, movements, and sounds. From the perspective of parents, it seems stubbornly uncharitable to entertain the possibility that newborns are conscious only in a neurological and not also in an experiential or phenomenological sense. Nevertheless, studies that have demonstrated the newborn's cognitive and other abilities and parental observations of the newborn's alert attention provide only "outside" evidence that newborns are experientially conscious. These studies and observations are based on the newborn's behavior, without any knowledge of what, if anything, the newborn is experiencing on the "inside."

Because the newborn is without language, it cannot report on what, if anything, it is experiencing. Is it not possible, therefore, that the only thing happening within the newborn is neurological processing of information followed by behavior that seems to be informed and motivated by phenomenal experiences but in fact is not? Behavioral studies and parental observations of newborns notwithstanding, is it not possible that the newborn is conscious only in a minimal, neurofunctional, and not yet in the full, neurophenomenological, sense?

Fortunately, neuroscientists are beginning to devise experiments that could provide an answer to the question about whether newborns are experientially conscious. Studies by Sid Kouider and colleagues have found evidence that infants as young as five months have experiences of a visual sort.[2] Kouider found that a known neurological signature of visual experiencing, which was discovered in working with adults, can be found in infants as young as five months, with the difference that the signature as found in five-month-old infants is weaker in expression and slower to appear. This evidence for experiential consciousness as early as five months is not evidence for such consciousness before five months. However, neither is it evidence against such consciousness before five months. Additional signatures of conscious experiencing may soon be discovered, and experimental strategies may soon be devised that will allow neuroscientists to confirm conscious experiencing in infants as young as newborns. One expert, commenting on Kouider's original findings in 2013, commented, "Although this group has studied five months and up, my suspicion would be that if we had different techniques, young infants—from birth on—would show the capacity of registering these sorts of stimuli."[3]

If these promising findings are added to the behavioral evidence cited earlier, the evidence available lends credibility to the view that the newborn is experientially conscious. The evidence is obviously incomplete. The view just stated is by no means established beyond a reasonable doubt. It is possible that the newborn is only a neurologically governed organism and, therefore, is not experientially conscious. Perhaps it takes some time after birth for the "lights to come on." The cosmos had a brief initial dark phase; perhaps human beings do so as well. However, the available evidence is such as to suggest that, if one needed to choose between the alternatives, the "more justified" alternative would be that the newborn is experientially conscious, albeit probably only in an obscure and inconstant way. Accordingly, we shall here adopt the alternative that is better, even though incompletely, supported by evidence and assume that, for the newborn, the lights (sounds, smells, sensations), although perhaps dim and flickering, are already on.

Does our assumption that the newborn is experientially conscious imply that the newborn's consciousness has the specific form of a unity of apperception? The answer is clearly "no," for the newborn's experiential consciousness might consist only of a succession of momentary experiences, each of which arises and disappears without there being a temporally unified subject whose experiences they are. Such momentary experiences might be the experiences of equally momentary subjects, each without relation to those that preceded it. Were this the case, consciousness, although consisting of conscious experiences, would not be a unified consciousness, and, therefore, would not have the form of a unity of apperception. What needs to be added to experiential consciousness to give it the form of a unity of apperception?

What is needed is memory, that which brings the past forward into the present. That newborns, and even fetuses, are capable of rudimentary memory is indicated by the fact that they habituate to repeated stimuli. Habituation is the tendency to respond preferentially to things that have not been experienced before. Clearly, this tendency presupposes at least primitive recognition memory. The newborn must record to memory what it has experienced earlier if it is to be able to distinguish which among things it is experiencing in the present are novel and which are not.

The newborn's memory ability indicates that the newborn's experiential consciousness, rather than consisting only of a succession of momentary experiences, is the consciousness of a temporally unified subject, a subject that has a memory record of past experiences and, therefore, can match present experiences with past experiences and in this way unify its experiences over time. In being temporally unified, this subject is self-identical—although perhaps not permanent—over time.[4] A subject that remembers is a subject that recognizes at least implicitly that it is experiencing again something that it, the very same subject, experienced before. An experiencing subject that remembers thus has a history, which it brings forward with it from the past into the present and in doing so unifies its experiences by holding them together under its temporally unified point of view.

In being such a unified unifier of its experiences, the newborn satisfies one of the two conditions for being a unity of apperception, the condition for being a *unity* of apperception. Let us now consider whether the newborn also satisfies the other condition, that for being a unity *of apperception,* an experiencing subject that is self-aware at least in the minimal sense of relating to the experiences it unifies in a proprietary way, recognizing them as "its" experiences, experiences that belong to it as parts of what it is.

The view that the newborn relates to its experiences in a proprietary way is supported by both empirical evidence and rational considerations. An important empirical finding is that the newborn coordinates multimodal information about itself in ways that allow it to distinguish between itself as a unified physical entity and its environment. Specifically, studies have shown that the newborn discriminates between self-touching and being touched and that it gives preferential attention to images of its body when those images represent what is happening to it tactilely.[5] Additionally, a study has shown that infants as young as five months can sense when the movements of animated characters they are viewing are out of synchrony with their heartbeats.[6] According to developmental theorists, facts such as these indicate that the newborn, owing to its own movements beginning in utero, has constructed a primitive body schema of itself as a unified, active physical entity. This schema is the basis of an implicit proprioceptive self-awareness, an immediate internal awareness by the newborn of itself as a bodily entity.[7] Such bodily self-awareness, such *apperception,* indicates that the newborn has a preverbal proprietary sense, a sense that some things belong to it as a bodily experiencer, whereas other things do not.

The rational considerations supporting the view that the newborn is a proprietary subject are these: (1) the newborn's body is more intimately near than other objects; (2) the newborn's body, unlike other objects, never goes away; and, most importantly, (3) the newborn's body, unlike other objects (so far as the newborn knows), is a sensorium, an object that is sensitive and responds to objects, including most importantly itself. The newborn's body, unlike other objects, is "closer than close," always present, and not only sensitive but also self-sensitive. These facts about the newborn's body indicate that the newborn is an embodied subject with a proprietary sense, an embodied subject with an immediate internal sense of itself.

Given our assumption that the newborn is experientially conscious, we are thus led to the conclusion that the newborn satisfies both conditions for being a unity of apperception. We have looked at evidence that indicates that the newborn is both a unified unifier and an appropriating owner of its experiences. However, if the newborn is for these reasons a unity of apperception, it is so only in a weakly constituted way. The need for this qualification is evident from the fact that the newborn tends to be strongly focused only when salient stimuli are present. The newborn sleeps a great deal and, when awake, tends to be unfocused and disengaged unless stimuli stand out in ways that attract its attention. From the perspective of our conception of the ego, this tendency of the newborn to be either asleep or unfocused and disengaged in the absence of salient stimuli indicates that the unifying-appropriating function, of which the ego is the organized form, is not robustly active at birth. From our perspective, the strength of the unifying-appropriating function fluctuates a great deal at birth, being weak for the most part but becoming more strongly active intermittently, in response to salient stimuli.

Having concluded that the newborn is a unity of apperception, we have half of the answer to our question about whether the newborn has an ego. So far, we can say that the newborn *does* have an ego at least in the sense of being what an ego is, a unity of apperception. Now we need to consider whether the newborn also has an ego in the sense of doing what an ego does, perform cognitive and practical functions.

The jury is out on the question of whether the newborn performs cognitive and practical functions. However, the preponderance of evidence, which we review in the next chapter, suggests that the ego's executive functions do not come online until shortly after the neonatal period. During the neonatal period, most if not all cognition and action are reflexive and automatic rather than intentional and self-initiated. If we are to go only so far as available evidence indicates, therefore, the safest position is this: executive functions of both cognitive and practical sorts, if active at all during the neonatal period, are so only in precursory ways.

Except for immediate conscious experiencing of objects and sensations, cognition during the neonatal period seems to be only unexperienced neurological processing of information received through the sensory systems. The processing of sensory data during the neonatal stage—as in all stages—is performed by perceptual and neurological systems working beneath the level of experiential consciousness and without the newborn's active participation. The same is true of the recording of sensory data to memory. It might be thought—and it might be true—that the newborn exercises some slight control at least over the direction and duration of its visual attention. Such control of attention is the first and most basic cognitive executive function to emerge. However, evidence reviewed in the next chapter indicates that voluntary control of visual attention does not begin to come online until after the neonatal stage, sometime between three or four and six months of age. Therefore, for present purposes, it is safest to say that the newborn's attention is primarily if not exclusively governed by salient stimuli to which the newborn is drawn rather than by the newborn itself acting in an intentional, self-initiated way. So far as we know, the newborn's cognition is not the cognition of an ego actively performing cognitive functions.

However, this conclusion is restricted to cognitive functions, leaving open the possibility that the newborn actively performs some practical functions, that it intentionally initiates some rudimentary actions in response to stimuli. Indeed, it seems as though the newborn does just this. The best candidates for such actions, such neonatal practical functions, are the newborn's responses to the caregiver, which are of two principal types, those by which the newborn orients itself toward the caregiver and those that seem to imitate the caregiver. Among the newborn's orienting behaviors are those by which the newborn turns toward the caregiver's breast, those by which it preferentially responds to the caregiver's smell and sound, those by which it fixes its attention on the caregiver's face, and those by which it seeks direct rather than averted contact with the caregiver's eyes.[8] These orienting responses resemble intentional actions in being selective in focus and supportive of the newborn's survival. Moreover, they are responses that soon evolve into intentional actions. This fact notwithstanding, these orienting behaviors are generally thought to be reflexive rather than self-initiated in character during the neonatal period.[9]

Better candidates for practical executive functions during the neonatal period are responses that seem to indicate imitation of the caregiver. The hypothesis that the newborn does genuinely imitate the caregiver and is in this way actively engaged in an intersubjective exchange has been supported by quite a few experimental studies. However, some critics have argued that the newborn's seeming imitations of the caregiver can be explained in a simpler way, as expressions of heightened arousal. Other critics have redesigned experiments used to test for imitation, presenting newborns with a wider range of behaviors to imitate, without finding evidence for imitation.[10]

It is indisputable that the newborn is preferentially aware of and self-interestedly responsive to the caregiver, as should be expected from an evolutionary point of view. This point made, it is not, as we have seen, clear that the newborn's preferential awareness of the caregiver is accomplished by active cognitive functions. Furthermore, as is more to the point here, it is not clear that the newborn's self-interested responses to the caregiver are to any extent accomplished by active practical functions. These responses might be only reflexive actions or, perhaps, only outer expression of internal bodily states produced in interaction with the caregiver. It certainly seems that the newborn's and caregiver's joined gazes, the newborn's incipient smiles, and the newborn's responses to the caregiver's expressions, movements, and sounds are indications of a truly interactive exchange. However, disagreements among experts in the field require us to withhold judgment. What we can say is that two-sided intentional exchanges between infant and caregiver, if not present during the neonatal stage, emerge very soon thereafter. As we shall see in the next chapter, such exchanges begin sometime in the third month.

We can now state the other half of the answer to our question about whether the newborn has an ego. Whereas the first half of the answer was on balance positive, the second half is on balance negative. Whereas we concluded earlier that the newborn, if experientially aware, is a unity of apperception, we conclude here that the newborn, if active as a cognitive and practical agency, is so only in precursory ways. Both halves of this answer can, I believe, be stated with justification if not with complete confidence. The first half is supported by behavioral evidence and might soon be confirmed by stricter scientific evidence as neuroscientists continue to investigate neurological signatures of experiential consciousness in young infants. The second half of the answer, as we shall see in the next chapter, is supported by both behavioral evidence and neuroscientific findings. Neither half of our answer is supported conclusively; nevertheless, both halves, I believe, are supported by a preponderance of currently available evidence.

Ego and Self-System

Because its consciousness is organized as a unity of apperception, the newborn has a self-system. This self-system, however, is only a minimal self-system, a self-system consisting of the ego alone. The ego is the root self of the self-system and, therefore, is the most basic component of the self-system. The ego for this reason precedes the other three components of the self-system. The ego at birth *does* appropriate for itself an exterior or Me side, of which it is apperceptively aware. We have seen that the newborn is aware of itself as a unified, active physical entity. However, this self-awareness does not yet qualify as a self-representation because the newborn, although aware of its body and body-based experiences from an internal point of view, is not, as is required for a self-representation, aware of its similarities and differences from others from an external point of view. As explained in chapter 9, a self-representation presupposes self-recognition, the ability to see oneself as others do; and self-recognition does not emerge until the second half of the second year. However, although the newborn's self-awareness is not yet a self-representation, it is the first, most basic foundation for what later will be the self-representation. The newborn's self-awareness is the most basic layer of implicit self-knowledge.

As for the other components of the self-system, the ego ideal and the superego, they (along with the shadow) presuppose a self-representation and, therefore, emerge only after the self-representation has emerged. They are not fully in place until the beginning of middle childhood. At birth, it is only the ego that is on scene, and even it, most likely, is on scene only as a unity of apperception and not yet as the executive agency of consciousness.

The Lifeworld—A Child-Centered Microcosm

Those who, before the 1970s, subscribed to the view that the newborn is unable to differentiate between itself and the world also subscribed to the view that the newborn's world is not a world in the proper sense of the term. The newborn's world, they thought, consists only of a jumble of sensations and impressions. Thus conceived, the newborn's world was compared to the precosmic chaos of Greek mythology, the unbounded, undifferentiated source out of which the cosmos, the bounded, structured world of cognizable objects, emerges. We now know that this view of the newborn's world, like the corresponding view of the newborn's inability to distinguish between itself and the world, is wrong.

We now know that the newborn's world—or, in our terms, *lifeworld*—is like ours in being bounded and structured, in being a cosmos rather than a chaos. However, the newborn's lifeworld is much less bounded and structured than ours. Developmentally, the newborn's lifeworld could not be farther removed from the lifeworld we live in as adults, and for this reason it is necessary to proceed with caution in describing it. Fortunately, we have learned basic facts about the newborn that allow us to infer in broad outline a few features of its lifeworld. I shall focus on the following three such facts: (1) the newborn's consciousness is limited to what is perceived in the present moment, (2) the newborn's eyesight is poor, and (3) the caregiver is the principal reality of the newborn's lifeworld.

There are two reasons that explain why the newborn's consciousness is limited to what is perceived in the present moment. The reason ordinarily given is that the newborn probably has no or at most only a negligible expectation that objects continue to exist after they cease being perceived, what is called "object permanence." We have already seen that the newborn, with the help of memory, recognizes objects that it has experienced before. Such recognition, however, does not mean that the newborn assumes that objects it has experienced before have continued uninterruptedly in existence since the last time it experienced them. Some developmental psychologists studying newborns have for this reason distinguished between object identity and object permanence, clarifying that newborns, in recognizing objects they have experienced before, may, in effect, recognize them only as self-identical objects, objects that are the same as objects they have experienced before, rather than as permanent objects, objects that have remained continuously in existence since the last time they were experienced.[11]

Accordingly, memory of objects experienced before does not imply an expectation of object permanence. Evidence suggests that expectation of object permanence emerges only gradually over the first year. Jean Piaget, the first to investigate the issue of object permanence, set the emergence of understanding of object permanence at approximately eight months because that is the age at which children begin to search for hidden objects. This view was challenged in the 1980s and 1990s, when investigators devised clever experiments that demonstrated that infants as young as 3½ months give preferential attention to events that seem to violate object permanence. Such attention indicates that the infants had expected object permanence and, therefore, were drawn to the novelty of a seeming violation of their expectation. With these findings, the conclusion was drawn that children have at least a slight expectation of object permanence at a much earlier age than Piaget believed, long before they are able physically to search for hidden objects.[12]

What do these findings imply about the newborn? Nothing conclusive. Lack of evidence for an expectation of object permanence before 3½ months is not evidence against at least a slight expectation before this time. It is possible, therefore, that the newborn has some slight expectation of object permanence. However, there are two reasons that explain why this possibility should not be considered evidence that the newborn's consciousness extends beyond what is perceived in the present moment.

The first of these reasons is that the newborn, as already noted, does not have voluntary control of its visual attention. The newborn's attention, it seems, is automatically drawn to the most salient stimulus in its field of view and for this reason is tied to what is going on in the present moment. If the newborn has an expectation of object permanence, it might experience a flicker of cognitive discomfort if a seeming violation of that expectation were to occur. However, after the moment of discomfort, the newborn would immediately be drawn to a new object, which would take hold of its attention. The newborn's consciousness, therefore, does not extend beyond what is perceived in the present moment because it is constantly commandeered by stimuli of the present moment. For the newborn, "in sight is in mind."

The second reason the newborn's consciousness is limited to the present moment is that the newborn lacks not only voluntary control of attention but also working memory, the ability to keep something in mind when it is no longer present to the senses. Evidence to be discussed in the next chapter indicates that working memory does not come online until the prefrontal cortex is sufficiently developed to support it, at approximately six months or shortly thereafter. Although the newborn retains past experiences unconsciously in recorded memory, it cannot retain them consciously in working memory. Working memory is like voluntary control of attention in being a basic cognitive executive function; and evidence indicates that both these functions come online only after the neonatal stage. Accordingly, the newborn is unable to extend its consciousness beyond what is perceived in the present moment not only because, without voluntary control of visual attention, what is in sight is in mind but also because, without working memory, what is out of sight is out of mind.

For the reasons just set forth, we conclude that the newborn's world extends only to the limits of vision and consists only of objects located within these limits. Objects outside the limits of vision are unknown to the newborn, either because the newborn has never seen them before or because, although the newborn has seen them before, they are now out of sight and, therefore, out of mind, having been replaced by something else that, having come into sight, is now in mind. So far as the newborn knows, the small space lying within its field of vision and the objects currently occupying this space are all that exists.

Some early theorists of child development used the image of an all-containing egg to depict this world of the newborn. Another image that has been used is that of a bubble. These images are seriously misleading because they suggest that the newborn is autistically self-encapsulated, cut off from the larger world. However, despite being misleading in this way, these images are helpful in at least the following way: they aptly depict the microcosmic all-inclusiveness of the newborn's lifeworld. They aptly convey the idea that, so far as the newborn knows, the world extends only as far as the eye can see.

It is important to rid the egg and bubble images of the suggestion that the newborn is cut off from the larger world. Prominent psychoanalysts, including both Freud and Margaret Mahler, were misled by this suggestion. For example, Freud, in a passage cited by Mahler, described the newborn as being self-encapsulated, as if in a bird's egg in which everything needed is available except the warmth provided by the mother.[13] Mahler accepted Freud's comparison and described the first few weeks of life as a "normal autistic phase," a phase during which the child is enclosed in an autistic shell and shows little response to the external world.[14] Mahler later retracted the idea of a normal autistic phase to accommodate emerging findings in the field of neonatal cognition.[15] Nevertheless, her view was representative of psychoanalytic thinking at the time. Moreover, it was hugely influential, both within and beyond the psychoanalytic community.

The misleading feature of the egg and bubble images is the material boundary—the shell of the egg, the membrane of the bubble—that not only spatially distinguishes what is inside the egg or bubble from what is outside but that also seals what is inside the egg or bubble from what is outside. The reason this feature of the images is misleading is that the newborn's egg or bubble world has only a visual-epistemic boundary, not a boundary that could function as a seal. The fact that the newborn does not understand that the world extends beyond its field of vision in no way places a barrier between the newborn and the larger world. Objects and people outside the newborn's lifeworld encounter no resistance in entering it. The newborn, therefore, is not cut off from the world beyond its egg or bubble. Indeed, having not yet developed psychological defenses, it is unguardedly open to the larger world.

Another fact that helps explain distinctive features of the newborn's lifeworld is that the newborn's vision is poor, falling far short of normal standards.[16] The newborn has difficulty bringing objects into focus, which means that its visual acuity is poor and, therefore, that objects have blurry features and boundaries. The newborn's depth perception is also poor. At birth, the eyes are not well coordinated with each other and, therefore, stereoscopic vision is minimal. The newborn can discern the distinctive features of objects, especially when they are in optimal viewing range (8 to 12 inches) and are boldly accented or outlined; and it is probably aware of some differences in distance and depth between objects that are close to it and to each other. In general, though, the newborn's visual acuity and depth perception are poor.

Poor vision is responsible for one other feature of the newborn's lifeworld: a limited color spectrum. Color perception, like visual acuity and depth perception, is far below normal standards at birth. The newborn has difficulty discriminating between colors that do not sharply contrast with each other. Although the newborn's world is not completely lacking in color, it is nonetheless a world in which differences of light and dark are more evident than differences of hue. Color perception develops quickly in the first few months; however, it is markedly undeveloped at birth. Overall, the newborn's lifeworld is visually impoverished. Poor vision causes the newborn to see a world that, in addition to extending only as far as the eye can see, has blurry objects, unclear gradations of depth, and only a basic color palette.

There is one object that appears within the newborn's lifeworld that is of special importance to the newborn: the caregiver. The newborn is keenly aware of the caregiver as an object that it experiences repeatedly within its small world, an object that, recognized because past experiences of the caregiver match present ones, possesses object identity if not object permanence in the newborn's eyes. The newborn is powerfully attracted to the caregiver. As already explained, it orients itself toward the caregiver by rooting instinctively for the caregiver's breast, by turning toward the caregiver's smell and voice, by attending preferentially to the caregiver's face, and by favoring direct rather than averted contact with the caregiver's eyes. Although its vision is poor, the newborn can focus on objects close to it; and it is especially drawn to the caregiver, who is the principal reality of its world.

The relationship between the newborn and the caregiver is intimate and complex. The newborn is drawn to the caregiver through all its senses; and the caregiver plies the newborn with pleasurable sensations and with expressions, movements, and sounds that seek to elicit responses from the newborn. The newborn responds to these attentions with an engaged gaze and, some believe, imitative expressions and movements. Whatever the status of these seemingly imitative behaviors, there can be no doubt that the newborn is exquisitely attuned to the caregiver. It is the caregiver who triggers the newborn's orienting responses, who captivates the newborn's attention, and who is most often at the center of the newborn's experience. Although we do not know whether the caregiver is a person with whom the newborn genuinely interacts, we do know that the caregiver is the primary reality of the newborn's lifeworld.

In sum, the newborn is an experiencing subject situated at the center of a small world, a microcosm that, so far as the newborn knows, contains all that exists. This microcosm is populated by one object that is always present, the newborn's own body, and by many other objects that appear, disappear, and sometimes reappear. The objects of the newborn's world are blurry and lacking in clear increments of depth and fine gradations of hue. Some of these objects, however, are sufficiently accentuated or outlined to attract the newborn and to take command of its attention. The most important of these objects, the principal reality of the newborn's lifeworld, is the caregiver, a being who attracts the newborn's attention through all its senses and who tries to communicate with the newborn with expressions, movements, and sounds. Although some newborns are unhealthy or neglected, most are healthy and cared for at least well enough. These fortunate newborns are favored in ways that we but not they can understand. From our perspective, these newborns are like little gods in worlds of their own, baby deities around whom all existence revolves and to whom a powerful and attractive being caters.

Conclusion

We have argued that the balance of evidence justifies the conclusion that the newborn has an ego, albeit only a minimal one, an ego that, although experientially aware and organized as a unity of apperception, probably does not yet perform cognitive or practical functions. We have also argued that the newborn, as such a minimal ego, has a self-system, albeit only a minimal one, a self-system consisting of the ego alone. Finally, we have argued that the newborn, so far as it knows, lives at the center of an all-inclusive microcosm the principal reality of which attends to its needs.

Chapter 7

Infancy

Something profound happens after approximately two months: the infant's relationship with the caregiver flowers into a reciprocity of mutual recognition. Whereas the newborn's smiling and seeming imitations of the caregiver may be expressions of endogenous or nonsocial exogenous triggers, it is otherwise with the infant's responses to the caregiver in the weeks leading to and following the end of second month. At approximately this time, the infant's smiles, vocalizations, and other behaviors unmistakably exhibit interactive exchanges with the caregiver. A large body of experimental literature documents this transition. Important findings reported are the emergence at this time of verifiable social smiling, rapt attention fixed on the caregiver, expressions of excitation, cooing, and distressed attempts to reengage the caregiver when the caregiver ceases interacting with the infant and assumes a still, neutral face.[1]

The infant's emerging sociality quickly evolves into exchanges between the infant and the caregiver during which each imitates the other's behavior. The caregiver imitates in exaggerated form one of the infant's expressions, movements, or sounds, and the infant responds with rapt attention, smiles, gurgling or cooing sounds, and, later, laughter. The caregiver again imitates the expression, movement, or sound, and the infant responds by repeating the expression, movement, or sound, prompting the caregiver to imitate it again, and so forth. To the observer it is evident that the infant no longer merely observes the caregiver as a fascinating object to gaze upon and has awakened to the caregiver as a being "like me," a being who, in addition to being experienced by the infant, experiences the infant in turn, responding to its expressions, movements, and sounds.[2] This mutual recognition of two "experiencers," each experiencing and responding to the other, is an unmistakable early form of intersubjectivity.

In awakening to the caregiver, the infant begins to focus on the caregiver more intensely and for increasing lengths of time. The caregiver, already the principal reality of the newborn's world, now becomes the eclipsing center of the infant's world. The infant is captivated by the caregiver and continues to be captivated by the caregiver until such time as the infant, by means of crawling, is able significantly to expand the range of its activities and interests. Accordingly, the infant's awakening to the caregiver as a being who experiences and responds to the infant marks the beginning of a stage that extends from approximately 2 months to 8 or 9 months (with crawling typically beginning between 7 and 10 months).

Strengthening of Ego and Activation of Executive Functions

The infant's awakening to the caregiver leads to a strengthening of the ego as a unity of apperception, as a unifying, proprietary experiencer. It does so because the caregiver now becomes a powerful, long-lasting stimulus, a stimulus that, according to our account, engages the unifying-appropriating function for longer stretches of time, thus strengthening this function and keeping the infant's attention riveted for longer stretches of time. Whereas the newborn tends to be focused only for brief interludes, as salient stimuli appear and disappear, the infant, in communicative interaction with the caregiver, can remain focused for extended periods. The infant still frequently lapses into weakly organized ego states. However, when awake and alert, and especially when focused on the caregiver, it spends much less time in these states than it did earlier, as a newborn.

The infant's awakening to the caregiver not only strengthens the ego as a unity of apperception but also activates it as an executive agency. This activation of executive functions is most evident in the infant's interactions with the caregiver. Although the newborn's seeming imitations of the caregiver might be only expressions of heightened arousal, the infant's responses to the caregiver beginning in the third month very soon evolve into voluntarily initiated actions. The caregiver provides a "scaffolding" for the infant-caregiver relationship by plying the infant with undivided attention, a happy face, baby talk, and imitations of the infant's behaviors intended to elicit repetitions of those behaviors from the infant.[3] In providing this scaffolding, the caregiver is at first primarily the active party in the infant-caregiver relationship, with the infant being primarily reactive. However, it does not take long before the infant-caregiver relationship evolves into a true interaction, with the infant not only reacting to the caregiver but also initiating actions that elicit reactions from the caregiver. The caregiver's imitations of the infant increasingly elicit from the infant not only responsive smiles and gurgling or cooing sounds but also actively initiated repetitions of the behaviors that the caregiver had imitated, repetitions that elicit further rounds of imitation from the caregiver. The caregiver's agency, focused on the infant and providing the infant with a scaffolding for its responses, in this way triggers the infant's agency. The infant's ego thus becomes an executive agency performing the most basic practical function, intentional, self-initiated action performed to produce an effect in the world.

As this most basic practical function emerges, so also do basic cognitive functions. The first and most basic of these functions is the voluntary control of visual attention. Precursors of such control—the ability easily to shift attention from one stimulus to another, the ability to maintain attention on a stimulus despite distracting stimuli, the ability to inhibit eye movement toward distracting stimuli, and the ability to anticipate where stimuli are moving or will reappear—emerge between 3 or 4 months and 6 months. These precursors then together evolve into voluntary control of attention proper from approximately 6 months to between 12 and 15 months.[4] Appearing along with or soon after voluntary control of visual attention are working memory, the ability to keep objects consciously in mind when they are no longer present to the senses, and cognitive inhibition, the ability to block previously established action tendencies and other influences that might interfere with a new cognitive task. Studies on the emergence of working memory and cognitive inhibition are cited later in the chapter.

With all these functions coming online, infancy is a stage during which the ego ceases being primarily if not exclusively an experiencing subject and becomes also and increasingly an agency performing cognitive and practical functions. Not long after the infant awakens to the caregiver, therefore, it clearly has a complete rather than only a minimal ego, which is to say, an ego that not only is what an ego is (a unity of apperception) but that also does what an ego does (perform cognitive and practical functions).

The Self-System

The infant's awakening to the caregiver does not change the self-system in the sense of adding new components to it. The self-system remains a minimal, ego-only self-system. However, a second step is taken in preparing the ground for the self-representation. This step is the emergence of a new kind of self-awareness, a self-awareness that is now added to the newborn's immediate internal self-awareness. To recall, the newborn, as a unity of apperception, has an immediate internal awareness of itself as an experience-near, always-present, self-experiencing body. This self-awareness is entirely subjective. The newborn experiences itself exclusively from the inside. It has no access to information about what it looks or sounds like from an external point of view. However, upon awakening to the caregiver, the infant gains access to just such information. It begins to see and hear itself reflected in the caregiver's imitative responses, which reproduce the infant's expressions, movements, and sounds in magnified form. The infant, in seeing the caregiver as a being "like me," thus sees the caregiver outwardly acting in ways that match the internal sensations it experiences when it acts in those ways, thus bringing those ways of acting into increasingly better focus for the infant. The caregiver's mirroring responses thus provide the infant with a completely new perspective on itself.[5]

In becoming aware of itself in this new way, the infant moves toward but does not yet achieve self-recognition proper. Although the infant focuses intently on its expressions, movements, and sounds as they are imitated by the caregiver, it does not yet think, let alone say, to itself, "Oh, that is what I look (or sound) like from the outside." Although the infant, with the help of the caregiver, has gained a new perspective on itself, it has not yet become aware *that* it is aware of itself. The infant's caregiver-mediated self-awareness, therefore, is not yet self-recognition. Again, on most accounts self-recognition proper begins to emerge only midway through the second year, when children start to notice that their reflections in mirrors are indeed reflections of themselves.

This point made, the more important point for present purposes is that the infant now has a new—external (caregiver-reflected)—source of information about itself. Processing the information that it derives from this new source, the infant begins prereflectively to match what it is now learning about itself from the outside with what it has already learned about itself from the inside. Accordingly, it now begins to match its externally reflected expressions, movements, and sounds with its internally experienced sensations and feelings, thus not only acquiring new information about itself but also bringing a new perspective to information previously acquired. Clearly, as this happens, the infant's self-awareness grows at a rapid pace.

This last point needs elaboration, for the infant's self-awareness grows at a rapid pace not only for the reasons already explained but also because the caregiver, as a reflecting mirror, is more specifically a "teaching" mirror. The scaffolding of undivided attention, a happy face, baby talk, and imitative behaviors that the caregiver brings to the infant-caregiver relationship makes the caregiver an intelligent mirror that is perfectly designed to teach the infant about itself. The caregiver responds selectively to the infant's expressions, movements, and sounds and imitates them in an exaggerated way, with reinforcing smiles and baby talk that the infant cannot help but notice. The caregiver is sensitive to the infant's growth in self-awareness and fosters such growth by responding to the infant in ways that best facilitate its self-discovery. The caregiver thus "shines the light of self-knowledge" on the infant, serving as both a guide and goad to the infant's growth in self-awareness. As noted in chapter 4, much of our self-knowledge is dependent on the mirroring feedback of others. This is especially true during infancy. The infant is highly dependent on the mirroring feedback of others, and the caregiver is ready and ideally suited to meet this need.

The infant's self-awareness is transformed in one other way in the months that follow awakening to the caregiver. The infant begins to be aware that things—including, presumably, itself—are like or unlike other things by virtue of belonging or not belonging to the same general categories. Studies based on the idea that habituation to a stimulus produces preference for novelty have established that rudimentary awareness of categories emerges between three or four months, when children demonstrate the ability to recognize many basic categories, such as "square," "triangle" "cat," "dog," "red," and "green," and a few superordinate categories, such as "animal" and "furniture."[6]

It may be that at this young age awareness of categories emerges from perceptual processes that sort things only according to their physical features. However, if this is true it is not long before infants begin grouping things in categories based on shared features of a nonperceptual, more abstract character. The work of Jean Mandler and colleagues has shown that such categorization begins as early as seven months if not before and is unmistakably in play between nine and fourteen months, when children begin performing category-appropriate actions even on highly dissimilar examples of categories, examples that would not have been grouped together on the basis of perception alone.[7] Although nine to fourteen months lies beyond the boundaries of the stage treated in this chapter, the point remains that categorical groupings of objects, including groupings not based on shared perceptual features, emerge during infancy.[8]

This early understanding of categories strongly suggests that the infant, perhaps beginning near the middle of the first year, is aware not only that objects generally resemble or differ from each other in kind but also that it, as a particular object, resembles or differs from other objects in kind. It suggests that the infant begins to be aware of itself not only as a bodily entity possessing particular features (parts, abilities, expressions, movements, sounds) but also as a bodily entity possessing general kinds of features, kinds by virtue of which it is like some things and unlike others.

It is unclear just which of its features the infant at this point becomes aware of as belonging to general categories. The fact that the infant is aware of the caregiver as a being "like me" suggests that it understands that it is close in kind to the caregiver. Because the infant has immediate bodily awareness of its own agency, it might also understand that it is close in kind to a cat or a dog, although less close to a cat or a dog than to the caregiver. For the same reason, the infant might understand that it is fundamentally different in kind from objects that do not display self-motion, for example, cups and pieces of furniture.

Whatever categorical information the infant might now gather about itself is added to the information that the infant gathers about itself from internal bodily self-awareness and caregiver-assisted reflected self-awareness. The infant's self-awareness thus now derives from three sources: the body, the caregiver, and emerging understanding of categories. Information from all these sources is now gathered, integrated, and recorded to memory as an archive of data that later, once self-recognition emerges, is transformed into the self-representation.

The Lifeworld—A Space of Child-Caregiver Intersubjectivity

The infant's awakening to the caregiver transforms not only the infant's self-awareness but also its lifeworld. The reciprocity of mutual recognition established between infant and caregiver opens a new dimension of the world for the infant: intersubjectivity. The world beyond the infant now consists not only of a physical space that the infant shares with other material objects but also an intersubjective space that the infant shares with another experiencer, another being "like me," another self.

Specifically, the intersubjective space that the infant enters is the space of primary or direct intersubjectivity, the intersubjectivity of the infant and caregiver sharing in the experience of each other. Primary intersubjectivity is to be distinguished from secondary or indirect intersubjectivity, which is the intersubjectivity of the infant and caregiver sharing in the experience of an object or game.[9] Whereas primary intersubjectivity is a relationship in which the infant's social agency is elicited and strengthened in interactions with the caregiver, secondary intersubjectivity is a relationship in which the infant, now an agent, is aware of the caregiver as a coagent in an interaction with an object or in a game. It is only primary intersubjectivity that emerges when the infant first awakens to the caregiver as another self. Evidence suggests that secondary intersubjectivity, although ordinarily emerging around nine or ten months, may begin to emerge as early as five months.[10] However, secondary intersubjectivity does not become a primary way in which the child interacts with the caregiver until after crawling and toddling begin.

In its newly revealed intersubjective dimension, the infant's lifeworld is essentially dyadic. It is a world of two-person, infant-caregiver inter-subjectivity. In time the infant interacts—smiles, vocalizes, and otherwise engages interactively—with other people who attend to it. Nevertheless, it is the caregiver who is the infant's primary partner in intersubjectivity. It is the caregiver with whom the infant spends the most time and with whom, therefore, the infant establishes an ongoing intersubjective connection rather than only fleeting intersubjective contact. The infant establishes its first genuine *relationship* with the caregiver. Moreover, this relationship is the center of the infant's world. Although the infant continues to observe objects and increasingly interacts with them, its interest in them diminishes relative to the sharp increase in its interest in the caregiver. The caregiver is a bright sun that outshines everything else.

The infant's lifeworld, transformed by emerging intersubjectivity, is transformed as well by rapidly improving vision. Improved vision changes the lifeworld by bringing objects into sharper focus, by throwing gradations of depth into relief, and by enlivening the world with a wide and richly variegated spectrum of colors. These changes occur rapidly along with the development of the eyes, eye muscles, and brain. According to most accounts, the child's eyesight, although by no means fully developed, is well along the way to normalcy by the end of the first year. By the end of the first year—and even by eight or nine months, the end of the stage under consideration here—the child has made a good deal of progress toward seeing the world as we do.[11]

The lifeworld undergoes one other important transformation during the months of infancy: improving understanding of object permanence extends the world beyond the limit of vision. At 7½ months children, after a brief delay, begin to search for objects they have seen being hidden from view, thus demonstrating not only an expectation of object permanence but also, now, the emergence of working memory, the ability to keep objects in mind, even if only briefly, after they are no longer present to the senses.[12] However, this emergence of working memory sets the stage for a serious error, first reported by Piaget. If, on repeated trials, a child of 7½ months watches as an object is hidden at location A and is able after a brief delay to retrieve the object at that location, the child is prone thereafter to search for the object at location A, even if it has just watched the object being hidden at a new location, B. If there is more than a two-second delay between the hiding of the object at B and the beginning of the search for the object, the child will search for the object at A, where it has seen and found it before.

The good news is that soon after falling prey to this "A-not-B error," as it is called, the child, between 7½ and 12 months, makes progress toward correcting it. The work of Adele Diamond and associates has shown that the delay time within which children are still able successfully to search for an object at location B goes up steadily after 7½ months until, at 12 months, children can manage a 10-second delay and still search for the object at B. The conclusion they draw from their studies is that the increased delay times before children revert to the A-not-B error indicate strides forward in both working memory (which lengthens the time that location B can be kept in mind) and cognitive inhibition (which blocks memories and action tendencies that would bias the search toward location A). Diamond and associates provide evidence that working memory and cognitive inhibition, two basic executive functions, grow steadily stronger as the prefrontal cortex becomes more active in the second half of the first year.[13]

It is unclear to what extent children transitioning from infancy to toddling understand that a world exists beyond the field of vision. Awareness of unperceived objects quite evidently is emerging. Children at this age, despite being prone to the A-not-B error, do look for hidden objects; and they are able to keep previously perceived objects in mind, even if only for brief periods. However, their understanding of the world beyond the field of vision remains quite limited because working memory and cognitive inhibition, although improving, are still weak, because only a small set of objects, those in the immediate environment, have been experienced, and because basic rule-governed ways in which objects are related (e.g., temporally, causally) and even basic ways in which objects can move (e.g., "invisibly," without being perceived to do so) are not yet understood.[14] Understanding of object permanence and how objects can affect each other and move is achieved only gradually. Suffice it here to say that beginning sometime in the second half of the first year the infant is increasingly aware of hidden, unperceived objects and, therefore, is increasingly aware that the world is not limited to what is seen.

Conclusion

In awakening to the caregiver, the infant ceases being a sleepy newborn in a world of its own and becomes a wide-eyed babe in a world of emerging intersubjectivity. The infant experiences both awe and delight as it awakens to the caregiver and begins to interact with the caregiver in playful exchanges. The infant takes special delight in the caregiver's imitative responses to its expressions, movements, and sounds, since these responses allow the infant to begin experiencing itself in a new way. They allow the infant, which hitherto had experienced itself only from an unfocused, internal point of view, as a congeries of sensations and feelings, to begin experiencing itself from a more focused, external point of view, as a set of expressions, movements, and sounds that match its internal sensations and feelings. The caregiver's responses thus provide the infant with one of two new types of self-awareness that emerge during infancy, the other being the self-awareness that emerges with initial understanding of categories.

The infant's awakening to the caregiver transforms the lifeworld by opening the dimension of intersubjectivity, a communicative space that the infant shares with the caregiver as a being "like me." The infant connects with the caregiver, who captivates the infant's attention, elicits the infant's agency, helps the infant see itself from an external point of view, and, in interacting with the infant in these ways, draws the infant into its first real relationship. As this happens, improving vision and improving understanding of object permanence also transform the lifeworld. Improving vision sharpens the features of objects, clarifies gradations of depth, and imbues the world with a full spectrum of colors. Concomitantly, improving understanding of object permanence has the effect, in effect, of extending the world beyond the field of vision, even if only in vague, poorly understood ways. In the period from approximately two months to eight or nine months, the infant awakens not only to the caregiver but also to a new world, a world with other selves, a profusion of colors, and expanded horizons.

Chapter 8

Early Toddling

Locomotion—crawling and then toddling—marks the beginning of a new stage of development. In enabling the child to pursue objects, locomotion increases the child's interest in them; and this increased interest in objects shifts the child's primary focus of attention from the caregiver to the object world. The caregiver thus ceases being the eclipsing center of the child's world and becomes an anchor and refuge for the child as it now moves away from the caregiver to explore the physical environment. The caregiver remains the child's primary partner in intersubjectivity, but intersubjectivity is now increasingly extended to the object world. The child and the caregiver now share not only in the experience of each other (primary intersubjectivity) but also, as coagents, in the experience of exploring and playing games with objects (secondary intersubjectivity).

As the child broadens its horizons in these ways, both the ego and the lifeworld undergo significant changes. The ego grows stronger as an experiencing subject, a unity of apperception, and becomes more active and capable as an executive agency, as is evident in the child's focused pursuit and avid study of objects. Concomitantly, the lifeworld becomes a realm full of fascinating objects to be discovered. These changes in the ego and the lifeworld occur at approximately eight or nine months—or, less strictly, whenever crawling begins—and are characteristic of the time between the beginning of crawling and the middle of the second year. They correspond to the crawling and early toddling phases of childhood. For convenience, I combine these phases and refer to them as the "early toddling stage" or the "stage of the young toddler," leaving it to the reader to include crawling within this stage.

Basic Executive Functions Strengthened, Growth in
Intuitive Understanding of Categories, and Emergence
of Intuitive Understanding of Basic Logical Relationships

The ego grows stronger as an experiencing subject because the child now gives keen attention to the object world, to which its mobility has given it access. The child's exploration of the object world requires sustained engagement of the unifying-appropriating function. Such engagement strengthens this function; and because the ego on its subject or I side just *is* the organized form of this function, it therefore strengthens the ego as well. The unifying-appropriating function, which had produced strongly organized ego states primarily when the child interacted with the caregiver, now also produces strongly organized ego states when the child pursues and studies objects. The child's heightened interest in objects keeps the child alertly focused and active, with the consequence that strongly organized ego states occur much more frequently than before.

Concurrent with this strengthening of the ego is a corresponding strengthening and further development of the ego's executive functions.[1] As we learned in the last chapter, the primary executive functions of a cognitive sort that come online during infancy are attention control, working memory, and cognitive inhibition. These executive functions are exercised in the young toddler's interactions with objects and, therefore, are strengthened and further developed because of these interactions. The young toddler's exploration of the object world thus helps the child improve control of its attention, increase the time it can retain absent objects in working memory, and block preestablished action tendencies and other influences that would interfere with focused exploration. Additionally, as we shall see presently, this further development of basic cognitive executive functions prepares the ground for other (nonexecutive, intuitive) forms of cognition that emerge during the early toddling stage.

As the young toddler's ego becomes more active and effective in the performance of basic cognitive functions, it becomes more active and effective in the performance of basic practical functions as well. Such advance is most evident in the young toddler's voluntary actions. Whereas the infant's voluntary actions depend on the scaffolding that the caregiver brings to the infant-caregiver interaction, the young toddler's voluntary actions occur without need of such scaffolding. Acting entirely on its own, the young toddler sets its eyes on objects, moves toward them, and then examines them enthusiastically. The young toddler thus increasingly acts on its own volition, pursuing objects and studying them with rapt fascination. The young toddler's voluntary actions are not yet goal-directed in the strict sense of pursuing objects with the expectation that they will be the cause or occasion of a desired outcome; nevertheless, they are goal-directed in the simple sense that they pursue objects as goals.[2] In being goal-directed in this sense, the young toddler's actions are examples of greatly improved self-initiation and control of action.

A new practical function that begins to emerge in the early toddling stage is impulse control, the first form of self-regulation. Numerous studies have demonstrated that 12-month-olds, when presented with a novel object or situation, will heed the caregiver's facial expression or tone of voice in deciding whether to explore the object or situation. This heeding of the caregiver's cues is known as "social referencing."[3] Young toddlers have begun to explore a world in which everything is new, and they frequently look to the caregiver or another adult for guidance. Young toddlers also control their behavior by taking cues from interactions between other people, known as "emotional eavesdropping." For example, children as young as 15 months can control the impulse to imitate an action performed by another person if they observe someone else expressing anger toward that person as she or he performs the action.[4] The young toddler takes this negative exchange between others as a cue to inhibit its own action. The young toddler in these ways takes the first steps toward inhibitory control of its actions.

In addition to these advances in executive functions, there are important advances in nonexecutive abilities that occur during the early toddling stage. These advances are steps forward in intuitive rather than executive cognition. One such advance is that the child continues to make progress in building a framework of categories. The most important example of this progress is that the child improves its understanding of how objects belonging to the same superordinate categories (e.g., animal, furniture) but different basic categories (e.g., dog, cat; table, chair) differ from each other on the basic level.[5] The child might now improve its understanding of how dogs and cats differ from each other as types of animals and how tables and chairs differ from each other as types of furniture. Early category formation is not always bottom-up, starting with basic categories and then building midlevel categories on top of these and then building superordinate categories on top of these. Superordinate and basic categories emerge together, with the former being sorted in highly abstract or global ways, according to how in general objects in these categories move, behave, or are used by human beings, and the latter being sorted primarily in a perceptual way, according to distinguishing physical characteristics. For example, the superordinate category "animal" might emerge in an abstract way as a group of self-moving nonhuman objects with faces; and the superordinate category "furniture" might emerge abstractly as a group of large objects in the house that remain stationary in their places. In contrast, the basic categories "dog" and "cat" might emerge solely from perceived differences in the physical characteristic of these animals; and the basic categories "table" and "chair" might emerge in the same way, solely from perceived physical differences.

Because basic categories are at first sorted primarily according to physical characteristics, more abstract ways of sorting these categories, such as according to their distinctive movements, behaviors, or functions, are initially vague. However, this vagueness begins being eliminated during the early toddling stage, when understanding of basic categories begins being enriched by the acquisition of more abstract knowledge of the objects belonging to these categories. For example, a young toddler who has already learned that dogs and cats are not the same because they look different might now also begin to learn that they are not the same because they act differently. Similarly, a young toddler who has already learned that tables and chairs are not the same because they look different might now also begin to learn that they are not the same because human beings use them differently. This more abstract sorting of basic categories, a lifelong task, has its beginnings during the early toddling stage.

The young toddler, like the infant, understands categories immediately and intuitively, not by any kind of executive analysis of similarities and differences. Its understanding of categories is based either on direct discernment (superordinate categories and all mid- and lower-level categories sorted by abstract characteristics) or on sense perception (basic categories, when first formed). However, although the young toddler's categories are thus the fruit of intuition, they are also the fruit of the ego's previous work as an executive agency performing cognitive functions. It is only by exercising attention control, working memory, and cognitive inhibition in its examination of objects that the young toddler is able intuitively to extract information about the objects, both abstract and concrete-perceptual information. The young toddler's taxonomic intuitions come to it only because it has paid keen attention to objects and has avidly studied their features and tested their powers. Basic executive functions thus play an indispensable adjunct role in the young toddler's growing intuitive understanding of categories.

Another important development in cognition beginning during the early toddling stage is the ability intuitively to grasp basic logical relationships. Studies have shown that children beginning as young as eight months can generalize and make statistical inferences of inductive sorts.[6] They can generalize that what has been learned about one instance of a category applies to other instances of that category and can infer statistically that, for example, the ratio of red and white ping-pong balls in a set of balls taken from a larger set should be the same as the ratio in the larger set. A recent study has shown that 10- to 13-month-old children can even make basic deductive inferences, specifically inferences of a transitive sort dealing with dominance relations. For example, they can infer that if a hippo puppet is dominant over a bear puppet and the bear puppet is dominant over an elephant puppet then the hippo puppet will be dominant over the elephant puppet.[7] This understanding of logical relationships, like the young toddler's understanding of categories, is the fruit of immediate intuition, not—as is true of executive cognition of a logical sort—the result of explicit, actively carried out inductive, statistical, or deductive inferences. Still, this initial understanding of logical relationships is a developmental advance of great importance. In addition to being an intuitive taxonomist, the young toddler is an intuitive logician, as, indeed, it has been called an "intuitive statistician" with specific respect to its ability to make statistical inferences.[8]

The young toddler's logical inferences, although intuitions rather than executive actions, are, like its growing understanding of categories, made possible only because the young toddler has been hard at work performing basic cognitive executive functions. The young toddler's logical inferences are possible only because the young toddler has exercised attention control, working memory, and cognitive inhibition in studying the objects that are the focus of its inferences. It is only by exercising these executive functions that the young toddler gathers the information about objects that it then intuitively extends to other objects of the same type or that it then intuitively uses in making statistical or deductive inferences. As with the young toddler's understanding of categories, the inspiration of intuition is possible only because of the "perspiration" of previous executive activity.

We learned in the last chapter that the emergence of working memory and cognitive inhibition improve the infant's understanding of object permanence to the point that the infant begins to understand that the world is populated not only by objects that are in view but also by objects that, having been in view, have gone out of view. This understanding that the world extends beyond the field of vision improves greatly during the early toddling stage. It does so primarily because the child is now insatiably interested in the world, enthusiastically exploring it on its own and keenly observing it when taken on walks or for rides by parents or other adults. Moreover, the strengthening of basic cognitive executive functions, along with the improvement of cognition and memory generally, contribute to the child's increasing understanding of the world beyond the field of vision. The young toddler thus makes great strides in understanding that the world is populated by objects of diverse sorts, many of which, from the perspective of the child's current location, are hidden or too far away to be seen.

Despite these strides, the young toddler's understanding of the world is still held back by limited memory ability, limited experience of objects, and incomplete understanding of how objects are related and what objects can do. To recall, we discussed studies in the last chapter that have found that children do not learn that objects can be related in rule-governed ways without being physically connected or that objects can move without being perceived to do so until near the end of the second year.[9] Consequently, although the young toddler makes great strides in understanding the contents and size of the world, it continues, effectively, to live in a small, child-centered world, a world that, although extending beyond the field of vision, does so in ways that are only vaguely and fleetingly understood.

The Self-System

One other noteworthy development occurring during the early toddling stage, this one pertaining to the self-system, is the continued gathering of information that later will be included within the self-representation. The child continues to gather internal sensory information about its body; caregiver-reflected information about its expressions, movements, and sounds; and preverbal categorical information about its features and powers. Indeed, the amount of information that the child gathers now increases rapidly because the child's ardent investigation of the object world provides it with a wealth of information not only about the objects it investigates but also about its own bodily self, which does the investigating. As the child crawls, toddles, and coordinates eye and hand movements in exploring the object world, it learns not only about objects other than itself but also about itself as an object interacting with other objects. The many new things that the child thus learns about itself are added to the body of information that later will make up the self-representation.

Separation Anxiety

An interesting phenomenon emerges at approximately eight months, near the beginning of the stage we are discussing: separation anxiety. The child begins to be distressed when the caregiver leaves the child alone or with strangers. The reason most often given for this anxiety is that the child's understanding of object permanence has developed to the point that the child begins to understand the possibility of object loss, the loss of the caregiver most importantly. In understanding that the caregiver exists when not perceived, the child understands that the caregiver's absences are not just interruptions of presence but are in fact departures to an unseen region, a region from which the caregiver might not return. Strongly attached to the caregiver and increasingly aware that absences could mean departure without return, the child experiences anxiety when the caregiver exits from view.

The young toddler's separation anxiety is not so severe as to undermine its interest in the object world. Although the child experiences distress when the caregiver is absent, it does not ordinarily cling to the caregiver when the caregiver is present, as it will begin doing near the middle of the second year. In fact, when the caregiver is present the child, although frequently looking to the caregiver for guidance or encouragement (social referencing), most often acts in a completely fearless way. Under the watchful eye of the caregiver, the child enjoys itself with reckless abandon as an intrepid explorer of the object world. For the young toddler, therefore, separation anxiety is not crippling. Although distressing, it is intermittent and relatively short in duration when it occurs.

The Lifeworld—A "Garden of Delight"

Given its confidence when the caregiver is present and its heightened interest in the object world, the young toddler takes the same kind of delight in the object world that, as an infant, it had taken in the caregiver. Using its rapidly developing motor skills, the young toddler investigates one object after another, manipulating, inspecting, tasting, and in general thoroughly examining each in turn. The child savors each new discovery, and it greatly enjoys sharing its discoveries with the caregiver. The child looks back to the caregiver with an object in hand, or it takes an object to the caregiver. This sharing of objects extends intersubjectivity beyond primary (dyadic) intersubjectivity, the intersubjectivity of child and caregiver sharing in the experience of each other, to secondary (triadic) intersubjectivity, the intersubjectivity of child and caregiver sharing in the examination of objects or in games with objects. The whole of the child's lifeworld is thus brought within the shared space of intersubjectivity.

Margaret Mahler, the preeminent psychoanalytic writer on early childhood, called the early toddling stage a time of "practicing" and described it as a period during which the child carries on a "love affair with the world," assuming the availability of the caregiver as anchor and refuge, as protector and home base for emotional refueling.[10] The young toddler, despite the vigilance of the caregiver, does frequently hurt itself. These mishaps, however, are most often only minor bumps and scratches. After hurting itself, the young toddler reaches for the caregiver for refueling and then immediately returns to exploring the world, with gusto and breathless anticipation of what it might discover next.

The young toddler's eagerness and delight in investigating objects suggest that the young toddler's lifeworld has a wondrous character. Three reasons, two factual and one conjectural, support this hypothesis. The first and most obvious reason, which is factual, is that almost everything in the child's world is something hitherto unexperienced and, therefore, something new and possibly exciting to play with. Just as the young infant, upon awakening to the caregiver, is immediately enthralled by this new being, this new self, so the young toddler, able for the first time to move on its own, is immediately enthralled by the wealth of new objects that are now within its reach.

The second reason helping to explain the wondrous character of the young toddler's lifeworld, this one also factual, is that the young toddler's senses are pristine. The young toddler's senses are not yet overridden by habits, narrowed by preestablished interests, or restricted in focus to properties of objects that identify them according to type. The young toddler has not yet acquired habits, and for this reason it is not prone to attend to objects only insofar as they play roles in established routines. The young toddler is not without strong interests, but its interests are those of the moment, fixed on objects in view, not interests formed in the past that might cause it to disregard objects in view. Finally, the young toddler, despite being an intuitive taxonomist, does not yet, as adults do, focus primarily on properties of objects that identify them according to type. Adults, in navigating the environment, frequently say to themselves, "Oh, another one of the those," without in any significant way attending to the things thus noticed. It is clearly otherwise with the young toddler. The fascination with which the young toddler investigates objects indicates that in each case it is primarily *this* object and only secondarily this *kind* of object to which the toddler is primarily attending. Given the pristine character of the young toddler's senses, objects are fresh, vivid, and rich in detail. They are worlds unto themselves, unique particulars with features and powers fully displayed.

The third reason helping to explain the wondrous character of the young toddler's lifeworld, this one conjectural, is that both the young toddler and its world are infused with freely mobile psychic energy. For the young toddler, a great deal of psychic energy remains unbound, unrestricted in its availability, because it is not yet held in reserve or assigned to specific needs or goals. The young toddler, therefore, has a great deal of free energy at its disposal to expend without constraint in the experience of the moment. The young toddler is for this reason exuberant in its exploring activities; and the objects it perceives are highly charged ("cathected") with energy, which amplifies, accentuates, and magnetizes them, transforming them into irresistible attractors. The young toddler is both aroused and enraptured, and the objects it discovers are both extraordinary and captivating. In sum, the lifeworld of the young toddler, I suggest, has a wondrous character, not only because it is full of new things to discover and because the toddler's senses are pristine, but also because freely mobile psychic energy both impassions the child and enchants its world.

Many have described early childhood as a time of childhood spirituality. This description is apt in conveying the idea that the young toddler lives in an Eden-like "garden of delight" overseen (assuming a female caregiver) by a goddess-like nurturer, guide, and protector. However, although the description is apt in conveying this idea, it should be amended to convey the additional idea that childhood spirituality has a dark side. We explore this dark side in the next chapter; and then, in chapter 10, we propose an explanation of how childhood spirituality comes to an end.

Conclusion

The early toddling stage is a time during which the ego again grows stronger as the subject of consciousness and becomes more capable as the executive agency of consciousness. The ego grows stronger as the subject of conscious-ness because mobile access to fascinating objects keeps it alertly focused. Concomitantly, the ego grows more capable as the executive agency of consciousness because exploration of the object world is accomplished by the exercise of cognitive and practical functions, and the exercise of these functions strengthens them and furthers their development. Cognitive functions already online thus become more effective; and practical functions develop in kind (initial forms of impulse control arise), independence (the child no longer needs to rely on the caregiver's promptings), and range (the child is no longer restricted by lack of mobility).

Mobile access to objects, in helping bring about these advances, also leads to growth in intuitive understanding of categories, especially basic categories, and to the ability intuitively to make basic logical inferences, including even deductive inferences. Additionally, mobile access to objects facilitates growth in self-awareness, since the young toddler, in exploring the object world, learns a great deal about itself both as an agency with causal powers over objects and as a bodily being subject to the causal powers of objects.

Mobile access to objects transforms the lifeworld by allowing the young toddler to become enthralled by objects, as earlier, as an infant, it was enthralled by the caregiver. Although the young toddler is sometimes anxious when the caregiver is absent and is heedful of the caregiver's cues, it is in general an intrepid explorer of the object world. It is obvious from its behavior that the young toddler takes delight in discovering objects. Moreover, theory provides reasons that help explain why this is so: the young toddler's lifeworld is a new frontier perceived with pristine senses and rendered irresistibly attractive by the young toddler's own freely mobile energy.

The lifeworld of the young toddler, although focused primarily on objects, is focused on people as well, especially on the caregiver. The caregiver is the young toddler's anchor and refuge and primary partner in intersubjectivity, not only the primary intersubjectivity of child and caregiver participating in imitative exchanges but also, now, the secondary intersubjectivity of child and caregiver sharing in the wonders of objects or in playful exchanges with objects. Drawn to the caregiver in these ways, the young toddler divides its time between the caregiver and the object world. Given strength by the caregiver as anchor and refuge, the young toddler confidently sets off on its own to investigate the world. Delighted by what it finds, the young toddler turns its attention back to the caregiver and delights in sharing its discovery with the caregiver and then delights further in the caregiver's delight in what it has found. Such is the experience of the young toddler, who, as we have suggested, lives in a close relationship with a protecting, loving caregiver in an irresistibly attractive garden of delight.

Chapter 9

Late Toddling and the Preschool Years

Thus far our approach to ego development has been primarily empirical. We have drawn on experimental studies to explain how the ego develops as subject and executive agency of consciousness. We continue with this approach here and throughout the rest of the book. However, beginning here and continuing in the next chapter, the empirical approach takes a back seat to the theoretical. It does so because we now adopt and modify theories explaining the emergence of two of the first forms of psychological self-defense—splitting, followed by repression—so that we can clarify the role these forms of self-defense play in the creation of the ego ideal, superego, and shadow and, therefore, in the completion of the self-system/shadow complex.

The Crisis-Adjustment Stage

It is generally understood that the period beginning near the middle of the second year and continuing into the third year is a difficult time for children. Often referred to as the "terrible twos," this late toddling period is characterized at the outset by the emergence of an acute ambivalence toward the caregiver. The child's ambivalence is explained by Margaret Mahler as arising out of the frustration the older toddler experiences in seeking rapprochement—a restored sense of closeness—with the caregiver.[1] As explained by Anni Bergman, an associate of Mahler's, this need for a closer relationship with the caregiver is itself caused at least in part by the formation of the self-representation.[2] With the formation of the self-representation, the child gains an understanding of itself as an embodied being different from others and thus becomes more aware of its separateness from others, including most importantly the caregiver.

The child, increasingly sensing its separateness from the caregiver, feels an increasingly strong need to reestablish closeness with the caregiver, only to discover that the caregiver does not respond as it hopes, expects, and demands.

> The fact that mothers were not always available began to cause frustration and dissatisfaction in the toddlers, who in this period became more sensitive to their mothers' presence and absence than they had been during practicing. A growing awareness of separateness and aloneness ensued, and miscommunication between mother and toddler often occurred. When mothers, despite their best efforts, could not satisfy their toddlers, both they and their children could become frustrated and angry. These observations led us to understand that a representational crisis was taking place that was not entirely contingent on the mother's behavior, or even her emotional availability. The formulation of the rapprochement conflict was based in part on the observation that even the most sensitive mothers could not be entirely available for the amount of sharing demanded by their toddlers, nor could they be fully prepared for the outbursts of anger directed at them by their toddlers.[3]

Near the middle of the second year, it seems, the child wants more from the caregiver than the caregiver can provide. The child wants to reestablish the close relationship with the caregiver that it enjoyed during the early toddling stage. That relationship, however, was in significant part predicated on the young toddler's unawareness of its separateness from the caregiver. Once the self-representation and, with it, awareness of separateness emerge, therefore, the closeness with the caregiver that characterized the early toddling stage is lost without the possibility of being restored. The older toddler desperately attempts to reestablish this lost closeness. However, its attempts fail and lead only to frustration and ambivalence toward the caregiver, who, from the child's perspective, seems to be the one who has changed.

The older toddler's need for rapprochement with the caregiver underlies a new, ambivalent, relationship with the caregiver. The child seeks to please the caregiver so that it can win the caregiver's attention, only, frequently, to be put off and enraged by the caregiver's seeming lack of concern. The child clings to the caregiver in the hope that the caregiver will share in a discovery or participate in a playful exchange, only, frequently, to find that the caregiver is inattentive or even sharp, thus leaving the child frustrated and prone to recoil from the caregiver and assert itself angrily. The sequence of behaviors is as follows: attempts to please the caregiver are followed by outbursts of anger, clinging is followed by defiance and pushing away, and selfless sharing is followed by unbridled self-assertion. The older toddler is riven with contradictions, alternating between obsequious overtures to the caregiver and temper tantrums directed against the caregiver.

The onset of the child's ambivalence toward the caregiver marks the beginning of a new stage, a stage during which the child's ambivalence emerges, intensifies, and then gradually wanes. This stage runs a long course, beginning in the period between approximately 15 and 24 months, when the child's ambivalence emerges and then quickly intensifies, and continuing through a relative long period into the preschool years, when the child's ambivalence wanes and finally disappears. We are indebted above all to Mahler for our understanding of this stage. She drew on psychoanalytic object-relations theory and her own extensive studies of children to explain how the stage in question unfolds through two subphases, which she called the "rapprochement" and the "road-to-object-constancy" subphases of the "separation-individuation process," the process during early childhood by which the child establishes boundaries and achieves independence from the caregiver.[4]

Mahler's rapprochement and road-to-object-constancy subphases will here be referred to, respectively, as the "crisis" and "adjustment" substages of a "crisis-adjustment" stage, the stage of early childhood that, again, runs from the beginning of the late toddling stage into the preschool years. We have changed Mahler's terminology for two reasons. The first is that "crisis" and "adjustment" are clearer than "rapprochement" and "road to object constancy." The second reason is that the ensuing exposition significantly modifies some of Mahler's views, reformulating them so that they better fit our primary themes. Specifically, we reformulate her views to explain more clearly how splitting, which emerges in the crisis substage of the crisis-adjustment stage, and repression, which gradually replaces splitting in the adjustment substage, together create the ego ideal, superego, and shadow, thus completing the formation of the self-system/shadow complex.

As the term suggests, the crisis-adjustment stage begins with a crisis, referred to by Mahler as the "rapprochement crisis," the crisis that results when the child is frustrated in its attempts to establish a closer relationship with the caregiver. This crisis, which defines the first substage of the crisis-adjustment stage, is of relatively brief duration and is soon followed by a longer period, the adjustment substage of the crisis-adjustment stage, during which the child's ambivalence and anger toward the caregiver subside and the child gradually reestablishes a stable, primarily positive relationship with the caregiver. The adjustment substage of the crisis-adjustment stage has no precise endpoint. Nevertheless, it can be said to come to an end later in the preschool years, during the transition from early to middle childhood, which occurs at four or five years of age.[5]

Executive Functions and Intuitive Understanding of Categories Combine—Symbolic Thinking and Symbol-Guided Action

Two new executive functions emerge during the crisis-adjustment stage, symbolic thinking and symbol-guided voluntary action, both of which are well known from Piaget's groundbreaking studies. Symbolic thinking, which Piaget classified as a type of preoperational thinking, is the use of representations to think about things, whether actual things, like the family dog, Winston, or generic things, perhaps an imagined dog that is not Winston or any other actual dog. For example, a boy who lives with Winston might engage in symbolic thinking by holding on to a stuffed animal so that he can think about Winston when Winston is somewhere else or by playing with the stuffed animal so that he can pretend that he is playing with Winston or so that he can pretend that he is playing with a generic dog. Although symbolic thinking can in principle use mental images as symbolic representations, mental images are fleeting; and for this reason, symbolic thinking in its early stages relies heavily on physical objects as symbolic representations.

Three important precursors of symbolic thinking are attention control, working memory, and the initial intuition of categories, all of which, as we have learned, emerge in the first year of life, well before the crisis-adjustment stage. Attention control and working memory are precursors of symbolic thinking because they are what allow symbolic thinking to maintain attention on representations of things when the things represented are not present to the senses. In turn, intuition of categories is a precursor of symbolic thinking because it is what allows symbolic thinking to represent not only actual things but also generic things. Symbolic thinking, therefore, requires both (1) that attention control, working memory, and intuition of categories each be well along in development and (2) that these three components of symbolic thinking be sufficiently integrated with each other that they can function seamlessly together.

To the extent that it relies on attention control and working memory, which are executive functions, symbolic thinking is itself an executive function, a new, higher-order executive function. The boy who lives with Winston performs an executive (ego-initiated) action on a symbolic representation when he holds on to a stuffed animal to keep Winston in mind. Even more, this boy performs a multitude of such actions when he manipulates the stuffed animal to pretend that he is playing with Winston (or with a generic dog). Symbolic thinking is thus an executive function because it is based on ego-initiated actions performed on symbolic representations, whether simple actions, such as sustained attention, or complex actions, such as those that involve significant manipulation of a representation.

Symbolic thinking is preoperational because the child, when thinking symbolically about things, is not thinking explicitly about the categories to which things belong as examples. In thinking about a dog, the child is not thinking explicitly about the features by virtue of which something is a dog. Nor is it thinking explicitly about how dogs are like or unlike things belonging to other categories. Such explicit thinking about categories is the task of operational thinking, which does not emerge in its first form until middle childhood. Symbolic thinking still focuses on categories only implicitly and intuitively. Although symbolic thinking is an executive function insofar as it relies on attention control and working memory, it otherwise—like logical (inductive, deductive) thinking—remains a form of intuitive cognition.

Symbolic representations multiply quickly as the child adds new categories to its cognitive repertoire, becomes better able to express itself in words, and improves its vocabulary. Aided by language, the child now "speaks its mind," putting into words symbol-based thoughts about which it is eager to communicate. The crisis-adjustment stage, continuing well into the preschool period, is a time during which language and, with it, symbolic representations develop at great speed. Symbolic thinking thus emerges in the crisis-adjustment stage and develops rapidly during the stage.

Turning from cognitive to practical functions, the most important new development is the emergence of symbol-guided action, which, as explained in the last chapter, is goal-directed action in the strict sense.[6] Symbol-guided action is action by which a child seeks out an object, not, as the young toddler does, because it is novel and, therefore, something to explore, but rather because the child knows from previous experience that the object does or contains something that the child wants to experience again or that the object can be used to do something that the child wants to do again. For example, an older toddler might (1) pick up a sound-making toy to hear again the amusing sound it makes when squeezed; (2) go to a box on the coffee table in which sweets are kept in search of a piece of candy; or, again, (3) pick up a stuffed animal to pretend that it is playing with a dog. Actions such as these are symbolically guided because the child uses symbolic representations of anticipated outcomes as guides to its behavior.

Just as symbolic thinking, in integrating attention control, working memory, and intuition of categories, brings into being a new, higher-order cognitive executive function, so symbol-guided action, in applying symbolic thinking to action, brings into being a new, higher-order practical executive function. Unlike the young toddler, who acts spontaneously in pursuit of interesting objects not knowing what it will experience, the older toddler acts with foresight to reproduce experiences it has had before. Unlike the young toddler, who relates to objects only as goals, as treasures to be discovered, the older toddler relates to objects not only as goals but also as means to anticipated ends.

The Self-System—Emergence of the Self-Representation

A major change in the self-system occurs near the middle of the second year: the self-representation quickly takes form. The consensus is that the self-representation takes form at this time because the middle of the second year is the time at which the child achieves self-recognition.[7] That self-recognition is achieved near the middle of the second year is confirmed by the classic mirror test of self-recognition.[8] In this test a rouge spot is placed on a child's face, and the child is then placed in front of a mirror. If the child is younger than 15 months, it most likely will not respond to the oddity of seeing a child in a mirror with a rouge spot on its face. In contrast, if the child is between 15 and 18 months, it more often than not will respond to the spot by self-consciously touching it. This touching reveals that the child finally understands that, in seeing its image in the mirror, it is seeing itself rather than another child. It reveals that the child has achieved self-recognition.

In achieving mirror self-recognition, the child understands that the image it sees in the mirror matches the information it has gathered about itself and, therefore, that in looking at the image in the mirror it is looking at itself. The time at which mirror self-recognition emerges, therefore, is the time at which the child ceases being merely implicitly aware of its experiences and attributes and becomes explicitly aware of them, as experiences and attributes that belong to it distinctively and thus differentiate it from others. In recognizing itself in its mirror image, the child sees itself from an external point of view, as others do. In seeing itself in this new way, the child understands and records to memory a representation of what it is like as an embodied being different from and independent of others. This representation is the self-representation.

As the child acquires language skills, it soon adds linguistic self-reference to self-recognition. It is the caregiver who is the child's primary language teacher, and the caregiver makes a special effort to teach the child words that will facilitate its self-understanding. With the help of the caregiver, therefore, the child who has just learned to recognize itself is soon able to use language to express itself *as a self*. Sometime after 24 months, the child begins to refer to itself by name and to use the pronouns "I," "me," and "mine," thus referring to itself and bringing its selfhood to the attention of others.[9] Soon after the child begins using these pronouns, it also begins using nouns and verbs to describe itself in simple ways, thus describing itself both in its particularity and as an instance of kinds.[10] For example, young Emily might now refer to her fingers as "Emily's fingers," these words used to designate both the particular things that are *Emily's* fingers and the kind of things that are Emily's *fingers*. Similarly, the child learns words referring to many of its other bodily parts and to its most-frequently repeated actions (e.g., getting up, getting down, walking, laughing, crying), thus learning how linguistically to ascribe to itself these parts and actions. In this way, the information now making up the child's self-representation begins being translated into language, and the child begins being able to use language not only for the purpose of direct self-reference but also for the purpose of self-description.

The self-representation that emerges near the middle of the second year and that is soon thereafter translated into language in the ways just discussed is a self-representation of a limited sort. The primary limitation is temporal: the self-representation is confined to the present moment. The child can recognize itself when it looks at its image in the mirror or at the moment it refers to or describes itself. In thus recognizing itself, however, the child does not yet understand that it is a temporally extended being with a course of life. Evidence discussed in the next chapter indicates that the self-representation of the older toddler is not yet an autobiographical self-representation, a self-representation by means of which the child understands and narrates its personal history. This fact notwithstanding, the self-representation *is* now in place for the first time. The information that the child has gathered about itself is now integrated within a representation by means of which it recognizes itself as a creature with distinctive features by virtue of which it differs from and is independent of others.

With the establishment of the self-representation, the self-system becomes a two-component, ego–self-representation self-system. The ego's object or Me side is now explicitly recognized and registered in a mental record, a record that is now added to the subject or I side of the ego as the second component of the self-system. The self-representation, thus recording the ego's object or Me side, is a representation of the ego's "actual" self, the self that the ego in fact recognizes itself to be. The ego does not yet have an ego ideal or superego. Functions that later will be performed by these two components of the self-system at this point begin being performed by the caregiver. The caregiver now begins to mold the child's behavior both by praising the child for its good behavior (thus laying the foundation for what later will become the ego ideal) and by chastising the child for its bad behavior (thus laying the foundation for what later will become the superego). The foundations of the ego ideal and the superego are thus laid down during the crisis-adjustment stage. However, these two components of the self-system do not themselves come online until the end of the stage, at or near the beginning of middle childhood. During the crisis-adjustment stage, the self-system remains a two-component self-system, a self-system consisting only of the ego as interior subject and executive agency of consciousness and the newly formed self-representation, a record of the ego's exterior, object or Me, side.

Crisis—Acute Ambivalence

To recall, the primary reason explaining why the older toddler's relationship with the caregiver becomes problematic is that the formation of the self-representation, in allowing the child to see how it differs from others, also brings the child to see how it is separate from others, most importantly how it is separate from the caregiver. This feeling of separateness stirs a desire for rapprochement with the caregiver, a desire that, as we have seen, leads to frustration with and ambivalence toward the caregiver and thus to a crisis in the child's relationship with the caregiver.

If the formation of the self-representation thus explains how the child's relationship with the caregiver becomes problematic and reaches a crisis, it does not explain how the crisis that emerges evolves as it subsequently unfolds. Let us, therefore, consider three reasons that help explain why the rapprochement crisis, after first emerging as a crisis of lost closeness with the caregiver, tends to evolve into a crisis of lost faith in the caregiver. These reasons help explain why the child's newly emerged need for restored closeness with the caregiver can trigger a return of separation anxiety, this time in the new and stronger form of abandonment anxiety.

We learned in the last chapter that, according to most accounts, separation anxiety first emerges at approximately eight months because the young toddler has begun to understand object permanence well enough to worry that the caregiver, when absent, might not return. Here we can add that the older toddler has not only this reason but also three other reasons for worrying about the caregiver's absences. The first of these reasons is that, after approximately 18 months, the child realizes that the world is significantly larger than it had previously understood. The older toddler's improved locomotive abilities have allowed it to explore further reaches of its immediate environment, and trips with adults outside the home have made the older toddler even more aware that the world consists of a multitude of spaces. In thus realizing that the world is larger than previously understood, the child of course does not yet have any idea of the real size of the world. The child's trips with parents might be isolated episodes that the child is unable accurately to integrate into its evolving understanding of the size of the world. The child's world might for this reason still be effectively quite small, perhaps including little more than the child's home and its immediate surroundings. Still, the child's world, however small, has grown significantly larger. The world now extends not only farther than the eye can see but, relative to what the child understood earlier, *much* farther. This expansion of the world could contribute to fear of object loss, in this case to fear that the caregiver, in exiting from view, might go far enough away to be unavailable in time of need.

The second reason why the older toddler might worry about the caregiver's absences is that the older toddler, unlike the young toddler, understands that the location of objects no longer in view is uncertain. As Piaget demonstrated, the child nearing two years of age begins to understand invisible displacement of objects, the fact that objects can move to new locations without being perceived to do so.[11] Before the middle of the second year, children look for an object at a specific location in space, either the location at which the object has most often been observed (8–12 months) or the location at which the object has most recently been observed (12–18 months). Before eighteen months, children are unable to understand that the position of an object in space is not tied to their previous perceptions of the object. This inability is overcome in the second half of the second year, when children begin to search for objects in places they have not observed them before.

Understanding invisible displacement could contribute to worry about object loss because it brings the child to understand that the caregiver, in exiting from view, is free to move about in the unperceived region of space and, therefore, is not tied to any location. When the caregiver is not in view, the child can now worry not only that the caregiver might have gone far away but also that the caregiver might have gone to an unknown location, a location at which the child has never perceived the caregiver. Understanding invisible displacement of objects might thus raise the worry that the caregiver's whereabouts cannot be known when the caregiver is out of sight.

The third and primary reason explaining the older toddler's worries about the caregiver's absences is that, with the onset of the rapprochement crisis, the child begins to sense that the caregiver's feelings for it have changed. The child is now the focus not only of the caregiver's love and protection but also of the caregiver's anger and discipline. The caregiver not only continues to play with the child and to keep it out of harm's way but also now begins to chastise the child. The caregiver had already intervened on the child's behavior in the early toddling stage, but these interventions were primarily attempts to prevent the child from hurting itself, not attempts to teach the child that it has misbehaved. It is otherwise in the late toddling stage, when the caregiver, responding to the child's constant demands for attention, its clinging, and, most of all, its temper tantrums, can become angry, conveying to the child, at least in words and tone if not also in disciplinary actions, that its behavior is unacceptable.

It is probably not a coincidence that the child's unacceptable behavior and the caregiver's disciplining responses come at a time when the child is old enough to learn from attempts to modify its behavior. In any case, the caregiver now not only praises or otherwise reinforces the child when it does something good but also, and of most relevance here, sternly corrects the child—whether by angrily saying "no, no," by taking away a toy, by disallowing a favorite activity, or by removing the child from interaction with others (time-out)—when it does something bad. The older toddler's constant demands and especially its out-of-control outbursts elicit responses from the caregiver that clearly inform the child that the caregiver is displeased.

The child thus experiences ambivalence toward the caregiver not only because it is frustrated by the caregiver's frequent failures to comply with its demands but also because it is frightened that the caregiver's feelings for it might have changed. The young toddler's separation anxiety, caused by initial fear of object loss, might for this reason return in the stronger form of abandonment anxiety, the fear that the caregiver, in exiting from view, might not *want* to return. The older toddler, therefore, might cling to the caregiver not only because, in becoming aware of its separateness, it desires greater closeness with the caregiver but also because, having been disciplined by the caregiver, it worries that the caregiver can no longer be relied on for love and protection.

Although we may never know all the causes that contribute to the rapprochement crisis, we do know that the causes at work produce dramatic changes in the child's behavior, changes that presumably express changes in the child's perception of the caregiver and the world. The child, who as a young toddler turned to the caregiver primarily for recreational exchanges and emotional refueling, now, as an older toddler, demands the caregiver's constant company, only, frequently, to explode in fits of temper when the caregiver does not do what the child wants. The child, who had acted as if the caregiver would always be available to attend to its needs, now clings to the caregiver and is fearful when the caregiver leaves, worrying that the caregiver might have gone far away to an unknown location, perhaps angry with the child and not wanting to return.

The child's behavior suggests that its perception of the world has changed. The world, which had been a treasure field to be explored with reckless abandon, is now a larger and more uncertain realm that the child is reluctant to explore without the caregiver constantly at its side. Like the older toddler's relationship with the caregiver, the older toddler's relationship with the world is complicated and ambivalent. The world remains attractive as a treasure field to be explored, but it is now perceived fearfully, not only because it has become larger and more uncertain, but also because it is now a world in which, the child worries, it might be left alone.

Splitting Emerges as Mechanism of Defense

This section follows Mahler's account of the rapprochement crisis. Emphasis is given to clarifying how her account is based on psychoanalytic object relations theory, especially its approach to the phenomenon of early child-hood splitting. Again, we will here be referring to Mahler's rapprochement subphase of the separation-individuation process as the "crisis" substage of the "crisis-adjustment" stage.

The rapprochement crisis is a dilemma of ambivalence that the child experiences in relation to the caregiver. On the one hand, the child wants a closer relationship with the caregiver; on the other hand, however, the child is now frustrated or angry with the caregiver for being inattentive and worried about or fearful of the caregiver for being absent or stern. The child thus finds itself in an ambivalent relationship with the caregiver that, according to psychoanalytic object relations theory, causes the child to perceive the caregiver in two starkly opposed ways. When the child is embraced and played with by the caregiver, it perceives the caregiver, as it probably had hitherto, as a kind and attractive being. However, when the child feels neglected or harshly treated by the caregiver, it now begins to perceive the caregiver as a cruel and repellent being. In thus perceiving the caregiver in these opposite ways, the child, in the language of object relations theory, "splits" its representation of the caregiver. It creates two opposite representations, one a representation of an all-good caregiver and the other a representation of an all-bad caregiver. With this splitting of the representation of the caregiver, the child in effect perceives the caregiver as two separate beings, one all good and the other all bad.

The child may split its representation of the caregiver because, cog-nitively, it is unable to do otherwise. The older toddler, given its cognitive limitations, might have no choice but to think that strongly conflicting perceived qualities cannot be the qualities of one being. However, even if the child does have the ability to understand that the caregiver, despite possessing strongly conflicting perceived qualities, is one being, it has a compelling reason for splitting the representation of the caregiver nonethe-less. The reason is that the child, faced with a larger and uncertain world and a caregiver who is frequently absent or stern, needs to believe that there is an all-good being to protect it. The child is in crisis and would be devastated if it had to acknowledge both that the world is large and uncertain and that the caregiver is not all good. It is understandable that an adult, feeling vulnerable in a vast and mysterious cosmos, would believe in an all-good divine protector. It is even more understandable that an older toddler, feeling vulnerable in a larger and uncertain world, would believe in an all-good human protector.

The child meets its need for an all-good human protector by dividing the caregiver into an all-good caregiver and an all-bad caregiver, the former possessing all and only the positive (reliable, nurturing, playful, protecting) qualities of the actual caregiver and the latter possessing all and only the negative (inattentive, absent, angry) qualities of the actual caregiver. This splitting of the representation of the caregiver is one of the first forms of psychological defense. The older toddler splits its representation of the caregiver so that it can allay fears that have arisen because of perceived changes in both the caregiver and the world. Splitting allows the older toddler to believe that, despite now living with an uncaring, cruel adult in a larger, uncertain world, there is a perfectly good adult on whom the child can rely always to give it the love and protection it needs.

The all-good and all-bad caregivers are well known in children's literature. The all-good caregiver is depicted as a perfect being who is completely devoted to the child, a constant companion who plays with the child and attends to its every need. Specifically, the all-good caregiver is depicted as a kind maiden, beautiful princess, or protective fairy godmother or as the child's true mother, an altruistic being who enjoys the child's company and can be relied on to rescue the child when it is in distress. In contrast, the all-bad caregiver is depicted as a malevolent being who pretends to be devoted to the child but in fact is burdened by the child and wants nothing to do with it. Specifically, the all-bad caregiver is depicted as an evil hag or wicked stepmother. The child believes that the all-good caregiver alone is the true caregiver and that the all-bad caregiver is an evil imposter.

A consequence of the splitting of the caregiver into two antithetical beings is that the child is forced, correspondingly, to split itself into two antithetical beings. In the terms of object relations theory, the splitting of the representation of the caregiver is at the same time a splitting of the self-representation. Wanting desperately to be attended to by the all-good caregiver, the child has a strong need to please the caregiver and to believe that, because it is pleasing to the caregiver, it can expect the caregiver's love and protection. The child's need for an all-good caregiver is thus at the same time a need for the child itself to be an all-good child. It would do the child little good if there were an all-good caregiver but the child was not loved by this caregiver. The child for this reason not only seeks to behave in ways that are pleasing to the caregiver but also begins to identify only with such behaviors. Of course, the child, having very little self-control, does frequently displease the caregiver. It flies into rages, asserts itself defiantly, acts in utterly selfish ways, and does other things that are characteristic of the so-called terrible twos. However, because the child identifies only with behaviors that are pleasing to the caregiver, it cannot accept these displeasing behaviors as its own. The child for this reason purges these behaviors from its self-representation and imputes them to a separate, all-bad child.

In this way, the child's self-representation, like its representation of the caregiver, is split in two. It is divided into opposite good-child and bad-child representations. Because the child identifies only with behaviors pleasing to the caregiver, it relates only to the good-child representation as self-representation. One might think that the good-child representation would better serve the child as an ego ideal, as a representation of an ideal self to be strived for rather than as a representation of an actual self believed to be already achieved. However, this would be to skip ahead in development. The good-child representation, as we shall see, does eventually evolve into the child's ego ideal. At this point, however, the child is unable to distinguish between actual and ideal selves and in any case is desperate to believe that it is in fact a perfectly good child. The child for these reasons relates to the good-child representation as self-representation, thus disowning its bad behaviors and attributing them to another child, an all-bad child frequently mistaken for the all-good child. The bad-child representation, like the bad-caregiver representation, refers to an imposter. The splitting of the self-representation is thus effectively a splitting of the child into two separate children. The child in effect becomes a split personality.

The splitting of the self-representation causes ego instability. This instability differs from the instability of the ego in the first months of life, which is an instability of a weakly organized subject of consciousness or unity of apperception. To recall, ego instability at the outset of life is evident when the newborn or young infant falls into dreamy states when not attending to salient stimuli or not engaged with the caregiver in communicative interaction. In contrast, ego instability during the late toddling stage is an instability of intrapsychic conflict. Splitting of the self-representation pulls the older toddler's ego in opposite directions, making it an interior subject or I with two opposite object or Me sides, one all good and the other all bad. The subject or I side of the older toddler's ego remains undivided and is now much more strongly constituted as a unity of apperception. Nevertheless, the object or Me side is divided in the manner indicated. The older toddler for this reason finds itself being shuttled back and forth between an all-good child and an all-bad child. It is repeatedly taken possession of by the all-bad child and then returned to the all-good child. From the all-good child's perspective, it may seem as if it is repeatedly abducted and forced to do the bidding of an imposter all-bad child, only to be released and returned repeatedly to its true all-good self, and thus restored to innocence and worthiness of the all-good caregiver's favor.

Along with the desires, frustrations, and fears that give rise to it, splitting is a chief feature of the crisis substage of the crisis-adjustment stage. Once splitting sets in, the child's overall experience is subject to dramatic shifts between positive and negative. The child's belief that there is an all-good caregiver and that it is an all-good child deserving of this caregiver's love and protection allows the child to pretend that all is well. However, the child is increasingly aware of the limitations of the caregiver, the size and uncertainty of the world, and, therefore, its own vulnerability. Awareness of these facts triggers a shift in perspective from positive to negative. The child suddenly sees itself as a victim of neglect or mistreatment; it sees the caregiver as indifferent or cruel; and it believes that another, all-bad, child is responsible for its misfortune. After such an episode of fear, anger, and dissociation, the child and the caregiver reconcile in loving embrace. This triggers a shift in perspective from negative back to positive. The all-good child and the all-good caregiver return, until the next episode of fear, anger, and dissociation. So it goes.

The splitting that occurs in the crisis substage of the crisis-adjustment stage is a temporary expedient that keeps the older toddler from being overwhelmed with fear once it has become more needy and vulnerable in its relationship with the caregiver and more aware of the size and uncertainty of the world. However, splitting is not a solution to the child's predicament. It is merely a fabrication that provides the child with short-term false hope. Indeed, splitting, rather than easing the child's predicament, in fact makes it worse because it allows the split-off bad child a completely free hand to act with unbridled self-assertion, thus further provoking the caregiver's disapproval and seeming withdrawal. For the child to overcome its existentially dire situation, therefore, it must improve its relationship with the caregiver, its lifeline; and to improve its relationship with the caregiver, the child must somehow eliminate its "terrible" behavior.

The child does just this during the adjustment substage of the crisis-adjustment stage. In the next chapter, we discuss two hypotheses that help explain how the child achieves self-control and thus improves its behavior during this substage. Here it suffices to say that the child's behavior does improve and so as well does its relationship with the caregiver, with the consequence that splitting is gradually overcome. As these developments unfold, the fear, conflict, and instability of the time of crisis gradually subside and a new stage of confidence, harmony, and stability gradually emerges.

Conclusion

The general character of the adjustment substage of the crisis-adjustment stage is sketched in table 9.1. More is then said about this substage in the next chapter, where we discuss the hypotheses that help explain how the child achieves self-control and thus improves its behavior. Here we need only recall that, unlike the crisis substage of the crisis-adjustment stage, which is relatively brief, the adjustment substage is quite long, lasting from approximately 24 to beyond 36 months, perhaps even to four if not five years of age, when middle childhood begins.

The fact that the crisis-adjustment stage is defined by the crisis of its first, relatively brief substage does not mean that it is a stage that has a negative emotional tone overall. On balance, the opposite is probably true. Although the crisis substage is beset with feelings of need, vulnerability, fear, and anger, the much-longer adjustment substage is a time when these feelings gradually wane and concord with the caregiver and confident enjoyment of the world return. Moreover, the crisis substage, although extremely difficult for some children, is probably less difficult for others, depending on personality and life circumstances. Not all two-year-olds are in constant meltdown.

In sum, the crisis-adjustment stage is a stage that, arising from cognitive advances that increase the child's sense of separateness and vulnerability, begins with ambivalence toward the caregiver, soon leads to crisis and splitting, and then gradually moves toward restored confidence, harmony, and stability.

Table 9.1. The Crisis-Adjustment Stage

Unfolding of stage	Age	Description
First substage: Crisis (emergence of ambivalence) (Mahler: rapprochement subphase of separation-individuation process)	15–18 months	Formation of the self-representation makes the child more aware of its separateness and, therefore, stirs a desire for restored closeness with the caregiver. This desire, however, brings into focus the caregiver's frequent absences and fluctuating moods, causing the child to experience frustration with and ambivalence toward the caregiver.
First substage: Crisis (intensification of ambivalence, splitting) (Mahler: rapprochement subphase of separation-individuation process)	18–24 months	Advances in cognition make the child better aware of the size and uncertainty of the world, thus increasing the child's desire for closeness with the caregiver and, therefore, exacerbating its frustration with and ambivalence toward the caregiver. Separation anxiety returns in the form of abandonment anxiety. Child alternates between clinging to the caregiver and asserting itself in out-of-control episodes of rage, defiance, and selfishness. Child splits both the representation of the caregiver and its own self-representation into two opposite representations, one all good and the other all bad. Only the all-good representations depict the "true" caregiver and the "true" child. The all-bad representations depict imposters.
Second substage: Adjustment (Mahler: road-to-object-constancy subphase of separation-individuation process)	24–36+ months	Child's behavior and relationship with the caregiver improve, with the consequence that splitting is gradually overcome. The all-good versus all-bad split in the representation of the caregiver gradually gives way to a unified representation according to which the caregiver is imperfect but nonetheless mostly good. Correspondingly, the all-good versus all-bad split in the self-representation gradually gives way to a unified self-representation according to which the child is imperfect but nonetheless mostly good. Finally, as these transformations occur, the child's sense of vulnerability gradually subsides, and the child begins once again to take fearless delight in the world, which now becomes a field of play.
End of stage	4 or 5 years; the beginning of middle childhood	Overcoming of splitting is complete. Child is now a mostly good child cared for by mostly good parents or guardians in a mostly safe world. Confidence, harmony, and stability are restored.

Chapter 10

Middle Childhood

The features that distinguish middle childhood as a stage do not appear all at once at the beginning of the stage. As explained in the last chapter, they are already in progress during the adjustment substage of the crisis-adjustment stage. The transition from the crisis-adjustment stage to middle childhood is for this reason gradual and cumulative. This fact should be kept in mind when in this chapter I speak of the distinguishing features of middle childhood as if they appear at the beginning of the stage. The point is that they appear *in fully established form* at the beginning of the stage.

Emergence of Inner Speech— Verbally Implemented Executive Functions

During the preschool years, children begin to divide spoken language into two types of speech: social speech (spoken communication with others) and self-directed speech, the first form of which is private speech, the speech by which children speak aloud to themselves. Lev Vygotsky, working in the 1920s and early 1930s, pioneered the study of self-directed speech.[1] According-ing to Vygotsky, private speech, as the first form of self-directed speech, is a precursor of silent inner speech. Private speech, he argued, is the vehicle by which children, in speaking aloud to themselves, gradually internalize social speech, thus transforming spoken communication with others into spoken communication with oneself, at first aloud and then silently, within. Vygotsky believed that this process of internalization from social to private to inner speech occurs in the transition from the preschool to the school years.

More recent studies confirm Vygotsky's overall view of self-directed speech, with some qualifications. Two qualifications that have come to light are that private speech performs more functions and is more enduring than Vygotsky realized and that it may take a bit longer into the school years than Vygotsky thought—perhaps as late as between ages six and eight—before inner speech becomes the primary type of self-directed speech.[2] Whatever the exact timing, it is in the early years of middle childhood that speech is internalized and thus becomes not only social and private but also inner speech.

Inner speech, frequently called "inner thinking," transforms the ego's executive functions. Soon after emerging, it becomes the voice with which the ego performs both cognitive and practical functions. A growing number of studies in recent years have explored how inner speech takes command of executive functions such as working memory, cognitive flexibility, planning, and self-control.[3] These studies indicate that inner speech plays an essential role in the performance and coordination of executive functions from its first appearance in middle childhood throughout the rest of life.

In middle childhood, the mastery of inner speech marks the transition from preoperational symbolic thinking and acting to what Piaget referred to as "concrete operational" thinking and acting. Here we briefly summarize Piaget's well-known account of concrete operational thinking, giving special emphasis to what recent research has shown to be the role of inner speech in this type of thinking and, therefore, in the type of acting based on it.

The concrete operational thinking that emerges in middle childhood is an *operational* thinking because the child's thinking about categories and logical relationships is no longer only implicit and intuitive and now, with the aid of inner speech, becomes explicit and active, as a higher-order cognitive executive function. The child, for example, now speaks to itself to confirm that objects do or do not belong to categories or to make logical inferences based on what it has learned about connections between objects and events. Piaget referred to this first form of operational thinking as *concrete* operational thinking to indicate that, although school-age children think explicitly and actively about categories and logical relationships, they do so only with respect to objects with which they are interacting. They think about categories and logical relationships only with reference to exemplifying instances, not yet in the abstract.

Because inner speech is highly abbreviated, using only key words or expressions, its use by school-age children in performing concrete operations of classificatory and logical sorts consists of brief observations that introduce the operation without needing to complete it. For example, it might consist of observations such as (1) "Jenny wears nice clothes" [left implicit: therefore her parents are rich]; (2) "That's not a lizard" [left implicit: because it doesn't have legs]; (3) "That's a black widow" [left implicit: therefore watch out, it's dangerous]; (4) "Most [of the balls in the gumball machine] are red" [left implicit: therefore I'll probably get a red one]; and (5) "Joe was in my room" [left implicit: therefore he took my baseball cards]. These examples illustrate how school-age children might use inner speech to group objects into categories and to make logical inferences without yet defining categories or expressing logical relationships abstractly.

As inner speech thus transforms cognitive functions, school-age children begin using it to think not only about life and events of the day generally but also about themselves specifically. It is by inner speech that school-age children think not only, for example, about the clothes they will wear to school, a birthday party they want to go to, and whether a friend will be allowed to spend the night, but also, for example, about their height and hair color, their gender and ethnicity, and their abilities and inabilities. In this latter role, as the voice by which children think about themselves specifically, inner speech is the voice by which children narrate—and thus verbally keep track of—their self-representations. Such narration of the self-representation is a major theme of this and ensuing chapters.

If school-age children speak to themselves in performing cognitive functions, they do so as well in performing practical functions, since action is guided by cognition. School-age children, therefore, speak to themselves, for example, in choosing between courses of action and in exploring means to desired ends. The symbol-guided action of the crisis-adjustment stage is thus here replaced with verbally guided action based on concrete operational cognition. It is noteworthy that school-age children, in using inner speech to plan and execute their actions, also use inner speech to motivate their actions. They speak to themselves to inspire themselves or to command themselves to act. Later, in discussing the self-system of middle childhood, we explain how these self-motivating voices of school-age children are related to and differ from the self-narrating voice they use in keeping track of their self-representations.

Perhaps the most important advance in practical functions that distinguishes middle childhood from the crisis-adjustment stage is greatly improved self-control. The self-control exercised by the school-age child is vastly superior to that of the older toddler, who is susceptible to outbursts of rage, defiance, and selfishness. Just how this advance in self-control is accomplished is a major topic of the present chapter. Later in the chapter, we discuss two hypotheses that help to explain the advance, the maturation hypothesis and the repression hypothesis. For present purposes, we need make only the following two points about this improved self-control: (1) it, like the features of middle childhood generally, is something that gradually emerges in the adjustment substage of the crisis-adjustment stage and is fully established only at the beginning of middle childhood, and (2) it marks a major step forward in the development of practical functions.

From Splitting to Integration of the Self-Representation

By the time a child has reached school age, it has outgrown the needs and overcome the fears that erupted during the crisis substage of the crisis-adjustment stage. It no longer feels the need for constant closeness with the caregiver, and it has grown comfortable in the larger, more uncertain world in which it lives. During the adjustment substage of the crisis-adjustment stage, the child gradually comes to see that the caregiver, although frequently harsh or absent, is nonetheless attentive enough, supportive enough, and reliable enough to meet its needs. Correspondingly, it gradually learns that the world, although large and uncertain, is mostly safe, at least in the neighborhood in which the child lives. These lessons are of first importance, for they help the child bring an end to splitting.

According to psychoanalytic object relations theory, splitting of the representation of the caregiver comes to an end because children, no longer plagued with the needs and fears that caused the older toddler's crisis, no longer need to cling to the idea of a perfectly loving and protecting caregiver. By the time a child has reached middle childhood it is able to accept the caregiver's limitations and discipline without splitting its representation of the caregiver because it now sees the caregiver in a more realistic light, as someone who, although not all good, is nonetheless "good enough." The all-good caregiver and the all-bad caregiver created and kept apart by splitting are in this way integrated and become, in the mind of the child, a single, imperfect but mostly good caregiver. In the terms of psychoanalytic object relations theory, this integration of the representation of the caregiver is "object constancy."

In integrating the representation of the caregiver, the child at the same time integrates its self-representation. According to object-relations theory, object constancy is at the same time self-constancy. The child's self-representation is integrated for the following two reasons: (1) because the child, in learning that the caregiver need not be all good to provide adequate love and protection, also learns that it need not be all good to expect the caregiver's love and protection; and (2) because the child—for reasons to be explained later—has now gained enough self-control that it is no longer prone to the unacceptable behaviors that the older toddler had imputed to the (split) all-bad child.

The first of the reasons just stated explains how the child is freed from the assumption that it must be all good, and the second explains how the child is able to be mostly good. Taken together, the two reasons explain how the child mends the split in its self-representation. The child, having reestablished a stable relationship with the caregiver and having greatly improved its self-control, can finally see that the caregiver does not need to be perfect and is in fact mostly good. With this insight, the child can also see that it does not need to be perfect either and that it can in fact, with effort, be mostly good as well. The child is thus able to integrate its self-representation and to begin thinking of itself as a single, imperfect but mostly good child worthy of the love and protection of a single, imperfect but mostly good caregiver. In thinking of itself and the caregiver in these ways, the child thinks about the world in corresponding fashion, as a world that, with the protection of a mostly good caregiver, does not need to be completely safe to be mostly safe.

Integration of the self-representation brings an end to the instability the ego had suffered because of splitting. The ego ceases being shuttled back and forth between an all-good child and an all-bad child, repeatedly abducted by the latter and then returned to the former. This is not to say that the ego ceases being pulled in opposite directions by conflicting feelings. Such crosscurrents are a normal part of life. Rather, the point is that the ego is no longer forced to serve as the self of two opposing self-representations, the "I" of two opposing "Me's," one all good and the other all bad. No longer divided in this way, the ego is now the self of a single (integrated) self-representation, the I of a single (imperfect but mostly good) Me.

The transition to middle childhood marks not only the integration of the self-representation but also the beginning of its transformation into a temporally extended, autobiographical self-representation. Carefully crafted studies have shown that children at approximately age four begin to understand that their current selves are continuations of their past selves and that their current selves will unfold into the future. For example, in studies using a time-delay variation of the classic mirror mark test for self-recognition, children were photographed or videotaped playing a game in which, unbeknownst to the children, stickers had been placed on their heads. After a short delay, the children were shown the photos or videotapes, with the result that few three-year-olds but most four-year-olds reached to their heads for the stickers. Moreover, most three-year-olds referred to their time-delayed images impersonally, using their names or third-person pronouns, whereas most four-year-olds referred to their time-delayed images using the first-person pronoun "me."[4] The implication is that in the year between ages four and five children finally begin to understand explicitly, what they previously sensed only implicitly, that their lives are temporally extended and that they possess self-identity over time.

They also begin to understand that their lives continue into the future. Studies have shown that between the ages of three and five children develop the ability to project themselves into possible future scenarios, imagining not only the scenarios but also *themselves* in the scenarios.[5] This ability, first present in three-year-olds, develops dramatically between ages four and five. The year between ages four and five for this reason seems to be an important transition period during which children go from understanding their past and future lives as consisting of only impersonal, disconnected episodes to understanding their past and future lives as belonging to them as temporally extended, chronologically unfolding persons. During this year, therefore, what had been merely episodic memories become truly autobiographical memories, and what had been merely episodic future imaginings become truly autobiographical imaginings. The year between ages four and five is thus the time during which the self-representation becomes a representation of a *course of life*.

The autobiographical self-representation of the school-age child emerges in interaction with adults, primarily parents. Developmental psychologists have shown that parents help the child come to an understanding of its course of life by presenting it with narrative frameworks within which the child's experiences fit together in time.[6] Focusing on memories, parents seek to elicit the child's recollection of past events by employing either a repetitive or an elaborative conversational style. They either repeat questions about a specific event in the past or, more often, help the child remember a past event by presenting cues about the place of the event and about what people said or did at the event. Either way, they help the child retrieve a memory, and then they initiate a verbal exchange with the child that helps the child better situate the memory in the context of family, relationships, events, and, therefore, time. Parents (and other adults) in these ways guide the child in the selection and interpretation of its memories—and of its experiences generally, past, present, and future—and, therefore, in the formation of its autobiographical self-representation.

Once inner speech emerges, children begin to speak to themselves about their lives, thus narrating their autobiographical self-representations. In a self-narrating voice, children now begin inwardly to predicate and deny things of themselves, past, present, and future. For example, a school-age child might say to itself such things as, (1) "I used to live with Grandma"; (2) "I don't like school"; (3) "I got 100% on the test; I'm smart"; (4) "I wish I were better at gymnastics"; and (5) "When school starts, I'll be in the fourth grade." In saying such things, the child is not narrating a life *story*; it is not attempting to give its life meaning or purpose. Life stories do not emerge until adolescence. School-age children, although able to place past, present, and possible future experiences into the temporal framework of a course of life, do not yet have the cognitive abilities needed to narrate their lives as unfolding stories about who they are, how they have grown and evolved, and what they want to do or become in future years.[7] The narration of the self-representation at this point, therefore, is only an inner recording of memories, facts, hopes, fears, and future imaginings that have been stitched together in keeping track of an unfolding course of life.

Emergence of Ego Ideal and Superego— Completion of Self-System

The overcoming of splitting has multiple consequences for the self-system. In addition to integrating the self-representation and restabilizing the ego, it creates the ego ideal and the superego (and the shadow, too). Freud was the first to set forth the notions of the ego ideal and the superego, although he did not always clearly distinguish between them, sometimes speaking of the ego ideal as if it were a part of the superego. The ensuing account of the ego ideal and the superego differs significantly from Freud's.[8] However, it agrees with Freud's account on the matter of developmental timing: the ego ideal and the superego are created in the preschool years leading to middle childhood. Accordingly, it is only at the beginning of middle childhood, at approximately age five, that all four components of the self-system—ego, self-representation, ego ideal, and superego—are finally in place.

To recall, whereas the self-representation is a mental record of the ego's actual self, the self that the ego understands itself to be as a matter of fact, the ego ideal is a mental record of the ego's ideal self, which, as we have defined it, is the self that the ego would be if it realized its highest hopes and realized as well those of its other desires that are compatible with its highest hopes. This distinction between actual and ideal selves is unknown to the child whose self-representation is split. The child during the crisis substage of the crisis-adjustment stage in effect conflates the actual and the ideal. Having split itself into all-good and all-bad selves and in identifying only with the former, the child during the crisis substage believes that it is in fact a perfectly good child. In contrast, the school-age child, although believing that it is mostly good, which is to say, good enough for a mostly good relationship with parents, knows that it is not perfectly good. It acknowledges that it possesses negative as well as positive features and that its positive features are less than perfectly good. It thus knows that it is not the ideal self that earlier, as a child with a split all-good self-representation, it had believed itself to be. The school-age child for this reason relates to this former ideal self in a new way, no longer as actual self and now as possible ideal self. The former all-good self-representation is thus projected as a goal and becomes the ego ideal, a new component of the self-system.

The development of inner speech eventually gives a voice to the ego ideal. Speaking to itself inwardly, the child encourages itself to be the best it can possibly be so that it can be as close as possible to what it believes its parents (or guardians) want it to be. For example, in this inspiring voice the child might say to itself such things as, (1) "If I study hard, I can get good grades"; (2) "If I practice, I might win an award at the dance recital"; (3) "If I earn enough merit badges, I can become an Eagle Scout"; (4) "If I do the dishes and take out the trash, mom and dad will be pleased"; and (5) "I'm going to try to be more like Mary [a child, often praised by parents, who seems accomplished and perfect]." Once the child, in overcoming splitting, begins to distinguish between actual and ideal selves and, in mastering inner speech, begins to speak silently to itself, it begins to speak to itself not only as self-narrator but also as inspiring motivator, not only in a voice that represents its mostly good actual self (the self-representation) but also in a voice that represents its perfectly good ideal self (the ego ideal).

It is inherent to the idea of the ego ideal that one seeks to emulate people who seem to embody one's ego ideal. Such people, therefore, are role models, people who show both that it is possible and what it is like to be what one ideally would like to be. Clearly, for the school-age child, it is parents who first serve as role models. It is parents who teach the child the ideal it should aspire to and who themselves seem to embody that ideal. To aspire to be a perfect child (as defined by parents) is to aspire to be as much like parents as it is possible for a child to be. If parents are thus the first role models during middle childhood, other role models emerge as school-age children grow older. According to studies, these role models include older friends or relatives, idealized figures depicted in popular media, entertainers, and athletes.[9] However, studies agree that even as these new role models emerge, it remains parents who are most often mentioned by school-age children as the people they most respect and admire.

The superego also emerges in the transition to middle childhood. The foundation of the superego begins being laid in the adjustment substage of the crisis-adjustment stage, when the older toddler, and then the preschooler, struggles to eliminate the outbursts of rage, defiance, and selfishness that provoke the disciplining actions of the caregiver. The child's struggle against these outbursts is its first major effort to regulate its behavior, where such self-regulation is the basic function of the superego. By the time the transition to middle childhood is complete, the child has made the following two major strides toward the formation of the superego: (1) it has accepted the fact that parental prohibitions against outbursts of unbridled self-assertion must be obeyed; and (2) it has (for reasons yet to be explained) achieved the self-control needed to comply with those prohibitions. The school-age child, having thus accepted the first and most basic rules of conduct imposed by parents and having achieved a good measure of self-control, has laid the foundation for the superego.

With the foundation thus laid, the superego proper emerges when, in the transition to middle childhood, the child internalizes parental prohibitions, adopting them as its own, and when the child finally understands not only *that* but also *why* it must comply with these prohibitions. Unlike the split older toddler, who believes that it is all good and that there is an all-good caregiver to love and protect it, the school-age child knows that it is not all good and that its parents, although mostly good, are also not all good. The school-age child for this reason understands that it must regulate its behavior to ensure that it remains mostly good, which is to say, good enough to remain in the good graces of mostly good but imperfect parents. Knowing that such self-regulation is required, the school-age child begins to monitor its behavior with parental expectations in mind. Having already accepted and internalized the most basic parental rules of expected behavior, those prohibiting outbursts of unbridled self-assertion, the child now accepts and internalizes additional such rules, rules that define, not ideal behavior (which is specified by the ego ideal), but rather behavior that parents in fact expect from the child. The fact that the child has now accepted and internalized this expanded set of parental rules indicates that the superego, the agency of self-discipline, is fully installed.

Initially, the superego may be active with only rudimentary private speech, a primary function of which is the self-regulation of behavior.[10] However, once self-directed speech is internalized, the superego becomes active with its distinctive inner voice. By age six or seven the child uses inner speech not only to think operationally, to narrate its life course, and to inspire itself to strive toward being a perfectly good child but also to discipline itself to behave at least acceptably well, as parents require. The child thus internalizes the voice of parental authority, putting pressure on itself to meet parental expectations, if not perfectly, as encouraged by the voice of the ego ideal, at least well enough to be a "good enough" child. The child, speaking to itself in the voice of the superego, now begins to command itself to do what its parents require it to do, to praise itself when it does, and to scold itself when it does not.

The ego ideal and the superego work together as complementary instruments of self-motivation. The ego ideal motivates by desire and inspiration, the superego by fear and discipline. The ego ideal works by force of attraction, by pulling the school-age child toward the realization of its highest hopes (to be a perfectly good child) and toward the satisfaction of its desires generally, insofar as they are compatible with its highest hopes. In other words, the ego ideal motivates the child to pursue its positive self-interest generally. In complementary fashion, the superego works by force of pressure, by exhorting the school-age child to avoid behaviors that would lead to unwanted consequences. In other words, the superego motivates the child to pursue its negative self-interest generally. The ego ideal is the carrot, the telic cause; the superego is the stick, the efficient cause. The ego ideal motivates actions that are thought to lead to happiness; the superego motivates actions that are thought to avoid unhappiness.

The addition of the ego ideal and the superego to the self-representation completes the self-system. The ego in a sense now has three selves, an actual self, corresponding to the self-representation; an ideal self, corresponding to the ego ideal; and a good enough self, corresponding to the superego. As the ego now has these three selves, it also has three inner voices representing these selves, a narrating voice representing the actual self, an inspiring voice representing the ideal self, and a disciplining voice representing the good enough self. The ego speaks to itself in its inspiring voice, which motivates it to be as good as it can possibly be; and it speaks to itself in its disciplining voice, which motivates it to be at least good enough to remain on good terms with parents. Then, having thus spoken *to* itself in these voices, the ego speaks *for* itself in its narrating voice to tell itself what in fact it believes itself to be. In being the voice with which the ego speaks for itself rather than only to itself, the narrator voice is the master voice of the self-system.

With its completion in the transition to middle childhood, the self-system becomes a stable basis for continuing development until adolescence. In later chapters, we explain how the self-system—as a complete, four-component system—is challenged during adolescence and then reconstituted in early adulthood and how it is then challenged and reconstituted again, repeatedly, in later stages of development. Table 10.1 recapitulates the discussion of the self-system thus far, summarizing the emergence of the self-system from

Table 10.1. The Formation of the Self-System

Component	Function, content	Newborn	Infant (8 weeks to 8 or 9 months)	Young toddler (8 or 9 months to approximately 18 months)	Older toddler and preschooler (18 to 36+ months)	School-age child (approximately 4 or 5 years to puberty)
Ego (self of self-system)	Subject and executive agency of consciousness	Ego present as subject of consciousness but might not yet be active as agency	Ego grows stronger as subject of consciousness and begins performing basic cognitive and practical functions as executive agency of consciousness	Ego grows stronger as subject of consciousness Basic executive functions, now employed in exploration of the object world, grow stronger First forms of impulse control emerge	Executive functions develop with emergence of symbol-based preoperational thinking and corresponding symbol-guided action Ego destabilized by splitting	Inner speech emerges as voice of executive functions, which develop to the level of concrete operational thinking and verbally premeditated intentional action Ego restabilized by repression, which replaces splitting as primary defense mechanism

continued on next page

Table 10.1. Continued.

Component	Function, content	Newborn	Infant (8 weeks to 8 or 9 months)	Young toddler (8 or 9 months to approximately 18 months)	Older toddler and preschooler (18 to 36+ months)	School-age child (approximately 4 or 5 years to puberty)
Self-representation	Representation of the worldly self that the ego believes itself to be—the ego as object or Me	No self-representation Immediate, implicit internal self-awareness	No self-representation Infant's implicit self-awareness brought into focus and further developed by the caregiver's imitations of the infant	Self-representation emerges Implicit self-awareness transformed into self-representation once explicit self-recognition emerges (15–18 months)	Self-representation is split into all-good and all-bad representations, with only the former accepted as *self*-representation (18–24 months) Split in self-representation gradually mends (24–36+ months)	Splitting overcome; self-representation is integrated as representation of a "mostly good" child Child begins using inner speech to narrate self-representation, now an autobiographical representation of a course of life
Ego ideal	Representation of the worldly self that the ego ideally would like to be	No ego ideal	No ego ideal	No ego ideal	No ego ideal Representation of all-good child is precursor of ego ideal	Representation of all-good child, no longer the self-representation, is projected as ego ideal Inner speech gives an (inspiring) voice to ego ideal

Superego	Ego as agency of self-discipline	No superego	No superego	No superego Child's struggle to control impulses responsible for the behavior of all-bad child lays foundation for superego	Superego emerges as child, having achieved greatly improved self-control, internalizes and thus adopts parental rules of required conduct Inner speech gives a (commanding, praising, blaming) voice to superego
Shadow (unconscious subsystem beneath self-system)	Psychic materials that have been repressed because they once posed serious threats to the ego	No shadow	No shadow	No shadow Representation of all-bad child is precursor of shadow	Shadow emerges Impulses (and cognitive content) responsible for behavior of the all-bad older toddler are repressed Neurological traces of repressed all-bad child remain as school-age child's shadow

birth, when only the ego is present, to the establishment of the complete self-system at the beginning of middle childhood.

Repression, the Achievement of Self-Control, and the Formation of the Shadow

Formed at the same time as the ego ideal and the superego is a psychic structure that Carl Jung called the "shadow." As explained in chapter 5, the shadow is a structure that, although not a component of the self-system, is inherently tied to it. It is the hidden underside of the self-system containing everything about the ego that the ego finds too threatening to acknowledge and thus accept as part of its conscious life. Jung focused on the shadow as it underlies the adult self-system and as it sometimes awakens and reveals itself to consciousness in the second half of life, during what he called the "individuation" process. We discuss this adult shadow and why it can, even if it ordinarily does not, manifest itself during midlife in chapters 12 and 13. Here the point is to explain the origins of the shadow in childhood. The first version of the shadow emerges long before adulthood. Like the first versions of the ego ideal and the superego, it emerges in the transition from early to middle childhood.

Discussion of the shadow brings us to the controversial topic of repression, the defense mechanism that creates the shadow. To set the context for a discussion of repression, we need to return to a question previously introduced but not yet answered, "How does the child moving from early to middle childhood achieve the self-control needed to eliminate the unbridled outbursts of the older toddler?" The default answer to this question is that the child achieves this self-control as part of the normal maturation process. Such maturation includes both neurological and experiential maturation. Neurologically, normal maturation includes the further development of the prefrontal cortex and executive functions and, therefore, the further development of top-down control of behavior. Experientially, normal maturation includes an increasing understanding on the part of the child that the caregiver, although frequently angry or absent, is kinder and more reliable than was feared; that the world, although large and uncertain, is safer than was feared; and that desires, although seemingly urgent, are often less dire and difficult to satisfy than was feared.

This maturation hypothesis is clearly correct as far as it goes. It quite evidently provides an explanation for much of the improvement in self-control in the preschool years. The question is whether the maturation hypothesis provides a complete explanation of the transformation that occurs. Psychoanalysis holds that it does not, arguing that a second hypothesis is needed, the repression hypothesis. Psychoanalysis maintains that self-control is achieved in the transition from early to middle childhood at least in part because repression removes from consciousness instinctual urges that, in early childhood, overpower the child and cause it to behave in ways that bring it into danger of parental punishment.[11] In eliminating such urges from consciousness, this repression—which Freud called "primal repression"—removes impulses that had overpowered the child and thus dramatically improves its self-control.[12]

According to the psychoanalytic view, therefore, early childhood repression helps to bring about greatly improved self-control because it removes overpowering instinctual—and, specifically, sexual—impulses from consciousness and thereby creates a condition of calm that allows the child to exercise its will much more effectively. Psychoanalysis refers to this condition of calm as "psychosexual latency" and holds that it obtains throughout middle childhood. Unlike the maturation hypothesis, this repression hypothesis is not clearly correct. Indeed, the consensus is that the hypothesis is suspect, if not discredited. Accordingly, since we will be formulating a revised version of the repression hypothesis, it is necessary that we look more closely at the original psychoanalytic version and the criticisms that have been brought against it.

Among the criticisms of the Freudian conception of repression, the following two are the most important: (1) there is no evidence of containment under pressure as seems to be implied by the idea that impulses, instinctual or other, are removed from consciousness by sustained repressive inhibition; and, more seriously, (2) the very notion of repression is inconsistent, presupposing both awareness and unawareness of what is repressed, awareness because the ego must at some level be aware of what it represses to know to repress it and to keep it repressed, and unawareness because repression removes what is repressed from consciousness.

The first criticism, that there is no evidence of containment under pressure, as seems to be implied by the notion of repressive inhibition, has teeth only if one subscribes to Freud's hydraulic conception of repression. According to this conception, repression is a sustained targeted inhibition (counterforce: "anticathexis" or "countercathexis") that, equal to or greater than the force of the impulses it represses, submerges these impulses beneath consciousness. Freud says,

> The process of repression is not to be regarded as an event which takes place *once*, the results of which are permanent, as when some living thing has been killed and from that time onward is dead; repression demands a persistent expenditure of force, and if this were to cease the success of the repression would be jeopardized, so that a fresh act of repression would be necessary. We may suppose that the repressed exercises a continuous pressure in the direction of the conscious, so that this pressure must be balanced by an unceasing counter-pressure.[13]

In Freud's view, impulses repressively removed from consciousness continue to assert themselves, their upsurge now blocked by the repressive downforce that contains them. In this view, the ego, in repressing threatening impulses, contains them under pressure in a psychic underworld, where they continue to be active, powerfully astir. Primal repression of instinctual impulses during early childhood is thus the "lid" that keeps threatening instinctual drives of the id contained.

This hydraulic conception of repression has long been considered suspect, and the criticism under discussion points to one of its major weaknesses: there is no evidence of a potentially explosive standoff between repressed impulses and a repressive counterforce that keeps them contained. The lack of such evidence has led theorists either to dismiss the notion of repression altogether or to reconceive it in a nonhydraulic way. We follow the latter course here and propose a conception of repression that, although agreeing with the original conception on the point that repression is a targeted inhibition of threatening impulses (and corresponding cognitive content), disagrees with the original conception on the point that such inhibition must lead to a standoff of force versus counterforce.

The conception of repression proposed here does away with the idea of force versus counterforce by holding that repression, rather than containing threatening impulses under pressure, instead depletes them of energy, thus weakening them, if not to the point of complete deactivation, at least to the point at which they no longer pose a significant threat to the ego. Repression in this way weakens threatening impulses until they become safe and manageable and, therefore, no longer need to be further repressed. At this point, impulses become safe because, even if still threatening to some degree, they are no longer strong enough to trigger behavior that might lead to dire consequences. Correspondingly, impulses become manageable because the ego now exercises at least adequate control over them, either by controlling them directly by exercise of will or, as we shall see, by controlling them indirectly by deploying defense mechanisms in addition to repression. In sum, the conception of repression proposed here holds that repression is a short-term inhibition that weakens what it targets rather than a long-term inhibition that contains what it targets.

Although the account of repression formulated thus far has focused on threatening impulses, it can be widened to apply to psychic content of any sort, including, most importantly, cognitive content, such as thoughts, images, perceptions, and memories. Repression targets anything within consciousness that is highly charged with negative energy, which is to say anything that is sensed to pose a serious threat to life or well-being. All psychic content of this sort provokes intense anxiety and is for this reason a candidate for repression, whether it be an impulse or associated thoughts, images, perceptions, or memories. In our conception, therefore, repression works simultaneously to reduce the energy available to impulses that trigger intense anxiety and, in a manner to be explained, to prevent the production of cognitive content associated with those impulses.

Recent work in neuroscience has shown that voluntary inhibition of thoughts and memories (occasioned by cue words) initiates neurological processes that impair the ability to retrieve the targeted thoughts and memories. This retrieval impairment has been shown to occur with neutral thoughts and memories, to occur more often and to a greater extent with negatively charged thoughts and memories, and to occur rarely if ever with positively charged thoughts and memories. Additionally, voluntary inhibition has also been shown to be effective in deterring behaviors associated with inhibited thoughts and memories. Furthermore, the efficacy of voluntary inhibition in impairing the ability to retrieve negatively charged thoughts and memories has been shown to be greater for people with a history of trauma in their lives than for people without such a history.[14]

This research has focused only on mildly aversive cognitive content, not on the highly threatening cognitive content that triggers repression as we have described it. Moreover, the research is still in its early stages and is not without skeptics. Nevertheless, the research offers a promising way of understanding how voluntary inhibition can initiate neurological responses that result in unconscious repression, where the repression is of a neurologically programed rather than hydraulic sort. The research provides a promising way of understanding how voluntary inhibition, if applied with strength and frequency, can be the initiating impetus leading to neurological changes that remove from consciousness not only highly charged threatening impulses but also the cognitive content associated with such impulses.

The neuroscientific research on repression cited in endnote 14 suggests that the process leading to repression can be understood from a neurological perspective to be a complex but primarily top-down reprogramming of brain areas responsible for producing impulses and memories. The prefrontal cortex, the primary seat of the ego's executive functions, sends inhibitory signals to these brain areas, primary among which are subcortical regions such as the amygdala (fear, strong negative affect) and the hippocampus (memory). The inhibitory signals sent from the prefrontal cortex, repeated with strength and frequency, recode the neurological regions that energize threatening impulses and that release related cognitive content in such ways that they greatly reduce the energy available to the impulses and impair the ability to retrieve the cognitive content. Eventually, the impulses, reduced in energy, recede into the background, and the cognitive content is no longer available to consciousness.

The foregoing discussion leads to the following generalizations: (1) that the inhibition leading to repression works neurologically, not hydraulically; (2) that this inhibition removes not only threatening impulses from consciousness but also the cognitive content that informs and inflames such impulses; (3) that threatening impulses are removed by energy reduction, which weakens them until they become safe and manageable; (4) that threatening cognitive content is removed by "retrieval impairment," which makes it unavailable to consciousness; and (5) that actions that had been based on threatening impulses and corresponding cognitive content disappear as the former grow weaker and as the latter becomes irretrievable. These conclusions indicate that repression is best approached from multiple perspectives, including most importantly psychological, neurological, and behavioral perspectives. Psychologically, repressive inhibition leads to energy reduction and retrieval impairment; neurologically, signals sent from executive areas of the brain reprogram subcortical regions; and behaviorally, actions based on threatening impulses and corresponding cognitive content cease to occur.

The conception of repression just set forth is henceforth referred to as the "energy-reduction" conception. This designation has the advantage of highlighting the most important point of contrast between the conception of repression presented here and the original psychoanalytic conception, namely, that repression, rather than being a long-term inhibition that contains the repressed, is a short-term inhibition that deenergizes the repressed.

However, this designation has the disadvantage of making no mention of the cognitive side of repression. To include the cognitive side, we would have been stuck with the "energy-reduction, retrieval-impairment" conception of repression or with a corresponding unattractive acronym, which would have been awkward. Accordingly, the reader should keep in mind that the shorter "energy-reduction" designation is intended to convey not only the impulse or energy-reduction side of repression but also the cognitive or retrieval-impairment side.

Let us now apply the energy-reduction conception of repression to the situation of the child caught in the throes of splitting. The process leading to repression might unfold as follows. The older toddler, fearing the loss of the caregiver in a world that has grown larger and more uncertain, begins mightily to resist the highly charged negative impulses, thoughts, and perceptions that, in provoking its temper tantrums, seem to be putting its relationship with the caregiver at risk. The child mobilizes all resources at its disposal against these impulses, thoughts, and perceptions because its struggle for self-control is seemingly a life-or-death matter, a matter of keeping or losing the caregiver, the child's lifeline. Initially, the child's attempts thus to inhibit threatening impulses and cognitive content do little good. The child, however, has no choice but to persevere, since it finds itself in a situation with seemingly dire consequences.

Fortunately, with perseverance the child eventually succeeds in resisting the expression of the targeted impulses, thoughts, and perceptions to some extent and, in doing so, in reducing the energy of the impulses and the frequency of the thoughts and perceptions. This initial success in repressive inhibition makes further success easier, since the impulses, thoughts, and perceptions still needing repression are now less energetic and frequent than they were before. Accordingly, each round of repressive inhibition is more successful than the previous until a point is reached at which targeted impulses are no longer strong enough and targeted thoughts and perceptions no longer frequent enough to provoke the unacceptable behaviors that had made their repression necessary. At this point, the impulses, thoughts, and perceptions that had seemed to be putting the child in danger recede from consciousness. The impulses, owing to energy reduction, become safe and manageable and thus withdraw from the forefront to the background of consciousness. The thoughts and perceptions, owing to retrieval impairment, cease being produced and are thus lost to consciousness. Correspondingly, the behaviors that had seemed to jeopardize the child's relationship with the caregiver cease to occur. Such is the repression hypothesis as we propose it here.

Why, it might be asked, cannot the same result be explained by the maturation hypothesis? The answer is that maturation takes time, and the older toddler does not have time or at least does not know that it has time. The child's existence is seemingly on the line. The child, therefore, must do something immediately and decisively to improve its relationship with the caregiver. Unfortunately, neurological growth, although rapid in early childhood, unfolds at its own pace. Moreover, relevant insights that maturation will confirm—that the caregiver is mostly good, that the world is mostly safe, and that cooperating with parents is the best way to satisfy desires—are not yet available to the child. Anyway, even if these insights were available, it is implausible that they would suffice on their own to subdue the impulses, thoughts, and perceptions that, to the child, seem to be jeopardizing its relationship with the caregiver. Adults who suffer from psychological disorders are helped only so much by learning that the impulses they feel impelled to act on are counterproductive and that the cognitive content that informs and inflames those impulses is irrational. A young child is less able to apply such insights effectively, especially when, owing to the pace of maturation, they are not yet available. The older toddler for this reason needs to take immediate and decisive action, and so, I suggest, it does. It begins to resist the impulses, thoughts, and perceptions that overwhelm it, as if its life were at stake.

As the child is engaged in this repressive effort, neurological growth and the insights of more mature experience do in time play a role, and in doing so they assist the child in its struggle for self-control. What at first was only desperate resistance to threatening psychic materials, therefore, increasingly becomes a process facilitated by neurological growth and maturing insight. As repression depletes threatening impulses of energy and impairs the ability to retrieve corresponding thoughts and perceptions, neurological growth makes it easier for the child to control its impulses, and emerging insights assuage the child's fears and help it understand that self-control and cooperation are in its interest. Repression and maturation in this way very likely work together to help the child overcome splitting and achieve self-control. Repression starts the process by strongly resisting threatening impulses, thus weakening them, and by interdicting corresponding thoughts and perceptions, thus decreasing the frequency with which they occur. Neurological growth and emerging insight then assist the process to completion. Without urgency, maturation on its own might be able to bring the child to the self-control characteristic of middle childhood. However, the older toddler, in the throes of the rapprochement crisis, faces what seems like life-threatening danger and needs to act. For this reason, it initiates a maximum inhibitory response, the kind needed for repression.

The discussion thus far suggests that early childhood repression plays a positive developmental role. The role it plays is by no means completely positive because, as is explained soon, it leaves behind the (childhood) shadow and restricts the availability of freely mobile psychic energy, negative consequences of considerable importance. Nevertheless, early childhood repression plays a necessary and, therefore, a *net* positive role *at the developmental juncture at which it occurs.* It does so not only because it helps the child gain self-control but also because, in doing so, it eliminates the issues that had plagued the older toddler, including the rapprochement crisis, the fear that the caregiver is not reliable, and splitting.

Early childhood repression eliminates these issues by solving (rather than hiding) the primary problems in the child's relationship with the caregiver. Most importantly, early childhood repression frees the child of the strongly negative impulses, thoughts, and perceptions that had exaggerated the caregiver's "bad" qualities, thus deaccentuating those qualities and allowing the child to see that the caregiver's good qualities greatly outweigh the bad. The child, freed of its own negativity toward the caregiver, thus sees much less negativity in the caregiver. In this way, the postrepression child relates to a very different caregiver than the prerepression child did. It relates to a caregiver who, no longer split into two caregivers, one all good and the other all bad, is now a single caregiver who on balance is much more good than bad. Early childhood repression, therefore, is not a means by which an earlier unhappy relationship between an all-bad child and an all-bad caregiver is hidden from view; rather, it is a means by which a mostly happy relationship between a mostly good child and a mostly good caregiver is achieved.

That early childhood repression plays a net positive developmental role at the time it occurs is not uncharacteristic of repression. Repression is frequently a trade-off; something is repressively removed from consciousness so that life can be made bearable or feasible and so that development can thus move forward. That which is lost can be essential or inessential to one's wholeness as a person. If essential, then what repression removes from consciousness may later need to be restored if development at that time is to move forward. In this way, repression, which might be necessary for developmental advance at one stage, can become an impediment to developmental advance at a later stage, thus requiring a later "return of the repressed" if development is once again to move forward. Clearly, many instances of repression merely remove something from consciousness without facilitating developmental advance in doing so. This fact notwithstanding, some types of repression can be necessary conditions of developmental advance when they occur, even though they may set the stage for a later return of the repressed.

One such type is the repression of traumatic memories, now called "memory amnesia." Although the notion of repressed memories met with a good deal of skepticism in the 1990s, when it was the focus of highly publicized legal cases, the notion continues to be widely accepted among mental health professionals, including 70% of clinical psychologists.[15] This wide acceptance of the notion is understandable because repression of traumatic memories is frequently necessary, especially for young people, if they are to extricate themselves from harms they have suffered and thus be able to move forward in development. However, the memories thus repressed might eventually need to be restored and the issues related to those memories worked through before developmental advance can occur at a later time.

A second type of repression that can be necessary for development advance at one time only to set the stage for a later return of the repressed is repression of impulses that are biologically or psychologically inherent to a person. Examples of such impulses are those related to sexual or gender orientation, personality type, emotional temperament, and intellectual or artistic aspirations. When social or family pressures require repression of impulses of any of these sorts, inherited parts of a person are left behind without being expressed, thus often causing persistent feelings of incompleteness, lack of fulfillment, or inauthenticity. Repression of inherent impulses is sometimes required in early adulthood as a precondition of performing adult social roles. It can, therefore, be developmentally necessary at that time, even though it leaves behind unresolved issues that might eventually need to be faced and worked through if development is to continue to move forward later in the adult years. We have more to say about repression of inherent impulses in ensuing chapters.

In mentioning the phenomenon of the return of the repressed, the question arises how repressed impulses can spring back to life, sometimes suddenly and powerfully, if, as we have hypothesized, repression of impulses works by energy reduction. The Freudian conception of repression provides a simple, if implausible, explanation of the return of the repressed. According to this explanation, repressed impulses sometimes spring back to life because the inhibitory counterpressure that contains them is weakened, thus allowing the impulses to erupt from confinement. Our energy-reduction conception of repression cannot explain the return of the repressed in this way, since, according to it, repressed impulses have been weakened and, therefore, are not highly charged and primed to reassert themselves.

Instead, the energy-reduction conception explains the return of the repressed in terms of a reactivation of the neurological programming that had been overwritten by repression. In this view, external triggers or developmental challenges are sometimes strong enough to reactivate the prerepression programming of brain centers responsible for impulse strength and memory retrieval, thus allowing these centers to reenergize repressed impulses and to resume production of repressed cognitive content. With prerepression neurological programming thus reactivated, what had been repressed returns to life, not because it has been loosed from confinement, but rather because it has been given a second life. Having been repressed by energy reduction and retrieval impairment, it is given a second life by energy restoration and retrieval repair. The return of the repressed, even in cases of sudden and powerful return, can be explained more plausibly in this way than by the release-from-containment metaphor.

Having made the case that early childhood repression is necessary for developmental advance and, therefore, that it plays a net positive role when it occurs, we need now to look at the other, negative, side of the story. One important negative consequence of early childhood repression is that it leaves behind the childhood shadow, which is the topic we are here preparing to explain. However, an even more important negative consequence is that it incurs a significant reduction in the amount of psychic energy at the child's disposal. Although early childhood repression does not cause psychosexual latency, as psychoanalysis maintains, it does cause an energetic calming of the child's experience generally. It has this effect because the energy available to the child's self-assertive impulses, which repression targets, is not energy reserved exclusively for those impulses. It is, rather, unbound or freely mobile psychic energy, energy that is available for all the child's actions and experiences.

In chapter 8, we introduced the hypothesis that it is just such energy that helps explain why the young toddler explores the object world with reckless passion and rapturous delight. Now we can add the companion hypothesis that it is the same energy that helps explain why the older toddler's displeasures are expressed in meltdowns of shrieking and flailing. The availability of unbound or freely mobile energy means that everything the toddler does or experiences is highly charged with energy. For the young toddler, who is interested above all in the object world, this energy potentiates curiosity into rapture; and for the older toddler, who has grown ambivalent toward the caregiver, it potentiates frustration into rage.

The unbound energy at the young and older toddler's disposal is a "nonspecific amplifier" of experience.[16] Not reserved for preassigned functions, this energy is available to intensify all the toddler's actions and experiences. The benefit of having such energy at its disposal is that the toddler is intensely alive. However, the cost is that the toddler, despite making some progress in impulse control, is vulnerable to emotional outpourings, whether enraptured or enraged, that are well beyond its ability to control. The young toddler has no need to control its rapture. However, the older toddler has an urgent need to control its rage. It is the older toddler's outbursts of rage, defiance, and selfishness that seem to be undermining its relationship with the caregiver, the child's lifeline. These outbursts, therefore, must be stopped. Repression comes to the rescue by dialing down the energy available for their expression and, as we have argued, by impairing the ability to retrieve the thoughts and perceptions (of the bad caregiver) that had helped incite them. The negative impulses that had overwhelmed the child are thus depleted of much of their energy; the negative cognitive content that had provoked the child's fury thus disappears; and, therefore, the child is able to exercise its will much more effectively. Repression in this way helps the child achieve self-control.

However, this improved self-control is achieved at a high price. The child overcomes its susceptibility to rage only by forfeiting its capacity for rapture. Early childhood repression, I suggest, in reducing the unbound energy available for actions and experiences with a negative energetic discharge, reduces the unbound energy available for all types of actions and experiences, including those with a positive energetic discharge. Early childhood repression in this way decreases the intensity of the child's life in all modalities and expressions. In this view, the enduring effect of early childhood repression is not that it decreases only instinctual or sexual energy, thus resulting in psychosexual latency. Rather, the enduring effect is that it decreases the unbound, freely mobile energy available to all actions and experiences, thus resulting in a marked reduction in the energy of the psychic atmosphere overall. This conclusion, although speculative to some degree, is here set forth as a follow-up hypothesis to the energy-reduction conception of repression.

This subduing of the psychic atmosphere marks a developmental transition from what is often called "early childhood spirituality" to the beginning of what might be called "ego-ascendancy." Early childhood is often spoken of as having a spiritual character because, as we have seen, young children live in the presence of a power greater than themselves, a power they are powerless to control, a power that can dissolve their boundaries in outpourings of emotional intensity. This power is intimately tied to the caregiver, who is thus the "goddess" of early childhood spirituality. Descriptions of early childhood spirituality ordinarily focus on the positive rather than the negative expressions of this "goddess power." They ordinarily highlight the raptures experienced by the young toddler as it explores the world in interaction with a loving, playful caregiver rather than on the rage experienced by the older toddler as it strives to reestablish closeness with the caregiver only to find that the caregiver is inattentive, absent, or "cruel." This association of early childhood spirituality with its positive rather than negative expressions is understandable, even though, in our view, it is the same power, unbound psychic energy, that is responsible for both. In any case, as we have proposed, early childhood repression brings about a marked reduction in the unbound energy available to the child, thus lowering the overall intensity of its experience and in this way bringing the period of early childhood spirituality to an end.

With early childhood spirituality thus coming to an end, a long period of ego ascendancy begins, a period during which the ego, having achieved stability, self-control, and well-defended boundaries, begins implicitly to think of itself as the sovereign power of the soul. Having successfully repressed its rage, and, with it, a power it was previously powerless to control, the ego gains confidence in its own power and assumes the stance, bordering on belief, that it is in charge within the soul. This presumption of sovereignty, although completely implicit and, therefore, not a recognized feature of the self-representation, is nonetheless basic to the ego's self-understanding, from middle childhood forward.

The thesis that the ego, from middle childhood forward, carries with it this presumption of sovereignty is here proposed without further defense and is not discussed again until part 3, which focuses on spiritual development. We return to the thesis in part 3 because many spiritual traditions maintain that the ego's presumption of sovereignty stands in the way of spiritual development. Spiritual traditions differ on how the ego is disabused of its presumption of being in charge within the soul, but they agree that the presumption is deeply rooted and must be removed if spiritual development is to unfold successfully to its conclusion. Many people have overplayed the idea of early childhood spirituality and have also overplayed the idea that this early spirituality comes to an end with the ascendancy of the ego, this author included. Nevertheless, these ideas, properly framed and qualified, are not without a good measure of truth.

The transition from early childhood spirituality to ego ascendancy is what in psychoanalysis is referred to as the transition from the preoedipal to the oedipal stage of life. This transition is described as the turning point at which a child is forced to turn away from an energetically powerful life of embodied, instinctual, and emotional intimacy with a female caregiver and is forced to begin living an energetically subdued life of reason (language), agency, self-control, and obedience to male authority. Our view agrees with this psychoanalytic view, albeit with four major provisos, two of which were explained in our discussion of psychoanalytic feminist theory in chapter 4. These two provisos are (1) that the caregiver of the preoedipal stage is be understood as female only because women historically have been assigned the primary role of caring for young children, as Dorothy Dinnerstein and Nancy Chodorow have argued; and (2) that the male authority of the oedipal stage is to be understood primarily in a symbolic way, as signifying the authority of male-dominant culture, irrespective of whether there is literally a male figure within the family who represents this authority, as Luce Irigaray and Julia Kristeva, following Jacques Lacan, have stressed.

As we learned in chapter 4, the paths of women's and men's ego development, despite unfolding in the same basic, "from-matriarchal-to patriarchal," direction, are already diverging during the preoedipal stage, owing to the historically female-centered character of this stage; and they continue to diverge in the oedipal and postoedipal stages, owing to the historically male-dominant character of these stages. We return to these differences in women's and men's ego development in part 3 of the book, where we discuss how differences in women's and men's ego development early in life are the bases of corresponding differences in their spiritual development later in life.

The other two provisos to the psychoanalytic account of the transition from the preoedipal to the oedipal stage concern early childhood repression, the intrapsychic side of the transition. Our account of this repression differs from the psychoanalytic account on the following two points: (1) that the outer cause of early childhood repression is the child's need to safeguard its relationship with the caregiver, not the child's need to capitulate to the wrath of a father figure; and (2) that the effect of early childhood repression is a pervasive energy reduction affecting the psychic atmosphere generally rather than a selectively focused reduction affecting only instinctual, especially psychosexual, drives. In our view, it is an irony that the child can safeguard its relationship with the caregiver only by separating itself from "her," only by turning away from the fully embodied, intensely alive, female-centered preoedipal world and submitting itself to the "father" and the male-dominant patriarchal world.

We can now turn to the second and most serious of the criticisms of the Freudian repression hypothesis, that the very notion of repression is inconsistent. Fortunately, this criticism, like the first, has teeth only if one assumes the hydraulic conception of repression. The ego must do what is logically impossible, keep its eye on threatening materials it has removed from view, only if those materials are still asserting themselves against the ego's repressive containment of them. However, the ego no longer needs to keep its eye on such materials after, as with impulses, energy reduction has weakened them, thus rendering them safe and allowing them to recede from view, or after, as with cognitive content, retrieval impairment has halted its production, thus rendering it inaccessible to consciousness. According to the energy-reduction conception of repression, although the ego must keep its eye on threatening materials during the time it is repressing them, it ceases needing to do so once these materials, successfully repressed, are safely manageable or no longer available.

Although repressed impulses can remain active and even threatening to some extent, they have been "tamed" by energy reduction and disconnected from inflaming cognitive content by retrieval impairment. For these reasons, repressed impulses ordinarily arise and disappear without commanding attention or significantly disturbing the flow of life. In response to external triggers, repressed impulses might on occasion be reenergized to an alarming extent and might for this reason require special efforts of self-regulation or even the employment of secondary defense mechanisms. For example, a child might become so angry with a parent that it needs to find a safe way to ventilate its anger, perhaps by displacing or sublimating it or otherwise dealing with it with secondary defense mechanisms. However, in most cases of this sort, when repressed impulses are stirred, the impulses that are energized remain safely manageable and, therefore, do not cause significant harm.

In sum, the energy-reduction conception of repression avoids the contradiction that plagues the Freudian conception by holding that the ego, although both aware and unaware of the threatening materials it represses, is not aware and unaware of these materials *at the same time*. The ego is vigilantly aware of the threatening materials it represses during the process of repressing them; then, once repression has rendered these materials either safely manageable or unavailable, the ego no longer needs to monitor them as it did before. These materials are thus repressively removed from consciousness not by forcibly submerging them beneath consciousness, which is impossible, but rather, in the case of threatening impulses, by deenergizing them so that they recede from view and, in the case of threatening cognitive content, by overwriting the neurological instructions needed for its retrieval.

Having defended the energy-reduction conception of repression, we can finally return to the point that occasioned the foregoing discussion of repression, namely, that repression is the cause of the shadow. In our view, repression creates the shadow in the transition from early to middle childhood because, in targeting the impulses, thoughts, and perceptions responsible for the older toddler's outbursts, it targets the split-off bad child, which, in being repressed, becomes the shadow. Corresponding to how the ego ideal replaces the split all-good child, the shadow thus replaces the split all-bad child. Corresponding to how the ego ideal is a transformation of the older toddler's all-good self from an actual, lived self into a projected, to-be-strived-for self, the shadow is a transformation of the older toddler's all-bad self—or, rather, negative alter ego or nonself—from an actual, lived self into a repressed, dead-and-forgotten self. The all-bad child that thus becomes the shadow is "dead" because repression has deprived it of the energy that had given it life, and it is "forgotten" because repression has made it impossible to retrieve its thoughts and perceptions (of the all-bad caregiver) from memory. In this way, I propose, what was the intensely alive all-bad child becomes a shade of the underworld, deprived of life and lost to memory.

Although the all-bad child, in the form of the shadow, is dead and forgotten, it is not expunged from existence. Traces of it are left behind, leaving open the possibility of its "resurrection." Specifically, neurological pathways established by the all-bad child's repeated outbursts are not dismantled. Repression causes the brain to overwrite the instructions governing these pathways so that problematic impulses are reduced in energy and corresponding cognitive content becomes irretrievable. However, this overwriting does not erase the original instructions that are overwritten. The original instructions remain as a default that can be restored to priority, especially under conditions of stress, when more advanced functioning tends to yield to more primitive. Impulses that had been subject to energy reduction can thus be reenergized, and cognitive content that had been rendered inaccessible can thus be retrieved. Accordingly, although the all-bad child, as the shadow of the school-age child, is dead and forgotten, its distinctive impulses, thoughts, and perceptions—and, therefore, its distinctive action tendencies—are preserved for possible reactivation, perhaps, as explained in the next chapter, during adolescence.

We should add that the shadow, like the self-representation, the ego ideal, and the superego, has a voice. The shadow's voice is ordinarily quiet when the shadow itself is quiet, as is the case during middle childhood. However, when the shadow awakens, as can happen when the self-system is unstable or undergoing stage-related change, the shadow's voice can emerge. Because the shadow consists of impulses and cognitive content that the ego had once perceived as dangers to its life or well-being, the voice of the shadow most often speaks to the ego in menacing ways, or at least it does so initially, in early stages of shadow awakening. In thus menacing the ego, the shadow voice typically—indeed, archetypally—speaks as an adversary and tempter. Speaking as an adversary, this voice challenges the ego's self-system by mocking features of the self-representation and by deriding goals of the ego ideal and rules of the superego. Concomitantly, speaking as a tempter, this voice undermines the ego's self-system by enticing the ego to act on impulses disavowed by the self-representation and proscribed by the ego ideal and the superego.

Although the voice of the shadow is thus most often the voice of an adversary and tempter, it can be—should the ego be ready to explore changes to its self-system—the voice of a counselor and guide. It can be a voice that leads the ego through needed but frightening periods of self-transformation, especially when the ego, at a developmental impasse, must face a return of the repressed if it is to continue to move forward in development. More is said about the voice of the shadow, both as adversary and tempter and as counselor and guide, in ensuing chapters, when we discuss stages during which shadow awakening sometimes occurs.

With the completion of the self-system and the creation of the shadow, repression replaces splitting as the child's primary means of self-defense. More precisely, repression of the shadow replaces splitting of the self-representation as the child's primary means of self-defense. Repression and splitting are similar in being defense mechanisms by which the child eliminates unwanted parts of itself. However, these two mechanisms differ in how they accomplish this end. When the child uses splitting, it eliminates unwanted parts of itself by dissociation, by allowing their expression but imputing them to someone else. In contrast, when the child uses repression, it eliminates unwanted parts of itself by energy reduction and retrieval impairment, by sapping their strength and making their cognitive content inaccessible.

The replacement of splitting with repression in the transition from early to middle childhood marks a major developmental advance. It does so because (1) it helps the child overcome the rapprochement crisis and splitting; (2) it improves the child's self-control and strengthens its boundaries; (3) it improves the child's relationship with the caregiver, thus helping the child to see both the caregiver and itself in a more realistic way; and (4) it creates a stable basis for the recently completed self-system, which itself is the basis for the child's continuing development. Developmental advance is not always a steady emergence of new strengths and abilities. It sometimes requires either repression or, as we shall see in ensuing chapters, a return of the repressed.

The Lifeworld—A Field of Play

As the child overcomes splitting, thus reestablishing a stable relationship with the caregiver and forging a complete, stable self-system, it also regains a confident footing in the world. The fact that the world is large and uncertain is no longer as daunting to the child as it was earlier, when the child, as an older toddler, experienced intensely ambivalent feelings for the caregiver, the child's lifeline. The child, therefore, now sheds much of its fear of the world, as, indeed, it was already in the process of doing during the adjustment substage of the crisis-adjustment stage. The child is now comforted by the understanding that at least its own immediate neighborhood, watched over by mostly good parents or guardians, is mostly safe. By the time middle childhood begins, therefore, the child no longer worries about what might happen to it when it pursues the attractions of the world.

The school-age child, like the young toddler, is an eager explorer of the world, which still has countless treasures to be discovered. However, the school-age child has already investigated its immediate surroundings and spends most of its time enjoying activities such as swimming and cycling; acting out imaginary scenarios with dolls, trucks, or other toys; and, most gratifying of all, participating in games or sports with other children. Accordingly, whereas the young toddler is motivated primarily by a desire to explore, the school-age child is motivated primarily by a desire to play. This difference in the motivations of the young toddler and the school-age child is reflected in their lifeworlds. Whereas the young toddler lives in a world of treasures to be discovered, the school-age child lives in a world of recreations to be enjoyed. Whereas the world of the young toddler is a garden of delight, the world of the school-age child is a field of play.

Because childhood play is intrinsically pleasurable, it need have no purpose beyond itself. However, it does in fact have a developmental purpose.

Studies by developmental and educational psychologists and by neuroscientists confirm the benefits of play during middle childhood.[17] These studies have shown that play, in exercising the body, mind, and imagination, helps the school-age child learn how to coordinate bodily movement, deliberate about alternative courses of action, think creatively, discover personal strengths, and get along with others. Middle childhood is a time of rapid development across all dimensions of growth, and it is by means of play that much of this development is achieved. It is on the field of play—whether at home, at a park, on vacation, or during recess at school—that we, as children, learn many of the basic lessons of life.

The school-age child, enjoying itself on the field of play and loved and protected by mostly good parents or guardians, lives a mostly good— indeed, relative to later stages, a very good—life. The school-age child is not a fearless explorer in a garden of delight, but neither is it a split personality in a frightening world. The school-age child is aware that the world is large and uncertain, and it understands that parents or guardians are not perfect. Still, the school-age child—assuming the absence of hardship, abuse, and medical issues—suffers little anxiety and enjoys life robustly, as most of us well remember.

Chapter 11

Adolescence

Adolescence is a transitional stage. From the perspective of ego development, this fact is most evident in the experimental character of the self-system and lifeworld. The self-system is experimental because, no longer a child's self-system, it is being refitted with more mature parts, parts that are being tested on a trial, temporary basis. The lifeworld is experimental because it is a rehearsal stage, a stage on which adolescents act as if they were adults without yet being adults. In these and other ways, adolescence is clearly a stage "on the way" and "in between." Rather than being a stage with a defining character of its own, it is a stage that is defined by the stages it lies between.

Rapidly Maturing Cognitive Functions, Challenges to Self-Control

Executive functions, seated in a maturing prefrontal cortex, develop rapidly during adolescence. Cognitive functions especially develop rapidly. Cognitive advances include improvements in mental processing speed, working memory, cognitive flexibility (ability to inhibit and override earlier cognitive routines), and cognitive agility (ability to shift attention between cognitive tasks).[1] These improved abilities underlie and make possible a more general cognitive advance of the first importance, the ability to think abstractly, the ability, as Piaget put it, to perform cognitive operations of a formal rather than only of a concretely exemplified sort.

According to Piaget, concrete operational thinking begins being replaced by formal operational thinking in the transition from middle childhood to adolescence. Although school-age children, thinking with the help of inner speech, group things by category and draw conclusions from premises, they do so only with concrete examples of the categories or premises in mind. In contrast, adolescents, using inner speech, can define and map relations among categories and draw conclusions from premises without any thought of concrete examples. In thus being able to think abstractly, adolescents are able as well to think in terms of possibilities, hypotheses, and principles. Freed from the need to anchor thought in concrete examples, adolescents can entertain multiple possibilities, generate alternative hypotheses, and grasp general principles without regard to which possibilities are actual or which hypotheses or principles are true.

Practical functions also advance during adolescence. The most important advance is the ability, based on the emergence of formal operational thinking, to plan and carry out complex goal-directed actions.[2] Overall, however, practical functions advance more slowly during adolescence than do cognitive functions. The major reason for this lag is that adolescents' ability to carry out goal-directed actions cannot keep up with their ability to plan them. Studies discussed below indicate that adolescents, although able to follow out planned courses of action when emotions are calm, are frequently unable to do so when faced with emotion-arousing choices, especially in risk-reward interactions with peers. The hormonal changes of puberty, along with heightened self-consciousness, intense emotionality, and peer pressure, make adolescents susceptible to impulsive behavior. Practical functions thus progress more slowly than cognitive functions because they are impeded by lapses in judgment and self-control.

Studies focusing on risk-taking during adolescence have investigated the neurological bases of the adolescent's struggle with self-control.[3] Evidence from these studies indicates that the brain undergoes a broad twofold development during adolescence. On the one hand, the prefrontal cortex develops in ways that make possible the advances in executive functions just discussed. On the other hand, subcortical regions of the brain, especially regions of the limbic system and basal ganglia responsible for desire and reward, exhibit surges of activity, especially in the context of interaction with peers. These surges in subcortical regions can be strong enough that the prefrontal cortex, despite its own development, is unable to exercise top-down control of arising feeling. Such problems with self-control indicate that the development of the brain during adolescence occurs without an effective connection between two of the primary areas undergoing change, the prefrontal cortex and the subcortical regions exhibiting surges of activity. Adolescents' struggles with self-control, thus rooted in changes occurring in a developing brain, are gradually overcome as adolescence moves toward adulthood and the connection between the prefrontal cortex and subcortical regions grows stronger.

The Experimental Character of the Self-System

We have already noted that the self-system of adolescence is experimental in character. Adolescents, no longer children, begin to think and act like adults without yet being adults. The self-system of adolescence, therefore, is neither a child's nor an adult's self-system but something in between. The self-system of middle childhood no longer "fits," and the self-system of early adulthood is not yet in place. As a *child's* self-system, the self-system of middle childhood becomes obsolete once the school-age child becomes an adolescent. Of course, not everything about this earlier self-system becomes obsolete, since parts based on race, ethnicity, gender, family, and many personal traits ordinarily remain constant. However, all parts attributable only to children do become obsolete, including child-defining features of the self-representation, the "perfectly good child" goal of the ego ideal, and norms of the superego that properly apply only to children.

Once the child becomes an adolescent, these child-specific parts of the self-system of middle childhood are removed and replaced with what we shall call "more mature" content, content that, characteristic of neither children nor adults, is of a transitional and distinctively adolescent sort. Perhaps the most important such content, at least in more technologically advanced countries today, is content based on membership in peer groups.[4] Peer groups facilitate growth by providing audiences before which adolescents can act in more mature ways without being constrained by parental supervision.[5] In thus facilitating growth, peer groups, as we shall see, are the basis of new, more mature features of the self-representation; new, more mature goals of the ego ideal; and new, more mature norms of the superego.

Some peer groups are anchored in the neighborhood (e.g., early teen same-sex friendship groups, loosely knit groups of neighborhood friends, gangs), but most are anchored in the school the adolescent attends. Such school-based peer groups include (1) groups related to student activities, such as student government, clubs, and sports teams; (2) smaller, more tightly organized groups of friends, called "cliques"; and (3) larger, more loosely organized groups, called "crowds," for example, in American high schools, groups of so-called brains, populars, jocks, preppies, surfers, partyers, greasers, and goths. Groups of all these sorts expect specific behaviors for membership, and crowds and gangs often prescribe entire microcultures of action, dress, and talk. Adolescents, wanting to belong, typically adopt the behaviors of a primary and one or more secondary peer groups. If adolescents are accepted by the groups to which they seek to belong, they can add membership in the groups as features of their self-representations. For example, an adolescent might thus become a "member of the smart crowd," an "honors student," and a "thespian" or, perhaps, a "surfer" and a "partyer" or, perhaps, as in the musical *West Side Story*, a "Jet" or a "Shark."

The expression "more mature" applies not only to the self-system of adolescents but also to the behavior that gives expression to this self-system. Adolescent behavior is more mature because it is no longer the behavior of a child and not yet the behavior of an adult. In between, it is the behavior of a child-no-longer who is striving to be an adult without yet knowing what it is like to be an adult. Adolescents, thus attempting to act in ways beyond their years, sometimes try too hard when imitating adult behavior. They sometimes pretend to be adults only awkwardly to caricature adult behavior, especially when attempting to be "cool" or otherwise savvy to the ways of the world. Notwithstanding such pretenses, most attempts by adolescents to act in more mature ways—excluding those that are antisocial or self-destructive in character—are important steps forward in the direction of adulthood. Adolescents, in acting in more mature ways, rehearse being adults and in this way make progress toward becoming adults.

As narrative approaches to developmental theory have shown, adolescence is the first stage in which the narration of the self-representation becomes the telling of a *life story*, a story about a life with beginning, turning points, and eventual end, with both continuity and change, and with both meaning-conferring themes and justifying purposes.[6] This life story is fashioned by the ego speaking in its narrator voice. Using this voice, adolescents edit features of their self-representations by distancing themselves from child-specific features they think they have outgrown, by attributing to themselves more mature features they have forged or are forging, and by "trying on" features that, according to their life stories, they might someday achieve.

The features of the self-representation that are the focus of this self-narration tend to change as adolescence unfolds through early adolescence (10–14 years), middle adolescence (15–17 years), and late adolescence

(18+ years).[7] Because early adolescence is a time of initial transition to adolescent life, the primary focus of self-narration during this time is on removing child-specific features from the self-representation and replacing them with more mature features based on peer groups, which during early adolescence tend to be small groups of same-sex friends. Because middle adolescence is a time of transition to the larger cohort of adolescent life, the primary focus of self-narration during this time is on forging more mature features for the self-representation that are based on larger peer groups, such as student-activity groups, cliques, and crowds. Finally, because late adolescence is a time of initial transition to adulthood, the primary focus of self-narration during this time is on forging more mature features for the self-representation that are precursors of adult features that might soon be added, features based on adult relationships, lifestyles, ideologies, or social roles.

Life stories emerge during adolescence for two major reasons, cognitive and motivational. Cognitively, adolescence is the time of life in which we first begin to think about our lives in the comprehensive, thematic, multicausal, and hypothetical ways that are necessary for narration of a life story.[8] Specifically, it is only during adolescence that we begin to organize our life experiences into temporally unified wholes of past, present, and projected future; to conceive of our lives as having coherent threads and themes; to explain our life circumstances as effects of multiple causes (e.g., personal choices, physical attributes, race, gender, social class); and to think hypothetically about our lives as having multiple possible continuations. It is only during adolescence that these and other cognitive abilities are sufficiently developed to allow the ego's narration of the self-representation to progress beyond simple autobiographical self-reporting to autobiographical self-authoring proper.

The motivational reason for the emergence of the life story in adolescence has been recognized by all authors on adolescence since Erik Erikson's groundbreaking work beginning in the 1950s, which explained that adolescence is the time when we are challenged by the issue of self-identity. We discuss Erikson's work and adolescent identity exploration presently. Here we need say only that, from our point of view, the primary motivational reason for the emergence of the life story in adolescence is that adolescence, as a transitional stage, is a time when the self-system and, therefore, the self-representation (or identity) is not stably defined. Adolescents, no longer children and not yet adults, are motivated to ponder what they are and might become. They are motivated to speak to themselves not only about their ongoing lives but also about their past and possible future lives.

As adolescents add more mature features to their self-representations, they refashion their ego ideals in a corresponding manner. They abandon the childhood ideal goal of being a perfectly good child and replace it with a more mature ideal goal related to their emerging life stories, especially as their life stories focus on peer groups to which they belong or want to belong. Accordingly, in early adolescence, when small, same-sex friendship groups are at the fore, the refashioning of the ego ideal brings into view the ideal goal of confidently giving expression to the interests and the styles of speech and dress of a few close friends. In turn, in middle adolescence, when school-activity groups, cliques, and crowds come to the fore, the refashioning of the ego ideal brings into view the ideal goal of being a successful actor on the larger stage of adolescent life. Finally, in later adolescence, when romantic relationships and preparation for adult life come to the fore, the refashioning of the ego ideal brings into view the ideal goal of being in an enviable relationship, of confidently giving expression to an adult lifestyle or ideology, or of being successful in an adult occupational role. These changes to the ego ideal during adolescence reflect the transitional character of adolescence as a stage. The ego ideal during adolescence shifts focus as adolescents distance themselves from parents, come under the influence of friends, seek to belong to larger peer groups, and, then, increasingly pay attention to the adult world they are about to enter.

Adolescents, in being attracted to ideal lives of the sorts just mentioned, admire people who seem best to exemplify those lives. We learned in the last chapter that admiring ideal role models goes hand in hand with having an ego ideal. Role models during adolescence tend for this reason to evolve together with the ego ideal. Accordingly, young adolescents tend to adopt as role models close same-sex friends who confidently act in ways that they would like to act. Adolescents in the middle teen years tend to adopt as role models peers who are popular in larger school-activity groups, cliques, or crowds. Finally, older adolescents tend to adopt as role models not only peers but also adults who enjoy high status in their relationships, who are respected for advocating an adult lifestyle or ideology, or who are successful in an adult occupational role. A vast body of research exists demonstrating the powerful influence that role models of these and other types can have on adolescents, for both good and bad.[9] The point here is that this influence of role models is tied to the ego ideal.

Given the transitional character of adolescence as a stage and the differing concerns of early, middle, and late adolescence as substages, it comes as no surprise that adolescents frequently change their life stories and, therefore, their ego ideals and role models as well. These changes may seem capricious, but they have a purpose, which is increasingly evident in later adolescence. Research indicates that the direction of change of the life story as adolescence approaches adulthood is toward greater coherence and complexity.[10] It is by means of narrative exploration of progressively more mature behaviors and beliefs that adolescents bring their possible future lives into progressively more unified and elaborated focus. It is by exploring a variety of life stories, by fantasizing about a variety of ideal goals, and by admiring a variety of role models that adolescents get a better idea of what they might be once they become adults.

The superego also becomes more mature during adolescence. In the early and middle teen years, as adolescents are distancing themselves from parents and coming under the influence of peers, they increasingly adopt peer-group norms as standards to be enforced by the superego. Adolescents are strongly motivated to belong to peer groups and, therefore, strive hard to meet peer-group standards. Seeking acceptance, they speak to themselves in the voice of the superego to motivate themselves to dress, talk, and act as peer groups require. Furthermore, because peer group memberships tend to change during adolescence, the job of the superego tends to change as well.[11] The superego for this reason must be ready to adapt to new assignments. Enforcing such changing peer-group standards is a primary task of the superego until later in adolescence, when attention begins to shift toward preparing for commitment to adult social roles.

The fact that the self-representation, life story, ego ideal, and superego change frequently during adolescence means that the ego is busy during this stage speaking to itself in all three voices of the self-system, the (master) narrating voice of the self-representation and life story, the inspiring voice of the ego ideal, and the disciplining voice of the superego. Speaking in the narrating voice, the ego is busy updating features of the self-representation, especially those representing peer-group memberships. In this voice, it is busy as well scripting story lines about possible ways in which life might unfold, at first in the immediate context of adolescent life and then, later in adolescence, in the context of the adult world that is by then coming into view. Additionally, speaking in the voice of the ego ideal, the ego is busy encouraging itself to strive for ideal goals, at first those representing success in interactions with peers and then, later in adolescence, those representing success in the adult world. Finally, speaking in the voice of the superego, the ego is busy enforcing a variety of norms, peer-group norms, reevaluated parental norms, and, later in adolescence, norms that are precursors to adult norms.

The Lifeworld—A Rehearsal Stage

The lifeworld of adolescence, like the self-system, is experimental in character. It is a rehearsal stage on which adolescents act in more mature ways before audiences of peers. This rehearsal stage has shifting locations depending on the peers making up the audience.[12] Generally, in early adolescence, the primary audience consists of a few same-sex friends, who meet not only at school but also at each other's homes, on the telephone (voice, texting), on social media sites, and, especially for boys, on multiplayer video gaming platforms. In middle adolescence the audience grows larger, consisting of peers belonging to school-activity groups, cliques, or crowds, which meet primarily at school and at large school-sponsored events. Cliques if not crowds also meet in such places as shopping malls, coffee shops, the beach, basketball courts, street corners, and social media sites. Finally, in later adolescence, as the influence of the peer groups of middle adolescence wanes, the location of the stage on which adolescents act shifts increasingly to places where romantic relationships and other adult interests and endeavors can be rehearsed, places such as restaurants, movie theaters, public forums, and houses of friends.

What all these adolescent meeting places have in common is the minimal presence if not absence of adults. If parents, teachers, or chaperones are present, they are expected to remain in the background so that adolescents can have spaces of their own in which to interact. In these spaces, adolescents are free to rehearse adult behavior and to feel like adults without being overseen by "real" adults. The lifeworld of adolescence is thus a shielded stage on which young people who are not yet adults can nonetheless act as if they were and in doing so make progress toward actually becoming adults. Just as testing more mature behaviors is inherent to adolescence, so, too, is the rehearsal stage on which these behaviors are tested.

In previous chapters, we discussed some of the ways in which the feedback of others is a primary source of self-knowledge in the early years of life. The importance of such feedback continues in adolescence, with the difference that it is now primarily peers rather than the caregiver or parents who provide the primary feedback. Adolescents, in attempting to act in more mature ways before audiences of peers, cannot know if they *are* what they are *trying to be* unless their "performances" are favorably received by peers. Peers thus serve as judges who authorize adolescents to add new, more mature features to their self-representations, features that previously were in doubt. We are all well familiar with this need of others to confirm features of our self-representations that we are unable to confirm on our own. Much of our self-knowledge is interpersonally grounded. This fact is especially evident during adolescence owing to the importance of peer-group acceptance during the stage.

Identity, Worth, and the Possibility of Shadow Awakening

G. Stanley Hall, an influential early writer on adolescence, is credited with the long-standing description of adolescence as a stage of "storm and stress."[13] This phrase was used to highlight the turmoil and instability that are frequently associated with the stage. Throughout much of the twentieth century, many writers on adolescence, especially psychoanalytic writers such as Anna Freud and Peter Blos, described adolescence in this way.[14] However, in recent decades researchers have concluded that the storm-and-stress motif greatly exaggerates the turbulence of adolescence.[15] According to their findings, adolescence is not ordinarily a stage of storm and stress but is rather a stage that can unfold either smoothly or turbulently depending on a variety of factors, including family dynamics, cultural norms, economic circumstances, and individual temperament.

Although adolescence is not ordinarily a stage of storm and stress, it *is* a stage fraught with difficult challenges, challenges that sometimes do lead to storm and stress. These challenges arise from many causes, the more important of which are sexual awakening, problems with self-control, and, from our perspective, a rapidly changing self-system and a lifeworld that is a rehearsal stage. We shall here briefly consider challenges that arise from the last two of these causes.

The principal challenges arising from a rapidly changing self-system are (1) losing a child's identity without thereby suffering an "identity crisis," and (2) losing a child's sense of value and justification without thereby suffering a crisis of lack of worth. In turn, the principal challenges arising from living in a lifeworld that is a rehearsal stage are (1) acting on this stage without being overly daunted by performance anxiety, and (2) acting on this stage without acting recklessly and thus undermining support systems or incurring adult responsibilities too soon.

Having shed child-specific features from the self-representation without having yet made the long-term identity commitments of early adulthood, the adolescent is without a firmly defined identity. Psychoanalyst Erik Erikson introduced the notion of the adolescent identity crisis to explain this existential phenomenon.[16] The term "crisis" can lead to misunderstanding because, as Erikson himself made clear, he used that term to mean *challenge*, a test that can but need not and ordinarily does not lead to a crisis in the sense of storm and stress. In any case, Erikson's signature contribution to our understanding of adolescence was that adolescence is a stage during which young people are challenged to engage in identity exploration so that they can get a better idea of what life might be like for them once they become adults.

According to Erikson, society supports adolescent identity exploration by granting adolescents what he called a "psychosocial moratorium." This moratorium is a period of freedom from expectation during which more mature identity possibilities can be tested without thereby making adult commitments and taking on adult responsibilities. Protected by this moratorium, adolescents can "search for self" without experiencing an existential crisis. Some adolescents do suffer significant anxiety, especially when they approach the time at which the moratorium for exploration expires. Nevertheless, protected by the moratorium, most adolescents are able to explore identity options safely, without risk of incurring regrettable life-changing consequences.

Adolescents also face a challenge with respect to self-esteem or self-worth. Studies generally agree that self-esteem declines in the transition from middle childhood to adolescence, but they disagree on what happens thereafter, during adolescence. Some studies have found that self-esteem declines not only in the transition to adolescence but also throughout adolescence. Other studies have found that self-esteem, after declining in the transition to adolescence, neither increases nor decreases significantly thereafter. Still other studies have found that, after declining in the transition to adolescence, self-esteem increases during middle adolescence, only to decline again in late adolescence, thus following an inverted "U" course.[17]

These findings are confusing. To make sense of them it is necessary to distinguish between explicit self-esteem, the conscious assessment of one's value based on how one presents oneself to others, and implicit self-esteem, one's underlying, unconscious sense of value. If this distinction is made, then studies finding that self-esteem, after declining in the transition to adolescence, follows an inverted "U" course must be understood to apply only to explicit self-esteem. This stipulation is needed because implicit self-esteem has been found to decrease in entering adolescence and to remain lower throughout adolescence.[18] Explicit and implicit self-esteem are frequently discrepant during adolescence because explicit self-esteem is contingent on peer-group approval and, therefore, can be exaggerated and fragile, narcissistically hiding an implicit sense of lack of value. Wanting to belong to peer groups and to be validated by peers as being more mature than they are, adolescents frequently present themselves as if they have more confidence and, therefore, more (explicit) self-esteem than is in fact true (implicitly, unconsciously).

The focus here is on decreased implicit self-esteem during adolescence. In what follows, we use our theoretical perspective to explain why implicit self-esteem tends to decrease in the transition to adolescence and to remain at a low level throughout adolescence, until commitment to adult social roles effectively brings an end to adolescent concerns about identity and worth.

An adolescent, no longer feeling like a mostly good *child* (self-representation of middle childhood), no longer aspiring to the goal of being a perfectly good *child* (ego ideal of middle childhood), and no longer driven to meet the norms required for being at least a good enough *child* (superego of middle childhood), is prone to feel a loss of previous justifying value and a corresponding loss of motivation to reestablish that value. Adolescents of course seek to earn justifying value, for example, by excelling in school, participating in extracurricular activities, working part-time jobs, and meeting if not exceeding the expectations of parents and peers. However, from our perspective, efforts such as these are made at least in part because adolescents, no longer enjoying a child's sense of justifying value, worry that their justifying value might be in question. Furthermore, it is characteristic of adolescence as a transitional stage that efforts such as these earn only a temporary value, a value that substitutes for lost childhood value until more enduring adult value, based on commitment to adult social roles, begins being achieved. The transitional character of adolescence thus renders adolescents prone to worries about their worth. As with worries about identity, these worries are not ordinarily a cause of storm and stress. Nonetheless, they are worries to which many adolescents are prone.

Ideas introduced earlier in this book bring into focus one other reason why adolescents might experience worries about their worth: shadow awakening. Studies of shadow awakening have been conducted primarily within the Jungian school and have focused on the shadow formed during early adulthood, as it sometimes awakens during midlife transition.[19] However, we learned in the last chapter that the shadow, like the ego ideal and the superego, is first formed long before adulthood, in the transition from early to middle childhood. This early formation of the shadow suggests the possibility of shadow awakening before midlife and specifically during adolescence.

The fact that adolescence is a stage during which the self-system of middle childhood is in large part dismantled suggests that it is also a stage during which the shadow underlying that self-system is more likely, even if not very likely, to awaken. Specifically, it suggests that the bad-child shadow, repression of which was necessary to consolidate the self-system of middle childhood, is more likely, even if not very likely, to awaken. We explore this possibility here, stressing that, in the absence of empirical studies, the possibility is discussed only theoretically, as an implication of ideas unique to this book.

In the last chapter, we learned that the shadow was created over the course of the crisis-adjustment stage when repression was introduced to eliminate the older toddler's outbursts of rage, defiance, and selfishness, which seemed to jeopardize the child's relationship with the caregiver. As the older toddler's violent outbursts were thus eliminated, the action tendencies created by them remained in the form of neurological pathways that, although repressively overwritten and deactivated, can be reactivated. The proposal here is that just such a reactivation sometimes occurs during adolescence. When it does, the bad-child shadow of middle childhood is awakened.

Among the changes to the self-system during adolescence, the one that most increases the chances of shadow awakening is the loss, already discussed, of those parts of the self-system that had provided the school-age child with its sense of justifying value, namely, the "mostly good child" feature of the self-representation, the "perfectly good child" goal of the ego ideal, and the "at least good enough child" requirement of the superego. These parts of the school-age child's self-system are of paramount importance during middle childhood. They have this importance because the school-age child knows that it could not survive without its parents, and these parts of the self-system are what provide the child with the sense that it has value in its parents' eyes and, therefore, that it can expect to be loved and protected by them.

However, once the school-age child becomes an adolescent, not only does it lose the parts of the self-system on which its sense of justifying value had been based; it also loses the incentive, fear that it could not survive without parents, that had made those parts of the self-system so important. The adolescent will soon be an adult and understands that independence from parents is imminent. Indeed, some adolescents believe that they are already mature enough to live on their own. Accordingly, whereas the school-age child has compelling reasons to continue being mostly good in its parents' eyes—which is to say, to avoid reverting to the behaviors of the all-bad child it had repressed—the adolescent does not.

This loss of reasons for not reverting to the behaviors of the all-bad child does not mean that the adolescent will fall prey to those behaviors. It does not mean that the childhood shadow is about to awaken. To recall, early childhood repression does not remove the impulses that had prompted the older toddler's outbursts by containing them under pressure. Rather, it deenergizes those impulses while at the same time impairing the ability to retrieve the thoughts, images, and perceptions that had provoked them. The repressed impulses of the childhood shadow, therefore, are not, as it were, lying in wait ready, once the school-age child's reasons for keeping them repressed are outgrown, to erupt on the scene of adolescent life. Instead, they remain only as weakened remnants of what they once were, remnants that must be reenergized in response to triggering stimuli if they are to regain anything close to their original intensity. To bring shadow impulses back to life, therefore, it is necessary not only that the school-age child's sense of justifying value and dependence on parents be outgrown but also that triggering stimuli reactivate the neurological pathways that, in early childhood, had given the impulses energy and had otherwise facilitated their expression.

The most obvious such stimuli are authority figures who seem to impose unfair expectations or restrictions on the adolescent. It is fortunate that most adolescents have good enough relationships with parents and other authority figures that conflicts serious enough to provoke the awakening of shadow impulses do not arise. However, some adolescents quite evidently feel strongly that they are victims of unfair treatment. Some feel strongly that parents or other authority figures are unfair to them, either because they expect them to do or be things they do not want to do or be or because they do not allow them to do or be things they want to do or be. These adolescents can understandably nurse resentments strong enough to rekindle shadow impulses.[20]

Adolescents in whom shadow impulses have awakened might begin to speak to themselves in the voice of the shadow, a voice that here challenges what is perceived to be unfair authority. The perceived authority can be either external or internal, either parents (or other authority figures) or the parent-based self-system of the school-age child to the extent that it has not been outgrown. Directed against the latter, the shadow voice, speaking silently, might now challenge what remains of parental authority within the self-system by saying, "You're not a child anymore; you shouldn't be expected to be the good little girl [or boy] your parents want you to be." In thus taking a stand against the self-system that is in the process of being outgrown, the shadow voice expresses itself as an adversary of that self-system, deriding its childish features and its parentally defined goals and rules. It can also express itself as a tempter, a voice that seeks to rationalize behaviors prohibited by parents by scoffing at the parents' reasons for prohibiting them and by otherwise making the behaviors seem attractive and safe.

In thus speaking against internalized parental authority, the shadow voice might also begin speaking aloud to the parents themselves. In the shadow voice, adolescents might begin saying such things as, "I'm old enough to make my own decisions; don't tell me what to do"; "You don't understand me; quit thinking you know what's best for me"; or "You're a hypocrite; you've done everything you won't let me do." The implications of such shadow speech are clear. Adolescents who speak to themselves or to parents in the voice of the shadow have begun to perceive the primary authority figures in their lives as oppressive powers, powers from which they must break free if they are to live their lives in their own ways.

The shadow voice can serve as a safety valve that helps adolescents avoid acting on shadow impulses. However, if awakening shadow impulses become strong enough, shadow speech can begin to incite shadow action. Should this happen, adolescents might respond to parents by furiously shouting at them or by rebelling against expectations or restrictions imposed by them or by acting with brazen disregard of their wishes and feelings. Growing resentments against perceived unfair treatment and corresponding awakening of shadow impulses can provoke violent outbursts of rage, defiance, or selfishness. Adolescents who fall prey to such shadow behavior might feel exhilarated in their assertion of independence, but they also might suffer from strong negative self-judgment. They might feel not only that they have lost the justifying value they had enjoyed as school-age children but also that in losing this value they have changed from being "mostly good" to being "all bad" in their parents' eyes.

Adolescents' shadow outbursts as just described resemble the raging, defiant, and selfish outbursts of the older toddler, the primary difference being that they occur in a more mature developmental context. The intensity and the violently oppositional character of some adolescent outbursts suggest that more is going on than an expression of frustration with what are perceived to be unfair expectations or restrictions. They suggest that issues from the past have reemerged. Adolescents who fall prey to shadow awakening are for this reason susceptible to unbridled self-assertion of a childish sort. It is an irony that, in their efforts to be adults, some adolescents end up acting like children, all-bad children. The raging, defiant, and selfish outbursts that jeopardized the older toddler's relationship with the caregiver return as hostile, rebellious, and uncaring actions that jeopardize the adolescent's relationship with parents or others. This at any rate is what is implied by our account of the origin of the shadow in childhood.

Sexual awakening might also play a role in shadow awakening. The hormonal changes of puberty produce powerful releases of energy, which may help reactivate the neurological pathways that charge shadow impulses. Moreover, the aggressive impulses that sometimes accompany sexual awakening have a close-enough affinity with the self-assertive impulses associated with the childhood shadow as possibly to feed energy to them, thus assisting them in awakening. The awakening of shadow impulses may thus have psychoenergetic as well as interpersonal and social triggers.

While on the topic of the shadow, we should note that adolescence is a time during which not only new sexual impulses but also new impulses of many other sorts emerge. Most of these impulses—henceforth: "adult impulses"—can be expressed without encountering opposition or causing distress. However, some adult impulses that emerge during adolescence *do* encounter opposition or cause distress, either because they are prohibited by society generally or because they are prohibited by a social group to which one belongs or because they are prohibited by discrimination against one's race, class, or gender or because they are prohibited by adverse circumstances such as poverty or disability. These prohibited impulses are discussed further in the next chapter. For present purposes, we need only note that these impulses can be problematic for the people who experience them and, therefore, can be candidates for repression. Repression in this case, should it occur, would target adult impulses and, therefore, would transform what had been a child's shadow into an adult's shadow. This transformation of the shadow of middle childhood into an adult shadow is discussed in the next chapter. The later awakening of the adult shadow, which sometimes occurs during midlife transition, is discussed in the chapter 13.

Although crises of identity and worth are not the norm during adolescence, they are not for that reason uncharacteristic of the stage. Because the self-system is the basis of both identity and worth, having a self-system that is in transition, as is the case during adolescence, has the effect of calling into question both identity and worth, as we have seen. It also has the effect of opening the door for a possible awakening of the childhood shadow, as we have proposed. Adolescents are for these reasons susceptible to existential anxieties about identity and worth, anxieties that can, even though they ordinarily do not, lead to storm and stress.

Having considered the challenges of adolescence that arise from having a self-system that is in transition, let us now consider the challenges that arise from living in a lifeworld that is a rehearsal stage. One of these challenges, noted earlier, is to avoid being overly daunted by performance anxiety. As novice actors rehearsing more mature roles before audiences of peers, adolescents are prone to self-consciousness, which is to say, stage fright. In extreme cases, this stage fright takes the form of social anxiety disorder (SAD). Studies indicate that adolescence is the stage during which the greatest number of new cases of SAD arise, owing both to the need to perform new roles before audiences of peers and to the emergence of social self-consciousness, consciousness of oneself as a social object seen by others.[21] For these reasons, adolescents experience trepidation when they step onto the rehearsal stage and are acutely aware of their "performances" on that stage.

Adolescents' stage fright is heightened by awareness that peers can be harshly critical. Adolescents, pretending to be more mature than they are, are fearful that peers will not be favorably impressed and might pass harsh judgment. Overcoming this fear requires courage. Fortunately, the desire to be accepted by peers is strong, and it ordinarily overrides stage fright. Clearly, the great majority of adolescents surmount performance anxiety and summon the courage to act on the rehearsal stage. In doing so, they perform their more mature roles sufficiently well to earn a good measure of the validation they seek.

In attempting to act in more mature ways, adolescents also face the challenge of acting like adults without thereby acting recklessly and thus undermining support systems or incurring adult responsibilities too soon. The need to rehearse adult roles can prompt actions that go too far, thus effectively bringing adolescence to an end. Sadly, some adolescents find themselves shouldering adult responsibilities because of unfortunate circumstances, such as poverty or living with a sick, disabled, or irresponsible parent or parents. These adolescents, wrestling with hardships, not only take on adult responsibilities but also think of themselves as being older than they are.[22] In contrast, other adolescents find themselves shouldering adult responsibilities because strong oppositional impulses prompted them to act recklessly, in ways that undermined their support systems. These adolescents, for example, do such things as drop out of school, break the law, get pregnant, run away from home, elope, or join a "bad crowd." Whatever the cause, unfortunate circumstances, reckless actions, or something else, taking on adult responsibilities too soon comes at the price of forfeiting the opportunity for growth that adolescence provides.

In wanting to act in more mature ways, adolescents are pushed toward a line beyond which adolescence, as a time for exploring adult roles without yet needing to take on adult responsibilities, comes to an end. The challenge for adolescents is to explore more mature ways of acting without crossing this line. Correspondingly, the challenge for parents is to oversee adolescents' "speed of growth," supporting their exploration of more mature ways of acting when such exploration is on schedule but otherwise applying a brake.[23] These are difficult challenges, as all of us who have been both adolescents and parents of adolescents know. Fortunately, the challenges in question are ordinarily met well enough, with the result that most adolescents, with the help of parents, exercise good enough judgment to keep from bringing adolescence to a premature end.

Conclusion

Many people look back on adolescence as a time during which they were intensely alive. Despite remembering such things as worries about identity and worth, moments of awkward self-consciousness and, perhaps, actions they now regret, many people also remember such things as the excitement of their first steps toward independence, the thrill of acting on the rehearsal stage, and the passion of their first romantic relationship. Additionally, many people remember the satisfaction of being a member of a close-knit group or groups of peers. Some even remember the satisfaction of receiving the admiring approval of peers, of being popular, stars on the rehearsal stage. If adolescence has a distinctive happiness—as delight in exploring the physical environment is the distinctive happiness of the early toddling stage, and as the pleasure of carefree play is the distinctive happiness of middle childhood—it is the satisfaction that comes from being a member of a peer group. As adults, although we enjoy intimacy with partners or lovers and companionship with friends, we miss the heady camaraderie that goes with being a member of a cohort of peers who both test and support each other as together they prepare for a new stage of life.

Chapter 12

Early Adulthood

In one sense adulthood begins when one becomes physically and sexually mature. In another sense it begins when one is old enough to make adult decisions and enjoy adult privileges. In still another sense adulthood begins when one takes on adult responsibilities by committing oneself to adult social roles. It is this third sense that is relevant to our topic. So far as significant changes to the ego, self-system, and lifeworld are concerned, one becomes an adult when one makes commitments to adult roles, such as wife or husband, mother or father, police officer or teacher, Republican or Democrat, Christian or Muslim, and so forth. In making such commitments, one ceases experimenting with possible identities and life stories and finally decides on or at least accepts an adult identity and life story for the long term.

The age at which people make commitments to primary adult roles—especially to job, relationship, and parenting roles—varies from person to person, with some people never making these commitments, either because they are unable or unwilling to do so. The age at which people make commitments to primary adult roles also varies from society to society. In premodern societies, commitments to such roles were ordinarily made early and without an opportunity for adolescent exploration of alternative options. Education was minimal in premodern societies, and one was most often expected to take on adult roles as dictated by one's gender, class, and family background. Much the same was true, especially for members of the working class, in modern Western societies up to the end of the nineteenth century. Then, as education through the secondary level became the norm, commitments to primary adult roles were postponed until the late teens, after finishing high school or the equivalent. Finally, in more recent times, from approximately mid-twentieth century to the present, commitments to primary adult roles have increasingly been postponed until after the completion of college. Indeed, the college years are now frequently referred to as a time of "emerging adulthood," a time during which a young person is living more independently and is studying, testing relationships, considering employment options, and otherwise preparing to make adult commitments.[1]

Given this variation in the age at which people make and, historically, have made commitments to adult social roles, it is impossible to stipulate a precise age range for such commitments and, therefore, for the beginning of early adulthood in the sense that concerns us here. Fortunately, this indefiniteness poses no difficulty for the ensuing discussion. It suffices for our purposes to work with flexible boundaries, defining early adulthood as a stage that can begin as early as the teens but that most often begins between ages 20 and 25 and that continues until midlife, to approximately age 40.

Cognitive Executive Functions— Peak and Beginning of Decline

Executive functions are fully developed early in adult life. Studies have shown that executive functions such as attention control, working memory, cognitive flexibility, formal operational thinking, and voluntary, goal-directed action peak between approximately ages 20 and 29 and decline thereafter.[2] The fact that executive functions begin to decline so early in adult life does not mean that cognitive and practical abilities decline overall. As explained more fully in the next chapter, two facts compensate for decline in executive functions. The first is that the brain is adaptable and can increase activation in areas devoted to executive functions or can redistribute executive functions to other areas. The second fact is that cognitive and practical abilities are grounded not only in executive functions but also in experience, learning, and acquired skills, often referred to as "crystallized intelligence." In the next chapter, we discuss studies that show that crystallized intelligence continues to grow over time, thus compensating for decline in executive functions. With these points made, the tracking of the growth of the ego's executive functions, which has been a central task of the book thus far, can now be considered complete. We continue to discuss the ego's cognitive and practical functions in ensuing chapters. However, the discussion in those chapters focuses on their decline rather than on their growth.

The Self-System Based on Adult Social Roles

Two commitments more than any others mark entry into adult life, commitment to a type of work and to a life partner. The first of these commitments typically involves an agreement, if not a formal contract, to engage in an activity, whether in the public or private sphere, that provides one with a livelihood by contributing to society in some way. The second commitment typically involves an agreement, if not a sworn vow, of partnership with someone with whom one will share the responsibilities of life. Not everyone enters adulthood by making one or both of these commitments; still, making a commitment to a type of work or to a life partner is the primary way in which one becomes a member of the adult world.

Commitment to work, to a life partner, to parenting, or to other adult social roles reconstitutes the self-system in a straightforward way. We begin by discussing this reconstitution theoretically, explaining how in our perspective the self-representation (and life story), ego ideal, and superego are transformed by commitments to adult roles. We then set forth a generalization implied by this theoretical account, namely, that commitment to adult social roles in early adulthood tends to bring an end to adolescent issues of identity and worth. Finally, we turn to the literature on adult identity development to see whether it confirms or disconfirms our generalization and, therefore, whether it confirms or requires qualifications to our account of the reconstitution of the self-system in early adulthood.

Commitment to adult roles reconstitutes the self-system by replacing the transitional, "more mature," features of the self-representation of adolescence with long-term features based on adult roles and by making corresponding changes to the life story, ego ideal, and superego. The primary features of the self-representation—and, therefore, the primary themes of the life story—thus become those that reflect the adult roles that one is now performing. Additionally, the primary goals of the ego ideal become those of succeeding ideally well in one's adult roles. Finally, the primary standards enforced by the superego become those that require at least adequate performance of one's adult roles. Commitment to adult social roles thus transforms the whole of the self-system.

Young adults, in making commitments to adult roles, identify with those roles, in effect *becoming* them. A young woman who takes a job with a real estate agency and gets married *becomes* a real estate agent and a wife. A young man who takes a job with a plumbing company and gets married *becomes* a plumber and a husband. A young woman and man who decide to have a child *become* a mother and a father. In committing themselves to these work-related, partnership, and parenting roles, young adults define themselves in new ways by adding new adult features to their self-representations. Young adults also commit themselves to a wide variety of other adult roles, thus adding yet other adult features to their self-representations. Most often, they commit themselves to roles associated with adult lifestyles, interest groups, and belief systems. As a simplifying generalization, we can say that whereas adolescents reconstitute their self-representations by making short-term commitments to peer-group roles, young adults reconstitute their self-representations by making long-term commitments to adult social roles.

The self-representation of early adulthood consists of many features other than its new role-related features. Most features of the young adult's self-representation are carried over from earlier stages of development. Examples include features that for most people change only slowly if at all over the course of life, such as body type, personality traits, gender, race, family lineage, ethnicity, language, and nationality. Other features frequently carried over from earlier stages are belief-based features, especially those acquired during the teenage years, when adolescents begin consciously to identify with or to reject beliefs of their parents. For example, an adolescent boy whose parents are, say, Mormon (Church of Jesus Christ of Latter-day Saints) in their religion and conservative in their politics might begin consciously to think of himself as a Mormon and a conservative. Furthermore, he might continue to think of himself as a Mormon and a conservative after becoming an adult, thus carrying over "Mormon" and "conservative" from his adolescent to his adult self-representation. Alternatively, this boy might reject the beliefs of the LDS Church and become a Buddhist; and he might reject conservative political views and become a socialist. In this case, the boy might carry over "Buddhist" or "socialist" from his adolescent to his adult self-representation, unless, of course, on becoming an adult, he were to return to the beliefs of his parents or to adopt religious or political beliefs different from any of the aforementioned.

An important philosophical point about the self-representation of early adulthood is that most of its features are responsibly owned, whether explicitly or tacitly, where "responsibly owned" means that they are owned as if, originally, they had been consciously chosen. That most features of the adult self-representation are responsibly owned in this sense is of course most evident in the case of features that, originally, *were* consciously chosen. For example, in today's world, young adults most often consciously choose to accept a job, to make a commitment to a life partner, and to become a parent, thus consciously adopting and taking responsibility for the corresponding role-based features of their self-representations. However, the point about responsible ownership applies as well to most features of the adult self-representation that were not consciously chosen, including most features that were biologically inherited, prereflectively acquired, or conferred by unforeseeable events, for example, being brown-eyed, biracial, right-handed, a Chicago Bears football fan, and a winner of the Presidential Medal of Freedom. Clearly, most people whose self-representations have features like these accept the features not only in the sense that they would allow that the features accurately reflect facts about them but also in the sense that they have at least tacitly identified with the features, thus adopting and, therefore, taking responsible ownership of them.

Another example of features of the adult self-representation that are responsibly owned even if, originally, they were not chosen are belief-based features like those considered in discussing the example of the adolescent boy whose parents were Mormons and political conservatives. The boy, in initially thinking of himself as a Mormon and a conservative, probably did not evaluate alternative belief systems and then decide that the beliefs of his parents were best. Rather, his Mormon beliefs and his conservative political beliefs probably emerged unconsciously, as part of being raised by Mormon, conservative parents. This fact notwithstanding, the boy, should he continue into adulthood to believe as his parents do, would automatically assume responsible ownership of his Mormon and his conservative beliefs on becoming an adult. He does not need to make a conscious commitment to these beliefs. No such commitment is necessary because one incurs responsibility for one's beliefs simply by becoming an adult. Society holds adults responsible for their beliefs. Exceptions are made for adults who have been brainwashed or who are mentally ill or incapacitated. Otherwise, if one is an adult of sound mind and believes X, one is responsible for believing X. It would be utterly odd to suggest otherwise.

The analysis just set forth applies as well to the scenario in which the adolescent boy turns away from the beliefs of his parents and consciously avows Buddhism and socialism in their place (assuming that he retains his Buddhist and socialist beliefs on becoming an adult). The fact that in this scenario the boy consciously adopts Buddhism and socialism before becoming an adult does not change the previous analysis because, under the psychosocial moratorium of adolescence, the boy's preadult beliefs in Buddhism and socialism are viewed as trial beliefs, beliefs for which the boy is not held responsible until he becomes an adult. The fact that adolescents are generally not held fully responsible for their beliefs, even when the beliefs are consciously chosen, highlights the corresponding fact that adults *are* held fully responsible for their beliefs.

We said that *most* features of the self-representation of early adulthood are responsibly owned because not all are. Some features, rather than being consciously chosen or even tacitly adopted, are acknowledged only of necessity, as representing "things that have happened to me" or "things that other people see in me" rather than as representing "things that I am." Some features of the adult self-representation are not only unchosen but also unwanted, and some of these may be impossible to remove. Extreme examples are "sexual abuse victim," "quadriplegic," and "outcast." Features of this sort might be descriptively accurate and acknowledged as such by the people whose features they are. Nevertheless, many people who acknowledge features such as these have not appropriated and thus identified with them as parts of what they are. Many if not most people who acknowledge features of this sort, therefore, bear no responsibility for them. No one—other than the Jean-Paul Sartre of *Being and Nothingness*—would argue otherwise.

It will be helpful to recall two general points about the formation of the self-representation made in chapter 4. The first is that the ego's choices in authoring the self-representation are frequently limited by unchangeable biological or social factors or by unforeseeable events. The second point is that although the ego's self-authoring choices are thus limited, the ego is nonetheless the responsible author of its self-representation overall. It is so because it has significantly different if not many different choices in most situations, because it tacitly accepts responsibility for most features of its self-representation that it did not consciously choose, and because, if it tried hard enough, it could remove at least some features of its self-representation that, however acquired, it does not want. The statement that the ego is the responsible author of its self-representation overall is only a generalization. One can imagine extreme situations in which the circumstances of one's life are almost completely wrested from one's control. Such cases, however, are rare. Most of us, although subject to many circumstances that cannot be changed, have enough control of our lives to be the responsible authors of our self-representations overall.

The general point that emerges from these observations is that the transition to early adulthood is a time when a person makes commitments to adult social roles, commitments that significantly reconstitute the self-representation. These commitments add distinctively adult features to the self-representation, either by adding features that reflect commitments to new adult roles or by assuming, even if only tacitly, adult responsibility for features of the self-representation carried over from adolescence. Whereas middle childhood is a stage during which we *discover* our identities by learning how we fit into society, and whereas adolescence is a stage during which we *explore* our identities by rehearsing more mature behaviors before audiences of peers, early adulthood is a stage during which we *establish* our identities by committing ourselves to adult social roles. Early adulthood is the stage of life during which we, although limited in our choices and sometimes forced to acknowledge things about ourselves that we wish were not true, become responsible authors of our self-representations.

Young adults, in authoring their self-representations, narrate life stories based on their adult social roles. Whereas most adolescents, in experimenting with multiple identity possibilities, narrate several corresponding life stories, most young adults, having made long-term commitments to a few primary social roles, narrate in broad outline a single life story based on those roles. For example, a young woman who has committed herself to the roles "teacher," "wife," "mother," and "Christian" might narrate a life story about a woman who goes to a university, marries a man she meets there, becomes an English teacher, helps raise several children, is devoted to the Christian faith, and, after many years of employment, enjoys a happy retirement with her husband, children, and, now, grandchildren.

Life stories like this one, first scripted at the beginning of early adulthood, are filled in and edited as new events occur, new interests emerge, and new possibilities come into view. Sometimes unexpected events are sufficiently life-changing—for example, a career-ending loss of a job, a divorce or death of a partner, a serious accident—that major revisions to a life story are necessary. Despite this fact, the life stories of most young adults, except for the filling in and editing just noted, remain much the same in broad outline at least until midlife, if not thereafter. Midlife, as we shall see in the next chapter, is a time during which some people, a minority, feel a strong need to rethink their life stories.

Commitment to adult social roles, in changing the self-representation and life story in the ways we have explained, at the same time changes the ego ideal and the superego in closely corresponding ways. The goals of the ego ideal now become those of succeeding ideally well in one's adult roles. For example, the young woman whose self-representation includes being a teacher, wife, mother, and Christian would have as her ideal goals being the *best possible* teacher, the *best possible* wife, the *best possible* mother, and the *best possible* Christian she can be. The young woman knows that she is not without shortcomings in the performance of her roles; nevertheless, she finds the thought of being a model of success in her roles an inspiring ideal. This ideal, although unlikely to be completely achieved, is nevertheless a continuing source of motivation. It is an attractor that inspires her to perform her social roles as well as she can.

In previous chapters, we learned that the ego ideal guides people in selecting role models. Attraction to an ideal goal is at the same time attraction to people who seem to have achieved that goal. It follows, therefore, that people selected as role models in early adulthood would ordinarily be those who seem to have succeeded ideally well in one or more of one's own social roles. The young woman we have been using as an example might for this reason greatly admire people who, she believes, are exemplary teachers, spouses, parents, or Christians. Young adults do often greatly admire people who succeed in roles different from their own. These people, however, are secondary role models; they are models of success generally, not models of success in one's own roles. These points are obvious, but they are worth making because they highlight once again the close—indeed logical—connection between the ego ideal and role models.

Commitment to adult social roles reconstitutes the superego by making society's standards for adequate performance in one's adult roles the primary standards enforced by the superego. Whereas the superego of middle childhood is an agency enforcing internalized parental standards and whereas the superego of adolescence is an agency enforcing internalized peer-group standards, the superego of early adulthood is an agency enforcing internalized adult social standards. Young adults, having committed themselves to adult social roles, hold themselves accountable to the standards set by society for adequate performance in those roles. Accordingly, they say to themselves such things as, "Daniel's not doing well in math. I should help him with his homework." "The project went well. The boss should be pleased." "Don't forget about the reception for Pastor Jefferson on Saturday." In speaking to themselves in these ways, young adults motivate themselves to meet social standards, if not perfectly, as the ego ideal encourages, at least well enough to maintain good standing in society.

Generalization—Adolescent Anxieties Wane

An important implication of the preceding analysis of how the self-system is transformed by commitment to adult social roles is that adolescent anxieties about identity and worth tend to wane in early adulthood. The reason is clear: these anxieties wane because commitment to adult roles by itself creates both a clearly defined identity and a clear justification of worth. As pertains to identity, the answer to the question "What am I?" is no longer in doubt because it now has the clear answer "I am X, Y, and Z" (fill in the adult roles). Correspondingly, as pertains to worth, the answer to the question "Am I earning justifying value?" is also no longer in doubt because it has the clear answer "I am earning justifying value because I contribute to society by performing adult roles X, Y, and Z." Generally speaking, whereas the adolescent's identity and worth are in transition and, therefore, in question, the young adult's identity and worth, anchored in long-term commitments to social roles, are not.

Let us now advance this generalization about waning adolescent anxieties and see to what extent it is supported by empirical studies. Let us begin by looking at known exceptions to the generalization to assess whether, added together, they provide enough counterevidence to overturn the generalization or whether they are instead exceptions that "prove the rule." Two exceptions are, first, the group of young adults who, for whatever reasons, do not make commitments to primary adult roles and, second, the group of young adults who postpone making such commitments because they are still exploring adult identity options. Eriksonian psychologist James Marcia uses the expression "identity diffusion" to describe those in the first group and "identity moratorium" to describe those in the second.[3]

Evidence from identity research shows that young adults in these two groups, without having made commitments to core features of an adult identity, are prone to identity anxiety.[4] Generally, the evidence indicates that such anxiety is greatest for those in the identity moratorium group, since they are striving for identity commitments and are anxious about not yet knowing what commitments they will be able to make. Those in the identity diffusion group do not suffer exactly this anxiety, since they have chosen not to commit themselves to adult social roles. However, they frequently suffer from anxiety about lacking a socially recognized identity or about lacking direction or purpose or about feeling isolated, outside the mainstream.

Fortunately, identity diffusion is not that common in early adulthood, and most young adults exploring identity possibilities do eventually make identity commitments, at least after finishing college. Evidence indicates that those who have made such commitments suffer less identity anxiety for having done so.[5] It shows that they suffer less identity anxiety not only if they make adult role commitments after a period of exploration (what Marcia calls "identity achievement") but also if they adopt adult roles—or have them chosen for them—without having engaged in much if any advance exploration (what Marcia calls "identity foreclosure"). The point here is that commitment to adult roles, whether by achievement or by foreclosure, has the effect of relieving identity anxiety.

A third exception to our generalization about the waning of adolescent anxieties is the group of young adults who, after making adult commitments, fail to sustain them for the long term. Commitment to adult roles is not a one-time thing. Role commitments and, therefore, adult identity continue to be put to the test and called into question as young adults face challenges related to role expectations, job security, intimacy issues, parenting responsibilities, and financial difficulties. Sometimes these challenges are serious enough that young adults need to change one or more of their role commitments during early adulthood. Still, the research on identity development most recently cited shows that most young adults meet the challenges of early adulthood sufficiently well to make progress toward a more strongly established sense of identity over the course of early adulthood. Reviewing the results of studies, a leading authority says, "Longitudinal, cross-sectional, and retrospective investigations of identity change from early through middle adulthood years point to a slow, ongoing transition of development toward identity achievement, identity certainty, greater self-knowledge, cohesion, and stability of commitments over time."[6] Research on identity development in early adulthood thus indicates that for most people adolescent identity anxiety, quieted in first making adult commitments, continues to wane thereafter and eventually ceases being an issue as the years of early adulthood unfold.

The studies cited thus far on the reduction of identity anxiety in early adulthood frequently acknowledge that what is true regarding identity anxiety is true regarding anxiety about one's worth or value as well. However, that young adults experience a reduction in anxiety about worth is independently verified by studies of the development of self-esteem, a close cousin of self-worth. These studies have shown that, after adolescence, self-esteem increases steadily for most people throughout the years of early adulthood, indeed throughout the rest of adult life, up to old age.[7] Since a primary factor on which self-esteem is based in early adulthood is how well one has performed in one's social roles—the very roles on which adult identity is based—it makes sense that increasing confidence in one's identity over the course of early adulthood would at the same time be an increasing confidence in one's worth or value. Multiple research streams, therefore, indicate that for most people both identity anxiety and anxiety about worth are quieted and then gradually disappear in early adulthood.

Finally, a fourth exception to the generalization under discussion, this one less well understood, is the group of young adults who want to make adult commitments but are unable to do so or are unable at least to sustain such commitments because they cannot control impulses that conflict with adult roles. These young adults, unable to control socially proscribed impulses, clearly suffer anxiety that they might never be able to establish a socially accepted adult identity or to enjoy a sense of having worth or value in the eyes of society. Fortunately, young adults who find themselves in this situation are a minority, as clearly follows from the evidence, already reviewed, that most young adults *do* make commitments to adult social roles and, after making such commitments, *do* sustain the commitments sufficiently well to enjoy steadily increasing confidence in identity and worth as the years of early adulthood unfold.

Repression and the Formation of the Adult Shadow

Having broached the subject of socially proscribed impulses and the need to control them if one is to perform adult social roles, we are brought again to the following two important themes of this book: repression and the shadow. These themes return here because, I suggest, many young adults experience impulses that, were they not repressed and relegated to the shadow, would make it impossible for them to perform required, chosen, or desired adult roles. Unfortunately, the literature on adult identity development has little to say about people who struggle with impulses that conflict with adult roles. Moreover, repression and the shadow in early adulthood are not well understood generally. For these reasons, in discussing repression and the shadow here, we proceed, as we have done in previous chapters, with a theoretical discussion only, without the support of empirical studies. As in earlier chapters, we here discuss repression and the shadow in terms of the energy-reduction conception of repression.

Impulses that might conflict with adult social roles and, therefore, that could be candidates for repression in early adulthood were touched on briefly in the last chapter. To recall, these impulses ordinarily first emerge during adolescence and for this reason are distinctively "adult" impulses. As such, they are impulses that, should they be repressed and thus relegated to the shadow, would belong to a distinctively adult shadow. Here our aim is to explain why repression of such impulses and, with it, the transformation of the shadow into an adult shadow are frequently necessary to eliminate conflicts with social roles and in this way secure the self-system of early adulthood.

It will be helpful to divide adult impulses of the sort under discussion into six major types, as set forth in text box 12.1. This division clarifies the wide variety of impulses that might be repressed in early adulthood and the many reasons they might need to be repressed. It also clarifies that, although many of these impulses are malign, harmful, or otherwise "bad," many others are, or at least can be, benign, beneficial, or otherwise "good."

Text Box 12.1
Impulses That Might be Repressed in Early Adulthood

1. *Impulses of malign intent:* Impulses that society has prohibited because they cause harm or death to others (e.g., predatory, pedophiliac, sadistic, hostile-aggressive, and murderous impulses).

2. *Impulses causing psychological distress to others:* Impulses that society has prohibited because they can lead to actions that have unnecessary negative effects on others (e.g., slanderous, exhibitionistic, voyeuristic, and stalking impulses).

3. *Impulses inconsistent with social cohesion:* Impulses that society has prohibited because they undermine social stability or trust (e.g., rebellious, larcenous, mendacious, and deceptive impulses).

4. *Impulses related to prohibited forms of sexual or gender expression:* Impulses that some societies have prohibited because they fall outside the boundaries of what those societies consider acceptable forms of sexual or gender expression (e.g., promiscuous and adulterous impulses, contrasexual impulses, and impulses associated with LGBTQ sexual or gender orientations).

5. *Impulses related to prohibited rights, aspirations, or forms of self-expression:* Impulses that are prohibited because to act on them would violate restrictions that society imposes on a race, gender, class, or caste or because to act on them would violate restrictions imposed by groups within society (e.g., by one's family, community, faith, or ideology).

6. *Impulses conflicting with adverse circumstances:* Impulses that, although not prohibited by society or by groups within society, nonetheless cannot be acted on because of adverse circumstances such as poverty, physical disability, or confinement.

The impulses listed in lines 4, 5, and 6 of text box 12.1 are noteworthy because they provide examples of impulses frequently repressed in early adulthood that are not inherently harmful and, if allowed expression, might contribute beneficially not only to the lives of those who experience them but also to society generally. We discuss impulses listed in lines 4 and 5 shortly. For the moment, it suffices to have set forth a classification of major types of impulses that might be repressed in early adulthood. It should be clear from text box 12.1 that the list of impulses set forth there is not complete. Indeed, it should be clear that in early adulthood almost any impulse, if strong enough, could be a candidate for repression for people in some circumstances.

Repression of recently emerged adult impulses (and corresponding cognitive content) in early adulthood transforms the childhood shadow into an adult shadow. Unlike the impulses of the childhood shadow, which are out-of-control self-assertive impulses that seemed to the older toddler to jeopardize its relationship with the caregiver, the impulses added to the shadow in early adulthood are adult impulses that seem to the young adult to jeopardize his or her chance of performing adult social roles and, therefore, of enjoying the rewards that come from performing those roles. Primary among such rewards that might be jeopardized are a socially accepted adult identity, a sense of worth as a contributing member of adult society, spousal and parental relationships, social status, income, and, generally, happiness as defined by society. In sum, the impulses making up the adult shadow consist of those of the childhood shadow plus any adult impulses that are repressed because they pose a risk to adult social roles by means of which young adults believe they will earn essential goods of life.

Unlike the childhood shadow, which is formed in response to prohibitions enforced by parents, the adult shadow is formed in response to prohibitions enforced by adult society, whether by adult society generally or by membership groups within society such as those based on family, community, faith, or ideology. Unlike the childhood shadow, therefore, which is primarily an antiparental shadow, the adult shadow is primarily an "antisocial" shadow. Scare quotes are used because, as already noted, not all adult shadow impulses are antisocial in the sense of being detrimental to society. This point stressed, it remains true that the adult shadow is antisocial in the sense that (except for impulses listed in text box 12.1, line 6) its expression would violate prohibitions imposed either by society generally or by membership groups within society.

Carl Jung is to be credited not only for being the first to formulate the notion of the shadow but also for clarifying that many shadow impulses can be beneficial. As is well known, he argued that contrasexual or opposite-gender impulses (text box 12.1, line 4), if expressed, can empower women, sensitize men, and thus create more common ground for communication between women and men. We can add that impulses related to LGBTQ rights (text box 12.1, line 4), if expressed, can lead to greater personal fulfillment and to social acceptance of a wider range of sexual and gender expressions. Additionally, impulses related to rights, aspirations, or self-expression (text box 12.1, line 5), if expressed, can enrich a person's experience and thus increase a person's value as a member of society. Impulses of these three types, when expressed, do not always lead to net beneficial outcomes. Nevertheless, they can and frequently do lead to such outcomes. The point is that these impulses, as well as many others that are sometimes banished to the shadow in early adulthood, need not be harmful either to the person whose impulses they are or to society. Although some shadow impulses are inherently dark, many are dark only because society or groups within society forbid them, thus depriving them of light.

The struggle to repress socially prohibited adult impulses is not always completely successful. Impulses that have been targeted for repression, especially those that are inherent to a person's biological or psychological makeup, often remain distressing to some degree even after they have been weakened and associated thoughts and fantasies have for the most part faded from view. Some repressed impulses, therefore, may require the deployment of secondary defenses to keep them from undermining social roles. Projection and reaction formation—which deal with threatening impulses by focusing on their presence in others rather than in oneself—are sometimes employed for this purpose, especially in dealing with impulses like those described in line 4 of text box 12.1. For example, puritanism in people struggling against prohibited sexual impulses and homophobia in people struggling specifically against prohibited same-sex impulses have been adduced, somewhat controversially, as conditions that use projection or reaction formation to avoid confronting threatening impulses.[8] Additionally, sublimation and rationalization—which deal with threatening impulses by rechanneling or reinterpreting them—are sometimes used as defenses against persisting threatening impulses like those described in lines 5 and 6 of text box 12.1. For example, people struggling to repress impulses related to denied or unachievable rights, aspirations, or forms of self-expression might find new aims for their impulses, refocusing them on ends that they are allowed to pursue or that they can achieve (sublimation). Alternatively, they might try to convince themselves that the original aims of these impulses are less attractive than they had previously believed (rationalization).

Because impulses inherent to a person's biological or psychological makeup are the most difficult to repress and keep repressed, they are the ones most likely to persist and require the assistance of secondary defense mechanisms. Moreover, even in cases when repression of inherent impulses is successful—which is to say, when the impulses have been greatly weakened and one no longer dwells on the thoughts and fantasies previously associated with them—the possibility exists that a powerful stimulus will trigger a return of the repressed. Such a return is especially likely when developmental or social circumstances change in ways that challenge the role-based self-system of early adulthood. More is said about the awakening of repressed adult impulses in the next chapter, which discusses conditions under which the adult shadow sometimes awakens during midlife.

Repression of threatening impulses during early adulthood is not always the dire struggle that the foregoing discussion might suggest. Moreover, the liberalization of social policy, especially the recognition of LGBTQ rights, in many democratic societies has meant that many fewer people are being forced to struggle against strongly experienced or deeply rooted parts of themselves as a condition of performing adult social roles. These facts notwithstanding, many young adults do experience impulses that, if acted on, would jeopardize important adult roles, impulses, therefore, that, together with associated thoughts and fantasies, need to be repressively removed from consciousness and banished to the shadow. In sum, I propose, many young adults have some repressive work to do to secure the foundations of their role-based self-systems.

Consolidation of the Role-Based Self-System

Once adult social roles have been adopted and impulses conflicting with them have been quieted, the foundations of the adult self-system are secured and this self-system serves as a stable foundation for long-term development. Early adulthood is a stage during which commitment to adult social roles creates strong core features for the self-representation and provides strong motivation to aspire to role-based goals (ego ideal) and to enforce role-based rules (superego). Moreover, as studies discussed in this chapter have shown, early adulthood is a stage during which most people enjoy an increasingly strong sense of both identity and worth. Finally, as studies to be discussed in the next chapter have shown, early adulthood is a stage during which most people eventually succeed well enough in their roles to be able, in looking back from the vantage point of midlife, to judge their lives favorably, as being on balance more good than bad.

This finding has dramatic exceptions, since some people, in approaching midlife, experience significant discontent with the lives they have been living. Nevertheless, most people who evaluate their lives from the vantage point of midlife see that, for them, early adulthood, considering both its successes and its failures, both its satisfactions and its disappointments, was on balance more good than bad. Most young adults, with stable self-systems, quiet shadows, and the benefits earned from performing their roles at least well enough, move forward in life with decreasing anxieties and with increasing confidence in themselves and the lives they are living.

The Lifeworld—A Workplace

The lifeworld of early adulthood, like the self-system, is shaped by adult social roles. In contrast to the lifeworld of adolescence, which consists of the gathering places in which adolescents rehearse more mature roles before audiences of peers, the lifeworld of early adulthood consists of the gathering places in which young adults perform the duties of their social roles. The world in which young adults live is thus a workplace, either a place of employment outside the home or a home in which household chores, parenting, or paid in-home work is done or, as is increasingly the case (especially for women), both. As a workplace, this adult lifeworld is a place in which meeting the responsibilities of one's social roles is the paramount concern. The lifeworld of early adulthood is for this reason governed by the reality principle.

The fact that the lifeworld of early adulthood is a workplace does not mean that it is only a place of work. Most young adults enjoy recreations, hobbies, social gatherings, cultural events, and vacations. The places in which activities like these occur also belong to the lifeworld of early adulthood. To use an analogy, the lifeworld of early adulthood is like a building that has two markedly different kinds of rooms, main rooms, in which job or parenting roles are performed, and side rooms, in which young adults can relax and pursue interests not related to their work. Moreover, the main rooms of this building should not be thought of as places only of dutiful performance of roles, since many young adults enjoy their work and enjoy as well the company of people with whom they work. With satisfaction thus to be found not only in the side rooms of our building but also, for many people, in the main rooms as well, the lifeworld of early adulthood is clearly a place of both work and pleasure. This point made, the lifeworld of early adulthood is, again, a place where meeting the responsibilities of one's work roles is the paramount concern.

The lifeworld of early adulthood is a place governed by the clock and calendar and by a daily agenda of work to be done. As for the clock, hours are divided into working hours, during which one performs one's primary roles, and leisure time, during which one is free to do as one pleases. As for the calendar, the week is divided into workdays and a day or two of respite from work; and the year is divided into a greater part devoted to work and shorter periods when work is not required, such as seasonal downtimes, contractually allowed vacation times, and government or religious holidays. The clock and calendar are thus structured to give priority to work while allowing time for rest and recreation.

The daily agenda is also determined by one's primary social roles, which dictate activities that tend to be similar each day of the workweek. For those working outside the home, the activities are the daily assignments of their employment; and for those working inside the home, the activities most often are keeping a house in order and taking care of children. As required by their social roles, most young adults, whether working outside or inside the home or both, tend during the workweek to perform tasks of the same general character from one day to the next. The teacher teaches, the plumber plumbs, the homemaker manages a home, looks after children, and sometimes does paid in-home work. The world of early adulthood is for this reason not only a world of clocks and calendars but also of "dailiness," of repetition of the similar, if not the same.

Although the dailiness of role responsibilities can be tedious, a "daily grind," it need not be. We have already noted that many young adults enjoy both their work and people with whom they work. Moreover, young adults perform their work-related roles not only to meet the responsibilities and enjoy the satisfactions of the day but also to make progress toward a better future. The goal toward which young adults work is long-term success in their roles as judged by society. They work so that at midlife or later they can look back and say that they have succeeded in what they set out to accomplish at the beginning of adulthood, if not ideally, as projected by their ego ideals, at least well enough.

Achieving success in one's roles is society's definition of happiness: "Across the lifespan, society often pushes a subtle message with a basic formula: Work hard, become successful, *then* you'll be happy. We hear it from our parents, teachers, employers, and even television ads. After a while, this way of thinking can become automatic. 'When I graduate from college . . . When I land my dream job . . . When I make six figures,' we think to ourselves, *then* I will be happy."[9]

Society defines happiness as succeeding in one's social roles because such success benefits society overall. Motivating people to pursue success in their roles motivates them to work hard over the long term and in this way to contribute as best they can to social well-being. In encouraging people to pursue success in their social roles, society provides an inducement by promising happiness as the reward. Society's definition of happiness as succeeding in one's social roles thus motivates young adults to persevere in their roles so that they can later enjoy happiness as the reward of their labor. We return to society's promise that happiness is achieved by succeeding in one's social roles in the next chapter, where we explain how differently people evaluate this promise when looking back on early adulthood from the vantage point of midlife.

Society's promise that success in one's roles leads to happiness is a guiding theme in young adults' life stories. Although most young adults live lives that are good enough in the present, they also look forward to a future when their lives will be better, when they will be happy in the sense of being well pleased in what they have accomplished in their social roles. In the lifeworld of early adulthood, happiness is something that is thought to be progressively earned and, therefore, something to be enjoyed in full only in due time, perhaps at midlife or thereafter.

Chapter 13

Midlife

Midlife, beginning at approximately age 40 and ending sometime between ages 55 and 60, is a time of life about which there is a good deal of disagreement. Some have described midlife as the low point in life, comparing it to the bottom of a U-shape curve, a slough of despond separating the relatively happier years that precede and succeed it.[1] Others, including the popular press, have amplified this negative conception of midlife by giving a great deal of attention to the phenomenon of midlife crisis, almost to the point of suggesting that crisis is characteristic of midlife as a stage. However, this negative conception of midlife has been challenged by a good deal of research. Studies supporting the U-shape curve account have been called into question by other studies indicating that the experience of dissatisfaction at midlife is not as pervasive, let alone as definitive of midlife, as proponents of the U-shape curve analysis have argued.[2] Moreover, other studies indicate that the incidence of crises during midlife is much lower than widely assumed.[3]

In the last chapter, we cited studies indicating that most people enjoy an increasingly strong sense of role-based identity over the course of early adulthood. We also cited evidence indicating that most people enjoy an increasing sense of self-esteem over the course of early adulthood. Consistent with these studies, other studies have found that most people have an overall favorable assessment of their lives at midlife and that some even experience midlife as the prime of life.[4] Most people at midlife believe that on balance their circumstances are more good than bad. Such a belief is understandable given that midlife is a time during which most people are more confident in their roles, more secure in their finances, and, with children becoming more self-sufficient and leaving home, better able to pursue their own interests.

Three Pathways through Midlife

Clearly, research on midlife is all over the map. Studies have established that crises are relatively rare during midlife, that identity achievement and self-esteem are relatively high at midlife, that a sizable percentage of people are happy during midlife, with some happier than they have ever been, and that life assessment overall is relatively high at midlife. However, studies have also established that many people experience significant dissatisfaction at midlife. What stands out in these conflicting findings is that there is no clear correlation between life assessment and life satisfaction at midlife. Many who at midlife assess their lives favorably—acknowledging that they have done at least reasonably well in their social roles and have reaped rewards in having done so—nonetheless experience significant dissatisfaction at midlife. Clearly, some people who have earned the goods that come with succeeding in social roles are still prone to dissatisfaction at midlife. These people, it seems, do not find the goods that come with success to be as satisfying as society had led them to expect. They acknowledge that they are doing well but say that they are unhappy nonetheless.

That many at midlife experience dissatisfaction even when they assess their lives favorably highlights what has been called the "paradox" of midlife, the fact that many people experience midlife not only in different but in *opposite* ways. Some, a minority, experience midlife as a greatly satisfying time of life and others, also a minority, experience midlife as a greatly dissatisfying time of life. On the one hand, research has found that most people assess midlife to be on balance more good than bad, with some of these people even experiencing midlife as the best time of life. On the other hand, there is no denying that dissatisfaction is a phenomenon strongly and properly associated with midlife.

The facts just set forth suggest that people at midlife can be divided into three groups according to their differing degrees of satisfaction and dissatisfaction. One group, which is relatively small, consists of those for whom midlife is much more satisfying than dissatisfying, including those for whom midlife is the prime of life. A second group, also relatively small, consists of those for whom midlife is much more dissatisfying than satisfying, including those for whom midlife is a time of crisis. The third group, this one much larger than the other two, consists of those for whom midlife is a time of neither great satisfaction nor deep dissatisfaction, as it is for people in the first two groups. For some in this third group, satisfactions outweigh dissatisfactions, but not, as for people in the first group, greatly so; and for others, dissatisfactions outweigh satisfactions but not, as for people in the second group, greatly so. Applying research findings, most of the people in this third group, with relatively strong identities and high self-esteem, assess their lives to be on balance more good than bad, even if a significant number of them find their lives to be less satisfying than they had hoped.

With this division of people at midlife into three groups, it follows as a rough generalization that there are three primary pathways through midlife: a less traveled pathway of satisfaction, on which satisfaction greatly outweighs dissatisfaction; a less traveled pathway of dissatisfaction, on which dissatisfaction greatly outweighs satisfaction; and the most traveled pathway of both satisfaction and dissatisfaction, on which neither satisfaction nor dissatisfaction greatly outweighs the other. Of these three pathways, the pathway of satisfaction can be said to represent a *culmination* of early adult life. On this pathway, one enjoys the fulfillment of the dreams of early adulthood because one has succeeded in one's social roles and has thus achieved life goods that are experienced to be greatly rewarding, just as society had promised they would be. In stark contrast, the pathway of dissatisfaction can be said to represent a *loss of faith* in early adult life. On this pathway, one is disillusioned of the dreams of early adulthood because one has fallen short of hoped-for success in one's roles or, if one has achieved success, because one has found the goods earned by success to be much less rewarding than society had promised they would be. Finally, in contrast to both of the preceding pathways, the pathway of both satisfaction and dissatisfaction can be said to represent a *continuation* of early adult life. On this pathway, one continues to pursue the dreams of early adulthood because one has succeeded in one's roles incompletely but nonetheless well enough, typically, that life assessment, if not life satisfaction as well, is on balance positive.

That there are these three pathways through midlife is not a mystery, for midlife, as the time at which the ambitions of youth begin to confront the realities of aging and decline, is a time during which people tend to look back and reflect on the lives they have lived. In thus reflecting, people at midlife tend to focus on the goals they set in early adulthood, asking whether they have achieved those goals, and, if so, whether their success is as rewarding as they thought it would be. Clearly, such reflection can lead to conclusions that match the perspectives of the people in the three groups we have distinguished. It is understandable that such reflection would lead some people, a minority, to conclude that midlife is a time that is greatly satisfying, other people, also a minority, to conclude that midlife is a time that is greatly dissatisfying, and still others, the majority, to conclude that midlife is a time that is neither greatly satisfying nor greatly dissatisfying but is instead a bit of both, with most people in this group assessing their lives to be good overall, even if less satisfying than they had hoped.

A comprehensive chapter on midlife would include an account of all three pathways we have distinguished. However, the present chapter focuses only on the pathway of dissatisfaction because it, much more than the other two pathways, can lead to significant changes to the self-system and life-world, which are primary themes of our account of ego development. The pathways of satisfaction and of both satisfaction and dissatisfaction are in different ways extensions of early adulthood, the former, again, representing a culmination and the latter a continuation of early adulthood. In contrast, the pathway of dissatisfaction, representing a loss of faith in early adult life, poses a serious challenge to the self-system and lifeworld of early adulthood, frequently requiring significant changes to them.

Declining Cognitive Executive Functions, Fluid versus Crystallized Intelligence, Postformal Thinking

Before turning to the pathway of dissatisfaction, we need briefly to discuss the status of the ego's executive functions during midlife. We reported in the last chapter that executive functions begin to decline by age 30 if not earlier but that this decline does not entail a decline in cognitive and practical abilities overall. One factor working against overall decline is that the brain reorganizes itself to mitigate the decline of executive functions. Neuroimaging studies have shown that many older adults continue to perform executive functions at a relatively high level because the prefrontal cortex and other regions of the brain correlated with the performance of executive functions in early adulthood increase in activation during midlife or because regions of the brain not correlated with the performance of executive functions in early adulthood are recruited to assist the regions that were, most often homolo-gous regions of the opposite hemisphere.[5] We now know that the brain is adaptable to a remarkable degree well into the second half of life and that this adaptability allows many people to slow the decline of executive functions.

A second reason why the decline of executive functions does not entail a decline of cognitive and practical abilities overall is that the decline of executive functions is offset by continued growth of intelligence more broadly. This trade-off is frequently described in terms of the distinction, first made by Raymond Cattell and further developed by John Horn, between fluid and crystallized intelligence.[6] Fluid intelligence is the ability to solve new problems by focusing attention, holding relevant information in mind, processing information quickly, and thus finding lines of thought or patterns of organization that lead to solutions. Fluid intelligence is related to ability in mathematics, reading comprehension, and written expression.[7] More generally, fluid intelligence is closely related to the exercise of cognitive executive functions. Cognitive executive functions are discrete abilities, whereas fluid intelligence is a more general problem-solving ability carried out by engaging cognitive executive functions. Given their close connection, fluid intelligence and cognitive executive functions follow a similar developmental path, emerging in early childhood, peaking in early adulthood, and declining thereafter.[8]

In contrast to fluid intelligence, crystallized intelligence is acquired understanding based on experience, study, or training. It is the storehouse of information and the repertoire of skills that one has already acquired and, therefore, can apply to situations similar to those one has experienced before. Crystallized intelligence, in being already acquired and ready-to-hand, differs fundamentally from fluid intelligence, which works in the moment to process new information, solve new problems, and learn new skills. Crystallized intelligence, differing from fluid intelligence in these ways, differs from it as well in following a developmental path that, rather than beginning to decline early in adulthood, continues to improve or at least remain at roughly the same level throughout adult life, even into old age.[9]

Accordingly, the trade-off that makes cognitive growth possible after executive functions (and fluid intelligence) begin to decline is one in which this decline is offset by continued growth of crystallized intelligence. The benefits of compensating for executive decline by making gains in crystallized intelligence are especially evident when one is performing tasks that one has performed many times before, tasks that rely on information and skills already acquired without, therefore, needing to rely heavily on executive functions to work out solutions on the fly. To be sure, as executive functions decline, one might find it more difficult to retrieve needed information, to retain multiple considerations in mind, to block distractions, and, generally, to process new information. However, such decline is most often more than offset by superior factual knowledge, a larger skill set, and more mature understanding of human nature and human affairs.

Adding to the cognitive gains provided by growth in crystallized intelligence is the emergence of what in the Piagetian tradition is called "postformal" cognition. Theories of postformal cognition emerged in the 1970s and were further developed and widely discussed in the 1980s and

1990s. Major contributors to postformal theory are Patricia Arlin, Michael Basseches, Michael Commons, Francis Richards, Jan Sinnott, and Gisela Labouvie-Vief.[10] These authors presented different approaches to postformal cognition, but they described it generally as a kind of cognition that is more sensitive to matters such as context, perspective, fallibility, ambiguity, contradiction, complexity, and interrelatedness.

Postformal cognition is the ability to understand that much of knowledge is based on context and perspective and, therefore, is interpretive at least to some degree rather than being exclusively factual; that theories are vulnerable to contradictions and, therefore, often need to be amended from the point of view of higher-order theories; and that knowledge generally grows toward deeper understanding of complexity and wider understanding of the interrelatedness of things. Clearly, many adults at midlife or later do not experience significant gains in cognition of this sort. Many continue to think in simpler terms, never considering the subtle issues of postformal cognition. Still, the possible emergence of postformal cognition, along with the further development of crystallized intelligence, is such that many adults at midlife or later, despite experiencing a decline in executive functions and fluid intelligence, enjoy cognitive abilities that on balance are superior to those they possessed during early adulthood.

Having thus far spoken primarily of cognitive abilities, we should add that what has been said about cognitive abilities applies to practical abilities as well, abilities such as making good decisions and achieving challenging goals. With the growth of crystallized intelligence and, perhaps, of postformal cognition as well, people during midlife can make decisions with a better understanding of the variables involved, especially the human variables; and they can achieve goals with more complete knowledge of the relations of means to ends. Except when facing new challenges, for which crystallized intelligence is of little use, adults in middle and later years of life can frequently make decisions more quickly and accomplish goals more efficiently than young adults can. In these and other ways, it is possible to age not only gracefully, as the developmental literature frequently says, but also with increasing abilities overall, well into one's senior years.

The Pathway of Dissatisfaction

Let us now turn to the pathway through midlife on which we will be focusing, that of dissatisfaction. The first point to make about this pathway is that many people at midlife experience frustration or disappointment in finding that their efforts to be successful in their social roles have not resulted in the happiness that society had led them to expect. Most who come to this realization do so out of a sense of frustration. They feel frustrated because they have not been as successful in their roles as they had hoped they would be. These people, feeling that their efforts have fallen short, may conclude that it is futile any longer to strive for the fulfillment of their dreams.

Others who come to the realization in question, a minority, do so from a sense of disappointment rather than frustration. These are people who *have* succeeded in their social roles, who *have* achieved or perhaps even surpassed their long-term goals, only to find that their accomplishments are not as satisfying as society had led them to expect. For these people, midlife is on balance "very good" so far as life assessment is concerned (they have done well) and on balance "very bad" so far as life satisfaction is concerned. These people, therefore, may ask themselves "Why was I so narrowly focused on success?" or "Is this all there is?" These people, dissatisfied despite their success, frequently begin to wonder where satisfaction might elsewhere be found.

In sum, whether by frustration or by disappointment, some people at midlife come to see that the pathway they embarked on in early adulthood has not led to the happiness that society had promised. These people, consequently, experience dissatisfaction at midlife, some seriously so. Ordinarily, their dissatisfaction is focused on job, relationship, or parenting roles, these roles being the primary ones in which most young adults strive for success and happiness. The examples most often cited of people who experience such dissatisfaction are those of men who, suffering midlife crises, quit their jobs, have affairs, or otherwise make decisions that change their lives in major ways. It is understandable that people would focus primarily on examples like these, but doing so is misleading, for two reasons: (1) because it suggests that midlife is characteristically a time of serious dissatisfaction if not crisis, and (2) because it suggests that midlife dissatisfaction is primarily a male phenomenon. We have already noted that the first of these suggestions is unfounded. We can now note that the second is as well.[11]

The traditional gender division of labor, which still prevails to a significant extent, lies behind differences in women's and men's midlife dissatisfaction. Because women throughout most of history have invested their efforts primarily in the roles of wife, homemaker, and family caregiver, their midlife dissatisfaction has been focused primarily on those roles and on the sense that, in having devoted themselves to those roles, they have left many talents and potentialities undeveloped. In contrast, because men throughout most of history have invested their efforts primarily in the roles of husband, worker (outside the home), and family provider, their midlife dissatisfaction has been focused primarily on those roles and on the sense that, in having devoted themselves to those roles, they have sacrificed opportunities for pleasure and adventure. The social roles of women and men have changed a good deal since the end of World War II, primarily because women have increasingly entered the workforce and pursued higher education. Moreover, there have always been women and men who have been exceptions to the generalizations just stated. Still, the traditional gender division of labor has by no means disappeared and neither, therefore, have corresponding differences in women's and men's midlife dissatisfaction.

Effects of Midlife Dissatisfaction on the Self-System

From our perspective, the most relevant consequence of midlife dissatisfaction is that it causes the self-system and the lifeworld to seem alien *to some extent or degree.* The qualifier is italicized not only to highlight the point that the seeming alienness of the self-system and the lifeworld during midlife is characteristically only partial, but also, by highlighting this point, to avoid having to repeat it. The point should be understood as implicit in the ensuing discussion. Later in the book, in chapter 16, we discuss a life stage (spiritual preawakening) in which dissatisfaction sometimes *is* so severe as to cause the self-system and lifeworld to seem completely alien, leading to the "death" of the self-system and to a "desolation" of the lifeworld. In this chapter, focusing on midlife, the point is that dissatisfaction during midlife, although sometimes quite serious, is rarely so serious as to have such dire consequences.

Signs that midlife dissatisfaction is causing the self-system to appear alien are a sense that one's self-representation no longer accurately reflects who or what one is and a corresponding decrease in the motivating power of the ego ideal and the superego. Regarding the former, people who suffer midlife dissatisfaction have begun to feel that their primary social roles no longer facilitate their self-expression or growth as well as they did earlier. These roles no longer "fit" well; they now seem confining. Correspondingly, the self-representation based on these roles seems out of date and obsolete to some degree; it seems less Me than it did before. Midlife dissatisfaction thus causes one to feel that one is not being fully authentic in one's social roles and, therefore, that one's role-based self-representation no longer reflects one's "whole" or "true" self.

As the self-representation of early adulthood thus becomes alien to some degree, so, too, does the corresponding life story. Evidence indicates that midlife is a time during which many people, although by no means all, begin to rethink their life stories.[12] Using inner speech, the narrator voice now begins to explore changes that might be made to the life story. The fact that midlife crises are relatively rare indicates that major changes, should they be contemplated, most often are not implemented. Still, the feeling that the self-representation no longer reflects one's whole or true self is at the same time a feeling that the story one has been narrating about oneself is no longer one's whole or true story. For this reason, people suffering midlife dissatisfaction are impelled to contemplate how they might revise their life stories to make them more authentically self-expressive and to give them better prospects for satisfying outcomes.

Midlife dissatisfaction renders the ego ideal alien because it causes the ideal goals of early adulthood to seem less attractive, thus decreasing the ego's commitment to them. The ego ideal is now caught between two sets of goals. It continues to motivate the pursuit of old goals, although now with much less persuasive power than before. However, in thus continuing to promote old goals, it now also begins to search for new goals. This search for new goals is part of the narrator's work in rethinking the life story. The narrator here begins to explore goals that might restore passion to life, goals that would either supplement or perhaps even replace old primary goals. Because goals that would replace old primary goals would require major changes to the life story, they are most often entertained only in fantasy. Again, the relatively rarity of midlife crises indicates that most major revisions to the life story, including those introducing major new life goals, do not get beyond the stage of fantasy exploration. Midlife dissatisfaction, therefore, splits the allegiance of the ego ideal between old goals, which are no longer as inspiring as they previously were, and new goals, many if not most of which are contemplated without being acted on.

As for the superego, midlife dissatisfaction renders it alien by making role-based duties seem less urgent or necessary. The inner voice that insists that one perform the assigned tasks of the day loses at least some of its authority. It may still issue most of the same commands it did before. However, these commands now have less force, for dissatisfaction makes it seem as if there is less at stake in either obeying or disobeying the superego. This is not to say that people suffering midlife dissatisfaction disobey the superego. Some do. Some, driven by extreme dissatisfaction, abandon their social roles and do things that, earlier, their superegos would not have allowed them to do. However, the relative rarity of midlife crises indicates that most people who suffer midlife dissatisfaction do not act out in these ways. Just as most continue to pursue the primary goals of early adulthood, even if with less motivation than before, most also continue to listen to the superego and to obey its commands, even if, now, primarily out of inertia or fear of consequences rather than out of respect for its authority.

In sum, the self-system of the person suffering midlife dissatisfaction consists of a self-representation that no longer fits well, a life story that has reached an impasse, and an ego ideal and a superego that have lost much of their power to motivate. The self-system, although rendered alien in these ways, ordinarily remains intact. Again, midlife dissatisfaction ordinarily renders the self-system only partially alien. The self-representation, although ill fitting, continues to be the primary vehicle of self-expression and growth; the life story, although stalled at an impasse, continues to be a work in progress; and the ego ideal and the superego, although weakened, continue to be the primary instruments of self-motivation. Nevertheless, the more important point is that the self-system has been undermined to a significant extent.

Midlife Dissatisfaction and the Possibility of Shadow Awakening

This undermining of the self-system can lead to shadow awakening. The likelihood of shadow awakening increases because loss of faith in social roles weakens the incentive to avoid impulses that were repressed as a condition of performing those roles. Those who in early adulthood had to repress parts of themselves so they could perform adult roles might for this reason, should they experience dissatisfaction at midlife, be especially prone to look back and feel misled by society's promise that success in social roles is rewarded with happiness. They might be especially prone to disillusionment of a bitter sort at midlife, perhaps feeling that society had cheated them not only by inducing them to work hard in pursuit of an impossible goal but also by requiring them to sacrifice important parts of themselves as a condition of doing so. Such feelings of disillusionment open the door for a return of the repressed.

The fact that the door has thus been opened for a return of the repressed does not mean that shadow impulses will reawaken. Shadow impulses are not contained under pressure, ready to spring forth once the original incentives that led to their repression disappear. Something more, therefore, is needed to stir them than midlife loss of faith in social roles. This something more is the presence of stimuli that trigger shadow impulses. It is plausible to assume that such stimuli *are* present during midlife. Stimuli that trigger repressed impulses most often do not go away when repression occurs. Rather, they simply lose their salience, especially when, in early adulthood, commitment to adult roles focuses attention on the challenges and benefits of those roles. Accordingly, assuming the presence of triggering stimuli, midlife loss of faith in social roles means that these stimuli can no longer be easily ignored. Stimuli that trigger shadow impulses thus regain salience; and as they do, they can stir shadow impulses, thus recharging them with energy.

Because each person's shadow is different, there is no way to state for any person which shadow impulses are most likely to reawaken at midlife. In the last chapter (text box 12.1) we presented a list of the six types of impulses that might be repressed in early adulthood and the reasons they might be repressed. Any of the impulses in that list, and many others besides, could be a candidate for reawakening at midlife for some people. Given this fact, it is impossible to present a typical account of midlife shadow awakening.

This point made, there are impulses that awaken during midlife that can plausibly be interpreted as reawakening shadow impulses. Consider the following scenarios: (1) a man who, when young, quit performing in a music group to opt for the security of a business career begins at midlife to experience a desire to be a musical performer again; (2) a woman who had identified with being heterosexual begins at midlife to experience strong attractions to women; and (3) a man who had been an ardent member of a faith community begins at midlife to question his faith and to explore alternative belief systems. Let us use these possible examples to explain more fully how shadow awakening might be experienced at midlife.

Perhaps the clearest indication that shadow awakening has begun is the emergence of the shadow voice. As we know, this voice tends at first to speak as an adversary to the self-system and as a tempter enticing the ego to yield to impulses that are prohibited by the self-system. Turning to our examples for illustration, the shadow voice emerging at midlife might begin to speak as follows:

1. "You've given 24/7 to the company. The work is tedious and unfulfilling. You've stuck with it to provide for the family. It's time to begin living your own life, even if it will be hard on the family for a while! You know that music is what you really love!"

2. "You've never been attracted to men. Stop denying it. John is a good man, but you know you don't love him. If you're ever going to find love, you need to follow your desires!"

3. "Why would God have given us minds of our own if not to think for ourselves? The teachings of the church are obviously out of touch with the times. It's better to admit that you don't know than to pretend that you do. Don't play along any longer!"

In speaking to themselves in these ways, the people in our examples might be dealing only with superficial midlife dissatisfaction, in which case they might quickly work through their shadow issues and soon be comfortable with their lives again. However, it is possible that their dissatisfaction is more serious, in which case the shadow voice might become more insistent, perhaps moving them to the brink of shadow action. The man who wants to return to music might begin to pursue performance opportunities and might consider quitting his job. The woman questioning her sexual orientation might find that she has fallen in love with a woman and might consider having an affair. The man doubting his faith might acknowledge his doubts to trusted friends and might consider moving away from his faith community.

Although the shadow voice tends at first to speak as an adversary and tempter, it sometimes later begins to speak as a counselor and guide. As a counselor, the shadow voice, which had been primarily a harsh critic of the status quo, becomes a source of ideas about how one might best embark on a new life path. At the same time, as a guide, the shadow voice, which had been primarily a goad to disobedience, becomes a source of discernment that brings into focus new life possibilities as they emerge. Such a transformation of the shadow voice occurs most often when shadow awakening facilitates developmental growth, as it does when it awakens impulses that, rooted in one's biological or psychological makeup, need to be acknowledged and integrated—and, therefore, allowed expression or brought under control—if one is to be psychologically whole.

We can now return to our examples to see how the shadow voice might evolve from a voice of an adversary and tempter into a voice of a counselor and guide. The man whose shadow voice derided his job might now begin to speak to himself as a counselor and guide by suggesting to himself how he might explain his passion for music to his family, how, without continuing his business career, he might provide for his family by supplementing income from musical engagements with a part-time job, or, perhaps, how he might negotiate a modus vivendi with his wife that would allow him to travel as a performer. The woman whose shadow voice challenged her sexual orientation might now begin to speak to herself as a counselor and guide by suggesting to herself how she might refashion her appearance, how she might open or end her marriage, how she might let others know about her sexual orientation, or how she might begin a relationship of a kind she has never experienced before. Finally, the man whose shadow voice sought to undermine his faith might now begin to speak to himself as a counselor and guide by suggesting to himself how he might best let his family know about his new perspective, how he might speak his mind forthrightly without offending those who still believe as he did, or, perhaps, how he might seek out new friends who believe as he now does.

Carl Jung, who first introduced the notion of the shadow, stressed the counseling and guiding functions of the shadow voice during midlife. Presupposing the traditional (essentialist, binary) understanding of male and female sexuality and gender differences, he argued that the shadow voice of a women is a man's voice and that the shadow voice of a man is a women's voice. Although there is much in Jung's account of such contrasexual or opposite-gender shadow awakening at midlife that is problematic, we should briefly discuss it here, both because it brought attention to a type of shadow awakening that can occur at midlife and because it has had an immense influence on all subsequent discussion of shadow awakening.

Jung held that contrasexual impulses, which are often repressed in early adulthood, often awaken at midlife. He believed that this midlife awakening of contrasexual impulses leads to a balancing of gender opposites. In his view, men at midlife frequently come under the influence of their feminine side or "anima," expressed in the voice of a female counselor and guide, and that women frequently come under the influence of their masculine side or "animus," expressed in the voice of a male counselor and guide. In Jung's account, a man's anima can elicit feminine powers that complement his masculine strengths; and a woman's animus can elicit masculine strengths that complement her feminine powers.

Jung's account of contrasexual shadow awakening at midlife can be understood in terms of society's promotion of an exaggerated gender dimorphism in its conventional definitions of "masculine," "feminine," "father," and "mother." These definitions have been subject to a great deal of criticism in recent decades for their stereotypical, restrictive, and binary character. Nevertheless, many young men and women still strongly identify with these definitions, believing that the more fully they embody them the better they will be able to attract desirable partners and the more effective they will be in performing parenting roles. For young adults who do strongly identify with these definitions, being male or female as defined by society becomes a core feature of their self-representations, a feature that excludes contrasexual impulses.

These prohibited impulses are disallowed expression and relegated to the shadow, where they remain until, for some, midlife loosening of gender-based features of the self-representation opens the door for their awakening. Midlife, as a time when youth slips away, when testosterone levels in men decline and the hormonal changes of female menopause occur, when parenting roles wind down, and when dissatisfaction with social roles can occur, is clearly a time when it is plausible to expect changes in the sense of what it means to be male or female.

Jung's account of contrasexual shadow awakening at midlife was a major contribution in its time. However, although some studies have supported his account, findings overall are mixed. Of most concern is that studies have not established that contrasexual awakening is as prevalent during midlife as Jung believed or even that it plays an important causal role in countering society's exaggerated gender dimorphism. Studies have confirmed that conventional male-female differences *do* decrease during midlife (at least for the reasons mentioned in the last paragraph).[13] However, studies have not confirmed that contrasexual awakening is always or even ordinarily a cause, let alone the primary cause, of this decrease. Although a good deal of personal testimony supports Jung's view, there is not enough evidence to know how often contrasexual awakening occurs during midlife or to what extent it is a contributing cause of midlife decrease in conventional male-female differences.

Another issue with Jung's account of contrasexual shadow awakening at midlife is that it does not consider the possible midlife awakening of sexuality or gender in forms other than those associated with the traditional view of male and female as inherent binary opposites. Limited to this traditional view, Jung believed that contrasexual awakening is "normal" during midlife and that it leads to a beneficial outcome, gender balancing, thus implying if not explicitly stating that the awakening of other forms of sexual or gender expression during midlife may not be normal and may not have beneficial outcomes. Jung was ahead of his time on feminist and on gay and lesbian issues. His thinking on feminist issues was progressive because he recognized the value of forms of thought and feeling traditionally associated with women; and his thinking on gay and lesbian issues was progressive because, in addition to opposing the criminalization of homosexuality, he defended homosexuality, if not as a form of sexuality, at least as a form of love.[14]

Nevertheless, judged from the perspective of our time, Jung was insensitive and uninformed in his understanding of the issues in question. His thinking on feminist issues was distorted by the stereotypical, binary assumptions of the traditional understanding of male-female differences; and his thinking on gay and lesbian issues was closed to the idea of homosexuality being anything more than an immature form of love. It is understandable that many feminists have been critical of Jung and that the LGBTQ community has found little of value in his writings. Nevertheless, Jung remains a pioneer of great importance so far as the phenomenon of midlife shadow awakening is concerned. He is to be credited for having explained how midlife can be a time when we become more complete and balanced human beings by integrating previously rejected parts of ourselves, including not only those related to sexuality or gender but also many others that are often sacrificed in early adulthood as the cost of being allowed to perform adult social roles.

When shadow impulses awaken during midlife, they can be disconcerting and can interfere with the performance of social roles. People who experience midlife crises and begin acting in uncharacteristic ways, perhaps exploring dramatically different interests, lifestyles, or relationships, might be responding not only to midlife dissatisfaction but also to shadow awakening. Such extreme actions reveal that midlife dissatisfaction can be more than just a disillusionment with social roles. They reveal that midlife dissatisfaction can also be a lifting of constraints that allows a recharging of repressed impulses, impulses that had remained quietly in the background when one was striving to succeed in one's social roles.

Despite the upheaval it can cause, midlife shadow awakening often facilitates psychological growth, as, again, it is most likely to do when it awakens impulses that are inherent to one's biological or psychological makeup. When impulses of these sorts are repressed, neither the internal sources nor, ordinarily, the external triggers of the impulses go away. The internal sources languish or fester; and the external triggers—whether the original triggers or substitutes for them—can enter one's life at any time and may never have left in the first place. Failure to address repressed impulses of such a deeply rooted sort can, therefore, have serious negative consequences, including feelings of incompleteness and inauthenticity, neurotic and somatic symptoms of a variety of sorts, and, eventually, the inability to move forward in development. We recalled earlier that repression may be the price one must pay in early adulthood to be allowed to perform adult social roles and thus pursue happiness as defined by society. Here we can add that shadow awakening may be the price one must pay at midlife to break through developmental arrest and thus move toward greater wholeness and authenticity.

Caution is needed because shadow awakening is not always a good thing. Some people harbor shadow impulses of an unwholesome, strongly antisocial sort. The reawakening of impulses of this sort during midlife—or at any other time—is problematic. Depending on the type and strength of such impulses, it might be that neither rerepression nor safe integration of the impulses is possible. Professional help might be needed to devise a plan for how to live with impulses that are antisocial and, perhaps, dangerous to others. It is not easy to have sympathy for people who experience impulses to commit heinous deeds. Nevertheless, people who have such impulses, who understand the heinous nature of their impulses, *and* who, perhaps with professional help, have done what is necessary to keep their impulses under control deserve, if not credit, at least acknowledgment for waging a difficult internal struggle for the sake of others.

The Lifeworld—A Place of Duty and Repetition of the Same

For those suffering midlife dissatisfaction, the lifeworld, like the self-system, is rendered alien to some extent. Dissatisfaction with one's social roles at midlife is at the same time a dissatisfaction with the lifeworld in which one performs those roles. Midlife dissatisfaction thus causes the lifeworld to lose much of its appeal. The lifeworld, which had been a place of satisfying engagement and hopeful prospects for the future, becomes a place that is stale and restricting, a place primarily of duty and repetition of the same. In extreme cases, the lifeworld affected by midlife dissatisfaction can seem like a prison, a world in which one is held captive because one has been committed to it for so long.

Just as midlife dissatisfaction does not render the self-system completely alien, neither does it render the lifeworld completely alien. Most people suffering midlife dissatisfaction remain sufficiently invested in their lifeworlds not to abandon them. However, if people suffering midlife dissatisfaction do not ordinarily abandon their lifeworlds, they do fantasize about more attractive alternatives. They imagine what it would be like to live in new places embarking on new endeavors, cultivating new relationships, or, simply, pursuing pleasure. These fantasies go hand in hand with the search for new goals for the ego ideal, discussed earlier. Both are expressions of being caught between the old and the new, between the life one has been living and a significantly different, more satisfying life that one might embark on.

People respond to midlife loss of interest in the lifeworld in a variety of ways. The best-known response is also the most extreme and, according to the research cited at the beginning of the chapter, the least common. This response is simply to abandon one's lifeworld in search of dramatic change, as sometimes happens during midlife crises. Most of us know of people who at midlife have quit their jobs or left their partners or walked away from an ideology or faith to explore new possibilities in work, relationship, or belief. Although such measures are extreme, that does not mean they are destined to have regrettable consequences. Abandoning roles that one has long performed can be the best response for some people, especially for those who are motivated by midlife dissatisfaction to deal with problems that predate midlife. For example, midlife dissatisfaction can provide the motivation needed finally to walk away from a job for which one was never well suited, to free oneself from a toxic relationship, and to disaffiliate oneself from an ideology or faith in which one no longer believes. For people who are thus aided by midlife dissatisfaction, beginning life anew in a significantly restructured lifeworld might turn out to be the best or the only way for them to overcome midlife dissatisfaction. In looking back, they might conclude that they did the right thing, at least for themselves.

A second response to midlife loss of interest in the lifeworld, this one less extreme and more common, is to find new sources of satisfaction that do not require one to abandon any of one's primary roles. For example, some people find new sources of satisfaction by doing such things as returning to school; adding a part-time job; cultivating old or new friendships; volunteering to work for charitable, civic, or political organizations; or embarking on craft, artistic, or writing projects. Clearly, doing things of these sorts can help reenliven a lifeworld with which one has become dissatisfied, thus enhancing its appeal and reducing the level of dissatisfaction overall. Moreover, with overall dissatisfaction thus reduced, one might begin to perceive the roles that had been the original focus of dissatisfaction in a new, more positive way.

The two responses to loss of interest in the lifeworld just described are well known because they are based on observable actions. Another response, this one less well known although perhaps more common, is to take no action and simply persevere in quiet desperation. Perhaps taking no action should not count as a response, since it allows dissatisfaction to unfold without doing anything to alleviate it. Nevertheless, nonaction is a response of a sort; indeed, it is a response that for most people leads to a positive outcome. This fact is confirmed by studies that have found that, in today's world, life after midlife is on balance a time of happiness for most people. We discuss these studies in the next chapter. The point here is that these studies indicate that time is on the side of those who suffer midlife dissatisfaction, even if they take no action to bring it to an end. In most cases perseverance on its own leads eventually to a lifting of dissatisfaction and, therefore, to renewed appreciation of one's life circumstances.

There is one more response to midlife loss of interest in the lifeworld that deserves consideration. This response is less well understood than the previous three because it is based on philosophical reflection, a kind of thinking to which many people are not inclined. This fact notwithstanding, philosophical reflection, I suggest, can be an effective response to midlife loss of interest in the lifeworld because it can lead to insights that reveal that one's dissatisfaction is often more a product of unrealistic aspirations or misleading assumptions than it is of one's actual midlife circumstances.

One such insight, which is especially helpful to those whose dissatisfaction at midlife is one of frustration for not having fully achieved their goals, is the realization that the long-term goals set in early adulthood tend to be unrealistic in the sense of being set higher than most people can achieve. There are two reasons why young adults tend to set their goals so high. The first is that it is the function of the ego ideal to do just this. The ego ideal projects an ideal way of living according to which one is—or, it is hoped, will become—highly successful in one's roles. The second reason is that many modern societies, promoting competitive individualism and upward mobility, encourage the belief that with enough effort one can be whatever one aspires to be, even if one's goals are set very high. Thus motivated by their ego ideals and encouraged by society, many young adults commit themselves to roles in pursuit of goals that, although achievable by some, are not realistically achievable by most.

This insight about aiming higher than most can reach can help people who have fallen short of their goals come to terms with the lives they have lived. Specifically, it can help them see that even though they have not fully achieved their original goals, they have nonetheless achieved a good deal. The insight about goals being set unrealistically high can thus help people see that their circumstances, although perhaps far from ideal, are good enough. People who have fallen short of their goals can in this way begin once again to perceive their lifeworlds in a positive way.

A second insight that can help alleviate loss of interest in the lifeworld is the realization that, and why, society's promise of happiness for those who succeed in their social roles is misleading. Society encourages the belief that success in one's roles is rewarded with happiness for the same reason it encourages the belief that with enough effort one can be whatever one wants to be. The reason is that both these messages motivate people to be as productive as they can possibly be and, therefore, to contribute to social well-being as much as they possibly can. However, both messages are misleading, for what promotes well-being for the collective is not always in the interest of the individual. Coming to this insight can also have a transforming effect on the lifeworld.

People who, having achieved their goals, experience midlife as the prime of life are not likely to question society's promise that happiness is the reward for succeeding in one's roles. For them, society's promise seems to have been fulfilled. However, those who experience dissatisfaction because they have fallen short of their goals and, even more, those who experience dissatisfaction despite having achieved their goals may well question this promise and might come to see that, and why, it is misleading. Those who have fallen short of their goals might come to see not only that they set their goals higher than most can reach but also that their pursuit of success had been motivated by a suspect definition of happiness. As for those who have achieved their goals without thereby achieving happiness, they are even more likely to arrive at the second of these insights. Having achieved success but not happiness, they are themselves "refutations" of society's promise equating happiness with success.

Initially, the insight that one has been misled by society's definition of happiness can deepen one's dissatisfaction. However, it can also soon lead to a renewal of interest in the lifeworld because it is an easy transition from the disillusioning insight that one has been misled about happiness to the inspiring insight that there is more to happiness than what one had been led to believe. This last insight is inspiring because it stirs a search for new sources of happiness, a search that frequently leads to the discovery that happiness can be found in many things that, although available to almost everyone, were underappreciated when one's primary focus had been on the pursuit of success. Things in which happiness might now be found are the beauties of nature, contemplation, gatherings with friends, hobbies, expanding one's knowledge, creative endeavors, and contributing to the welfare of others or future generations. In better appreciating goods like these, people who suffer dissatisfaction at midlife—whether out of frustration, because they have fallen short of their goals, or out of disappointment, because they have achieved their goals without thereby achieving happiness—often find that their living circumstances, rather than being stale and restricting, are rich in sources of happiness.

Conclusion

There is no single or best way of responding to midlife dissatisfaction. Some people need to abandon their roles and venture into new lifeworlds. Others need only find new activities in which they can find satisfaction, activities that supplement rather than replace their primary roles. Still others find that the healing effect of time suffices to bring an end to dissatisfaction. Yet others deal with dissatisfaction by reflecting on the goals they set in early adulthood and on why they pursued them. Only a minority of people who struggle with midlife dissatisfaction abandon one or more of their primary roles. Most work through midlife dissatisfaction by supplementing their roles with new activities, by benefiting from the passage of time, or both. Some, those who are inclined to philosophical reflection, work through midlife dissatisfaction by thinking more deeply about the reasons for their dissatisfaction and in this way coming to see that their lives are richer in sources of satisfaction than they had thought.

Chapter 14

Retirement

Medical advances in the twentieth century greatly lengthened the average lifespan. Benefiting from this progress, most people living in developed countries can now expect to live not only well beyond middle age but also well into their senior years. The lengthening of the lifespan has perhaps most dramatically increased the number of years people can expect to live between the time they retire and the time they begin to experience the decline in abilities characteristic of advanced old age. These years are increasingly being recognized as making up an important stage of life: the stage of the retired senior.

The stage of the retired senior can be defined as the time when (1) one has retired in the sense of having ceased to perform full-time job or parenting roles, and (2) one is senior in age but not yet limited by significant age-related decline. Because retirement occurs earlier for some people and later for others and because significant decline also occurs earlier for some people and later for others, there are no definite age boundaries marking the beginning and end of the stage of the retired senior. However, approximate boundaries are clear enough. In developed countries at the present time the stage ordinarily begins in the middle to late sixties and ordinarily lasts at least until the middle to late seventies if not until the early to middle eighties.

Retirement is like midlife in being a stage with multiple pathways. We learned in the last chapter that midlife has three major pathways, a pathway of satisfaction, a pathway of dissatisfaction, and a pathway of both satisfaction and dissatisfaction. In this chapter, we propose that the stage of the retired senior has four primary pathways or at least that it does so currently in the developed countries in which the stage has recently emerged.

We refer to these pathways as "succumbing to loss," "enjoying freedom," "meeting the challenge," and "answering the call."

The discussion of the stage of the retired senior in this chapter assumes that retired seniors have the financial resources needed to live relatively comfortable lives and that they are in relatively good health. Sadly, these assumptions fail to describe the circumstances of many retired seniors. This fact notwithstanding, the assumptions are adopted here because they make it possible to explain why a basic shared fact of retired life—that one is no longer performing full-time job or parenting roles—is the starting point for markedly different pathways through the retirement years. Retired seniors who live comfortably and enjoy good health can choose among alternative pathways, whereas retired seniors lacking resources or suffering poor health frequently cannot.

Studies cited in the last chapter documenting a trade-off between declining executive functions (and fluid intelligence) on the one hand and growing crystallized intelligence on the other hand apply not only to people at midlife but also to retired seniors. Executive functions continue to decline during the retirement years, owing both to the vulnerability of the prefrontal cortex to aging and to deterioration of connections between the prefrontal cortex and other brain regions with which the prefrontal cortex interacts.[1] However, offsetting this decline in executive functions is the continuing growth of crystallized intelligence, at least for those retired seniors who pursue new learning and acquire new skills. Although older adults do significantly less well on cognitive tasks requiring the processing of new information, a good short-term memory, and the ability to analyze new situations, they can do better than younger adults on many cognitive tasks, for example, those involving vocabulary, stored information, comprehension, recognition of similarities, and even arithmetic.[2]

Additionally, growth in postformal cognition, especially as pertains to human affairs, can grow during retirement, thus increasing a senior's "wisdom of age." Retired seniors may worry about declining abilities to recall names and facts, to block distractions, to sustain focused attention, and to respond quickly to challenges they have not faced before. These worries, however, can be allayed if retired seniors reflect on the large body of knowledge and large repertoire of skills they have acquired over the course of their lives. Like people during midlife, people in their retirement years have an advantage in crystallized intelligence that can more than offset the disadvantage of declining executive functions and fluid intelligence. The retirement years can be a time of both serious intellectual study and effective practical endeavor, a time during which cognitive and practical abilities remain strong overall and can even improve.

The discussion that follows is divided into two parts. The first part explains more fully the most general ways in which retirement changes the self-system and lifeworld, those that apply to everyone who retires. The second part then explains four markedly different ways in which retired seniors have responded to these changes, ways that have led them to follow four markedly different pathways through the retirement years.

Self-System and Lifeworld—Changes That Apply to Everyone

Retirement changes the self-system by deleting from it those features of the self-representation, those goals of the ego ideal, and those duties of the superego that had been based on preretirement job or parenting roles. To facilitate discussion of these changes, beginning with those to the self-representation, let us consider the case of a woman who has just retired from a career as a police officer and is no longer performing the role of caregiver for her children, who are now grown.

Clearly, in retiring, this woman would to a significant extent relinquish the features "police officer" and "mother" from her self-representation. The qualification "to a significant extent" is needed because previous job or parenting features of the self-representation characteristically "linger" in a meaningful but diminished and fading way.[3] However, even when these features linger, it remains true that, in retiring, seniors relinquish much of the sense of *being* what previously, when they were still performing their primary roles, they had little doubt they *were*. This removal or attenuation of core features of the self-representation can be distressing. However, it is less often a cause of distress today than it was in earlier years, before the extension of the lifespan made possible by advances in medicine, as we shall see.

The loss of preretirement job or parenting features from the self-representation requires major revisions to the life story. Having relinquished the roles that had given their life stories their basic plotlines, retired seniors must rethink who they are and what they are supposed to do. This rethinking is a challenge because the retirement years in developed societies today have no preassigned expectations. Unlike traditional societies, in which seniors ordinarily have well-defined kinship roles, responsibilities, and privileges, societies like ours have no conventions stipulating what one is supposed to be or do during retirement. Some researchers have for this reason used the term "normless" to describe the stage of the retired senior, indicating by the term that the stage has no definition other than the negative one of being a stage in which full-time job or parenting roles are no longer being performed.[4] Accordingly, it is up to each retired person to create her or his own retirement story. In this chapter, we set forth the distinctive themes of the life stories corresponding to each of the four pathways through the retirement years we discuss.

In removing features of the self-representation that had been based on job or parenting roles, retirement at the same time removes corresponding ideal goals from the ego ideal. Once the police officer and mother has retired from the police department and has finished raising her children, she ceases striving to be a model police officer and mother. Almost all retirees continue to pursue ideal goals, both goals carried over from preretirement years and new goals. However, all retirees cease pursuing the core ideal goals they had pursued since the beginning of adulthood, those based on job or parenting roles. These core goals of the ego ideal, like the corresponding features of the self-representation, are deleted from the self-system.

Also deleted from the self-system are those duties that the superego had enforced to ensure at least adequate performance of preretirement job or parenting roles. If one has retired from a job as a police officer, one no longer needs to prod oneself to make it to work on time or to avoid mistakes in law-enforcement procedure. If one's children are grown and living independently, one no longer needs to give oneself pep talks to prepare meals for them, to get them off to school, to drive them to extracurricular activities, and the like. Before retirement, enforcing duties like these is the main job of the superego. After retirement, however, the superego is relieved of these duties. It continues as before to enforce other duties of daily life, and for most people it enforces new duties dictated by their retirement pathway. Nevertheless, the superego "retires" from the chief duties it had earlier performed.

Understandably, retired seniors, in reflecting on the changes to the self-system just discussed, are prompted to ask themselves questions about their identity, purpose, and justification. Corresponding to the loss of core features of their self-representations, retired seniors are prompted to ask, "Now that I am no longer an X [fill in job or parenting roles], what am I?" Corresponding to the loss of core goals of the ego ideal, they are prompted to ask, "Now that I no longer strive to be an ideal X, what is my purpose?" Finally, corresponding to the loss of core duties of the superego, they are prompted to ask, "Now that I no longer must do what an X is supposed to do, what, if anything, should I do [to earn justifying value as a member of society]?" The ways in which retired people respond to these questions—henceforth referred to as "the three questions of retirement"—determine the pathway through the retirement years they will follow.

Retirement changes the lifeworld in ways that correspond closely to the changes in the self-system just discussed. Corresponding to the removal of job or parenting components from the self-system is a relocation of the lifeworld from the center to the margins of the social world. In ceasing to perform full-time job or parenting roles and in growing older in a youth-oriented society, retired seniors are moved, whether suddenly or gradually, from the hub to the periphery of society. Having ceased performing major roles on the main stage of life, they find themselves on a side stage on which roles have not been assigned.

Although retired seniors share a space on the margins of the social world, they do not for that reason live in the same lifeworld. On the contrary, they live in markedly different lifeworlds because they perceive their shared living space in markedly different ways. Their differing perceptions correspond to the pathways through the retirement years we discuss. As we shall see, retired seniors who find themselves on the pathway of succumbing to loss live in a lifeworld of "idleness and isolation," those who pursue the pathway of enjoying freedom live in a lifeworld of "leisure or recreation," those who choose the pathway of meeting the challenge live in a lifeworld of "commitment and responsibility," and those who are drawn to the pathway of answering the call live in a lifeworld of "devotion or practice."

Having described the most general changes to the self-system and lifeworld that occur when one retires, we can now consider why retired seniors respond to these changes in such different ways, thus following different pathways and living in different lifeworlds during the retirement years. For purposes of exposition, the four pathways and corresponding lifeworlds sketched below are presented in extreme form. Few people follow just one pathway and live in its corresponding lifeworld as emphatically as the ensuing discussion would suggest. Nevertheless, we have chosen to describe the four pathways and their lifeworlds in extreme form so that their distinguishing features and primary differences can be seen as clearly as possible, in bold outline.

Four Pathways, Four Lifeworlds

Pathway of Succumbing to Loss, Lifeworld of Idleness and Isolation

Some people experience retirement as a distressing loss of what had been their primary roles. Typically, these are people who were strongly identified with their job or parenting roles and enjoyed the status and benefits that went with them. Such people are understandably despondent when they retire, especially when they believe that there is little to look forward to in their retirement years. For people in this group, the three questions of retirement are deeply troubling because they accentuate the sense of loss of identity, purpose, and justification they experience. As we shall see, this response to retirement, which was once quite common, is much less so now. Nevertheless, there are still people who experience retirement primarily in a negative way, as a loss of their preretirement life.

Research indicates that differences in how men and women experience retirement is to a great extent determined by differences in the roles from which they retire and how they perceived those roles before they retired.[5] Before the last quarter of the twentieth century, most primary social roles were assigned by gender. Most men worked outside the home and for this reason were more susceptible, if they experienced retirement primarily as a loss, to a sense of having lost identity, purpose, and justification conferred by a job in the public workplace. In contrast, most women worked within the home and for this reason were more susceptible, if they experienced retirement primarily as a loss, to a sense of having lost identity, purpose, and justification conferred by being a homemaker and caregiver of growing children.

This traditional gender arrangement has been giving way for many years, beginning in the years of World War II and picking up pace in the 1960s, 1970s, and thereafter. However, this arrangement has by no means disappeared. Although most women now work outside the home, they continue in many households to perform most of the caregiving roles and to take most responsibility for managing the household and maintaining family and friendship relationships. The traditional gender arrangement, therefore, still affects how men and women experience retirement, including men and women who experience retirement in the negative way we are describing here.

People who experience retirement primarily as a loss are prone to reconstruct the self-system in a negative way. The self-representation becomes a representation of someone who used to be an X (fill in job or parenting roles) but who now is "no longer an X." The self-representation is thus refashioned in a way that leaves the retired person without a sense of satisfying identity. Although some sense of "being an X" may linger, what is most evident to those on the pathway under discussion is that a previous, highly valued identity (and corresponding sense of purpose and justification) has been lost. This loss of identity is reflected in the life story. The inner narrator now focuses primarily on the past, with few and primarily negative things to say about the present and future. In effect, the life story is over. The narrator feels like an outsider looking back on a previous life.

As the self-representation and life story are transformed in these ways, the ego ideal ceases functioning for the most part. People whose primary focus is on the loss of their preretirement roles feel as though there is little left to strive for. The primary goals of the preretirement years have been deleted from the ego ideal without being replaced with new ones, thus leaving the retired person with a sense of purposelessness. As for the superego, it, too, like the self-representation, life story, and ego ideal, becomes primarily negative, now often speaking in a harsh, punitive tone. Without previous job or parenting duties to perform, there is little left for the superego to do other than be critical of the retired person for being idle. The superego voice for this reason chides the retired person for no longer contributing to society and, therefore, for lacking justifying value. The whole of the self-system is thus reconstructed in a negative way.

Corresponding to this negative reconstruction of the self-system is a negative reconstruction of the lifeworld. For seniors who experience retirement primarily as a loss, the margins of the social world to which they have been moved are experienced as a space in which they merely pass time, bereft of social function and cut off from valued relationships. These seniors, therefore, live in a lifeworld of idleness and isolation, a lifeworld in which they are confined and left with nothing meaningful to do. This lifeworld is most often the home. For people who retire from a job in the public workplace, the home, which had been a haven for physical and emotional rejuvenation, now becomes a place of incarceration. For people whose primary role was that of a homemaker and caregiver, the home, which had been a place of engagement bustling with children, now becomes an empty nest.

Fortunately, such a one-sidedly negative response to retirement is now quite rare. We have already noted that many retired people continue to identify with their preretirement roles, although less strongly than they did before retiring. These people, therefore, continue to enjoy some sense of satisfying identity, even if only in a qualified "I am a retired X" way. More importantly, the extension of the lifespan made possible by advances in medicine has changed the meaning of retirement in a way that mitigates the sense of loss that some people feel. Retirement is no longer associated with the nearness of the end of life and is now seen as the beginning of a new and perhaps lengthy stage of life. This perception of retirement as the beginning of a new stage helps retired seniors to dwell less on the past and focus more on the future.

Recent studies have found that most people, rather than experiencing retirement primarily in the negative way we have described in this section, instead experience it as a trade-off of losses and gains, where gains include goods such as greater autonomy, more leisure time, and relief from job or parenting stress. Additionally, an increasing number of studies have found that, with the lengthening of the lifespan, negative emotions tend to decrease in one's senior years and, therefore, that overall life satisfaction or mental well-being tends to increase after retirement, at least until advanced old age.[6] These latter studies indicate that the retirement years can be the best years of life, thus providing solace for people who are persevering through midlife dissatisfaction and, more pertinent here, providing positive prospects for people who are about to retire from roles they have valued and will sorely miss. However, despite this positive news, it remains true that some people experience retirement as a painful loss, whether only temporarily or for an extended time.

Pathway of Enjoying Freedom, Lifeworld of Leisure or Recreation

Opposite to people who experience retirement primarily as a loss are people who experience it primarily as freedom from job or parenting responsibilities. Some of these people may have enjoyed their preretirement roles but enjoy their newfound freedom more. Others, however, may have felt alienated or, perhaps, even demeaned in their preretirement roles and, upon retiring, feel only relief in being free of them. In either case, people who experience retirement primarily as freedom from previous responsibilities welcome the changes that retirement brings. This positive perspective is reflected in both the self-system and the lifeworld. The self-system is reconstructed in ways that reflect freedom from previous responsibilities and, therefore, freedom to do as one pleases. The lifeworld is reconstructed in corresponding fashion, becoming a place in which one, free from the demands of preretirement life, is at last free to enjoy leisure or recreation.

Seniors enjoying the freedom of retired life may regret having lost previous role-related features of their self-representations. The police officer and mother, upon retiring, might feel relief in being free of police and parenting responsibilities but still miss having "police officer" and "mother" as core features of her self-representation, even if these features still linger to some extent. In her case, retirement might be a better-than-even trade-off, an exchange of valued features of identity for greater autonomy, more leisure time, and relief from job and parenting stress. For her, the exchange of previous identity for freedom might thus be a net gain. In contrast, people who felt alienated or, perhaps, demeaned in their preretirement roles would understandably feel unqualified relief in no longer having their self-representations tied to those roles. Not only would they no longer have to do something they did not like doing; they would no longer have to be something they did not like being. For these people, the exchange of previous identity for freedom would be an unqualified gain.

For seniors whose primary focus is on freedom, the life story becomes a story of a person who, having worked hard for many years, can now enjoy the fruits of his or her labor. The life story is now about a person who looks forward to a stress-free, enjoyable retirement, the kind often described as "the golden years." Clearly, such a story is the opposite of the story of the person who experiences retirement primarily as a loss. Nevertheless, both stories give expression to the same underlying changes to the self-system and lifeworld: the removal of those components of the self-system that had been based on job or parenting roles and the relocation of the lifeworld from the center to the margins of the social world.

Unlike seniors who experience retirement primarily as a loss, seniors who experience retirement primarily as freedom do not feel as though their lives are without purpose. The removal of previous job or parenting goals from their ego ideals does not leave them with a sense that they have nothing left to strive for. These seniors, therefore, are happy for the most part to live with fewer goals. They do still pursue ideal goals. For example, although the retired police officer and mother no longer aspires to be a model police officer and a model mother, she may still aspire to ideal goals unaffected by retirement, perhaps those of being a model spouse or partner, a model grandmother, and a model caregiver of elderly parents. The point is that the removal of preretirement goals from the ego ideal does not have a significantly negative effect on the retired person's well-being. The newfound sense of freedom outweighs any sense of loss of purpose.

It also outweighs any sense of loss of justification that might emerge from no longer performing job or parenting roles. Just as seniors whose primary focus is on freedom are happy to have fewer goals to pursue, they also are happy to have fewer duties to perform. The fact that they no longer perform full-time job or parenting roles does not cause them to feel idle or lacking in justification. For them, therefore, the question of justification is not an anguishing concern. Should it arise, the question can ordinarily be answered without difficulty. The retired police officer and mother might say, "I paid my dues. I served as a police officer for thirty-seven years and raised two children, who are now adults making their own contributions to society. I deserve time to do as I please." Seniors who experience retirement as freedom continue to speak to themselves in the voice of the superego. The superego continues to work as the enforcer of prudence generally and of honesty, fidelity, household chores, payment of bills, and the like specifically. However, the superego now has a much lighter workload because it is no longer charged with the task of enforcing the stressful duties of full-time job or parenting roles.

Like the self-system, the lifeworld of people who experience retirement as freedom reflects a lifting of preretirement responsibilities. The lifeworld of these people, therefore, is any place that allows them to do as they please, whether their preference is leisure or recreation or both. Specifically, it is a place in which retired people can do such things as meet with family and friends, read books, pursue hobbies, undertake projects, or travel. Such a lifeworld can take many physical forms. It can be a home, social gathering place, vacation spot, craft studio, workshop, flower garden, or study. Whatever form it takes, this lifeworld of leisure or recreation is the reward given to retired people for having met their social obligations at least passably well.

PATHWAY OF MEETING THE CHALLENGE, LIFEWORLD OF COMMITMENT AND RESPONSIBILITY

Many people, rather than experiencing retirement primarily as a loss or as freedom, instead experience it primarily as a challenge to reinvent themselves. These people feel challenged to replace the parts of their lives that were lost when they retired. Responding to this challenge, these people seek to add new features to their self-representations, new goals to their ego ideals, and new duties to their superegos. They seek to reinvent themselves by committing themselves to new social roles and by using these new roles to reconstruct their self-systems.

In this effort to reinvent themselves, these seniors do such things as take on part-time jobs, join boards or councils, volunteer for charitable work, care for grandchildren, devote themselves to an art form, and go back to school. These new roles serve as the bases for the reconstruction of the self-system. Identification with the new roles creates new features for the self-representation, features such as "zoo guide," "school board member," "hospice worker," "grandmother" or "grandfather," "portrait painter," and "philosophy student." In thus adding new role-based features to their self-representations, seniors seeking to reinvent themselves replace preretirement features with new features of the same general type, features that allow them to continue to contribute to society, either directly or indirectly (e.g., by further training or education). The difference is that full-time job or parenting roles have been replaced by roles better suited to the realities of retired life.

Commitment to new roles of the sort described assigns the inner narrator the task of adding a new chapter to the life story. This new chapter is like the one that preceded it in being a story about a person who has made commitments to social roles. This chapter, however, is shorter because seniors making commitments to new roles do so with a shorter future in view. They know that their new roles, or others that might replace them, will last only as long as health and stamina allow. The new chapter of the life story that is now narrated, therefore, is a relatively brief sequel to the chapter that preceded it.

Commitment to new social roles reconstitutes the ego ideal by creating new ideal goals to pursue. Seniors seeking to reinvent themselves replace goals that had been based on job or parenting roles with goals based on newly adopted retirement roles. The ego ideal, therefore, now reflects the desire to succeed ideally well in one's roles, say, as zoo guide, school board member, hospice worker, grandmother or grandfather, portrait painter, or philosophy student. The ego ideal, like the self-representation and life story, is thus a new version of its precursor, with the difference that it is adapted to a more limited future and to other realities of retired life.

The superego is also a new version of its precursor. It continues to function by enforcing the duties of social roles and of everyday life. However, because the senior who experiences retirement as a challenge has replaced preretirement job or parenting roles with new roles, many of the duties enforced by the superego are now new duties. The superego thus now enforces such duties as being on time for a shift at the zoo, being prepared for a school board meeting or hospice visit, being available to babysit grandchildren, or being dedicated to one's art or schoolwork. In enforcing these new duties, the superego, as it did before retirement, issues commands, metes out criticism, and offers praise to ensure, if not ideal, at least good enough performance of social roles. The superego thus continues to motivate activity that benefits society in some way.

In continuing to act in ways that benefit society, the retired person has a ready answer to the question of justification. Should the question arise, the retired person can say, "Of course I'm living as I should; I'm working a part-time job [or doing volunteer work or caring for grandchildren or producing art or studying and improving my mind]." The person who experiences retirement as a challenge continues to contribute to society and, therefore, continues to earn justifying value in the eyes of society. This earned value ensures that the question of justification, should it arise, will not pose a problem.

The lifeworld of the retired person taking on new social roles, like the self-system, is a new version of its preretirement precursor. Although all retired people are relocated to the margins of the social world, those who experience retirement as a challenge remain on the public stage, the difference being that they are no longer on the main public stage, on which full-time job or parenting roles are performed, and are now on a side stage, on which, characteristically, roles of shorter duration and with lighter responsibilities are performed. Despite thus being located on a side stage, the lifeworld of retired people seeking to reinvent themselves is like the lifeworld that preceded it in being a place of commitment and responsibility. It is a new version of the preretirement lifeworld adjusted to the realities of retired life.

Pathway of Answering the Call, Lifeworld of Devotion or Practice

Some people respond to the questions of retirement by experiencing a call to spiritual life. In the Hindu tradition, retirement is referred to as the stage of the "forest dweller." In this stage a person, having finished the work of the householder, withdraws from work and family responsibilities to devote full time to the pursuit of spiritual liberation. The West has no similar conception of retirement as being primarily a spiritual stage. Nevertheless, there are many people in the West who experience retirement as an opportunity finally to give their full attention to spiritual life.

Devotion to spiritual life in retirement is immediately reflected in the self-system. Regarding the self-representation, those of its features that had been based on job or parenting roles are now replaced with features that reflect that the primary focus of life has turned to the spiritual quest. Such a transformation is evident in answers that might now be given to the first of the three questions of retirement. In asking the question, "Now that I am no longer an X, what am I?" the retired person called to spiritual life might say, "I am a Jew [or Christian or Muslim] living a life of obedience, surrender, and service to God" or "I am a Hindu living a life of yogic practice [or renunciation or devotion to a guru or god]" or "I am a Buddhist living a life of nonattachment and loving kindness [or commitment to the Bodhisattva vow]." These answers indicate that retired people called to spiritual life identify themselves primarily with their spiritual belief, service, or practice.

As the self-representation is reconstituted as a primarily spiritual self-representation, the life story is rewritten in corresponding fashion. The ego's narrator voice, no longer needing to give primary attention to the responsibilities of work or family, now gives primary attention to matters of ultimate concern, matters pertaining to the state and destiny of the soul. The narrator voice might for this reason give primary attention to matters such as doubt versus faith, pride versus humility, desire versus nonattachment, sin versus surrender, or ignorance versus enlightenment. These matters of concern govern what is narrated about the primary activities of the day, which might include charitable or missionary work, service to a religious community, performance of devotional rituals, or practice of a spiritual discipline, such as prayer, yoga, or meditation. For many seniors called to spiritual life, the life story becomes less a story about life in this world than about life, perhaps eternal life, in another world, with this world being only a staging ground for the other world. In these and other ways, the life story of retired seniors whose highest priority is spiritual life is a story about a person living a life of spiritual belief, service, or practice as guided by matters of ultimate concern.

The ego ideal and the superego are also transformed by the call to spiritual life, as is evident in answers that might be given to the second and third questions of retirement. Asking themselves the second question—"Now that I no longer strive to be an ideal X, what is my purpose?"—retired people called to spiritual life might respond by saying that their purpose is to achieve a closer relationship with God, higher states of consciousness, or, ultimately, salvation, liberation, or enlightenment. Such goals, projected as ideals, now become the primary goals of the ego ideal.

As for the third question—"Now that I no longer need to discipline myself to do what an X is required to do, what, if anything, should I discipline myself to do?"—retired people called to spiritual life might respond by saying that they should now discipline themselves to be more committed in belief, more compassionate in service, or more diligent in practice. These answers indicate that the question of justification has become a question of whether one is trying as best one can to meet the challenges of the spiritual quest. More generally, they indicate that the superego has become the guardian, the protector and enforcer, of spiritual life.

For seniors called to spiritual life, the lifeworld on the margins of the social world is a place dedicated to spiritual pursuit. Such a place—whether a church or sanctuary, a hermitage or ashram, a monastery or convent, a forest dwelling or mountain top, or, perhaps most often, a private residence—is set apart from the mundane world. It is set apart not only because it is located on the margins of the social world but also because it is a place that is sensed to have a sacred character. The lifeworld is here a place in which one seeks or serves God or the divine. It is a place in which spirit is felt to dwell and in which, it seems, time impinges on eternity.

Conclusion

Retired seniors belong to the same stage of life not only because they are close in age but also because they share a self-system from which core role-related components have been removed and because they share a living space on the margins of the social world. However, despite these fundamentals in common, retired seniors are a heterogeneous group because they respond in markedly different ways to the questions that retirement poses. Some respond negatively, feeling that they have lost identity, purpose, and justification. Others respond positively, feeling that they have finally gained the freedom to live their lives as they please. Others respond by feeling a need to reinvent themselves by forging a new identity, purpose, and justification. Still others respond by feeling a need to devote themselves to spiritual life. There is no common mold for retired seniors. Those fortunate enough to enjoy adequate means and good health are free to chart their own pathways through the retirement years.

Chapter 15

Old Age

The medical advances of the twentieth century have made it much more difficult to say just when old age begins. Old age for this reason is best defined functionally rather than chronologically. Thus defined, old age is the time of life when physical or cognitive decline has advanced far enough to place significant limitations on one's ability to live independently, specifically limitations on one's ability to see, hear, walk, remember, or perform cognitive tasks. In developed countries today, such decline might not become evident until the early eighties and for a few does not become evident until the late eighties or even early nineties. Regrettably, for some, those who suffer from medical issues, especially Alzheimer's, such decline becomes evident much earlier.

Reflective Self-Understanding

Executive functions and fluid intelligence continue to decline in old age. This decline, however, is most often gradual. Dementia, including Alzheimer's, sometimes accelerates cognitive decline during old age, but it is not considered part of the normal aging process. The normal aging process, although indeed one of declining ability to recall names and facts, process new information, assess unfamiliar options, and calculate future consequences, is normally a matter of gradual rather than precipitous decline in executive functions and fluid cognition, especially for those who remain physically, socially, and intellectually active.[1]

Although crystallized intelligence may suffer attrition in some areas—frequently because of lack of use—it can be supplemented in others. Knowledge and skills acquired in the past may be lost to some extent, but new knowledge and skills can be acquired. Studies indicate that marked decline in crystallized intelligence is correlated with serious illness and physical deterioration leading to death, not old age itself.[2] Most old people today, therefore, continue to age gradually and gracefully, without significant loss of lucidity or judgment, beyond the retirement years into advanced old age.

In addition to being a time when new knowledge and skills can be acquired, old age is a time when a special kind of cognition can emerge, a kind that is frequently said to flower in old age: wisdom. In speaking about the wisdom of old age, it should be stressed immediately that this wisdom is not the postformal cognition that is often said to be a kind of wisdom that emerges in life's more mature years. As noted in earlier chapters, this kind of wisdom begins to emerge long before old age, with intuitive understanding of human nature of a postformal sort already emerging as the fruit of experience by midlife if not earlier. Moreover, some cognitive skills frequently associated with postformal cognition—such as understanding of complexity, contextuality, ambiguity, and fallibility—may be in decline, along with executive functions and fluid intelligence generally, in old age.

Rather than postformal cognition, the wisdom distinctive of old age is the wisdom of *reflective self-understanding*. This kind of wisdom is distinctive of old age because it is near the end of life that one is most inclined to look back on one's life and submit it to review. Before old age, people tend to live either as if life will go on forever (children, adolescents, young adults) or as if life, even with its approaching end coming into view, will go on long enough to allow for major new endeavors (middle-aged adults, many retirees). However, in arriving at old age, people are forced to acknowledge that the end of life is near; and as they accept this fact, many are prompted to reflect on the lives they have lived.

Erik Erikson, in his well-known account of the stages of life, brought scientific attention to reflective self-understanding as it can emerge in old age by calling it the distinctive "virtue" of old age.[3] According to Erikson, the pursuit of reflective self-understanding during old age is what allows us to avoid despair in the face of death. In achieving such self-understanding, or wisdom, we achieve what Erikson called "integrity," where integrity is the acceptance of the whole of one's life just as one lived it, even if there is much that one would do differently if given a chance to live life again. "It [integrity] is the acceptance of one's one and only life cycle as something that had to be and that, by necessity, permitted of no substitutes."[4] Erikson's account of reflective self-understanding may seem dated from the perspective of current theories, which stress the social construction of meaning and the neuroscientific study of the brain. It remains important, however, because it provides a needed whole-life, existential-philosophical perspective for understanding cognition in old age.[5]

As Erikson makes clear in the statement just quoted, reflective self-understanding as it emerges in old age is more than a cognitive achievement. It is an achievement not only of self-understanding but also, for many, of self-acceptance. Old people, in submitting their lives to review, seek not only to understand but also to come to terms with the lives they have lived. Many people achieve a good deal of personal self-insight before old age. However, these people are young enough to be able to postpone facing the issue of self-acceptance. Although the need for self-acceptance is present throughout life, it understandably grows stronger as one approaches the end of life. Old people tend for this reason to be more strongly motivated, when they submit their lives to review, to focus their inquiry not only on self-understanding but also on self-acceptance.

That the wisdom of reflective self-understanding is a distinctive possibility of old age does not mean that all or even that most old people are wise in this sense. Unfortunately, many old people suffer from health issues or other hardships that require them to devote almost all their energy to the challenges of the day. Other old people suffer cognitive losses that make significant self-inquiry impossible. Moreover, studies indicate that some old people have no interest or see no point in self-inquiry.[6] The wisdom of reflective self-understanding for these reasons should not be considered an expectable achievement of old age. Still, it is a *characteristic* achievement, for it is the kind of wisdom that old age more than any other stage of life elicits. Although midlife often elicits a review of the achievements of early adulthood, only old age provides the complete archive of life experiences and the urgent end-of-life incentive to elicit a life review that might lead to reflective self-understanding as Erikson defined it.

Adjustments to the Self-System in Old Age

The self-system changes in response to the realities of old age, especially the following three, which are the most pronounced: declining abilities, contracting life boundaries, and nearness of the end of life. The self-representation changes to reflect these realities by becoming a representation of a person who is unable to do many of the things younger people do, who is cut off from much of life as it occurs in the outside world, and who knows that the time remaining in life is relatively short. These changes to the self-representation should not be taken to imply that old people have primarily a negative outlook on their lives, although some do. The point is that old people face realities that force them to change their self-representations in profound ways.

The ego's narration of the life story continues in old age and reflects the changes to the self-representation just noted. The realities of old age frame the life story and determine its primary points of focus. Declining abilities bring into focus increasing dependence on others; contracting life boundaries bring into focus increasing separation from others; and nearness of the end of life brings into focus the past and, for some, a possible afterlife. With these points of focus, it is important to reiterate that old people need not have primarily a negative outlook on their lives. The life story of old age, despite focusing on difficult realities, does not need to be a sad story, as we shall see.

For some, especially those who suffer serious illness or infirmity, those who have major regrets about the past, those who have been removed from their families and placed in elder care facilities, and those who feel they have nothing left to live for, the life story of old age *is* a sad story. Indeed, for people in the last of these groups, the story is not only sad but also finished. These people, feeling that they are just waiting to die, stop narrating their life stories, a fact referred to as "narrative foreclosure."[7] However, for many if not most old people, especially those who have lived interesting or productive lives and have supportive families or friends, the life story can be primarily positive. For example, it can be a story about enjoying the activities of the day, about reliving past adventures, about taking pride in accomplishments, about looking forward to visits from family or friends, and, for some, about anticipating a happy afterlife.

For those old people who place their lives in review, the life story reverses its temporal perspective. It ceases any longer being primarily a story about how one's life is unfolding into the future and becomes primarily a story about how one lived in the past. The life story now recapitulates earlier stages of life so that they can be interpreted as chapters of a whole-life story. This whole-life story, like previous stage-specific stories, is narrated by the ego speaking to itself in inner dialogue. However, in old age the narration of the life story is also frequently performed outwardly, either, as was traditionally the practice, as part of a generational transmission of history and wisdom or, as is increasingly occurring today, as a spoken or written exercise of self-examination. The benefits for old people in telling or writing a life story are now well understood. Robert Butler, using the expression "life review," was the first to bring these benefits to the attention of clinicians.[8] Since Butler, many studies of life reviews have appeared, and many people have been trained to assist old people in doing a life review or, as it is also called, a guided autobiography.[9]

According to the literature, the benefits of doing a life review can include (1) greater appreciation of the goods of life, especially those associated with family, friends, and past experiences or accomplishments; (2) release from feelings of grievance, regret, and disappointment; (3) insight into how the stages of one's life fit together in the story of one's whole life; and (4) a sense that one's life, whatever its shortcomings, was good enough to merit acceptance if not affirmation.[10] A life review can thus lead to gratitude, peace of mind, self-understanding, and self-acceptance. Of course, not all old people benefit in these ways from doing a life review. Some strongly regret things they have done or failed to do and become distressed or depressed, at least temporarily, when reviewing their lives.[11] Nevertheless, according to those who have studied the subject, the great majority of people who do a life review report that they greatly benefited from the exercise, especially when they communicated their life stories to others, whether in oral or written, private or published form.

Of the components of the self-system, the ego ideal is the one most affected by the realities of old age. Indeed, the ego ideal ceases to function for the most part and, effectively, is deleted from the self-system. There are two primary reasons for this major change to the self-system. The first is that there is less point in striving for ideal goals when the end of life is near. Indeed, there is less point in striving for goals of any sort other than those that can be achieved in the near future. Goals for this reason are greatly reduced in number, with only urgent, short-term goals remaining on the agenda. However, and this is the second reason for the deletion of the ego ideal, urgent, short-terms goals are, effectively, imperatives of the present rather than aspirations for the future, which means that the only remaining goals of the ego ideal have, effectively, been reduced to duties of the superego. Given that little time remains for the old person, it is, therefore, almost exclusively the superego that does the work of self-motivation.

Among high-priority goals that are thus reduced to duties, two are primary and can be considered distinctive of old age as a stage. These duties pertain to "getting one's affairs in order." The first such duty is to get one's personal affairs—one's finances, correspondence, and final arrangements—in order. To enforce this duty, the superego may begin to urge old people to pay debts and reorganize assets, to get in touch with people with whom they have unfinished business, to rewrite wills, and to clarify preferences for final care. In performing these duties, old people discharge obligations and achieve peace of mind knowing that their personal affairs will not cause difficulties for others when they are gone.

As the superego moves old people to get their personal affairs in order, it might also move them to get their inner lives, their souls, in order. Many old people are urged by the superego to address and, if possible, resolve feelings of grievance, guilt, or disappointment stemming from actions of the past.[12] Not all old people feel a need to address matters such as these. Again, some old people are unable to carry out a life review or have no interest in doing one. However, many old people are motivated by the superego to reflect on their lives to resolve matters like those mentioned. Speaking in its characteristic voice, the superego advises these people to look back on their lives, not only to take satisfaction in those things that turned out well but also to come to terms with those things that did not, especially relationships that ended with regrets. In motivating old people to address these unresolved issues, the superego performs one of its last major developmental tasks.

In addition to enforcing duties arising from the nearness of the end of life, the superego continues to enforce the familiar duties of the day. Primary among these duties are those of self-care and caring for others. With declining abilities, old people are increasingly dependent on others. Nevertheless, there is much they can still do for themselves and for others as well. Accordingly, the superego has the task of exhorting old people to be as independent as their abilities allow and to help others as their means allow. For example, it might urge old people politely to decline offers of help when they can do something on their own; and it might urge them to help others so far as they can, perhaps with financial gifts but at least with kindness and expressions of gratitude. These duties of the day, along with those arising from the nearness of the end of life, are important duties of the superego during old age.

How Old Age Transforms the Lifeworld

The lifeworld as well as the self-system is transformed by the three realities of old age we have discussed. Declining abilities make the lifeworld of old age a place in which there are fewer things to do. Whether old people enjoy their daily activities or feel bored because they have little to do, they understand that the activities available to them are far fewer and more dependent on the help of others than in earlier years. Additionally, contracting boundaries make the lifeworld of old age a place even farther removed from the center of the social world than was the world of the retired senior. Many old people enjoy social gatherings outside the home and get-togethers with family or friends. Nevertheless, even they understand that their circle of social life has shrunk and is smaller than it was in earlier years. Finally, nearness of the end of life makes the lifeworld of old age a world in which the past rather than the future is the primary temporal dimension beyond the present. Without a significant future to look forward to and, frequently, with waning interest in the present, many old people turn their attention to the past to engage their minds. In this way, the past, which before old age had always receded from view, springs back into view, presenting itself for reflective examination.

It is important to note that, just as the life story of old age need not be a sad story, neither does the lifeworld of old age need to be a grim reality. Undeniably, it is a grim reality for some. Fortunately, for many old people, perhaps most, the lifeworld of old age, if not a greatly satisfying world, is at least a world with many goods to appreciate. As noted previously, many old people enjoy the activities of the day, gatherings outside the home, and visits with family and friends; and many find pleasure in remembering earlier experiences or accomplishments. The extent to which the lifeworld of old age is grim or bright depends greatly on finances, health, family, and friends; and it also depends greatly on the character of the life one has lived.

Recollecting the Past—An Example of a Life Review

Old people who reflect on their lives in pursuit of self-acceptance ask themselves "existential" questions. These are questions that can help old people come to terms with their lives. Unless a life review is being done with a professional memoirist, these questions are rarely asked explicitly. Most often, they play a role only implicitly, in the form of feelings of concern that guide life reviews and only later might lead to insights that provide answers to explicit questions. There is no formula for knowing which questions will come to the fore in a life review. Nevertheless, here are some that could play prominent roles: "Did I follow my own course in life?" "Did I achieve my goals?" "Did I meet my responsibilities?" "Was I kind and generous?" "Did I accomplish anything of which I can be proud?" "Should I have taken more risks?" and "Should I have taken more time to enjoy the pleasures of life?" None of these questions is essential, asked in all life reviews. Any one could be a primary or secondary question in a life review.

The text that follows presents an account of a possible life review. This life review differs from most others in three ways. First, it differs because it poses the guiding existential questions explicitly. Second, it differs because it has selected questions (the first three in the list just set forth) that are closely tied to components of the self-system and, therefore, that have direct relevance to themes of this book. Third, the life review that follows differs from most life reviews because, for convenience, it is based on a fictional life review, that of Ivan Ilych in Tolstoy's novella *The Death of Ivan Ilych*. However, although the life review set forth here differs from other life reviews in these ways, it has the advantage of presenting in clearly delineated fashion principal concerns of many life reviews.

DID I FOLLOW MY OWN COURSE IN LIFE?

This question—let us call it the "question of authenticity"—is tied to the self-representation and the life story. It asks, in effect, whether the self-representation and corresponding life story as they evolved over the course of life were truly self-authored or were instead scripted primarily by external factors, such as other people, society, and unplanned events. Because such external factors play major roles in the formation of anyone's self-representation, the question of authenticity can be restated to ask, "Did I remain true to myself even when I sought the validating attentions of others?" "Did I give expression to myself in selecting and performing [largely prescribed] social roles?" and "Was my identity still authentically my own even as events unexpectedly changed the course of my life?" Again, like other questions that might be asked in life reviews, it is unlikely that old people ask these questions in the ways formulated here. Nevertheless, the need to believe that one has to a significant extent lived one's own life, rather than having lived only as society or events dictated, can be a guiding concern for many people doing a life review. It is understandable that a primary objective of a life review would be to learn the extent to which one lived one's own life, from the inside out, even when one's life was at the same time being determined for one by social and other external factors, from the outside in.

Ivan Ilych was unable to arrive at a positive answer the question of authenticity. Before becoming ill and facing imminent death, he had been a successful magistrate in the judicial system of Tsarist Russia. He was a man of high accomplishment and good reputation. However, when, in facing death, he began to place his life in review, he realized that he had failed to follow his own course at major turning points in his life, having instead allowed social expectations or the perceived judgments of others to make important decisions for him. Ivan saw such inauthenticity in his choice of the woman he married, who was considered a good match for a person of his rank and ambition; in his pursuit of career, in which he always strived for greater prestige or at least higher pay; and in his attempts to live in a style that would impress others. Ivan suffered a good deal of anguish in coming to see the inauthenticity of his life, regretting that he had so often failed to follow his own course.

DID I ACHIEVE MY GOALS?

This question—let us call it the "question of success"—is tied to the ego ideal. It asks whether one was successful in achieving the goals one set for oneself, regardless of what they were and how they might have changed over the course of one's life. Clearly, for most people, the primary goals that would come to the fore in a life review would be those that were set in early adulthood related to work, primary relationships, and parenting. With these goals in mind, an old person doing a life review might pose the question of success by asking, "Did I accomplish what I set out to achieve in my job [or career]?" "Did I have a good relationship with my spouse(s) [or partner(s)]?" or "Did I do a good job in caring [or providing] for my family?" Of course, quite a few people pursue goals other than those related to work, relationships, and parenting. Some pursue moral or spiritual goals. For these people, the question of success might take a form such as, "Did I live a virtuous life?" "Did I treat others as I would have wanted them to treat me?" or "Was I a good Christian [Jew, Muslim, Hindu, Buddhist, etc.]?" Whatever the ideal goals were, the person asking the question of success asks whether she or he achieved or at least came reasonably close to achieving those goals.

Ivan, in his life review, was able to answer the question of success in a way that might bring satisfaction, even pride, to many people. Yes, he had been successful in his judicial career and was well respected by others.

He had made what was regarded as a good marriage and had provided well for his family. From the point of view of others, he had indeed lived a successful life. However, Ivan, in his life review, found little satisfaction in the success he had achieved because, as already noted, he saw in it primarily his own inauthenticity, his willingness to allow society and other people to make his choices for him. Furthermore, Ivan, in his life review, came to have other major regrets. He realized that his professional ambition had caused him to miss many of the pleasures of life. Even worse, he realized that his ambition had caused him to relate to others primarily in impersonal or self-interested ways. Ivan thus realized that he had missed much of the joy of life and had failed to treat others with the respect, kindness, and consideration they deserved. Ivan's life review was more difficult than most life reviews. He experienced a good deal of regret for the life he had lived.

Did I Meet My Responsibilities?

This question—let us call it the "question of conscience"—is tied to the superego. Whereas the questions of authenticity and success ask about specific aspects of one's life, the question of conscience asks about one's life generally. It asks whether one lived one's life "in the right way," where for most people "the right way" means the way generally prescribed by society. Thus understood, the question of conscience might take such forms as, "Did I meet my responsibilities in my job [or as a spouse, partner, or parent]?" "Did I avoid harming others?" "Was I a law-abiding citizen?" and "Was my life free of serious wrongdoing?" Whatever form it takes, the question of conscience asks whether, irrespective of one's answers to other life-review questions, one at least "did what one ought," what social norms required.

A negative answer to the question of conscience might make it impossible for an old person to arrive at self-acceptance in a life review. To conclude that one did not live one's life in the right way is to swallow a bitter pill. However, to conclude that one did do what was expected of one can go a long way toward arriving at self-acceptance. Some old people no doubt use a positive answer to the question of conscience as a rationalization to hide regrets that might arise in reflecting on other life-review questions. Ivan Ilych did just this. He used the fact that he had done everything *comme il faut*, as social standards dictated, as a rationalization to try to hide regrets about his inauthenticity, his failure to enjoy life, and his failure to treat others better. Ivan was not successful in this attempt to hide his regrets. Despite trying to reassure himself with the thought that he had lived his life as society required, he continued to be tormented by his perceived failures. Before he died, he had to face those failures and try to come to terms with them.

Most old people, despite having some regrets about how they lived their lives, are not as hard on themselves as Ivan was. Most people for this reason probably find more comfort in a positive answer to the question of conscience than Ivan did. They probably find it easier to acknowledge their mistakes and still conclude that, having done what was expected of them, they lived their lives at least well enough. They might conclude, "Although I could have lived a better life, I tried as best as I could. I met my responsibilities. That is good enough." It is unrealistic to expect perfection of oneself. Although honest self-review is frequently difficult, it can lead to an understanding of just this fact and, therefore, to an understanding that mistakes, even big ones, need not stand in the way of self-acceptance. Ivan had to experience more anguish than most in reaching self-acceptance. The story suggests that he finally came to terms with his life only minutes before its end.

Conclusion

Life reviews do not always lead to satisfying outcomes, to self-acceptance or self-affirmation rather than distress or despair. Some old people may be able to arrive at a satisfying outcome with a positive answer to just one life-review question, perhaps the question of authenticity or the question of success or, more likely, the question of conscience. However, other old people might be harder on themselves, requiring positive answers to two or more life-review questions, perhaps, in asking them, only to arrive at negative answers instead. These people might find their life reviews anguishing ordeals, as Ivan Ilych did. Although some old people might find reflecting on their lives a relatively trouble-free exercise, most do not.

Most old people have significant regrets about the lives they lived. However, such regrets do not ordinarily preclude self-acceptance at the end of a life review. Reflection leads to understanding, and understanding, often if not always, leads to reconciliation, even if only after considerable anguish. Old age is a time suited for examining the entire course of one's life so that one can see how one lived, why one lived as one did, and what, if anything, one should have done differently. This reflective review, as a distinctive developmental possibility of old age, helps many people bring their lives to a close, if not with deeply satisfying affirmation, at least with acceptance and peace of mind.

Part III

Rethinking the Ego's Role in Spiritual Life

Chapter 16

Spiritual Preawakening

All the stages of development discussed thus far are stages that everyone who lives long enough can expect to live through. In contrast, the stages to be discussed in this and the next three chapters are "exceptional" stages, in the two main meanings of that term. They are rare, stages that few live through; and they are extraordinary, stages with both pronounced, dramatic experiences and profound developmental gains. The stages in question are four stages of spiritual development: spiritual preawakening, awakening, growth, and maturity.

The ensuing account of ego development through these four spiritual stages is set apart from the rest of the text here in part 3 for three reasons. The first is that the focus of inquiry is now restricted to a specific sphere of life: spirituality. We are now focusing on stages of ego development only insofar as they are more fundamentally stages of spiritual development. The second reason is that most spiritual traditions are critical of the ego, for reasons that pertain specifically to spirituality. Most criticisms allege that the ego, in one way or another, is an impediment to spiritual life. For example, it is argued that the ego is something the presumed reality of which stands in the way of liberation or enlightenment (Advaita Vedanta, Buddhism) or the "thinking" and "doing" of which stand in the way of the fullness and spontaneity of life (Taoism, Zen) or the weakness, waywardness, or sinfulness of which stands in the way of a life of obedience, faith, or surrender (Judaism, Christianity, Islam). Part 3 defends the ego against criticisms such as these and argues that the ego plays an indispensable role in spiritual life.

The third reason the ensuing account of spiritual development is set apart from the rest of the text is that it is based on a disputed assumption, namely, that there exists a spiritual reality—here called "spirit"—in relation to which spiritual development unfolds. This assumption, obviously, is controversial. Although it has had countless adherents, it has also had strong and persuasive critics, principally atheists and agnostics. Atheists have argued that rational arguments and empirical evidence rule out the existence of spirit, with high probability if not complete certainty. In contrast, agnostics have argued that arguments and evidence do not rule out the existence of spirit but do not sufficiently support it either. An important point made by both atheists and agnostics is that those who affirm the existence of spirit conceive it in widely different, conflicting ways. This diversity and incompatibility of conceptions of spirit, atheists and agnostics have argued, casts doubt on the existence of the thing being conceived. More is said about competing conceptions of spirit below.

Points to Keep in Mind in Reading Part 3

Although there have been many accounts of spiritual development, there is no consensus on the nature or number of stages of spiritual development. Moreover, no account specifying discrete stages can do justice to everyone's experience. Some people do not acknowledge spirituality as a part of their lives. Others report that spirituality has been part of their lives since childhood. Others report that spirituality is a part of their lives that emerges, recedes, reemerges, and so forth, without evidently being a developmental phenomenon. Still others report that spirituality, upon emerging in their lives, unfolds gradually and without discernible stage transitions.

Clearly, no account of spiritual development specifying discrete stages can accurately describe the experience of any of these people. No such account, therefore, can be considered universally applicable. This qualification applies to the account of spiritual development presented here, which for this reason is not intended to apply to everyone. The reader needs to keep this point in mind because for stylistic reasons the ensuing account is presented without qualification, as if it were universally applicable when it most definitely is not.

Another point to keep in mind is that the ensuing account of spiritual development is intended only as a hypothetical model. The account is based on a good deal of cross-cultural research and encapsulates views that have wide acceptance. Nevertheless, it cannot claim to be anything more than a proposal, a proposal based on the author's decision to divide spiritual development into the four stages noted earlier and to focus on the primary themes of this book, the ego and its self-system and lifeworld. This point is also important to keep in mind because, again, the ensuing account of spiritual development is set forth without qualification, not only as if it were universally applicable but also as if it were unproblematically factual.

Because this book is about the ego, it is appropriate that, in discussing spiritual development, it puts the ego at center stage. In discussing spiritual stages, therefore, the ensuing account explains how they appear to the ego undergoing them, how the ego, by exercising its executive functions, responds to the challenges that spiritual stages present, and how spiritual stages in turn bring about changes in the ego's self-system and lifeworld. In thus putting the ego at center stage, the account of spiritual development set forth here might seem suspect to some. Specifically, it might raise concerns about gender and cultural differences. These issues are addressed shortly.

A further point to keep in mind is that the account of spiritual development set forth here presents stages of spirituality as they would be experienced by the ego *in their most extreme expression.* The ensuing account of spiritual development, therefore, not only puts the ego at center stage; it also puts the ego's spiritual experience under a magnifying glass, thus exaggerating it. Spiritual preawakening is described as a stage during which the ego hungers desperately for spirit while despairing that it will ever be able to find spirit. Spiritual awakening is described as a stage during which spirit, having been an invisible attractor, suddenly manifests itself to the ego as a radically unfamiliar higher power, a supreme "other" that takes charge of the ego's life and holds the ego in thrall. Spiritual growth is then described as a stage during which the drama of spiritual awakening gradually subsides over a long period of spiritual transformation, during which the ego is nurtured and guided by spirit and thus grows closer to spirit and increasingly able to give expression to spirit. Finally, spiritual maturity is described as a stage during which the ego is completely integrated with spirit and, therefore, works in seamless unity with spirit as the vehicle for its expression in the world.

The exaggerated character of this account of spiritual development should be evident. Few are so spiritually hungry and yet so unable to discern the closeness of spirit as the ego we describe in the stage of spiritual preawakening. Few are so suddenly awakened by spirit and so prone to experience spirit as other, overpowering, and eclipsing as the ego we describe in the stage of spiritual awakening. Few undergo such a long transformation under the nurturing and guiding influence of spirit as the ego we describe in the stage of spiritual growth. Finally, few are so seamlessly integrated with spirit as the ego we describe in the stage of spiritual maturity.

Clearly, such an extreme account of the ego's spiritual development is not typical. It may accurately describe the experience of only a few people. Nevertheless, although not typical, such an account *is* ideal-typical in the sense that it presents in bold—and, therefore, clear—outline essential aspects of the ego's experience in each of the four stages of spiritual development we discuss. It describes in bold outline the status and role of the ego in each of these stages, the principal ways in which the ego relates to spirit in each stage, the chief types of challenges the ego faces in each stage, and the markers that indicate to the ego that it is moving from one spiritual stage to the next. To avoid confusion, therefore, the reader should keep in mind not only that the ensuing account of spiritual development is not intended to apply to everyone and is only hypothetical is character but also that it is exaggerated, understanding that it is exaggerated in the (idealizing) manner and for the (clarifying) purpose indicated.

The other points that need to be kept in mind pertain to gender and cultural differences. Regarding the former, it is important to understand that any account that describes spiritual development from the ego's perspective is in danger of describing it in a gender-biased way, specifically in a way that better reflects men's than women's experience. This danger exists because, as we learned in chapter 4, the notion of the ego as it has emerged in patri-archal societies more accurately represents men's than women's subjectivity. Accordingly, before we can proceed with our account of spiritual develop-ment, we need to explain why it describes not only men's but also women's experience, even if in some places it better describes men's experience and in other places better describes women's.

To recall, we concluded in chapter 4 that the ego, although perhaps not gendered at birth, becomes gendered almost immediately thereafter in response to interpersonal and social influences. Moreover, we concluded that in patriarchal societies—in which men have governed and women have cared for young children—women's and men's egos have inevitably been shaped similarly in some ways and differently in others. Women's and men's egos have been shaped similarly for the following two reasons: (1) both girls and boys, in beginning their ego development, are required to turn *away* from the original bases of life: the body, instincts, emotions, and relationship (with a goddess-like female figure); and (2) both girls and boys, in continuing their ego development, are required to turn *toward* later-developing forms of life: language ("reason"), agency, control of emotions, and obedience (to male authority). In patriarchal societies, both girls and boys thus follow a "from-matriarchal-to-patriarchal" course of ego development. This course requires both girls and boys to leave behind the original preoedipal or "matriarchal" bases of life and then to submit themselves to forms of life that are associated with expectations and values of patriarchal society.

However, the course of ego development just described shapes women's and men's egos not only similarly but also differently. In chapter 4 we discussed reasons why women's egos, although shaped like men's in the ways just summarized, have been shaped with less rigid individuating boundaries, less one-sided identification with rational and volitional faculties, less strict constraints on emotions, and greater remaining connection with the bases of life that were at the fore at the outset of life. We also discussed reasons why men's egos, although shaped like women's in the ways just summarized, have been shaped with more rigid individuating boundaries, more one-sided identification with rational and volitional faculties, stricter constraints on the emotions, and greater alienation from the bases of life that were at the fore at the outset of life.

These similarities and differences between women's and men's ego development have clear implications for spiritual development if one assumes, as we do, that spiritual development leads not to the fulfillment of only one, spiritual, dimension of humanness but rather to the fulfillment of humanness in all its dimensions. On this assumption, spiritual development, under the leadership of awakened spirit, must restore and integrate the original bases of life from which ego development required us to turn away. That is, it must restore and integrate the full embodiment, the robust instinctual life, the sensitive emotional attunement, and the radical openness to relationship that were at the fore early in life. Clearly, women's greater remaining connection to and men's greater alienation from these original bases of life imply that spiritual development in patriarchal societies will differ significantly for women and men. The primary implied differences are stated in text box 16.1.

The ensuing account of spiritual development focuses primarily on the similarities between women's and men's experience set forth in text box 16.1 and only secondarily on the corresponding differences set forth there. In doing so, it gives primary attention to the fact that both women's and men's egos have developed in the same basic direction, *away* from the embodied, instinctual, emotional, relational, and female-centered bases of preoedipal life and *toward* the rational, agentic, disciplined, individuated, and male-governed forms of adult life. In giving primary attention to these similarities

Text Box 16.1
Differences in Women's and Men's Ego
Development and Corresponding Differences
in their Spiritual Development

1. Men, alienated from the original (preoedipal, "matriarchal") bases of life, are prone to conceive of spirit in a one-sidedly male way, as a supreme subject and executive agency, as a transcendent heavenly father with an all-knowing mind and an all-powerful will.

2. Women, socialized as members of patriarchal society, are prone to conceive of spirit similarly while at the same time, given their greater affinity with the original bases of life, being prone to conceive of spirit differently, as a body-based goddess of surpassing wisdom and unconditional love.

3. Men, having been shaped with more rigid ego boundaries, are prone during the stage of spiritual preawakening to experience spirit as something from which they are cut off and, therefore, as something unmanifest and unknown.

4. Women, socialized as members of patriarchal society, are prone during the stage of spiritual preawakening to experience spirit similarly while at the same time, having been shaped with less rigid ego boundaries, being prone to experience spirit differently, as something that, although unmanifest and unknown, is nonetheless near and felt or sensed.

5. Men, in awakening to spirit, are initially prone to experience it as a supernatural power that is "wholly other" in provenance and harsh in effect, as a sovereign power that, like the father figure of the oedipal stage, disciplines the ego by sternly correcting its misbehavior.

6. Women, socialized as members of patriarchal society, are prone to experience spirit similarly while at the same time, given their greater affinity with the original bases of life, being prone to experience spirit differently, as a supernatural power that, although initially like the oedipal father figure in being other, sovereign, and harsh, is also, and more fundamentally, like the preoedipal caregiver in being kindred, supportive, and kind.

7. Men, although initially prone to experience spirit as a male power that metes out stern justice (humbling, purgative afflictions), are prone eventually, given their residual connections with the original bases of life, to experience spirit as a female power that dispenses tender love (supportive, empowering consolations).

8. Women, socialized as members of patriarchal society, are prone to experience spirit similarly while at the same time, given their greater affinity with the original bases of life, being prone to experience spirit differently, as a power that, although a source of both stern justice and tender love, is ultimately more nurturing than disciplining, more consoling than afflicting, and more female than male in character.

9. Men, given their greater alienation from the original bases of life, tend initially to perceive the return to these bases—and, with it, the shift to the female aspect of spirit—in an exaggeratedly negative way, as a threat to the achievements of ego development. Specifically, men tend initially to perceive the female aspect of spirit as an alien, primitive, engulfing power.

10. Women, given their greater affinity with the original bases of life, tend initially to perceive the return to these bases—and, with it, the shift to the female aspect of spirit—in a more positive way, as a redemptive restoration of what had been left behind during ego development. Specifically, women tend initially to perceive the female aspect of spirit as a power that is more kindred than alien, more wise than primitive, and more embracing than engulfing.

11. Men, given their greater alienation from the original bases of life, tend to undergo a longer and more difficult adjustment to the female aspect of spirit during the stage of spiritual growth than women do.

12. Women, given their greater affinity with the original bases of life, tend to undergo a shorter and less difficult adjustment to the female aspect of spirit during the stage of spiritual growth than men do.

13. Finally, both men and women, in approaching spiritual maturity, are prone to experience spirit as something that, no longer gendered in patriarchally defined ways—either as a sovereign male disciplinarian or as a nurturing female caregiver—transcends gender categories and is essential to the full humanness of all people.

Summary

In their spiritual development, both women and men experience both the male (disciplining, afflicting, oedipal, patriarchal) and the female (nurturing, consoling, preoedipal, matriarchal) aspects of spirit, with the former aspect being foremost in initial awakening and the latter aspect coming to the fore as spiritual development unfolds. With this similarity, men tend to experience the male aspect of spirit in a more pronounced and prolonged way than women do; and women tend to experience the female aspect of spirit sooner and, initially, in a more positive way than men do. These differences in women's and men's spiritual development reflect corresponding differences in their ego development. Turning points in ego development that set women and men on paths that diverge are revisited in reverse during spiritual development, thus setting women and men on paths that converge. This at any rate is true in patriarchal societies, in which men have governed and women have cared for the young.

between women's and men's ego development, the ensuing account assumes but gives less attention to the fact that men's egos have developed in this from-matriarchal-to-patriarchal direction in a more pronounced and one-sided way than women's egos have and, therefore, that women's egos remain more connected with the original (matriarchal) bases of life than men's do.

In thus focusing primarily on similarities, the ensuing account of spiritual development begins with women and men as adults, as they have been shaped by patriarchal society. With this starting point, it is understandable that spiritual development at the outset would have primarily a male point of view, seeing spirit as an all-powerful god who holds the ego accountable to patriarchal laws. However, it is also understandable that spiritual development would later—once it begins to restore the original bases of life left behind during ego development—begin to take on primarily a female point of view, seeing spirit as a caring goddess who nurtures and guides the ego as it experiences a resurgence of embodied, instinctual, emotional, and intimately relational life.

Spiritual development as conceived here thus reverses the course that ego development characteristically takes in patriarchal societies. Whereas ego development in patriarchal societies unfolds in a "from matriarchal-to-patriarchal" direction, spiritual development in patriarchal societies unfolds in a "from-patriarchal-to-matriarchal" direction. As it unfolds in this direction, spiritual development restores to full expression the embodied, instinctual, emotional, and relational life that was at the fore at the beginning of life; and it integrates the ego and its developed executive functions with this life. Once this process of restoration and integration is complete, spirit ceases being seen primarily through either male or female lenses and begins being seen as a power that, shared by everyone, is essential not only to fulfilled spirituality but also to fulfilled humanness.

Clearly, the approach to spiritual development just described is greatly simplified. Because our approach begins from the standpoint of the adult ego as it has been shaped by patriarchal society, the treatment of early spiritual development most likely simplifies women's experience more than men's, underplaying important ways in which women's experience differs from men's, as set forth in text box 16.1. Oppositely, because our approach then proceeds to describe spiritual development as it returns to matriarchal origins, the treatment of later spiritual development most likely simplifies men's experience more than women's, underplaying important ways in which men's experience differs from women's, again, as set forth in text box 16.1. Our approach to spiritual development thus not only exaggerates the ego's experience but also simplifies it, for the sake of clarifying its foremost aspects at each spiritual stage, including its gendered aspects as they have appeared in societies in which men have governed and women have cared for the young.

Because spiritual development follows a course that is the reverse of ego development, it can be said to describe—and here I modify an expression introduced by psychoanalyst Ernst Kris—a "regression in the service of integration."[1] According to our account, spiritual development begins from where we are, as adult members of patriarchal society. Using the terminology already introduced, it thus begins from a patriarchal stage (spiritual preawakening), during which one is alienated from and searching for spirit as an all-powerful "heavenly father," who is felt but not seen. It then proceeds backward through an oedipal stage (spiritual awakening), during which spirit becomes manifest as a power that, like the oedipal father figure of psychoanalytic theory, seems to be more other than kindred, more sovereign than caring, and more disciplining than nurturing. Spiritual development then continues in reverse through a preoedipal or matriarchal stage (spiritual growth), during which a seeming change of object from a male to a female divine parent occurs and during which spirit seems increasingly to be a power that is more kindred than other, more caring than sovereign, and more nurturing than disciplining. Only then does spiritual development reach a stage (spiritual maturity) at which the male and female guises of spirit and the contrary effects corresponding to these guises recede into the background. We follow the course of regression in the service of integration in this and ensuing chapters.

To avoid misunderstanding, it is important here clearly to indicate the ways in which regression in the service of integration is and is not regressive. A first point to stress is that regression in the service of integration is regressive *only* in the sense that it revisits conditions of life similar to those of early stages of ego development and in doing so restores bases of life that had been at the fore during those stages. A second point to stress is that regression in the service of integration ordinarily is *not* regressive in the strict sense of requiring a sacrifice of abilities achieved during ego development. Specifically, it ordinarily requires no loss of or impairment to the ego's developed executive functions. These functions are challenged during regression in the service of integration, but they ordinarily survive the "journey" intact. Finally, a third point to stress, this one implied by the previous two, is that regression in the service of integration, in restoring bases of life left behind during ego development without ordinarily sacrificing any of the achievements of ego development, is in most cases a process with an *entirely positive* outcome. Regression in the service of integration, although reversing the course of ego development, thus leads to higher—more inclusive, more integrated—stages of development. Using the term "regression" is risky and can lead to serious misunderstanding unless the points just made are kept clearly in mind.

Yet another point to keep in mind is that the account of spiritual development set forth here, in putting the ego at center stage, might be said to reflect major Western spiritual traditions better than major Asian traditions. Might not our approach to spiritual development, in focusing on the unfolding of the ego-spirit relationship, apply better to the Abrahamic faiths, which focus on the unfolding of the person-God or people-God relationship, than to Asian traditions such as Advaita Vedanta, Buddhism, Taoism, and Zen, which are skeptical of the ego generally and often sharply critical of executive functions associated with the ego?

How can our account of spiritual development apply to Advaita Vedanta and Buddhism, which challenge the notion of an abiding individual self (or ego) and argue that we must relinquish our attachment to the idea of such a self if liberation or enlightenment is to be possible? Furthermore, how can our account of spiritual development apply to Taoism and Zen, which, in addition to being skeptical of the ego generally, describe the ego's executive functions almost entirely in negative ways? Major points of emphasis for Taoism and Zen are that (active, especially operational) thinking interferes with the immediacy and fullness of experience and that (will-initiated, intentional) acting interferes with the spontaneous unfolding of life. Rather than such thinking and acting, Taoism and Zen favor being alertly aware with a still mind ("without thinking") and allowing events to unfold of their own accord ("without acting)." Given that the ensuing account of spiritual development puts the ego and its executive functions at center stage, it is unclear how, if at all, it can apply to traditions like the ones just mentioned. Nevertheless, I suggest that it does apply to these traditions, albeit primarily in a negative way, by setting forth a challenge to them.

It challenges Asian traditions that call into question the existence of the ego because, according to our account, the ego is present in all known spiritual states, including those in which it seems to be absent. In chapter 3, we argued that the ego is present even in such allegedly egoless states as the fertile emptiness described by Buddhism, in which there seems to be only spontaneously arising psychomental phenomena, and the *samādhi* and *jhāna* states described by Hinduism and Buddhism, respectively, in which there seem to be only egolessly absorbed states of consciousness. The primary reason presented in chapter 3 for concluding that an ego is present in these seemingly egoless states—namely, that the later recollection of these states by the ego indicates that the ego was present at least as a bare experiencer when the states occurred—applies as well to other apparently egoless states described by Asian traditions. It applies even to mystical states of seemingly egoless illumination or egoless emptiness, states in which, for example, it seems as if there is nothing other than the limitless radiance of Brahman (Advaita Vedanta) or the unclouded clarity of *shūnyatā* (Buddhism). How could liberated or enlightened souls recall such experiences if they were not there (as egos) to experience them in the first place?

Generally stated, the ensuing account of spiritual development challenges traditions skeptical of the ego's existence by providing reasons for believing (1) that the ego exists as the subject and executive agency of consciousness not only before but also after liberation or enlightenment has been achieved; (2) that the ego is present in all (known, remembered) spiritual states, even if only as a functionally disengaged experiencer; and (3) that the ego, as we shall see, plays an indispensable role in all stages of spiritual development.

The ensuing account of spiritual development also presents a challenge to traditions, such as Taoism and Zen, that stress nonthinking and nonacting.

From our perspective, these traditions devalue the ego's executive functions in an unjustified way because they focus on the misuse rather than the proper use of these functions. We agree with these traditions that people who are driven always to be exercising executive functions, people, that is, who are unable to "let be" and thus allow things to reveal themselves in their immediacy and fullness or who are unable to "let go" and thus allow life to unfold of its own accord, are missing much that is essential to life. However, we disagree with these traditions to the extent that, in valorizing immediacy, fullness, and spontaneity, they devalue thinking and acting.

In the place of such a one-sided approach, the ensuing account of spiritual development recommends a both-and or, more precisely, a "sometimes one and sometimes the other" approach. No one would dispute that it is often appropriate to quiet the mind and savor the immediacy and fullness of the moment or to disengage the will and allow life to unfold spontaneously. However, it seems obvious that it is just as often appropriate to investigate and think about things and to take charge of events. Immediacy, fullness, and spontaneity are essential; however, so also are the ego's executive functions. The challenge to traditions such as Taoism and Zen is clear: the ego and its cognitive and practical functions need to be given credit, not only for the essential role they play in life generally but also for the essential role they play in spiritual life specifically.

The challenges just set forth may be too polemical. Clearly, it is important to acknowledge that *attachment* to the ego can interfere with experiencing spiritual realities beyond the ego and that *overuse* of executive functions can interfere with appreciating the immediacy, fullness, and spontaneity of life. However, this point made, it is fair to say that the criticisms of the ego presented by the Asian traditions just discussed are extreme and, I believe, deserving of the challenges we have posed. That the ego is a subject that is irreducible to what it experiences and an agency always ready to perform essential cognitive and practical functions is, I propose, a fact not only of prespiritual but also of fully realized spiritual life.

A final point to keep in mind is that the account of spiritual development presented here may have little or no applicability to indigenous spiritual traditions. Views frequently associated with indigenous spirituality—that the earth is the source of life; that everything is interconnected in a self-balancing ecosystem of life; that objects, plants, and animals have animating spirits with which we can communicate; that ancestors are present in the spirit world; and that shamans cross over into the spirit world—are sufficiently different from the views set forth in this book to indicate that it would be a mistake to try to apply our account of spiritual development to indigenous spirituality, even as a challenge. To be sure, our account of spiritual development should have implications for any spirituality in which the ego is present, including, it would be imprudent to assume otherwise, indigenous spirituality. Moreover, the definition of "spirit" set forth in the next section is broad enough to include spirit as it is often understood—as an animating spirit or spirits—in indigenous traditions. Nevertheless, there are too many differences between the account of spiritual development presented here and conceptions of spiritual life in indigenous traditions to venture a thesis about how the former might bear upon the latter.

There is a great deal to learn from writers who stress the diversity of spiritual experience across genders, cultures, and traditions. However, there is danger if emphasis on diversity leads to skepticism of any attempt to search for unifying themes. Proponents of diversity have exposed biases—theocentric, Christocentric, relational, Eurocentric, masculinist, hierarchical, dualistic, and other—that frequently distort attempts to compare different spiritual paths. The importance of exposing such biases and thus clarifying differences between spiritual paths cannot be overstated. However, as differences are thus better understood, commonalities remain to be explored, with due caution. The search for commonalities is as important as the search for differences. The two inquiries are complementary. Difference without commonality is complete unlikeness, and commonality without difference is sameness.

Knowing that people who present accounts of spiritual development focusing primarily on commonalities run the risk of overlooking important differences, I again stress the cautionary points set forth in this section. The reader should keep in mind that the ensuing account of spiritual development is not meant to apply to everyone or even to apply equally to those to whom it does apply. The reader should also keep in mind that the account is hypothetical in character and is presented as a conceptual model only, a model that, like all models, highlights some things while failing to consider others. Additionally, the reader should keep in mind the gender and cultural differences we have discussed in this section, remembering that the ensuing account of spiritual development applies to men better than women in some respects and to women better than men in others, applies to main Asian traditions primarily as a challenge, and applies to indigenous traditions unclearly if at all. Finally, and most importantly, the reader should keep in mind that the ensuing account of spiritual development both exaggerates and simplifies the ego's experience for explanatory purposes. If I seem here to be placing quite a few qualifications on the ensuing account of spiritual development, that is because I believe that it has important things to say, if not to most people, let alone to everyone, at least to many.

How Is Spirit to Be Conceived?

We have already noted that the idea of spirit has been called into question because spirit has been conceived in numerous, conflicting ways. To avoid such skepticism, spirit is here conceived in a minimal way, a way that leaves unspecified the ontological status of spirit (e.g., whether it is supernatural or natural, immortal or mortal), the specific form or forms of spirit (e.g., whether it is personal or impersonal, humanlike or non-humanlike), the numerical character of spirit (e.g., whether it is many, one, or many-in-one [a duality, trinity, quaternity, etc.]), and the possible earthly or cosmic functions of spirit (e.g., whether it is a creator, destroyer, ruler, judge, protector, redeemer, or liberator). Leaving all these possible facts about spirit unspecified, spirit as conceived here assumes only two things about spirit: that it exists and that it possesses causal powers that can produce a wide range of experiences that we classify as spiritual.

Spirit as conceived in this minimal way is consistent with all and preferential to none of the following conceptions of spirit: (1) that it is a nondual impersonal radiance of which the natural world and individual souls are manifestations (Advaita Vedanta, Mahayana Buddhism); (2) that it is an impersonal intelligence that orders the cosmos and human affairs (Taoism, Stoicism); (3) that it is a supreme personal deity or earthly manifestation or messenger of such a deity (Vaishnavism and Shaivism in Hinduism, the Abrahamic faiths); (4) that it is a power expressed in a pantheon of personal deities (polytheism); (5) that it is a power expressed in the spirits of objects, plants, and animals (indigenous spiritualities); (6) that it is a numinously charged archetype of the human psyche (Carl Jung); (7) that it is a cosmic energy that can be tapped by the human psyche (Wilhelm Reich); (8) that it is psychic energy in a particular mode or modes of expression (this author in previous publications); and (9) that it is a sensed power that arises from a distinctive pattern of electrochemical activity in the brain (contemporary scientific naturalists). Again, without affirming or denying any of these conceptions of spirit, spirit as conceived here holds only that spirit exists and possesses causal powers that can produce a wide range of experiences that we classify as spiritual.

Adopting a distinction often made by writers on spiritual development, spiritual stages are here divided into two basic types, those that unfold primarily because of the efforts of the spiritual seeker and those that unfold primarily because the causal powers of spirit are working on or within the spiritual seeker. Let us call these two types of spiritual stages "ego-driven" and "spirit-driven" stages, respectively. Only spirit-driven stages are considered in this account of spiritual development.

Spiritual stages of the ego-driven type ordinarily precede stages of the spirit-driven type. In being ego-driven, these stages emerge primarily from the ego's exercise of executive functions in searching or preparing itself for spirit, for example, in praying, meditating, practicing a form of yoga, disciplining the emotions or appetites, surrendering the will, or imitating the life of a spiritually revered being. In contrast, spiritual stages of the spirit-driven type—and this is the reason, as previously noted, they are extraordinary—emerge primarily from spirit's transforming influence on the ego (and the ego's response to this influence). Accordingly, the stages of spiritual development treated in this and the next three chapters presuppose that the ego has entered sufficiently within spirit's sphere of influence that spirit has begun playing the leading role in the ego's spiritual life. These stages, again, are spiritual preawakening, awakening, growth, and maturity.

Spirit-driven spirituality has been described as "infused," "mystical," "awakened," and "passive," the last description being seriously misleading.[2] In what follows I dispense with these terms and, leaving stages of ego-driven (preinfused, premystical, etc.) spirituality out of the discussion, refer to the stages of spirit-driven spirituality simply as the four stages of spirituality. Adopting this usage, all ensuing references to stages of spiritual development are to those extraordinary stages in which it is primarily spirit rather than the ego that drives and directs the spiritual process.

Spiritual Preawakening

We can now begin our account of the four stages of spiritual development. To facilitate the exposition, we start with an overview of the terrain. Table 16.1 presents a summary of the chief features of each of the four stages and how they relate to corresponding features of the other stages. Most of what is summarized in table 16.1 will become clear only in the exposition that follows in this and the next three chapters. Nevertheless, the overview set forth in table 16.1 should be helpful as a rough guide to what is to come. It should also be helpful as a recapitulation for those who have read through to the end of part 3. Once finished with part 3, the reader can return to the table for a refreshed and now much clearer overview.

Table 16.1. Four Stages of Spiritual Development

	Spiritual preawakening	Spiritual awakening	Spiritual growth	Spiritual maturity
Outer manifestation of spirit	*Transcendent spirit* Spirit is an unseen cosmic attractor that, sensed but not seen, is the cause and desideratum of the ego's spiritual hunger.	*Numinous spirit* Spirit is an overawing supernatural power that darkens the atmosphere of the world and daunts and eclipses the ego.	*Radiant spirit* Spirit is a supernatural radiance that beautifies and sacralizes the world and uplifts the ego.	*Native spirit* Spirit is a radiance that, no longer to any degree otherworldly in perceived character, is the beautifying-sacralizing light of the earth.
Inner manifestation of spirit	*Enfolded spirit* Spirit is an unseen interior attractor, a "black hole" in psychic space that stirs spiritual hunger and pulls the ego inward, toward the deep center of the psyche.	*Sovereign spirit* Spirit awakens within the soul and asserts its supremacy over the ego. Sovereign spirit's role as agency of purgative discipline comes to the fore.	*Caring spirit* Spirit's sovereignty and disciplining function recede and spirit's nurturing, comforting, and guiding functions come to the fore.	*Inherent spirit* Spirit is no longer other to the ego and is now joined with the ego as a single self, such that the ego is the ego of spirit and spirit is the spirit of the ego.
Regression in the service of integration	*Withdrawal from the world in preparation for spirit* Withdrawal from world is precursor to retracing stages of ego development.	*Oedipal stage* Sovereign spirit recapitulates role of oedipal father figure, disciplining the ego and purging it of tendencies that conflict with spirit.	*Preoedipal stage* Caring spirit recapitulates role of preoedipal caregiver, guiding and protecting the ego as it returns to fully embodied, instinctual, emotional, and relational life.	*Ego-spirit integration* Regression in the service of integration comes to an end; spiritual maturity achieved.

	Proximity of planes	Rupture of planes	Merging of planes	Fusion of planes
Supernatural and natural planes	Supernatural and natural planes are close enough that the former exerts a gravitational pull on the latter without yet manifesting itself directly within the latter. Spirit is sensed but not seen.	Supernatural breaks through into natural plane and manifests itself directly, as sovereign spirit within the soul and as numinous spirit within the world.	Supernatural and natural planes begin to join, with supernatural plane thus being "naturalized" and natural plane "supernaturalized."	Supernatural and natural planes fuse as "naturally supernatural" world, a world in which there is no longer any distinction between supernatural and natural planes.
Spirit's effects within the soul	The gravitational pull of spirit draws the ego out of the world, causing it to lose all appetite for the goods of the world and to hunger for something sensed but not seen.	Spirit awakens within the soul, potently energizing the ego's experience and causing consolations and afflictions. Spirit disciplines the ego with purgative afflictions when its actions conflict with spirit's expression.	Spirit, in potently energizing the ego's experience, now causes gentler consolations and afflictions. Spirit transforms the ego in ways that facilitate its growth as a vehicle of spirit's expression.	Spirit potently energizes ego's experience without any longer causing afflictions or even consolations. Spirit, integrated with the ego, no longer needs to transform it. Interior experience stabilizes at a higher, potently energized equilibrium.
Spirit's effects within the body	As the gravitational pull of spirit draws the ego out of the world, the body suffers a flagging of instinctual desire.	Spirit awakens instinctual desire and can cause bodily sensations and movements that are physical analogues of the consolations and afflictions that spirit causes within the soul. Soul and body begin to open to each other.	Soul and body continue to open to each other. Ego returns to fully embodied, instinctual, emotional, and relational life. Ego and soul are increasingly anchored in the body as locus of upwelling spirit.	Complete integration of ego and spirit is complete integration of soul and body. Soul and body are now fully open to and united with each other.

continued on next page

Table 16.1. Continued.

	Spiritual preawakening	Spiritual awakening	Spiritual growth	Spiritual maturity
Spirit's transformation of the self-system	Withdrawal from world causes "dying to self." Self-representation becomes a lifeless mask. Ego ideal loses power to inspire; superego loses power to command. Ego is motivated only by spiritual hunger.	Awakened spirit, as sovereign spirit, reduces ego to secondary status within the soul. Ego now authors the self-representation under the supervision of spirit. Ego ideal becomes goal of living a heroic or saintly spiritual life. Superego becomes spirit's assistant disciplinarian.	Spirit elevates the ego to the status of spirit's junior partner in spiritual life. Self-representation becomes a record of spirit and the ego's shared life. Ego ideal becomes goal of living a life that is both fully spiritual and realistically human. Superego becomes spirit's assistant guardian.	Ego and spirit are integrated as a single self. Self-representation becomes a record of the life of this integrated self. Ego ideal is the realized ideal of a fully spiritual, realistically human life. Superego is no longer spirit's assistant disciplinarian or guardian, for spirit and ego now act with one will.
Spirit's effect on the shadow	Dying to self allows shadow impulses to stir. Shadow impulses no sooner stir than they are caught in the gravitational pull of spirit and, like worldly desires generally, wither and die.	Awakening spirit, in energizing both soul and body, awakens shadow impulses, this time without the possibility of rerepression, thus bringing an end to the shadow.	What was the shadow is now in the process of being assimilated within a more inclusive self-representation.	Last vestiges of shadow disappear.

	Desert	Dark wood	Forest clearing	Home
Spirit's transformation of the lifeworld	As ego is drawn out of the world, it loses interest in the world, which, consequently, becomes arid and flat, a barren tract.	Numinous spirit permeates the world, darkening it with an overcast sky. Numinous spirit's amplifying, accentuating, and magnetizing effects imbue the world with an eerie and transfixing supernatural beauty.	Radiant spirit breaks through overcast sky, illuminating the ground below with shafts of wondrous, soothing light. Radiant spirit's amplifying, accentuating, and magnetizing effects imbue the world with a gleaming and inviting supernatural beauty.	Naturally supernatural union of sky and earth; dwelling place of both spirit and humans. The extraordinary beauty bestowed by spirit's amplifying, accentuating, and magnetizing effects is no longer to any degree otherworldly in perceived character and is now seen to be the world's own beauty.
Ego's spiritual journey	Ego wanders in a desert searching for something sensed but not seen.	Ego is lost in a dark wood. There seems to be no way out of the wood.	Ego is guided out of darkness by a light that, shining through an overcast sky and forest canopy, illumines the ground below.	Following the light shining in the forest clearing, ego arrives at the edge of forest and finally returns home.

The first of the four stages of spiritual development, spiritual preawakening, is the subject of this chapter. The most remarkable thing about this stage is its paradoxical nature. The stage is the opposite of what it seems. Spiritual preawakening, as the name indicates, is a stage that prepares for an awakening of spirit in one's life. As such, it is a stage with promising potential. However, to the person undergoing it, spiritual preawakening seems to be the very opposite. As Søren Kierkegaard, drawing on a biblical phrase, described it, spiritual preawakening seems to be a "sickness unto death." Kierkegaard was referring specifically to the despair that is a primary affliction of spiritual preawakening. However, despair is only one of the many afflictions of the "illness" of spiritual preawakening. Others are loss of appetite for the goods of the world, a "dying" to one's sense of self, and a feeling that one is no longer at home in the world. It is characteristic of the stage of spiritual preawakening that these afflictions, and others as well, grow steadily worse. From the sufferer's perspective, it seems that the prospects of the stage are not good and become bleaker as the stage unfolds. Despite appearances, however, the stage moves in the direction of spirit, such that the more severe the afflictions, the more seemingly bleak the prospects, the closer one is to spiritual awakening. The paradox of spiritual preawakening is that the closer one is to the goal of the stage, the further from the goal one seems to be.

That spiritual preawakening moves toward spirit despite seeming to move away is evident in yet another affliction of the stage. This affliction, which distinguishes spiritual preawakening from conditions that might otherwise resemble it, is spiritual hunger. The person undergoing spiritual preawakening suffers from a relentless need for something unknown. Having lost appetite for the goods of the world, the person undergoing spiritual preawakening hungers for something more than the world—or at least something more than the *known* world—can offer. Only something supernatural, it seems, could remedy the afflictions of the stage. However, what the person undergoing spiritual preawakening does not understand is that spiritual hunger, although seemingly an affliction indicating the absence of spirit, is in fact a sign indicating the nearness of spirit. Paradoxically, the more desperate the hunger for spirit and the more it seems that spirit is absent, the closer one is to spirit.

The bleakness of the stage of spiritual preawakening can be mitigated with spiritual counseling. A spiritual director can explain that the afflictions of the stage are caused by spirit and, therefore, indicate the opposite of what they seem. In this vein, a spiritual director can explain that loss of appetite for the world and spiritual hunger are indications that one has come within spirit's sphere of influence. Additionally, a spiritual director can explain that not being able to find that for which one desperately yearns is not an indication of the remoteness of spirit, for it is precisely the closeness of spirit that explains the intensity of the yearning. Unfortunately, not everyone in the stage of spiritual preawakening is fortunate enough to have a good spiritual director. Since we are here presenting the extreme case of spiritual preawakening, we do not assume the presence of a spiritual director to mitigate the afflictions of the stage.

The stage of spiritual preawakening has been described in the major religions of the world. In Hinduism, it is the stage of renunciation (*sannyāsa*), which for some begins late in life—after stages of schooling, adult social responsibilities, and retirement—but for others begins much earlier, in response to a call to devote themselves entirely to the search for liberation. In Buddhism, spiritual preawakening is the stage during which one, having begun to sense that the world we live in (*samsāra*) is "unsatisfactory," afflicted with suffering (*dukkha*), begins to take up in earnest the Eightfold Noble Path in search of enlightenment. As depicted in the well-known Zen Ox-Herding Pictures, spiritual preawakening is the first of the ten pictures, the picture in which a man who has left his village searches in unfamiliar territory for an ox that is nowhere to be seen.

From a biblical perspective, spiritual preawakening is often associated with the desert experience, a trial of passage through hostile terrain in which one encounters demons, hungers for spiritual sustenance, and searches for one's true spiritual home. It has also been described as "dying to self" or "dying with Christ," a stage of development during which one forsakes the world and undergoes suffering in preparation for spiritual rebirth. Finally, perhaps the best-known description of spiritual preawakening from a biblical perspective is that of Saint John of the Cross, who, in *Dark Night of the Soul*, described it as the "night of the senses," a time when one loses one's appetite for life, dies to one's old sense of self, struggles with dark impulses, and searches desperately for God.

World-Weariness

The loss of appetite for the world experienced by people in the stage of spiritual preawakening is a special type of life dissatisfaction. Since we already know from chapter 13 that midlife is a time during which life dissatisfaction is a significant issue for some people, it will be helpful here to recall the discussion of that chapter so that we can be as clear as possible about how the dissatisfaction characteristic of spiritual preawakening differs from that of midlife.

To recall, for those who experience it, midlife dissatisfaction is an unhappiness about one's life that is limited in scope, restless in mood, and worldly in focus. It is limited in scope because it is a dissatisfaction with one's specific life circumstances, typically with circumstances related to one's primary social roles. It is restless in mood because the person who suffers it feels compelled to explore in imagination, if not in action, changes that might alleviate her or his dissatisfaction. Finally, midlife dissatisfaction is worldly in focus because the changes explored are worldly in nature. People suffering midlife dissatisfaction explore changes in such things as their lifestyles, friendships, and recreations and sometimes in their jobs and close relationships.

In contrast, the dissatisfaction characteristic of spiritual preawakening is global in scope, despairing in mood, and spiritual in focus. It is global in scope in two ways, first, because it is a dissatisfaction with life itself rather than with only a specific set of life circumstances, and, second, because it is a sickness unto death that afflicts the body as well as the soul. As the soul suffers a loss of appetite for the goods of the world, the body suffers a corresponding flagging of instinctual desire, including desire for food, sex, and life itself. In thus being global in scope, the dissatisfaction characteristic of spiritual preawakening is despairing in mood, for the person suffering the dissatisfaction cannot imagine any changes in worldly circumstances that could possibly alleviate the dissatisfaction. Finally, the dissatisfaction characteristic of spiritual preawakening is spiritual in focus because it is accompanied by a hunger for something more than the known world can offer, as if only something supernatural could alleviate the dissatisfaction. Given these ways in which it differs from midlife dissatisfaction, let us call the dissatisfaction characteristic of spiritual preawakening "world-weariness."

How is world-weariness to be explained? Before turning to our own hypothesis, that it is caused by spirit, let us first consider other possible hypotheses. Having already explained how world-weariness differs from midlife dissatisfaction, we can say that it is unlikely that the cause or causes of midlife dissatisfaction are sufficient to explain world-weariness. As identified in chapter 13, the primary cause of midlife dissatisfaction is a disillusionment that some people experience in realizing that, despite having worked hard to succeed in their social roles, they have not achieved happiness, either because they have not achieved the level of success they set out to achieve or because they have achieved this level (or better) but without achieving happiness in doing so. This disillusionment can cause people at midlife to lose faith in the lives they have been living and to begin searching for happiness in new ways.

The disillusionment underlying midlife dissatisfaction does not explain the global, despairing, or spiritual features of world-weariness. Although it explains dissatisfaction with social roles and related life circumstances, it does not explain global dissatisfaction with life itself. Nor does it explain the withering of instinctual desire characteristic of world-weariness. Additionally, midlife disillusionment does not explain the despair of world-weariness, for those who suffer midlife dissatisfaction are hopeful that changes in their lives will relieve their dissatisfaction. Finally, midlife disillusionment does not explain the spiritual hunger characteristic of world-weariness. Except in cases in which midlife dissatisfaction and world-weariness overlap, people suffering midlife dissatisfaction hunger only for improved life circumstances, not for something unseen and unknown. For these reasons, the disillusionment about success and happiness that sometimes occurs at midlife, although perhaps a contributing cause of world-weariness in some instances, cannot plausibly be considered a primary let alone a sufficient cause. Many Jungians and this author in previous publications need to be corrected on this point.[3]

A second hypothesis is that world-weariness is a form of depression and for this reason can be explained by the same cause or causes that are responsible for depression. This hypothesis is highly implausible if by depression one means situational depression. Situational depression is caused by unfortunate circumstances (e.g., unemployment, separation from a spouse or partner, death of a loved one) and is typically remedied by improved circumstances or by the passage of time. Clearly, situational depression lacks the distinguishing features of world-weariness. It is neither a global nor a despairing nor a spiritual dissatisfaction. It is a response only to specific unfortunate circumstances; it is a despondency that falls short of despair; and it is not associated with spiritual hunger. Because situational depression differs from world-weariness in these ways, it seems reasonable to conclude that the unfortunate circumstances that cause situational depression are not responsible for world-weariness.

World-weariness has much more in common with clinical depression, which afflicts not only people in unfortunate circumstances but also people in fortunate circumstances. Clinical depression is like world-weariness in being both a global and a despairing dissatisfaction. Like world-weariness, clinical depression is a dissatisfaction with life itself rather than only with specific life circumstances and, therefore, is a dissatisfaction that afflicts not only the soul, which loses motivation to act, but also the body, which suffers a flagging of instinctual desire. Furthermore, clinical depression, like world-weariness, is despairing because it seems as though nothing in the world could possibly remedy it.

However, despite resembling world-weariness in these ways, clinical depression differs from world-weariness in lacking an evident spiritual dimension. Whereas world-weariness is a condition in which one has lost one's appetite for the world *because* one has begun hungering for spirit instead, clinical depression is a condition in which one has simply lost one's appetite for the world. This statement is too strong because there no doubt are many gradations of each condition, and the two conditions may overlap in some cases. Proper diagnosis is difficult. Nevertheless, there are cases in which the two conditions clearly do not overlap, and in these cases the difference is the unmistakable presence of spiritual hunger in world-weariness and its apparent absence in clinical depression.

The difference between clinical depression and world-weariness is further evident in the fact that people suffering clinical depression experience lassitude and inactivity, whereas people suffering world-weariness do not. Clinically depressed people most often lack energy; and although they frequently suffer from insomnia, they also frequently suffer from the opposite, the tendency to sleep long hours or at least to remain in bed. In contrast, people suffering world-weariness, despite having lost their appetite for the world, are energetic and active. They are so because something drives them in their search for the unknown that, they believe, can alone cure their dissatisfaction. As we shall see, that which drives them is nothing other than the unknown for which they are searching.

The prevailing view is that clinical depression is caused by chemical imbalances in the brain and for this reason requires medication as part of an effective therapy. Such chemical intervention might not be appropriate as a treatment for world-weariness, since it does not address the spiritual dimension of world-weariness. Clinical depression is remedied when one regains one's previous interest and engagement in life, when one becomes one's "old self" again. Such an outcome might not and perhaps should not be considered the remedy for world-weariness, since with this outcome the spiritual hunger of world-weariness would disappear without having been satisfied. The chemical imbalances in the brain that cause clinical depression may indeed be in play in many instances of world-weariness, but another cause or other causes seem to be essentially in play as well.

Let us now turn to the hypothesis that will guide our account: that there is such a thing as spirit and that the four stages of spirituality we are considering are stages during which spirit, rather than the ego, plays the leading causal role. According to this hypothesis, the unknown for which the world-weary person hungers is not a figment of the world-weary person's imagination but is rather spirit itself acting on the world-weary person in such a way as to cause the distinguishing features of world-weariness: global dissatisfaction, despair, and spiritual hunger.

Given these features of world-weariness, it follows from our hypothesis that the specific causal role played by spirit during the stage of spiritual preawakening is that of an *unseen attractor.* As an unseen attractor, spirit works as an invisible power that exerts a gravitational pull on the world-weary person, a pull that causes the world-weary person to lose appetite for the world (global dissatisfaction), to feel ill without hope of worldly remedy (despair), and to search for something unknown (spiritual hunger). The world-weary person suffers global dissatisfaction and despair and is driven by spiritual hunger because, adopting the assumption of spirit causation, there is an invisible power, spirit, the pull of which has these effects on the world-weary person.

The world-weary person is thus drawn to something sensed but not seen. This fact indicates that the ego has somehow moved within spirit's sphere of influence. Although spirit may work as an unseen attractor before the stage of spiritual preawakening, it is only during this stage that the gravitational power of spirit begins to have dramatic, unmistakable effects on the ego: withdrawal from the world, relentless spiritual hunger. Although the ego worries that spirit cannot be found—perhaps because spirit is unreachably remote or perhaps because it is merely a fictional projection of the imagination—the fact is that spirit is so close as to be "palpably inevident." Spirit is palpably *inevident* as *unseen* attractor and *palpably* inevident as unseen (but nonetheless sensed) *attractor.* To make this point in other terms, we can say that the "supernatural" plane of spirit and the "natural" plane of the ego and this world have drawn near enough to each other that the gravitational pull of the former is beginning to be felt within the latter but not so near that the former has begun to manifest itself directly within the latter. Let us refer to this nearness of spirit and ego, of supernatural and natural planes, as a "proximity of planes."

Inner and Outer Expressions of Spirit—
Enfolded and Transcendent Spirit

Spirit has both inner and outer expressions, expressions that, as we shall see, change in closely interrelated ways over the course of spiritual development.

For those whose spirituality is primarily inward in focus, it is the inner expression of spirit that is primary; for those whose spirituality is primarily outward in focus, it is the outer expression of spirit that is primary; and for those whose spirituality is both inwardly and outwardly focused, it is the inner and outer expressions of spirit together, in their complementarity, that are primary.

For those whose spirituality is primarily inward in focus, spirit as unseen attractor is most often conceptualized as an interior core of spiritual life hidden deep within the soul. This interior core is hidden because it is concealed beneath or behind tiered "layers" of the embodied soul. In the West, such layers are ordinarily identified with the physical body as vehicle of the soul and the interior faculties of the soul, including the sensory system, the imagination, the will, and the intellect. In Asian traditions, corresponding layers of the embodied soul are referred to as "sheaths" (*koshas*) in Hinduism and as "aggregates" (*khandas*) in Buddhism, the latter based closely on the former. For example, according to Hinduism, the sheaths of the soul are (1) the sheath of the physical body (*annamaya-kosha*), (2) the sheath of vital energy (*prānamaya-kosha*), (3) the sheath of the sensory-intentional mind (*manomaya-kosha*), (4) the sheath of the intellect (*vijñānamaya-kosha*), and (5) the sheath of subtle karmic tendencies (*samskāras*), referred to as the sheath of "bliss" (*ānandamaya-kosha*). Despite some differences in details, these Western and Asian accounts of the layers of the soul agree that the layers overlie the interior core of spiritual life, enfolding and covering it, layer by layer, and thus hiding it.

Let us call this interior core of spiritual life "enfolded spirit" to indicate that it is an invisible attractor covered and hidden by layers of the embodied soul. As an invisible attractor, enfolded spirit beckons and sometimes produces discernible effects without revealing itself directly. It is an invisible center of psychic gravity that, when one is subject to its influence, stills the mind, stirs spiritual hunger, and draws one inward, toward something sensed but not seen. Enfolded spirit is in these ways like a black hole in psychic space, a source of concentrated gravity that, although unseen, can be known by its influence on things that are close enough to it to be affected by it. In the case of enfolded spirit, the effects of its influence are evident in those who are close enough to it to be in the zone of the proximity of planes.

For those whose spirituality is primarily outward in focus, spirit as unseen attractor is most often conceptualized as a supernatural power hidden in natural objects or places or as a god or goddess hidden above or beneath the earth or sea. Let us call such outer, hidden forms of spirit "transcendent spirit." Examples of transcendent spirit are almost uncountably many, including the spirit-animated objects and places of indigenous spiritualities, which exude a power that can be felt but not seen (except by shamans); the personal gods and goddesses of polytheistic religions, who are said to reside out of sight on mountain tops or beneath the earth or sea; and the monotheistic gods of the Abrahamic faiths, who are said to reside high in the heavens beyond the cover of the clouds. These supernatural beings influence our lives and draw us to them even when they do not show themselves to us directly.

In Hinduism, although the focus theologically is frequently on the underlying mystical unity of all existence and, therefore, on the immanent presence of the divine, the focus devotionally is often on the transcendent absence of a divine being, who is hidden and either longed for lovingly by the devotee (*viraha bhakti*) or scolded by the devotee for being neglectful or for having abandoned the devotee (*virodha bhakti*).[4] Similarly, in the Abrahamic faiths, spirit as unseen attractor is described as a *deus absconditus*, a god who does not show his face and reveals himself only occasionally and indirectly, through voices, miracles, messengers, prophets, or, in Christianity, a human incarnation. Otherwise, this hidden god remains remote, concealing his full glory. Martin Luther explained how this god invites, tests, and strengthens our faith, drawing us close to him as an unseen attractor for whom we yearn.

When subject to the gravitational pull of unseen spirit, whether enfolded spirit or transcendent spirit, one is brought to a halt, silenced, and partially enveloped by a power that is felt but not seen. Responding to the inner pull of enfolded spirit, one feels as if one has come under the influence of a power hidden deep within the soul, a power that disengages one's faculties, quiets one's mind, and then draws one into states of semiabsorption. Correspondingly, responding to the outer pull of transcendent spirit, one feels as if one has come upon the dwelling place of a supernatural power or being, the unseen influence of which disengages one's faculties, captivates one's attention, and then holds one in thrall. Such dwelling places are natural phenomena from which, it seems, a supernatural power emanates, a power that is felt but not seen. Whether in the presence of enfolded spirit within or transcendent spirit without, one feels as if one has come under the influence of an unseen power that stills and tethers the mind and draws one ever deeper within its sphere.

Such experiences are markedly out of the ordinary and suggest that one is undergoing profound change. This suggestion is not without warrant, since the experiences just described are initial effects of spirit working in its role as unseen attractor. People who have begun to be affected by spirit's gravity are understandably fascinated by what is happening to them. However, they might also be distressed, for the effects of spirit's gravity can stir worries that one is subject to influences that cannot be controlled. Again, spiritual counseling can mitigate the afflictions of spiritual preawakening, in this case worries about mental instability. A spiritual director can explain that states like the ones just described are expectable, normal phenomena because, owing to the proximity of planes, spirit has begun to have a discernible gravitational effect within or on the soul.

As pertains specifically to the inwardly felt effects of enfolded spirit, both Western and Asian spiritual traditions have described a stage of interior practice during which, in our terms, the gravitational pull of enfolded spirt becomes discernible in states of disengaged quiet that deepen into states of semiabsorption. This stage is the second of five broad stages of interior practice recognized by both Western and Asian traditions. The five stages are summarized in text box 16.2.

Spiritual preawakening, when inwardly directed, is quite evidently correlated with the second of the five stages summarized in text box 16.2. The disengaged quiet of the second stage and, even more, the semiabsorptions that sometimes occur during this stage strongly indicate that one has begun being drawn into more interior layers of the soul or, as Saint Teresa of Avila says, more interior "mansions" or "dwelling places" within the soul. The fact that states of disengaged quiet and states of semiabsorption emerge without having been produced by the ego indicates that the transition from ego-driven to spirit-driven spirituality has begun.

In sum, world-weariness can be focused either inwardly, on the soul, or outwardly, on the world. The world-weary person may be drawn toward an unseen attractor thought to be hidden deep within the soul (enfolded spirit) or may search for an unseen attractor thought to be hidden within or beyond the cosmos (transcendent spirit). In either case, the world-weary person has lost all appetite for the world and hungers for one thing only: the unseen attractor that is both the cause and the goal of the spiritual search.

How World-Weariness Affects the Self-System

Let us now consider how world-weariness affects the self-system. Again, it is helpful to compare world-weariness with midlife dissatisfaction. The major point of comparison here is that both world-weariness and midlife dissatisfaction cause the self-system to seem alien to some degree. Alike in having

Text Box 16.2
Five Stages of Interior Practice

1. *Effortful, unsteady attention.* During this stage, one must exercise will to overcome distractions and drowsiness and thus to achieve alert, steady attention, either one-pointed attention directed to a selected object (image, idea, theme) or open awareness of psycho-mental phenomena as they arise spontaneously within conscious-ness. Interior practice of the one-pointed sort is "concentrative" meditation or prayer; interior practice of the open sort is "open-ing" meditation or prayer, as we have called it. Concentrative and opening meditation or prayer in this initial stage of interior practice, requiring effort of will, are forms of ego-driven interior practice. It is the ego that takes the initiative in combating distractions and drowsiness and thus in keeping attention alert and steady, whether in a one-pointed or open way.

2. *Disengaged inwardness; effortless, steady attention.* During this stage, the ego is drawn inward. As this happens, distractions dis-appear, and drowsiness ceases to be a problem. Except for alert attention, executive functions are disengaged and stilled, leaving the ego quietly composed. With this composure, alert attention becomes effortless and steady, whether attention is one-pointedly directed to a selected object or openly mindful of what arises within consciousness. As the pull inward increases, states of disengaged inwardness can evolve into states of semiabsorption, which can be semiabsorptions in objects of concentrative meditation or prayer or in psychomental phenomena as they arise in open meditation or prayer. Sometimes states of semiabsorption are objectless. It may seem as if, rather than being semiabsorbed in anything discrete or discernible, one is instead semienveloped by something indefi-nite and hidden, an unseen attractor within. The pull inward that occurs during this stage of practice indicates that one has begun moving toward more interior and subtle layers (faculties, sheaths, aggregates) of the soul. In our terms, this stage of interior practice marks the transition from ego-driven meditation or prayer to spir-it-driven meditation or prayer. Enfolded spirit, as unseen attractor, has disengaged and quieted the ego and will soon play the leading causal role in the ego's interior experience. Were the ego to try at this point to resume cognitive or volitional activity, it would disrupt the spirit-caused inward pull distinctive of this transitional stage of interior practice.

3. *Extraordinary states of consciousness.* During this stage, the effort-less, steady attention of the previous stage ends and states of powerful absorption and excitation occur. Because these states are extraordinary in character, this third stage of interior practice is the one most frequently associated with infused, awakened, or mystical spirituality. From our perspective, this third stage indicates that enfolded spirit, having drawn the ego within its "event hori-zon," is now actively in charge of the ego's interior life. Here it is unmistakably evident that it is spirit's causal influence that is dra-matically absorbing and exciting the ego. Absorptions are now full absorptions rather than semiabsorptions. It seems as if the ego has disappeared without remainder into that in which it is absorbed. In contrast to these states of absorption, states of pleasurable or painful excitation also occur. These states, which are often referred to as "consolations" and "afflictions" respectively, are similar in some respects and opposite in others. Examples are ecstasy and agony, bliss and frenzy, rapture and rupture, and inspiration and intoxication. Whether one experiences primarily absorptions or exci-tations during this third stage of spiritual practice depends on many factors, including perhaps most importantly the type of interior practice one performs.

> NOTE: Dramatic absorptions occur more often during intense concentrative meditation, for example, the *samādhi* meditation of Hinduism and the closely similar *jhāna* meditation of Buddhism. Dramatic excitations occur more often during emotionally charged devotional meditation or prayer, for example, *bhakti* practices in Hinduism and many contemplative practices in Christianity. Finally, less dramatic absorptions and excitations occur in opening practices of a non-devotional, non-theistic sort, for example, Buddhist insight meditation and other practices of steadfast atten-tion to whatever presents itself within consciousness.

4. *Higher equilibrium.* During this stage, extraordinary states of con-sciousness gradually disappear and consciousness restabilizes at a higher level of energy, clarity, and composure. In arriving at this stage, the ego has withdrawn into the most interior, subtle layer of the soul and is nearing the goal of interior practice. In our terms, this fourth stage of interior practice is the last stage that can be said to be spirit-driven because during this stage spirit begins pri-

marily to act *through* the ego rather than any longer, as before, *on* it. This fourth stage of interior practice, therefore, is a transitional stage between spirit-driven meditation or prayer and fully spiritual consciousness.

5. *Liberation, enlightenment, union.* During this stage, the journey inward moves through and beyond the most interior layer of the soul, thus reaching the core of the psyche, spirit's realm. This movement is variously conceived as a passage from the most interior sheath of the soul into the fourth and highest state of consciousness, *turīya* (liberation: Hinduism), as a passage from the most interior layer of aggregates of the soul into the unconditioned realm of *nirvāna* (enlightenment: Buddhism), and as a passage from the most interior faculty of the soul into the full presence of God, Spirit, or Christ within (mystical union: mystical traditions in the Abrahamic faiths).

this general effect, the two forms of dissatisfaction differ in the degree to which they render the self-system alien. Whereas midlife dissatisfaction renders the self-system only partially alien, world-weariness renders the self-system completely alien. In making this point, the reader is again reminded that the account of world-weariness presented here sets forth the extreme case.

That world-weariness renders the self-system completely alien is reflected in the self-representation, the ego ideal, and the superego. Regarding the self-representation, let us recall that midlife dissatisfaction renders it alien to some degree by causing one to feel that role-related features of the self-representation no longer "fit" well. One senses that the self-representation no longer fully reflects who or what one is. In contrast, world-weariness, in rendering the self-representation completely alien, makes it seem as if the self-representation, rather than no longer fitting well, no longer fits at all. The self-representation ceases altogether being a vehicle of self-expression and growth. It ceases altogether being Me. Although world-weary people may continue to perform the social and other roles on which their self-representations are based, they no longer feel like themselves in doing so. Worldly roles have become only scripts for an actor who no longer "lives" them, and the self-representation based on these roles has become only an actor's mask. The self-representation in this way "dies," becoming a lifeless façade.

World-weariness has much the same effect on the ego ideal. Whereas midlife dissatisfaction renders only the ideal goals associated with primary social roles alien and ordinarily does so only partially, world-weariness renders all worldly goals alien and does so completely. People suffering midlife dissatisfaction, although much less inspired by the goals associated with their social roles, are still strongly inspired by goals, as is evident in the fact that they fantasize about new goals that might restore passion to their lives. In contrast, people suffering world-weariness, having lost all appetite for the world, do not fantasize about new worldly goals. Suffering from a global dissatisfaction, world-weary people are indifferent to the world. For them, everything is "equal," equally uninspiring. The ego ideal is thus disempowered as an agency of self-motivation and, like the self-representation, dies. In the place of the ego ideal, it is spiritual hunger that now motivates the world-weary person.

The superego, too, is rendered alien, although not completely. The qualification is necessary because world-weary people continue to speak in the superego voice to ensure that they are heedful of the interests of others. However, having lost their appetite for the world, world-weary people are no longer concerned about their own interests, that is, their own *worldly* interests. For them, the spiritual quest has replaced the pursuit of worldly interests. Consequently, since the pursuit of worldly interests had been the primary job of the superego, the superego has much less work to do. It does not go silent, but it has much less to say. Overall, it withers away and, like the self-representation and ego ideal, dies. The ego thus loses both the inspiring motivation of the ego ideal and, for the most part, the impelling motivation of the superego. Again, it is spiritual hunger that is now the primary motivator in the ego's life.

The death of the self-system caused by world-weariness—let us call it "dying to self"—closely resembles the clinical condition known as "depersonalization." However, the similarity is not complete. The two conditions differ in one essential way, the same way in which world-weariness differs from clinical depression. The difference is that, whereas depersonalization, like clinical depression, is primarily a psychological condition, dying to self, like world-weariness, is primarily a spiritual condition. Dying to self is not only a psychological condition in which an old self becomes alien and dies; it is also and primarily a spiritual condition in which a new self, a spiritual self, is gestating under the influence of unseen spirit. Dying to self is like depersonalization in being a shedding of the self-system; however, it differs from depersonalization in being a shedding that not only strips the ego of its worldly clothing but also, in doing so, renders the ego naked to the transforming influence of spirit.

This contrast between dying to self and depersonalization, like the earlier contrast between world-weariness and clinical depression, is overstated. Dying to self and depersonalization have many gradations, and these two conditions probably overlap in some cases. Still, the main point is that dying to self is primarily a spiritual condition, whereas depersonalization is not. Dying to self is a condition in which the death of the self-system and spiritual hunger are both primary symptoms, whereas depersonalization is a condition in which the death of the self-system is the primary if not only symptom.

Shadow Awakening

Dying to self is a prelude to shadow awakening, a recurring theme of this book. We learned in previous chapters that adolescence and midlife are stages during which shadow awakening is more likely to occur than during other stages. Here we can add that the same is true in the case of spiritual preawakening. Indeed, spiritual preawakening is not only a stage during which shadow awakening is more likely to occur than during other stages; it is a stage during which shadow awakening is more likely to occur than not. Unlike adolescence and midlife, during which shadow awakening occurs frequently but is not the norm, spiritual preawakening is a stage during which shadow awakening is the norm.

The world-weary person, having died to self, no longer relates to the self-representation as Me and, therefore, is no longer motivated to defend the self-representation against impulses that conflict with it, including most importantly those that had been repressed and relegated to the shadow. Shadow impulses for this reason can easily be awakened during spiritual preawakening, needing only to be stirred and thus energized by tempting or provoking stimuli. Moreover, because the death of the self-system during spiritual preawakening is a *complete* death, a death in which all features of the self-representation have been rendered completely alien, the door is open for an awakening of the *entire* shadow. Whereas shadow awakening during adolescence tends to be an awakening primarily of childish impulses that challenge authority figures, and whereas shadow awakening during midlife tends to be primarily an awakening of adult impulses that conflict with social roles, shadow awakening during spiritual preawakening is potentially an awakening of all repressed impulses. Shadow awakening during spiritual preawakening thus tends to be wider in scope than during adolescence and midlife. Interestingly, as we shall see, it also tends to be less intense and less likely to be acted on.

Shadow awakening as it occurs during spiritual preawakening is exclusively negative in perceived character, for two reasons. First, it is *negative* in perceived character because, as is true of shadow awakenings generally when they first occur, it stimulates impulses that the ego finds threatening, indeed so threatening as previously to have repressed them. Second, shadow awakening during spiritual preawakening is *exclusively* negative because, for reasons explained presently, it has no chance of evolving from shadow awakening into shadow integration. Such an evolution does occur during spiritual stages; however, it does so during the stage of spiritual awakening, not the stage of spiritual preawakening. As we shall see in the next chapter, spiritual awakening brings the shadow to life one more time, this time the final time, for it awakens the shadow in such a way that the ego has no choice but to integrate it within a more comprehensive self-representation.

It follows from the fact that shadow awakening during spiritual preawakening is exclusively negative in perceived character that the voice of the shadow as it emerges during spiritual preawakening is an exclusively negative voice. The voice of the shadow during spiritual preawakening speaks only as an adversary and tempter; it does not get a chance to begin speaking as a counselor and guide. Accordingly, the ego, alienated from the self-system, begins to speak to itself as an adversary of the self-system, perhaps taunting itself for being inauthentic (in the features of its self-representation), naïve (in the goals of its ego ideal), and meekly conformist (in the norms of its superego). In the shadow voice, the ego might say to itself such things as "You hypocrite; you know that the self you've presented to others is only a mask, not your true self" or "You fool; you've pursued goals that society set for you, not your own goals" or "You coward; you've allowed conventional morality to stifle your strength and creativity." At the same time, the ego might speak to itself as a tempter, enticing itself to yield to impulses that are denied by its self-representation and disallowed by its ego ideal and superego. It might say to itself, "You know what you really want. You've deceived others. Don't deceive yourself any longer."

Speaking to itself in these ways, the ego is confronted with the possibility that the shadow rather than the self-system represents its true self. Concluding that the self-representation, which has died, is only a false façade and that the ego ideal and superego, which have lost the power to motivate, are only socially programed agencies, the ego is now faced with the prospect of admitting that it is the opposite of what it had previously believed itself to be. However, if the self-system does not represent the ego's true self, neither does the shadow. The fact is that both are partially true selves. The world-weary person thus goes from one partial truth to an opposite partial truth mistakenly thinking that it has gone from something wholly false to something that might be wholly true. The world-weary person, thus faced with the prospect of acknowledging the shadow as the true self, is in a trying situation, to say the least.

Interestingly, such an encounter with the shadow does not indicate that shadow impulses are about to awaken strongly enough to cause serious psychic turmoil, let alone strongly enough to impel the ego to act on them. Shadow awakening as it occurs during spiritual preawakening tends to be less intense than shadow awakenings in other stages of development. The reason for this curious fact is that world-weariness, in causing loss of appetite for the world, deprives shadow temptations of much of the appeal they would otherwise have. When shadow awakening occurs, therefore, the forbidden fantasies it triggers tend not to arouse intense desire or emotion. These fantasies tempt the world-weary person with forbidden *worldly* goods, and worldly goods, even forbidden ones, are not what the world-weary person wants. As we know, the only thing the world-weary person wants is something unknown, something that is different from anything the known world can offer. The world-weary person believes that only this unknown X, not any worldly goods, not even those that would satisfy shadow impulses, is sufficient to cure world-weariness.

Shadow impulses, therefore, in being stirred, compete futilely with unseen spirit for the world-weary person's allegiance. These impulses *do* make their case. However, like the worldly desires that preceded them, they are sapped of strength by the stronger pull of unseen spirit. In this way the shadow, like the self-system before it, eventually dies. This death of the shadow is the reason shadow awakening during spiritual preawakening cannot evolve into shadow integration and, correspondingly, why the shadow voice cannot evolve from the voice of an adversary and tempter into a voice of a counselor and guide. The shadow no sooner asserts itself menacingly than the undertow of unseen spirit deprives it of energy and puts it back to sleep.

To summarize, the sequence is this: (1) world-weariness causes the self-system to die; (2) this death of the self-system opens the door for an awakening of the shadow; (3) shadow impulses are stirred and the shadow begins to speak in a negative voice, deriding the ego's self-system and tempting the ego with forbidden fantasies; (4) the ego listens to the shadow voice but tends not to follow its urgings, since to do so would be to pursue worldly goods, which are not what the ego really wants; (5) shadow impulses, having been stirred and given a voice, are caught in the gravitational undertow of unseen spirit, which saps them of energy; and, consequently, (6) the shadow, like the self-system before it, dies. Once the shadow dies, all that remains of the self-system and its underpinnings is the ego itself as a unity of apperception and executive agency. The ego, stripped of a self-representation, ego ideal, and superego and without even a shadow to contend with, stands alone as a naked, disconnected subject, a bare spectator looking out on a world to which it no longer belongs.

The shadow awakening of spiritual preawakening is often described in spiritual literature as an encounter with demons, gods, goddesses, or superhuman forces associated with death, the underworld, or distant lands. These dark powers are both adversaries and tempters of spiritual seekers. They are adversaries because they put spiritual seekers to the test by exposing their flaws and weaknesses, by mocking their spiritual aspirations, and by challenging their spiritual strength. At the same time, these dark powers are tempters because the primary way in which they put spiritual seekers to the test is by tempting them with worldly goods. Succumbing to such temptation proves that a seeker is unready for spiritual life.

Examples of encounters with such dark powers are (1) young Nachiketa's meeting with Yama, the Lord of Death, who offered Nachiketa all manner of worldly goods in an attempt to avoid answering Nachiketa's question about the secret of death and the fate of the soul (Hinduism: *Katha Upanishad*); (2) Siddhartha Gautama's confrontation with the demon Mara, who tested the future Buddha's meditative resolve by threatening him with horrific creatures, tempting him with beautiful women, and mocking the futility of his efforts (Buddhism); (3) the hero's journey of classical mythology, on which a hero-to-be travels into the underworld or to distant lands, where he is challenged with temptations, tasks, or trials that measure his readiness to be transformed by supernatural power; and (4) Jesus's desert encounter with Satan, who tested Jesus's pride and faith and finally offered Jesus all the kingdoms of the world if only Jesus would worship him. These and other accounts suggest that an encounter with seemingly superhuman powers emerging from shadowy or distant realms is frequently a preparation for entry into spiritual life. In our terms, it is an indication that world-weariness has run its course and that spiritual awakening is soon to occur.

Lifeworld—Aridity, Unreality, Desolation

The effect of world-weariness on the lifeworld is in some ways like the effect of midlife dissatisfaction on the lifeworld. Both render the lifeworld alien to some degree. Both cause the lifeworld to lose its appeal. However, with this similarity, there is an even greater difference. The difference is that whereas midlife dissatisfaction affects the lifeworld only locally and partially, world-weariness affects it globally and completely. Midlife dissatisfaction affects only the lifeworld within the boundaries of one's social roles, which ordinarily loses much but not all its appeal. Furthermore, as this local lifeworld diminishes in appeal, possible lifeworlds beyond local boundaries increase in appeal, presenting themselves to the imagination as greener pastures in which one might again find satisfaction in life. In contrast, world-weariness affects the entire lifeworld, both within and beyond the boundaries of social roles; and it does so completely, divesting it of all appeal.

In thus losing all appeal, the world of world-weariness appears arid and flat. The more the world-weary person loses motivation to act in the world, the more the world is divested of inspiring peaks and frightening valleys, of energetically charged positive and negative values. The world in this way ceases attracting the ego's interest. Nothing stands out to be pursued or avoided. The only thing that attracts the ego's interest is the unknown for which it yearns, and this unknown is seemingly not of this world. Accordingly, like what happens to the world-weary person's self-representation, which becomes a lifeless façade, the world-weary person's world becomes a lifeless desert. The world-weary person's world is for this reason perhaps not a *life*world properly so called.

The desert in which the world-weary person wanders seems unreal. It is hard to find just the right word to describe this apparent unreality of the lifeworld. "Derealization" would work nicely, but it is already used to describe a clinical condition from which the apparent unreality of the world we are describing needs to be contrasted. "Devitalization" would work, but it lacks poetic power and gives no hint of the hidden spiritual dimension of the condition of the world we are discussing. For these reasons, we shall call the apparent unreality of the world caused by world-weariness "desolation." "Desolation" is a word frequently used in spiritual literature to describe the bleak and seemingly hopeless condition of those who have lost contact with God. We shall take advantage of the poetic power and spiritual connotations of this word by using it to describe a world that seems lifeless and destitute, bereft of meaning, value, and hope.

Desolation resembles the clinical condition of derealization. Both are conditions in which the world seems arid and flat. However, despite this similarity, the two conditions differ in an essential way, the same way in which world-weariness differs from clinical depression and dying to self differs from depersonalization. The difference is that whereas derealization, like clinical depression and depersonalization, is primarily a psychological condition, desolation, like world-weariness and dying to self, is primarily a spiritual condition. Although desolation resembles derealization in being a condition in which the world seems arid and flat, only desolation is a condition that prepares the world to be regenerated with new, spiritual, life and values. As is true of world-weariness and clinical depression, and as is true of dying to self and depersonalization as well, desolation and derealization probably overlap in some cases. Nevertheless, the difference already stated remains: derealization is primarily a psychological condition, desolation primarily a spiritual condition.

The First Stage of Regression in the Service of Integration

We earlier described spiritual development as a process of "regression in the service of integration." We can now say that the stage of spiritual preawakening is the first stage of this process. Let us call this first stage "withdrawal from the world in preparation for spirit" to indicate both the perceived character of the stage (loss of appetite for the world, dying to self, desolation of the world) and the unseen goal of the stage (the awakening of spirit). In the next two chapters, we explain how spirit, upon awakening, leads the ego through the next two stages of regression in the service of integration, the first of which returns the ego to conditions like those that prevailed during the oedipal stage of development and the second of which returns the ego to conditions like those that prevailed during the preoedipal stage. As we shall see, this return of the ego to conditions like those that prevailed early in life leads to the following two important developmental outcomes: (1) it restores to full expression embodied, instinctual, emotional, and relational bases of life that were to a significant extent left behind during ego development, and (2) it thus allows the ego to integrate its developed executive functions with these essential bases of life. With spirit leading the way, regression in the service of integration thus leads ultimately to a higher integration of ego and spirit, soul and body, reason and feeling, and self and others. Once this goal is achieved, regression in the service of integration ends and the stage of spiritual maturity begins. The reader can consult tables 16.1 and 16.2 for a preview of these developments.

Table 16.2. Regression in the Service of Integration

	Spiritual preawakening	Spiritual awakening (oedipal stage)	Spiritual growth (preoedipal stage)	Spiritual maturity
Relationships	Ego drawn inward by enfolded spirit, an invisible attractor that quiets and stills the mind.	Ego submits inwardly to spirit in the form of sovereign spirit, which, like an oedipal father figure, is a godlike judge and disciplinarian.	Ego comes under the inward influence of spirit in the form of caring spirit, which, like the preoedipal caregiver, is a goddess-like nurturer, guide, and protector.	Ego inwardly integrated with spirit as inherent spirit, which, without losing any of its power, loses its godlike and goddess-like—and therewith its gendered—guises.
Psychospiritual bases of life	Spirit is sensed but has not yet awakened. Original (embodied, instinctual, emotional, and relational) bases of life, which were left behind during ego development, are not yet restored to full expression.	Spirit awakens and reenlivens original bases of life.	Ego adjusts to both spirit and the fullness of embodied, instinctual, emotional, and relational life.	Ego is fully integrated with spirit and with restored embodied, instinctual, emotional, and relational life.
Direction of change	Withdrawal from world; dying to self; desolation of world.	Return to bases of life and to relationships like those at the fore during original oedipal stage.	Return to bases of life and to relationships like those at the fore during original preoedipal stage.	Higher integration of ego and spirit, soul and body, executive functions and restored embodied, instinctual, emotional, and relational life.

Conclusion

Spiritual preawakening has two completely opposite sides. On one side, it is a stage of dying, despair, and desolation, a stage during which one is "sick unto death," bereft of hope, and lost in a lifeless and unreal world. On the other side, however, spiritual preawakening is a stage that is under the direct influence of unseen spirit and for this reason is a stage during which, appearances to the contrary, dying is a precursor to rebirth, despair is a precursor to renewal of hope, and desolation is a precursor to regeneration.

Although spiritual preawakening has these two sides, only the first side, that of dying, despair, and desolation, is apparent. This, at any rate, is true in the extreme case, when the afflictions of the stage are severe and not mitigated by spiritual counseling. In this extreme case, the other side of spiritual preawakening, the side of approaching rebirth, renewal, and regeneration, is hidden. People undergoing spiritual preawakening know only that the self they were is no longer familiar to them, that they are seemingly without hope of finding that for which they yearn, and that the world has become arid and flat. Their condition seems dire. However, the more dire their condition seems, the closer they are to spirit. This is the paradox of spiritual preawakening.

Chapter 17

Spiritual Awakening

As world-weariness unfolds in the direction of increasing dissatisfaction, alienation, and loss of reality, it approaches an inversion point at which the process of dying to self and withdrawal from the world gives way to the awakening of spirit. It is at this point that the hidden side of the stage of spiritual preawakening is revealed. What had seemed to be only a stage of dying, despair, and desolation is now seen also to have been a stage of spiritual gestation preceding spiritual birth. Accordingly, as the first stage of spiritual development reaches its end, the inversion occurs. Spirit ceases being an unseen attractor and becomes a manifest presence within the soul and the world. What had been a yearned-for unknown nowhere to be found now becomes a superenergetic power that pervades one's entire life, both within and without. This breakthrough of spirit marks the beginning of the second stage of spiritual development, the stage of spiritual awakening.

We should step aside for a moment to note that our decision to present the stages of spiritual development as they would be experienced in extreme form takes the risk of suggesting that spiritual awakening is inherently a single dramatic occurrence that brings world-weariness to a sudden end. This suggestion is wrong. Most people, rather than experiencing a single "big" awakening, probably experience a sequence of smaller awakenings, awakenings that grow in power and insight and that only gradually bring world-weariness to an end. Acknowledging this fact, the description in the previous paragraph, although potentially misleading, is warranted because it clarifies the factors in play in spiritual awakening by presenting them in bold outline. It describes spiritual awakening as it would be experienced in the (unlikely) event that all factors in play were present in full force at the same time. This point made, the exposition in this and the next two chapters continues to describe spiritual development as it would unfold in its most extreme form.

Spirit Manifests Itself as a Supernatural Power

When the ego first awakens to spirit, it experiences spirit as a radically unfamiliar energy, an energy that arrives from an unknown source and affects the ego in strange ways. The ego for this reason cannot help but sense that spirit, experienced both inwardly, in the soul, and outwardly, in the world, is a supernatural power of otherworldly origin. It seems as if spirit, although now powerfully active *in* the soul and the world, is not itself *of* the soul or the world. It seems, that is, that spirit is a power that is emphatically other, completely different in type and effect from anything the ego can remember having experienced before. This perceived otherness of spirit, of course, is a matter of degree. Some people may experience spirit in its initial awakening in ways that seem less emphatically other than others do. As explained in the last chapter (text box 16.1), women more than men might sense that awakened spirit, appearance to the contrary, is a power with which they are somehow familiar and to which they are somehow akin. Still, we are right in emphasizing the supernatural perceived character of spirit in its initial awakening because spirit at this point is experienced as something markedly different from the phenomena of the natural world.

The sense that spirit is supernatural in character is a consequence not only of its radical unfamiliarity but also of its potency. Inwardly, spirit intensifies the ego's experience across all modalities; and outwardly, spirit amplifies, accentuates, and magnetizes objects and their qualities, thus imbuing everything with an eerie, transfixing beauty. Mystics and contemplatives from many spiritual traditions have reported that spiritual awakening is typically accompanied by highly energetic, extraordinary experiences, best-known among which are interior experiences that we shall call "consolations of heightened stimulation." For example, the potency of spirit can euphorically stimulate the ego by causing it to experience surges of exultation, flashes of inspiration, swoons of ecstasy, and flights of rapture. After having suffered the afflictions of world-weariness, people who upon awakening experience consolations such as these may cry with tears of relief and newfound hope. They may even leap to the conclusion that, with the arrival of spirit, they have achieved the goal of spiritual life.

This conclusion is premature, for two reasons. The first and more obvious reason is that spiritual awakening is only the beginning, not the culmination, of awakened spiritual life. The second, less obvious reason is that any consolations the ego might experience at the beginning of spiritual awakening are misleading because spiritual awakening has its own afflictions. These afflictions, if not evident at first, soon emerge and tend to grow in number and severity. Indeed, these afflictions can eventually grow to the point at which they outweigh consolations, with such a predominance of afflictions over consolations being the norm in extreme cases of spiritual awakening.

The ensuing account of spiritual awakening uses two familiar metaphors in describing the newly awakened ego, that of a spiritual subject (in the political sense of "subject") and that of a spiritual child. The metaphor of a spiritual subject is used because the newly awakened ego, having just come into the presence of a "higher power," is very much like a subordinate subject in relation to this power. The metaphor of a spiritual child is used because the ego, upon being spiritually awakened, is new to spiritual life and, therefore, in need of spirit's parentlike supervision and support. The ego will in time grow into a spiritual youth, a junior partner of spirit maturing under spirit's care, and will eventually become a spiritual adult, a mature vehicle of spirit's expression in the world. During spiritual awakening, however, the ego is a babe whose eyes have just opened in a new world.

Spirit Asserts Itself as the Sovereign Power of the Soul

Spiritual awakening transforms the entire self-system, including not only the self-representation, ego ideal, and superego but also, and most profoundly, the ego itself. The ego is transformed because the awakening of spirit within the soul reduces the ego to secondary status within its own domain. The ego, which had long acted as if it were the sovereign power of the soul, is reduced in status to being the subject of a superior power, awakened spirit. What happens here is in significant respects the reverse of what happened in early childhood when, as explained in chapter 10, repression brought the period of childhood spirituality to an end and ushered in the long period of ego ascendancy. Unlike what happened then, when the ego initially achieved self-control and thus took charge of the soul, the ego is here divested of much of its self-control and shown in dramatic fashion that it is the lesser of two powers present within the soul. In awakening to spirit, therefore, the ego is disabused of its long-held presumption of being the sovereign power of the soul. The power of awakened spirit so exceeds that of the ego that it is immediately evident to the ego that it is now the subject of a higher sovereign.

Let us for this reason refer to spirit as it initially awakens within the soul as "sovereign spirit." Sovereign spirit is the successor to enfolded spirit, the inner expression of spirit during the stage of spiritual preawakening. In its inner expression, therefore, spirit is now transformed from an unseen gravitational attractor hidden deep within the soul into the manifest sovereign power of the soul, a power that arises from the deep center of the soul where, earlier, it had lain hidden.

Consolations and Afflictions during Spiritual Awakening

We have noted that consolations of heightened stimulation frequently accompany initial spiritual awakening. These consolations are so often mentioned in writings on spiritual awakening that many people do not know that spiritual awakening is often a stage primarily of afflictions and is characteristically such a stage in extreme cases. That afflictions might prevail over consolations during spiritual awakening becomes evident once it is clarified that the ego, as a spiritual child, is not a pristine innocent ready to live an exemplary spiritual life. The newly awakened ego, although a spiritual child, is a worldly adult; and as a worldly adult, it has many deep-seated tendencies that put it at odds with spirit. As a worldly adult, the ego is long accustomed, and, therefore, attached, to being the sovereign power of the soul. Moreover, it harbors impulses (especially former shadow impulses) and is fettered by defense mechanisms and by engrained habits that obstruct or oppose spirit's expression. These impediments to spirit's expression are challenged by awakened spirit, which means that the spiritual child, rather than being like a beaming infant, is instead more like a resistant, willful two-year-old whose unacceptable behavior must be corrected. The newly awakened ego's spiritual immaturity, therefore, rather than implying that the newly awakened ego is spiritually innocent, implies that the newly awakened ego is burdened with impediments to spiritual life that must be purged. It is the job of sovereign spirit to purge these impediments, which it does by subjecting the ego to afflictions when it obstructs or opposes spirit.

The newly awakened ego impedes the expression of spirit not only in the ways just mentioned but also in being susceptible to pride. One type of pride that frequently emerges during spiritual awakening is the pride of feeling superior because one is spiritually awakened. Let us call this the pride of "spiritual superiority." Those who fall prey to pride of this type experience gratification in knowing that others are aware that spirit has awakened within them. They are for this reason prone not to hide this fact and even to put it on display, for example, by making a show of consolations during group meditation or prayer, by exaggerating acts of devotion, observance, charity, or penance, or even by "humbly" denying the fact of being spiritually awakened. Challenging this type of spiritual pride is an important task of sovereign spirit in its purgative role. It is also an important task of a spiritual director.

A second type of pride that can emerge during spiritual awakening is the pride of acting as if spirit's power were one's own power. The newly awakened ego, despite attempting to surrender to spirit, is still attached to the idea of being the sovereign power of the soul and is thus susceptible to acting as if it were the source of the spiritual power active within it. Those who fall prey to pride of this type experience gratification in leading others to believe that the spiritual power active within them belongs to them uniquely and, therefore, is to be credited to them. In thus deceiving others, these people frequently fall prey to self-deception, taking pleasure in the thought that they are spiritually powerful and wise beings. Let us for this reason call this the pride of "spiritual deception." This type of pride is especially problematic. Challenging it is another important task of sovereign spirit in its purgative role. A good spiritual director will respond to this type of pride with harsh disapproval.

In succumbing to spiritual pride of either of the types described, the ego seeks to use the power of spirit to its own advantage. In doing so, the ego brings itself into conflict with spirit, the power of which is not for the ego to exploit. The ego's attempts to take advantage of spirit, therefore, do not come to a good end. Spirit punishes the ego by striking it down or by afflicting it in other ways that teach it the imprudence of its pride. Given spirit's superior power and the ego's desire to be relieved of afflictions, the inevitable direction of change during the stage of spiritual awakening is toward greater acceptance of spirit as the sovereign power of the soul. However, the temptations of pride are such that the ego frequently acts contrary to this direction of change. When it does, the consequences are unpleasant, and the ego is thus taught that attempts to exploit spirit—as is true also of attempts to obstruct or resist spirit—succeed only in increasing its own suffering.

It is not easy for the ego to surrender to spirit's sovereignty. The ego knows that it must do so, since it is aware that spirit's power is far superior to its own. The ego for this reason attempts to surrender to spirit and even takes pleasure in doing so when spirit graces it with consolations. However, the ego frequently cannot help but fight against spirit when spirit challenges its lingering presumption of sovereignty, overrides its impulses, defenses, or habits, or strikes down its pride. When spirit overpowers the ego in these ways, the ego struggles to protect itself from spirit's advances, but always to no avail. Spirit is always the superior power. It is inevitable, therefore, that the ego will eventually—perhaps only after a long while—adjust to its subordinate status and begin to cooperate with spirit not only when spirit dispenses consolations but also when it metes out afflictions.

In sum, spirit afflicts the ego by disciplining it and thereby purging it of tendencies to obstruct, oppose, or exploit spirit. When spirit challenges the ego's lingering presumption of sovereignty, the ego feels powerless and defeated; when spirit overrides the ego's impulses, the ego feels constrained and frustrated; when spirit breaks through the ego's defenses, the ego feels wounded and violated; when spirit disables the ego's habits, the ego feels incapacitated and paralyzed; when spirit strikes down the ego's pride, the ego feels chastised and humbled; and when spirit otherwise encroaches upon the ego's space or asserts itself against the ego, the ego feels vulnerable and weak. All these afflictions caused by spirit, as sovereign spirit, can be understood as ways in which spirit disciplines the ego to purge it of impediments to spiritual life. Using our metaphors, they are ways in which spirit disciplines its unruly subject, a recalcitrant spiritual child, to purge it of its obstinate, defiant, and arrogant tendencies. Given the purgative aim of these afflictions, let us call them "afflictions of purgative discipline." Afflictions of this type are distinctive of spiritual awakening as a stage.

Spirit's purgative role has been described in many ways in the world's religions. Some accounts emphasize punishment, as in karmic or God-authorized retribution (in a future life or afterlife), whereas other accounts emphasize purgation as a cleansing or removal of impediments to spiritual life, as in "burning of karmic seeds" (Hinduism, yoga), "uprooting of defilements" (Buddhism), and "purgation of sins" (Christianity, especially Roman Catholicism). From our perspective it suffices to say that spirit, in afflicting the ego in the ways indicated, is an agency of punishment—better: corrective discipline—and purgation at the same time. Spirit is an agency of corrective discipline because it afflicts the ego to correct its "misbehavior." At the same time, it is an agency of purgation because, in thus afflicting the ego, it gradually purges the ego of tendencies that impede spirit's expression within the soul. The newly awakened ego is an unruly subject in need of the purgative discipline of spirit, its sovereign "lord" or "master."

A second type of affliction that occurs during spiritual awakening is a type caused when the potency of spirit stimulates the ego beyond what it can tolerate. When the potency of spirit thus exceeds the ego's limits, the ego feels wildly excited, inflamed, inflated, or swept away and, generally, out of control. What earlier had been consolations of heightened stimulation can in this way be transformed into afflictions, which we shall call "afflictions of painful overstimulation." For example, exultation can be transformed into frenzy, inspiration into intoxication, ecstasy into agony, rapture into rupture (the feeling of being inflated to the bursting point), and, generally, consoling empowerment into afflicting impairment. The literature on infused spirituality from all major world religions attests that interior life during spiritual awakening can have an intensely double-edged character.

Sometimes spirit, in painfully overpowering the ego—whether with afflictions of purgative discipline or of painful overstimulation—can cause the ego to worry that it is endangered by spirit. Spirit can so assail the ego that it not only challenges the ego's self-assertions, thwarts the ego's impulses, breaks through the ego's defenses, disables the ego's habits, and strikes down the ego's pride but also arrests the ego's executive functions, rendering the ego unable to think or act. Additionally, spirit can so stimulate the ego that, when raptures become ruptures, the ego feels utterly "blown away," so inflamed and inflated as seemingly to lose cohesion as a unity of apperception. When thus assailed, arrested, or overstimulated by spirit, the ego may worry that, rather than having experienced a spiritual breakthrough, it has instead suffered a psychological breakdown. In such "spiritual emergencies," as they are called, the ego might worry that spirit, in its potency, is damaging if not destroying necessary defenses, action routines, faculties, or boundaries. The guidance of a spiritual director can help alleviate such worries. A good spiritual director can explain that the effects of spirit causing concern are most often temporary spiritual afflictions that will disappear once the ego is better adjusted to spirit's sovereignty and potency. However, the qualification "most often" suggests the possibility that spiritual awakening can have persisting pathological outcomes under some conditions. More is said on this topic in chapter 19.

In experiencing both consolations and the hopes that go with them and afflictions and the fears that go with them, the newly awakened ego is understandably ambivalent toward spirit. This ambivalence is expressed in the inconsistent ways in which the newly awakened ego responds to spirit, sometimes surrendering to spirit, other times obstructing or resisting spirit, and yet other times attempting to exploit spirit's power. We have already noted that the newly awakened ego knows that it must surrender to spirit and succeeds in doing so when spirit rewards it with consolations. Nevertheless, the ego remains prone to obstruct, resist, and exploit spirit and in these ways to incur the afflictions of spirit's purgative discipline. Additionally, the ego enjoys many consolations of heightened stimulation only, owing to the potency of spirit, frequently to have these consolations be turned into afflictions of painful overstimulation. The newly awakened ego is thus strongly conflicted in its relationship with spirit, seeking, impossibly, to enjoy the "good" that spirit brings while avoiding the "bad."

Dramatic consolations and afflictions of the types we have described are characteristic of spiritual awakening as a stage. Consolations frequently draw the most attention when spiritual awakening first occurs but are misleading because, as already explained, it is not long before afflictions characteristic of spiritual awakening emerge. In extreme cases of spiritual awakening—when spirit awakens abruptly and with great intensity and when the ego is burdened with many impediments to spirit's movement—the afflictions characteristic of spiritual awakening eventually become predominant, thus outweighing consolations and causing concern about the possible dangers of the process that is unfolding.

The Awakening of Spirit within the Body

We have noted that the energy of awakened spirit intensifies the ego's experience across all modalities. In doing so, it reenlivens the soul, awakening it from the "death" it had suffered during the stage of spiritual preawakening. What had been a dying to self thus now becomes a spiritual rebirth of self, as everything within the soul that had withered and died in response to the gravitational pull of transcendent or enfolded spirit is stimulated and thus reawakened by the potency of sovereign spirit.

This return to life is not limited to the soul. It extends to the body as well. When spirit reenlivens the soul, it also "resurrects" the body, reenergizing it and stirring instinctual and other bodily desires, which had flagged during spiritual preawakening. This simultaneous awakening of spirit in soul and body suggests that the protective insulation that had shielded psyche from soma has been removed. Soul and body are now open to each other and much more evidently act or respond in unison, as, for example, happens when impactful thoughts, rather than being confined to the soul, are immediately felt in the body.

With this opening of soul and body to each other, awakened spirit works in both at the same time, thus energizing not only the ego's psychological experiences but also its physical experiences. Additionally, working in both soul and body, awakened spirit purges not only the ego's psychological defenses but also the physical blockages and knots that are their underlying bases. Spirit's awakened presence in the body might for this reason be experienced as a current of energy that stimulates bodily centers, breaks through bodily obstructions, and dissolves bodily tensions. As spirit thus works in the body, one might experience a variety of unusual sensations (e.g., chills, horripilation), postures (yoga postures), movements (tics, spasms, hopping, dancing), facial gestures, and vocalizations. These unusual phenomena are physical analogues of the consolations and afflictions that spirit causes within the soul. They indicate that awakened spirit is superstimulating bodily centers, thus causing consolations of heightened stimulation or afflictions of painful overstimulation, and forcibly removing obstacles to its movement, thus causing purgative afflictions.

Among spiritual traditions, physical phenomena like the ones just mentioned are best known in writings on hatha and kundalini yoga, in which they are referred to as *kriyās* (cleansing actions). However, most spiritual traditions acknowledge that unusual somatic phenomena can accompany spiritual awakening. Since we are here presenting the extreme case of spiritual awakening, assuming sudden and intense awakening, it is appropriate to include the phenomena just mentioned in our discussion.

The Shadow Awakens without the Possibility of Rerepression

As spirit is thus reenlivening soul and body, it reawakens desires that had withered when the gravitational pull of spirit had drawn the ego out of the world. Included among these desires are not only those that were active in the ego's everyday life before the stage of spiritual preawakening but also those associated with the shadow impulses that had stirred briefly at the end of that stage, only soon thereafter, like desires generally, to wither and die. With the shadow thus being reawakened by the psychophysical movement of spirit, spiritual awakening is, like adolescence, midlife, and spiritual preawakening, a stage during which shadow awakening is more likely to occur than during other stages. Indeed, spiritual awakening, like spiritual preawakening, is a stage during which shadow awakening can be considered the norm. However, the shadow awakening that occurs during spiritual awakening is unique because it is an awakening that brings an end to the shadow.

This awakening brings an end to the shadow because it removes the possibility of rerepressing shadow impulses. Repression—as is true of all the ego's defenses—conflicts with the free movement of spirit and, therefore, is a target of spirit's purgative discipline. Spirit thus eliminates vestiges of previous shadow repression and prohibits any attempts by the ego to rerepress shadow impulses. Attempts to reengage defenses, especially the root defense of repression, or to rebuild defensive infrastructures, especially the bodily bases of repression, incur painful afflictions. These afflictions teach the ego the imprudence of trying to defend itself against the movement of spirit, whether in the soul or in the body.

The ego, therefore, in experiencing the reawakening of shadow impulses, has no choice but to work with them, allowing expression to those that are beneficial and consciously controlling those that are not. Furthermore, it has no choice but to do these things *as spirit requires,* learning moment to moment from spirit's guidance, which during spiritual awakening means learning moment to moment from spirit-caused consolations ("do that") and spirit-caused afflictions ("don't do that"). The awakening of spirit thus reawakens shadow impulses in a way that brings an end to the shadow, which, no longer repressible, begins being integrated within the self-representation and the self-system generally. The shadow is thus eliminated as an unconscious subsystem lying beneath the self-system.

Self-System Is Reenlivened and Transformed by Sovereign Spirit

In reenlivening soul and body, awakened spirit reenlivens the self-system, in all its components, the ego, self-representation, ego ideal, and superego. As for the ego, we have learned that awakened spirit demotes it to secondary status within the soul, dismantles its defenses, and disables many of its habits. More to the point here, we have also learned that spirit injects the ego with energy that potently stimulates it, either pleasurably so, by causing consolations, or painfully so, by causing afflictions. Thus stimulated by spirit, the ego recovers from the world-weariness it had suffered during spiritual preawakening and is restored not just to life but to highly energized, intense aliveness.

In thus returning the ego to life, awakened spirit returns the ego's self-representation to life. The ego begins again to invest itself in the self-representation, reappropriating it and relating to it once again as Me, as what I *am*. The self-representation, which during the stage of spiritual preawakening had been reduced to a lifeless mask, in this way becomes once again a *lived* self-representation. However, the self-representation that is thus brought back to life is no longer what it was before world-weariness led to its death, for spiritual awakening changes the self-representation in three important ways.

First, it changes the self-representation by making it a record not only of the ego's worldly life but also of its awakened spiritual life. The ego, in authoring the self-representation, now records not only the ordinary facts of the day but also such facts as spirit's presence and sovereignty within the soul, spirit's movement within both soul and body, spirit's consoling and afflicting effects, and, most importantly, the ego's need to conform and surrender to spirit. The ego's new relationship with spirit thus transforms the self-representation because the ego now conceives of itself in a fundamentally new way, as a subordinate subject that, newly awakened to spirit, is in the process of being purgatively transformed by spirit.

A second way in which spiritual awakening changes the self-representation is that it brings the self-representation under spirit's editorial supervision. The ego remains the author of the self-representation (and of the life story), but it now revises the self-representation by altering, deleting, or adding features as required by spirit. In remaining the author of the self-representation, the ego continues to bear primary responsibility for it as a record of its life. However, spirit has now staked a claim on the ego's life and, therefore, on its self-representation, both of which it is now refashioning in its own image. Spirit-caused consolations are now encouraging the ego to strengthen features of the self-representation that facilitate spirit's expression; and spirit-caused afflictions are now forcing the ego to modify or delete features that in any way work against spirit's expression. The ego is still the author of the self-representation, but it now has a demanding editor, an editor who requires extensive, difficult revisions to the previous script.

Finally, a third way in which spiritual awakening changes the self-representation is that it broadens its scope to include parts of the ego's life that the ego had previously hidden from view. The awakening of shadow impulses that cannot be rerepressed forces the ego to find ways to integrate shadow impulses within its life and, therefore, within its self-representation. The ego must either embrace shadow impulses or find ways to bring them under control. Either way, the ego must acknowledge the impulses and include them within its self-representation, which thus becomes a more inclusive and accurate record of its life.

Awakened spirit reenlivens the ego ideal by assigning it a new ideal goal, that of living a perfect spiritual life. The ego, having only just awakened to spirit, is ignorant of what is and is not possible in spiritual life. Furthermore, the ego, in perceiving spirit as a supernatural power, naively imagines that an ideal spiritual life would be a life with supernatural and, therefore, superhuman virtues. Such a life, the ego imagines, would not be held back by human weaknesses and for this reason would be heroic or saintly in spiritual character. The fact that such a life exceeds what is realistically possible does not deter the newly awakened ego, which believes that this ideal life *can* be achieved, if not by its own efforts, then by its own efforts supernaturally assisted by the grace of spirit. However, the fact that the ego thus strives for an ideal life that is not realistically possible is not the most important point here. The most important point is that the ego *is* striving for a new ideal goal. This fact indicates that the ego ideal has been reenlivened as an instrument of telic or inspiring motivation.

Awakened spirit reenlivens the superego by assigning it a new task of great urgency, that of enforcing obedience to spirit. Although the ego now aspires to spiritual perfection, it knows that such perfection will be realized, if at all, only in the distant future. The ego, therefore, does not chastise itself for falling short of its ideal goal. Instead, it requires of itself only that it obey spirit's imperatives as they emerge in daily life. The ego does at times succeed in obeying spirit and praises itself for having done so. However, owing to its spiritual immaturity, the ego more often fails to obey spirit and is left to chastise itself for having obstructed or resisted spirit or for having attempted to exploit spirit in some way. However, whether the ego succeeds or fails in its attempts to obey spirit is not the most important point here. The most important point is that the ego *is* now exhorting itself to obey spirit. This fact indicates that the superego has been reenlivened as an instrument of efficient or impelling motivation.

The praise and blame meted out by the superego play an important role in disciplining the newly awakened ego in its relationship with spirit. However, they play only a secondary role compared with the consolations and afflictions meted out by spirit. These dispensations of spirit—especially the afflictions, which are foremost in extreme cases of spiritual awaking—bring the ego into compliance with spirit much more powerfully than anything the superego can say or do. Spirit is for this reason a more powerful disciplinarian than the superego. Spirit's disciplining actions, therefore, are primary and the superego's secondary. The superego is now an assistant disciplinarian the job of which is to keep the ego from suffering the purgative discipline of spirit. Like a mother who disciplines a child so that the child can avoid the sterner discipline of the father, the superego now disciplines the ego so that it can avoid the sterner discipline of spirit. In this way, the superego and spirit become cooperating agencies of efficient or impelling motivation.

Lifeworld—Numinous Spirit and the Dark Wood

Spiritual awakening, like all the stages of spiritual development we are considering, has not only an inner but also an outer expression. It transforms not only the ego and its self-system but also the lifeworld. We have already referred to the inner expression of spirit during the stage of spiritual awakening as "sovereign spirit." Let us now borrow the term "numinous" from the German theologian and philosopher of religion Rudolf Otto and refer to the corresponding outer expression as "numinous spirit."[1] Corresponding to the inner expression of spirit as a seemingly supernatural power that reenlivens the soul in ways that stimulate and purge the ego is an outer expression of spirit as a seemingly supernatural power that reenlivens the world in ways that enthrall and overawe the ego. In both the soul and the world, spirit expresses itself as a power arriving seemingly from another world that potently energizes everything it touches and in relation to which the ego is weak and vulnerable. Enfolded and transcendent spirit of the stage of spiritual preawakening thus give way, respectively, to sovereign and numinous spirit in the stage of spiritual awakening.

To avoid misunderstanding, we should here repeat that we are taking no position on the ontological status of spirit. Specifically, we are taking no position on whether spirit in fact exists "out there" in the world, whether as transcendent spirit or as numinous spirit or, to anticipate the next two chapters, as radiant spirit or as native spirit. It is possible that spirit only seems to exist in these outer forms because the person in whom spirit is active projects it outwardly, thus making it appear as if it were also in the world. In this case, spiritual development would be something that happens exclusively within the soul and body but seems also to happen in the world because it alters how the world is perceived. This possibility, like the possibility that spirit exists first and primarily in the world and is present in human beings only secondarily, is neither affirmed nor denied in this account. We are assuming only that spirit is something that exists and plays a causally essential role in spiritual development.

With the emergence of numinous spirit, the world, which had been desolated during the stage of spiritual preawakening, is regenerated with the potent energy of spirit. It is supercharged with an energy that dramatically enhances objects and their qualities and that potentiates the atmosphere of the world. Corresponding to how spirit within the soul intensifies experience across all modalities, spirit within the world amplifies, accentuates, and magnetizes all that is outwardly perceived. The moon is still a silver crescent or globe, but its light is now brighter and more riveting as it stands out against the inky blackness of the night sky. The ocean shore is still composed of countless grains of sand, but these grains are now more defined, singular, and fascinating, each a world unto itself. The cheetah is still a creature of grace, speed, and power, but these features of the cheetah are now extraordinary, as if surpassing what is possible in nature. Everything in the sky and on the earth is now invested with an energy that heightens its potency, felt significance, and allure.

During spiritual awakening, spirit, as numinous spirit, has not only amplifying, accentuating, and magnetizing effects but also, owing to its radically unfamiliar and overawing perceived character, a "haunting" effect. Spirit imbues the world with a frightening, inauspicious aura. Objects may appear distorted in exaggerated, menacing, and mesmerizing ways. If one were to undertake an inventory of the world, the list of objects and their qualities would not have changed. However, the description of the objects and their qualities would have changed a great deal, indicating profound, disturbing differences in the felt significance of objects and the potency of their qualities. In contrast to the lifeworld of the stage of spiritual preawakening, which is lifeless and unreal, the lifeworld of the stage of spiritual awakening is superalive and surreal. It is uncanny: strange, ominous, fascinating.

Numinous spirit is experienced within the world not only indirectly, through its effects on objects and their qualities, but also directly, as an overawing energetic presence that can be encountered "face to face." Otto described spirit as it is encountered in this way as a *mysterium tremendum et fascinans*.[2] Otto also used the term we have adopted from him, "numinous," to refer to this manifestation of spirit. The difference between Otto's and our use of "numinous" is that Otto's use refers primarily to the direct outer manifestation of spirit as an overawing energetic presence, whereas our use refers not only to this direct manifestation but also to the indirect manifestation of spirit as the power that amplifies, accentuates, and magnetizes objects and their qualities in eerie and ominous ways.

Numinous spirit is a *mysterium,* a mysterious power, because, as Otto says, it is "wholly other" (*das ganz Andere*). Like sovereign spirit, numinous spirit is completely unlike anything with which we are familiar in the natural world. As a *mysterium,* numinous spirit seems to have arrived in this world from a world beyond. It seems as if an invisible cosmic boundary separating supernatural and natural planes has been breached, allowing an ominous otherworldly power to enter this world. The supernatural plane, which during the stage of spiritual preawakening had drawn close enough to the natural plane for spirit's gravitational power to affect the ego, has now broken through into the natural plane, manifesting itself directly to the ego. What had been a proximity of planes has thus given way to what Mircea Eliade called a "rupture of planes."[3] As within, so without, it seems as if boundaries have been violated by a supernatural power, a power that, within, is "not of the soul" and that, without, is "not of this world."

As a *mysterium,* numinous spirit is more specifically a *mysterium tremendum,* a mysterious power of overawing immensity. It is, according to Otto, a power before which one is eclipsed and made small, as if nothing. This overawing immensity of numinous spirit is the outer correlate of the overpowering potency of sovereign spirit within the soul. Just as the potency of sovereign spirit can seem dangerous, so also can the immensity of numinous spirit. The potency of sovereign spirit can seem dangerous because, when the ego is overstimulated by sovereign spirit, it feels as though it could easily burst and thus lose self-cohesion. Correspondingly, the immensity of numinous spirit can seem dangerous because, when the ego is in the presence of numinous spirit, it feels as if it could easily be seized or swallowed and thus lose self-possession. Numinous spirit is for this reason a daunting power.

In religious literatures, numinous spirit is frequently described as an angry god who reveals himself in frightening ways. In Indo-European mythologies, this god is most often a sky god who, like Indra (Vedic), Zeus (Greek), Thor (Norse), and Perun (Slavic), creates storms over the earth and throws down thunderbolts from on high. A similar conception of an angry sky god is found in the Abrahamic faiths. The following passage from Psalms dramatically describes how God, when his anger is provoked, can unleash his wrath: "Then the earth shook and trembled; the foundations also of the hills moved and were shaken, because he was wroth. There went up a smoke out of his nostrils, and fire out of his mouth devoured: coals were kindled by it. He bowed the heavens also, and came down: and darkness was under his feet. . . . He made darkness his secret place; his pavilion round about him were dark waters and thick clouds of the skies."[4]

Numinous spirit is also described in religious literatures as a power that can be dangerous to those who experience it directly. The Ark of the Covenant, a chest in which sacred artifacts were enclosed and through which, it was thought, God's presence in the world was manifested, was said to be a source of a power so great that it could be lethal to anyone who touched it or attempted to look inside. Additionally, God withheld his face because people would die if they were exposed directly to his power: "And he said, Thou canst not see my face: for there shall no man see me, and live"[5] The transition from transcendent spirit of the stage of spiritual preawakening to numinous spirit of the stage of spiritual awakening is thus a transition from a form of spirit that is unseen and seemingly remote to a form of spirit that is beginning to reveal itself in dark, ominous, and frightening ways.

Although numinous spirit is dark and seemingly dangerous, it is irresistibly fascinating. It is not only a *mysterium tremendum* but also a *mysterium fascinans*. Numinous spirit magnetizes things in the world because it is itself magnetically attractive. One cannot look away from numinous spirit, even when threatened by it. The newly awakened ego is for these reasons ineluctably drawn to numinous spirit, just as it is fascinated by whatever it energizes. Responding to the magnetism of numinous spirit, the newly awakened ego is frequently spellbound or otherwise held in thrall by a power that has made the world potently, eerily, and ominously captivating.

A metaphor that conveys the lifeworld of numinous spirit—which is to say, the lifeworld of the stage of spiritual awakening—is that of a wooded area darkened by stormy clouds. This metaphor has been used in mythic and spiritual literatures to convey the idea of a frightening but mesmerizing realm in which one feels exposed to invisible supernatural forces, dangerous forces that could reveal themselves suddenly. One can wander into such a wood without forewarning. In Dante's *Comedy*, the pilgrim Dante, halfway through life, suddenly found himself lost in a dark wood from which escape was blocked by menacing creatures. From our point of view, this dark wood seems inescapable because it is overcast and permeated throughout by numinous spirit. Wherever one goes, one meets with numinous spirit working its ominously shrouding and captivating, its eerily amplifying, accentuating, and magnetizing effects.

The Second Stage of Regression in the Service of Integration

Spiritual awakening as it occurs within soul and body is the second stage of regression in the service of integration, which we have described as a second oedipal stage. The ego, having been drawn out of the world by the gravitational pull of transcendent or enfolded spirit, is awakened inwardly and disciplined by the power of sovereign spirit. That the newly awakened ego is subject to the discipline of sovereign spirit gives the stage of spiritual awakening a relational character like that of the oedipal stage of early child-hood. Both stages are defined by an authority figure disciplining a child. To be sure, the authority figure during spiritual awakening is sovereign spirit, not a literal or symbolic human authority figure; and the child during spiritual awakening is a spiritual child, not a literal child. Nevertheless, the presence of an authority figure requiring obedience from a child is the same.

Additionally, spiritual awakening is like the original oedipal stage in being a transitional stage during which the underlying embodied, instinc-tual, emotional, and relational bases of life are experienced, if not fully, as is characteristic of the preoedipal stage, then at least in a highly energetic way. Granted, the ego during spiritual awakening is *returning* to these bases of life rather than, as was the case during the original oedipal stage, *leaving them behind.* Nevertheless, the fact that bases of life that were still powerfully in play during the first oedipal stage are returning to powerful expression during spiritual awakening is a striking similarity between these two stages.

In sum, we can say that the stage of spiritual awakening and the first oedipal stage are alike in sharing much the same authority-obedience, adult-child relational structure and in being powerfully in touch with the embodied, instinctual, emotional, and relational bases of life. These two stages differ greatly in that spiritual awakening moves "backward," over old ground, for the purpose of spiritual development, whereas the first oedipal stage moves "forward," over new ground, for the purpose of ego development. Nevertheless, the two stages are similar in the ways indicated, sufficiently so to warrant our description of spiritual awakening as a second oedipal stage.

Conclusion

The ego undergoing spiritual awakening faces many challenges. The principal challenge is to learn how to live in the immediate presence of spirit without either resisting spirit or losing self-cohesion or self-possession to spirit. The ego must learn how to surrender to spirit's supremacy without thereby being swept away or burst by (sovereign) spirit's potency or captivated or engulfed by (numinous) spirit's immensity. Meeting this challenge is the major task of the next, third, stage of spiritual development, the stage of spiritual growth.

Chapter 18

Spiritual Growth

The supremacy of spirit's power and the resistance of the ego to this power recede into the background as the stage of spiritual awakening ends and the stage of spiritual growth begins. They do so not because spirit's power decreases in strength and thus ceases to be supreme but rather because the ego is much more receptive and much better adjusted to spirit. By the time the stage of spiritual growth begins, the ego has been transformed by spirit's purgative discipline to the point at which its receptivity to spirit significantly exceeds its resistance. Moreover, by this time the ego has become better accustomed to the potency of spirit and, therefore, is less often overstimulated by it in destabilizing ways. For these reasons, the ego is better able to experience spirit's movement in soul and body without suffering consolations so intense or afflictions so painful as significantly to disrupt the flow of life.

From Sovereign Spirit to Caring Spirit

The ego in the stage of spiritual growth continues to experience consolations and afflictions and, sometimes, even the unusual somatic phenomena caused by spirit's movement in the body. However, afflictions and disconcerting somatic phenomena become less pronounced, decrease in frequency, and in these ways wane during the stage of spiritual growth. In contrast, consolations increase in frequency, at least initially, although, as we shall see, they eventually wane as well. The transition from the stage of spiritual awakening to the stage of spiritual growth thus ushers in a reversal in the weightings of consolations and afflictions. It leads from a stage in which afflictions had outweighed consolations (the stage of spiritual awakening, at least in extreme cases) to a stage in which consolations outweigh afflictions (the stage of spiritual growth).

This reversal is reflected in the ego's experience of spirit. Within soul and body, the ego now begins to experience spirit less often as sovereign spirit, an overpowering disciplinarian and purgative power, and begins increasingly to experience spirit as *caring* spirit, a consoling nurturer, guide, and protector. From the perspective of gender, it might here seem as if an angry father god is fading into the background and a loving mother goddess is emerging into the foreground. In terms of regression in the service of integration, it might seem as if a stage similar to the oedipal stage of development is fading into the background and a stage similar to the preoedipal stage is emerging into the foreground.

It is important to stress that this overall transformation from sovereign to caring spirit, from tough to tender love, is a gradual rather than sudden reversal. It is a reversal that leads from a diminishing preponderance of discipline and purgation over care and support to an increasing preponderance of care and support over discipline and purgation and, correspondingly, from a diminishing preponderance of afflictions over consolations to an increasing preponderance of consolations over afflictions. As the harsh "justice" of sovereign spirit gradually recedes into the background, the gentle "mercies" of caring spirit gradually emerge into the foreground.

Consolations and Afflictions during Spiritual Growth

To illustrate this pattern of change, let us look more closely at what happens with consolations and afflictions. As we have seen, both consolations and afflictions are present during the stage of spiritual awakening, with afflictions (of purgative discipline and painful overstimulation) predominating over consolations (of heightened stimulation), at least in extreme cases. Moreover, because the ego is to a great extent resistant to spirit and lacks adjustment to spirit's potency during spiritual awakening, both the consolations and the afflictions that occur during this stage tend to disrupt the flow of life. Consolations of heightened stimulation push the ego to the limit of what it can endure, frequently pushing too far, thus being transformed into afflictions of painful overstimulation; and afflictions of purgative discipline tend to arrest or disarm the ego in painful and debilitating ways.

In contrast, once the stage of spiritual awakening ends and the stage of spiritual growth begins, spirit begins to cause more consolations than afflictions, and both consolations and afflictions become less disruptive. Spirit at this point begins to cause more consolations than afflictions not only because afflictions decrease in frequency but also because, with the ego's better adjustment to the potency of spirit, what had been afflictions of painful overstimulation are transformed into consolations of heightened stimulation. Moreover, as consolations thus begin to outnumber afflictions, both consolations and afflictions become less disruptive. Consolations of heightened stimulation become less disruptive because, with the ego's continuing adjustment to spirit's potency, they become less explosive and overpowering and more enlivening and empowering. Afflictions of purgative discipline become less disruptive because, with the ego now more receptive to spirit, they become less painfully purgative and more gently instructive in character. Finally, afflictions of painful overstimulation become less disruptive because, with the ego now better adjusted to spirit's potency, they tend to overstimulate the ego less painfully and eventually, as just explained, cease even being afflictions and become consolations (which themselves tend to become less disruptive). In sum, both the consolations and the afflictions of the stage of spiritual growth evolve in such a way that they become increasingly more gentle than harsh, increasingly more empowering that overpowering, and increasingly more instructive than punishing. The consolations of the stage of spiritual growth might for this reason be called consolations of "caring support" and the afflictions of the stage might be called afflictions of "caring correction."

In time, as the stage of spiritual growth approaches the stage of spiritual maturity, not only afflictions but also consolations decrease in frequency and, finally, disappear. Both consolations and afflictions are symptoms of spiritual immaturity. They indicate that the ego is not yet fully in conformity with the movement of spirit or not yet fully adjusted to spirit's potency and, therefore, is still being transformed by spirit, whether in ways that are pleasing and empowering (consolations) or painful and overpowering (afflictions). Accordingly, although consolations and even afflictions continue well into the stage of spiritual growth, they gradually disappear over the course of the stage.

Among the many ways in which caring spirit has been described, three are most common, as a comforter, counselor, and guardian, which is to say, as a power or being that provides nurture, guidance, and protection. Representing one or more of these three functions, depictions of caring spirit having been numerous and diverse across cultures. In monotheistic, dominantly patriarchal societies, caring spirit has been conceived primarily in male terms, for example, as a loving heavenly father, a male incarnation of such a deity, a loving male spirit, and a male spiritual lover.[1] In contrast, in polytheistic, less dominantly patriarchal societies, caring spirit has more often been conceived in female terms, for example, as a goddess of fertility, love, or wisdom, a warrior goddess providing guidance and protection, and a nurturing divine mother. The ensuing discussion abstracts from the myriad cultural variations on the theme of spirit as caregiver and focuses on caring spirit in general terms. The purpose here is to explain how the ego's relationship with caring spirit, with spirit-as-comforter, spirit-as-counselor, and spirit-as-guardian, is reflected in the self-system and lifeworld.

Caring Spirit's Transformation of the Self-System

The ego's relationship with caring spirit is reflected in all components of the self-system, including most evidently the ego itself, which again undergoes a change in status in relation to spirit. The ego, having been demoted in status by sovereign spirit, is promoted in status by caring spirit. Having been demoted from being the (presumed) sovereign power of the soul to being only a subordinate subject of sovereign spirit, the ego is now promoted to being a junior partner of caring spirit. Spirit, as caring spirit, does still sometimes discipline the ego firmly. However, such treatment of the ego is now increasingly rare. For the most part, spirit treats the ego as a junior partner needing nurture, guidance, and protection rather than firm discipline. The ego is still subordinate to spirit and sometimes still disobeys spirit. However, it is now more intimately akin to spirit and much more cooperative with spirit. Spirit in turn, therefore, now treats the ego more gently and benevolently.

The ego records its new status in relation to spirit in the self-representation. For example, the ego might record changes like these: (1) that it is no longer newly awakened to spirit and is now much more closely interactive with spirit; (2) that it is much less frightened of spirit and is now much more welcoming of spirit; (3) that it is much less resistant to spirit and is now much more yielding to spirit; and (4) that it is much less afflicted by spirit and is now much more consoled by spirit. These and other facts pertaining to the ego's greatly improved relationship with spirit are recorded in the self-representation, which thus becomes a representation of someone increasingly living a life of spirit, as a junior partner of spirit, be it as a youthful companion, loyal follower, friend, or lover of spirit.

As the ego thus records its growing closeness with spirit in the self-representation, it also records the growing closeness of soul and body.

Spirit now flows through both soul and body with increasing smoothness and integration. With the ego now better adjusted to the potency of spirit, spirit less frequently overstimulates the ego in disruptive ways, whether in the soul or in the body. With most obstacles to the movement of spirit having been purged, spirit now flows more easily, both in the soul and in the body. Additionally, with the insulation that had shielded the soul from the body having been removed, the psychic and somatic expressions of spirit begin to merge, and spirit gradually ceases being a split current flowing separately through the soul and the body and increasingly becomes a unified current flowing through a unified embodied soul. Spirit still potently energizes the ego's experience across all modalities and still causes consolations and afflictions, many of which are still perceived to occur primarily within either the soul or the body, as primarily psychological or physical consolations or afflictions. Nevertheless, the direction of change is clear. Spirit's movement is increasingly gentle, smooth, and psychophysically integrated.

The ego records these facts in the self-representation by no longer thinking of itself as undergoing spiritual purgation within two spheres, the soul and the body, and instead thinking of itself as undergoing spiritual rejuvenation and growth within one sphere, the embodied soul. The ego now understands that it is undergoing a transformation that is not only psychospiritual in character, leading to ego-spirit integration, but that is also psychophysical in character, leading to soul-body integration. It is, therefore, aware that its transformation by spirit is not only raising it to the fullness of spiritual life but also returning it to the fullness of embodied (instinctual, emotional, relational) life. The ego records all these facts in the self-representation.

The self-representation, in reflecting the changes in the ego's life just described, becomes even more a shared product of the ego and spirit than it was during the stage of spiritual awakening. During spiritual awakening, the ego remained the sole author of the self-representation but revised it (and the life story) to implement changes mandated by awakened spirit. To recall, spirit, as sovereign spirit, is a demanding editor requiring the ego to make extensive, frequently unwanted changes to the record of its life. In contrast, during the stage of spiritual growth, spirit works with the ego in a closer, more mutual, and more supportive way, more often suggesting minor changes to the self-representation that the ego welcomes than demanding major changes that the ego resists.

Indeed, spirit, as caring spirit, works so closely with the ego as to be coauthor with the ego of the self-representation. Caring spirit and the ego are joined closely enough to be partners in a common life and, therefore, to be partners as well in the task of keeping the record of this life. During the stage of spiritual growth, therefore, the collaboration between the ego and spirit with respect to the self-representation is more a collaboration between a junior (narrating) author and a senior (inspiring) coauthor than, as it was during the stage of spiritual awakening, a collaboration between an author and a highly critical editor. In this way, the self-representation becomes not only the ego's but also spirit's self-representation.

Unlike the self-representation, which reflects the ego's relationship with caring spirit generally, in all its functions, the ego ideal reflects the ego's relationship with caring spirit primarily in its guiding function. The ego ideal is tied to spirit-as-counselor, to spirit insofar as it is the source of spiritual insight. The ego during the stage of spiritual awakening, a spiritual child, makes its way on the spiritual path blindly, without its own spiritual vision. The newly awakened ego is unable to see on its own how best to move forward on the spiritual path and, therefore, must rely on sovereign spirit to guide it with consolations and afflictions, rewards and punishments. Even less is the newly awakened ego able to see the goal toward which the spiritual path leads and, therefore, must rely on a merely imagined, unrealistic ego ideal, that of living a life of superhuman spiritual heroism or saintliness.

In contrast, the ego during the stage of spiritual growth has learned enough from spirit's consolations and afflictions to begin to see the spiritual path with its own eyes, guided by spirit's wisdom. Accordingly, with the help of caring spirit in its role as counselor, the ego now begins to see not only the next steps it must take on the spiritual path but also the ideal goal toward which this path leads. At first, the ego's emerging spiritual vision is poor, but it becomes increasingly sharp as the stage of spiritual growth unfolds, thus bringing the spiritual path and its goal ever more clearly into view. This spiritual vision that emerges during the stage of spiritual growth is often referred to as "discernment."

In thus beginning to *see* rather than, as before, only to imagine the ideal goal of awakened spiritual life, the ego begins to bring into focus a new ego ideal. Emerging spiritual discernment in this way disabuses the ego of its former naïve ideal of spiritual heroism or saintliness and reveals to it that an ideal spiritual life always remains "merely" human. The ego ideal that gradually emerges during the stage of spiritual growth, therefore, is that of achieving spirit's purposes as best one can given not only one's abilities as empowered by spirit but also one's inescapable weaknesses as a human being. With each new step on the spiritual path, therefore, the ego now consults with spirit-as-counselor, and spirit-as-counselor responds by helping the ego better discern what is ideally possible—not only in the here and now but also, increasingly, in the future—in pursuing a life that is not only fully spiritual but realistically human as well. In this way, awakened spiritual vision helps bring into view the more fitting ego ideal of *fully spiritual humanness*, which is an ideal of spiritual courage that, although not always heroic, is steadfast and strong and of spiritual compassion that, although not always saintly, is generous and kind. This new ego ideal is only a work in progress during the stage of spiritual growth. It is fully articulated only when, interestingly, it is fully realized, when spiritual growth culminates in spiritual maturity.

With the emergence of spiritual discernment, the ego makes rapid progress on the spiritual path and, therefore, is increasingly able to give expression to spirit in the world. The ego is not yet a mature vehicle for spirit's expression and, therefore, is still being transformed by spirit so that it can further improve in this role. Nevertheless, the ego during the stage of spiritual growth is increasingly able not only to see with spirit's wisdom but also to act in the world with spirit's power. Correspondingly, spirit during the stage of spiritual growth is increasingly able to use the ego as the instrument of its worldly expression. During this stage, although spirit continues to act *on* the ego, by continuing to transform it within the soul, it also, and increasingly, acts *through* the ego, by using the ego to express itself in the world.

This use of the ego by spirit reveals that spirit is in its way as dependent on the ego as the ego is on spirit. Just as the ego needs spirit's wisdom and power to move forward effectively on the spiritual path, so spirit needs the ego's sense perception and mental and volitional faculties to express itself effectively in the world. The stage of spiritual growth is thus a time during which the ego and spirit are in the process of completing each other by each providing for the other what it lacks on its own. Spirit is in the process of completing the ego by imparting to it spiritual discernment and empowering grace. In turn, the ego is in the process of completing spirit by giving it a conscious perspective, executive functions, and knowledge of the world. That the ego thus completes spirit should be more than enough to establish the case that the ego plays an essential and primarily positive role in spiritual development.

As this process of mutual completing unfolds, the ego's perception of spirit changes profoundly. Whereas the newly awakened ego, in awe of spirit, tends to overestimate spirit, perceiving it as something limitless in wisdom and power, the ego undergoing spiritual growth begins to see spirit more accurately. It continues to see spirit as something that is great, indeed. However, it now also sees spirit as something that is unable on its own to perceive the world, to think logically or operationally about the world, and, therefore, to act effectively in the world, with head as well as heart, with informed forethought as well as caring impulse. In this way, it becomes clear to the ego undergoing spiritual growth that it and spirit are transforming each other. What had seemed to be only a process of spirit "spiritualizing" the ego is now seen as also having been a process of the ego "humanizing" spirit. The culmination of this process by which ego and spirit complete each other is explored in the next chapter, in which spiritual maturity is described as a stage of full ego-spirit integration.

Unlike the ego ideal, which reflects caring spirit primarily in its guiding function, the superego reflects caring spirit primarily in its protecting function. To recall, the superego during the stage of spiritual awakening protects the ego by being spirit's "assistant disciplinarian," by disciplining the ego to protect it from incurring the stronger discipline of (sovereign) spirit. The superego does on occasion still discipline the ego in this fashion during the stage of spiritual growth. However, for the most part it now protects the ego in the same way that caring spirit does, less often by punishing the ego when it strays from the spiritual path, more often by rewarding the ego when it moves forward on the spiritual path, and, generally, by correcting the ego's behavior with gentle, caring instruction. The role of the superego during the stage of spiritual growth, therefore, can be described as that of being caring spirit's "assistant guardian." The superego is now a guardian whose assignment is to protect the ego from going astray in the same way that caring spirit would, with tender rather than with tough love.

The superego is now able to correct the ego's behavior with gentle, caring instruction because, should it fail in its assignment as assistant guardian, the consequences would not be serious. Should it be necessary for spirit to step in, spirit would also correct the ego with gentle, caring instruction. Accordingly, the superego now corrects the ego more through cautions, praise, and reminders than, as before, through alarms, reprimands, and commands. The superego and spirit continue to work together as agencies that correct the ego's course when it strays from the spiritual path, the superego as secondary agency working under the direction of spirit as primary agency. Now, however, they work together more as benevolent guardians who correct the ego with gentle encouragements and nudges than as stern overlords who correct the ego with harsh discipline.

Lifeworld—Radiant Spirit and the Forest Clearing

The kinship that the ego enjoys with caring spirit within the soul is reflected outwardly in the ego's experience of spirit as an energetic presence in the world. Corresponding to the inner transformation of spirit from sovereign spirit into caring spirit is an outer transformation of spirit from numinous spirit into *radiant* spirit. The supernatural energy that enlivens the world undergoes a transformation in perceived character, gradually changing from an ominous, daunting, murky, shrouding energy into an auspicious, comforting, gleaming, revealing energy. Although this energy, spirit, is still otherworldly in appearance, its seeming otherworldliness is now inviting and resplendent rather than daunting and dark. It may seem as if shafts of light have broken through a covering of clouds, bathing the ground below in hope-inspiring, glorious luminescence. The lifeworld of the stage of spiritual growth is thus a world open to a supernatural radiance that descends from the heavens to illumine the earth and to uplift the spirits of those who live on the earth.

Like numinous spirit before it, radiant spirit amplifies, accentuates, and magnetizes everything it touches. For this reason, the world of radiant spirit, like that of numinous spirit, is a world of pronounced qualities, heightened significance, and fascinating allure. The similarities stop here, however; for, again, radiant spirit is positive (inviting, resplendent) in all the ways in which numinous spirit is negative (daunting, dark). Radiant spirit, therefore, charges the world in appealing rather than disturbing ways. Whereas the world charged with the energy of numinous spirit is eerily captivating, the world charged with the energy of radiant spirit is wondrously entrancing.

Let us recall that the numinous lifeworld of the stage of spiritual awakening exhibits characteristics of a rupture of planes. It seems as if an invisible cosmic boundary separating natural from supernatural realms has been breached, allowing an otherworldly power, a *mysterium tremendum et fascinans,* to enter this world. In contrast, the radiant lifeworld of the stage of spiritual growth exhibits characteristics of a *merging of planes.* It seems as if what was a rupture of planes has become an opening between previously separate realms that are now in the process of joining. The realms that are joining are not yet fully open to each other and, therefore, have not yet fully merged into one realm. The radiance that descends upon the earth does not yet properly belong to the earth; it remains an energy of seemingly otherworldly provenance. However, although the two realms have not yet fully merged, they are at least in progress toward this end. The light of the heavens now reaches the earth below, and the earth below is now open to the heavens above.

Because the world of radiant spirit is a transitional space, a space lying between the shrouded, alien realm of the stage of spiritual awakening and the clear, native ground of the stage of spiritual maturity (next chapter), it is not well represented in spiritual literatures as a world distinct from those that precede and succeed it. There is, however, a metaphor that captures it nicely and is frequently used to describe it. Corresponding to the idea of a dark wood, which has been used as a metaphor to depict a lifeworld threateningly overcast by numinous spirit, is the idea of a forest clearing, which has been used as a metaphor to depict a lifeworld invitingly open to radiant spirit. Juxtaposing these two ideas, we can say that, once the stage of spiritual growth begins, the overcast skies of the dark wood begin to clear, allowing light from above to break through parting clouds and reach the ground below. This light, like caring spirit, nurtures, guides, and protects the ego. It nurtures the ego by transforming its fears into hope; it guides the ego by revealing the path to the forest's edge; and it protects the ego by leading it from the dangers of the forest to the safety of "home." Radiant spirit in these ways performs in the outer world the functions that caring spirit performs within the embodied soul.

The Third Stage of Regression in the Service of Integration

The stage of spiritual growth is the third stage of regression in the service of integration. Having been drawn out of the world by transcendent or enfolded spirit and then inwardly awakened and disciplined by sovereign spirit, the ego is nurtured, guided, and protected by caring spirit. Caring spirit's nurture, guidance, and protection of the ego during the stage of spiritual growth correspond closely to the preoedipal caregiver's nurture, guidance, and protection of the child at the outset of life. Accordingly, just as spiritual awakening and the original oedipal stage have much the same relational structure, so, too, do spiritual growth and the original preoedipal stage. Additionally, the stage of spiritual growth and the original preoedipal stage are alike in being stages during which the embodied, instinctual, emotional, and relational bases of life are experienced immediately and in their fullness. To be sure, the stage of spiritual growth and the original preoedipal stage differ profoundly in that the former moves backward, retracing old ground for the purpose of spiritual development, whereas the latter moves forward, exploring new ground for the purpose of ego development. Nevertheless, the two stages are similar, similar enough, I believe, to justify describing the stage of spiritual growth as a second preoedipal stage.

Conclusion

The stage of spiritual growth is a time when the ego lives in intimate relationship with caring spirit within the embodied soul and in the immediate presence of radiant spirit in the outer world. Caring spirit, as comforter, counselor, and guardian, nurtures, guides, and protects the ego as it grows in the direction of spiritual maturity. Correspondingly, radiant spirit, as we have just seen, nurtures, guides, and protects the ego as it brings light into darkness and in this way leads the ego from darkness to light.

Chapter 19

Spiritual Maturity

Spiritual maturity is achieved once the ego and spirit are fully integrated. Within the embodied soul, full integration of ego and spirit is evident when spirit ceases almost entirely acting *on* the ego—whether as a power that invisibly attracts the ego, a power that harshly disciplines and purges the ego, or a power that gently nurtures, guides, and protects the ego—and begins almost exclusively acting *through* the ego. In terms used here, this point is reached when spirit ceases being experienced as enfolded spirit or as sovereign spirit or even as caring spirit and begins being experienced as *inherent* spirit, a power that, expressed through the ego, is the ego's own spiritual life. Correspondingly, in the outer world, full integration of ego and spirit is evident when spirit ceases being experienced as a power that is to any degree otherworldly in character—whether as an unseen object of spiritual hunger, as a *mysterium tremendum et fascinans,* or even as an earth-illuminating, soul-uplifting power—and begins being experienced as a power that belongs properly to this world. In terms used here, this point is reached when spirit ceases being experienced as transcendent spirit or as numinous spirit or even as radiant spirit and begins being experienced as *native* spirit, a power fully at home in and fully integrated with the natural world.

The achievement of full ego-spirit integration marks yet another transformation of the self-system, including another transformation of the ego. The ego again undergoes a change in status in relation to spirit. Having been an unruly subject or child of (sovereign) spirit and then a youthful companion or partner of (caring) spirit, the ego is now a spiritual adult fully joined to spirit in a higher union, which is sometimes described as the "spiritual marriage." In this union, ego and spirit work together seamlessly,

447

with spirit no longer correcting the ego and the ego no longer resisting or obstructing spirit. In this union, ego and spirit belong to each other as mutually completing, mutually facilitating sides of a larger self. This goal of full ego-spirit integration is the *telos* toward which spiritual development tends and the defining mark of spiritual maturity.

How Spiritual Development Can Fail to Reach Its Goal

Before explaining the goal of full ego-spirit integration in more detail, we should note that spiritual development does not always reach its goal. Spiritual development sometimes derails or runs into roadblocks. It does so either because a person in whom spirit has awakened never fully adjusts to spirit or because a person who has fully adjusted to spirit for some reason still falls prey to impulses that violate spiritual values. Regarding the first of these possibilities, we noted earlier (chapter 17) that some people, in experiencing spiritual awakening, suffer what are called "spiritual emergencies." These emergencies are conditions in which one is overwhelmed and rendered dysfunctional to some extent by awakened spiritual energy. Since the 1980s, a good deal of literature has emerged on the topic of spiritual emergencies, thanks especially to the work of Christina and Stanislav Grof.[1] Additionally, the American Psychiatric Association in 1994 added the diagnostic category "religious or spiritual problem" to the Association's *Diagnostic and Statistical Manual* (DSM-IV).[2] This category recognized difficulties that are distinctively spiritual or religious in character and, therefore, should not be reduced to any of the standard categories of psychological disorder.

Fortunately, most spiritual difficulties, including spiritual emergencies, are temporary. They eventually subside, allowing spiritual development to proceed on a more auspicious course. This point made, we should acknowledge that some spiritual difficulties are enduring and can be serious. Some people, in experiencing spiritual awakening, suffer not just temporary spiritual emergencies or other problems but chronic spiritual "illnesses." Work in the field of transpersonal psychology has given us a much better idea of how spiritual difficulties, although irreducible to psychological disorders, can nonetheless overlap with them. On the spiritual side, causes contributing to such overlapping might be sudden and intense spiritual awakening. On the psychological side, causes contributing to such overlapping might be a rigid, fragile defense system and, especially, proneness to schizophrenia, bipolar disorder, or borderline disorder. Should spirit awaken suddenly and with great intensity in a person suffering or prone to any of the psychological conditions just mentioned, it is understandable that full adjustment to spirit might not be possible. In such cases, it is understandable that spiritual awakening might lead to chronic psychological issues and, perhaps, significant dysfunction.

Spiritual development can also diverge from the goal of full ego-spirit integration when a person, although fully adjusted to awakened spirit, nonetheless still falls prey to impulses that violate spirit's outreaching, life-affirming values. Such violations of spirit's values can happen when the ego, awakened by spirit, is played upon by strong impulses of a problematic character. Remember that spiritual awakening reenlivens instinctual and other impulses, including impulses that had been repressed and relegated to the shadow. Moreover, as we have learned, it reenlivens shadow impulses in a way that does not allow their rerepression. Although we have taken pains to explain that shadow impulses are often beneficial, the more important point here is that they can be harmful, even malign. Should, for example, impulses of an aggressive, destructive, or predatory sort be deeply rooted in a person's personality or, perhaps, DNA, they can, if awakened, cause chronic impulse-management challenges and lead to behaviors that are not only unacceptable to society but also contrary to spirit's values. It would be naive to assume that awakened spirit would always be able to prevail over such impulses, let alone exempt a person from being prone to them.

In speaking of ethically inappropriate behavior in the context of spirituality, one thinks immediately of people in positions of spiritual authority who have sexually exploited those who trust them. Acknowledging this problem, it is important to keep an open mind about sexuality in the context of spirituality because sexuality and spirituality are closely intertwined. A good case can be made, as I have argued in earlier books, that repression of sexuality blocks the expression of spirit and, oppositely, that awakening of spirit, which circulates as a potently stimulating energy in soul *and body*, intensifies sexual desire. Be this as it may, the more pertinent fact here is that both sexuality and spirituality are inherent to our natural endowment and should for that reason be compatible. Strong sexual desire and a powerfully awakened spiritual life should not be enemies. This statement, however, is only an abstract proposition, which does not imply that sexual self-control in the service of spiritual values is easy. Accordingly, it should not be a surprise that people of developed or awakened spirituality are frequently alleged to have engaged in inappropriate behavior, sexual or other. No one, especially those in positions of spiritual authority, should be considered immune.

Having considered ways in which spiritual development can be fraught with psychological or ethical complications, let us now focus on spiritual development that achieves its *telos:* a state of ego-spirit integration so thorough that the ego and spirit belong to each other as sides of a single, larger self.

Difficulties in Understanding Ego-Spirit Integration

We need to explain the statement that the ego and spirit belong to each other as sides of a single, larger self. To begin, let us reformulate this statement to clarify what we shall call "the two perspectives of ego-spirit integration." The two perspectives are those of the ego and of spirit, if, for the purpose of argument, we can assign spirit a perspective. Beginning with spirit's perspective, we can reformulate our statement as follows: from the perspective of spirit, the ego belongs to spirit, as spirit's ego; and from the perspective of the ego, spirit belongs to the ego, as the ego's spirit. Of these two perspectives, the perspective of spirit is unproblematic and should be clear, for it is a fundamental teaching of most spiritual traditions. Most traditions hold that spiritual maturity is attained only after one has so yoked or surrendered oneself to spirit that one becomes a vehicle for spirit's expression in the world. Most spiritual traditions hold that the ego should "give" itself to spirit so that, eventually, it "belongs" to spirit, as spirit's ego.

If ego-spirit integration from spirit's perspective is unproblematic, this integration from the ego's perspective—that spirit belongs to the ego, as the ego's spirit—is not. Ego-spirit integration from the ego's perspective is controversial and is often repudiated by spiritual traditions, especially by those that, like the Abrahamic faiths, have stressed the dual character of the human-God, ego-spirit relationship. Understandably, many people have been alarmed by the statement that spirit belongs to the ego. This kind of statement has gotten mystics in trouble countless times over the centuries. The trouble arises because the statement suggests spiritual pride, specifically the pride of spiritual deception, which was explained in chapter 17. A person who says "spirit is my spirit" seems to be pridefully arrogating spirit, pretending that she or he is the source rather than only a vehicle of spirit. The worry about such pride, which is warranted in the context of spiritual awakening, is unwarranted in the context of spiritual maturity.

It is unwarranted because the sense in which a spiritually mature person says that spirit is my spirit is profoundly different from the sense in which a person newly awakened to spirit might say the same thing. The difference rests on the fact that a spiritually mature person, having been thoroughly transformed—afflicted, consoled, struck down, uplifted, humbled, empowered, and, finally, embraced—by spirit, knows full well that spirit is "through me," not "from me" or "by me." For this reason, a spiritually mature person, in saying that spirit is my spirit, is not pridefully arrogating spirit but is rather saying much the same thing as a person who says about his or her family, "This is my family." Furthermore, just as families are shared by all who belong to them, so spirit is shared by all human—and, perhaps, by all living—beings. A spiritually mature person, therefore, says not only that spirit is *my* spirit but also that spirit is *our* spirit. In sum, it is because spirit has embraced the spiritually mature ego as its ego that the spiritually mature ego is able to embrace spirit is its spirit.

The Spiritually Mature Self-System

The two perspectives of ego-spirit integration are reflected throughout the self-system. Spirit's perspective is recorded in the self-representation in the ego's understanding that, as the subject of consciousness, it belongs to spirit as spirit's experiencing point of view and that, as the executive agency of consciousness, it belongs to spirit as spirit's cognitive and practical faculties. The ego now understands that spirit sees with the ego's eyes, thinks with the ego's (active, operational) mind, and acts with the ego's (intentional) will, which now belong to spirit as its own eyes, mind, and will. The fact that the ego belongs to spirit in these ways is recorded in the self-representation.

In understanding that it belongs to spirit in the ways mentioned, the ego understands that even its self-representation belongs to spirit. It understands that this record of its life belongs also to spirit as a record of spirit's life. The ego now sees that the self-representation is a record of spirit's itinerary and unfolding expression within the soul. The self-representation thus now reflects spirit's journey from its beginning as an invisible attractor hidden deep within the soul, to its awakening as a manifest power within the soul, to its transformation of the ego in its roles as sovereign and caring spirit, to its increasing use of the ego's eyes, mind, and will to express itself in the world, to, finally, its complete integration with the ego, as its own ego. However, if the ego understands that the self-representation has thus become spirit's self-representation, it does not for that reason cease thinking of the self-representation as its own self-representation.

The ego continues to think of the self-representation as its own self-representation because it has recorded in the self-representation not only spirit's but also its own perspective on ego-spirit integration, that spirit belongs to the ego, as the ego's spirit. Not only does the ego now understand that it belongs to spirit, as spirit's eyes, mind, and will; it also now understands that spirit belongs to it, as its own spiritual wisdom and power. The ego now understands that spirit's ego-informed, ego-executed actions are its own spirit-discerned, spirit-empowered actions. It thus becomes clear to the ego that the self-representation, despite now being spirit's self-representation, remains its own self-representation, as the self-representation of a two-sided self both sides of which are united as the owner of the self-representation.

With spiritual maturity achieved, the self-representation once again has a single author. To recall, before spiritual awakening, the ego, although greatly influenced by interpersonal and social factors and by unforeseen events, is the sole responsible author of the self-representation. Then, during spiritual awakening, the ego remains the sole author, but spirit asserts itself in the role of a demanding editor who requires the ego to make extensive, unwelcome changes to the self-representation, Then, during spiritual growth, the ego and spirit become partners in a common life and, therefore, coauthors of the self-representation, with the ego working as junior (narrating) author and spirit as senior (inspiring) author. Finally, during spiritual maturity, the ego and spirit unite as a single self and, as this self, become the sole author of the self-representation.

As the ego and spirit thus unite as the author of the self-representation, they record to the self-representation the following basic fact about their integration: that each completes the other. During the stage of spiritual growth, it becomes increasingly evident not only that the ego needs spirit but also that spirit needs the ego. As the ego sees that it is acquiring spirit's wisdom-guided discernment and enlivening, life-affirming power, it also sees that spirit is acquiring its, the ego's, ability to perceive, know, and act in the world. This process of each acquiring the other's strengths and abilities comes to an end once the stage of spiritual growth ends and the stage of spiritual maturity begins. At this point, the larger self of ego-and-spirit understands—and records to the self-representation—that the ego's faculties, functions, and acquired knowledge on the one hand and spirit's wisdom and power on the other have been integrated seamlessly with each other, each now completing the other. Full ego-spirit integration is thus an integration of a fully spiritualized ego with fully humanized spirit.

Because the ego and spirit are now integrated in this mutually completing way, they no longer inflame or impede each other, as is indicated in the disappearance of the consolations and afflictions that had occurred during the stages of spiritual awakening and spiritual growth. These "passions of the soul" disappear because they are consequences of the spiritually immature ego's lack of adjustment to spirit's potency and lack of compliance with spirit's expression. They are ways in which spirit pleasurably or painfully overstimulates the ego when it is not yet adjusted to spirit's potency and ways in which spirit overpowers the ego when it obstructs, resists, or attempts to arrogate spirit. Accordingly, once spiritual maturity is achieved, with the ego fully adjusted to spirit's potency and in complete compliance with spirit's expression, what were consolations and afflictions disappear or, rather, occur only rarely and in minimal ways. What were consolations remain only as slight stirrings, and what were afflictions remain only as gentle nudges.

As ego-spirit integration is thus recorded in the self-representation, so also is soul-body integration. We already know that the unusual somatic phenomena that sometimes occur when newly awakened spirit flows through the body decrease in frequency and become less pronounced during the stage of spiritual growth, finally disappearing as spiritual growth approaches spiritual maturity. We also know that spiritual awakening removes the insulation that had shielded the soul from the body, thus exposing each to the other and in time, during the stage of spiritual growth, gradually integrating soul and body as a unified embodied soul. This gradual integration of soul and body reaches its goal when the flow of spirit is no longer turbulent to any degree and is completely unified. That is, it reaches its goal when the flow of spirit ceases causing psychological or physical disturbances (consolations, afflictions) and when it ceases to any extent being split into two flows, one moving through the soul and the other through the body, and becomes a completely unified flow moving through a completely unified embodied soul. All these ways in which the soul and the body are integrated as a two-sided unity are fully achieved and recorded in the self-representation once the stage of spiritual maturity begins.

With soul-body integration achieved, the soul is anchored in the body, and the body is the seat of the soul. Everything that had been psychological, of the soul, is now physical as well. Desires and feelings are clearly felt within the body, and even thoughts are felt within the body to the extent that they trigger energetic responses. Additionally, spirit's movement now enhances the ego's awareness of bodily states, states such as relaxation and tension, movement and blockage, vitality and lethargy, and, generally, good and ill health. In these ways, the soul is no longer separate from the body, and the body is now part of the soul. Just as the ego is now the ego *of* spirit and spirit now the spirit *of* the ego, so also the soul is now the soul *of* the body and the body is now the body *of* the soul. This integration of soul and body, like the integration of ego and spirit, is recorded in the self-representation.

Ego-spirit, soul-body integration restabilizes the ego's experience, thus establishing a new baseline for defining what is "normal" and "ordinary." As before spiritual awakening, so now, with spiritual maturity achieved, the ego's internal life moves forward on an even keel, without significant turbulence. However, this new equilibrium is in one respect fundamentally different from the equilibrium that preceded it, for it is an equilibrium of a spiritually awakened, potently energetic sort. The fact that the ego is no longer swept away, arrested, or struck down by spirit does not mean that spirit's power has decreased in strength. Rather, it means that the ego is fully adjusted to and aligned with spirit and, therefore, works with spirit effectively, in harmonious union. The ego's experience is indeed extraordinary in its spiritual wisdom and power, but it is nonetheless ordinary in the sense of being free of the intense consolations and afflictions of the stage of spiritual awakening and even of the gentler consolations and afflictions of the stage of spiritual growth.

Like the self-representation, the ego ideal of the spiritually mature ego reflects the full integration of ego and spirit. The ego ideal that gradually emerges during the stage of spiritual growth—that of fully spiritual human-ness—comes clearly into view once spiritual growth culminates in spiritual maturity. To recall, the ego during the stage of spiritual growth, guided by spirit-as-counselor, has its spiritual eyes opened. It receives the gift of discernment. The ego's spiritual vision, thus awakened, gradually improves until, on achieving spiritual maturity, the ego no longer needs to consult with spirit-as-counselor. Spirit-as-counselor is no longer needed because by this time spirit's wisdom, consultation with which had sharpened the ego's spiritual vision, is now the ego's own wisdom. The ego now possesses its own wisdom-guided spiritual vision with which to see what it must do if it is to live a life that is both fully spiritual and realistically human.

Once the ego is fully endowed with spirit's wisdom, the ego ideal becomes not only the ego's but also spirit's ideal. The ego's ideal goal is now seen to be precisely the goal toward which spirit had all along been working since it awakened within the soul. The ego now sees that its mature spiritual ideal, humanness fully spiritualized, is nothing other than the realization of spirit's ideal aim, spirituality fully humanized. In this way the ego ideal, like the self-representation, ceases being a component of only the ego's self-system and becomes a component of a self-system belonging to a larger self in which the ego and spirit are joined as one. Because the ego is now spirit's ego and spirit now the ego's spirit, not only the self-representation but also the ego ideal belongs properly, and equally, to both the ego and spirit, as coessential sides of a single self.

The superego of the spiritually mature ego also reflects full ego-spirit integration. Such integration is evident in the fact that the superego, in correcting the ego's behavior, is no longer spirit's assistant in doing so. The superego is no longer spirit's assistant disciplinarian, as it was during the stage of spiritual awakening, or even spirit's assistant guardian, as it was during the stage of spiritual growth. The superego is no longer spirit's assistant in these ways because, with ego-spirit integration achieved, any correction of the ego by spirit would be a correction of the ego by itself. Anyway, the spiritually mature ego is no longer in need of further correction from spirit because, having already been purged and transformed by spirit, it acts in harmonious union with spirit. By the time spiritual maturity is achieved, spirit has finished its correction of the ego and, therefore, the superego ceases to serve as spirit's assistant "corrections officer."

The fact that the superego no longer serves as spirit's assistant corrections officer does not mean that it has nothing to do. There are many matters of daily life that have no relation to spiritual values; and the superego still has a role to play in cautioning, lecturing, and rewarding the ego so that it acts in prescribed ways in dealing with these matters. However, when spiritual values are at stake—especially those of kindness, decency, generosity, and humility—the spiritually mature ego is entirely in accord with spirit. So far as matters of spiritual importance are concerned, the ego is not only sighted with spirit's wisdom but also strengthened by spirit's power.

How Spiritually Mature People Are Perceived by Others

Throughout part 3, we have taken no position on the ontological status of spirit other than to say that it exists and possesses the causal powers needed to affect the ego in the ways we have described in discussing the stages of spiritual development. Having thus assumed that spirit exists and possesses distinctive causal powers, we now need to address the following important implication of this assumption: that spiritually mature people, in giving outer expression to spirit, outwardly affect other people in the same kinds of ways that, before spiritual maturity, spirit had inwardly affected them. Spiritually mature people—and to a lesser extent, people growing in spirit and people recently awakened to spirit—are conduits of spirit. According to our assumption about the causal powers of spirit, this fact implies that spiritually mature people affect others in distinctively spiritual ways. More precisely, it implies that spiritually mature people affect others *who are sensitive to spirit or who are themselves spiritually awakened* in distinctively spiritual ways.

Assuming this qualification, we can say that spiritually mature people, in giving outer expression to spirit, affect others in ways that cause others to perceive them either as mysterious attractors or as harsh disciplinarians or as caring senior partners or as loving brothers or sisters in spirit. Generally, people in the stage of spiritual preawakening perceive spiritually mature people as mysterious attractors. People in this stage are sensitive to and irresistibly attracted to spirit but not yet able to perceive spirit directly. In turn, people in the stage of spiritual awakening tend to perceive spiritually mature people as harsh disciplinarians. People in this stage, although awakened to spirit, are resistant and ill-adjusted to spirit and, therefore, tend to perceive spiritually mature people as disapproving superiors who wield daunting power. In turn, people in the stage of spiritual growth tend to perceive spiritually mature people as caring senior partners. People in this stage are more receptive, more surrendered, and better adjusted to spirit and, therefore, tend to perceive spiritually mature people as comforters, counselors, and guardians. Finally, people who are themselves spiritually mature tend to perceive spiritually mature people as loving brothers or sisters in spirit. People in this final stage of spiritual development are fully integrated with spirit and, therefore, tend to meet with spirit as expressed through others on equal, mutually outreaching and affirming terms.

According to our account of spirit as a causally efficacious power, spiritually mature people have these effects on others not only because their words and actions attract, challenge, support, or embrace others but also, and chiefly, because spirit itself, as an energetic reality, is expressed through their words and actions, indeed, by their very presence. In giving outer expression to spirit, spiritually mature people thus affect others in ways that are characteristic of the four stages of spiritual development.

The point just made can be restated to say that spiritually mature people emanate spirit's "love," which has four different, stage-related expressions, as a seductive, tough, tender, and self-affirming love. Spirit's love is experienced by those in the stage of spiritual preawakening as a seductive love, for in this stage spirit is an unseen object of desire that stirs spiritual yearning and draws the ego ever closer to spirit. Spirit's love is experienced by those in the stage of spiritual awakening as a tough love, for in this stage spirit acts on the ego primarily as a disciplining, purging, and eclipsing higher power. In turn, spirit's love is experienced by those in the stage of spiritual growth as a tender love, for in this stage spirit nurtures, guides, and protects the ego. Finally, spirit's love is experienced by those in the stage of spiritual maturity as a self-affirming love, for in this stage spirit meets with itself in others in a fully expressed, self-affirming way. Spiritually mature people, in giving outer expression to spirit, thus love others in spirit's fourfold way, which means that they are not only sighted with spirit's wisdom and strengthened with spirit's power but also gifted with spirit's love.

The Lifeworld—Native Spirit in a Naturally Supernatural World

Corresponding to the inner integration of ego and spirit and of soul and body is an outer integration of world and spirit: the world and spirit, the natural and the supernatural realms, unite as one. The process leading to this end, begun in the stage of spiritual growth, here achieves culmination. Spirit as it is present in the world loses the last vestiges of otherworldliness and becomes a supernatural power that belongs properly to the natural world. This union of the heavens above with the earth below brings into being a world in which the supernatural has been fully naturalized and, therefore, the natural has been fully supernaturalized or, rather, a world in which the distinction between natural and supernatural has been surpassed.[3] The heavens and the earth have now come together to form a single world. What began as a proximity of planes and then became a rupture of planes and then became a merging of planes is now a *fusion* of planes. The world as perceived by the spiritually mature person is, therefore, a "naturally supernatural" world, a world in which the radiance of the heavens is completely at home nurturing the soil of the earth and in which spirit, no longer transcendent, numinous, or even radiant spirit, is native spirit.

The naturally supernatural world just described is exquisitely beautiful. Owing to the causal properties of spirit, it is a world with amplified qualities, accentuated significance, and irresistible allure. The naturally supernatural world of the stage of spiritual maturity is not alone in being charged with spiritual energy in these ways. The ominously supernatural world of the stage of spiritual awakening and the radiantly supernatural world of the stage of spiritual growth are also imbued with spiritual energy, and they, too, are exquisitely beautiful for this reason. However, the beauty of these worlds seems otherworldly. It is not yet the inherent beauty of this world.

The beauty of the ominously supernatural world of the stage of spiritual awakening, although extraordinary, suggests the presence of an alien power. In this world, spirit, as numinous spirit, amplifies, accentuates, and magnetizes objects and their qualities in ways that make them appear dark and menacing. The beauty of this world is striking, but it is frightening as well. In contrast, the beauty of the radiantly supernatural world of the stage of spiritual growth is glorious and uplifting rather than frightening. Nevertheless, the beauty of this world, bestowed by the light of radiant spirit, is still otherworldly in perceived character. Radiant spirit shines through overcast skies as if from a far-off celestial realm. Although *in* this world, radiant spirit and the beauty it bestows on the world are not properly *of* this world.

It is only in the naturally supernatural world of the stage of spiritual maturity that spirit, as native spirit, belongs properly to this world and, therefore, that the extraordinary beauty produced by spirit's causal powers also belongs properly to this world, as an inherent beauty restored by spirit rather than as an otherworldly beauty overlaid by spirit. In thus being an inherent rather than otherworldly beauty, the beauty of the naturally supernatural world is paradoxically both extraordinary and ordinary. It is extraordinary because it is a beauty that has been amplified, accentuated, and magnetized by spirit; and it is ordinary because it is a beauty without dramatically shifting, seemingly otherworldly aspects. Gone are the overcast sky of the stage of spiritual awakening and the breakthrough of celestial light of the stage of spiritual growth. As within the soul and the body, in which consolations and afflictions have given way to a new, more powerful equilibrium, so within the world, in which stormy clouds and cloud-piercing shafts of light have given way to a new, more radiant calm, to a clear, still sky shining on open, fertile ground. Within both the embodied soul and the world, the extraordinary is thus also ordinary.

In addition to being exquisitely beautiful, the naturally supernatural world of the stage of spiritual maturity is a world of sacred value. The celestial realm, which had been thought to be the source of sacred value, is no longer disconnected from the earth. In the naturally supernatural world, one does not need to look upward to a transcendent realm in search of sacred value. The earth is open to the heavens and, therefore, is saturated with sacred value. Keenly aware of the sacredness of the earth, the spiritually mature person affirms the earth, appreciating its beauty, majesty, and profusion of life; its fragility, finitude, and contingency; its *perfection*—just as it is. Too often religions, in placing sacred value in a remote realm above the earth, have devalued the earth as a lower, profane, if not evil, plane of existence. Those who live in the naturally supernatural world of the stage of spiritual maturity do not succumb to this devaluing of the earth. They know how precious the earth is and understand what great good fortune it is to live on earth, even if only for a fleeting moment of cosmic time.

Finally, the naturally supernatural world of the stage of spiritual maturity is "home." Because one does not need to look beyond the earth to find sacred value, one feels completely at home on the earth. Just as spirit is now native spirit, so the earth is now native ground. Having wandered in a desert without knowing where to go, having been lost in a dark wood from which escape seemed impossible, and having come to a forest clearing the light of which revealed the way out of the forest, the spiritual seeker has finally returned home. This home is a place of exquisite beauty and sacred value belonging to both humans and the divine.

Such a home, a fusion of earthly and heavenly planes, is described in spiritual literature as a paradisiacal realm reserved for those who have pleased their god or gods. Examples of such a realm are (1) the Elysian Fields and Isles of the Blessed, which, originally conceived by the Greeks, are places of winterless beauty and bounty in which heroes and other worthy souls enjoy themselves after mortal life; (2) the New Jerusalem, as described in the Book of Revelation, a place where all who have been redeemed through faith will finally gather; and (3) the Buddha-fields or "pure lands" of Mahayana Buddhism, paradisiacal realms of enlightenment into which those who remain mindful of a Buddha or bodhisattva are eventually reborn.

The philosopher Martin Heidegger set forth a powerful description of the naturally supernatural world in his essay "Building Dwelling Thinking."[4] To borrow Heidegger's term, our earth, as a naturally supernatural world, is where one "dwells." To dwell is to live on the earth as part of what Heidegger called the "gathering of the fourfold," the gathering of sky, earth, gods, and mortals. The gathering of sky and earth corresponds to what we have called the fusion of supernatural and natural planes. The heavens, having opened, are no longer an otherworldly realm apart from earth and are now the heavens, the radiant sky, *of the earth*. To dwell on the earth is thus to be at home on the earth as it is bathed in the beautifying, sacralizing light of the sky.

The gathering of gods and mortals is the dwelling on earth not only of humans but also of spirit, as native spirit. The overcoming of natural-supernatural dualism is at the same time an overcoming of human-divine estrangement. Spirit no longer resides in a celestial realm apart from the earth; the gods no longer live high in the sky or on mountain tops. As the pre-Socratic philosopher Heraclitus said when guests unexpectedly found him warming himself by the fire, "Here, too, are gods." The gods live among us; immortals and mortals are thus gathered. The spiritually mature person, then, is a mortal who dwells on earth in the presence of the divine.

The Goal of Regression in the Service of Integration

Regression in the service of integration withdraws the ego from the world, purges it of impediments to the expression of spirit, returns it to conditions of life like those that prevailed in early stages of development, promotes its growth in spirit, and, finally, leads it to the stage of spiritual maturity. Arriving at spiritual maturity, the ego is fully united with spirit, as, too, is the soul with the body, the supernatural with the natural, and the heavens with the earth. That regression in the service of integration leads to such a goal indicates that, despite its backward or regressive movement, it is developmentally progressive overall. Regression in the service of integration moves backward so that it can retrieve what is needed to spiral up to higher ground.

Conclusion

The primary purpose of part 3 has been to explain how the ego plays an essential and much more positive role in spiritual life than is generally acknowledged. In response to those who argue that the ego's role in spiritual life is problematic because the notion of the ego has better described men's than women's subjectivity, I hope to have shown that just this fact reveals that there are important differences in women's and men's spiritual development that must be taken into account if we are to understand what women and men share in their spiritual lives. As we have seen, asymmetries in women's and men's ego development that set women and men on paths that diverge are revisited in reverse during spiritual development, thus setting women and men on paths that converge.

In response to those who argue that liberated or enlightened life is without an ego, I hope to have shown that the ego is present in all known spiritual states and in all spiritual stages, at least as an "experiencer," an observing unity of apperception, if not also as an executive agency performing cognitive and practical functions. Although the ego can blind us to greater realities beyond ourselves, we should not let the beholding of these realities (by the ego) blind us to the ego.

In response to those who argue that the ego's executive functions should play little or no role in spiritual life because they inevitably interfere with the immediacy, fullness, or spontaneity of spiritual life, I hope to have shown that spiritual life without ego functions would be completely ineffectual. I hope to have shown that spirit and the ego are complementary sides of spiritual life, each providing for the other what it cannot provide for itself. Spirit without the ego's conscious perspective and executive functions would be as incomplete as the ego without spirit's wisdom, power, and love.

Finally, in response to those who argue that the ego plays primarily a negative role in spiritual development because it is susceptible to unwholesome influences or because it is self-willed or because it is inherently prone to sin, I hope to have shown that, whatever weaknesses the ego might have, it still plays an indispensable role in all stages of spiritual development and an increasingly important role as these stages unfold. Although the ego at first might have to struggle against engrained tendencies that obstruct, resist, or try to exploit spirit, it increasingly surrenders to spirit, joins with spirit, facilitates spirit, and, finally, in reaching spiritual maturity, unites with spirit as the instrument by which it expresses itself in the world.

In part 1 of the book, I argued that the ego and the spontaneity of consciousness are coessential sides of conscious life generally. Correspondingly, here in part 3, I have argued that the ego and spirit—together with the soul and the body—are coessential sides of spiritual life specifically.

Postscript

Because this book has been about the ego, it is appropriate that we have put the ego at center stage in setting forth the stages of spiritual development here in part 3. However, we could have written part 3 from spirit's rather than the ego's perspective, which would have been an interesting exercise. If the ego experiences trials, breakthroughs, consolations, and afflictions on the way to spiritual maturity, imagine what it must be like for spirit!

Notes

Introduction

1. Whether to abbreviate "revised conception of the ego" in this introduction was a difficult decision. In the end, I decided that the advantage (simpler, more efficient exposition) clearly outweighed the disadvantage (repetition of an unattractive abbreviation).

2. *Principles of Philosophy* I.32 (Descartes, 1985–1991, vol. 1, p. 204).

3. Although, according to Descartes, the soul is active when it exercises the will to operate on, say, a thought, image, or impulse, it is completely passive *in the original moment of experiencing* the thought, image, or impulse. Descartes's account of the passivity of the perceiving intellect is summarized in chapter 1.

4. The idea of individual self-authorship was first espoused by existentialist philosophers, some of whom were highly critical of the traditional notion of the ego. The idea only later became associated with the traditional notion of the ego when postmodernists, stressing the social construction of the self, took aim at that notion.

5. Self-identity does not imply permanence or uninterruptedness over time, as we explain in chapters 3 and 6.

6. I adopt the italicized term from Francisco J. Varela (1996).

7. The distinction between I and Me sides of the self was introduced by James in 1890 and then played a prominent role in the work of sociologist George Herbert Mead. James introduced the distinction in *Principles of Psychology,* using the terms "I" and "me" to describe the two sides of the ego that hitherto had been called the pure or transcendental ego (which James refers to as "I") and the phenomenal or empirical ego (which James refers to as "me"). James sums up his account by saying, "The consciousness of Self [or ego] involves a stream of thought, each part of which as 'I' can 1) remember those which went before, and know the things they knew; and 2) emphasize and care paramountly for certain ones among them as 'me,' and appropriate to these the rest" (1890/1950, vol. 1, p. 400).

8. In chapters 6 through 8, we discuss forms of self-awareness that precede and prepare the way for the formation of the self-representation; and in chapters

9 and 10, we discuss forms of incentive and disincentive that precede and prepare the way for the ego ideal and the superego, respectively. As we shall see, the self-representation emerges only after self-recognition proper—as, for example, in mirror self-recognition—emerges, in the second half of the second year. In turn, the ego ideal and the superego emerge only after the self-representation has emerged, in the transition from early to middle childhood. The point here is that, *once the self-representation has emerged,* it becomes the ego's primary instrument of self-knowledge; and *once the ego ideal and the superego have emerged,* they become the ego's primary instruments of self-motivation.

Chapter 1

1. *Meditations,* Third Meditation (CSM II, 24). All quotations from Descartes's work are from the standard English translation, *The Philosophical Writings of Descartes,* 3 vols., edited and translated by J. Cottingham, R. Stoothoff, and D. Murdoch, with vol. 3 (correspondence) also translated by A. Kenny, Cambridge University Press, 1985–91. Following common practice, references to the first two of these volumes use the abbreviations CSM I and CSM II, and references to the third volume the abbreviation CSMK.

2. *Meditations,* Second Meditation (CSM II, 17–18).

3. *Objections and Replies,* Fifth Set of Replies (CSM II, 246).

4. *Principles of Philosophy* I.51 (CSM I, 210).

5. *Meditations,* Third Meditation (CSM II, 30).

6. *Meditations,* Sixth Meditation (CSM II, 59).

7. *Passions of the Soul* I.30 (CSM I, 339).

8. *Principles of Philosophy* I.52 (CSM I, 210).

9. Descartes maintained that the converse is true as well, that a thinker requires thinking, *actual* thinking, *actual* consciousness, not just the ability to think or the ability to be conscious. Descartes believed that the ego can never be completely without thought because, in his view, actually having experiences or actually performing actions is as essential to the ego's existence as actually being extended is essential to the existence of material substances. For Descartes, an incorporeal thinking thing and actual thinking, the ego and actual conscious awareness, necessarily go together. On this point, see Descartes's letter to Guillaume Gibieuf of January 19, 1642 (CMSK, 203), and his letter to Antione Arnauld of June 4, 1642 (CMSK, 355).

10. *Objections and Replies,* Fourth Set of Replies (CSM II, 171).

11. *Principles of Philosophy* I.32 (CSM I, 204).

12. *Meditations,* Second Meditation (CSM II, 20–22).

13. *Meditations,* Fourth Meditation (CSM II, 39, 40).

14. *Objections and Replies,* Second Set of Replies (CSM II, 117).

15. *Objections and Replies,* Sixth Set of Replies (CSM II, 292).

16. Later in the chapter, we explain that in the last years of his life Descartes seems to have rethought his conception of the will, moving toward an exclusively elective conception, a conception according to which the will is set in motion only by the ego, as the ego's autonomous instrument of action.

17. In *Discourse* (1637), Descartes, without mentioning the Stoics, recommends the Stoic approach to life as the third maxim of a general moral code for how best to live one's life. Descartes then elaborated on this maxim in his correspondence with Princess Elisabeth in 1645, using Seneca's *On the Happy Life* as a text for their exchange. Finally, Descartes presented the theoretical basis for explaining how one can achieve a life of reason, self-mastery, and peace of mind in *Passions of the Soul,* a book that grew out of his correspondence with Princess Elisabeth.

18. The Stoics did not in fact have a conception of the will properly so called. Nevertheless, they did set forth an idea that played an essential role in the emergence of the notion of the will: the idea that action is based on the soul's giving or withholding assent to an impulse. This idea was later incorporated within the notion of the will as the soul's ability to move the will actively or electively, whether, minimally, by assenting to an impulse or, more fully, by exercising autonomous, agent-initiated choice. More is said about Stoicism's contribution to the emergence of the notion of the will in the next chapter.

19. *Meditations,* Third Meditation (CSM II, 36).

20. In *Comments on a Certain Broadsheet* (CSM I, 304), Descartes acknowledged that sensory phenomena such as pains, colors, and sounds are also innate in the sense that they are generated within the mind when it is affected by material objects. However, Descartes gave little attention to these phenomena, since he believed that, unlike purely intellectual innate ideas, they are cognitively "obscure" and, therefore, unreliable as sources of knowledge.

21. Siren, hippogriff: *Meditations,* Third Meditation (CSM II, 26); winged horse, triangle inscribed in square: *Objections and Replies,* First Set of Replies (CSM II, 83–84); sun larger than it appears: *Meditations,* Third Meditation (CSM II, 27) and letter to Marin Mersenne of June 16, 1641 (CSMK, 183).

22. See especially the letters to Henricus Regius of May, 1641 (CSMK, 182), and Denis Mesland of May 2, 1644 (CSMK, 232). The wax and seal analogy is in the letter to Mesland.

23. *Principles* I.45 (CSM I, 207–8).

24. In *Passions,* Descartes notes that the ego's passive experiencing of its own actions is an exception to the stipulation that passions are effects of material causes (I.19 [CSM I, 335–36]). Actions of the soul are at the same time passions because when the ego performs an action it can at the same time be—indeed, *always is,* Descartes thought—aware of itself doing so. In witnessing its own actions, the ego experiences them as passions, passions caused by the (incorporeal) ego itself rather than by any material cause or causes. Later in *Passions,* Descartes speaks of an inner joy or sense

of well-being—similar to the serenity extolled by Stoics—as an example of a kind of feeling that is "produced in the soul only by the soul itself" (II.147 [CSM I, 381]).

25. *Passions* I.18 (CSM I, 335).

26. Examples of active or executive cognition of this scientific sort are the line of reasoning, already discussed, that leads to the invented idea that the sun is larger than it appears and the inference, discussed in *Rules* (CSM I, 47–48), that proceeds from the premises that water is thinner than earth and air thinner than water to the conclusion that whatever exists beyond atmospheric air (ether) is thinner yet.

27. Fixing attention: *Passions* I.43 (CSM I, 344); summoning innate ideas: *Objections and Replies,* Third Set of Objections with Replies (CSM II, 132); recalling memories: *Passions* I.42 (CSM I, 343–44); eliciting mental images: *Passions* I.43 (CSM I, 344).

28. *Passions* I.41 (CSM I, 343).

29. *Passions* I.41 (CSM I, 343).

30. CMSK, 245.

31. *Passions* I.41 (CSM I, 343).

32. *Passions* I.50 (CSM I, 348).

33. *Passions* II.52 (CSM I, 349).

34. In *Passions,* Descartes's account of the ego's control of passions that refer to the soul focuses primarily on feelings and desires, and the discussion here follows Descartes in this regard. However, it should be kept in mind that spontaneously arising mental images, such as those of fantasy, daydreaming, and night dreaming, are also passions that refer to the soul. Unlike actively elicited mental images, which are a joint product of the ego's active attempts to bring them forth and the responding movement of animal spirits in nerve pathways and the brain (*Passions* I.43 [CSM I, 344]), spontaneously arising mental images are caused by the movement of animal spirits without any prior efforts on the ego's part (*Passions* I.21 [CSM I, 336]). Spontaneously arising mental images are passions of the same type as feelings and desires, and for this reason they should be subject to the same kind of control as feelings and desires. Although Descartes does not make the point, it is noteworthy that spontaneously arising mental images typically give expression to feelings and desires, such that any degree of control that the ego might gain over the latter should extend to the former as well.

35. Letters to Princess Elisabeth of September 1, 1645 (CSMK, 264), and September 15, 1645 (CSMK, 266).

36. *Passions* I.50 (CSM I, 348).

37. *Passions* I.50 (CSM I, 348).

Chapter 2

1. *Phaedo* 105 c–e.

2. *De Anima* III.v, 430a10–25.

3. Descartes, although believing that macroscopic objects are made up of microscopic particles, held that, as extended substances, even these microscopic particles are in principle always further divisible. Descartes thus denied the existence of indivisible atoms, and he denied the existence of a void as well. According to Descartes, material bodies do not move through a void but rather through other material bodies, which they displace in doing so.

4. In a letter to Henricus Regius dated January 1642, Descartes criticized substantial forms bluntly, describing them as occult explanatory hypotheses that not even their advocates understand (CMSK, 208–9). In a footnote to the preface to the French edition of *Principles of Philosophy*, Descartes, more diplomatically, quoted the following statement from his *Meteorology*: "I regard the minute parts of terrestrial bodies as being all composed of one single kind of matter, and believe that each of them could be divided repeatedly in infinitely many ways, and that there is no more difference between them than there is between stones of various different shapes cut from the same rock. . . . But to keep the peace with the philosophers, I have no wish to deny any further items which they may imagine in bodies over and above what I have described, such as their 'substantial forms,' their 'real qualities,' and so on. It simply seems to me that my arguments will be all the more acceptable in so far as I can make them depend on fewer things" (CSM I, 187n2).

5. Menn (1998), who stresses Descartes's similarities to Augustine, presents an account of the principal figures and their positions in this debate.

6. For Saint Paul's references to outer and inner dimensions of human life, see 2 Cor. 4:16; Eph. 3:14–16; Romans 7:22–23.

7. *De Trinitate* XII.1.

8. *Confessions* III.vi.10.

9. CSM I, 315.

10. CSMK, 182 (italics in original).

11. There are forms of executive or active cognition other than discursive (or operational) thinking. For example, attention control, working memory, task switching, warding off distractions, and actively eliciting ideas, images, or memories are forms of executive cognition but are not discursive in character because they are not multistep operations leading from starting points to end points.

12. *Posterior Analytics* I.vi, 74b5 (Aristotle, ca. 350 BCE/1957b, p. 53).

13. *Posterior Analytics* I.ii, 71b20–23 (Aristotle, ca. 350 BCE/1957b, p. 31).

14. In *De Anima* (III.v, 430a) Aristotle suggests that the intellect has a side (later known as the active or agent intellect) that is active in producing intuition of universal truths in a manner that is like the way physical light is active in producing vision of material things. The light of the intellect renders universal truths intelligible in a manner that is like the way in which the light of the sun renders material things visible.

15. CSM II, 4.

16. *Phaedo* 79c–80c.

17. The Averroistic view that we share a single universal intellect ran afoul of the Church because it is inconsistent with the Church's teaching that each person has an immortal soul that is unique to that person and, therefore, numerically distinct from all other immortal souls. The Averroistic position was rejected in 1311 (during the Council of Vienne) and, in more detail, in 1513 (during the Fifth Lateran Council).

18. Aristotle, in speaking of what came to be known as the active intellect, also spoke of a part of the intellect that is the passive complement of the active intellect, what came to be called the passive (or potential or material) intellect. According to Aristotle, these two parts of the intellect go together because the active intellect, in illuminating universal truths or intelligible forms, requires a medium in which to illuminate them. The passive intellect is this medium. The active and passive intellects are thus related as form to matter, although the matter of the passive intellect is not the matter of physical objects. Because the active and passive intellects are related as a complementary pair, Averroes, but not Avicenna, concluded that not only the former but also the latter is incorporeal, immortal, and universal.

19. *Summa Theologiae* I.Q76.A3.

20. *Summa Theologiae* I.Q76.A3; I.Q76.A5.

21. *Summa Theologiae* I.Q76.A3. Reply to Objection 1.

22. *Summa Theologiae* I.Q77.A8.

23. 439 a–d.

24. *Passions* I.47 (CSM I, 345–46).

25. Fowler (1999) presents an excellent account of these Platonic difficulties and a well-informed general discussion of Descartes's attempts to make his positions conform to teachings of the Church. The rest of this section is indebted to Fowler's exposition.

26. *Objections and Replies,* Fourth Set of Objections (CSM II, 143).

27. See the letter to Regius of January 1642 (quoted in part below), the letter to Regius of December 1641 (CSMK, 200), and *Objections and Replies,* Fourth Set of Replies (CSM II, 156–57 & 160).

28. CSMK, 207–8, revised by Fowler (1999, 328). Fowler's revision of the CSMK translation brings out more clearly Descartes's view that the human soul *alone* is to be considered a substantial form.

29. *City of God* XI.26 and elsewhere.

30. *De Trinitate* XV.12.21.

31. See Menn (1998) and O'Neill (1996) for details on Descartes's access to Augustine's thought.

32. *Objections and Replies,* Fourth Set of Replies (CSM II, 171).

33. *Confessions* 10.8.15.

34. Two influential studies of the historical emergence of the notion of the will are Dihle (1982) and Frede (2011).

35. *Confessions* I.1 (Augustine, 354–430/1997, p. 3).

36. *Summa Theologiae* I–II.Q8.A1

37. *Confessions* VIII.9

38. For Augustine, memory is not only that by which we remain in touch with our personal and historical origins but also that by which we remain in touch with our ontological origins: God. It is by memory—which is like Plato's recollection but without the assumption of reincarnation—that we retrieve the universal truths that God makes innately accessible to us; and it is by memory that we eventually find our way back to God.

39. Aquinas's conception of memory as an incorporeal power of the soul pertains only to the memory of universal principles and intelligible forms. Aquinas, an Aristotelian rather than, like Augustine, a Platonist, held that memory of universal principles and intelligible forms is a retention of them in the intellect after they have been intuitively grasped from information provided by the senses, a retention that allows the intellect later to bring them forth from within itself, without needing to return to sense experience to retrieve them again. *Summa Theologiae* I.Q79.A6.

40. Locke is an interesting case. His conception of the will evolved from a purely desiderative to a purely elective conception, as is evidenced in revisions to his *Essay on Human Understanding*. Beginning with a conception that equated willing to preferring, Locke came to conceive of willing as "a particular determination of the mind whereby, barely by thought, the mind endeavours to give rise, continuation, or stop to any action which it takes to be in its power. This, well considered, plainly shows that the *will* is perfectly distinguished from *desire;* which, in the very same action, may have a quite contrary tendency from that which our *will* sets us upon" (II.xxi.30). For this analysis of the evolution of Locke's conception of the will, see Rickless (2020).

Chapter 3

1. Question 3 is the exception. It is included here because it is a question of the same type as the other four and because it is a question that leads to one of the key ideas of our revised conception of the ego.

2. Hume, 1739–1740/1888, p. 252.

3. See, especially, the second section of the chapter on the transcendental deduction of the categories in the *Critique of Pure Reason* (second edition), "Transcendental Deduction of the Pure Concepts of the Understanding" (Kant, 1787/1998, pp. 245–66).

4. The distinction between self-identity (being the same thing at both an earlier and a later time) and permanence (remaining uninterruptedly in existence from an earlier to a later time) is crucial in talking about the ego as an experiencing subject. Later in the chapter, we explain how the ego can possess self-identity as an experiencing subject even though it might be intermittent rather than permanent in its existence.

5. Kant, 1787/1998, pp. 247–48. Boldface in translation corresponds to emphasis in original German.

6. Kant, 1787/1998, p. 453. Boldface in translation corresponds to emphasis in original German.

7. Strawson, 1966/2005, p. 17.

8. The background and subsequent development of James's I-Me distinction were discussed in note 7 of the introduction.

9. In chapter 9, we explain that the self-representation emerges in the second half of the second year, after the child has achieved self-recognition proper, the ability to see itself from an external perspective. In chapters 6 through 8, we discuss forms of self-awareness—awareness by the ego of its exterior or Me side—that precede the emergence of the self-representation.

10. Kant, 1787/1998, p. 247. Boldface in translation corresponds to emphasis in original German.

11. I adopt the term "neurophenomenology" from Varela (1996).

12. Distinguishing between unbound or anonymous experiences on the one hand and bound or owned experiences on the other raises the question of whether experiences of the former type are even possible. We consider this question later in the chapter.

13. Kant argued that the synthesizing activity that produces the ego as an experiencing subject does so by organizing the data of experience according to basic concepts or "categories of understanding." He did not offer a corresponding account of how this activity at the same time produces the ego as owner and executive agency of consciousness. These matters are profound and, perhaps, inherently obscure in their depths.

14. Sartre, 1937/1957, pp. 98–99.

15. Kant, 1787/1998, p. 246. Boldface in translation corresponds to emphasis in original German.

16. Nir & Tononi, 2010.

17. See Mutz & Amir-Homayoun (2017) for a literature review.

18. C. G. Jung spoke of a dreaming ego, saying, "In most dreams, for instance, there is still some consciousness of the ego, although it is a very limited and curiously distorted ego known as the dream-ego. It is a mere fragment or shadow of the waking ego. Consciousness exists only when psychic contents are associated with the ego, and the ego is a psychic complex of a particularly solid kind. As sleep is seldom quite dreamless, we may assume that the activity of the ego-complex seldom ceases entirely; its activity is as a rule only restricted by sleep" (Jung, 1948/1969b, p. 306).

19. Bain, 1855, p. 359.

20. Two states of consciousness might be considered exceptions to this generalization. These states, discussed earlier, are those of (functionally disengaged) expansive openness and (functionally arrested) deep absorption. In the former state,

it seems that, although the spontaneity of conscious is active producing thoughts, images, and impulses, the ego is inactive because it has ceased performing executive functions. In the latter state, it seems that both the spontaneity of consciousness and the ego have been arrested, since in this state the ego is absorbed in a single and seemingly unchanging object of consciousness. Appearances to the contrary, it is unlikely that the ego ever comes to a complete standstill in either of these states. In the state of expansive openness, the ego is not like a mirror, which is completely unaffected by and unresponsive to the images it reflects. Rather, the ego, even though seemingly stationary as a witness to the spontaneity of consciousness, probably suffers microfluctuations and performs microactions in response to the phenomena it witnesses, fluctuations and actions that are too quick and slight to be noticed. In the state of deep absorption, although the ego is immobilized by an attractor (the object or energy in which it is absorbed), it is probably never rendered completely inert. In this state, too, unnoticed microfluctuations and microactions probably occur. These statements express probabilities only, not certainties. However, if our primary hypothesis, that the ego is the organized form of the unifying-appropriating function, is correct, it follows that the underlying nature of the ego prohibits it from ever coming to a complete standstill. More on this point in a moment.

21. Since John Locke, many have considered continuity of memory to be a necessary condition for the self-identity of the ego. In our view, memories are part of the exterior side of the ego, not the interior side, and, therefore, can be erased without destroying the ego's self-identity on its interior side. The interior side of the ego, as the organized form of the unifying-appropriating function, can for this reason remain self-identical even if the ego were to lose its memories, in somewhat the same way as a computer's spinning or solid-state drive remains self-identical even if the data recorded on it are erased.

22. National Park Service, 2020.

23. Thompson (2015) presents an interesting account of how contemporary neuroscience might be brought to bear upon the possibility of dreamless sleep as described in these Asian philosophies.

Chapter 4

1. These are the defense mechanisms that Anna Freud selected from her father's work for discussion in her classic *The Ego and the Mechanisms of Defense* (1936/1977).

2. Freud was already in the process of correcting himself on this matter in *The Ego and the Id* (1923/1961), where he stressed that the ego has the power not only to defend itself from threatening instinctual impulses but also to mediate between the demands of the id and the superego. He continued this corrective course in *Inhibitions, Symptoms, and Anxiety* (1926/1959), where he acknowledged that the ego has extensive power over the id.

3. Hartmann, 1939/1958.

4. The issue of the ego's sovereignty or lack thereof is revisited later in the book, in chapter 10 and then again in chapters 16 through 19. In chapter 10, we explain the origin of the ego's presumption of sovereignty in the transition from early to middle childhood, when repression helps the child achieve self-control. Then, in chapters 16 through 19, we set forth an account of four stages of spiritual development—spiritual preawakening, awakening, growth, and maturity—and explain how the ego is disabused of its presumption of sovereignty during the stage of spiritual awakening, when it must surrender to a higher spiritual power, a higher spiritual sovereign.

5. Nietzsche, 1886/1996, p. 24.

6. Heidegger, 1975/1988, p. 64.

7. Sartre offered another reason for rejecting the Cartesian idea of an exclusively interior psychic space: there is no interior ego to support such a space in existence. As explained in the last chapter, Sartre reported that at the center of consciousness, where an interior ego is supposed to reside, there is instead a "hole in being," what we have referred to as the "space of spontaneity." For Sartre, because there is thus no interior ego to support consciousness in existence, consciousness can exist only by being the consciousness *of* something beyond consciousness, something in the world. Consciousness thus presupposes prereflective engagement in the world as a condition of its existence.

8. Merleau-Ponty, 1945/1962, p. xiii.

9. Washburn, 1995, 2003.

10. There is a sense in which, for Jung, the personal unconscious has a wider scope, including not only those parts of the ego's personal history that, owing to their threatening character, the ego has excluded from consciousness but also all parts that, in Freud's term, are "preconscious," that is, not currently in consciousness even though the ego has not excluded them from consciousness (Jung, 1954/1969a §382).

11. For example, Jung held that the shadow contains contrasexual archetypes—the archetype of the female (anima) in men and the archetype of the male (animus) in women—and, at its deepest level, the archetype of evil. Jung's view that these archetypes are universal in the sense of being more a product of the species' evolution than of a person's social and cultural development is controversial.

12. Bierstedt, 1963, p. 200.

13. Stolorow & Atwood, 1992.

14. Gergen, 2000.

15. Lacan, 1949/2006, pp. 75–81.

16. For Lacan, the law of the father that requires the child to turn away from the caregiver is a symbolic authority rather than a literal father; and the "phallus" that is central to the oedipal drama is a symbol of primacy and power rather than a literal penis.

17. Kristeva, 1974/1984, pp. 46–51.

18. This is the title of a section of *Speculum of the Other Woman* (Irigaray, 1974/1985a, pp. 133–46).

19. Irigaray, 1995, p. 8.

20. Irigaray, 1981/1991b, pp. 40–41.

21. Kristeva, 1980/2002b, pp. 371–82.

22. Kristeva, 1974/1984.

23. Kristeva, 2010, 79–94.

24. Irigaray, 1981/1991c, p. 50.

25. Irigaray, 1991a, p. 117.

26. Irigaray, 1985b, p. 212.

27. Kristeva, 1984/2002a, pp. 349–50.

28. Chodorow, 1978, p. 133.

29. Chodorow, 1978, pp. 130, 133, 167, 212.

30. Dinnerstein, 1976/1999, p. 76.

31. Dinnerstein, 1976/1999, p. 104.

32. Dinnerstein, 1976/1999, p. 155.

33. Chodorow, 1978, pp. 92–110.

34. Chodorow, 1978, pp. 125–29.

35. Chodorow, 1978, p. 206.

36. Chodorow, 1978, p. 14.

37. Brentano, 1874/1995.

38. For the distinction between derivative and original intentionality, see Haugeland (1981, 2002). For a similar distinction, see Searle (1980, 1983, 1992).

39. Chalmers, 1995.

40. Wilber, 1995, 1997.

Chapter 5

1. American psychoanalyst Harry Stack Sullivan (1953/1977, 1954/1970) used the term "self-system" in elaborating his interpersonal psychiatry. For Sullivan, the self-system consists of all interpersonal strategies for avoiding anxiety and protecting self-esteem. As such, the self-system does not correspond to any agency or apparatus of classical psychoanalysis: "It is not a thing, a region, or what not, such as superegos, egos, ids, and so on" (1953/1977, p. 167). Rather, the self-system is a "dynamism"—a set of self-organizing and self-defending functions—by means of which a person protects a core sense of acceptable selfhood from threatening interpersonal input. It consists of all the "security operations"—the strategies of selective inattention, the alert systems, the precautions, the avoidances, and the like—that provide this protection. The conception of the self-system in this book differs considerably from Sullivan's, principally by focusing on self-knowledge and self-motivation rather than on self-esteem.

2. In chapters 6 through 8, we discuss forms of self-awareness that precede the self-representation.

3. Dan P. McAdams especially has contributed to our understanding of the role played by self-narration in the forging and development of the self. We draw on McAdams's work in ensuing chapters.

4. Freud introduced the notion of the ego ideal in "On Narcissism: An Introduction" (1914), describing the ego ideal as a strived-for state of perfection that might replace the sense of narcissistic perfection that was enjoyed during infancy. When Freud introduced the notion of the superego in *The Ego and the Id* (1923), he spoke of the ego ideal and the superego almost as if they were equivalent notions, notions of an inner agency by which the ego submits itself to ideals and standards of conduct generally. After 1923, Freud had little to say about the ego ideal and, when he did discuss it, he spoke of it as if it were a part or function of the superego.

5. A similar notion is found in the work of Harry Stack Sullivan (1953/1977). Sullivan introduced the notion of the "not me," which, like the Jungian shadow, consists of those parts of a person that cannot be acknowledged because to do so would undermine the person's sense of self or well-being.

6. To avoid misunderstanding, I am not suggesting that shadow awakening is the norm during adolescence and midlife, only that it is something that is more likely to occur during these stages than during most other stages, for reasons explained in chapters 11 and 13. The matter is otherwise with the stages of spiritual preawakening and awakening, during which, I argue in chapters 16 and 17, shadow awakening is the norm rather than the exception.

Chapter 6

1. The more important studies reporting these findings are well known and do not need to be cited here. In the course of the chapter, I give specific attention to the newborn's ego, self-system, and lifeworld, and studies bearing on these matters are cited.

2. Hochmann and Kouider, 2022; Kouider et al., 2013.

3. Louise Newman, director of the Centre for Developmental Psychiatry and Psychology at Monash University, quoted in Jackson-Webb (2013).

4. The qualification is necessary because, as we explained in chapter 3, self-identity does not imply permanence, uninterrupted existence over time. The argument here is that memory indicates that the newborn, as an experiencing subject, is a self-identical subject over the times its memory reaches, even if it exists as an experiencing subject only intermittently rather than continuously over these times.

5. Bahrick, 1995, 2010, 2013 (processing and coordinating of multimodal information about the body in infancy); Rochat & Hespos, 1997 (newborn's ability

to distinguish self-touch from external touch); Filippetti et al., 2013 (newborn's preferential attention to images of its own body).

    6. Maister et al., 2017.

    7. Gallagher & Meltzoff, 1996; Rochat, 2012, 2019.

    8. Farroni et al. (2002) performed a study demonstrating newborns' preference for direct eye contact.

    9. Shultz, Klin, & Jones, 2018.

    10. For those who have argued that the newborn does in fact imitate the caregiver as one side of an intersubjective exchange, see Meltzoff & Moore, 1977, 1983, 1997, 1998a; Nagy & Molnar, 2004; and Trevarthen, 2005, 2011. For those who hold that the newborn's seeming imitation of the caregiver is in fact only an expression of arousal, see Anisfeld, 2005; and Jones, 2009. For a study finding no evidence of imitation, see Oostenbroek et al., 2016.

    11. Meltzoff & Moore, 1998b; Moore & Meltzoff, 2009.

    12. Baillargeon, 1993, 2004; Spelke et al., 1992.

    13. S. Freud, 1911/1958, p. 220n.

    14. Mahler, Pine, & Bergman, 1975.

    15. Coates, 2004; Pine, 2004.

    16. Farroni & Menon (2008) provide a summary of research findings. Zimmermann et al. (2019) provide a timeline of vision milestones in the first years of life based on a literature review.

Chapter 7

    1. Messinger & Fogel, 2007 (social smiling); Lavelli & Fogel, 2005 (attention on caregiver, excitation, cooing); Bertin & Striano, 2006, and Tronick et al., 1978 (responses to caregiver's neutral, still face); Rochat & Passos-Ferreira, 2008, 2009, and Shultz, Klin, & Jones, 2018 (general discussion of transition to social interaction at approximately two months).

    2. Andrew N. Meltzoff (Meltzoff, 2007; Meltzoff & Brooks, 2007) explains that the infant's ability to see the caregiver as a being "like me" is the foundation on which intersubjective and social life is built.

    3. Stephens & Matthews, 2014.

    4. Reynolds & Romano (2016) provide a general review of studies of the emergence of voluntary control of visual attention. For studies of the emergence of precursors to voluntary control, see Atkinson et al., 1992, and Hood & Atkinson, 1993 (ability to shift attention); Richards, 1985, 1989, 1997 (sustained attention); M. H. Johnson, 1995 (ability to inhibit eye movement); Haith, Hazan, & Goodman, 1988, Adler & Haith, 2003, and Canfield & Haith, 1991 (ability to anticipate movement or reappearance of stimuli). For the development of voluntary control

of visual attention after six months, see Colombo, 2001; Colombo & Cheatham, 2006; and Courage, Reynolds, & Richards, 2006.

5. This account of the infant's new, caregiver-mediated self-awareness closely follows Philippe Rochat's account (2004, 2007).

6. Mandler, 2004, 2007; Owen & Barnes, 2021; Quinn & Eimas, 1996; and, for color vision in infancy, Bornstein, 2006; Bornstein, Kessen, & Weiskopf, 1976; Franklin & Davies, 2004.

7. Mandler, 2000; Mandler & McDonough, 1996, 1998.

8. Philosophers might prefer the term "categorial" to "categorical," since, for them, the latter term is used primarily in logic to refer to assertoric or unqualified propositions and the categorical syllogisms based on them. Philosophers often use the term "categorial" in referring specifically to basic categories of reality or thinking, such as Aristotelian or Kantian categories, respectively. However, both "categorial" and "categorical" include "of or pertaining to categories" among their established meanings, and the latter term is much more widely used.

9. The distinction between primary and secondary intersubjectivity was introduced into the field of infant studies by developmental psychologists Colwyn Trevarthen and Penelope Hubley (Hubley & Trevarthen, 1979; Trevarthen & Hubley, 1978).

10. Fogel & DeKoeyer (2007) document the transition from primary to secondary intersubjectivity through four stages, beginning at 26 to 32 weeks and ending at 38 to 40 weeks, when secondary intersubjectivity is fully established. Grossman & Johnson (2010) report beginnings of secondary subjectivity as early as five months.

11. Farroni & Menon, 2008; Zimmerman et al., 2019.

12. Reynolds & Romano (2016) and Buss, Ross-Sheehy, & Reynolds (2018) review studies on working memory. Evidence indicates that working memory emerges as early as six months, when infants' anticipatory eye movements indicate that they can keep in mind (for up to three seconds) a location at which a stimulus has appeared before (Gilmore & Johnson, 1995; Reznick et al., 2004).

13. Diamond, 1985, 1990, 2006; Diamond and Doar, 1989.

14. See Diamond (2006) for a review of her and others' work showing that it is not until between 9 and 12 months that children begin to grasp more abstract, rule-governed relations between objects, such as the causal relation between choosing an object of one kind and thereby obtaining another object of a different, desired kind. Moreover, even then children can learn such relations between objects only if the chosen and desired objects are physically attached in some way. It is not until the end of the second year that children begin to understand that abstract, rule-governed relations between objects do not depend on the objects being physically attached. It is also not until approximately this time that children begin to understand invisible movements of objects, as Piaget (1954) discovered in his classic studies of children's cognitive development.

Chapter 8

1. Studies—Devine, Hughes, & Ribner, 2019; Miller & Marcovitch, 2015; Wiebe, Lukowski, & Bauer, 2010—confirm overall continued development of executive functions in the second year. However, uniform improvement across functions is not consistently evident in test results until near the middle of the second year. Given the inconsistent results for children in the first half of the second year, developmental psychologists—Devine, Hughes, & Ribner, 2019; Garon, Bryson, & Smith, 2008; Miyake & Friedman, 2012; Miyake et al., 2000—have raised the question of whether different executive functions, rather than being expressions of a common higher-order ability, are perhaps abilities that are joined but partially dissociable or are abilities that are at first separate and only gradually coalesce as an integrated multicomponent skill.

2. Kenward et al. (2009), Klossek, Russel, & Dickinson (2008), and Klossek, Yu, & Dickinson (2011) conducted experiments that showed that children do not pursue goals in this stricter sense until they are at least two years old.

3. Klinnert, 1984; Mumme, Fernald, & Herrera, 1996; Sorce et al., 1985.

4. Although most work on emotional eavesdropping in early childhood focuses on 18-month-olds, some studies (Repacholi et al., 2014) have demonstrated impulse control based on emotional eavesdropping as early as 15 months.

5. For this and ensuing points about category development in the stage under discussion, see Mandler, 2000, 2008, and Mandler & McDonough, 2000.

6. For studies of young toddlers' ability to generalize from one to other instances of a category, see Baldwin, Markman, & Melartin, 1993, and Mandler & McDonough, 1996. For studies of young toddlers' ability to make statistical inferences, see Denison & Xu, 2014, and Xu & Garcia, 2008.

7. Gazes, Hampton, & Lourenco, 2015.

8. Xu & Garcia, 2008.

9. See chapter 7, endnote 14 for the relevant studies.

10. Mahler, Pine, & Bergman, 1975. Practicing is a subphase of what Mahler called the "separation-individuation process," the process during early childhood by which the child establishes boundaries and achieves a representation of itself as an embodied being independent of the caregiver. We discuss the two subphases of the separation-individuation process that follow practicing in the next chapter.

Chapter 9

1. Mahler, Pine, & Bergman, 1975.

2. Bergman & Harpaz-Rotem, 2004.

3. Bergman & Harpaz-Rotem, 2004, p. 558.

4. Mahler, Pine, & Bergman, 1975. According to Mahler, the rapprochement and road-to-object-constancy subphases of the separation-individuation process are preceded by "hatching" and "practicing" subphases, the latter subphase corresponding to the stage of the young toddler, the topic of the last chapter.

5. According to Mahler (McDevitt & Mahler, 1980), the road-to-object-constancy subphase of the separation-individuation process (our adjustment substage of the crisis-adjustment stage) is open-ended, extending well beyond 36 months and even to the end of the oedipal stage, the conclusion of which, in psychoanalytic theory, marks the beginning of middle childhood.

6. Kenward et al., 2009; Klossek, Russel, & Dickinson, 2008; Klossek, Yu, & Dickinson, 2011.

7. Diehl et al., 2011; Harter, 2012.

8. The mirror test was first used with chimpanzees by Gordon G. Gallup, Jr. (1970) and was then used with human children by Beulah Amsterdam (1972). See Lewis & Brooks-Gunn (1979).

9. Lanza & Flahive, 2008.

10. Harris & Chasin, 2004.

11. Piaget, 1954.

Chapter 10

1. Vygotsky, 1934/1986.

2. Alderson-Day & Fernyhough, 2015; Diaz & Berk, 1992; Flavell et al., 1997; Geva & Fernyhough, 2019; Winsler, 2009. We continue sometimes to talk aloud to ourselves when, for example, we attempt to solve new problems, to motivate ourselves to do things that we resist or fear, and to recall things that do not come immediately to mind.

3. See Alderson-Day & Fernyhough (2015) and Winsler (2009) for literature reviews.

4. Povinelli, Landau, & Perilloux, 1996; Povinelli et al., 1999; Povinelli & Simon, 1998. Fivush (2011) presents a review of studies on the prerequisites and emergence of biographical memory in childhood and adolescence.

5. Atance, 2008; Atance & Meltzoff, 2005; Atance & O'Neill, 2005.

6. Fivush, 1991, 1994, 2011; Nelson, 1993, 2003; Welch-Ross, 1997.

7. Reese et al., 2011.

8. The ensuing account explains the genesis of these two components of the self-system in terms of splitting and its overcoming rather than in terms of infantile narcissism and its psychic imprint (Freud's early explanation of the ego ideal) or in terms of the Oedipus complex and its resolution (Freud's explanation of the superego).

9. Anderson & Cavallaro, 2002; Bricheno & Thornton, 2007. Teachers, as parent surrogates, are often mentioned as important role models during middle childhood. However, Brichino & Thornton did not find evidence for this common view.

10. Day & Smith, 2013.

11. S. Freud, 1915/1957, 1926/1959.

12. Kernberg, 1976, 1987.

13. S. Freud, 1915/1957, p. 151 (italics in original).

14. Anderson & Green (2001) demonstrated that voluntary inhibition of cognitive content such as cued thoughts and memories leads to retrieval impairment. Anderson (2006) then explained the relevance of this fact for the phenomenon of repression. Building on the work of Anderson and Green, others (Depue, Banich, & Curran, 2006; Joorman et al., 2005) demonstrated that voluntary inhibition of cognitive content leads to retrieval impairment not only when the content is emotionally neutral but also and even more so when it is negatively charged. Lambert, Good, & Kirk (2010) confirmed this finding, showing as well that voluntary inhibition does not lead to retrieval impairment when the cognitive content is positively charged. Herbert & Sütterlin (2012) then confirmed that voluntary inhibition has similar effects on behavioral responses correlated with cognitive content. Finally, Hulbert & Anderson (2018) have shown that people with a history of trauma or adversity are better than others at using voluntary inhibition to block the intrusion of unwanted thoughts and memories. The growing evidence for the efficacy of voluntary inhibition in removing cognitive content and corresponding feelings and behavior from consciousness is reviewed by Anderson & Hanslmayr (2014). Most of the studies just cited report findings on the neurological underpinnings of voluntary inhibition as a mechanism that can lead to repression. Ceylan & Dönmez (2012) review these findings and present a hypothetical account of the neural systems and causal pathways involved in repression. Finally, Boag (2018) offers a recent neural-dynamic account of repression that draws on neuroscientific studies.

15. Otgaar et al., 2019.

16. I borrow this expression from Stanislav Grof (1975).

17. The literature explaining how play facilitates learning during childhood is vast. For a review of recent neuroscientific studies, see Liu et al. (2017).

Chapter 11

1. Luna et al., 2004 (mental processing speed, cognitive flexibility, working memory); Crone, 2009 (overview); Huizinga, Dolan, & van der Molen, 2006 (working memory, cognitive agility); Jensen, 2006 (mental processing speed); Kail & Ferrer, 2007 (mental processing speed); Conklin et al., 2007 (working memory).

2. Gestsdottir & Lerner, 2008; Luciana et al., 2009.

3. Casey, Getz, & Galvan, 2008; Galvan et al., 2006; Hare et al., 2008; Jensen & Nutt, 2015; Steinberg, 2007.

4. In many preindustrial areas today, as was true more generally in the pre-industrial past, most adolescents are required by their families or by social custom to take on adult roles, thus precluding any opportunity to explore identity options before making adult commitments.

5. The ensuing account of adolescent peer groups is based on Brown (1990, 2004).

6. Habermas & Bluck, 2000; Habermas & de Silveira, 2008; McAdams, 1985, 1993.

7. Adolescence is ordinarily divided into the three stages just noted, each stage having its distinctive set of motivations and concerns. See Barrett, 1996; Christie, 2005; SAHRC, 2013a, 2013b, 2013c.

8. Habermas & Bluck, 2000; Habermas & Reese, 2015.

9. Hurd & Zimmerman (2011) present a literature review.

10. Habermas & Paha, 2001 (increasing coherence); McAdams et al., 2006 (increasing complexity). The time between late adolescence and early adulthood has expanded in recent decades as increasing numbers of people have pursued postsecondary education. These bridge years of "emerging adulthood" are discussed in the next chapter.

11. Brown & Larson, 2009 (changing peer relationships during adolescence).

12. The ensuing account of the changing locations at which adolescents meet is based on Connolly, Furman, & Konarski (2000), Dunphy (1963), Fishman (2019), and Lenhart (2015).

13. Hall, 1904.

14. A. Freud, 1958; Blos, 1962, 1967.

15. Arnett, 1999; Offer, Ostrov, & Howard, 1981.

16. Erikson, 1959, 1963, 1968.

17. Robins et al. (2002) cite many conflicting studies on rising or falling self-esteem during adolescence and themselves report evidence of falling self-esteem not only in the transition to adolescence but also thereafter, throughout adolescence. Orth, Erol, & Luciano (2018) and Orth, Trzesniewski, & Robins (2010) cite studies indicating a fall in self-esteem in the transition to adolescence but report no significant rise or fall in overall self-esteem during adolescence. Cai et al. (2014) report findings that confirm the inverted U-shape course, but only for explicit, not implicit, self-esteem. Pickhardt (2010) discusses the kinds of self-esteem issues that characteristically occur in early adolescence and the kinds that characteristically occur in late adolescence.

18. Cai et al., 2014.

19. Recent studies have shown that the Jungian view associating midlife with shadow awakening is overstated. These studies are cited in chapter 13, where we discuss the data indicating that shadow awakening during midlife is significantly cor-

related only with people, a minority, who experience midlife as a time of pronounced dissatisfaction with their social roles. As for shadow awakening during adolescence, we shall be proposing that it, too, is experienced only by a minority, specifically by adolescents who perceive parents or other authority figures as adversaries or who have bleak prospects for the future. In general, we shall be proposing that neither midlife nor adolescence is a stage during which shadow awakening is expectable in the sense of being the rule rather than an exception but that both are stages during which shadow awakening is relatively more likely to occur than during (most) other stages. "Most" was inserted because, as explained in chapters 16 and 17, there are two stages in which shadow awakening *is* the rule rather than the exception, the stages of spiritual preawakening and spiritual awakening.

20. We face a chicken-and-egg situation here. Do resentments cause the awakening of shadow impulses or does the awakening of shadow impulses cause resentments? The answer is probably a bit of both. The most likely scenario is that growing resentments begin to stir shadow impulses, which then fuel and amplify resentments, which in turn further inflame shadow impulses, and so forth.

21. Rankin et al., 2004 (self-consciousness during adolescence); Kessler et al., 2005 (onset of anxiety disorders); Somerville, Jones, & Ruberry, 2013 (neurological correlates of self-consciousness during adolescence); Haller et al., 2015 (cognitive neuroscience and SAD during adolescence); Leigh & Clark, 2018 (SAD during adolescence).

22. Johnson & Mollborn, 2009.

23. Pickhardt, 2010; Walsh, 2014.

Chapter 12

1. Arnett, 2000; Schwartz et al., 2013.

2. Cepeda et al., 2001; Craik & Bialystok, 2006; De Luca et al., 2003; Zelazo, Craik, & Booth, 2004.

3. Marcia, 1966, 1980.

4. Kroger & Marcia, 2011; Luyckx et al., 2008; Ryeng, Kroger, & Martinussen, 2013; Schwartz et al., 2009, 2011, 2013; Waterman, 2007.

5. Fadjukoff, Pulkkinen, & Kokko, 2016; Kroger, 2015, 2017.

6. Kroger, 2015, p. 10 (online version).

7. Orth, Erol, & Luciano, 2018; Orth, Robins, & Widaman, 2012; Orth, Trzesniewski, & Robins, 2010.

8. Homophobia is a controversial phenomenon insofar as it is thought to be a defense against acknowledging one's own same-sex attraction rather than to be only an expression of a society's negative attitude toward homosexuality. Adams, Wright, & Lohr (1996), Guerra Meneses (2015), and Weinstein et al. (2012) found homophobia to be significantly correlated with same-sex attraction; MacInnis &

Hodson (2013) and Meier et al. (2006) did not. However, empirical studies amply demonstrate—Brown & Malcolm (2002), Fingerhut, Peplau, & Ghavami (2005), and Mayfield (2001)—that homophobia, or homonegativity, is frequently internalized by people who experience same-sex attraction and for this reason is often an impediment that these people struggle to overcome in their identity development as gay, lesbian, or bisexual persons.

9. Walsh, Boehm, & Lyubomirsky, 2018.

Chapter 13

1. Blanchflower, 2020; Blanchflower & Oswald, 2008. The U-shape curve analysis was popularized by Jonathan Rauch (2014).

2. Frijters & Beatton, 2012; Laaksonen, 2018; Steptoe, Deaton, & Stone, 2014.

3. The scientific literature addresses the dramatic disparity between the widespread belief that midlife is a time of crisis and the relatively small percentage of people who report a midlife crisis in the context of empirical studies. Studies indicate that midlife crises are decidedly more the exception than the rule, occurring, depending on the study, in from approximately 25% to less than 10% of the population. See Brim, Ryff, & Kessler, 2004; McCrae & Costa, 1990; Rosenberg, Rosenberg, & Farrell, 1999; Wethington, 2000; and Wethington, Kessler, & Pixley, 2004.

4. In 1990, the John D. and Catherine T. MacArthur Foundation established the Research Network on Successful Midlife Development, directed by Orville Brim. The results of this ten-year study (Brim, Ryff, & Kessler, 2004) indicate that most people have primarily a positive assessment of their lives at midlife. Earlier studies with similar findings are Deutscher, 1968; Estes & Wilenski, 1978; Lowenthal, Thurnher, & Chiriboga, 1975; and Neugarten & Datan, 1974.

5. Cabeza, 2002; Cabeza et al., 2002; Greenwood, 2007; Rajah & D'Esposito, 2005; Berlingeri et al., 2010.

6. Cattell, 1943; Horn, 1980.

7. Tawfik & Hoffman, 2018.

8. Baltes, 1987; Bosworth, Schaie, & Willis, 1999; Hartshorne & Germine, 2015; Horn, 1980.

9. Baltes, 1987; Bosworth, Schaie, & Willis, 1999; Hartshorne & Germine, 2015; Horn, 1980.

10. For retrospective overviews and assessments of the contributions of postformal theories, see Commons & Richards, 2002; Despotović, 2014; and Marchand, 2002.

11. Wethington, 2000; Wethington, Kessler, & Pixley, 2004.

12. McAdams, 1993, 2014.

13. Much of the research on gender issues at midlife has been focused on David Gutmann's (1987, 1997) studies supporting what he calls the "crossover effect," the presumed tendency for women to become more assertive and agentic and men more receptive and affiliative at midlife, once their parenting responsibilities wind down. Gutmann's research has been challenged, and other studies of how one's sense of gender might shift at midlife have arrived at inconsistent results. See Parker & Aldwin (1997) for a review of studies and an interpretation of inconsistencies.

14. Jung's writings on homosexuality are sparse and scattered. One of the more important pieces is the essay "The Love Problem of a Student" (1928/1970), in which Jung describes homosexuality as an expression of sexuality that frequently occurs with salutary effects during adolescence but is best left behind when one comes of age. Hopcke (1989) reviews Jung's writings on sexuality and summarizes their major themes.

Chapter 14

1. Dennis & Cabeza, 2008, Grady, 2008, and Park & Reuter-Lorenz, 2009 (literature reviews of cognitive and related neurological decline in the aging brain); Bennett & Madden, 2014 (localized neurological decline versus decline in interconnectedness of brain regions in the aging brain); Fjell et al., 2017 (cognitive decline and decline in interconnectedness of brain regions in the aging brain).

2. Harada et al., 2013; Hartshorne & Germine, 2015.

3. Reitzes and Mutran (2006) refer to this phenomenon as "lingering identity," which, not exclusive to retirement, is characteristic of role-change generally, especially work-related role change (Wittman, 2019).

4. Kim & Moen, 2001.

5. Barnes & Perry, 2004; Kubicek et al., 2011; TIAA, 2016.

6. For studies indicating a trade-off of losses and gains, see Calvo & Sarkisian, 2011; Ross & Drentea, 1998; and Schmitt et al., 1979. For studies indicating a general increase in life satisfaction or mental well-being, see Carstensen et al., 2000; Charles, Reynolds, & Gatz, 2001; Lacey, Smith, & Ubel, 2006; Scarf, 2008; and Thomas et al., 2016.

Chapter 15

1. Dause & Kirby, 2019; McFall, McDermott, & Dixon, 2019.

2. Bosworth & Schaie, 1999; Cooney, Schaie, & Willis, 1988.

3. Erikson, 1959, 1963.

4. Erikson, 1963, p. 268.

5. Edmondson (2015) brings together studies from many disciplines that demonstrate the enduring importance of meaning-of-life issues, especially for old people, who engage such issues from a whole-life perspective.

6. Coleman, 1986.

7. Mark Freeman (2001) introduced this term to describe the life stories of old people who feel that their lives are over and, therefore, that there is nothing left for them other than to wait to die. For studies of this group, see Bohlmeijer et al. (2011) and van Wijngaarden, Leget, & Goossensen (2015).

8. Butler, 1963.

9. Birren & Deutchman, 1991; Lewis & Butler, 1974.

10. Birren & Svensson, 2013; Haber, 2006; Haight, 1991; Tyrrell, 2012; Wong & Watt, 1991.

11. Birren and Svensson (2013) and Tyrrell (2012) report that most people who experience such regrets work through them and reach a good measure of self-acceptance by the time they finish their reviews.

12. Birren and Svensson, 2013; Tyrrell, 2012.

Chapter 16

1. In earlier works, I have called this process "regression in the service of transcendence." "Integration" works better than "transcendence" in the context of this book.

2. "Passive," a term sometimes used in Catholic contemplative writings, is misleading because, as the Catholic tradition itself maintains, the ego is an actively responsible partner in spirit-driven transformation. Although spirit affects the ego in powerful ways, it does not thereby divest the ego of a responsible role in relation to spirit. During the so-called passive stages of spirituality, the ego, exercising its executive functions, is almost always able either to resist or cooperate with spirit and, therefore, is almost always responsible for either obstructing or facilitating its own spiritual transformation.

3. The general Jungian view is that the first half of life is the time during which the ego develops by differentiating itself from the Self, the underlying psychic source from which it emerges, and that the second half of life is the time during which the ego undergoes a spiritual return to and reintegration with the Self. In this Jungian view, midlife is the time at which the ego's worldly ambitions give way to dissatisfaction and to a hunger for something more than the known world can offer. The problem with this view is that the evidence, as we have seen, indicates that most people do not experience pronounced dissatisfaction at midlife and that those who do ordinarily experience a worldly dissatisfaction with specific life circumstances, accompanied by restlessness for change, rather than a global dissatisfaction with life itself, accompanied by despair and spiritual hunger. Although the evidence

is thus unfriendly to the general Jungian view, it should not be taken to undermine the view completely. It is possible, as already stated, that midlife dissatisfaction is a contributing cause of world-weariness for those who are ready to make the turn toward spirituality in their lives.

4. Ellis, 2009; Hardy, 1983.

Chapter 17

1. Otto, 1917/1950. Otto derived "numinous" from the Latin *numen*, meaning supernatural divine power.

2. Otto, 1917/1950.

3. Eliade, 1969.

4. Psalm 18:7–11 (KJV).

5. Exodus 33:20 (KJV).

Chapter 18

1. The fact that caring spirit has been conceived primarily in male terms in monotheistic, patriarchal societies indicates that the female side of the divine is often disguised or hidden in these societies. Feminist scholars in the study of religion have unmasked this fact, thus clarifying the archetypally female side of the divine, which, in our view, is expressed most evidently in the stage of spiritual growth.

Chapter 19

1. Grof & Grof, 1989, 1990.

2. For a discussion of the significance of and the process leading to the introduction of the category of religious or spiritual problem in DSM-IV, see Turner et al., 1995.

3. The idea and the expression "natural supernaturalism" are taken from M.H. Abrams (1971).

4. Heidegger, 1971, pp. 145–61.

References

Abrams, M. H. (1971). *Natural supernaturalism: Tradition and revolution in romantic literature.* Norton.

Adams, H. E., Wright, L. W. Jr., & Lohr, B. A. (1996). Is homophobia associated with homosexual arousal? *Journal of Abnormal Psychology,* 105(3), 440–45. https://doi: 10.1037//0021-843x.105.3.440

Adler, S. A., & Haith, M. M. (2003). The nature of infants' visual expectations for event content. *Infancy,* 4(3), 389–421. https://doi: 10.1207/S15327078IN0403_05

Alanen, L. (2003). *Descartes's concept of mind.* Harvard University Press.

Alanen, L. (2013). The role of will in Descartes' account of judgment. In K. Detlefsen (Ed.), *Descartes' Meditations: A critical guide* (pp. 176–99). Cambridge University Press.

Alderson-Day, B., & Fernyhough, C. (2015). Inner speech: Development, cognitive functions, phenomenology, and neurology. *Psychological Bulletin,* 141(5), 931–65. https://doi: 10.1037/bul0000021

Amsterdam, B. (1972). Mirror self-image reactions before age two. *Developmental Psychobiology,* 5(4), 297–305. https://doi.org/10.1002/dev.420050403

Anderson, J. K., & Cavallaro, D. (2002). Parents or pop culture? Children's heroes and role models. *Childhood Education,* 78(3), 161–68. https://doi.org/10.1080/00094056.2002.10522728

Anderson, M. C. (2006). Repression: A cognitive neuroscience approach. In M. Mancia (Ed.), *Psychoanalysis and Neuroscience* (pp. 327–49). Springer.

Anderson, M. C., & Green, C. (2001). Suppressing unwanted memories by executive control. *Nature,* 410(6826), 366–69. https://doi: 10.1038/35066572

Anderson, M. C., & Hanslmayr, S. (2014). Neural mechanisms of motivated forgetting. *Trends in Cognitive Sciences,* 18(6), 279–92. https://doi: 10.1016/j.tics.2014.03.002

Anisfeld, M. (2005). No compelling evidence to dispute Piaget's timetable of the development of representational imitation in infancy. In S. Hurley & N.

Chater (Eds.), *Perspectives on imitation: From neuroscience to social science* (pp. 107–31). MIT Press.

Aristotle. (1957a). *On the soul* (W. S. Hett, Trans.). The Loeb Classical Library. (Original work published 350 BCE)

Aristotle. (1957b). *Posterior analytics* (H. Tredennick, Trans.). The Loeb Classical Library. (Original work published 350 BCE)

Armstrong, D. M. (1968). *A materialist theory of mind* (Rev. ed.). Routledge.

Arnett, J. J. (1999). Adolescent storm and stress, reconsidered. *American Psychologist, 54*(5), 317–26. https://doi: 10.1037//0003-066x.54.5.317

Arnett, J. J. (2000). Emerging adulthood: A theory of development from the late teens through the twenties. *American Psychologist, 55*(5), 469–80. https://doi: 10.1037//0003-066X.55.5.469

Atance, C. M. (2008). Future thinking in young children. *Current Directions in Psychological Science, 17*(4), 295–98. https://doi.org/10.1111/j.1467-8721.2008.00593.x

Atance, C. M., & Meltzoff, A. N. (2005). My future self: Young children's ability to anticipate and explain future states. *Cognitive Development, 20*(3), 341–61. https://doi: 10.1016/j.cogdev.2005.05.001

Atance, C. M., & O'Neill, D. K. (2005). The emergence of episodic future thinking in humans. *Learning and Motivation, 36*(2), 26–144. https://doi: 10.1016/j.lmot.2005.02.003

Atkinson, J., Hood, B., Wattam-Bell, J., & Braddick, O. (1992). Changes in infants' ability to switch visual attention in the first three months of life. *Perception, 21*(5), 643–53. http://doi: 10.1068/p210643

Augustine, of Hippo, Saint, 354–430. (1997). *The confessions* (M. Boulding, Trans.). Ignatius Press.

Bahrick, L. E. (1995). Intermodal origins of self-perception. In P. Rochat (Ed.), *The self in infancy: Theory and research* (pp. 349–73). North-Holland-Elsevier.

Bahrick, L. E. (2010). Intermodal perception and selective attention to intersensory redundancy: Implications for typical social development and autism. In G. Bremner & T. D. Wachs (Eds.), *Blackwell handbook of infant development* (2nd ed.) (pp. 120–66). Blackwell Publishing.

Bahrick, L. E. (2013). Body perception: Intersensory origins of self and other perception in newborns. *Current Biology, 23*(23), R1039–R1041. https://doi.org/10.1016/j.cub.2013.10.060

Baillargeon, R. (1993). The object concept revisited: New directions in the investigation of infants' physical knowledge. In C. E. Granrud (Ed.), *Visual perception and cognition in infancy* (pp. 265–315). Erlbaum.

Baillargeon, R. (2004). Infants' reasoning about hidden objects: Evidence for event-general and event-specific expectations. *Developmental Science, 7*(4), 391–414. https://doi: 10.1111/j.1467-7687.2004.00357.x

Baillargeon, R., Spelke, E. S., & Wasserman, S. (1985). Object permanence in five-month-old infants. *Cognition, 20*(3), 191–208. https://doi.org/10.1016/0010-0277(85)90008-3

Bain, A. (1855). *The senses and the intellect*. John W. Parker and Son.

Baldwin, D. A., Markman, E. M., & Melartin, R. L. (1993). Infants' ability to draw inferences about nonobvious object properties: Evidence from exploratory play. *Child Development*, 64(3), 711–28. https://doi.org/10.2307/113 1213

Baltes, P. B. (1987). Theoretical propositions of life-span developmental psychology: On the dynamics between growth and decline. *Developmental Psychology*, 23(5), 611–26. https://doi.org/10.1037/0012-1649.23.5.611

Barnes, H., & Parry, J. (2004). Renegotiating identity and relationships: Men and women's adjustments to retirement. *Aging & Society*, 24(2), 213–33. https://doi.org/10.1017/S0144686X0300148X

Barrett, D. E. (1996). The three stages of adolescence. *The High School Journal*, 79(4), 333–39. http://www.jstor.org/stable/40364502

Bennett, I. J., & Madden, D. J. (2014). Disconnected aging: Cerebral white matter integrity and age-related differences in cognition. *Neuroscience*, 276, 187–205. https://doi: 10.1016/j.neuroscience.2013.11.026

Berger, P. L., & Luckmann, T. (1966). *The social construction of reality: A treatise in the sociology of knowledge*. Anchor Books.

Bergman, A., & Harpaz-Rotem, I. (2004). Revisiting rapprochement in the light of contemporary developmental theories. *Journal of the American Psychoanalytic Association*, 52(2), 555–70. https://doi: 10.1177/00030651040520020301

Berlingeri, M., Bottini, G., Danelli, L., Ferri, F., Traficante, D., Sacheli, L., Colombo, N., Sberna, M., Sterzi, R., Scialfa, G., & Paulesu, E. (2010). With time on our side? Task-dependent compensatory processes in graceful aging. *Experimental Brain Research*, 205(3), 307–24. https://doi.org/10.1007/s00221-010-2363-7

Bertin, E., & Striano, T. (2006). The still-face response in newborn, 1.5-. and 3-month-old infants. *Infant Behavior and Development*, 29(2), 294–97. https://doi: 10.1016/j.infbeh.2005.12.003

Bierstedt, R. (1963). *The social order: An introduction to sociology* (2nd ed.). McGraw-Hill.

Birren, J. E., & Deutchman, D. E. (1991). *Guiding autobiography groups for older adults: Exploring the fabric of life*. The Johns Hopkins University Press.

Birren, J. E., & Svensson, C. (2013). Reminiscence, life review, and autobiography: Emergence of a new era. *The International Journal of Reminiscence and Life Review*, 1(1), 1–6.

Blanchflower, D. G. (2020). Is happiness U-shaped everywhere? Age and subjective wellness in 132 countries. Working paper 26641, National Bureau of Economic Research. https://www.nber.org/papers/w26641.

Blanchflower, D. G., & Oswald, A. J. (2008). Is well-being U-shaped over the life cycle? *Social Science & Medicine*, 66(8), 1733–49. https://doi.org/10.1016/j.socscimed.2008.01.030

Blos, P. (1962). *On adolescence: A psychoanalytic interpretation*. Free Press.

Blos, P. (1967). The second individuation process of adolescence. *The Psychoanalytic Study of the Child*, 22(1), 162–86. https://doi.org/10.1080/00797308.1967.11822595

Boag, S. (2006). Freudian repression, the common view, and pathological science. *Review of General Psychology*, 10(1), 74–86. https://doi.org/10.1037/1089-2680.10.1.74

Boag, S. (2018). Freudian repression, the unconscious, and the dynamics of inhibition. Routledge.

Bohlmeijer, E. T., Westerhof, G. J., Randall, W., Tromp, T., & Kenyon, G. (2011). Narrative foreclosure in later life: Preliminary considerations for a new sensitizing concept. *Journal of Aging Studies*, 25(4), 364–70. https://doi.org/10.1016/j.jaging.2011.01.003

Bornstein, M. H. (2006). Hue categorization and color naming: Physics to sensation to perception. In N. Pitchford & C. P. Biggam (Eds.), *Progress in colour studies: Vol. 2. Psychological aspects* (pp. 35–68). John Benjamins.

Bornstein, M. H., Kessen, W., & Weiskopf, S. (1976). Color vision and hue categorization in young human infants. *Journal of Experimental Psychology: Human Perception and Performance*, 2(1), 115–29. https://doi.org/10.1037/0096-1523.2.1.115

Bosworth, H. B., & Schaie, K. W. (1999). Survival effects in cognitive function, cognitive style, and sociodemographic variables in the Seattle Longitudinal Study. *Experimental Aging Research*, 25(2), 121–39. https://doi.org/10.1080/036107399244057

Bosworth, H. B., Schaie, K. W., & Willis, S. L. (1999). Cognitive and socio-demographic risk factors for mortality in the Seattle Longitudinal Study. *Journal of Gerontology*, Series B: *Psychological Sciences*, 54B(5), 273–82. https://doi.org/10.1093/geronb/54B.5.P273

Brentano, F. (1995). *Philosophy from an empirical standpoint* (A. C. Rancurello, D. B. Terrell, & L. L. McAlister, Trans.). Routledge. (Original work published 1874)

Bricheno, P., & Thornton, M. (2007). Role model, hero or champion? Children's views concerning role models. *Educational Research*, 49(4), 383–96. https://doi.org/10.1080/00131880701717230

Brim, O. G., Ryff, C. D., & Kessler, R. C. (Eds.). (2004). *How healthy are we? A national study of well-being at midlife*. University of Chicago Press.

Brown, B. B. (1990). Peer groups and peer cultures. In S. S. Feldman & G. R. Elliott (Eds.), *At the threshold: The developing adolescent* (pp. 171–96). Harvard University Press.

Brown, B. B. (2004). Adolescents' relationships with peers. In R. N. Lerner & L. Steinberg (Eds.), *Handbook of adolescent psychology* (pp. 363–94). John Wiley & Sons.

Brown, B. B., & Larson, J. (2009). Peer relationships in adolescence. In R. M. Lerner & L. Steinberg (Eds.), *Handbook of adolescent psychology* (pp. 74–103). John Wiley & Sons.

Brown, C. J., & Malcolm, J. P. (2002). Correlates of internalized homophobia and homosexual identity formation in a sample of gay men. *Journal of Homosexuality*, 43(2), 77–92. https://doi.org/10.1300/J082v43n02_05

Buss, A. T., Ross-Sheehy, S., & Reynolds, G. D. (2018). Visual working memory in early development: A developmental cognitive neuroscience perspective. *Journal of Neurophysiology*, 20(4), 1472–83. https://doi.org/10.1152/jn.00087.2018

Butler, R. N. (1963). The life review: An interpretation of reminiscence in the aged. *Psychiatry*, 26(1), 65–76. https://doi.org/10.1080/00332747.1963.11023339

Cabeza, R. (2002). Hemispheric asymmetry reduction in older adults: The HAROLD model. *Psychology and Aging*, 17(1), 85–100. https://doi:10.1037//0882-7974.17.1.85

Cabeza, R., Anderson, N. D., Locantore, J. K., & McIntosh, A. R. (2002). Aging gracefully: Compensatory brain activity in high-performing older adults. *NeuroImage*, 17(3), 1394–402. https://doi: 10.1006/nimg.2002.1280

Cai, H., Wu, M., Luo, Y., & Yang, J. (2014). Implicit self-esteem decreases in adolescence: A cross-sectional study. *PLOS ONE*, 9(2), e89988. https://doi.org/10.1371/journal.pone.0089988

Calvo, E., & Sarkisian, N. (2011). Retirement and well-being: Examining the characteristics of life course transitions. Working Paper #2, Public Policy Institute at Universidad Diego Portales. Available at SSRN: https://ssrn.com/abstract=2527997

Canfield, R. L., & Haith, M. M. (1991). Young infants' visual expectations for symmetric and asymmetric stimulus sequences. *Developmental Psychology*, 27(2), 198–208. https://doi.org/10.1037/0012-1649.27.2.198

Carstensen, L. L., Pasupathi, M., Mayr, U., & Nesselroade, J. R. (2000). Emotional experience in everyday life across the adult life span. *Journal of Personality and Social Psychology*, 79(4), 644–55. https://doi.org/10.1037/0022-3514.79.4.644

Casey, B. J., Getz, S., & Galvan, A. (2008). The adolescent brain. *Developmental Review*, 28(1), 62–77. https://doi: 10.1016/j.dr.2007.08.003

Cattell R. B. (1943). The measurement of adult intelligence. *Psychological Bulletin*, 40(3), 153–93. https://doi.org/10.1037/h0059973

Cepeda, N. J., Kramer, A. F., de Sather, G., & Jessica C. M. (2001). Changes in executive control across the lifespan: Examination of task-switching performance. *Developmental Psychology*, 37(5), 715–30. https://doi.org/10.1037/0012-1649.37.5.715

Ceylan, M. E., & Dönmez, A. (2012). Neurobiology of repression: A hypothetical interpretation. *Integrative Physiological and Behavioral Science*, 46(3), 395–409. https://doi: 10.1007/s12124-012-9197-8

Chalmers, D. (1995). Facing up to the problem of consciousness. *Journal of Consciousness Studies*, 2(3), 200–219. https://doi:10.1093/acprof:oso/9780195311105.003.0001

Chappell, V. (1994). Descartes's compatibilism. In J. Cottingham (Ed.), *Reason, will, and sensation: Studies in Descartes's metaphysics* (pp. 177–90). Clarendon Press.

Charles, S. T., Reynolds, C. A., & Gatz, M. (2001). Age-related differences and change in positive and negative affect over 23 years. *Journal of Personality and Social Psychology*, 80(1), 136–51. https://doi.org/10.1037/0022-3514.80.1.136

Chodorow, N. (1978). *The reproduction of mothering: Psychoanalysis and the sociology of gender*. University of California Press.

Christie, D. (2005). Adolescent development. *The BMJ*, 330(7486), 301–04. https://doi: 10.1136/bmj.330.7486.301

Coates, S. W. (2004). John Bowlby and Margaret S. Mahler: Their lives and theories. *Journal of the American Psychoanalytic Association*, 52(2), 571–601. https://doi: 10.1177/00030651040520020601

Coleman, P. (1986). The past in the present: A study of elderly people's attitudes to reminiscence. *Oral History Society*, 14(1), 50–59.

Colombo, J. (2001). The development of visual attention in infancy. *Annual Review of Psychology*, 52, 337–67. https://doi: 10.1146/annurev.psych.52.1.337

Colombo, J., & Cheatham, C. L. (2006). The emergence and basis of endogenous attention in infancy and early childhood. *Advances in Child Development and Behavior*, 34, 283–322. https://doi.org/10.1016/S0065-2407(06)80010-8

Commons, M. L., & Richards, F. A. (2002). Four postformal stages. In J. Demick & C. Andreoletti (Eds.), *Handbook of adult development* (pp. 199–219). Kluwer Academic/Plenum Publishers. https://doi.org/10.1007/978-1-4615-0617-1_11 rg/10.1007/978-1-4615-0617-1_11

Conklin, H. M., Luciana, M., Hooper, C. J., & Yarger, R. S. (2007). Working memory performance in typically developing children and adolescents: Behavioral evidence of protracted frontal lobe development. *Developmental Neuropsychology*, 31(1), 103–28. https://doi: 10.1207/s15326942dn3101_6

Connolly, J., Furman, W. D., & Konarski, R. (2000). The role of peers in the emergence of heterosexual romantic relationships in adolescence. *Child Development*, 71(5), 1395–408. https://doi: 10.1111/1467-8624.00235

Cooney, T. M., Schaie, K. W., & Willis, S. L. (1988). The relationship between prior functioning on cognitive and personality dimensions and subject attrition in longitudinal research. *Journal of Gerontology: Psychological Sciences*, 43(1), P12–P17. https://doi.org/10.1093/geronj/43.1.P12

Courage, M. L., Reynolds, G. D., & Richards, J. E. (2006). Infants' attention to patterned stimuli: Developmental changes from 3 to 12 months of age. *Child Development*, 77(3), 680–95. https://doi: 10.1111/j.1467-8624.2006.00897.x

Craik, F. I. M., & Bialystok, E. (2006). Cognition through the lifespan: Mechanisms of change. *Trends in Cognitive Science*, 10(3), 131–38. https://doi.org/10.1016/j.tics.2006.01.007

Crone, E. A. (2009). Executive functions in adolescence: Inferences from brain and behavior. *Developmental Science*, 12(6), 825–30. https://doi: 10.1111/j.1467-7687.2009.00918.x

Dause, T. J., & Kirby E. D. (2019). Aging gracefully: Social engagement joins exercise and enrichment as a key lifestyle factor in resistance to age-related cognitive decline. *Neural Regeneration Research,* 14(1), 39–42. https://doi: 10.4103/1673-5374.243698

Day, K. L., & Smith, C. L. (2013). Understanding the role of private speech in children's emotion regulation. *Early Childhood Research Quarterly,* 28(2), 405–14. https://doi: 10.1016/j.ecresq.2012.10.003

De Luca, C. R., Wood, S. J., Anderson, V., Buchanan, J., Proffitt, T. M., Mahony, K., & Pantelis, C. (2003). Normative data from the Cantab. I: Development of executive function over the lifespan. *Journal of Clinical and Experimental Neuropsychology,* 25(2), 242–54. https://doi: 10.1076/jcen.25.2.242.13639

Denison, S., & Xu, F. (2014). The origins of probabilistic inference in human infants. *Cognition,* 130(3), 335–47. https://doi: 10.1016/j.cognition.2013.12.001

Dennis, N. A., & Cabeza, R. (2008). Neuroimaging of healthy cognitive aging. In F. I. M. Craik & T. A. Salthouse (Eds.), *The handbook of aging and cognition* (pp. 1–54). Psychology Press.

Depue, B. E., Banich, M. T., & Curran, T. (2006). Suppression of emotional and non-emotional content in memory: Effects of repetition of cognitive control. *Psychological Science,* 17(5), 441–47. https://doi: 10.1111/j.1467-9280.2006.01725.x

Descartes, R. (1985–1991). *The Philosophical Writings of Descartes* (Vols. 1–2, J. Cottingham, R. Stoothoff, & D. Murdoch, Eds. and Trans.; Vol. 3, J. Cottingham, R. Stoothoff, D. Murdoch, & A. Kenny, Trans.). Cambridge University Press.

Despotović, M. (2014, December). Knowledge and cognitive development in adulthood. *Andragoške studije,* 354–5415(2), 39–60. Institut za pedagogiju i andragogiju. UDK 374.7, 159.922.62

Deutscher, I. (1968). The quality of postparental life. In B. L. Neugarten (Ed.), *Middle age and aging* (pp. 263–68). University of Chicago Press.

Devine, R. T., Hughes, C., & Ribner, A. (2019). Measuring and predicting individual differences in executive functions at 14 months: A longitudinal study. *Child Development,* 90(5), e618-e636. https://doi: 10.1111/cdev.13217

Diamond, A. (1985). Development of the ability to use recall to guide action, as indicated by infants' performance on AB. *Child Development,* 56(4), 868–83. https://doi.org/10.2307/1130099

Diamond, A. (1990). The development and neural bases of memory functions as indexed by the AB and delayed response tasks in human infants and infant monkeys. *Annals of the New York Academy of Sciences,* 608(1), 267–317. https://doi.org/10.1111/j.1749-6632.1990.tb48900.

Diamond, A. (2006). The early development of executive functions. In E. Bialystok & F. I. M. Craik (Eds.), *Lifespan cognition: Mechanisms of change* (pp. 70–95). Oxford University Press.

Diamond, A., & Doar, B. (1989). The performance of human infants on a measure of frontal cortex function, the delayed response task. *Developmental Psychobiology,* 22(3), 271–94. https://doi: 10.1002/dev.420220307

Diaz, R. M., & Berk, L. E. (Eds.). (1992). *Private speech: From social interaction to self-regulation.* Erlbaum.

Diehl, M., Youngblade, L. M., Hay, E. L., & Chui, H. (2011). The development of self-representations across the lifespan. In K. L. Fingerman, C. A. Berg, J. Smith, & T. C. Antonucci (Eds.), *Handbook of life-span development* (pp. 622–46). Springer Publishing.

Dihle, A. (1982). *The theory of will in classical antiquity.* University of California Press. https://doi.org/10.1525/9780520313101

Dinnerstein, D. (1999). *The mermaid and the minotaur: Sexual arrangements and human malaise.* Other Press. (Original work published 1976)

Dirix, C. E. H., Nijhuis, J. G., Jongsma, H. W., & Hornstra, G. (2009). Aspects of fetal learning and memory. *Child Development, 80*(4), 1251–58. https://doi: 10.1111/j.1467-8624.2009.01329.x

Dunphy, D. C. (1963). The social structure of urban adolescent peer groups. *American Sociological Association, 26*(2), 230–46. https://doi.org/10.2307/2785909

Edmondson, R. (2015). *Ageing, insight and wisdom: Meaning and practice across the lifecourse.* Policy Press.

Eliade, M. (1969). *Yoga: Immortality and freedom.* Princeton University Press.

Ellis, T. B. (2009). I love you, I hate you: Toward a psychology of the Hindu *deus absconditus. International Journal of Hindu Studies, 13*(1), 1–23. https://doi:10.1007/s11407-009-9067-2

Erikson, E. (1959). Identity and the life cycle. *Psychological Issues, 1*(1), 1–171.

Erikson, E. (1963). *Childhood and society* (2nd ed.). W. W. Norton.

Erikson, E. (1968). *Identity, youth, and crisis.* W. W. Norton.

Estes, R. C., & Wilenski, H. L. (1978). Life cycle squeeze and the morale curve. *Social Problems, 25*(3), 277–92. https://doi: 10.1525/sp.1978.25.3.03a00050

Fadjukoff, P., Pulkkinen, L., & Kokko, K. (2016). Identity formation in adulthood: A longitudinal study from age 27 to 50. *Identity: An International Journal of Theory and Research, 16*(1), 8–23. https://doi.org/10.1080/15283488.2015.1121820

Fairbairn, W. R. D. (1952). A revised psychopathology of the psychoses and psychoneuroses. In W. R. D. Fairbairn, *An object-relations theory of the personality* (pp. 28–58). Basic Books.

Farroni, T., Csibra, G., Simion, F., & Johnson, M. H. (2002). Eye contact detection in humans from birth. *Proceedings of the National Academy of Sciences of the United States of America, 99*(14), 9602–5. https://doi.org/10.1073/pnas.152159999

Farroni, T., & Menon, E. (2008, December). Visual development and early brain development. *Encyclopedia of Early Childhood Development.* http://www.child-encyclopedia.com/brain/according-experts/visual-perception-and-early-brain-development

Filippetti, M. L., Johnson, M. H., Lloyd-Fox, S., Dragovic, D., & Farroni, T. (2013). Body perception in newborns. *Current Biology, 23*(23), 2413–16. https://doi: 10.1016/j.cub.2013.10.017

Fingerhut, A. W., Peplau, L. A., & Ghavami, N. (2005). A dual-identity framework for understanding lesbian experience. *Psychology of Women Quarterly, 29*(2), 129–39. https://doi.org/10.1111/j.1471-6402.2005.00175.x

Fishman, A. (2019, January 22). Video games are social spaces. *Psychology Today.* https://www.psychologytoday.com/us/blog/video-game-health/201901/video-games-are-social-spaces

Fivush, R. (1991). The social construction of personal narratives. *Merrill-Palmer Quarterly, 37*(1), 59–81.

Fivush, R. (1994). Constructing narrative, emotion, and self in parent-child conversations about the past. In U. Neisser & R. Fivush (Eds.), *The remembering self: Construction and accuracy in the self-narrative* (pp. 136–57). Cambridge University Press. https://doi.org/10.1017/CBO9780511752858.009

Fivush, R. (2011). The development of autobiographical memory. *Annual Review of Psychology, 62*, 559–82. https://doi-org.proxysb.uits.iu.edu/10.1146/annurev.psych.121208.131702

Fjell, A. M., Sneve, M. H., Grydeland, H., Storsve, A. B., & Walhovd, K. B. (2017). The disconnected brain and executive function decline in aging. *Cerebral Cortex, 27*(3), 2303–17. https://doi.org/10.1093/cercor/bhw082

Flavell, J. H., Green, F. L., Flavell, E. R., & Grossman, J. B. (1997). The development of children's knowledge of inner speech. *Child Development, 68*(1), 39–47. https://doi.org/10.2307/1131923

Fogel, A., & DeKoeyer-Laros, I. (2007). The developmental transition to secondary intersubjectivity in the second half year: A microgenetic case study. *Journal of Developmental Processes, 2*(2), 63–90.

Fowler, C. F. (1999). *Descartes on the human soul: Philosophy and the demands of Christian doctrine.* Kluwer Academic Publishers.

Franklin, A., & Davies, I. R. L. (2004). New evidence for infant colour categories. *British Journal of Developmental Psychology, 22*(3), 349–77. https://doi:10.1348/0261510041552738

Frede, M. (2011). *A free will: Origins of the notion in ancient thought* (A. A. Long, Ed.). University of California Press.

Freeman, M. (2001). When the story's over: Narrative foreclosure and the possibility of self-renewal. In M. Andrews, S. D. Sclater, C. Squire, & A. Treacher (Eds.), *Lines of narrative: Psychosocial perspectives* (pp. 81–91). Routledge.

Freud, A. (1958). Adolescence. *The Psychoanalytic Study of the Child, 13*(1), 255–78. https://doi.org/10.1080/00797308.1958.11823182

Freud, A. (1977). *The writings of Anna Freud: Vol. 2. The ego and the mechanisms of defense* (Rev. ed.). International Universities Press. (Original work published 1936)

Freud, S. (1957). Repression. In J. Strachey (Ed.), *Standard edition of the complete psychological works of Sigmund Freud* (Vol. 14). Hogarth Press. (Original work published 1915)

Freud, S. (1958). Formulations on the two principles of mental functioning. In J. Strachey (Ed.), *Standard edition of the complete psychological works of Sigmund Freud* (Vol. 12). Hogarth Press. (Original work published 1911)

Freud, S. (1959). *Inhibitions, symptoms, and anxiety.* In J. Strachey (Ed.), *Standard edition of the complete psychological works of Sigmund Freud* (Vol. 20). Hogarth Press. (Original work published 1926)

Freud, S. (1961). *The Ego and the Id.* In J. Strachey (Ed.), *Standard edition of the complete psychological works of Sigmund Freud* (Vol. 19). Hogarth Press. (Original work published 1923)

Frijters, P., & Beatton, T. (2012). The mystery of the U-shaped relationship between happiness and age. *Journal of Economic Behavior & Organization,* 82(1–2), 525–42. https://doi.org/10.1016/j.jebo.2012.03.008

Gallagher, S., & Meltzoff, A. N. (1996). The earliest sense of self and others: Merleau-Ponty and recent developmental studies. *Philosophical Psychology,* 9(2), 211–33. https://doi.org/10.1080/09515089608573181

Gallup, G. G., Jr. (1970). Chimpanzees: Self-recognition. *Science,* 167(3914), 86–87. https://doi: 10.1126/science.167.3914.86

Galvan, A., Hare, T. A., Parra, C. E., Penn, J., Voss, H., Glover, G., & Casey, B. J. (2006). Earlier development of the accumbens relative to orbitofrontal cortex might underlie risk-taking behavior in adolescents. *Journal of Neuroscience,* 26(25), 6885–92. https://doi: 10.1523/JNEUROSCI.1062-06.2006

Garon, N., Bryson, S. E., & Smith, I. M. (2008). Executive function in preschoolers: A review using an integrative framework. *Psychological Bulletin,* 134(1), 31–60. https://doi: 10.1037/0033-2909.134.1.31

Gazes, R. P., Hampton, R. R., & Lourenco, S. F. (2015). Transitive inference of social dominance by human infants. *Developmental Science,* 20(2), 1–10. https://doi.org/10.1111/desc.12367

Gergen, K. (2000). *The saturated self* (2nd ed.). Basic Books.

Gestsdottir, S., & Lerner, R. M. (2008). Positive development in adolescence: The development and role of intentional self-regulation. *Human Development,* 51(3), 202–24. https://doi.org/10.1159/000135757

Geva, S., & Fernyhough, C. (2019). A penny for your thoughts: Children's inner speech and its neuro-development. *Frontiers in Psychology,* 10, 1708. https://doi.org/10.3389/fpsyg.2019.01708

Gilmore, R. O., & Johnson, M. H. (1995). Working memory in infancy: Six-month-olds' performance on two versions of the oculomotor delayed response task. *Journal of Experimental Child Psychology,* 59(3), 397–418. https://doi.org/10.1006/jecp.1995.1019

Gonzalez-Gonzalez, N. L., Suarez, M. N., Perez-Piñero, B., Armas, H., Domenech, E., & Bartha, J. L. (2006). Persistence of fetal memory into neonatal life. *Acta Obstetricia et Gynecologica Scandinavica,* 85(10), 1160–64. https://doi.org/10.1080/00016340600855854

Grady, C. L. (2008). Cognitive neuroscience of aging. *Annals of the New York Academy of Sciences, 1124*(1), 127–44. https://doi: 10.1196/annals.1440.009

Greenberg, J. R., & Mitchell, S. A. (1983). *Object relations in psychoanalytic theory.* Harvard University Press.

Greenwood, P. M. (2007). Functional plasticity in cognitive aging: Review and hypothesis. *Neuropsychology, 21*(6), 657–73. https://doi.org/10.1037/0894-4105.21.6.657

Grof, C., & Grof, S. (Eds.). (1989). *Spiritual emergency: When personal transformation becomes a crisis.* Tarcher.

Grof, C., & Grof, S. (1990). *The stormy search for self: A guide to personal growth through transformational crisis.* Tarcher.

Grof, S. (1975). *Realms of the human unconscious.* Viking Press.

Grossman, T., & Johnson, M. H. (2010). Selective prefrontal cortex responses to joint attention in early infancy. *Biology Letters, 6*(4), 540–43. https://doi: 10.1098/rsbl.2009.1069

Guerra Meneses, A. (2015). Same-sex attraction in homophobic men: The role of impulsive processes. *Archive ouverte UNIGE.* https://archive-ouverte.unige.ch/unige:81099

Gutmann, D. (1987). *Reclaimed powers: Toward a new psychology of men and women in later life.* Basic Books.

Gutmann, D. (1997). *The human elder in nature, culture, and society.* Westview Press.

Haber, D. (2006). Life review: Implementation, theory, research, and therapy. *International Journal of Aging and Human Development, 63*(2), 153–71. doi: 10.2190/DA9G-RHK5-N9JP-T6CC

Habermas, T., & Bluck, S. (2000). Getting a life: The development of the life story in adolescence. *Psychological Bulletin, 126*(5), 748–69. https://doi.org/10.1037/0033-2909.126.5.748

Habermas, T., & Paha, C. (2001). The development of coherence in adolescents' life narratives. *Narrative Inquiry, 11*(1), 35–54. https://doi.org/10.1075/ni.11.1.02hab

Habermas, T., & Reese, E. (2015). Getting a life takes time: The development of the life story in adolescence, its precursors and consequences. *Human Development, 58*(3), 172–201. https://doi:10.1159/000437245

Habermas, T., & de Silveira, C. (2008). The development of global coherence in life narratives across adolescence: Temporal, causal, and thematic aspects. *Developmental Psychology, 44*(3), 707–21. https://doi: 10.1037/0012-1649.44.3.707

Haight, B. K. (1991). Reminiscing: The state of the art as a basis for practice. *International Journal of Aging & Human Development, 33*(1), 1–32. https://doi: 10.2190/F8YP-D4X5-MV9M-CGMH

Haith, M. M., Hazan, C., & Goodman, G. S. (1988). Expectation and anticipation of dynamic visual events by 3.5-month-old babies. *Child Development, 59*(2), 467–79. https://doi.org/10.2307/1130325

Hall, G. S. (1904). *Adolescence: Its psychology and its relation to physiology, anthropology, sociology, sex, crime, religion, and education* (Vols. 1–2). Prentice-Hall.

Haller, S. P., Cohen Kadosh, K. C., Scerif, G., & Lau, J. Y. (2015). Social anxiety disorder in adolescence: How developmental cognitive neuroscience findings may shape understanding and interventions for psychopathology. *Developmental Cognitive Neuroscience, 13*, 11–20. https:// doi: 10.1016/j.dcn.2015.02.002

Harada, C. N., Natelson, L., Marissa. C., & Triebel, K. L. (2013). Normal cognitive aging. *Clinics in Geriatric Medicine, 29*(4), 737–52. https://doi.org/10.1016/j.cger.2013.07.002

Hardy, F. (1983). *Viraha-Bhakti: The early history of Krsna devotion in South India.* Oxford University Press.

Hare, T. A., Tottenham, N., Galvan, A., Voss, H. U., Glover, G. H., & Casey, B. J. (2008). Biological substrates of emotional reactivity and regulation in adolescence during an emotional go-nogo task. *Biological Psychiatry, 63*(10), 927–34. https://doi: 10.1016/j.biopsych.2008.03.015

Harris, M., & Chasin, J. (2004). Developments in early lexical comprehension: A comparison of parental report and controlled testing. In J. Oates & A. Grayson (Eds.), *Cognitive and language development in children.* Blackwell.

Harter, S. (2012). *The construction of the self: Developmental and sociocultural foundations* (2nd ed.). Guilford Press.

Hartmann, H. (1958). *Ego psychology and the problem of adaptation* (D. Rapaport, Trans.). International Universities Press. (Original work published 1939)

Hartshorne, J. K., & Germine, L. T. (2015). When does cognitive functioning peak? The asynchronous rise and fall of different cognitive abilities across the life span. *Psychological Science, 26*(4), 433–43. https://doi: 10.1177/0956797614567339

Haugeland, J. (1981). Semantic engines: An introduction to mind design. In J. Haugeland (Ed.), *Mind design: Philosophy, psychology, artificial intelligence.* MIT Press.

Haugeland, J. (2002). Authentic intentionality. In S. Matthias (Ed.), *Computationalism: New directions.* MIT Press.

Heidegger, M. (1971). *Poetry, language, thought* (A. Hofstadter, Trans.). Harper & Row.

Heidegger, M. (1988). *The basic problems of phenomenology* (Rev. ed.) (A. Hofstadter, Trans.). Indiana University Press. (Original work published 1975)

Herbert, C., & Sütterlin, S. (2012, August 1). Do not respond! Doing the think/no-think and go/no-go tasks concurrently leads to memory impairment of unpleasant items during later recall. *Frontiers of Psychology, 3*(269), 1–6. https://doi.org/10.3389/fpsyg.2012.00269

Hochmann, J.-R., & Kouider, S. (2022). Acceleration of information processing en route to perceptual awareness in infancy. *Current Biology, 32*(5), 1206–10.e3. https://doi: 10.1016/j.cub.2022.01.029.

Hood, B. M., & Atkinson, J. (1993). Disengaging visual attention in the infant and adult. *Infant Behavior and Development, 16*(4), 405–22. https://doi.org/10.1016/0163-6383(93)80001-O

Hopcke, R. H. (1989). *Jung, Jungians & homosexuality.* Shambhala.

Horn, J. L. (1980). Concepts of intellect in relation to learning and adult development. *Intelligence, 4*(4), 285–317. https://doi.org/10.1016/0160-2896(80)900 25-2

Hubley, P., & Trevarthen, C. (1979). Sharing a task in infancy. In L. C. Uzgiris (Ed.), *Social interaction during infancy: New directions for child development* (Vol. 4, pp. 57–80). Jossey-Bass.

Huizinga, M., Dolan, C. V., & van der Molen, M. W. (2006). Age-related change in executive function: Developmental trends and a latent variable analysis. *Neuropsychologia, 44*(11), 2017–36. https://doi.org/10.1016/j. neuropsychologia.2006.01.010

Hulbert, J. C., & Anderson, M. C. (2018). What doesn't kill you makes you stronger: Psychological trauma and its relationship to enhanced memory control. *Journal of Experimental Psychology: General, 147*(12), 1931–49. https://doi: 10.1037/xge0000461

Hume, D. (1888). *A treatise of human nature* (L. A. Selby-Bigge, Ed.). Clarendon Press. (Original work published 1739–1740)

Hurd, N. M., & Zimmerman, M. (2011). Role models. In R. J. R. Levesque (Ed.), *Encyclopedia of adolescence.* Springer. https://doi.org/10.1007/978-1-4419-1695-2_230

Irigaray, L. (1985a). *Speculum of the other woman* (G. G. Gill, Trans.). Cornell University Press. (Original work published 1974)

Irigaray, L. (1985b). *This sex which is not one* (C. Porter, Trans.). Cornell University Press. (Original work published 1977)

Irigaray, L. (1991a). Questions to Emmanuel Levinas: On the divinity of love. In R. Bernasconi & S. Critchley (Eds.), *Re-reading Levinas* (pp. 109–18). Indiana University Press.

Irigaray, L. (1991b). The bodily encounter with the mother. In M. Whitford (Ed.), *The Irigaray reader* (pp. 34–46). Basil Blackwell. (Original work published 1981)

Irigaray, L. (1991c). "Women-mothers, the silent substratum." In M. Whitford (Ed.), *The Irigaray reader* (pp. 47–52). Basil Blackwell. (Original work published 1981)

Irigaray, L. (1995). The question of the other. *Yale French Studies, 87,* 7–19. https://doi.org/10.2307/2930321

Jackson-Webb, F. (2013). *Babies develop conscious perception from five months of age.* The Conversation. https://theconversation.com/babies-develop-conscious-perception-from-five-months-of-age-13588

James, W. (1950). *The principles of psychology* (Vols. 1–2). Dover Publications. (Original work published 1890)

Jayasekera, M. Y. (2010). *The will in Descartes' thought* [Unpublished doctoral dissertation]. University of Michigan. https://deepblue.lib.umich.edu/bitstream/handle/2027.42/78972/mjayas_1.pdf;sequence=1

Jensen, A. R. (2006). *Clocking the mind: Mental chronometry and individual differences.* Elsevier.

Jensen, F. E., & Nutt, A. E. (2015). *The teenage brain: A neuroscientist's survival guide to raising adolescents and young adults.* HarperCollins.

Johnson, M. H. (1995). The inhibition of automatic saccades in early infancy. *Developmental Psychobiology, 28*(5), 281–91. https://doi: 10.1002/dev.420280504

Johnson, M. K., & Mollborn, S. (2009). Growing up faster, feeling older: Hardship in childhood and adolescence. *Social Psychology Quarterly, 72*(1), 39–60. https://doi.org/10.1177/019027250907200105

Johnson, S. P. (2010). How infants learn about the visual world. *Cognitive Science, 34*(7), 1158–84. https://doi: 10.1111/j.1551-6709.2010.01127.x

Jones, S. J. (2009). The development of imitation in infancy. *Philosophical Transactions of the Royal Society B, 364*(1528), 2325–35. https://doi: 10.1098/rstb.2009.0045

Joorman, J., Hertel, P. T., Brozovich, F., & Gotlib, I. H. (2005). Remembering the good, forgetting the bad: Intentional forgetting of emotional material in depression. *Journal of Abnormal Psychology, 114*(4), 640–48. https://doi: 10.1037/0021-843X.114.4.640

Jung, C. G. (1969a). On the nature of the psyche (R. F. C. Hull, Trans.). In H. Read, M. Fordham, & G. Adler (Eds.), *The collected works of C. G. Jung: Vol. 8. Structure and dynamics of the psyche* (2nd ed., pp. 159–234). Princeton University Press. (Original work published 1954) https://doi.org/10.1515/9781400850952.159

Jung, C. G. (1969b). The psychological foundations of belief in spirits (R. F. C. Hull, Trans.). In H. Read, M. Fordham, & G. Adler (Eds.), *The collected works of C. G. Jung: Vol. 8. Structure and dynamics of the psyche* (2nd ed., pp. 301–18). Princeton University Press. (Original work published 1948) https://doi.org/10.1515/9781400850952.300

Jung, C. G. (1970). The love problem of a student (R. F. C. Hull, Trans.). In H. Read, M. Fordham, & G. Adler (Eds.), *The collected works of C. G. Jung: Vol. 10. Civilization in transition* (2nd ed., pp. 97–112). Princeton University Press. (Original work published 1928) https://doi.org/10.1515/9781400850976.97

Kail, R. V., & Ferrer, E. (2007). Processing speed in childhood and adolescence: Longitudinal models for examining developmental change. *Child Development, 78*(6), 1760–70. https://doi: 10.1111/j.1467-8624.2007.01088.x

Kant, I. (1998). *Critique of Pure Reason* (P. Guyer & A. W. Wood, Trans.). Cambridge University Press. (Original work published in its second edition in 1787)

Kenward, B., Sholtons, S., Holmberg, J., Johansson, A., & Gredebäck, G. (2009). Goal directedness and decision making in Infants. *Developmental Psychology, 45*(3), 809–19. https://doi: 10.1037/a0014076

Kernberg, O. (1976). *Object-relations theory and clinical psychoanalysis.* New York: Jason Aronson.

Kernberg, O. (1987). The dynamic unconscious and the self. In R. Stern (Ed.), *Theories of the unconscious and theories of the self.* Analytic Press.

Kessler, R. C., Berglund, P., Demler, O., Jin, R., Merikangas, K. R., & Walters, E. E. (2005). Lifetime prevalence and age-of-onset distributions of DSM-IV disorders in the National Comorbidity Survey Replication. *Archives of General Psychology,* 62(6), 593–602. https:// doi: 10.1001/archpsyc.62.6.593

Kim, J. E., & Moen, P. (2001). Moving into retirement: Preparation and transitions in late midlife. In M. E. Lachman (Ed.), *Handbook of midlife development.* John Wiley & Sons.

Klinnert, M. D. (1984). The regulation of infant behavior by maternal facial expression. *Infant Behavior and Development,* 7(4), 447–65. https://doi.org/10.1016/S0163-6383(84)80005-3

Klossek, U. M. H., Russel, J., & Dickinson, A. (2008). The control of instrumental action following outcome devaluation in young children aged between 1 and 4 years. *Journal of Experimental Psychology: General,* 137(1), 39–51. https:// doi: 10.1037/0096-3445.137.1.39

Klossek, U. M. H., Yu, S., & Dickinson, A. (2011). Choice and goal-directed behavior in preschool children. *Learning and Behavior,* 39(4), 350–57. https:// doi.org/10.3758/s13420-011-0030-x

Kouider, S., Stahlhut, C., Gelskov, S. V., Barbosa, L. S., Dutat, M., de Gardell, V., Christophe, A., Dahaene, S., & Dahaene-Lambertz, G. (2013). A neural marker of perceptual consciousness in infants. *Science,* 340(6130), 376–80. https://doi: 10.1126/science.1232509

Kristeva, J. (1984). The mirror and castration: Positing the subject as absent from the signifier (M. Waller, Trans.). In J. Kristeva, *Revolution in Poetic Language* (pp. 46–51). (Original work published 1974)

Kristeva, J. (2002a). Julia Kristeva in conversation with Rosalind Coward. In K. Oliver (Ed.), *The portable Kristeva* (pp. 333–50). Columbia University Press. (Original work published 1984)

Kristeva, J. (2002b). Interview with Elaine Hoffman Baruch on feminism in the United States and France. In K. Oliver (Ed.), *The portable Kristeva* (pp. 371–82). Columbia University Press. (Original work published 1980)

Kristeva, J. (2010). *Hatred and forgiveness* (J. Herman, Trans.). Columbia University Press.

Kroger, J. (2015). Identity development through adulthood: The move toward "wholeness." In K. C. McLean & M. Syed (Eds.), *The Oxford handbook of identity development* (pp. 65–80). Oxford University Press. Available online at https://www.researchgate.net/publication/275337420_Identity_development_through_adulthood_The_move_toward_wholeness

Kroger, J. (2017). Identity development in adolescence and adulthood. *Developmental Psychology,* 18(3), 341–58. https://doi:10.1093/acrefore/9780190236557.013.54

Kroger, J., & Marcia, J. E. (2011). The identity statuses: Origins, meanings, and interpretations. In S. J. Schwartz, K. Luyckx, & V. L. Vignoles (Eds.), *Handbook of identity theory and research* (Vol. 1). Springer.

Kubicek, B., Korunka, C., Raymo, J. M., & Hoonakker, P. (2011). Psychological well-being in retirement: The ethics of personal and gendered contextual resources. *Journal of Occupational Health Psychology,* 16(2), 230–46. https:// doi:10.1037/a0022334

Laaksonen, S. (2018). A research note: Happiness by age is more complex than U-shaped. *Journal of Happiness Studies,* 19(2), 471–82. https://doi.org/10.1007/s10902-016-9830-1

Lacan, J. (2006). The mirror stage as formative of the *I* function as revealed in psychoanalytic experience (B. Frank, Trans.). In J. Lacan, *Écrits* (pp. 75–81). W. W. Norton. (Original work published 1949)

Lacey, H. P., Smith, D. M., & Ubel, P. A. (2006). Hope I die before I get old: Mispredicting happiness across the adult lifespan. *Journal of Happiness Studies,* 7(2), 167–82. https://doi.org/10.1007/s10902-005-2748-7

Lambert, A. J., Good, K. S., & Kirk, I. J. (2010). Testing the repression hypothesis: Effects of emotional valence on memory suppression in the think—no think task. *Consciousness and Cognition,* 19(1), 281–93. https://doi: 10.1016/j.concog.2009.09.004

Lanza, J. R., & Flahive, L. K. (2008). *LS guide to communication milestones.* LinguiSystems.

Lavelli, M., & Fogel, A. (2005). Developmental changes in the relationship between the infant's attention and emotion during early face-to-face communication: The 2-month transition. *Developmental Psychology,* 41(1), 265–80. https://doi.org/10.1037/0012-1649.41.1.265

Leigh, E., & Clark, D. M. (2018). Understanding social anxiety disorder in adolescents and improving treatment outcomes: Applying the cognitive model of Clark and Wells. *Clinical Child and Family Psychology Review,* 21(3), 388–414. https://doi.org/10.1007/s10567-018-0258-5

Lenhart, A. (2015, August 6). Teens, technology, and friendships. Pew Research Center. https://www.pewresearch.org/internet/2015/08/06/teens-technology-and-friendships/

Lewis, M., & Brooks-Gunn, J. (1979). *Social cognition and the acquisition of self.* Plenum.

Lewis, M. I., & Butler, R. N. (1974). Life-review therapy: Putting memories to work in individual and group psychotherapy. *Geriatrics,* 29(11), 165–73.

Lillevoll, K. R., Kroger, J., & Martinussen, M. (2013). Identity status and anxiety: A meta-analysis. *Identity,* 13(3), 214–27. doi:10.1080/15283488.2013.799432

Liu, C., Solis, S. L., Jensen, H., Hopkins, E. J., Neale, D., Zosh, J. M., Hirsh-Pasek, K., & Whitebread, D. (2017, November). Neuroscience and learning through play: A review of the evidence. The LEGO Foundation, DK. https://doi: 10.13140/RG.2.2.11789.84963

Lowenthal, M. F., Thurnher, M., & Chiriboga, D. (1975). *Four stages of life.* Jossey-Bass.

Luciana, M., Collins, P. F., Olson, E. A., & Schissel, A. M. (2009). Tower of London performance in healthy adolescents: The development of planning skills and associations with self-reported inattention and impulsivity. *Developmental Neuropsychology,* 34(4), 461–75. https://doi: 10.1080/87565640902964540

Luna, B., Garver, K. E., Urban T. A., Lazar, N. A., & Sweeney, J. A. (2004). Maturation of cognitive processes from late childhood to adulthood. *Child Development,* 75(5), 1357–72. https://doi: 10.1111/j.1467-8624.2004.00745.x

Luyckx, K., Schwartz, S. J., Goossens, L., Soenens, B., & Beyers, W. (2008). Developmental typologies of identity formation and adjustment in female emerging adults: A latent class growth analysis approach. *Journal of Research on Adolescence,* 18(4), 595–619. https://doi.org/10.1111/j.1532-7795.2008.00 573.x

MacInnis, C. C., & Hodson, G. (2013). Is homophobia associated with an implicit same-sex attraction? *Journal of Sex Research,* 50(8), 777–85. https://doi: 10.1080/00224499.2012.690111

Mahler, M. S., Pine, F., & Bergman, A. (1975). *The psychological birth of the human infant.* Basic Books.

Maister, L., Tang, T., & Tsakiris, M. (2017, August 8). Neurobehavioral evidence of interoceptive sensitivity in early infancy. https://doi. 10.7554/eLife.25318

Mandler, J. M. (2000). Perceptual and conceptual processes in infancy. *Journal of Cognition and Development,* 1(1), 3–36. https://doi.org/10.1207/ S15327647JCD0101N_2

Mandler, J. M. (2004). Thought before language. *Trends in Cognitive Sciences,* 8(11), 508–13. https://doi: 10.1016/j.tics.2004.09.004

Mandler, J. M. (2007). On the origins of the conceptual system. *American Psychologist,* 62(8), 738–51. https://doi: 10.1037/0003-066X.62.8.741

Mandler, J. M. (2008). On the birth and growth of concepts. *Philosophical Psychology,* 21(2), 207–30. https://doi: 10.1080/09515080801980179

Mandler, J. M., & McDonough, L. (1996). Drinking and driving don't mix: Inductive generalization in infancy. *Cognition,* 59(3), 307–35. https://doi. org/10.1016/0010-0277(95)00696-6

Mandler, J. M., & McDonough, L. (1998). On developing a knowledge base in infancy. *Developmental Psychology,* 34(6), 1274–88. https://doi: 10.1037//0012-1649.34.6.1274

Mandler, J. M., & McDonough, L. (2000). Advancing downward to the basic level. *Journal of Cognition and Development,* 1(4), 379–403. https://doi: 10.1207/ S15327647JCD0104_02

Marchand, H. (2002). Some reflections on postformal stage. *Behavioral Development Bulletin,* 11(1), 39–46. http://dx.doi.org/10.1037/h0100490

Marcia, J. E. (1966). Development and validation of ego-identity status. *Journal of Personality and Social Psychology,* 3(5), 551–58. https://doi.org/10.1037/ h0023281

Marcia, J. E. (1980). Identity in adolescence. In J. Adelson (Ed.), *Handbook of adolescent psychology* (pp. 159–87). Wiley.

Matuz, T., Rathinaswamy, B., Govindan, H. P., Siegel, E. R., Muenssinger, J., Murphy, P., Ware, M., Curtis, L. L., & Eswaran, H. (2012). Habituation of visual evoked responses in neonates and fetuses: A MEG study. *Developmental Cognitive Neuroscience, 2*(3), 303–16. https://doi.org/10.1016/j.dcn.2012.03.001

Mayfield, W. (2001). The development of an internalized homonegativity inventory for gay men. *Journal of Homosexuality, 41*(2), 53–75. https://doi: 10.1300/J082v41n02_04

McAdams, D. P. (1985). *Power, intimacy, and the life story.* Dorsey Press.

McAdams, D. P. (1993). *The stories we live by: Personal myths and the making of the self.* William Morrow.

McAdams, D. P. (2014). The life narrative at midlife. *New Directions for Child and Adolescent Development,* (145), 57–69. https://doi.org/10.1002/cad.20067

McAdams, D. P., Bauer, J. J., Sakaeda, A. R., Anyidoho, N. A., Machado, M. A., Magrino-Failla, K., White, K. W., & Pals, J. L. (2006). Continuity and change in the life story: A longitudinal study of autobiographical memories in emerging adulthood. *Journal of Personality, 74*(5), 1371–400. https://doi: 10.1111/j.1467-6494.2006.00412.x

McCrae, R. R., & Costa, P. T. (1990). *Personality in adulthood.* Guilford.

McDevitt, J. B., & Mahler, M. S. (1980). Object constancy, individuality, and internalization. In S. I. Greenspan & G. H. Pollock (Eds.), *The course of life: Psychoanalytic contributions toward understanding personality development: Vol. I. Infancy and early childhood* (pp. 407–23). Mental Health Study Center, NIMH.

McFall, P. G., McDermott, K. L., & Dixon, R. A. (2019). Modifiable risk factors discriminate memory trajectories in non-demented aging: Precision factors and targets for promoting healthier brain aging and preventing dementia. *Journal of Alzheimer's Disease, 70*(S1), S101–S108. https://doi:10.3233/JAD-180571

Meier, B. P., Robinson, M. D., Gaither, G. A., & Heinert, N. J. (2006). A secret attraction or defensive loathing? Homophobia, defense, and implicit cognition. *Journal of Research in Personality, 40*(4), 377–94. https://:10.1016/j.jrp.2005.01.007.

Meltzoff, A. N. (2005). Imitation and other minds: The "like me" hypothesis. In S. Hurley & N. Chater (Eds.), *Perspectives on imitation: From neuroscience to social science: Vol. 2. Imitation, human development, and culture.* MIT Press.

Meltzoff, A. N. (2007). The "like me" framework for recognizing and becoming an intentional agent. *Acta Psychologica, 124*(1), 26–43. https://doi: 10.1016/j.actpsy.2006.09.005

Meltzoff, A. N., & Brooks, R. (2007). Intersubjectivity before language: Three windows on preverbal sharing. In S. Bråten (Ed.), *On being moved: From mirror neurons to empathy* (pp. 149–74). John Benjamins.

Meltzoff, A. N., & Moore, M. K. (1977). Imitation of facial and manual gestures by human neonates. *Science,* 198(4312), 75–78. https://doi.org/10.1126/science.198.4312.75

Meltzoff, A. N., & Moore, M. K. (1983). Newborn infants imitate adult facial gestures. *Child Development, 54*(3), 702–9. https://doi.org/10.2307/1130058

Meltzoff, A. N., & Moore, M. K. (1997). Explaining facial imitation: A theoretical model. *Early Development and Parenting*, 6(3–4), 179–92. https://doi.org/10.1002/(SICI)1099-0917(199709/12)6:3/4<179::AID-EDP157>3.0.CO;2-R

Meltzoff, A. N., & Moore, M. K. (1998a). Infant intersubjectivity: Broadening the dialogue to include, imitation, identity and intention. In S. Bråten (Ed.), *Intersubjective communication and emotion in early ontogeny* (pp. 47–62). Cambridge University Press.

Meltzoff, A. N., & Moore, M. K. (1998b). Object representation, identity, and the paradox of early permanence: Steps toward a new framework. *Infant Behavior & Development*, 21(2), 201–35. https://doi.org/10.1016/S0163-6383(98)90003-0

Menn, S. (1998). *Descartes and Augustine*. Cambridge University Press.

Merleau-Ponty, M. (1962). *Phenomenology of Perception*. Routledge & Kegan Paul. (Original work published 1945)

Messinger, D. S., & Fogel, A. (2007). The interactive development of social smiling. In R. V. Kail (Ed.), *Advances in child development and behavior* (Vol. 35, pp. 327–66). Elsevier Academic Press.

Miller, S. E., & Marcovitch, S. (2015). Examining executive function in the second year of life: Coherence, stability, and relations to joint attention and language. *Developmental Psychology*, 51(1), 101–14. https://doi.org/10.1037/a0038359

Miyake, A., & Friedman, N. P. (2012). The nature and organization of individual differences in executive functions: Four general conclusions. *Current Directions in Psychological Science*, 21(1), 8–14. https://doi: 10.1177/0963721411429458

Miyake, A., Friedman, N. P., Emerson, M. J., & Witzki, A. H. (2000). The unity and diversity of executive functions and their contributions to complex "frontal lobe" tasks: A latent variable analysis. *Cognitive Psychology*, 41(1), 49–100. https://doi: 10.1006/cogp.1999.0734

Moore, M. K., & Meltzoff, A. N. (2009). Numerical identity and the development of object permanence. In S. P. Johnson (Ed.), *Neoconstructivism: The new science of cognitive development* (pp. 61–83). Oxford University Press.

Mumme, D. L., Fernald, A., & Herrera, C. (1996). Infants' responses to facial and vocal emotional signals in a social referencing paradigm. *Child Development*, 67(6), 3219–37. https://doi.org/10.2307/1131775

Munakata, Y., & Stedron, J. M. (2002). Memory for hidden objects in early infancy. In J. W. Fagen & H. Hayne (Eds.), *Advances in infancy research* (Vol. 2, pp. 25–69). Erlbaum.

Mutz, J., & Amir-Homayoun, J. (2017). Exploring the neural correlates of dream phenomenology and altered states of consciousness during sleep. *Neuroscience of Consciousness*, 2017(1), 1–12. https://doi.org/10.1093/nc/nix009

Nagy, E., & Molnar, P. (2004). Homo imitans or homo provocans? Human imprinting model of neonatal imitation. *Infant Behavior & Development*, 27(1), 54–63. https://doi.org/10.1016/j.infbeh.2003.06.004

National Park Service. (2022). *Yellowstone: Current geyser activity.* https://www.nps. gov/yell/planyourvisit/geyser-activity.htm

Nelson, K. (1993). Events, narratives, memory: What develops? In C. A. Nelson (Ed.), *Memory and affect in development: Minnesota symposium on child psychology* (Vol. 26, pp. 1–24). Erlbaum.

Nelson, K. (2003). Narrative and self, myth and memory: Emergence of the cultural self. In R. Fivush & C. A. Haden (Eds.), *Autobiographical memory and the construction of a narrative self: Developmental and cultural perspectives* (pp. 3–28). Erlbaum.

Neugarten, B. L., & Datan, N. (1974). The middle years. In S. Arieti (Ed.), *American handbook of psychiatry: Vol. 1. The foundations of psychiatry* (pp. 135–59). Basic Books.

Nietzsche, F. (1966). Beyond good and evil: Prelude to a philosophy of the future (W. Kaufmann, Trans.). Vintage Books. (Original work published 1886)

Nir, Y., & Tononi, G. (2010). Dreaming and the brain: From phenomenology to neurophysiology. *Trends in Cognitive Science,* 14(2), 88–100. https://doi. org/10.1016/j.tics.2009.12.001

Oakes, L. M. (2009). Categorization skills and concepts. In J. B. Benson & M. M. Haith (Eds.), *Language, memory, and cognition in infancy and early childhood* (pp. 91–101). Academic Press.

Offer, D., Ostrov, E., & Howard, K. I. (1981). *The adolescent: A psychological self-portrait.* Basic Books.

Oliver, K. (Ed.). (2002). *The portable Kristeva.* Columbia University Press.

O'Neill, W. (1966). Augustine's influence upon Descartes and the mind/body problem. *Revue d'Etudes Augustiniennes et Patristiques,* 12(3–4), 255–61. https:// doi.org/10.1484/J.REA.5.104125

Oostenbroek, J., Suddendorf, T., Nielsen, M., Redshaw, J., Kennedy-Costantini, S., Davis, J., Clark, S., & Slaughter, V. (2016). Comprehensive longitudinal study challenges the existence of neonatal imitation in humans. *Current Biology,* 26(10), 1334–38. https://doi: 10.1016/j.cub.2016.03.047

Orth, U., Erol, R. Y., & Luciano, E. C. (2018). Development of self-esteem from age 4 to 94 years: A meta-analysis of longitudinal studies. *Psychological Bulletin,* 144(10), 1045–80. https://doi.org/10.1037/bul0000161

Orth, U, Robins, R., & Widaman, K. (2012). Life-span development of self-esteem and its effects on important life outcomes. *Journal of Personality and Social Psychology,* 102(6):1271–88. doi:10.1037/a0025558

Orth, U., Trzesniewski, K. H., & Robins, R. W. (2010). Self-esteem development from young adulthood to old age: A cohort-sequential longitudinal study. *Journal of Personality and Social Psychology,* 98(4), 645–58. http://doi: 10.1037/ a0018769

Otgaar, H., Howe, M. L., Patihis, L., Merckelbach, H., Lynn, S. J., Lilienfeld, S. O., & Loftus, E. F. (2019). The return of the repressed: The persistent and problematic claims of long-forgotten trauma. *Perspectives on Psychological Science,* 14(6), 1072–95. https://doi.org/10.1177/1745691619862306

Otto, R. (1950). *The idea of the holy* (2nd ed.) (J. W. Harvey, Trans.). Oxford University Press. (Original work published 1917)

Owen, K., & Barnes, C. (2021). The development of categorization in early childhood: A review. *Early Child Development and Care,* 191(1), 13–20. https://doi:10.1080/03004430.2019.1608193

Park, D. C., & Reuter-Lorenz, P. A. (2009). The adaptive brain: Aging and neurocognitive scaffolding. *Annual Review of Psychology,* 60(1), 173–96. https://doi:10.1146/annurev.psych.59.103006.093656

Parker, R. A., & Aldwin, C. M. (1997). Do aspects of gender identity change from early to middle adulthood? Disentangling age, cohort, and period effects. In M. Lachman & J. James (Eds.), *Multiple paths of midlife development.* University of Chicago Press.

Piaget, J. (1954). *The construction of reality in the child* (M. Cook, Trans.). Basic Books. https://doi.org/10.1037/11168-000

Pickhardt, C. E. (2010, September 6). Adolescence and self-esteem: Teach adolescents how to maintain healthy self-esteem. *Psychology Today.* https://www.psychologytoday.com/us/blog/surviving-your-childs-adolescence/201009/adolescence-and-self-esteem

Pine, F. (2004). Mahler's concepts of "symbiosis" and separation-individuation: Revisited, reevaluated, refined. *Journal of the American Psychoanalytic Association,* 52(2), 511–33. https://doi: 10.1177/00030651040520021001

Place, U. T. (1956). Is consciousness a brain process? *British Journal of Psychology,* 47(1), 44–50. https://doi.org/10.1111/j.2044-8295.1956.tb00560.x

Povinelli, D. J., Landau, K. R., & Perilloux, H. K. (1996). Self-recognition in young children using delayed versus live feedback: Evidence of a developmental asynchrony. *Child Development,* 67(4), 1540–54. https://doi.org/10.2307/1131717

Povinelli, D. J., Landry, A. M., Theall, L. A., Clark, B. R., & Castille, C. M. (1999). Development of young children's understanding that the recent past is causally bound to the present. *Developmental Psychology,* 35(6), 1426–39. https://doi.org/10.1037/0012-1649.35.6.1426

Povinelli, D. J., & Simon B. B. (1998). Young children's understanding of briefly versus extremely delayed images of the self: Emergence of the autobiographical stance. *Developmental Psychology,* 34(1), 188–94. https://doi.org/10.1037/0012-1649.34.1.188

Quinn, P. C., & Eimas, P. D. (1996). Perceptual organization and categorization in young infants. In C. Rovee-Collier & L. P. Lipsitt (Eds.), *Advances in infancy research* (Vol. 10, pp. 1–36). Ablex.

Rajah, M. N., & D'Esposito, M. (2005). Region-specific changes in prefrontal function with age: A review of PET and fMRI studies on working and episodic memory. *Brain,* 128(9), 1964–83. https://doi.org/10.1093/brain/awh608

Rankin, J. L., Lane, D. J., Gibbons, F. X., & Gerrard, M. (2004). Adolescent self-consciousness: Longitudinal age changes and gender differences in two cohorts. *Journal of Research on Adolescence,* 14(1), 1–21. https://doi.org/10.1111/j.1532-7795.2004.01401001.x

Rauch, J. (2014, December). The real roots of midlife crisis. *Atlantic.* https://www.theatlantic.com/magazine/archive/2014/12/the-real-roots-of-midlife-crisis/382235/

Rauch, J. (2018). *The happiness curve: Why life gets better after 50.* St. Martin's Press.

Reese, E., Haden, C. A., Baker-Ward, L., Bauer, P., Fivush, R., & Ornstein, P. A. (2011). Coherence of personal narratives across the lifespan: A multidimensional model and coding method. *Cognitive Development,* 12(4), 424–62. doi: 10.1080/15248372.2011.587854

Reid, T. (1788). *Essays on the active powers of man.* J. Bell and G. G. J. & J. Robinson.

Reitzes, D. C., & Mutran, E. J. (2006). Lingering identities in retirement. *The Sociological Quarterly,* 47(2), 333–59. https://doi.org/10.1111/j.1533-8525.2006.00048.x

Repacholi, B. M., Meltzoff, A. N., Rowe, H., & Toub, T. S. (2014). Infant, control thyself: Infants' integration of multiple social cues to regulate their imitative behavior. *Cognitive Development,* 32, 46–57. https://doi.org/10.1016/j.cogdev.2014.04.004

Reynolds, G. D., & Romano, A. C. (2016). The development of attention systems and working memory in infancy. *Frontiers in Neuroscience,* 10, article 15. https://doi.org/10.3389/fnsys.2016.00015

Reznick, J. S., Morrow, J. D., Goldman, B. D., & Snyder, J. (2004). The onset of working memory in infants. *Infancy,* 6(1), 145–54. https://doi: 10.1207/s15327078in0601_7

Richards, J. E. (1985). The development of sustained visual attention in infants from 14 to 26 weeks of age. *Psychophysiology,* 22(4), 409–16. https://doi.org/10.1111/j.1469-8986.1985.tb01625.x

Richards, J. E. (1989). Development and stability in visual sustained attention in 14, 20, and 26 week old infants. *Psychophysiology,* 26(4), 422–30. https://doi.org/10.1111/j.1469-8986.1989.tb01944.x

Richards, J. E. (1997). Effects of attention on infants' preference for briefly exposed visual stimuli in paired-comparison recognition-memory paradigm. *Developmental Psychology,* 33(1), 22–31. https://doi.org/10.1037/0012-1649.33.1.22

Rickless, S. (2020). Locke on freedom. In E. N. Zalta (Ed.), *The Stanford encyclopedia of philosophy.* (Spring 2020 ed.). Stanford University. https://plato.stanford.edu/archives/spr2020/entries/locke-freedom/

Robins, R. W., Trzesniewski, K. H., Tracy, J. L, Potter, J., & Gosling, S. D. (2002). Global self-esteem across the life span. *Psychology and Aging,* 17(3), 423–34. https://doi.org/10.1037/0882-7974.17.3.423

Rochat, P. (2001). *The infant's world.* Harvard University Press.

Rochat, P. (2003). Five levels of self-awareness as they unfold early in life. *Consciousness and Cognition,* 12(4), 717–31. https://doi:10.1016/S1053-8100(03)00081-3

Rochat, P. (2004). Emerging co-awareness. In G. Bremner & A. Slater (Eds.), *Theories of infant development* (pp. 258–83). Blackwell Publishing. https://doi.org/10.1002/9780470752180.ch10

Rochat, P. (2007). Intentional action arises from early reciprocal exchanges. *Acta Psychologica,* 124(1), 8–25. https://doi.org/10.1016/j.actpsy.2006.09.004

Rochat, P. (2012). Primordial sense of embodied self-unity. In V. Slaughter & C. A. Brownell (Eds.), *Early development of body representations* (pp. 3–18). Cambridge University Press.

Rochat, P. (2019, March 28). Self-unity as ground zero of learning and development. *Frontiers in Psychology.* https://doi.org/10.3389/fpsyg.2019.00414

Rochat, P., & Hespos, S. J. (1997). Differential rooting response by neonates: Evidence for an early sense of self. *Early Development and Parenting,* 6(3–4), 105–12. https://doi: 10.1002/(SICI)1099-0917(199709/12)6:3/43.0.CO;2-U

Rochat, P., & Passos-Ferreira, C. (2008). From imitation to reciprocation and mutual recognition. In J. A. Pineda (Ed.), *Mirror neurons systems: The role of mirroring processes in social cognition* (pp. 191–212). Humana/Springer.

Rochat, P., & Passos-Ferreira, C. (2009). Three levels of intersubjectivity in early development. In A. Carassa, F. Morganti, & G. Riva (Eds.), *Enacting intersubjectivity: Paving the way for a dialogue between cognitive science, social cognition, and neuroscience* (pp. 173–90). da Larioprint.

Rosenberg, S. D., Rosenberg, H. J., & Farrell, M. P. (1999). The midlife crisis revisited. In S. L. Willis & J. D. Reid (Eds.). *Life in the middle: Psychological and social development in middle age* (pp. 47–73). Academic Press.

Ross, C. E., & Drentea, P. (1998). Consequences of retirement activities for distress and the sense of personal control. *Journal of Health and Social Behavior,* 39(4), 317–34. https://doi.org/10.2307/2676341

Ryeng, M. S., Kroger, J., & Martinussen, M. (2013). Identity status and self-esteem: A meta-analysis. *Identity,* 13(3), 201–13. https://doi.org/10.1080/15283488.2013.799431

Ryle, G. (1949). *The concept of mind.* Hutchinson's University Library.

SAHRC [State Adolescent Health Resource Center]. (2013a, June 17). Understanding adolescence: Early adolescence. http://www.amchp.org/programsandtopics/AdolescentHealth/projects/Documents/SAHRC%20AYADevelopment%20EarlyAdolescence.pdf

SAHRC [State Adolescent Health Resource Center]. (2013b, June 17). Understanding adolescence: Middle adolescence. http://www.amchp.org/programsandtopics/AdolescentHealth/projects/Documents/SAHRC%20AYADevelopment%20MiddleAdolescence.pdf

SAHRC [State Adolescent Health Resource Center]. (2013c, June 17). Understanding adolescence: Late adolescence. http://www.amchp.org/programsandtopics/AdolescentHealth/projects/Documents/SAHRC%20AYADevelopment%20LateAdolescentYoungAdulthood.pdf

Sartre, J.-P. (1956). *Being and nothingness* (H. Barnes, Trans.). Philosophical Library. (Original work published 1943)

Sartre, J.-P. (1957). *The transcendence of the ego* (F. Williams & R. Kirkpatrick, Trans.). Farrar, Strauss and Giroux. (Original work published 1937)

Scarf, M. (2008). *September songs: The good news about marriage in the later years.* Riverhead Books.

Schmitt, N., White, J. K., Coyle, B. W., & Rauschenberger, J. (1979). Retirement and life satisfaction. *Academy of Management Journal,* 22(2), 282–91. https://doi.org/10.5465/255590

Schwartz, S. J., Beyers, W., Luyckx, K., Soenens, B., Zamboanga, B. L., Forthun, L. F., Hardy, S. A., Vazsonyi, A. T., Ham, L. S., Kim, S. Y., Whitbourne, S. K., & Waterman, A. S. (2011). Examining the light and dark sides of emerging adults' identity: A study of identity status differences in positive and negative psychosocial functioning. *Journal of Youth and Adolescence,* 40(7), 839–59. https://doi.org/10.1007/s10964-010-9606-6

Schwartz, S. J., Zamboanga, B. L., Luyckx, K., Meca, A., & Ritchie, R. A. (2013). Identity in emerging adulthood: Reviewing the field and looking forward. *Emerging Adulthood,* 1(2), 96–113. https://doi: 10.1177/2167696813479781

Schwartz, S. J., Zamboanga, B. L., Weisskirch, R. S., & Rodriguez, L. (2009). The relationships of personal and ethnic identity exploration to indices of adaptive and maladaptive psychosocial functioning. *International Journal of Behavioral Development,* 33(2), 131–44. https://doi.org/10.1177/0165025408098018

Searle, J. (1980). Intrinsic intentionality. *Behavioral and Brain Sciences* 3(3), 450–57. https://doi.org/10.1017/S0140525X00006038

Searle, J. (1983). *Intentionality: An essay in the philosophy of mind.* Cambridge University Press.

Searle, J. (1992). *The rediscovery of the mind.* MIT Press.

Shultz, S., Klin, A., & Jones, W. (2018). Neonatal transitions in social behavior and their implications for autism. *Trends in Cognitive Sciences,* 22(5), 452–69. https://doi.org/10.1016/j.tics.2018.02.012

Slater, A., Morison, V., & Rose, D. (1983). Locus of habituation in the human newborn. *Perception,* 12(5), 593–98. https://doi: 10.1068/p120593

Slater, A., Morison, V., & Rose D. (1984). Habituation in the newborn. *Infant Behavior and Development,* 7(2), 183–200. https://doi.org/10.1016/S0163-6383(84)80057-0

Somerville, L. H., Jones, R. M., & Ruberry, E. J. (2013). The medial prefrontal cortex and the emergence of self-conscious emotion in adolescence. *Psychological Science,* 24(8), 1554–62. https://doi.org/10.1177/0956797613475633

Sorce, J. F., Emde, R. N., Campos, J. J., & Klinnert, M. D. (1985). Maternal emotional signaling: Its effect on the visual cliff behavior of 1-year-olds. *Developmental Psychology,* 21(1), 195–200. https://doi.org/10.1037/0012-1649.21.1.195

Spelke, E. S., Breinlinger, K., Macomber, J., & Jacobson, K. (1992). Origins of knowledge. *Psychological Review, 99*(4), 605–32. https://doi.org/10.1037/0033-295X.99.4.605

Steinberg, L. (2007). Risk taking in adolescence: New perspectives from brain and behavioral science. *Current Directions in Psychological Science, 16*(2), 55–59. https://doi.org/10.1111/j.1467-8721.2007.00475.x

Steiner, K. L., & Pillemer, D. B. (2018). Development of the life story in early adolescence. *Journal of Early Adolescence, 38*(2), 125–38. https://doi: 10.1177/0272431616659562

Stephens, G., & Matthews, D. (2014). The communicative infant from 0–18 months: The social-cognitive foundations of pragmatic development. In D. Matthews (Ed.), *Trends in language acquisition research: Vol. 10. Pragmatic development in first language acquisition* (pp. 13–35). John Benjamins Publishing Company. https://doi.org/10.1075/tilar.10.02ste

Steptoe, A., Deaton, A., & Stone, A. A. (2014, November 6). Subjective well-being, health, and ageing. *The Lancet.* https://doi.org/10.1016/S0140-6736(13)61489-0

Stolorow, R. D., & Atwood, G. E. (1992). The myth of the isolated mind. In R. D. Stolorow & G. E. Atwood, *Contexts of being: The intersubjective foundations of psychological life* (pp. 7–28). Routledge.

Strawson, P. F. (2005). *The bounds of sense: An essay on Kant's* Critique of Pure Reason. Routledge. (Original work published 1966)

Sullivan, H. S. (1940). *Conceptions of modern psychiatry.* W. W. Norton.

Sullivan, H. S. (1970). *The psychiatric interview.* W. W. Norton. (Original work published 1954)

Sullivan, H. S. (1977). *The interpersonal theory of psychiatry.* W. W. Norton. (Original work published 1953)

Tawfik, S. H., & Hoffman, M. F. (2018). Fluid intelligence. In E. B. Braaten (Ed.), *The SAGE encyclopedia of intellectual and developmental disorders.* SAGE Publications. https://dx.doi.org/10.4135/9781483392271

Thomas, M. L., Kaufmann, C. N., Palmer, B. W., Depp, C. A., Martin, A. S., Glorioso, D. K., Thompson, W. K., & Jeste, D. V. (2016). Paradoxical trend for improvement in mental health with aging: A community-based study of 1,546 adults aged 21–100. *Journal of Clinical Psychiatry, 77*(8), e1019–e1025. https://doi: 10.4088/JCP.16m10671

Thompson, E. (2015). *Waking, dreaming, being: Self and consciousness in neuroscience, meditation, and philosophy.* Columbia University Press.

TIAA. (2016). Voices of experience: Insights on life in retirement. https://www.tiaa.org/public/pdf/2016-voices-full-report.pdf

Trevarthen, C. (2005). First things first: Infants make good use of the sympathetic rhythm of imitation, without reason or language. *Journal of Child Psychotherapy, 31*(1), 91–113. https://doi.org/10.1080/00754170500079651

Trevarthen, C. (2011). What is it like to be a person who knows nothing? Defining the active intersubjective mind of a newborn human being. *Infant and Child Development,* 20(1), 119–35. https://doi.org/10.1002/icd.689

Trevarthen, C., & Hubley, P. (1978). Secondary intersubjectivity: Confidence, confiding, and acts of meaning in the first year. In A. Lock (Ed.), *Action, gesture, and symbol: The emergence of language* (pp. 183–229). Academic Press.

Tronick, E., Als, H., Adamson, L., Wise, S., & Brazelton, B. (1978). The infant's response to entrapment between contradictory messages in face-to-face interaction. *Journal of the American Academy of Child & Adolescent Psychiatry,* 17(1), 1–13. https://doi: 10.1016/s0002-7138(09)62273-1

Turner, R. P., Lukoff, D., Barnhouse, R. T., & Lu F. G. (1995). Religious or spiritual problem: A culturally sensitive diagnostic category. *Journal of Nervous and Mental Disease,* 183(7), 435–44. https://doi: 10.1097/00005053-199507000-00003

Tyrrell, M. O. (2012). *Become a memoirist for elders: Create a successful home business* (J. Barker-Nunn, Ed.). Memoirs, Inc.

van Wijngaarden, E., Leget, C., & Goossensen, A. (2015). Ready to give up on life: The lived experience of elderly people who feel life is completed and no longer worth living. *Social Science and Medicine,* 138, 257–64. https://doi.org/10.1016/j.socscimed.2015.05.015

Varela, F. J. (1996). Neurophenomenology: A methodological remedy for the hard problem. *Journal of Consciousness Studies,* 3(4), 330–49.

Vygotsky, L. S. (1986). *Thought and language* (A. Kozulin, Trans.). MIT Press. (Original work published 1934)

Walsh, D. (2014). *Why do they act that way? A survival guide to the adolescent brain for you and your teen* (2nd ed.). Atria Paperback.

Walsh, L. C., Boehm, J. K., & Lyubomirsky, S. (2018, August 14). Is happiness a consequence or cause of career success? *LSE Business Review* https://blogs.lse.ac.uk/businessreview/2018/08/13/is-happiness-a-consequence-or-cause-of-career-success/

Washburn, M. (1994). *Transpersonal psychology in psychoanalytic perspective.* State University of New York Press.

Washburn, M. (1995). *The ego and the dynamic ground: A transpersonal theory of human development* (2nd ed.). State University of New York Press.

Washburn, M. (2003). *Embodied spirituality in a sacred world.* State University of New York Press.

Waterman, A. S. (2007). Doing well: The relationship of identity status to three conceptions of well-being. *Identity: An International Journal of Theory and Research,* 7(4), 289–307. https://doi.org/10.1080/15283480701600769

Weinstein, N., Ryan, W. S., Cody, R. D., Przybylski, A. K., Legate, N., & Ryan, R. M. (2012). Parental autonomy support and discrepancies between implicit and explicit sexual identities: Dynamics of self-acceptance and defense. *Journal of Personality and Social Psychology,* 102(4), 815–32. https://doi.org/10.1037/a0026854

Welch-Ross, M. K. (1997). Mother-child participation in conversations about the past: Relations to preschoolers' theory of mind. *Developmental Psychology,* 33(4), 618–29. https://doi.org/10.1037/0012-1649.33.4.618

Wethington, E. (2000). Expecting stress: Americans and "midlife crisis." *Motivation and Emotion,* 24(2), 85–103. https://doi.org/10.1023/A:1005611230993

Wethington, E., Kessler, R. C., & Pixley, J. E. (2004). Turning points in adulthood. In O. G. Brim, C. D. Ryff, & R. C. Kessler (Eds.), *How healthy are we? A national study of well-being at midlife* (pp. 586–613). University of Chicago Press.

Whitford, M. (Ed.). (1991). *The Irigaray reader.* Basil Blackwell.

Wiebe, S. A., Lukowski, A., F., & Bauer, P. J. (2010). Sequence imitation and reaching measures of executive control: A longitudinal examination in the second year of life. *Developmental Neuropsychology,* 35(5), 522–38. https://doi:10.1080/87565641.2010.494751

Wilber, K. (1995). *Sex, ecology, spirituality: The spirit of evolution.* Shambhala.

Wilber, K. (1997). An integral theory of consciousness. *Journal of Consciousness Studies,* 4(1), 71–92.

Winsler, A. (2009). Still talking to ourselves after all these years: A review of current research on private speech. In A. Winsler, C. Fernyhough, & I. Montero (Eds.), *Private speech, executive functioning, and the development of verbal self-regulation* (pp. 3–41). Cambridge University Press. https://doi.org/10.1017/CBO9780511581533.003

Wittgenstein, L. (1953). *Philosophical investigations.* Blackwell.

Wittman, S. (2019). Lingering identities. *Academy of Management Review,* 44(4), 724–45.

Wong, P. T., & Watt, L. M. (1991). What types of reminiscence are associated with successful aging? *Psychology and Aging,* 6(2), 272–79. https://doi:10.1037/0882-7974.6.2.272

Xu, F., & Garcia, V. (2008). Intuitive statistics by 8-month-old infants. *Proceedings of the National Academy of Sciences of the United States of America,* 105(13), 5012–15. https://doi.org/10.1073/pnas.0704450105

Zelazo, P. D., Craik, F. I. M., & Booth, L. (2004). Executive function across the life span. *Acta Psychologica,* 115(2–3), 167–83. https://doi: 10.1016/j.actpsy.2003.12.005

Zimmermann, A., de Carvalho, K. M. M., Atihe, C., Zimmermann, S. M. V., & de Moura Ribeiro, V. L. (2019). Visual development in children aged 0 to 6 years. *Arquivos Brasileiros de Oftalmologia,* 82(3), 173–75. https://doi.org/10.5935/0004-2749.20190034.

Index

www.ingramcontent.com/pod-product-compliance
Lightning Source LLC
Chambersburg PA
CBHW030855270326
41929CB00008B/422